OSPF Network Design Solutions
Second Edition

Thomas M. Thomas II, CCIE No. 9360

Cisco Press

Cisco Press
201 West 103rd Street
Indianapolis, IN 46290 USA

OSPF Network Design Solutions, Second Edition

Thomas M. Thomas II

Copyright© 2003 Cisco Systems, Inc.

Published by:
Cisco Press
201 West 103rd Street
Indianapolis, IN 46290 USA

Printed in the United States of America 1 2 3 4 5 6 7 8 9 0

First Printing April 2003

Library of Congress Cataloging-in-Publication Number: 2001095162

ISBN: 1-58705-032-3

Warning and Disclaimer

This book is designed to provide information about the Open Shortest Path First (OSPF) protocol. Every effort has been made to make this book as complete and as accurate as possible, but no warranty or fitness is implied.

The information is provided on an "as is" basis. The authors, Cisco Press, and Cisco Systems, Inc. shall have neither liability nor responsibility to any person or entity with respect to any loss or damages arising from the information contained in this book or from the use of the discs or programs that may accompany it.

The opinions expressed in this book belong to the author and are not necessarily those of Cisco Systems, Inc.

Trademark Acknowledgments

All terms mentioned in this book that are known to be trademarks or service marks have been appropriately capitalized. Cisco Press or Cisco Systems, Inc. cannot attest to the accuracy of this information. Use of a term in this book should not be regarded as affecting the validity of any trademark or service mark.

Feedback Information

At Cisco Press, our goal is to create in-depth technical books of the highest quality and value. Each book is crafted with care and precision, undergoing rigorous development that involves the unique expertise of members from the professional technical community.

Readers' feedback is a natural continuation of this process. If you have any comments regarding how we could improve the quality of this book, or otherwise alter it to better suit your needs, you can contact us through email at feedback@ciscopress.com. Please make sure to include the book title and ISBN in your message.

We greatly appreciate your assistance.

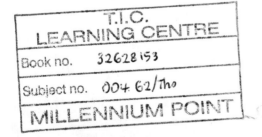

Publisher	John Wait
Editor-In-Chief	John Kane
Cisco Representative	Anthony Wolfenden
Cisco Press Program Manager	Sonia Torres Chavez
Manager, Marketing Communications, Cisco Systems	Scott Miller
Cisco Marketing Program Manager	Edie Quiroz
Executive Editor	Brett Bartow
Acquisitions Editor	Amy Moss
Production Manager	Patrick Kanouse
Development Editor	Christopher Cleveland
Project Editor	San Dee Phillips
Copy Editor	Progressive Publishing Alternatives
Technical Editors	Henry Benjamin, Matthew Birkner, Rick Burts, Daniel Golding, John Hammond, Cary Riddock
Team Coordinator	Tammi Ross
Book Designer	Gina Rexrode
Cover Designer	Louisa Adair
Indexer	Tim Wright

Corporate Headquarters
Cisco Systems, Inc.
170 West Tasman Drive
San Jose, CA 95134-1706
USA
www.cisco.com
Tel: 408 526-4000
 800 553-NETS (6387)
Fax: 408 526-4100

European Headquarters
Cisco Systems International BV
Haarlerbergpark
Haarlerbergweg 13-19
1101 CH Amsterdam
The Netherlands
www-europe.cisco.com
Tel: 31 0 20 357 1000
Fax: 31 0 20 357 1100

Americas Headquarters
Cisco Systems, Inc.
170 West Tasman Drive
San Jose, CA 95134-1706
USA
www.cisco.com
Tel: 408 526-7660
Fax: 408 527-0883

Asia Pacific Headquarters
Cisco Systems, Inc.
Capital Tower
168 Robinson Road
#22-01 to #29-01
Singapore 068912
www.cisco.com
Tel: +65 6317 7777
Fax: +65 6317 7799

Cisco Systems has more than 200 offices in the following countries and regions. Addresses, phone numbers, and fax numbers are listed on the
Cisco.com Web site at www.cisco.com/go/offices.

Argentina • Australia • Austria • Belgium • Brazil • Bulgaria • Canada • Chile • China PRC • Colombia • Costa Rica • Croatia • Czech Republic
Denmark • Dubai, UAE • Finland • France • Germany • Greece • Hong Kong SAR • Hungary • India • Indonesia • Ireland • Israel • Italy
Japan • Korea • Luxembourg • Malaysia • Mexico • The Netherlands • New Zealand • Norway • Peru • Philippines • Poland • Portugal
Puerto Rico • Romania • Russia • Saudi Arabia • Scotland • Singapore • Slovakia • Slovenia • South Africa • Spain • Sweden
Switzerland • Taiwan • Thailand • Turkey • Ukraine • United Kingdom • United States • Venezuela • Vietnam • Zimbabwe

About the Author

Thomas M. Thomas II is a self-proclaimed Network Emergency Repair Dude, or NERD for short, and a country boy who is CCIE No. 9360 as well as being a certified Cisco Systems instructor and holding CCNP, CCDA, and CCNA certifications and claims he never works because he loves what he does. Tom is the founder of NetCerts.com (now CCPrep.com) and the International Network Resource Group (www.inrgi.net) where he remains on the board of directors in an advisory capacity, providing vision and focus. He was previously an Instructor for Chesapeake Computer Consultants, Inc. (CCCI), and a course developer for Cisco Systems. He has also authored the first edition of *OSPF Network Design Solutions* and a variety of other networking books designed to help his fellow engineers. Tom is currently working as a senior network consultant designing and implementing Voice-over-IP and Data networks wherever he can as a part of US Networks, Inc. (www.usnetworksinc.com). Tom currently lives in Raleigh, NC, with his family, and although he is not in the country, he humorously observes that you can see it from his home.

About the Technical Reviewers

Henry Benjamin , CCIE No. 4695, holds three CCIE certifications (Routing and Switching, ISP Dial, and Communication and Services). Formerly with the Cisco Systems CCIE global team, Henry is now an independent consultant for a large security firm in Australia. He has served as a proctor for the CCIE Lab exams and is the author of *CCNP Practical Studies: Routing* from Cisco Press and *CCIE Routing and Switching Exam Cram* from Coriolis.

Matthew H. Birkner, CCIE No. 3719, is a technical leader at Cisco Systems, specializing in IP and MPLS network design. He has influenced multiple large carrier and enterprise designs worldwide. Matt has spoken at Cisco Networkers on MPLS VPN technologies in both the United States and EMEA over the past few years. Matt, a "Double CCIE," authored the Cisco Press book, *Cisco Internetwork Design*. Matt holds a B.S.E.E. from Tufts University, where he majored in electrical engineering.

Rick Burts, CCIE No. 4615, has over 20 years experience with computers and computer networks. Rick is a certified Cisco Systems instructor and a CCIE (Routing/Switching). He has taught a variety of Cisco courses and helped develop an OSPF course for Mentor Technologies. Rick is a consultant and has helped many customers with OSPF as their network routing protocol. He is a senior consultant with Chesapeake NetCraftsmen (www.netcraftsmen.net). In his current position, Rick deals with network design, implementation, and troubleshooting issues and teaches a few courses.

Daniel L. Golding is peering manager in America Online's Internet Architecture group. Dan is responsible for ensuring worldwide Internet connectivity for all AOL Time Warner subscribers and properties. His particular areas of expertise include internetwork peering and routing policy design. He has a long history of involvement with various Internet service providers, particularly in the area of backbone engineering. Dan is also a frequent speaker at North American Network Operator's Group (NANOG) meetings and has been a network engineer for over six years.

John Hammond has been an instructor and course developer for Juniper Networks for the past two years. Prior to that he was a member of the teaching staff of Chesapeake Computer Consultants, Inc., a Cisco Training Partner. John has been involved in many aspects of networks since 1990.

Cary Riddock, CCNP, CSS1, has worked as an network engineer for some of the largest companies in Houston, Texas and Central Florida over the last six years. He is very active in the IT Security Field and is currently pursuing CCSP and CISSP certifications. His resume includes co-authoring *MCNS* for Cisco Press and is a contributing author for various network security publications.

Dedications

I want to dedicate this book to my family for their ever-faithful support and understanding during the many nights and weekends I spent writing. An extra special thank you goes to my wife Rose, daughter Rebekah, and son Daniel who never voiced anything but encouragement and support.

Without the support of my family and their faith in me I would never have been able to completely rewrite this book.

I had my faith in the Lord and the knowledge that my family knew I could improve upon my book in this new edition to keep me going.

I want to reaffirm a few words of special meaning to my wife and I who have been married for over 15 years…

Always

Forever

Endlessly

Until Eternity

Acknowledgments

I am very grateful to the group of talented people that were assembled to make this book a reality. Through their knowledge, dedication, and hard work, this book has become more than I ever thought possible.

The most important acknowledgment must go to my wife, Rose, who put up with me writing all night after working all day. Her unwavering support was the single greatest factor in my ability to complete the book you now hold in your hands.

Writing this book allowed me to assemble a team of technical professionals who have helped me make this book more than I thought possible. I had the privilege to be a part of an awesome team during this time. Thank you all for your insight and friendship.

I have to recognize the extraordinary group of publishing professionals who helped guide me through the process: Amy Moss, a true and dear friend of many years now; and Chris Cleveland who is always busy but always has time to help me.

Contents at a Glance

Contents

Icons Used in This Book

Throughout this book, you will see the following icons used for networking devices:

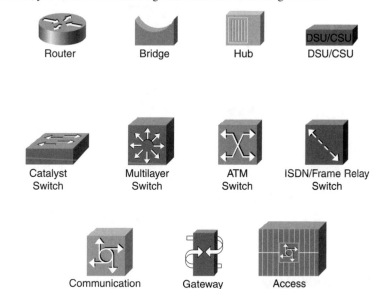

The following icons are used for peripherals and other devices:

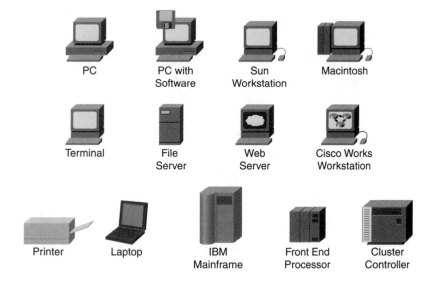

The following icons are used for networks and network connections:

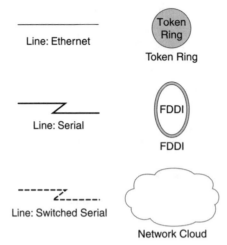

Command Syntax Conventions

The conventions used to present command syntax in this book are the same conventions used in the Cisco IOS Software Command Reference. The Command Reference describes these conventions as follows:

- Vertical bars (|) separate alternative, mutually exclusive elements.

- Square brackets [ ] indicate optional elements.

- Braces { } indicate a required choice.

- Braces within brackets [{ }] indicate a required choice within an optional element.

- **Boldface** indicates commands and keywords that are entered literally as shown. In actual configuration examples and output (not general command syntax), boldface indicates commands that are manually input by the user (such as a **show** command).

- *Italics* indicate arguments for which you supply actual values.

Introduction

OSPF is in use in numerous networks worldwide. OSPF is also one of the most widely tested on protocols if you choose to pursue a networking certification. From a technical perspective, the overwhelming presence of OSPF ensures that almost everyone will encounter it at some point in their career. A result of these facts is that everyone should understand OSPF including how it operates, how to configure it, troubleshooting, and—most importantly—how to design a network that will use OSPF. You can see that everyone will be exposed to OSPF to some degree, and because it is highly likely that your family is surfing the Internet and having their packets pass over a network that is OSPF enabled, it is clear to me that they, too, might benefit from this book, so consider getting them a copy as well.

Who Should Read This Book?

This book is not designed to be a general networking topics book; although, it can be used for that purpose. This book is intended to tremendously increase your knowledge level with regards to OSPF. Personnel responsible for understanding OSPF should read this book. You might need to understand OSPF because you are a programmer, network manager, network engineer, studying for certification, and so on.

How This Book Is Organized

Although this book can be read cover-to-cover, it is designed to be flexible and allow you to easily move between chapters and sections of chapters to cover just the material that you need more information on. If you do intend to read them all, the order in the book is an excellent sequence to use:

- **Chapter 1, "Networking and Routing Fundamentals"**—Those of us responsible for programming, managing, maintaining, troubleshooting, and ensuring the operation of the network will appreciate this chapter as the building blocks of interworking are reviewed.

- **Chapter 2, "Introduction to OSPF"**—This chapter helps you understand the basic types of routing protocols, their characteristics, and when it is best to use a certain protocol and uses that information to build a deeper understanding of how to implement them in your network.

- **Chapter 3, "OSPF Communication"**—This chapter introduces you to how OSPF communicates between routers running OSPF. This chapter covers *how* the link-state information is then entered into the link-state database through OSPF's use of Link-State Advertisement (LSA) and the various internal OSPF protocols that define and allow OSPF routers to communicate.

- **Chapter 4, "Design Fundamentals"**—The foundation of understanding the purpose for using OSPF and its operation as discussed in previous chapters is further expanded as the discussion of OSPF performance and design issues are expanded. Within each of the design sections, a series of "golden design rules" are presented. These rules can help you understand the constraints and recommendations of properly designing each area within an OSPF network. In many cases, examples are presented that draw upon the material presented, to further reinforce key topics and ideas.

- **Chapter 5, "Routing Concepts and Configuration"**—This is going to be a fun chapter that will challenge you, the reader, and me, the author, to keep you interested in the different. We are going to look at all the OSPF features, knobs, and functionality that are possible.

- **Chapter 6, "Redistribution" and Chapter 7, "Summarization"**—Redistribution and summarization are interesting concepts, and these chapters decipher and demystify the challenges you face when one routing algorithm is redistributed into another, when one of those protocols is OSPF (of course), or when the OSPF routing table is optimized through summarization.

- **Chapter 8, "Managing and Securing OSPF Networks"**—The management of your OSPF network is just as important as the security. In fact, a case could be made that proper network management is the most important aspect of having your network operate smoothly.

- **Chapter 9, "Troubleshooting OSPF"**—This chapter builds upon the design theories and OSPF communication processes as discussed throughout the book prior to this chapter. The basis for this chapter is how to go about monitoring OSPF to ensure it is operating correctly and what to do if it is not. There are certain troubleshooting procedures and techniques that you can use to determine the causes of a network problem, which are covered as well.

- **Chapter 10, "BGP and MPLS in an OSPF Network"**—This chapter covers some of the evolving OSPF extensions and new capabilities as OSPF grows to embrace new technologies such as Multiprotocol Label Switching (MPLS). This chapter begins this discussion by reviewing the difference between an IGP and an EGP routing protocol, and then looks at how OSPF interacts with BGP.

OSPF Fundamentals and Communication

CHAPTER 1

Networking and Routing Fundamentals

Achievement: Unless you try to do something beyond what you have already mastered, you will never grow. — Successories

In recent years, the growth of networks everywhere has accelerated as many organizations move into the international business arena and join the Internet community. This expansion continues to drive the development, refinement, and complexity of network equipment and software, consequently resulting in some unique issues and exciting advances. You rarely see an advertisement that does not contain the famous www prefix. In my hometown, one of the local news stations now displays the e-mail address of its reporters as they deliver the news! Is this the new economy in action, or is it just another example of too much information? At least the media are feeding on their own now!

Can you imagine modern business or life without computers, fax machines and services, e-mail, Internet commerce, automatic teller machines, remote banking, check cards, or video conferencing? Even more importantly, today's children think that these tools are commonplace and that business cannot be done without them when they get to our age. I hate to admit it, but I can clearly remember a time without the Internet and when Novell ruled the office; however, nothing stands still in our industry, and some of us have known that for quite a while.

Gordon Moore of Intel made an interesting observation in 1965, just 6 years after he invented the first planar transistor. He observed that the "doubling of transistor density on a manufactured die every year" would occur. Now almost 40 years later, his statement has become known as *Moore's law,* and it has continued to hold true. According to Intel

There are no theoretical or practical challenges that will prevent Moore's law from being true for another 20 years; this is another five generations of processors.

In 1995, Moore updated his prediction to indicate that transistor density would double once every two years. Using Moore's law to predict transistor density in 2012, Intel should have the capability to integrate 1 billion transistors on a production die that will be operating at 10 GHz. This could result in a performance of 100,000 MIPS. This represents an increase over the Pentium II processor that is similar to the Pentium II processor's speed increase over the 386 chip. That is impressive considering the sheer number of transistors on a chip that you can hold in your hand! Figure 1-1 depicts Moore's law.

Figure 1-1   *Moore's Law*

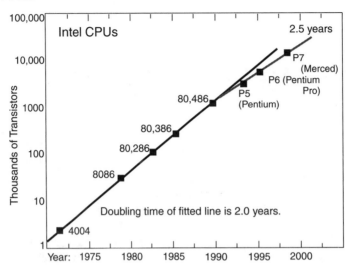

Foundations of Networking

Many advanced features are being supported by the physical hardware through the application of Moore's law. Those of us responsible for networking these many devices follow a theoretical framework that allows the required functionality to be deployed within our networks. This framework is more commonly known as the OSI reference model.

OSI stands for *open system interconnection,* where open system refers to the specifications surrounding the model's structure as well as its nonproprietary public availability. Anyone can build the software and hardware needed to communicate within the OSI structure. If you know someone that has written a script to access information in a router, at some level, he is following the OSI reference model.

Why Was the OSI Reference Model Needed?

Before the development of the OSI reference model, the rapid growth of applications and hardware resulted in a multitude of vendor-specific models. In other words, one person's solution would not work with anyone else's because there was no agreed-upon method, style, process, or way for different devices to interoperate. In terms of future network growth and design, this rapid growth caused a great deal of concern among network engineers and designers because they had to ensure that the systems under their control could interact with every standard. This concern encouraged the International Organization of Standardization (ISO) to initiate the development of the OSI reference model.

The work on the OSI reference model was initiated in the late 1970s and came to maturity in the late 1980s and early 1990s. The ISO was the primary architect of the model that is in place today.

Characteristics of the OSI Layers

Figure 1-2 demonstrates how the layers are spanned by a routing protocol. You might also want to contact Network Associates, as its protocol chart shows how almost every protocol spans the seven layers of the OSI reference model. Figure 1-2 provides a good illustration of how the seven layers are grouped in the model. For a better picture of how protocols are positioned in the OSI reference model, visit to the following websites and request a copy of the applicable posters:

Acterna (aka W&G) offers free OSI, ATM, ISDN, and fiberoptics posters at www.acterna.com/shared/forms/poster_form.html.
Network Associates offers its Guide to Communications Protocols at www.sniffer.com/dm/protocolposter.asp.

Figure 1-2   *How a Routing Protocol Spans the OSI Model*

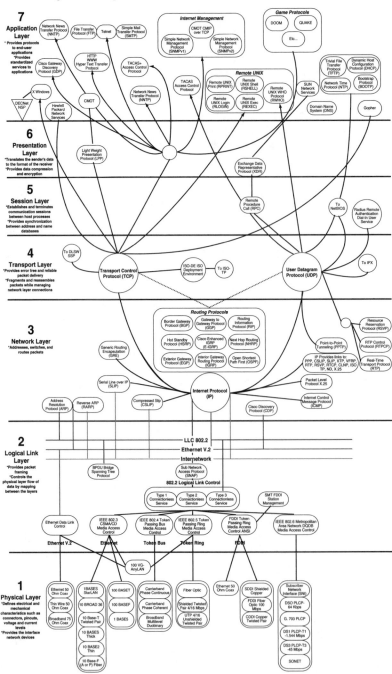

Table 1-1 outlines an effective mnemonic tool to help you remember the seven OSI layers and their order, working either from Layer 7 down or from Layer 1 up.

Table 1-1   *Mnemonics Used to Remember OSI Layers*

OSI Layer (Upper to Lower)	Mnemonic	OSI Layer (Lower to Upper)	Mnemonic
Application (Layer 7)	All	Physical (Layer 1)	Please
Presentation (Layer 6)	people	Data Link (Layer 2)	do
Session (Layer 5)	seem	Network (Layer 3)	not
Transport (Layer 4)	to	Transport (Layer 4)	take
Network (Layer 3)	need	Session (Layer 5)	sales
Data Link (Layer 2)	data	Presentation (Layer 6)	peoples
Physical (Layer 1)	processing	Application (Layer 7)	advice

Understanding the Seven Layers of the OSI Reference Model

The seven layers of the OSI reference model can be divided into two categories: upper layers and lower layers. The upper layers are typically concerned only with applications, and the lower layers primarily handle data transportation. The sections that follow examine the three upper layers, the four lower layers, and the functions of each.

Upper Layers

The upper layers of the OSI reference model—5, 6, and 7—are concerned with application issues. They are generally implemented only in software programs. The application layer is the highest layer and is closest to the end user. Both users and application layer processes interact with software programs that contain a communications component so that the application can interact with the OSI model effectively. The sections that follow review the functions of each upper layer in detail.

NOTE   The term *upper layer* is often used to refer to any higher layer, relative to a given layer. The opposite, *lower layer,* is used to refer to any layer below the one being discussed.

Layer 7—Application

The application layer essentially acts as the end-user interface. This is the layer where interaction between the mail application (cc:Mail, MS Outlook, and so on) or communications package (Secure CRT for Telnet or FTP Voyager for FTP) and the user occurs. For example, when a user wants to send an e-mail message or access a file on the server, this is where the process starts. Another example of the processes that occur at this layer are network file system (NFS) use and the mapping of drives through Windows NT.

Layer 6—Presentation

The presentation layer is responsible for the agreement and translation of the communication format (syntax) between applications. For example, the presentation layer enables Microsoft Exchange to correctly interpret a message from Lotus Notes. A historical example of why the presentation layer is needed is when a sender is transmitting in EBCDIC (8-bit) character representation to a receiver that needs ASCII (7-bit) character representation. Another example of the actions that occur in this layer is the encryption and decryption of data in Pretty Good Privacy (PGP).

Layer 5—Session

The session layer responsibilities range from managing the application layer's transfer of information to the data transport portion of the OSI reference model. An example is Sun's or Novell's Remote Procedure Call (RPC), which uses Layer 5.

Lower Layers

The lower layers of the OSI reference model—1, 2, 3, and 4—handle data transport issues. The physical and data link layers are implemented in hardware and software. The other lower layers are generally implemented only in software. These lower layers are the ones that network engineers and designers need to focus on to be successful. The sections that follow review the functions of each of the lower layers in detail.

Layer 4—Transport

The transport layer is responsible for the logical transport mechanism, which includes functions conforming to the mechanism's characteristics. For example, the transmission control protocol (TCP), a logical transport mechanism, provides a level of error checking and reliability (through sequence numbers) to the transmission of user data to the lower layers of the OSI reference model. This is the only layer that provides true source-to-destination, end-to-end connectivity through the use of routing protocols such as open shortest path first (OSPF) or the file transfer protocol (FTP) application as examples of TCP.

Contrast the presence of TCP with the user datagram protocol (UDP), which is an unreliable protocol that does not have the additional overhead that provides error checking and reliability like TCP. Some common examples of UDP-based protocols are Trivial File Transfer Protocol (TFTP) and Simple Network Management Protocol (SNMP). The most common usage of UDP is streaming media solutions, such as Real Audio.

Layer 3—Network

The network layer determines a logical interface address. Routing decisions are made based on the locations of the Internet protocol (IP) address in question. For example, IP addresses establish separate logical topologies, known as *subnets*. Applying this definition to a LAN workstation environment, the workstation determines the location of a particular IP address and where its associated subnet resides through the network layer. For example, there might be subnet 10.10.10.x, where the customer service people have their workstations or servers, and another subnet 10.20.20.x, where the finance people have their servers or workstations. IP addressing is discussed in more detail later in the section "Internet Protocol Addressing." Until then, remember that a logical IP address can have three components: network, subnet, and host.

Layer 2—Data Link

The data link layer provides framing, error, and flow control across the network media being used. An important characteristic of this layer is that the information that is applied to it is used by devices to determine if the packet needs to be acted upon by this layer (that is, proceed to Layer 3 or discard). The data link layer also assigns a media access control (MAC) address to every LAN interface on a device. For example, on an Ethernet LAN segment, all packets are broadcast and received by every device on the segment. Only the device whose MAC address is contained within this layer's frame acts upon the packet; all others do not.

It is important to note at this point that serial interfaces do not normally require unique Layer 2 station addresses, such as MAC addresses, unless it is necessary to identify the receiving end in a multipoint network. On networks that do not conform to the IEEE 802 standards but do conform to the OSI reference model, the node address is called the data link control (DLC) address. For example, in Frame Relay, this Layer 2 address is known as the data-link connection identifier (DLCI).

MAC addresses are 6 bytes or 48 bits in size, of which 24 bits are dedicated for Organization Unique Identification (OUI) and 24 bits are for unique identification. See the Institute of Electrical and Electronic Engineers (IEEE) website for more information.

The IEEE assigns Ethernet address blocks to manufacturers of Ethernet network interface cards. The first 3 bytes of an Ethernet address are the company ID, and the last 3 bytes are assigned by the manufacturer. Table 1-2 shows an example of an Ethernet address that is assigned to Cisco Systems.

Table 1-2   *Example Ethernet Address*

Organization Unique ID			Assigned by Cisco		
00	00	0C	01	23	45

When discussing MAC addresses, some people refer to the Organization Unique IDs as the vendor ID or OID. All are correct; however, the IEEE uses the term shown in Table 1-2.

Layer 1—Physical

The physical layer, the lowest layer of the OSI reference model, is closest to the physical network medium (for example, the network cabling that connects various pieces of network equipment). This layer is responsible for defining information regarding the physical media, such as electrical, mechanical, and functional specifications to connect two systems. The physical layer is composed of three main areas: wires, connectors, and encoding. Figure 1-3 shows the relationship among the seven layers.

Figure 1-3   *Detailed OSI Layer Relationships*

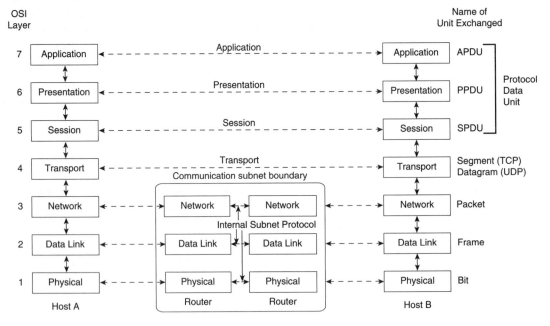

OSI Reference Model Layers and Information Exchange

The seven OSI layers use various forms of control information to communicate with their peer layers in other computer systems. This control information consists of specific requests and instructions that are exchanged between peer OSI layers. Control information typically takes one of two forms:

- **Headers**—Appended to the front of data passed down from upper layers
- **Trailers**—Appended to the back of data passed down from upper layers

OSI layers are not necessarily required to attach a header or trailer to upper-layer data, but they typically do.

Headers, Trailers, and Data

Headers (and trailers) and data are relative concepts, depending on the layer that is analyzing the information unit at the time.

For example, at the network layer, an information unit consists of a Layer 3 header and data, known as the *payload*. At the data link layer (Layer 2), however, all the information passed down by the network layer (the Layer 3 header and the data) is treated simply as data. In other words, the data portion of an information unit at a given OSI layer can potentially contain headers, trailers, and data from all the higher layers. This is known as *encapsulation*. Figure 1-4 shows the header and data from one layer that are encapsulated in the header of the next-lowest layer.

Figure 1-4   *OSI Packet Encapsulation Through the OSI Layers*

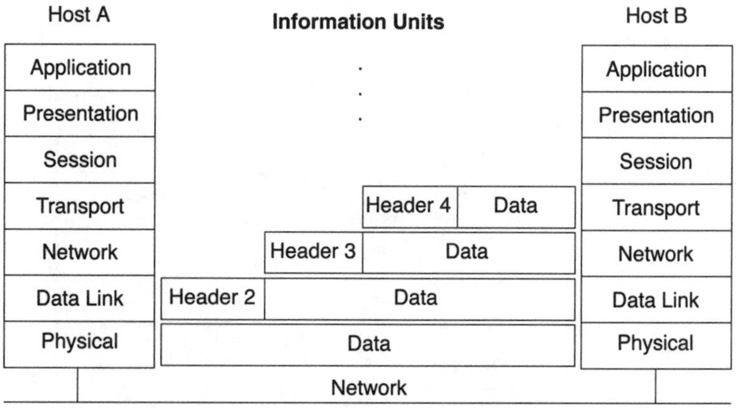

This discussion described the framework that is used to tie networks together. There are now hundreds of online and print references that spend even more time discussing the OSI model, but for this text, the level of discussion presented here is appropriate. However, note that how networks communicate has not been discussed. The following section reviews the basic principles of TCP/IP—the de facto standard for communication on the Internet.

TCP/IP Protocol Suite

A *protocol* is a set of rules and conventions that govern how devices on a network exchange information. This section discusses one of the more commonly used protocol suites: TCP/IP. This discussion does not provide sufficient information for an in-depth study of TCP/IP. Nevertheless, TCP/IP needs to be covered to some degree so that you can better understand the overall operation of network protocols; these discussions are expanded in later chapters concerning OSPF.

The TCP/IP protocol suite is also referred to as the TCP/IP stack, and it is one of the most widely implemented internetworking standards in use today. The term TCP/IP literally means *Transmission Control Protocol/Internet Protocol*. TCP and IP are the two core protocols that exist within the TCP/IP protocol suite, and their place in the TCP/IP protocol stack is clarified in the following paragraphs.

TCP/IP was originally developed for ARPAnet, a U.S. Government packet-switched WAN, over 25 years ago. Although at the time, the Internet was a private network and TCP/IP was designed specifically for use within that network, TCP/IP has since grown in popularity and is one of the most open protocols available for use in networks today. This growth and popularity is primarily due to TCP/IP's capability to connect different networks regardless of their physical environments. This has made TCP/IP today's de facto standard on the Internet and in the majority of today's networks, large and small.

TCP/IP is not 100 percent compatible with the OSI reference model; however, TCP/IP can run over OSI-compliant lower layers, such as the data link and physical layers of the OSI model. TCP/IP can communicate at the network layer as well using IP. Essentially, layers 3 and below in the OSI reference model are close to the original TCP/IP structure. Figure 1-5 illustrates this mapping of layers between the OSI model and the TCP/IP protocol.

Figure 1-5   *OSI Model–to–TCP/IP Mappings*

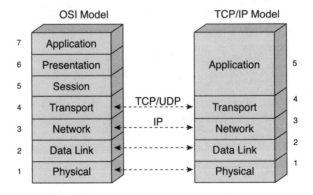

TCP/IP Functions

Whereas OSI was a structure for networks, you can consider TCP/IP the language of the networks. When combined, networks create a diverse and powerful network—the Internet. This section reviews the major functionality of TCP/IP in general and then TCP and IP in turn.

The term *segment* describes a unit of data at the TCP layer. At the IP layer, it is called a *packet,* and at the lower layers, it is called a *frame.* The various names are shown in Figure 1-3.

If a message is too large for the underlying network topology, it is up to the IP layer to fragment the datagram into smaller parts. For example, Ethernet frame sizes differ from what is allowable in Token Ring; therefore, IP handles the size changes as needed.

Different paths might be available through the Internet, between a source and a destination station. Fragments of a datagram might take different paths through a network. So, when messages arrive at the destination station, the IP protocol stack must sequence them and reassemble them into their original datagram. Each datagram or fragment is given an IP header and is transmitted as a frame by the lower layers.

NOTE   In addition to the two network layer protocols (IP and Internet control message protocol [ICMP]) and the two transport layer protocols (TCP and UDP), the TCP/IP suite includes a cluster of protocols that operates at the upper layers, such as FTP, Telnet, and so on.

Some of these are TCP/IP-specific, and some are protocols that can run with TCP/IP but originate elsewhere; however, discussion of these advanced protocols is beyond the scope of this book.

A good resource for further reading on the subject of TCP/IP is *TCP/IP Illustrated,* Volume 1, by Richard Stevens. It is somewhat dated in its examples, but the text is definitive. Also, by the time you read this, Stevens's second edition should be published. Hopefully, the high standards of the original volume will be maintained because Mr. Stevens has regretfully passed away and did not revise the first edition.

TCP Overview

Within this suite of protocols, TCP is the main transport layer protocol that offers connection-oriented transport services. TCP accepts messages from upper-layer protocols and provides the messages with an acknowledged reliable connection-oriented transport service to the TCP layer of a remote device. TCP provides five important functions within the TCP/IP protocol suite:

- Provides format of the data and acknowledgments that two computers exchange to achieve a reliable transfer
- Ensures that data arrive correctly
- Distinguishes between multiple destinations on a given machine

- Explains how to recover from errors
- Explains how a data stream transfer is initiated and when it is complete

IP Overview

IP is the main network-layer protocol. It offers unreliable, connectionless service because it depends on TCP to detect and recover from lost packets when TCP is being used. Alternatively, when UDP is used, there is no recovery of lost packets because UDP does not have that capability. IP provides three important functions within the TCP/IP protocol suite:

- Defines the basic format and specifications of all data transfer used throughout the protocol suite
- Performs the routing function by choosing a path to the required destination over which data is to be sent
- Includes the previously mentioned functions as well as those covering unreliable packet delivery

Essentially, these functions cover how packets should be processed, what error message parameters are, and when a packet should be discarded.

Types of Network Topologies

The preceding sections discussed the evolution of today's advanced networks and the building blocks that have evolved to make them what they are today—that is, the OSI reference model and the TCP/IP protocol. The sections on the OSI reference model described the essential means of how data is transported between the various layers that are running on all intranet devices. The TCP/IP section reviewed the protocols' characteristics. This section addresses the media that operates in your network. The sections that follow review both LAN and WAN topologies.

Local-Area Networks

LANs connect workstations, servers, legacy systems, and miscellaneous network-accessible equipment, which are, in turn, interconnected to form your network. The most common types of LANs are as follows:

- **Ethernet**—A communication system that has only one wire with multiple stations attached to the single wire; the system operates at a speed of 10 Mbps. Ethernet is currently traditionally found based on copper wire. You can contrast this with Fast Ethernet and Gigabit Ethernet, which have been developed on both copper wire and fiberoptic cabling.

- **Fast Ethernet**—An improved version of Ethernet that also operates with a single wire with multiple stations. However, the major improvement is in the area of speed; Fast Ethernet operates at a speed of 100 Mbps.

- **Gigabit Ethernet**—Yet another version of Ethernet that allows for operational speeds of 1 Gbps. The functional differences between copper- and fiber-based Gigabit Ethernet can affect design and operation.

- **Token Ring**—One of the oldest "ring" access techniques that was originally proposed in 1969. It has multiple wires that connect stations by forming a ring and operates at speeds of 4 Mbps and 16 Mbps. Token Ring is mentioned here as a courtesy to IBM (its creator); it is rarely used today.

- **Fiber distributed data internetworking (FDDI)**—A dual fiberoptic ring that provides increased redundancy and reliability. FDDI operates at speeds of 100 Mbps. FDDI is still in use, but Gigabit Ethernet and Synchronous Optical Network (SONET), mentioned in the next section, might make FDDI obsolete.

Figure 1-6 shows a typical Ethernet LAN.

Figure 1-6   *Typical Ethernet LAN*

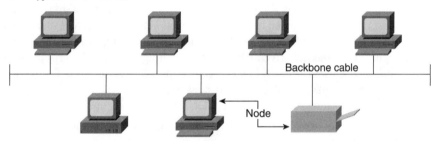

For further information on this subject, visit the following website:

www.ethermanage.com/ethernet/ethernet.html

Wide-Area Networks

WANs are used to connect physically separated applications, data, and resources, thereby extending the reach of your network to form an intranet. The ideal result is seamless access to remote resources from geographically separated end users. The most common types of WAN connectivity technologies include the following:

- **Frame Relay**—A good, connection-oriented, frame-switched protocol for connecting sites over a WAN. Frame Relay is a great solution for enterprise networks that require a multipoint WAN media.

- **Leased lines**—A dedicated connection from two distinct points that commonly uses the point-to-point protocol to provide various standards through encapsulation for IP traffic between serial links.

- **Asynchronous transfer mode (ATM)**—ATM is an International Telecommunications Union–Telecommunication Standardization Sector (ITU-T) standard for cell relay. Information is conveyed in small, fixed-size cells. ATM is a high-speed, low-delay multiplexing and switching technology that can support any type of user traffic, including voice, data, and video applications that are defined by the American National Standards Institute (ANSI) and International Telecommunication Union-Telecommunication Standardization Sector (ITU-T) standards committees for the transport of a broad range of user information. ATM is ideally suited to applications that cannot tolerate time delay, as well as for transporting IP traffic.

- **Integrated Systems Digital Network (ISDN)**—Consists of digital telephony and data transport services using digitization over a specialized telephone network. The future of ISDN is in question because of the development of digital subscriber line and cable modem technologies.

- **Digital subscriber line (DSL)**—An always-on Internet connection that is typically billed monthly, usually for a fixed price and unlimited usage. DSL, when installed as a wall socket, looks much like a phone socket. In the United States, the wall socket is, in fact, a phone socket and, for the popular residential type of DSL (asymmetric digital subscriber line [ADSL]), the phone wiring does indeed carry phone and data signals. The key advantage of DSL over dial-up modems is its speed. DSL is from several to dozens of times faster than a dial-up modem connection. DSL is also a great way to save money compared to pay-per-minute ISDN data lines or expensive T1 lines.

- **Cable modem**—Refers to a modem that operates over the ordinary cable TV network cables. Because the coaxial cable used by cable TV provides much greater bandwidth than telephone lines, a cable modem can be used to achieve extremely fast access to the World Wide Web. The term "Cable Modem" is a bit misleading, as a Cable Modem works more like a LAN interface than as a modem. Basically, you just connect the Cable Modem to the TV outlet for your cable TV, and the cable TV operator connects a Cable Modem Termination System (CMTS) in his end (the Head-End).

- **SONET**—An optical fiber-based network created by Bellcore in the mid-1980s. It is now an ANSI standard. The international equivalent of SONET is synchronous digital hierarchy (SDH). SONET defines interface standards at the physical layer of the OSI seven-layer model. The SONET ANSI standard defines a hierarchy of interface rates that allow data streams of different rates to be multiplexed from optical carrier (OC) levels, from 51.8 Mbps (about the same as a T-3 line) to 2.48 Gbps. The international equivalent of SONET, standardized by the ITU, is called SDH. SONET is considered to be the foundation for the physical layer of broadband ISDN (BISDN). Asynchronous transfer mode runs can also run on top of SONET as well as on top of other technologies.

- **Dense wave division multiplexing (DWDM)** — An optical multiplexing technique that is used to increase the carrying capacity of a fiber network beyond what can currently be accomplished by time-division multiplexing (TDM) techniques. DWDM replaces TDM as the most effective optical transmission method. Different wavelengths of light are used to transmit multiple streams of information along a single fiber with minimal interference. Using DWDM, up to 80 (and theoretically more) separate wavelengths or channels of data can be multiplexed into a light stream that is transmitted on a single optical fiber. DWDM is also sometimes called wave division multiplexing (WDM). Because each wavelength or channel is demultiplexed at the end of the transmission back into the original source, different data formats being transmitted at different data rates can be transmitted together. DWDM will allow SONET data and ATM data to be transmitted at the same time within the optical fiber.

These WAN technologies are only briefly covered in this book. However, their connectivity and protocol characteristics are compared. Figure 1-7 shows some of the basic differences and choices that are considered when switching is involved.

Figure 1-7   *Available WAN Technology Options*

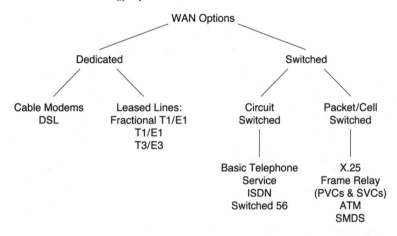

Table 1-3 summarizes the various carrier speeds and characteristics. This information is a good reference going forward and as the industry develops higher speeds.

Table 1-3 *Carrier Rates and Transmission Characteristics**

Digital Signal (DS) Name	Circuit Bit Rate	Number of DS0s Used	Equivalent T-Carrier Name	Equivalent E-Carrier Name
DS0	64 Kbps	1	-	-
DS1	1.544 Mbps	24	T-1	-
-	2.048 Mbps	32	-	E-1
DS1C	3.152 Mbps	48	-	-
DS2	6.312 Mbps	96	T-2	-
-	8.448 Mbps	128	-	E-2
-	34.368 Mbps	512	-	E-3
DS3	44.736 Mbps	672, or 28 DS1s	T-3	-
-	139.264 Mbps	2048	-	E-4
DS4/NA	139.264 Mbps	2176	-	-
DS4	274.176 Mbps	4032	-	-
-	565.148 Mbps	4 E-4 Channels	-	E-5
SONET Signal	**Bit Rate**	**SDH Signal**	**SONET Capacity**	**SDH Capacity**
OC–1 (STS-1)	51.84 Mbps	STM–0	28 DS–1s or 1 DS–3	21 E1s
OC–3 (STS-3)	155.52 Mbps	STM–1	84 DS–1s or 3 DS–3s	63 E1s or 1 E4
OC–12 (STS–12)	622.08 Mbps	STM–4	336 DS–1s or 12 DS–3s	252 E1s or 4 E4s
OC–48 (STS–48)	2.488 Gbps	STM–16	1344 DS–1s or 48 DS–3s	1008 E1s or 16 E4s
OC–192 (STS–192)	10 Gbps	STM–64	5376 DS–1s or 192 DS–3s	4032 E1s or 64 E4s
OC-256	13.271 Gbps	-	-	-
OC-768	40 Gbps	-	-	-

*STS-1 is electrical equivalent of OC-1

STS-1 = OC1 = 51.84 Mbps (base rate)

STS-3 = OC3 = STM-1 = 155 Mbps

STS-9 = OC9 = STM-3 = 9 times base rate (not used)

STS-12 = OC12 = STM-4 = 622 Mbps

STS-18 = OC18 = STM-6 = 18 times base rate (not used)

STS-24 = OC24 = STM-8 = 24 times base rate (not used)

STS-36 = 0C36 = STM-12 = 36 times base rate (not used)

STS-48 = OC48 = STM-16 = 2.5 Gbps

E1 = 32 64-kbps channels = 2.048 Mbps

E0 = 64 kbps

4 * E1 = E2

4 * E2 = E3

E3 = 34 Mbps in or around

STM = synchronous transport module (ITU–T)

STS = synchronous transfer signal (ANSI)

OC = optical carrier (ANSI)

Although an SDH STM–1 has the same bit rate as the SONET STS–3, the two signals contain different frame structures.

IP Addressing

This section discusses IP addressing methodology, basic subnetting, variable-length subnet masking (VLSM), and classless interdomain routing (CIDR).

In a properly designed and configured network, communication between hosts and servers is transparent. This is because each device that uses the TCP/IP protocol suite has a unique 32-bit IP address. A device reads the destination IP address in the packet and makes the appropriate routing decision based on this information. In this case, a device might be either the host or server using a default gateway or a router using its routing table to forward the packet to its destination. Regardless of what the device is, the communication is easily accomplished and transparent to the user as a result of proper IP addressing.

IP addresses can be represented as a group of four decimal numbers, each within the range of 0 to 255. Each of these four decimal numbers is separated by a decimal point. The method of displaying these numbers is known as *dotted decimal notation.* Note that these numbers can also be displayed in both the binary and hexadecimal numbering systems. Figure 1-8 illustrates the basic format of an IP address as determined by using dotted decimal notation.

Figure 1-8   *IP Address Format as Determined by Dotted Decimal Notation*

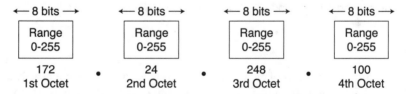

IP addresses have two primary logical components, network and host portions, the difference and use of which is extremely important. A third component, the *subnet,* is also used. A network address identifies the logical network and must be unique; if the network is to be a part of the Internet, the network must be assigned by American Registry for Internet Numbers (ARIN) in North America, Réseaux IP Européens (RIPE) in Europe, and Asia Pacific Network Information Centre (APNIC) in Asia. A host address, on the other hand, identifies a host (device) on a network and is assigned by a local administrator.

Consider a network that has been assigned an address of 172.24. An administrator then assigns a host the address of 248.100. The complete address of this host is 172.24.248.100. This address is unique because only one network and one host can have this address.

NOTE	In many cases when dealing with advanced networking topics such as OSPF, the latest trend is to write IP addresses as follows: x.x.x.x/8 or /16 or /24. This has become an accepted method of shorthand for IP addressing. The number to the right of the slash (/) represents the number of bits in the subnet mask.

Class A Addresses

In a Class A address (also known as /8), the first octet contains the network address and the other three octets make up the host address. The first bit of a Class A network address must be set to 0. Although mathematically it would appear that there are 128 possible Class A network addresses (the first bit is set to 0), the address 00000000 is not available, so there are only 127 such addresses. This number is further reduced because network 127.0.0.0 is reserved for loopback addressing purposes and 10.0.0.0 is a reserved private range. This means that only 126 Class A addresses are available for use. However, each Class A address can support 126 networks that correspond to 16,777,214 node addresses per Class A address.

NOTE	IP addresses or masks of either all 1s or all 0s in each octet are not usually allowed or used in a classful network implementation. The introduction of CIDR now allows most service providers to assign addresses in /19 or /20. Cisco has made exceptions in using all 1s or all 0s, but for this discussion, consider this practice as being not allowed.

Class B Addresses

In a Class B (also known as /16) address, the network component uses the first two octets for addressing purposes. The first 2 bits of a Class B address are always 10; that is, 1 and 0, not ten. The address range would then be 128.0.0.0 to 191.255.255.255. This makes available the first 6 bits of the first octet and all 8 bits of the second octet, thereby providing 16,384 possible Class B network addresses. The remaining octets are used to provide over 65,534 hosts per Class B address.

Class C Addresses

In a Class C (also known as /24) address, the first three octets are devoted to the network component. The first 3 bits of a Class C address must be 110. The address range would then be 192.0.0.0 to 223.255.255.255. This leaves 5 bits of the first octet and 8 bits of the second and third octets, thereby providing 2,097,152 possible Class C addresses. The node address is determined by the last octet, which provides 254 nodes per network.

Class D Addresses

Class D addresses are special addresses that do not refer to individual networks. The first 4 bits of these addresses are 1110. The address range would then be in the range of 224 to 239. Class D addresses are used for multicast packets, which are used by many different protocols to reach multiple groups of hosts (such as ICMP router discovery or Internet group membership protocol [IGMP], which is gaining in popularity since its release in Cisco IOS Software Release 11.2).

Consider these addresses as being preprogrammed within the logical structure of most network components in that when they see a destination address of this type within a packet, the address triggers a response. For example, if a host sends a packet out to the destination IP address 224.0.0.5, all routers (using OSPF) on this address's Ethernet segment respond.

Class E Addresses

Addresses in the range of 240.0.0.0 to 255.255.255.255 are termed Class E addresses. The first octet of these addresses begins with the bits 1111. These addresses are reserved for future additions to the IP addressing scheme. These future additions might or might not come to fruition with the advent of IP version 6 (IPv6).

In most networks, the assigned IP addresses have been broken into parts that logically relate to different areas. For example, part of an IP address identifies a particular network, part identifies a subnet (that is, subnetwork), and part identifies a specific host within that subnetwork (that is, a subnet).

The following three blocks of IP address space for private networks have been reserved according to RFC 1918, "Address Allocation for Private Internets":

- **10.0.0.0–10.255.255.255**—Single Class A network numbers
- **172.16.0.0–172.31.255.255**—Contiguous Class B network numbers
- **192.168.0.0–192.168.255.255**—Contiguous Class C network numbers

NOTE	You can also write these three networks as 10/8, 172.16/12, and 192.168/16, using the slash method to represent the address.

How IP Addresses Are Used

Routers examine the most significant or left-most bit of the first octet when determining the class of a network address. This technique of reading IP addresses (also known as the *first octet rule*) is discussed further as the different classes of addresses are defined.

Table 1-4 provides information regarding the different IP address classes. Note that in the format column, N equals the network number and H equals the host number. Also, for Class A addresses, one address is reserved for the broadcast address and one address is reserved for the network.

Table 1-4   *IP Address Quick-Reference Information*

Class	Format	Purpose	High-Order Bit	Address Range	Network/Host Bits	Maximum Number of Hosts
A	N.H.H.H	Large organizations	0	1.0.0.0–126.255.255.255	7/24	16,777,214 $(2^{24} - 2)$
B	N.N.H.H	Medium organizations	10	128.0.0.0–191.255.255.255	14/16	65,534 $(2^{16} - 2)$
C	N.N.N.H	Small organizations	110	192.0.0.0–223.255.255.255	22/8	254 $(2^{8} - 2)$
D	N/A	Multicast	1110	224.0.0.0–239.255.255.255	N/A	N/A
E	N/A	Experimental	11110	240.0.0.0–254.255.255.255	N/A	N/A

Tables 1-5 through 1-7 list the number of hosts and subnets for Class A, B, and C IP addresses. For the subnets and hosts, all 0s and 1s are excluded.

Table 1-5   *Host/Subnet Quantities for Class A IP Addresses*

Number of Bits	Subnet Mask	Effective Subnets	Effective Hosts
2	255.192.0.0	2	4,194,302
3	255.224.0.0	6	2,097,150
4	255.240.0.0	14	1,048,574
5	255.248.0.0	30	524,286
6	255.252.0.0	62	262,142
7	255.254.0.0	126	131,070
8	255.255.0.0	254	65,534

Table 1-5   *Host/Subnet Quantities for Class A IP Addresses (Continued)*

Number of Bits	Subnet Mask	Effective Subnets	Effective Hosts
9	255.255.128.0	510	32,766
10	255.255.192.0	1022	16,382
11	255.255.224.0	2046	8190
12	255.255.240.0	4094	4094
13	255.255.248.0	8190	2046
14	255.255.252.0	16,382	1022
15	255.255.254.0	32,766	510
16	255.255.255.0	65,534	254
17	255.255.255.128	131,070	126
18	255.255.255.192	262,142	62
19	255.255.255.224	524,286	30
20	255.255.255.240	1,048,574	14
21	255.255.255.248	2,097,150	6
22	255.255.255.252	4,194,302	2

Table 1-6   *Host/Subnet Quantities for Class B IP Addresses*

Number of Bits	Subnet Mask	Effective Subnets	Effective Hosts
2	255.255.192.0	2	16,382
3	255.255.224.0	6	8190
4	255.255.240.0	14	4094
5	255.255.248.0	30	2046
6	255.255.252.0	62	1022
7	255.255.254.0	126	510
8	255.255.255.0	254	254
9	255.255.255.128	510	126
10	255.255.255.192	1022	62
11	255.255.255.224	2046	30
12	255.255.255.240	4094	14
13	255.255.255.248	8190	6
14	255.255.255.252	16,382	2

Table 1-7 *Host/Subnet Quantities for Class C IP Addresses*

Number of Bits	Subnet Mask	Effective Subnets	Effective Hosts
2	255.255.255.192	2	62
3	255.255.255.224	6	30
4	255.255.255.240	14	14
5	255.255.255.248	30	6
6	255.255.255.252	62	2

NOTE   You can derive the maximum number of hosts in each of the address classes by doing the following calculation: N.H.H.H for H * H * H = total number of hosts, where (256 * 256 * 256) – 2 = 16 million, N is the network number, and H is the host. (The calculation actually results in 16,777,214 but is rounded to 16 million.)

Figure 1-9 shows the various IP address classes by network and host components.

Figure 1-9   *IP Addresses by Class*

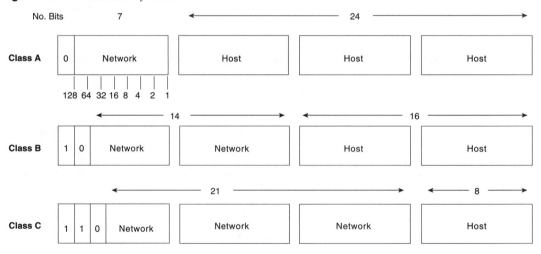

The IP addresses that are assigned to most networks have been broken into parts that logically relate to the different areas of each network. For example, part of an IP address identifies a particular network, part identifies a subnet (that is, a subnetwork), and part identifies a specific host within that subnetwork (that is, a host).

Role of IP Addresses

IP uses a hierarchical addressing structure. A router simply sends the packet to the next hop in the route to reach its destination. For example, if a packet has a destination IP address of 172.24.50.10, the router begins with the first octet (172) and searches its routing tables for it. When a match is found, the router then adds the next octet (24) to its search until enough information is learned so that the router can send the packet to its next destination. This router behavior is known as the *longest match rule*.

If the router does not have enough information to route the packet, the packet is dropped. Routers make their hierarchical decisions based on the network and host components of an IP address, as demonstrated in Figure 1-10.

Figure 1-10   *Example of a Hierarchical IP Address*

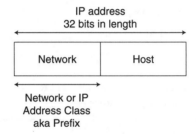

Another good example of the hierarchical addressing technique used by routers is your phone number. For example, if the phone number 919-779-*xxxx* is dialed, the phone system knows that 919 is located in North Carolina, 779 is in the Raleigh area, and the last four numbers are assigned to a residence. An interesting side note here is that the telephone system is also running out of numbers, hence the implementation of the new toll-free extension, 888. Even in the use of phone numbers, you can see how technology has depleted the "bank" of possible numbers as a result of the use of modems, pagers, cellular phones, personal 800 numbers, and multiple phone lines in a residence.

How IP Addresses Are Read

Routers examine the most significant or left-most bit of the first octet when determining the class of a network address. This technique of reading IP addresses (also known as the *first octet rule*) is discussed further as the different classes of addresses are defined.

A router usually has an interface to which it connects. This interface is assigned an IP address and subnet mask. Devices trying to reach a host within the network that are assigned to that interface are routed through the interface. For example, consider a Token

Ring interface with an IP address of 172.24.248.100. The router knows that packets going into or coming out of network 172.24.0.0 need to interact with this interface.

IP Subnet Addressing

The need for subnetting has resulted in the massive growth of networks in the past decade. As the available address space rapidly continues to shrink, network managers need to use the existing space more efficiently; hence, subnetting was born.

Additional benefits to using subnetting are as follows:

- Efficient use of available network addresses
- Flexibility in planning network growth and design
- Capability to contain broadcast traffic
- Availability of local administrative control

NOTE   *Broadcast traffic* is defined as data packets that are sent to all nodes on a network. Broadcasts are identified by a broadcast address of all 1s.

To better understand subnets, consider them to be extensions of the network number. Essentially, you are reassigning part of what is officially the host address space to act as an additional network address.

Use the following steps to assign addresses in a subnetted network:

Step 1   Define the subnet mask.

Step 2   Assign an address to each subnet.

Step 3   Assign IP addresses to each node.

In many organizations, subnets divide one large network into a number of smaller networks. For example, the previously mentioned Class B network (172.24.0.0) can be subdivided into 256 subnets: 172.24.0.0, 172.24.1.0, 172.24.2.0, and so on. Each subnet would have 254 hosts per subnet.

NOTE   According to RFC 1812, Section 5.3.5.3, all-subnet broadcast is no longer supported, so an all 1s subnet is now allowed.

Subnet Masking

Subnet masks use the same representation technique that regular IP addresses use. However, the subnet mask has binary 1s in all bits that specify the network field. Essentially, a subnet mask is a 32-bit number that is applied to an IP address to override the default network or node address convention. The subnet mask also tells the router which octets of an IP address to pay attention to when comparing the destination address of a packet to its routing table.

For example, for the subnet 172.24.1.0 to be properly configured, you must apply a mask of 255.255.255.0. This gives you a complete IP subnet address of 172.24.1.0255.255.255.0. If you were to then apply this to an Ethernet interface of a router, and a packet came into the router with a destination address of 172.24.1.30, the router would be able to route the packet appropriately because it knows (through the assigned IP address and mask) that any packet destined for the network 172.24.1.0 is to be sent out the router's Ethernet interface.

All class addresses have default subnet masks because the subnet bits come from the high-order bits of the host field. The following list provides the default subnet masks that are used for each class of IP address:

- **Class A** — 255.0.0.0 default mask
- **Class B** — 255.255.0.0 default mask
- **Class C** — 255.255.255.0 default mask

These default masks have a binary 1 in every position that corresponds to the default network address component of the appropriate IP address class.

Now that you are familiar with the technical explanation of subnet masking, further discussion is in terms that are easier to understand. The most important thing to remember about subnet masks is that you cannot assign IP addresses with no consideration. The question then becomes, "Why should I use subnetting on my network?" You should do so to route across your network. Then you might ask, "Why route?" Complicated and convoluted, isn't it?

For the purpose of this discussion, assume that you have a large Ethernet segment that is so full of users that the collisions occurring on it are negatively impacting the users' and the segments' performance. The easy fix is to use a bridge that enables you to split the network but retain connectivity. The problem here is that bridges use MAC addresses to make decisions on where to forward packets. However, if the bridge does not know where to send a packet, it resorts to broadcasting it to everyone. Your slow, busy Ethernet segment will have been split into two segments; your network performance should increase as a result. The problem is that as you begin to connect more segments, you end up with broadcasts flowing all across the network to the point that the intranet might come to a standstill. Large amounts of broadcasts, such as those described here, are typically called *broadcast storms,* which are a bad thing. What is needed is a piece of hardware with more intelligence — the router, which can segment multiple broadcast domains.

In general terms, the router connects multiple networks and makes decisions on if it should forward packets based on the packets' addresses. The router has been designed to drop all packets if it does not know where to forward them; hence, there are no more out-of-control broadcasts.

For example, suppose you have network 172.24.0.0 out interface #1 of your router and network 10.37.0.0 out interface #2. First, IP addresses must be assigned to each router interface—assume xxx.xxx.1.1—and at least one PC would need to be on each network. Figure 1-11 demonstrates this scenario.

Figure 1-11 *Basic Subnetting Example*

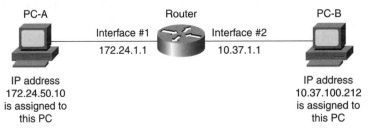

A router does not learn about every available address. Instead, the router believes that if interface 1 has an IP address of 172.24.1.1255.255.0.0, all packets destined for the 172.24.0.0 network must be located on that interface. To recap, if the router receives a packet that is not destined to either of the networks it knows about (in this case, 172.24.0.0 or 10.37.0.0), that packet is dropped (erased) from the router's memory.

If PC A is trying to communicate with PC B, the packet's destination IP address will be 10.37.100.212. So, how does the router know that this IP address is located in the same network as the IP address that is assigned to its interface (10.37.1.1)? Simply put, the subnet mask must be entered. Therefore, when you assign the IP address 10.37.1.1 to interface 2, you must also specify a subnet mask.

TIP   Every interface in a router must be assigned a local subnet mask. Fortunately, Cisco routers do not accept an IP address without a mask.

If you assigned a subnet mask of 255.255.0.0 to interface 2, you are telling the router when it needs to make a routing decision on a packet if the first two octets of the destination IP address match (10.37). The router then forwards the packet out interface 2. This is because, when designing a subnet mask, 255 in a subnet mask indicates that the router needs an exact match, whereas 0 means that this octet's value is not important.

If you give that interface a subnet mask of 255.255.255.0, you are telling the router to look only at the first three octets of the destination IP address when it needs to make a routing decision. This is because, as previously discussed, the first three octets for a natural Class C address define the network number.

You can use subnet masks in different ways to segment your network, but that goes beyond the scope of this book. If you are interested in learning more about basic subnetting techniques, refer to the RFCs that are mentioned in the next section. Before moving on, you must be aware of some restrictions when using subnets.

Subnetting Restrictions

Typically, you run into several restrictions in a traditional subnetted network,; however, when using VLSM along with a protocol that supports VLSM (such as OSPF or Border Gateway Protocol [BGP]) several of these restrictions disappear. However, if older, non-VLSM routing protocols (such as Routing Information Protocol [RIP] Version 1) are in use, these restrictions must still be observed.

For identical subnet masks, a router assumes that the subnet mask, which has been configured, is valid for all subnets. Therefore, a single mask must be used for all subnets within a network. Different masks can be used for different networks.

A subnetted network cannot be split into isolated portions because all subnets must be contiguous. Within a network, all subnets must be able to reach all other subnets without passing traffic through other networks.

For further discussion or examples on this topic, refer to the following sources:

- RFC 791, "Internet Protocol"
- RFC 950, "Internet Standard Subnetting Procedure"
- RFC 1219, "On the Assignment of Subnet Numbers"
- RFC 1700, "Assigned Numbers"
- RFC 1918, "Address Allocation for Private Internets"

You can find all RFCs online at the following website:

www.isi.edu/in-notes/rfc*xxxx*.txt

where *xxxx* is the number of the RFC.

Explaining the Need for VLSM and CIDR

VLSM is defined as the capability to specify a different subnet mask for the same network number on different subnets. VLSM can help optimize available address space.

CIDR is a technique that is supported by BGP-4 and based on route aggregation. CIDR enables routers to group routes to reduce the quantity of routing information that is carried by the core routers. With CIDR, several IP networks appear to networks outside the group as a single, larger entity.

Why are VLSM and CIDR needed? This answer is this: IP address depletion. This means that the current IP address scheme, which is known as IPv4, is beginning to run out of IP addresses. This is an unacceptable situation that many network engineers deal with every day. CIDR and VLSM are only interim solutions but are nonetheless effective. CIDR was needed because too many specific network numbers were filling the Internet routing table a few years ago. CIDR was invented to solve this problem and save the Internet from collapse.

NOTE   Not only is address depletion an issue, but also many networks are faced with large routing tables that need to be reduced in size to enable smoother network and router operation.

When this addressing scheme was first designed many years ago, the engineers most likely believed that it would be sufficient. Nevertheless, the recent explosive growth of the Internet and corporate intranets has made new technology and strategies necessary to deal with this looming problem. The situation becomes even more critical when you consider that corporations of all sizes are beginning to use the Internet as a means of revenue. It's an exciting time for our field when you consider that less than fifteen years ago, computers and networks were things of ponderous size with only specific applications. This is a time of constant change and advancement, and it is interesting to consider what the world of technology will be like for the next generation.

One of the most interesting enhancements on the horizon is IP version 6 (IPv6), also known as IP next generation (IPng), which is in its developmental stage. This is a move to improve the existing IPv4 implementation, which is quickly reaching critical mass. The proposal was released in July 1992 at the Boston Internet Engineering Task Force (IETF) meeting. IPv6 tackles issues such as the IP address depletion problem, quality of service capabilities, address autoconfiguration, authentication, and security capabilities.

NOTE   IPv6 is shipping today in Cisco IOS Software Release 12.2 T. Visit the following website: www.cisco.com/warp/public/cc/pd/iosw/prodlit/pfgrn_qp.htm

Because these issues are facing us in the here and now, it is in response to these concerns that the technologies of VLSM and CIDR were developed. Not only do these techniques enable us to better use the remaining IP addresses, but also they have enabled large networks to continue growing without the routers becoming saturated by the various routes within the network. A prime example of this is the Internet. This example will be discussed in further detail, but keep it in mind as you read through these sections.

Several items used within the discussions of VLSM and CIDR are important to discuss before preceding any further.

Route Summarization

Route summarization, also known as *aggregation* or *supernetting,* is a method of representing a series of network numbers in a single summary address that is advertised to other routers. For example, assume that a router knows about the following networks that are attached to it:

      172.24.100.0/24
      172.24.101.0/24
      172.24.102.0/24
      172.24.103.0/24

The router would summarize that information to other routers by saying "I know how to get to these networks in the summarization 172.24.100.0/22." Subnetting essentially extends the prefix to the right by making the router know a specific IP addresses; summarization, on the other hand, reduces the prefix to the left, thereby enabling the router to advertise only the higher-order bits. Figure 1-12 demonstrates how subnetting and route summarization differ.

Figure 1-12 *Comparison of Subnetting and Route Summarization*

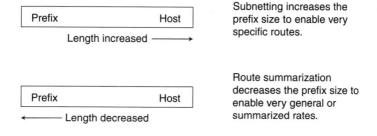

TIP   Refer to Chapter 3 of Cisco's "Internetwork Design Guide" for an overview that describes the best practices concerning summarization. You can also visit the following website:
      www.cisco.com/univercd/cc/td/doc/cisintwk/idg4/

An example of route summarization is CIDR, which is discussed in detail later in this chapter. The following requirements enable route summarization to work properly:

- Multiple IP addresses must share the same high-order bit to be properly summarized.

- Routing tables and protocols must base their routing decisions on a normal 32-bit IP address and a variable prefix length.

- Routing protocols must carry this prefix (such as /16, which translates into a 255.255.0.0 mask) with the 32-bit IP address in the routing table.

- Remember, not all routing protocols can carry a subnet mask; those that don't are referred to as *classful routing protocols.* The following sections discuss classful and classless routing protocols.

Classful Routing

Classful routing always summarizes routes by the major network numbers. RIP and Interior Gateway Routing Protocol (IGRP) are protocols that use this type of routing. They are called classful because they always consider the network class. This automatic summarization is always done at network boundaries.

Impact of Classful Routing

The use of classful routing has some considerable impact on a network. For one thing, subnets are not advertised to a different major network. In addition, noncontiguous subnets are not visible to each other. Figure 1-13 illustrates how classful routing and subnetting can affect your network.

Certain techniques have been developed to assist in overcoming this problem: IP unnumbered, secondary addressing, and using OSPF. Further discussion of classful routing and the issues surrounding its use (that is, discontiguous subnets) are beyond the scope of this book.

Figure 1-13 *How Classful Routing and Subnetting Affect the Network*

Each router has a subnet that it attaches to,
but in a classful environment, they cannot
and will not be advertised because the subnets
are not on a classful boundary

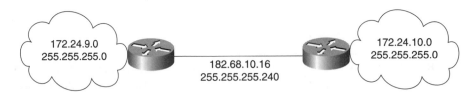

172.24.9.0
255.255.255.0

182.68.10.16
255.255.255.240

172.24.10.0
255.255.255.0

Classless Routing

Classless routing differs from classful routing in that the prefix length is transmitted. This prefix length is evaluated at each place it is encountered throughout the network. In other words, it can be changed to advertise routes differently at different locations within a network. This capability of classless routing enables more efficient use of IP address space and reduces routing traffic. A good example of this type of routing is OSPF. Classless routing has the following characteristics:

- One routing entry might match a block of host, subnet, or network addresses.
- Routing tables can be much shorter.

- Switching performance can be faster unless Cisco express forwarding (CEF) is used.
- Routing protocol traffic is reduced.

VLSMs

The basic concept of VLSMs is to provide more flexibility by dividing a network into multiple subnets. The trick to using this technique is ensuring that you have an adequate number of hosts allocated per subnet.

NOTE   Not every protocol supports VLSM. If you decide to implement VLSM, make sure that you are using a VLSM-capable routing protocol, such as OSPF, BGP, Enhanced IGRP (EIGRP), Intermediate System-to-Intermediate System (IS-IS), and RIP Version 2 (RIP-2).

OSPF and static routes support VLSMs. With VLSMs, you can use different masks for the same network number on different interfaces, which enables you to conserve IP addresses for better efficiency. VLSMs do this by allowing both big subnets and small subnets. As previously mentioned, you need to ensure that the number of hosts is sufficient for your needs within each subnet.

In Example 1-1, a 30-bit subnet mask is used, leaving 2 bits of address space reserved for serial line host addresses. There is sufficient host address space for two host endpoints on a point-to-point serial link.

Example 1-1   *VLSM Demonstration*

```
interface ethernet 0
ip address 131.107.1.1 255.255.255.0
! 8 bits of host address space reserved for Ethernet hosts
interface serial 0
ip address 131.107.254.1 255.255.255.252
! 2 bits of address space reserved for serial lines
! System is configured for OSPF and assigned 107 as the process number
router ospf 107
! Specifies network directly connected to the system
network 131.107.0.0 0.0.255.255 area 0.0.0.0
```

As Example 1-1 demonstrates, VLSM is efficient when used on serial lines because each line requires a distinct subnet number, even though each line has two host addresses. This requirement wastes subnet numbers. However, if you use VLSM to address serial links in a core router, you can save space. In Figure 1-14, the regular subnet 172.24.10.0 is further subnetted with 6 additional bits. These additional subnets make 63 additional subnets available. VLSM also enables the routes within the core to be summarized as 172.24.10.0.

Figure 1-14 *VLSM Conserves Subnets*

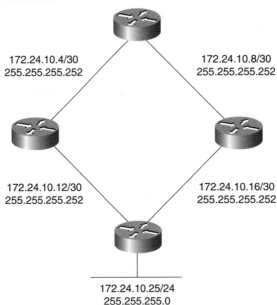

172.24.10.4/30
255.255.255.252

172.24.10.8/30
255.255.255.252

172.24.10.12/30
255.255.255.252

172.24.10.16/30
255.255.255.252

172.24.10.25/24
255.255.255.0

Most early networks never had their IP addresses assigned to them in a way that would enable network engineers to group them in blocks. Instead, they had been assigned as needed, so massive renumbering projects would need to be performed—not one of the most popular pastimes of anyone involved in networking. However, although hindsight is 20/20, remember the past when considering the future and newer technology, such as IPv6. Otherwise, you might end up doing quite a lot of static routing and odd configuring just to keep your network stable.

VLSM Design Guidelines and Techniques

To assist you when designing the use of VLSM within your network, consider the following guidelines:

- Optimal summarization occurs with contiguous blocks of addresses.

- If small subnets are grouped, routing information can be summarized.

- Group VLSM subnets so that routing information can be consolidated.

- Allocate VLSM by taking one regular subnet and subnetting it further.

- Avoid using two different classful subnet masks inside a given network address.

In conclusion, you might ask yourself why there are questions about implementing VLSM. As previously mentioned, VLSM is not supported by every protocol, although it is supported by OSPF, EIGRP, ISIS, and RIP-2. So these newer protocols might have to coexist with older protocols that do not support VLSM and would have trouble routing. In addition, the use of VLSM can be difficult. If it is not properly designed, it can cause the network to not operate properly, and it increases the complexity of troubleshooting any network.

CIDR

VLSM was a step up from subnetting because it relayed subnet information through routing protocols. This idea leads directly into this section on CIDR, which is documented in the following RFCs: 1517, 1518, 1519, and 1520. CIDR is an effective method to stem the tide of IP address allocation as well as routing table overflow. Without the implementation of CIDR in 1994 and 1995 in RFC 1817, the Internet would not be functioning today because the routing tables would have been too large for the routers to handle.

The primary requirement for CIDR is the use of routing protocols that support it, such as RIP-2, OSPFv2, and BGP-4. CIDR can be thought of as advanced subnetting. The subnetting mask, previously a number with special significance, becomes an integral part of routing tables and protocols. A route is no longer just an IP address that has been interpreted according to its class with the corresponding network and host bits.

Validating a CIDRized Network

The routing tables within the Internet have been growing as fast as the Internet itself. This growth has caused an overwhelming utilization of Internet routers' processing power and memory utilization, consequently resulting in saturation.

Between 1988 and 1991, the Internet's routing tables doubled in size every 10 months. This growth would have resulted in about 80,000 routes by 1995. Routers would have required approximately 25 MB of dedicated RAM to keep track of them all, and this is just for routers with a single peer. Through the implementation of CIDR, the number of routes in 1996 was about 42,000. Today, the routing table is about 100,000 routes at the core of the Internet. Without CIDR to aggregate these routes, the routing table size of a BGP-speaking router would be approximately 775,000 routes. This would shut down most common BGP-speaking routers due to memory utilization requirements, and the CPU would be degraded.

The major benefit of CIDR is that it enables continuous, uninterrupted growth of large networks. CIDR enables routers to group routes to reduce the quantity of routing information that is carried by a network's routers. With CIDR, several IP networks appear to networks outside the group as a single, larger entity. CIDR eliminates the concept of Class A, B, and C networks and replaces this concept with a generalized IP prefix.

Some of the benefits of using CIDR within your network are as follows:

- Reduces the local administrative burden of updating external route information
- Saves routing table space in routers by using route aggregation

- Reduces route-flapping and convergence issues
- Reduces CPU and memory load on a router
- Enables the delegation of network numbers to customers or other portions of the network
- Increases efficiency in the use of available address space

What Do Those Slashes Mean?

The terms /16 and /24 refer to the number of bits of the network part of the IP address. A former Class B address might appear as 172.24.0.0/16, which is the same as 256 Class Cs, which can appear as 192.200.0.0/16. A single Class C appears as 192.201.1.0/24 when using CIDR. This new look to IP addresses consists of an IP address and a mask length. A mask length is often called an *IP prefix*. The mask length specifies the number of left-most contiguous significant bits in the corresponding IP address.

For example, the CIDRized IP address of 172.24.0.0/16 indicates that you are using 172.24.0.0255.255.0.0. The /16 is an indication that you are using 16 bits of the mask when counting from the far left. Figure 1-15 demonstrates how CIDR defines its mask.

Figure 1-15 *Example of CIDR Addressing*

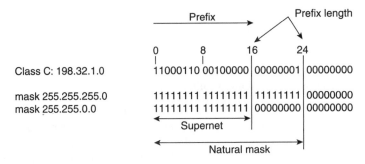

Important CIDR Terms

A network is called a supernet when the IP prefix contains fewer bits than the network's natural mask. For example, the Class C address 200.34.5.0 has a natural mask of 255.255.255.0. This address can also be represented in CIDR terms as 200.34.0.0/16. Therefore, because the natural mask is 24 bits and the CIDR mask is 16 bits (16 – 24), this network is referred to as a *supernet*. Simply put, supernets have an IP prefix that is shorter than the natural mask.

This enables the more specific contiguous networks—such as 200.34.5.0, 200.34.6.0, and 200.34.7.0—to be summarized into the one CIDR advertisement, which is referred to as an *aggregate.* Simply put, aggregates indicate any summary route. Figure 1-16 demonstrates how CIDR can be used to benefit your network by reducing routing tables.

Figure 1-16   *Example of CIDR Benefits on Routing Tables*

IP Classless

Use IP classless in your routers and use a default route inside your autonomous system. The **ip classless** command prevents the existence of a single subnet route from blocking access through the default route to other subnets. For those of you who are running Cisco IOS Software Release 12.0 and later, IP classless is enabled by default. IP classless causes the router to forward packets that are destined for unknown subnets to the best supernet route possible, instead of dropping them. In other words, if a specific route is not available, a less-specific route will be taken, provided that one exists. This is opposite to the old classful idea, in which if a specific route did not exist, the packets were dropped.

CIDR Translation Table

Table 1-8 provides basic CIDR information.

Table 1-8   *CIDR Translation Table*

CIDR	Dotted Decimal Format	Inverse Dotted Decimal Format
/1	128.0.0.0	127.255.255.255
/2	192.0.0.0	63.255.255.255
/3	224.0.0.0	31.255.255.255
/4	240.0.0.0	15.255.255.255
/5	248.0.0.0	7.255.255.255
/6	252.0.0.0	3.255.255.255
/7	254.0.0.0	1.255.255.255
/8	255.0.0.0	0.255.255.255
/9	255.128.0.0	0.127.255.255

Table 1-8 *CIDR Translation Table (Continued)*

CIDR	Dotted Decimal Format	Inverse Dotted Decimal Format
/10	255.192.0.0	0.63.255.255
/11	255.224.0.0	0.31.255.255
/12	255.240.0.0	0.15.255.255
/13	255.248.0.0	0.7.255.255
/14	255.252.0.0	0.3.255.255
/15	255.254.0.0	0.1.255.255
/16	255.255.0.0	0.0.255.255
/17	255.255.128.0	0.0.127.255
/18	255.255.192.0	0.0.63.255
/19	255.255.224.0	0.0.31.255
/20	255.255.240.0	0.0.15.255
/21	255.255.248.0	0.0.7.255
/22	255.255.252.0	0.0.3.255
/23	255.255.254.0	0.0.1.255
/24	255.255.255.0	0.0.0.255
/25	255.255.255.128	0.0.0.127
/26	255.255.255.192	0.0.0.63
/27	255.255.255.224	0.0.0.31
/28	255.255.255.240	0.0.0.15
/29	255.255.255.248	0.0.0.7
/30	255.255.255.252	0.0.0.3
/31	255.255.255.254	0.0.0.1
/32	255.255.255.255	0.0.0.0

Manually Computing the Value of a CIDR IP Prefix

To manually compute the CIDR IP prefix, refer to the following example, with a 5-bit-long subnet:

166.38.0.0/19

Compute the CIDR IP prefix as follows:

1 The four octets represent 32 bits.

2 This example is using only 19 bits.

3 The first two octets use 16 bits. The third octet uses only 3 bits. Five remaining bits are not used, as follows:

128	64	32	16	8	4	2	1
x	x	x	1	1	1	1	1

4 Add the remaining 5 bits using the binary conversion: $16 + 8 + 4 + 2 + 1 = 31$.

5 Add 31 to the octet, where the value was computed from $(0 + 31 = 31)$.

6 The final output of this CIDR block is 166.38.0.0 through 166.38.31.255.

Case Study: VLSMs

In 1987, RFC 1009 was published with the purpose of specifying how a subnetted network could use more than one subnet mask. As discussed earlier in this chapter, when an IP network is assigned more than one subnet mask, it is considered a network with variable-length subnet masks because the subnet masks (prefixes) have varying lengths.

If you recall, the use of VLSM brings benefits to a network and routing that allow for increased routing optimization in the form of a smaller and more concise routing table, known as route aggregation, as well as more efficient use of an organization's assigned IP address space.

A /16 network with a /22 extended-network prefix permits 64 subnets (2^6), each of which supports a maximum of 1022 hosts ($2^{10}\times2$). See Figure 1-17.

Figure 1-17 *Using a VLSM Extended-Network Prefix*

This is fine if the organization wants to deploy a number of large subnets, but what about the occasional small subnet that contains only 20 or 30 hosts? Because a subnetted network could have only a single mask, the network administrator was still required to assign the 20 or 30 hosts to a subnet with a 22-bit prefix. This assignment would waste approximately 1000 IP host addresses for each small subnet deployed. Limiting the association of a network number with a single mask did not encourage the flexible and efficient use of an organization's address space.

One solution to this problem was to allow a subnetted network to alter its subnet mask through the use of VLSM. Assume that in Figure 1-17, the network administrator is allowed to configure the 130.5.0.0/16 network with a /26 extended-network prefix. See Figure 1-18.

Figure 1-18   *Considerably Extending the Network Prefix with VLSM*

A /16 network address with a /26 extended-network prefix permits 1024 subnets (2^{10}), each of which supports a maximum of 62 hosts ($2^{6\times2}$). The /26 prefix would be ideal for small subnets with less than 60 hosts, while the /22 prefix is well suited for larger subnets containing up to 1000 hosts. This is VLSM in action, that is, several different masks in use within a network. The next section takes a look at how you can take an IP address range and subnet it into many different sizes so that you can meet the needs of every part of your organization.

Route Aggregation

VLSM also allows the recursive division of an organization's address space so that it can be reassembled and aggregated to reduce the amount of routing information at the top level. Conceptually, a network number is first divided into subnets, some of the subnets are further divided into sub-subnets, and those are further divided as well. This allows the detailed structure of routing information for one subnet group to be hidden from routers in another subnet group.

In Figure 1-19, the 11.0.0.0/8 network is first configured with a /16 extended-network prefix. The 11.1.0.0/16 subnet is then configured with a /24 extended-network prefix, and the 11.253.0.0/16 subnet is configured with a /19 extended-network prefix. Note that the recursive process does not require the same extended-network prefix to be assigned at each level of the recursion. Also, the recursive subdivision of the organization's address space can be carried out as far as the network administrator needs to take it.

Figure 1-19   *Dividing a Network Prefix with VLSM*

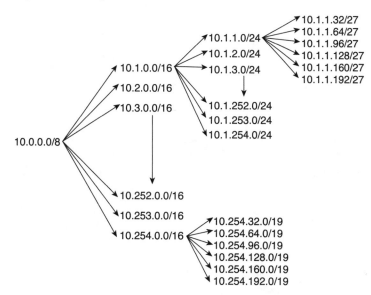

Figure 1-20 illustrates how a planned and thoughtful allocation of VLSM can reduce the size of an organization's routing tables and conserve IP address space. Notice how Routers F and G are able to summarize the six subnets behind them into a single advertisement (10.1.1.0/24 and 10.1.2.0/24, respectively) and how Router B (10.254.0.0/26) is able to aggregate all the subnets behind it into a single advertisement. Likewise, Router C is able to summarize the six subnets behind it into a single advertisement (10.1.0.0/16). Finally, the subnet structure is not visible outside of the organization, because through the use of VLSM and aggregation, Router A injects a single route into the global Internet's routing table—10.0.0.0/8 (or 10/8).

Figure 1-20   *VLSM in Action*

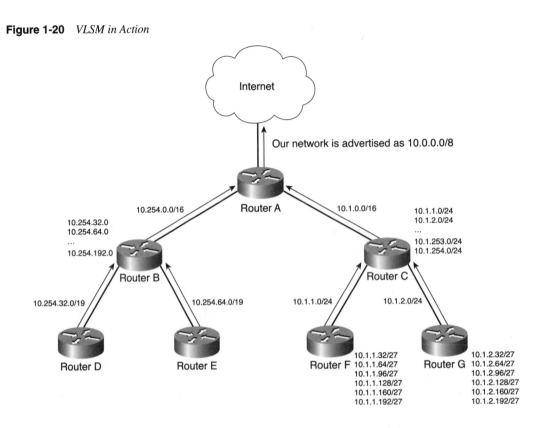

Summary

This chapter was either a quick foundation or a brief review on the fundamentals of networking and routing. All networks require a certain amount of common information with which to operate. Early discussion focused on learning about the structure of networking as found in the OSI reference model. Upon this structure, the TCP/IP protocol suite was presented; this protocol suite is the de facto communication standard of the Internet.

The discussion about IP addressing provided an overview of how addresses are classified. Several commonly used techniques were presented to help you better manage your IP addresses: subnet masking, VLSM, and CIDR. You also learned about the physical layout of networks. This chapter also established the physical foundations and needs for past, current, and future networks.

CHAPTER 2

Introduction to OSPF

It seems appropriate in this chapter to share with you a caption from a small picture that my wife gave me when we celebrated our 13th wedding anniversary. I keep it on my desk to remind myself of the "bigger picture." My daughter also likes it because it has a picture of a family of dolphins swimming, and it struck a chord that I felt was essential to have in my life:

The Essence of Family—from the Successories Collection

The family is a harbor of safety in an ocean of change. It is an association established in nature and guided by enduring principles of fellowship. It is where we first learn our potential, and face our responsibilities. In this kinship we find the strength to swim together and, eventually, the courage to swim apart.

This chapter introduces you to Open Shortest Path First (OSPF), a link-state routing protocol. You should know how to define a routing protocol and understand which protocol is best to use in your network. The purpose of this book is to teach you how to use and implement OSPF as the protocol of choice. However, you must also take an objective view of OSPF to understand why it is the best choice.

This chapter helps you understand the basic types of routing protocols, their characteristics, when it is best to use a certain protocol, and how to use that information to build a deeper understanding of how to implement routing protocols in your network. I wish every network used OSPF. However, each network has it own needs, but OSPF can almost always meet them. This chapter covers the following objectives:

- **What is a routing protocol?**—This section discusses fundamental portions of understanding routing protocols, beginning with the difference between routed and routing protocols. You also learn about distance vector protocols and how they operate. In addition, this section extensively discusses the fundamentals of link-state protocols because OSPF falls within this category of protocols.

- **Selecting a routing protocol**—One of the most practical objectives required by all network designers is the ability to understand how to select a routing protocol. This section presents this information, comparing and contrasting three different routing protocols using real-world concerns.

- **OSPF overview and functional environment**—This section discusses the earliest appearance and creation of the shortest path first (SPF) algorithm and its evolution into the OSPF routing protocol. This functional environment of OSPF is a key element in understanding OSPF. It is within this environment that all discussions are based. This section discusses the following basic aspects of where and how OSPF functions:
    - Network types
    - Router identification
    - Adjacencies
    - Designated routers
    - Protocols within OSPF
    - Link-state advertisements
- **OSPF routing hierarchy**—OSPF's capability to perform as a hierarchical routing protocol makes it a good candidate in many large networks. As a result of this capability, OSPF supports a variety of techniques and designations that make operation much smoother. This section discusses the types of OSPF routers and hierarchical design techniques, including how OSPF separates a network into a hierarchy through the use of areas and autonomous systems.

What Is a Routing Protocol?

A routing protocol can be analyzed as a process. A protocol is formalized through the Request for Comments (RFC) process. This process involves open written commentary on a proposed technology in an effort to bring about standardization of that technology. An example of a routing protocol standard would be OSPF as defined in RFC 2328.

NOTE   You can find all RFCs online at the following website:

www.isi.edu/in-notes/rfc*xxxx*.txt

where *xxxx* is the number of the RFC. If you do not know the number of the RFC, you can search by topic at the following site:

www.rfc-editor.org/cgi-bin/rfcsearch.pl

The basic reason you are studying this topic is to understand how, through the use of OSPF, you can get packets from one host to another over a network. This process can be summarized, from a router's perspective, as consisting of two steps, forwarding and routing:

- **Forwarding**—Refers to the process of a router receiving a packet on an interface and then knowing which interface to retransmit that packet out of so that the packet can continue to its destination. However, forwarding is entirely dependent on the router knowing where to send the packet; if it does not know this, it just discards the packet.

- **Routing**—For the router to know in which direction to forward packets, it requires a route or road map that illustrates the path from source to destination. This route can be generated by either a static or dynamic configuration; at this point, you need to be concerned with only the dynamic aspect of routing. OSPF is a dynamic routing protocol, and when a router is running OSPF, it dynamically develops routes to all destinations within a network. You can view these routes when you view a router's routing table.

The following are broad categories of protocols:

- **Routed protocols**—Protocols that forward data via routers. A router must be able to interpret the logical network as specified by the routed protocol for the router to operate properly. The most commonly known routed protocol is Internet protocol (IP); other examples include AppleTalk and DECnet. Routed protocols rely on the routing protocols for transport over a LAN or WAN.

- **Dynamic routing protocols**—Protocols that accomplish dynamic routing with a routing algorithm. A dynamic routing protocol supports a routed protocol and maintains routing tables. A dynamic routing protocol dynamically exchanges information about paths or topology of the network by distributing routing information throughout a network. Examples of dynamic routing protocols include OSPF, interior gateway routing protocol (IGRP), and routing information protocol (RIP).

A routed protocol such as IP is used as the method of communication between devices on a network. Using a selected routing protocol, such as OSPF, which is supported by the routed protocol, such as IP, you can build the network so that every device can communicate. For example, as previously mentioned, IP is a routed protocol that can use either OSPF or RIP as its routing protocol.

In summary, a dynamic routing protocol is a set of standardized rules that allow routers to determine routes. The routing protocol builds routing tables that tell the router the optimal path to a destination. Routing protocols compare numeric values known as *metrics* to determine the optimal route (sometimes referred to as *path*). Metrics are numeric values that represent route path characteristics. Metrics can be thought of as costs; therefore, the numeric value is explained as the cost of transiting a link. This information is then stored in the routing table to be used by the router when determining the best route to a destination network.

Basic Routing Protocol Operation

Consider an example of a router that is initially configured with two networks to which it directly connects. The router has only these two networks in its routing tables. However, other networks beyond the initial two are not entered into the routing table because they do not directly connect to the router. So how does the router recognize these other networks? This can be accomplished in the following ways:

- **Static routing**—A manually defined and installed type of route within the router as the only path to a given destination. This type of routing forces the destination within routing tables. This type of routing also takes precedence over routes chosen by dynamic routing protocols. Figure 2-1 shows an example of where to place a static route and how a static route is used. Static routing is not an effective stand-alone solution in a medium- to large-sized network because the work needed to make the network run something is very large. The most common use of static routes is in stub networks, as shown in Figure 2-1. In conjunction with a dynamic routing protocol such as OSPF, this synergy works well.

Figure 2-1   *Placement of Static Routes*

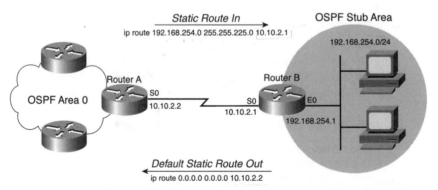

- **Default routing**—A type of route within the router that is manually defined as the path to take when no route to the destination is known. The router to which this information is sent is also known as the router or gateway of last resort. Figure 2-2 shows the use of a default route, which can make routing easy.

  In Figure 2-2, all traffic that Router B receives is forwarded to Router A's S0 interface if it is not for the E0 network, 192.168.254.0/24.

- **Dynamic routing**—Uses routing algorithms that analyze incoming routing update messages from one or more routing protocols to determine the optimal path to a destination. This type of routing has the greatest advantage in that routing automatically adapts to a change in the network's topology.

Figure 2-2 *Placement of a Default Route*

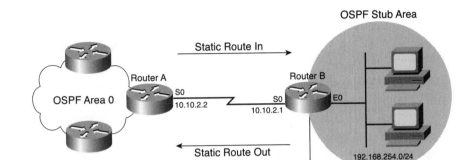

Dynamic routing is the most commonly used method of routing. Associated with this type of routing are several terms and characteristics that define how it operates, such as convergence and accuracy.

In dynamic routing, the routing table must consistently reflect accurate and up-to-date information concerning the network topology. The amount of time that it takes for changes to be reflected in every network router's routing table is known as the *convergence time.* Convergence, in this context, is the act of approaching the state where all routing tables have congruent information and are in steady state.

Having a routing protocol with a fast convergence time is desirable because disruption of routing can occur during the time that a router spends calculating the new optimal path.

Link-State Versus Distance Vector Routing Protocols

This section describes the two most common and relevant routing protocols that TCP/IP has available for use, namely RIP and OSPF. Controversy surrounds the debate over link-state versus distance vector routing algorithms regarding which is better.

NOTE   Link-State and distance vector routing protocols are also known as *interior gateway protocols (IGPs);* this concept is discussed later in the discussion of OSPF and border gateway protocol (BGP) interoperability. Chapter 7, "Summarization," discusses OSPF/BGP interoperability in greater detail.

An IGP is a classification that describes the use of a dynamic routing protocol to exchange routing information within an autonomous system (AS). Examples of common IGPs include IGRP, OSPF, Intermediate System-to-Intermediate System (IS-IS), and RIP. You can contrast an IGP with an exterior gateway protocol (EGP) such as BGP.

Link-State Routing Protocols

Link-state algorithms (also known as shortest path first algorithms) flood only incremental changes that have occurred since the last routing table update. During this incremental update, each router sends only that portion of the routing table that describes the state of its own links, as opposed to its entire routing table.

Link-state routing protocols require routers to periodically send routing updates to their neighboring routers in the internetwork. In addition, link-state routing protocols are quick to converge their routing updates across the network in comparison to distance vector protocols.

The speed at which they converge makes link-state protocols less prone to routing loops than distance vector protocols. However, link-state protocols also require more CPU power and system memory. One of the primary reasons that additional CPU power and memory are needed is that link-state protocols are based on the distributed map concept, which means that every router has a copy of the network map that is regularly updated. In addition to the size of the routing table, the number of routers in an area and the number of adjacencies amongst routers also has an affect on router memory and CPU usage in link-state protocols. These factors were obvious in the old fully meshed asynchronous transfer mode (ATM) networks, where some routers had 50 or more OSPF adjacent peers and performed poorly.

Link-state protocols are based on link-state algorithms, which are also called shortest path first (SPF) algorithms or Dijkstra algorithms. "SPF in Operation," later in this chapter, covers the SPF algorithm in more detail.

A simple way to understand how link-state technology operates is to picture the network as a large jigsaw puzzle; the number of pieces in your puzzle depends on the size of your network. Each piece of the puzzle holds only one router or one LAN. Each router "draws" itself on that jigsaw piece, including arrows to other routers and LANs. Those pieces are then replicated and sent throughout the network from router to router (via link-state advertisements [LSAs]), until each router has a complete and accurate copy of each piece of the puzzle. Each router then assembles these pieces by using the SPF algorithm.

NOTE The principle of link-state routing is that all the routers within an area maintain an identical copy of the network topology. From this map, each router performs a series of calculations that determine the best routes. This network topology is contained within a *link-state database,* where each record represents the links to a particular node in the network.

Each record contains the following pieces of information:

- Interface identifier
- Link number
- Metric information regarding the state of the link

Armed with that information, each router can quickly compute the shortest path from itself to all other routers.

The SPF algorithm determines how the various pieces of the puzzle fit together. Figure 2-3 illustrates all of these pieces put together in operation.

Figure 2-3   *Link-State Operation*

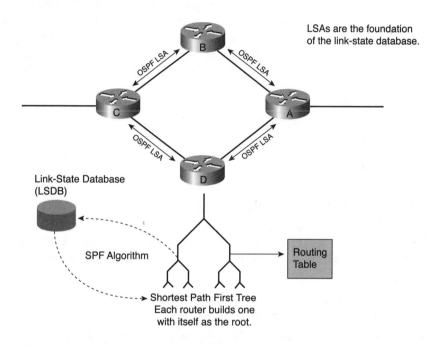

Link-state protocols such as OSPF flood all the routing information when they first become active in link-state packets. After the network converges, they send only small updates via link-state packets.

OSPF Characteristics

OSPF is a link-state protocol in which all routers in the routing domain exchange information and thus know about the complete topology of the network. Because each router knows the complete topology of the network, the use of the SPF algorithm creates an extremely fast convergence. Other key characteristics of OSPF are as follows:

* Provides routing information to the IP section of the TCP/IP protocol suite, the most commonly used alternative to RIP.

* Sends updates to tables only, instead of entire tables, to routers.

* Is a more economical routing protocol than RIP over time because it involves less network traffic.

The "It Depends Rule"

I occasionally invoke a rule I invented that I call the "It Depends Rule," and I am invoking it now! OSPF is usually more efficient than RIP in exchanging routing information when a network is stable; however, for this rule to hold true, it depends on network events. For example, during an external convergence event, OSPF could flood more traffic than RIP. Consider that RIP carries 25 routes per update; on the other hand, OSPF floods a single LSA per external route that is affected by the convergence event. So, provided that you have a (relatively) stable environment, OSPF involves less traffic, and over time, it is statistically more economical than RIP. Using a single LSA per external route is inefficient, but OSPF was never designed to be an EGP. Therefore, I recommend an OSPF/BGP deployment when large numbers of external routers are present.

Another popular type of dynamic routing protocol that is based on the Dijkstra SPF algorithm is IS-IS. The use of IS-IS versus OSPF has been hotly debated.

Integrated Intermediate System-to-Intermediate System

IS-IS is an OSI link-state hierarchical routing protocol that is based on work originally done at Digital Equipment Corporation for DECnet/OSI (DECnet Phase V). This protocol floods the network with link-state information to build a complete, consistent picture of network topology.

The International Organization for Standardization (ISO) has developed the following routing protocols for use in the Open System Interconnection (OSI) protocol suite:

- Intermediate System-to-Intermediate System (IS-IS) protocol
- End System-to-Intermediate System (ES-IS) protocol
- Interdomain routing protocol (IDRP)

For more information on IDRP or ES-IS, start with the RFCs, which can be found at www.ietf.org.

The American National Standards Institute (ANSI) X3S3.3 (network and transport layers) committee was the motivating force behind ISO standardization of IS-IS, which was originally developed to route in ISO connectionless network protocol (CLNP) networks. A version has since been created that supports both CLNP and IP networks. It is usually referred to as *integrated IS-IS;* this is the version discussed here.

OSI routing protocols are summarized in several ISO documents; those dealing with IS-IS are as follows:

- ISO 10589: Standards definition for IS-IS
- RFC 1195: Intermediate IS-IS

Distance Vector Routing Protocols

Distance vector means that information sent from router to router is based on an entry in a routing table that consists of the distance and vector to destination—distance being what it "costs" to get there and vector being the "direction" to get to the destination.

Distance vector protocols are often referred to as Bellman-Ford protocols because they are based on a computation algorithm described by R. E. Bellman; the first description of the distributed algorithm is attributed to Ford and Fulkerson. Distance vector algorithms (also known as Bellman-Ford algorithms) call for each router to send its entire routing table, but only to its neighbors. The neighbor then forwards its entire routing table to its neighbors, and so on. Figure 2-4 illustrates this routing table forwarding process.

Figure 2-4   *Distance Vector Operation*

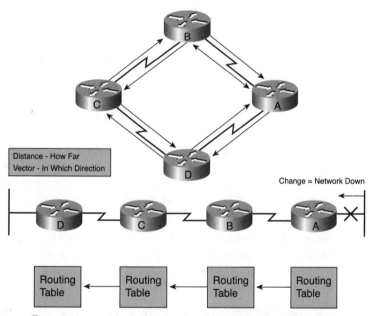

As Figure 2-4 illustrates, whenever a change to the network occurs, this causes the entire routing table to be sent from neighbor to neighbor in order for the network to reconverge in response to the network event (network down). What is not shown is the periodic sending of the routing table between neighbors—a mechanism that double-checks that the routing information each router has is valid.

Routing Information Protocol Characteristics

RIP v1 is a distance vector protocol designed at Berkeley in the late 1960s that is still widely deployed today. In this protocol, the router only exchanges routing information from the connected neighbors. Key characteristics of RIP are as follows:

- RIP broadcasts every 30 seconds to maintain network integrity.

- RIP maintains routing tables, showing the number of hops between routers, and is limited to a 15-hop count.

- A router using RIP passes its entire routing table to each directly connected neighbor router that it knows of.

A detailed discussion about RIP is not very relevant in a book dedicated to OSPF, but if you want to learn more on RIP v1 and v2, consider the following resources:

- *Routing TCP/IP*, Volume I, by Jeff Doyle. Chapter 5 is dedicated to RIP.

- Routing information protocol (RIP) at cisco.com:

    www.cisco.com/univercd/cc/td/doc/cisintwk/ito_doc/rip.htm

- RFC 2453 RIP Version 2, published in 1998

Conclusion

Link-state algorithms send small updates everywhere; distance vector algorithms send large updates only to neighboring routers. Because they create a consistent view of the internetwork, link-state algorithms are somewhat less prone to routing loops than are distance vector algorithms. When a network is in stable or steady state, link-state protocols allow for smooth routing.

On the downside, link-state algorithms can cause significant, widespread control traffic, for example, when a network event occurs and the event must be flooded throughout the network. The main concern in today's networks is the amount of flooding that can happen as networks grow ever larger.

Link-state algorithms are also computationally difficult compared to distance vector algorithms, requiring more CPU power and memory than distance vector algorithms. However, this has become less of an issue as router-processing capabilities have improved.

Link-state algorithms can therefore be more expensive to implement and support. Despite their differences, both algorithm types perform well in circumstances and networks that suit their strengths and recognize their limitations.

Selecting a Routing Protocol

Network designers and engineers frequently ask, "Which routing protocol should I use?" This section compares the two link-state protocols that are discussed in this chapter—IS-IS and OSPF. However, consider the following issues before selecting a routing protocol:

- **Operational considerations**—Determine how easy it is to manage a network over time. These considerations include how to determine a protocol's capability to adapt to changes, how to minimize disruptions to the network, and how to troubleshoot problems.

- **Technical considerations**—Assist in determining whether a given protocol is capable of supporting a particular set of network requirements.

- **Business considerations**—Defined as business priorities and policies that influence network design decisions. These types of considerations can originate from any area within a company and can be the keystones to the success of the network.

Operational Considerations

Table 2-1 shows a matrix of operational issues to consider when selecting a routing protocol.

Table 2-1   *Important Operational Considerations*

	OSPF	IS-IS
Protocols Supported	IP	IP, ISO, CLNP
Routing Hierarchies	Supported	Supported
IP Address Management	Required	Required
IP Encapsulation Support	Yes	No (OSI Layer 2)
Available Resources	Yes	No

Protocols Supported

Historically, all routed protocols have had their own independent routing protocols: AppleTalk uses Routing Table Maintenance Protocol (RTMP), Novell uses Internetwork Packet Exchange (IPX) RIP, and IP uses RIP, IGRP, or OSPF. This is conceptually simple to understand, but it is often difficult to implement. Yet, it is necessary for network engineers to design and operate networks that support multiprotocol environments. Therefore, they need to be able to manage a mix of routing protocols.

OSPF supports only the TCP/IP protocol suite. Although TCP/IP is the most popular suite in use today, it is not the only one being used. The inability of a routing protocol to support other protocols can be a detriment to legacy networks or networks with unique routing needs.

When IS-IS was created, the protocol designers asked a significant question: Why can't one routing protocol handle multiple routed protocols? Consequently, integrated IS-IS was enhanced to support both OSI CLNP and TCP/IP networks. In addition, integrated IS-IS supports other network protocols; this can be of great benefit in a multiprotocol network.

Routing Hierarchies

The key to building large networks is to introduce a logical hierarchy. Problems related to complexity and scale can be addressed with the proper use of hierarchy. Having a hierarchical network can provide you with many benefits—most notably, route summarization and reduced SPF calculation—thus giving your network a faster convergence time.

OSPF was the first major routing protocol to support hierarchical networking (areas) within a single routing domain (AS). OSPF supports two levels of hierarchy: a backbone area (Area 0) and other connected areas. OSPF routers carry full topology information about the backbone and connectivity information about all of the areas. Within each area, OSPF routers exchange full topology information about that area because the boundaries of areas fall within a router. This results in router interfaces being bound to areas. Because a router has multiple interfaces, it can be in multiple areas as well. However, this design would require the router to run separate SPF calculations for each area; therefore, you should design the network appropriately.

Integrated IS-IS uses the same two levels of hierarchy as OSPF; however, the two protocols differ in the quantity of information that is carried inside each area. Within an area, integrated IS-IS routers send all traffic that needs to go out of the area to the nearest IS-IS Level 2 router. OSPF, on the other hand, injects all the connectivity information about the other areas into each area. This enables every router in an OSPF area to choose the optimal area border router (ABR) for traffic that needs to go out of its area.

IS-IS area boundaries are segmented on a link between two routers; therefore, a router is typically only in one area. However, it is hard to deploy true hierarchical network architecture with IS-IS for several reasons, one of which is that IS-IS operates best with very large areas with at least one router in an area for it to operate properly. This is one of the factors that causes ISPs to deploy a single IS-IS area as their core, although many ISPs are now reconsidering OSPF.

IP Address Management

The key to a successful hierarchical network structure is proper IP address management. If addresses are assigned appropriately, it is possible to summarize routing information. The two significant reasons to summarize routes follows:

- Summarization localizes the effects of topology changes and thus contributes to network stability.

- Summarization reduces the amount of routing information that is carried by all routers.

These reasons simplify network administration and troubleshooting, in addition to reducing the resources that are consumed by the routing protocol (CPU, memory, and so on).

TIP   Each area used by OSPF or integrated IS-IS should have a contiguous set of network or subnet numbers assigned to it. The area border routers should summarize that set of addresses with an address mask. Summarization provides substantial benefits for your network.

IP Encapsulation Support

OSPF is a TCP/IP-based protocol and fully supports IP. On the other hand, IS-IS is a native OSI protocol and must still be implemented using ISO addressing for the IS-IS aspects of its operation. IS-IS allows the forwarding of IP packets although not specifically designed to do so.

Available Resources

You must be pragmatic when selecting a routing protocol. Resources should be available to assist network engineers at all levels of competence to help them understand the idiosyncrasies of the protocol that you want to implement.

OSPF is much more widely implemented and understood through the use of books (like this one), which explain to you the importance and functions of OSPF while providing practical examples to enhance your understanding. The standards surrounding OSPF are extremely well written thanks to the OSPF Working Group in the Internet Engineering Task Force (IETF); however, the specification does not include a lot of explanation on the "how" and "why."

IS-IS is deployed in some places, but compared to OSPF, it is still considered a niche protocol. Some ISPs are running it, but almost no enterprise networks are using it as of this writing. The IS-IS specification uses ISO language and terms and not IP.

If formal classroom instruction is of interest to you, several dedicated OSPF courses are available; however, few are available on IS-IS.

Technical Considerations

Table 2-2 provides a list of technical issues to consider when selecting a routing protocol.

Table 2-2   *Important Technical Considerations: IS-IS Versus OSPF*

	OSPF	IS-IS
Fast Convergence	Yes	Yes
Routing Updates	Fast, change only	Fast, change only
VLSM Support and CIDR	Yes	Yes
Load Sharing	Yes, equal cost	Yes, equal cost
Metric Range	0–65,535	0–1023
Static Metric Pieces	Sum of bandwidth	Sum of bandwidth
Dynamic Metric Pieces	None	None
Scalability	Very Strong	Strong
Physical Media Support	All types	Most, but some issues
Extensibility	Yes w/Opaque LSAs	Yes

Fast Convergence

All routing protocols have three important characteristics when dealing with the issue of convergence:

1 Detecting that a change has occurred

2 Adapting to that change

3 Updating the network topology to reflect the change

IS-IS and OSPF detect certain types of network changes instantly. In general, any change that can be detected by a physical change (such as loss of carrier) is detected immediately by any routing protocol.

In addition, both routing protocols use hello packets as keepalives and to detect other failures (such as the loss of an adjacent router or the degradation of an interface to the point where it should no longer be used). Both protocols cause adjacent routers to exchange information periodically.

After the routing protocol has detected the topology change, it needs to adjust the routing tables to accommodate the new topology. OSPF and integrated IS-IS both have mechanisms for updating routing tables. If the topology change were within the area, all the existing routes affected by the change would be discarded and a new routing table would be generated. In general, OSPF and integrated IS-IS converge in less than 2 seconds. The amount of CPU time required to do the recompilation is strongly affected by the number of routes and the amount of redundancy in the network.

Routing Updates

All routing protocols exchange routing information dynamically. The three most important questions concerning the operation of routing updates are as follows:

- **When are they sent?**—All three routing protocols exchange periodic hellos and full topology information when a router starts up and periodically thereafter, depending how they are configured. RIP floods the full topology table every 30 seconds. OSPF floods the full topology table every 30 minutes. Integrated IS-IS floods the full topology table every 15 minutes to ensure synchronization.

- **What is in them?**—Within an area, OSPF and integrated IS-IS exchange changed link-state information. Between areas, OSPF and integrated IS-IS exchange changed routes.

- **Where are they sent?**—Changed information in a RIP network is broadcast to all of its neighbors after the network has finished updating its topology. Changed information in OSPF and integrated IS-IS propagates throughout the area in which the change occurred. If route summarization is not done, change information might also propagate to the backbone and into other areas.

VLSM and CIDR Support

OSPF and integrated IS-IS include support for variable-length subnet masks (VLSMs) and classless interdomain routing (CIDR). VLSM is required to support route summarization. In addition, VLSM and CIDR also enable network administrators to use their address space more effectively.

Load Sharing

Today's networks are commonly designed with redundant paths. This has two positive benefits: rerouting in case of failure and load sharing. All routing protocols supported by Cisco provide load sharing across as many as six equal-cost paths. The default for OSPF is to use four equal-cost paths, but if you have more, you must configure OSPF to use them.

Metrics

The quality of route selection is essentially controlled by the value of the metrics placed upon the various routes. Two components are important in how a routing protocol uses metrics: the range of the values the metric can express and how the metric is computed.

OSPF uses a flat metric with a range of 16 bits. This results in OSPF having a metric range that is from 0 to 65,535. By default, OSPF metrics are assigned as an inverse of the bandwidth available on an interface—normalized to give the Fiber Distributed Data Interface (FDDI) a metric of 1. OSPF computes the cost of a path by summing the metrics for each hop on that path.

Integrated IS-IS uses a flat metric. The metric range is 0 to 1023. By default, all integrated IS-IS metrics are 10. Network administrators need to configure nondefault values. Integrated IS-IS computes the cost of a path by summing the metrics for each hop on that path.

Scalability

In IS-IS, ISO 10589 states that 100 routers per area and 400 L2 routers should be possible. The biggest scaling issue now seems to be the overhead of the flooding in large meshed networks, for example, flat ATM clouds with many attached routers that form a full mesh.

OSPF, on the other hand, scales well regardless of the size of the network. However, to make the network operate optimally, you should implement physical and logical areas as needed.

Physical Media Support

Both OSPF and IS-IS support point-to-point links and LANs in similar ways. However, IS-IS has no nonbroadcast multiaccess (NBMA) support and expects the router operating system to present the NBMA network as either a LAN or a set of point-to-point links; this can be problematic. OSPF can overcome this issue, but with Cisco routers, considerable configuration is needed.

Extensibility

Protocols must be able to grow and expand to meet the ever-changing and evolving network environment. OSPF has been able to do this through the recent inclusion of opaque LSAs; however, all routers must understand these LSAs to effectively adapt to the dynamic network environment. IS-IS floods unknown LSAs and ignores them.

Both protocols support traffic engineering, so networks can benefit from Multiprotocol Label Switching (MPLS) regardless of which protocol is chosen.

Business Considerations

Table 2-3 documents business issues to consider when selecting a routing protocol.

Table 2-3 *Important Business Considerations for Routing Protocol Selection*

	Integrated IS-IS	OSPF
Standard-Based	Yes	Yes
Multivendor Environments	Yes	Yes
Proven Technology	Yes	Yes

Standards

Many companies prefer to use protocols that are based on standards whenever possible; this is strongly recommended in every network. Networks running without the protocols and standards will eventually cause problems.

OSPF is a standard protocol that was developed by a committee of the IETF as an alternative to the RIP protocol. OSPF is defined in RFC 2328.

IS-IS is a standard protocol that was developed by the ISO. IS-IS is defined in International Standard 10589. Integrated IS-IS is a standard extension to IS-IS, which was developed by the IETF. Integrated IS-IS is defined in an Internet Draft.

Multivendor Environments

Large networks being designed today do not have the luxury of assuming a single vendor environment. It is common to have portions of a network that are provided by one vendor and other portions that are provided by another. You can use several techniques to permit multivendor environments. The most common technique is to use the same routing protocol on all the routers. To compare the viability of OSPF versus IS-IS for a multivendor environment, consider the following:

- Every major routing vendor implements OSPF.
- Integrated IS-IS is implemented by most of the major router vendors.

Proven Technology

OSPF has been available for several years from all the major routing vendors and is being deployed in an increasing number of networks ranging from very simple to very complex.

Integrated IS-IS has been available from Cisco for several years and is being deployed in a number of significant networks. OSPF is the routing protocol of choice of almost everyone. IS-IS is the routing protocol of choice for networks that need to support both OSI and IP. Integrated IS-IS is the standard routing protocol for DECnet Phase V networks.

TIP   You can find additional IS-IS information in the Cisco Press book *IS-IS Network Design Solutions*, written by Abe Martey.

SPF Overview

OSPF is a link-state routing protocol. Such protocols are also referred to in the literature and technical documents as SPF-based or distributed database protocols. This section discusses the developments in link-state technologies that have influenced the evolution of the OSPF protocol.

What Is a Link-State Protocol?

OSPF is a link-state protocol. For example, you can think of a link as being an interface on the router. The state of the link is a description of that interface. This description would include the interface's IP address and mask, and the type of network to which it is connected. This information is compiled for all the routers in your network into a link-state database, and the SPF algorithm is run against that data. Link-state derives from the indication of a link, in that a link has either an up status or a down status.

The first link-state routing protocol was developed for use in the ARPAnet packet-switching network. This protocol formed the starting point for all other link-state protocols. The homogeneous ARPAnet environment (that is, single-vendor packet switches connected by synchronous serial lines) simplified the design and implementation of the original protocol.

SPF in Operation

The ARPAnet used one of the first distance vector routing protocols. This protocol evolved into RIP, which is still in use today. Serious limitations were encountered with RIP as networks grew. This caused a demand for a new protocol that could run within an AS and had the capability to grow (scale) to a large-sized network comprised of many routers and network links.

Into this gap stepped OSPF version 1, published as Request for Comments (RFC) 1131 in October 1989 by the OSPF Working Group of the IETF. OSPF made use of the famous Dijkstra algorithm. This algorithm was not new and had not been created specifically to fill the demand of the networking community. This mathematical formula was initially created to demonstrate the ARMAC computer in 1956, over 30 years before OSPF was considered.

Edsger W. Dijkstra was born in 1930 in Rotterdam, the Netherlands. Born into a scientifically oriented family, he quickly excelled and achieved his Ph.D. in computer science in 1959 from the University of Amsterdam, Holland. By the time he was 32, Dijkstra achieved a full professorship in mathematics at Eindhoven University. His achievement remains extremely impressive to this day.

Dijkstra's most remembered contributions to the computer world are his algorithms, specifically the shortest path algorithm. Dijkstra did not consider his algorithm very remarkable at the time, and many years passed before he published it. Today, his algorithm is being applied to road building, communications routing, and the airline industry. His algorithm was even altered slightly to determine the most inexpensive way to wire a computer. The goal of Edsger Dijkstra's shortest path algorithm is to find the shortest route between two points through a series of nodes, as originally described in his paper outlining the algorithm. However, in routing, we translate the term *node* into *router.*

Consider the following example to describe the operation of the shortest path first algorithm in basic terms.

Suppose you are trying to find the shortest path in time between the cities of Raleigh and Boston. In between these cities are a number of other cities (routers) that might provide the best route to your final destination.

In this example, you want to determine the shortest path (cost) that is required to reach Boston while exploring every road (link) that each new city provides along the way. As you know, some roads (links) are better than others. These roads might be faster, bigger, or less traveled. To determine the shortest, (call it the fastest) path (route) from Raleigh to Boston, assign each road (link) a numerical value that reflects its speed.

Because computers only understand the importance of numbers and not opinions regarding path desirability, you need to manually assign these values to the paths to help the protocol do its job. A router can understand that a path with a value of 50 is more efficient than a path with a value of 100.

This example obviously refers to OSPF, so in the example, OSPF will collect all the link information on how to get from Raleigh to Boston. Then, the SPF algorithm will calculate the shortest path (see Figure 2-5). The sequence to find this minimum time value (shortest path) is as follows:

Figure 2-5   *SPF in Action*

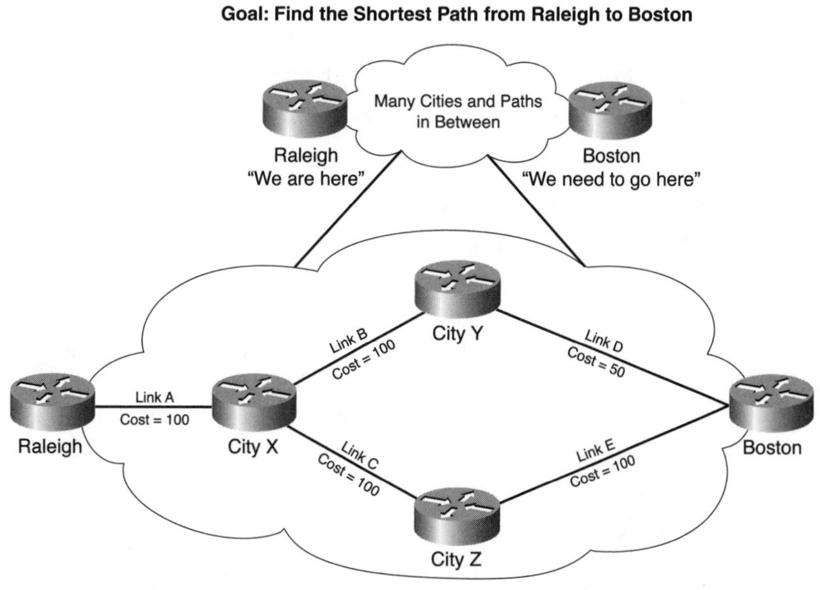

Goal: Find the Shortest Path from Raleigh to Boston

1 Begin in the city of origin (Raleigh). The time (distance) needed to reach Raleigh is 0 (because you are there).

2 Raleigh knows (via OSPF) that one connection to another city heads toward Boston. This connection to City X has a cost of 100 because it is a nice two-lane road. Place this link information in a database for future reference:

   Link A—Costs 100—Goes to City X—Link is up

3 City X tells you that there are two paths leaving it. As OSPF examines these links, it learns the following:

Link B — Costs 100 — Goes to City Y — Link is up

Link C — Costs 100 — Goes to City Z — Link is up

Place both entries into the database, and continue to search for Boston.

4 City Y tells you that it has a connection to Boston via a brand new expressway; place that information in the database as well:

Link D — Costs 50 — Goes to Boston — Link is up

At this point though, you also learned that City Z has a link to Boston as well.

Link E — Costs 100 — Goes to Boston — Link is up

Faced with two links to Boston, the SPF algorithm must compute which is the shortest path.

5 OSPF turns to its database. (Don't you think you should give this database a name? Well because you're tracking data regarding the many links (cost and status such as up/down, call it the *Link-state Database [Topological]*) and reviews what it knows:

Path A — Costs 100 — Goes to City X — Link is up

Path B — Costs 100 — Goes to City Y — Link is up

Path C — Costs 100 — Goes to City Z — Link is up

Path D — Costs 50 — Goes to Boston — Link is up

Path E — Costs 100 — Goes to Boston — Link is up

OSPF has discovered two paths to Boston, but which one should you use? You don't know which is the shortest. However, the SPF in OSPF can determine the shortest path for you.

6 OSPF now invokes the SPF algorithm and builds a map of all the links from Raleigh to Boston. This map can be visualized with Raleigh as the root (bottom) of a tree that has all these limbs (links) that go to many cities (destinations) (see Figure 2-6). Turn the book on its side so the figure looks like a tree.

Although this is a nice picture of a tree, computers prefer to treat this information mathematically:

Path 1: Link A (100) + Link B (100) + Link D (50) = Cost (250)

Path 2: Link A (100) + Link C (100) + Link E (100) = Cost (300)

Now the SPF algorithm compares these two paths and determines which is the shortest so that you can drive to Boston (transmit a packet). SPF chooses Path 1 because it has a lower cost than Path 2.

7 The shortest path is Path 1.

Figure 2-6   *SPF Tree*

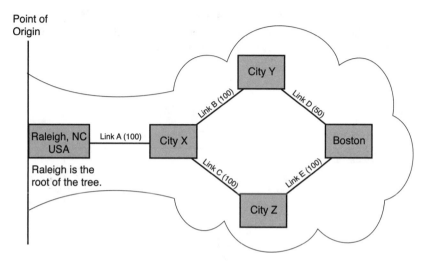

8   Path 1 is now inserted into the car's computer (route table), so it can tell you (the packet) how to get to Boston using the shortest possible path.

This example helps demonstrate the algorithm's name. Another important factor in its operation is how SPF converges. Using the preceding example, everything would change if the link between City X and Boston went down. The need to understand why this has happened and how traffic (packets) is redirected to the link through City Z is crucial. This concept is called convergence.

Reviewing the Link-State Database

The principle of link-state routing is that all the routers within a network maintain an identical copy of the network topology. From this map, each router performs a series of calculations that determine the best routes. This network topology is contained within a database, where each record represents the links to a particular node in the network.

Each record contains several pieces of information: an interface identifier, a link number, and metric information regarding the state of the link. With that information, each router can quickly compute the shortest path from itself to all other routers.

Essentially, OSPF converges in $0(M.\log M)$ iterations, where M is the number of links. This is far superior to the distance vector Bellman-Ford algorithm, which converges in $0(N.M)$ iterations, where N is the number of nodes.

SPF Functions

Assume that you have the network shown in Figure 2-7 with the indicated interface costs. To build the shortest-path tree for RTA, you would have to make RTA the root of the tree and calculate the smallest cost for each destination.

Figure 2-7 *SPF Functions*

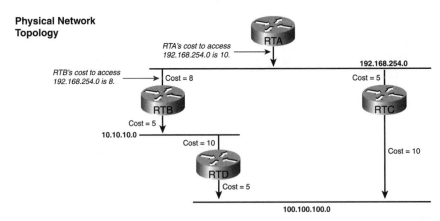

Figure 2-7 shows the view of the network as seen from RTA. Note the direction of the arrows in calculating the cost. For example, the cost of RTB's interface to network 192.168.254.0 is not relevant when calculating the cost to 10.10.10.0. RTA can reach 10.10.10.0 via RTB with a cost of 15 (10+5). RTA can also reach 100.100.100.0 via RTC with a cost of 20 (10+10) or via RTB with a cost of 20 (10+5+5). In case equal-cost paths exist to the same destination, Cisco's implementation of OSPF keeps track of up to six next hops to the same destination.

After the router builds the shortest-path tree, it starts building the routing table accordingly. Directly connected networks are reached via a metric (cost) of 0, and other networks are reached according to the cost calculated in the tree.

Before discussing the origins of the OSPF protocol, you should review its key characteristics. These characteristics and the protocol's many labels serve as a short review and as an introduction to future concepts.

The OSPF protocol is also known by the following definitions or labels:

- Link-state routing protocol
- Shortest path first (SPF) protocol
- Interior gateway protocol
- Distributed routing protocol

OSPF also has the following operational characteristics:

- Features open architecture
- Dynamically adjusts to changes in network topology
- Features adjustable distance metrics
- Features type of service (TOS) routing
- Supports hierarchical systems
- Features load balancing
- Provides security features
- Supports three kinds of connections or networks:
  - Point-to-point
  - Multiaccess networks with broadcasting
  - Multiaccess networks without broadcasting
- Determines routing by computing a graph, abstracting the topology of the network by using the shortest-path algorithm
- Segments the network through the use of autonomous systems and areas for ease of management and traffic
- Features multicasts rather than broadcasts
- Allows the use of virtual links
- Supports VLSM and CIDR

Full and Partial SPF Calculations

The Cisco Systems implementation of the SPF algorithm allows for quicker ways to calculate routes. This change has resulted in two types of SPF calculations: full and partial. The full SPF calculation operates as discussed so far this chapter.

The full SPF algorithm is run only when there is a topology change, as expressed in router link-state advertisements (LSAs), not for summary LSAs. Summary LSAs cause a partial SPF to be run.

In OSPF, partial SPF relates to external and summary LSAs' change only. Basically, if a network flap occurs via an external or summary LSA, you run partial SPF. In other words, partial SPF is invoked when topology of the area did not change but some IP prefix flapped.

An IP prefix change inside the area invokes the full SPF recalculation.

Verifying SPF Operation

As previously discussed, it can be important to monitor flooding with OSPF. Whenever an LSA is received, SPF could recalculate. You can see how OSPF is operating by executing a **show ip ospf** process id command. This command can be used to determine the number of times the SPF algorithm has been executed. It also shows the link-state update interval, assuming no topological changes have occurred. Example 2-1 shows an example of the **show ip ospf** command, with the highlighted area representing the total number of SPF calculations.

Example 2-1   *Displayed Output from the* **show ip ospf** *Command*

```
HAL9000#show ip ospf 100
 Routing Process "ospf 100" with ID 10.10.10.10
 Supports only single TOS(TOS0) routes
 SPF schedule delay 5 secs, Hold time between two SPFs 10 secs
 Number of DCbitless external LSA 0
 Number of DoNotAge external LSA 0
 Number of areas in this router is 1. 1 normal 0 stub 0 nssa
    Area BACKBONE(0) (Inactive)
        Number of interfaces in this area is 1
        Area has no authentication
        SPF algorithm executed 13 times
        Area ranges are
        Link State Update Interval is 00:30:00 and due in 00:09:05
        Link State Age Interval is 00:20:00 and due in 00:19:05
        Number of DCbitless LSA 0
        Number of indication LSA 0
        Number of DoNotAge LSA 0

HAL9000#
```

Furthermore, for partial SPF, because only summary or external LSAs are affected, you can also execute either a **debug ip ospf spf inter** command or a **debug ip ospf spf external** command to monitor the partial SPF. You can specify an access list to filter calculations only for an LSA with specific LSA ID.

OSPF Routing Hierarchy

One of most important features within the OSPF protocol is its capability to use a hierarchical routing structure. Remember the following characteristics when considering how OSPF operates within this type of hierarchical structure:

- Structure must exist or be created in order for OSPF to operate properly.

- Explicit topology has precedence over addressing.

An AS is a group of areas sharing a common routing strategy that fall under a common administrative domain. Autonomous systems are identified by a unique number. Autonomous systems' numbers can be either public or private, depending on your needs. Autonomous systems' numbers are assigned by American Registry for Internet Numbers (ARIN) in North America, Réseaux IP Européens (RIPE) in Europe, and Asia Pacific Network Information Centre (APNIC) in Asia. An AS number is not required to use OSPF, as single-homed enterprises are considered to be part of their upstream ISP's AS. The routing of information within an AS takes place in one of three ways:

- If the source and destination addresses of a packet reside within the same area, *intra-area routing* is used.

- If the source and destination addresses of a packet reside within different areas but are still within the AS, *inter-area routing* is used.

- If the destination address of a packet resides outside the AS, *external routing* is used.

Hierarchical Network Design Techniques

When designing your OSPF network, the following factors are supported by OSPF and are currently accepted network design theories:

- A three-tiered backbone approach allows fast convergence and economy of scale.

- Never use more than six router hops from source to destination (see the following note).

- Use 30 to 100 routers per area. (This can be adjusted depending on factors discussed later.)

- Do not allow more than two areas per Area Border Router (ABR) in addition to the ABR's connection to area 0. Otherwise, the ABR must keep track of too many link-state databases.

NOTE   The Cisco Systems network recommends that you have no more than six hops from source to destination when designing a hierarchical enterprise network. This has some validity; however, in practice, the number of hops you can see depends on what a network is trying to accomplish. Large, long-haul international networks by nature have more than six hops.

Routing Types Within an OSPF Network

OSPF can use three types of routes:

- Intra-area
- Inter-area
- External

The following sections provide general descriptions of these route types. As you move further into designing and implementing OSPF networks, you will be exposed to these different types of routes.

Intra-Area Routing

Intra-area routing describes routes to destinations within a logical OSPF area. Intra-area routes in OSPF are described by router (Type 1) and network (Type 2) LSAs. When displayed in the OSPF routing table, these types of intra-area routes are designated with an "O."

Inter-Area Routing

Inter-area routing describes destinations that require travel between two or more OSPF areas and still fall within the same AS. These types of routes are described by network (Type 3) summary LSAs. When routing packets between two nonbackbone areas, the backbone is used. This means that inter-area routing has pieces of intra-area routing along its path, for example:

1 An intra-area path is used from the source router to the area border router.

2 The backbone is then used from the source area to the destination area.

3 An intra-area path is used from the destination area's area border router to the destination.

When you put these three routes together, you have an inter-area route. Of course, the SPF algorithm calculates the lowest cost between these two points. When displayed in the OSPF routing table, these types of routes are indicated with an "O IA," as demonstrated in Example 2-2.

Example 2-2 *Discerning OSPF Route Types in an OSPF Routing Table*

```
Sydney#show ip route
Codes: C - connected, S - static, I - IGRP, R - RIP, M - mobile, B - BGP
       D - EIGRP, EX - EIGRP external, O - OSPF, IA - OSPF inter area
       N1 - OSPF NSSA external type 1, N2 - OSPF NSSA external type 2
       E1 - OSPF external type 1, E2 - OSPF external type 2, E - EGP
       i - IS-IS, L1 - IS-IS level-1, L2 - IS-IS level-2, ia - IS-IS inter area
       * - candidate default, U - per-user static route, o - ODR
       P - periodic downloaded static route
```

Example 2-2   *Discerning OSPF Route Types in an OSPF Routing Table (Continued)*

```
Gateway of last resort is not set

     20.0.0.0/24 is subnetted, 1 subnets
O IA    20.20.20.0 [110/2] via 192.168.254.100, 00:01:48, FastEthernet0/0
     10.0.0.0/24 is subnetted, 1 subnets
C       10.10.10.0 is directly connected, FastEthernet0/1
C     192.168.254.0/24 is directly connected, FastEthernet0/0
     30.0.0.0/24 is subnetted, 1 subnets
O IA    30.30.30.0 [110/2] via 192.168.254.101, 00:01:48, FastEthernet0/0
Sydney#
```

External Routes

External routing information can be gained by OSPF through a number of means. The most common means is through redistribution from another routing protocol. This is discussed in detail in Chapter 6, "Redistribution." This external route information must then be made available throughout the OSPF AS in order for it to be of use. The AS boundary routers (ASBRs) do not summarize the external routing information, but ASBRs flood the external route information throughout the AS. Every router receives this information, with the exception of stub areas.

NOTE	Summarization at ASBR happens only when configured with an outbound distribute list or an OSPF Summary statement, but this not the default. By default, Cisco routers let all external routes in without summarization.

The types of external routes used in OSPF are as follows:

- **E1 routes**—E1 routes' costs are the sum of internal and external (remote AS) OSPF metrics. For example, if a packet is destined for another AS, an E1 route takes the remote AS metric and adds all internal OSPF costs. They are identified by the E1 designation within the OSPF routing table.

- **E2 routes**—E2 routes are the default external routes for OSPF. They do not add the internal OSPF metrics; they use the remote AS only, regardless of where they are in the AS. For example, if a packet is destined for another AS, E2 routes add only the metrics from the destination AS associated with reaching the destination.

TIP	Multiple routes to the same destination use the following order of preference: intra-area, inter-area, E1, and E2.

OSPF Areas

Areas are similar to subnets in that the routes and networks contained within can be easily summarized. In other words, areas are contiguous logical segments of the network that have been grouped together. Through the use of areas within OSPF, the network is easier to manage and provides a marked reduction in routing traffic. These benefits are gained because the topology of an area is invisible to other routers outside of the area.

Areas also allow the routers contained within them to run their own link-state database and SPF algorithm. A router runs one copy of the link-state database for each area to which it is connected.

A typical scenario for many networks as they grow and more sites are added is that the benefits of OSPF begin to degrade. For example, the link-state database continues to grow in size as the size of the network and the number of routers grow. At some point, this becomes inefficient.

The flooding of LSAs from a large number of routers can also cause congestion problems. To solve these problems, begin by segmenting your AS into multiple areas. As you group routers into areas, consider limiting the number of routers per area. Each router then has a link-state database, with entries for each router in its area. This substantially increases the efficiency of your OSPF network.

Characteristics of a Standard OSPF Area

The following list provides general characteristics of an OSPF area:

- Areas contain a group of contiguous hosts and networks.
- Routers have a per-area topological database and run the same SPF algorithm.
- Each area must be connected to the backbone area known as area 0.
- Virtual links can be used to connect to area 0 in emergencies.
- Intra-area routes are used for routes within to destinations within the area.

Standard Area Design Rules

Consider the following requirements when designing an OSPF area:

- A backbone area, known as area 0, must be present.
- All areas must have a connection to the backbone area, even stub areas.
- The backbone area must be contiguous.
- Only use virtual links as an emergency temporary measure.

Area 0: The OSPF Backbone Area

A backbone area is the logical and physical structure for the AS and is attached to multiple areas. The backbone area is responsible for distributing routing information between nonbackbone areas. The backbone must be contiguous, but it need not be physically contiguous; backbone connectivity can be established and maintained through the configuration of virtual links. This is discussed in further detail in Chapter 4, "Design Fundamentals."

Stub Areas

An area is referred to as a stub area when there is commonly a single exit point from that area, or if external routing to outside of the area does not have to take an optimal path. A stub is just what it sounds like: a dead end within the network. Packets can enter and leave only through the ABR. Why would you ever need such an area? The reason is network size. By building stub areas, you can reduce the overall size of the routing tables within the routers that are inside an OSPF stub area. Stub areas have the following functional and design characteristics:

- External networks, such as those redistributed from other protocols into OSPF, are not allowed to be flooded into a stub area. Specifically, the ABR stops LSA Types 4 and 5. Therefore, no router inside a stub area has any external routes.

- Configuring a stub area reduces the link-state database size inside an area and reduces the memory requirements of routers inside that area.

- Routing from these areas to the outside world is based on a default route. Stub areas do contain inter-area and intra-area routes because the ABR injects a default route (0.0.0.0) into the stub area.

- Stub areas typically have one ABR; this is the best design. However, you can have additional ABRs, but this might cause suboptimal routing.

All OSPF routers inside a stub area must be configured as stub routers because whenever an area is configured as stub, all interfaces that belong to that area start exchanging OSPF Hello packets with a flag that indicates that the interface is part of an OSPF stub area. This is actually just a bit in the Hello packet (E bit) that gets set to 0. All routers that have a common area must to agree on that flag. For example, all the routers in a stub area must be configured to recognize that the area is a stub. If the routers don't agree, they cannot become neighbors and routing does not take effect.

Stub areas have certain restrictions applied to their operation. This is because they have been designed not to carry external routes, and any of the situations in the following list can cause external links to be injected into the stub area. These restrictions are as follows:

- Stub areas cannot be used as a transit area for virtual links.

- An ASBR cannot be internal to a stub area.

- OSPF allows certain areas to be configured as stub areas, but the backbone area cannot be a stub area.

- LSA Types 4 and 5 are not allowed in a stub area.

TIP   An extension to a stub area is called a *totally stubby area*. Cisco Systems indicates this type of stub area by adding a **no-summary** keyword to the stub area configuration within the router. A totally stubby area is one that blocks external routes and summary routes (inter-area routes) from going into the area. This way, only intra-area routes exist, and a default route of 0.0.0.0 is injected into the area.

Not-So-Stubby Areas

Not-so-stubby areas (NSSAs) are defined in RFC 1587, "The OSPF NSSA Option." NSSAs can be useful for ISPs and large institutions that need to connect to a remote site that runs a different routing protocol. NSSAs allow OSPF to import external routes into a stub area. This is a direct design violation of a regular stub area, and that is why a new RFC was introduced. By defining this new type of area, a new LSA type (Type 7) was also intro-duced. Using the new LSA, OSPF can now handle this apparent contradiction of importing external routes into a stub area.

NSSAs are useful for instances where you have no Internet transit link and you have to redistribute a legacy RIP network into a stub area, but you still have only a single exit point to other OSPF areas. There are many applications for this because many devices do not speak OSPF (or do not speak it well); these devices can speak RIP.

Figure 2-8 illustrates a typical NSSA network topology.

Figure 2-8   *NSSA Topological Example*

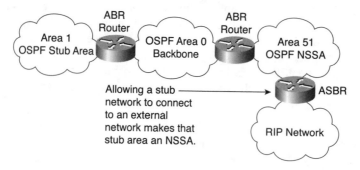

OSPF Operational Environment

This section describes the basic characteristics and features of the OSPF operational environment. The features and characteristics of its operation and design define the environment in which OSPF operates. Simply put, the operational environment of OSPF is defined as the network architecture in which the protocol can function correctly.

RFC 1793, "Extending OSPF to Support Demand Circuits," provides an example that concerns adding to OSPF the capability to operate in demand-based circuits. Until this RFC was published and implemented, OSPF did not function properly when dealing with circuits such as ISDN. Now that the protocol has been adjusted to operate properly when dealing with demand-based circuits, the functional environment of the protocol has expanded.

With that example in mind, turn your attention to the four router types and the three network types that OSPF recognizes.

Types of OSPF Routers

Four different types of routers designate the hierarchical routing structure used by OSPF. Each router has a unique role and set of defining characteristics within the hierarchy. Figure 2-9 shows a typical OSPF network, with multiple areas containing the different types of OSPF routers.

Figure 2-9   *Types of OSPF Routers*

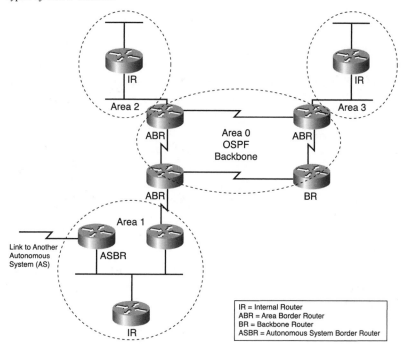

IR = Internal Router
ABR = Area Border Router
BR = Backbone Router
ASBR = Autonomous System Border Router

The following sections provide general descriptions for the four types of OSPF routers.

Internal Routers

Internal routers (IRs) are routers whose directly connected networks all belong to the same OSPF area. These types of routers have a single link-state database because they belong to only one area.

Area Border Routers

ABRs are attached to multiple OSPF areas, so there can be multiple ABRs within a network. ABRs have multiple instances of the link-state database because of this. The ABR has one database for each area that is summarized and then presented to the backbone for distribution to other areas.

Routers located on the border of one or more OSPF areas and that connect those areas to the backbone network are known as ABRs, which are considered to be members of both the OSPF backbone and the attached areas. The ABRs therefore maintain multiple link-state databases that describe both the backbone topology and the topology of the other areas. An ABR sends summary LSAs to the backbone area, and to be considered an ABR, the router must be connected to the backbone.

Autonomous System Boundary Routers

ASBRs are connected to more than one AS and exchange routing information with routers in another AS. ASBRs advertise the exchanged external routing information throughout their AS. Every router within an AS knows how to get to each ASBR with its AS. ASBRs run both OSPF and another routing protocol, such as RIP or BGP. ASBRs must reside in a nonstub OSPF area.

TIP   When using Cisco routers, the **redistribution** command is often used to bring two routing protocols together. BGP can also be used to bring multiple autonomous systems together. For additional information on this protocol and its use, see *Internet Routing Architectures, Second Edition*, by Sam Halabi.

ASBRs deal with external routes. One way that an ASBR can be configured or activated in OSPF is to add the **redistribute static** or **redistribute connected** command within the OSPF routing process.

Backbone Routers

Routers whose interfaces connect them only to the backbone area are considered backbone routers (BRs). BRs do not have an interface to the other OSPF areas, because if they did, they would be considered ABRs.

OSPF Network Types

Figure 2-10 illustrates the four different network types within which OSPF operates.

Figure 2-10   *OSPF Network Types*

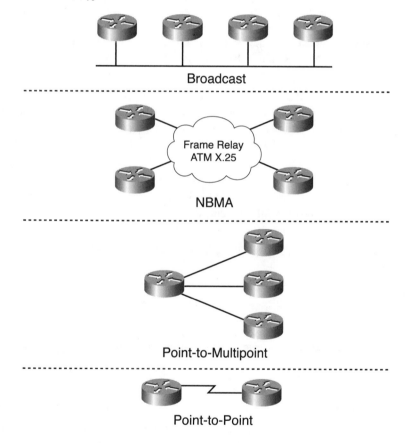

The following list explains the characteristics of the OSPF network types as illustrated in Figure 2-10:

- **Broadcast**—A network type that connects two or more OSPF routers over a broadcast media such as Ethernet or FDDI. Neighbor relationships are developed using OSPF Hellos; from that, a designated router (DR) and backup designated router (BDR) are formed via adjacencies to them.

NOTE   The next section fully explains OSPF neighbor relationships, adjacencies, and DRs.

- **Nonbroadcast multiaccess (NBMA)**—NBMA networks do not allow broadcasts by default; examples include frame relay, ATM, or X.25 networks. NBMA networks also have the potential for multiple adjacencies, but because they do not all send broadcasts, they cannot guarantee the proper relationships will form.
- **Point-to-multipoint**—A method of configuring NBMA networks that allows OSPF to operate as if the routers were connected via point-to-point links instead of via an NBMA network. There are no DRs or BDRs in this configuration because each link is treated as a point-to-point link.
- **Point-to-point**—A single circuit that connects two OSPF routers, which allows a single-neighbor relationship to be built. Some examples of this are leased lines running Point-to-Point Protocol (PPP) or High-Level Data Link Control (HDLC). There are no DRs or BDRs in this network type.

Configuring the OSPF network type is done at the interface level of a router, as demonstrated in Example 2-3.

Example 2-3   *Configuring the OSPF Network Type*

```
HAL9000(config-if)#ip ospf network ?
  broadcast               Specify OSPF broadcast multi-access network
  non-broadcast           Specify OSPF NBMA network
  point-to-multipoint     Specify OSPF point-to-multipoint network
  point-to-point          Specify OSPF point-to-point network
```

Router Identification

Every router running OSPF within a network must have a unique router ID (RID). This identification is a 32-bit number that identifies one router to another router within an AS. The RID is used by the OSPF link-state database (LSDB) as a method of tracking each router within the AS and the links that are associated with it.

This identification number is unique to each OSPF router. You can use several methods to determine how your network decides upon the OSPF RID.

To determine the RID, OSPF uses the following process:

Step 1   Has the RID been manually set using the **ospf router-id** command? If not proceed to Step 2.

Step 2   If loopback interfaces are present, the highest loopback IP address in use is used. If only a single loopback address is in use, this IP address is used. If a loopback interface is not present, go to next step.

Step 3   Set the RID as the highest IP address on one of the router's active interfaces.

Configuring a loopback address on the Cisco router has the added benefit of being much more stable than the default method of using the highest IP address present on the router, because a loopback address cannot go down or lose connectivity, which would result in the need to update routing tables. The interface is essentially a software-based interface that can be used for many additional purposes, such as summarizing IP address ranges or troubleshooting. Loopback addresses are reachable, provided they fall within the advertised IP address category.

TIP

When configuring the IP address for your loopback interface, remember that a "real" IP address uses valuable address space. The alternative is to use an unregistered or private IP address, which is essentially a made-up IP address that is not part of your network's normal IP address range. Refer to RFC 1918 if you decide to use this method.

Neighbors

OSPF considers two routers that have an interface located on a common network as *neighbors*. When OSPF discovers its neighbors, this is the first step of discovering the network and building a routing table. This process begins with the router learning the router identification numbers of its neighbors via multicast Hello packets.

Hello packets are transmitted every 10 seconds for broadcast and point-to-point interfaces and every 30 seconds on NBMA interfaces. Hello packets are sent to a multicast destination address of 224.0.0.5 (AllSPFRouters); this allows all routers running OSPF to receive and process the Hello packets.

A neighbor relationship begins when the routers exchanging Hello packets see their own RID in the other router's Hello packet and they agree upon the following:

* Hello/dead transmission intervals

* Area ID number

* Subnet mask (for multiaccess networks)

- Stub area flag (described earlier)

- Authentication type and password

The output in Example 2-4 helps you determine the neighbor relationships that your router has formed. In this example, the router HAL9000 has a relationship with all the other routers to which it is attached.

Example 2-4   *Determining Router OSPF Neighbor Relationships*

```
HAL9000#show ip ospf neighbor

Neighbor ID      Pri   State          Dead Time   Address          Interface
192.168.254.102   1   FULL/BDR       00:00:37    192.168.254.102 Ethernet0
192.168.254.100   1   FULL/DROTHER   00:00:32    192.168.254.100 Ethernet0
192.168.254.101   1   FULL/DROTHER   00:00:34    192.168.254.101 Ethernet0
HAL9000#
```

TIP   To build stable OSPF neighbor relationships, ensure that the number of routers per LAN is small. Use the **priority** command to organize which is the DR, and avoid having the same router as the DR for more than one link through the use of the **ip ospf priority** command.

Adjacencies

For adjacencies to form, OSPF must first have discovered its neighbors. Adjacencies are formed for the purpose of exchanging routing information. Not every neighboring router forms an adjacency. The conditions under which OSPF forms adjacencies are as follows:

- Network connectivity is point-to-point.

- Network connectivity is achieved through a virtual link.

- The router is the DR.

- The neighboring router is the DR.

- The router is the BDR.

- The neighboring router is the BDR.

Adjacencies control the distribution of routing updates in the sense that only routers adjacent to the one sending an update process the update. Chapter 3, "OSPF Communication," discusses the forming of adjacencies in more detail.

Neighbor Versus Adjacent OSPF Routers

This is a common question that should be explained easily yet is often not. Think of it this way. You live next to many different people, and you are considered *neighbors* to them as a result. You might wave at them when you drive to the store, but you are not close friends.

In certain circumstances, you become close friends with people with whom you were first neighbors. These close friends become known as *adjacent;* you talk to each other over the fence in the summer, have them over for dinner—that kind of thing. You essentially have a stronger level of communication with them.

You can determine which other routers you are adjacent with by using the **show ip ospf interface** command, as demonstrated in Example 2-5.

Example 2-5   *Determining Router Adjacencies*

```
HAL9000#show ip ospf interface
Ethernet0 is up, line protocol is up
  Internet Address 192.168.254.253/24, Area 0
  Process ID 100, Router ID 192.168.254.253, Network Type BROADCAST, Cost: 10
  Transmit Delay is 1 sec, State DR, Priority 1
  Designated Router (ID) 192.168.254.253, Interface address 192.168.254.253
  Backup Designated router (ID) 192.168.254.102, Interface address 192.168.254.102
  Timer intervals configured, Hello 10, Dead 40, Wait 40, Retransmit 5
    Hello due in 00:00:06
  Neighbor Count is 3, Adjacent neighbor count is 3
    Adjacent with neighbor 192.168.254.102  (Backup Designated Router)
    Adjacent with neighbor 192.168.254.100
    Adjacent with neighbor 192.168.254.101
  Suppress hello for 0 neighbor(s)
Serial0 is down, line protocol is down
  OSPF not enabled on this interface
HAL9000#
```

Designated Routers

OSPF builds adjacencies between routers for purposes of exchanging routing information. However, when OSPF has to deal with NBMA or broadcast networks, a problem presents itself. In these types of networks, there are multiple routers, which would result in too many adjacencies. To combat superfluous adjacencies, the Designated Router (DR) was introduced.

OSPF designates a single router per multiaccess network to build adjacencies among all other routers. You can calculate the number of adjacencies needed as follows:

Number of adjacencies needed = $[n(n-1)]/2$

where n is the number of routers on a common wire

For example, assume that you have 5 routers:

$[5 * (5-1)]/2 = 10$ adjacencies

As another example, assume that you have 10 routers:

$[10 * (10-1)]/2 = 45$ adjacencies

A DR is elected by OSPF's Hello protocol. The presence of a DR reduces the number of adjacencies that are formed, which in turn reduces the amount of routing protocol traffic and router overhead.

DRs are beneficial, but how does OSPF figure out which router on a network is the DR? The following steps describe how OSPF determines which router will be the DR.

NOTE   The steps that describe how a DR is elected assume that no DRs already exist on that network. If this is not the case, the process alters slightly; refer to RFC 2328 for additional information.

Figure 2-11 illustrates the process of selecting which router becomes the DR and BDR.

Figure 2-11   *Electing a DR*

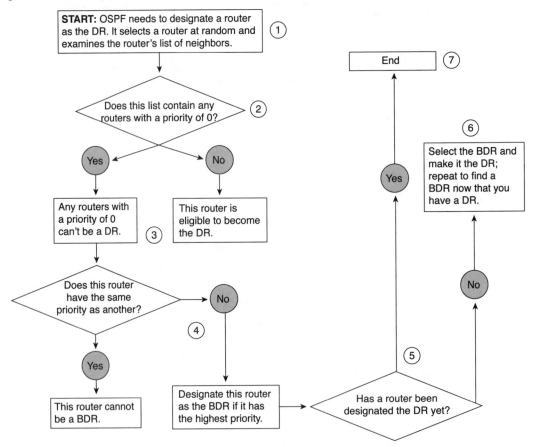

The process illustrated in Figure 2-11 uses the following steps:

1 OSPF selects a router at random and examines its list of neighbors; call this Router T. This list of router neighbors consists of all the routers that have begun a bidirectional communication among themselves. This communication is referred to as two-way and is the most advanced state of communication that neighboring routers can achieve without forming an adjacency.

2 Router T removes from that list all routers that are ineligible to become the DR. This would consist of routers that have an OSPF-assigned routing priority of 0. The process of altering the default priority is discussed later in this section. Proceed to the next step with the remaining routers on the list.

3 The BDR, which is chosen first, is determined through calculations on which router has the highest priority. If more than one router has the same priority value, OSPF takes the router with the highest router ID to break the tie.

4 Priority values can be defined or allowed to default. If a DR already exists, any router is ineligible for election at this point.

5 If no other router has declared itself to be the DR, assign the newly commissioned BDR to become the DR.

6 If Router T is now the new DR, the process begins again to identify which router functions as the BDR.

   For example, if Router T is the DR, it is ineligible for election when Step 3 is repeated. This ensures that no Router declares itself both the DR and the BDR. As a result of these calculations, Router T has become the DR and the router's OSPF interface state is set accordingly. For example, the DR has a new interface state of DR and the BDR has an interface state of DR other.

7 The DR now begins sending Hello packets to begin the process of building the necessary adjacencies with the remainder of the network's routers.

Case Study: Adding a New OSPF Router to a Network

This case study provides a scenario that covers most of the information presented in this chapter. Suppose that a new OSPF router is added to a network. With this scenario, follow the case study to understand the ramifications of how adding a new OSPF router would affect an operating network. Refer to Figures 2-12 through 2-15, which detail each step of the process as it occurs in the following sequence:

1 A new OSPF router is added to the network.

2 This new router immediately transmits a multicast Hello packet by using the all-OSPF routers multicast address of 224.0.0.5. At this point, the router does not know if there is a DR (see Figure 2-12).

Figure 2-12   *Adding a New Router*

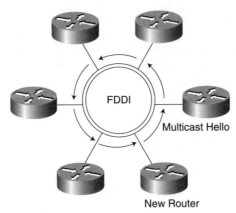

3 The DR and BDR respond to the new router with a unicast Hello packet that is
specifically addressed to it. This begins the process of building an adjacency (see
Figure 2-13).

Figure 2-13   *DR and BDR Respond*

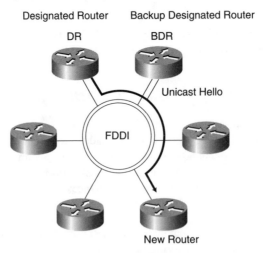

4 After the adjacency has been established with the DR, the new router sends a router LSA (Type 1) to the DR describing the specific links it has available and the status of these links. During this time, the BDR is also listening to see if the DR responds, thus proving that the BDR is operational (see Figure 2-14).

Figure 2-14   *Router LSA Is Sent*

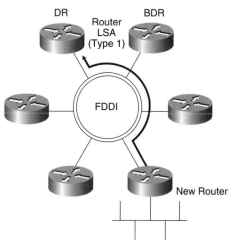

5 The BDR continues to listen, thereby ensuring that the DR is operating. The DR sends out a multicast (224.0.0.5) network LSA to the entire network, informing them of the new routes available as a result of the new router. All routers must then respond with an acknowledgment so that the DR knows that they have received the new information (see Figure 2-15). If the DR fails, the BDR becomes the DR, and another election takes place to determine the new BDR.

Figure 2-15   *Network LSA Is Sent*

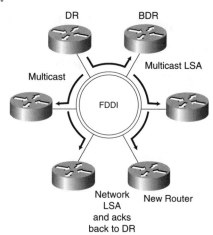

At this point, the new router has been fully identified to all other routers within the network. This information also includes any networks the new router can reach.

In certain OSPF networks, you want to force the determination of which router is to be the OSPF DR and BDR. For example, perhaps you have some routers that have larger processors and more memory, in which case you would want to make them the DRs. In addition, perhaps you are preparing for a certification lab test. In these cases, you use a command, applied on a per-interface basis, known as **ip ospf priority**.

The default value is 1, so the higher the router priority, the more likely it is to become the DR or BDR. This command can also be used to guarantee that a router does not become the DR by setting the priority to zero.

NOTE   Router priority is configured only for interfaces to multiaccess networks (in other words, not for point-to-point networks).

For example, to set the router priority value to 5, you enter the following commands:

```
interface ethernet 0
ip ospf priority 5
```

It is important to understand that the order in which routers join an OSPF area can have an effect on which routers are elected as the DR and BDR. Specifically, an election is necessary only when a DR or BDR does not exist in the network. As a router starts its OSPF process, it checks the network for an active DR and BDR. If they exist, the new router becomes a DR other; in other words, it does not become the DR or the BDR, regardless of its priority or router ID. Remember, the roles of DR and BDR were created for efficiency; new routers in the network should not force an election when roles are already optimized.

Case Study: Developing the Link-State Database

Earlier in this chapter, you learned how LSAs were used to send information about the links between OSPF routers. These LSAs are stored in the router in a database with each LSA as a record in that database.

Figure 2-16 shows the OSPF network topology for this case study.

Figure 2-16 *OSPF Network Topology for Link-State Database Case Study*

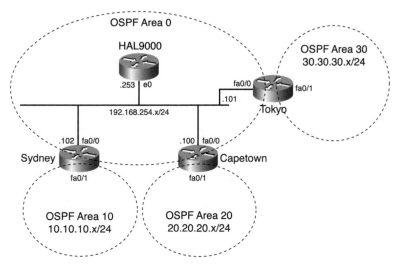

Example 2-6 shows entries generated by the **show ip ospf database** command from the router HAL9000.

Example 2-6 *Viewing the LSA Database for the HAL9000 Router*

```
HAL9000#show ip ospf database
        OSPF Router with ID (192.168.254.253) (Process ID 100)
                Router Link-states (Area 0)
Link ID          ADV Router       Age       Seq#        Checksum Link count
192.168.254.100 192.168.254.100 649        0x80000003 0x75C    1
192.168.254.101 192.168.254.101 651        0x80000003 0x55B    1
192.168.254.102 192.168.254.102 582        0x8000000A 0xF461   1
192.168.254.253 192.168.254.253 1486       0x80000051 0xD669   1
                Net Link-states (Area 0)
Link ID          ADV Router       Age       Seq#        Checksum
192.168.254.253 192.168.254.253 1346       0x80000006 0x355B
                Summary Net Link-states (Area 0)
Link ID          ADV Router       Age       Seq#        Checksum
10.10.10.0       192.168.254.102 648        0x80000002 0xBC91
20.20.20.0       192.168.254.100 1312       0x80000001 0x61D1
30.30.30.0       192.168.254.101 651        0x80000002 0xEF23
HAL9000#
```

Notice how the output here shows no information on the other areas in Figure 2-16. This is because the HAL9000 router is a backbone router and has no other interfaces in areas other than area 0. Contrast the output in Example 2-6 for the HAL9000 router with the output generated from the same command on the Tokyo router in Example 2-7.

Example 2-7   *Viewing the LSA Database for the Tokyo Router*

```
Tokyo#show ip ospf database
        OSPF Router with ID (192.168.254.101) (Process ID 100)
                Router Link-states (Area 0)
 Link ID          ADV Router      Age        Seq#        Checksum Link count
 192.168.254.100 192.168.254.100 903         0x80000003 0x75C    1
 192.168.254.101 192.168.254.101 903         0x80000003 0x55B    1
 192.168.254.102 192.168.254.102 836         0x8000000A 0xF461   1
 192.168.254.253 192.168.254.253 1740        0x80000051 0xD669   1
                Net Link-states (Area 0)
 Link ID          ADV Router      Age        Seq#        Checksum
 192.168.254.253 192.168.254.253 1601        0x80000006 0x355B
                Summary Net Link-states (Area 0)
 Link ID          ADV Router      Age        Seq#        Checksum
 10.10.10.0       192.168.254.102 902         0x80000002 0xBC91
 20.20.20.0       192.168.254.100 1567        0x80000001 0x61D1
 30.30.30.0       192.168.254.101 904         0x80000002 0xEF23
                Router Link-states (Area 30)
 Link ID          ADV Router      Age        Seq#        Checksum Link count
 192.168.254.101 192.168.254.101 904         0x80000002 0xCC6D   1
                Summary Net Link-states (Area 30)
 Link ID          ADV Router      Age        Seq#        Checksum
 10.10.10.0       192.168.254.101 826         0x80000005 0xC684
 20.20.20.0       192.168.254.101 1566        0x80000001 0x65CB
 192.168.254.0    192.168.254.101 1421        0x80000007 0x7B84
Tokyo#
```

NOTE   In many cases, people use the term *topological database* to describe the link-state database. That is technically incorrect because RFC 2328 on OSPF v2 refers to the table as the link-state database.

Each of these entries in Example 2-7 has a meaning in the LSA as defined in the following list:

- **Heading and introduction**—Cisco routers present you with a good bit of information about what you are viewing prior to giving you the LSA entries. The first part tells you what the RID is for, what router you have executed the command on, and what OSPF routing process this database is for. Cisco routers can run multiple and separate instances of OSPF.

- **Area information**—If you recall, a router like an ABR maintains a separate link-state database (LSDB) for each OSPF area. This part of the example reveals the type of LSA and for which OSPF area the LSDB relates:

- **Link ID**—RID of the router sending the LSA.

- **ADV router**—Identifies the advertising router by its RID that originated the LSA.

- **Age**—Age of the LSA in seconds.

- **Seq#**—Sequence number of the LSA and is included within the LSA and the database to prevent old or duplicate information.

- **Checksum**—Ensures that the LSA checks out.

- **Link count**—Number of interfaces that OSPF is running on for the router that transmitted the LSA. This field is present only in a Type 1 router LSA.

Figure 2-17 shows a network with eight routers, all running OSPF and with several of the interfaces associated with different costs (indicated by thicker lines for easy reference).

Figure 2-17   *Sample OSPF Network*

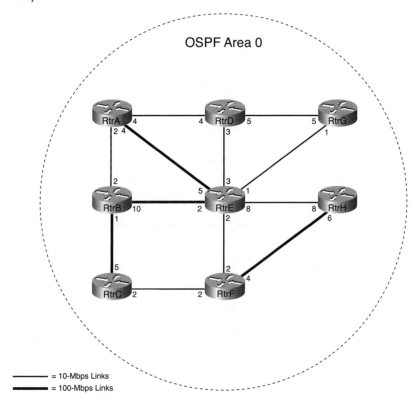

When viewing this network, note that cost is placed on a link per outgoing interface. For example, for RtrA, it would cost 4 to go directly to RtrE in the center of the network. However, if you were in RtrE, it would cost 5 to go directly to RtrA. Therefore, cost is considered to be interface-based and is applied in an outgoing direction.

With the given network, OSPF develops a link-state database based on the topology shown in Figure 2-17. In this network, it is assumed that all the routers belong to a single OSPF area, so each router has an identical copy of the database and no other. This example uses area 0.

NOTE   To make the table more legible, the names of the routers in Figure 2-17 have been abbreviated as RA for RtrA, RB for RtrB, and so on.

Table 2-4 shows the link-state database for each router in the OSPF network in Figure 2-17. This table consists of several parts, each of which represents the contents of the link-state database for each of the routers in Figure 2-17. The Router ID column identifies each of the routers. The layout of the link-state database is a result of OSPF building the link-state database with itself as the root of the tree. The next column, Neighbor, contains all the other routers to which the root router is directly connected (that is, its neighbors). The third and final column indicates the cost for the root router to reach its neighbor.

For example, consider Router A (RA). It has three neighbors: B, D, and E. The cost to reach B is 2, the cost to reach E is 4, and so on.

Table 2-4   *Link-State Database by Router for the OSPF Network*

Router ID	Neighbor	Cost
RA	RB	2
RA	RD	4
RA	RE	4
RB	RA	2
RB	RC	1
RB	RE	10
RC	RB	5
RC	RF	2
RD	RA	4
RD	RE	3
RD	RG	5
RE	RA	5
RE	RB	2
RE	RD	3
RE	RF	2
RE	RG	1
RE	RH	8
RF	RC	2
RF	RE	2
RF	RH	4
RG	RE	1
RH	RE	8
RH	RF	6

At this point, the network is not nearly converged. The next step is to go through that entire process. Dijkstra's algorithm was adapted for use when routers are running the SPF algorithm. This process starts with the router having already created a link-state database, as shown in Table 2-4. The process is described in the following steps:

1 A router begins the process of creating the SPF tree database by adding itself as the root of the SPF tree (recall Figure 2-6). When the router starts as the root, it enters itself as its own neighbor, with a cost of 0.

2 All entries in the link-state database that describe links to the root router's neighbors are added to the candidate database.

NOTE   A *candidate database* is a working database that OSPF creates during this process to expedite the calculation of the SPF tree entries from which the router derives the routing table.

---

3 The cost from the root router to each link in the candidate database is calculated. The link in the candidate database with the lowest cost is moved to the tree database. If two or more links are an equally low cost from the root, choose one.

NOTE   The *tree database* is the output of the root router running the SPF algorithm on the candidate database. When the algorithm is completed, the tree database contains the shortest path.

---

4 The neighbor RID of the link that was just added to the tree database is examined. With the exception of any entries whose neighbor ID is already in the tree database, information in the link-state database describing that router's neighbors is added to the candidate database.

5 If entries remain in the candidate database, return to Step 3. If the candidate database is empty, the SPF algorithm is stopped. The SPF calculations are finished and successful when a single neighbor ID entry is in the tree database that represents every router in the OSPF area.

Table 2-5 summarizes the process and results of applying Dijkstra's algorithm to build a shortest-path tree for the network in Figure 2-17.

In Table 2-5, the columns each represent various processes on how the network converges. The first column represents the potential candidate entries into the link-state database; after the calculations, these entries are entered into the tree database. The Description column explains the events that are occurring.

Table 2-5   *SPF Algorithm Applied to the Database of Table 2-4*

Candidate Entries	Cost to Root	Tree Database	Description
-	-	RA,RA,0	RA adds itself to the SPF tree as root.
RA,RB,2 RA,RD,4 RA,RE,4	2 4 4	RA,RA,0	The links and their costs to all of RA's neighbors are added to the candidate list.
RA,RD,4 RA,RE,4 RB,RC,1 RB,RE,10 RD,RE,7	4 4 3	RA,RA,0 RA,RB,2	(RA,RB,2) is the lowest-cost link on the candidate list, so it is added to the tree. All of RB's neighbors, except those already in the tree, are added to the candidate list. Note that there are three paths to RE. (RA,RE,4) is a lower-cost link to RE than (RB,RE,10) or (RD,RE,7), so the last two links are dropped from the candidate list.
RA,RD,4 RA,RE,4 RC,RF,2	4 4 5	RA,RA,0 RA,RB,2 RB,RC,1	(RB,RC,1) is the lowest-cost link on the candidate list, so it is added to the tree. All of RC's neighbors, except those already on the tree, become candidates.
RA,RE,4 RC,RF,2 RD,RE,3 RD,RG,5	4 5 7 9	RA,RA,0 RA,RB,2 RB,RC,1 RA,RD,4	(RA,RD,4) and (RA,RE,4) are both a cost of 4 from RA; (RC,RF,2) is a cost of 5. (RA,RD,4) is added to the tree, and its neighbors become candidates. Two paths to RE are on the candidate list; (RD,RE,3) is a higher cost from RA and is dropped.
RC,RF,2 RD,RG,5 RE,RF,2 RE,RG,1 RE,RH,8	5 9 6 5 12	RA,RA,0 RA,RB,2 RB,RC,1 RA,RD,4 RA,RE,4	(RF,RE,1) is added to the tree. All of RE's neighbors not already on the tree are added to the candidate list. The higher-cost link to RG is dropped.
RE,RF,2 RE,RG,1 RE,RH,8 RF,RH,4	6 5 12 9	RA,RA,0 RA,RB,2 RB,RC,1 RA,RD,4 RA,RE,4 RC,RF,2	(RC,RF,2) is added to the tree, and its neighbors are added to the candidate list. (RE,RG,1) could have been selected instead because it has the same cost (5) from RA. The higher-cost path to RH is dropped.
RF,RH,4		RA,RA,0 RA,RB,2 RB,RC,1 RA,RD,4 RA,RE,4 RC,RF,2 RE,RG,1	(RE,RG,1) is added to the tree. RG has no neighbors that are not already on the tree, so nothing is added to the candidate list.
		RA,RA,0 RA,RB,2 RB,RC,1 RA,RD,4 RA,RE,4 RC,RF,2 RE,RG,1 RF,RH,4	(RF,RH,4) is the lowest-cost link on the candidate list, so it is added to the tree. No candidates remain on the list, so the algorithm is terminated. The shortest-path tree is complete when RA has a complete tree with all the shortest links to all other routers in the network.

RtrA from Figure 2-17 is running the SPF algorithm, using the link-state database of Table 2-5. Figure 2-18 shows the shortest-path tree constructed for RtrA by this algorithm. After each router calculates its own tree, it can examine the other routers' network link information and add the stub networks to the tree fairly easily. From this information, entries can be made into the routing table.

Figure 2-18 *SPF Results*

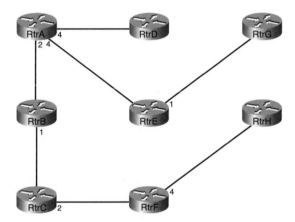

Case Study: OSPF Network Evolution and Convergence

The preceding two case studies reviewed the link-state database and how it was developed. This case study takes some concepts that were introduced in this chapter and shows how a simple OSPF network evolves and converges.

MatrixNet, a high-tech graphics firm that does specialized animations for the movie industry, has approached you to implement OSPF in its core network. The network is connected via Ethernet between the three routers, as shown in Figure 2-19.

Figure 2-19   *MatrixNet OSPF Core Network*

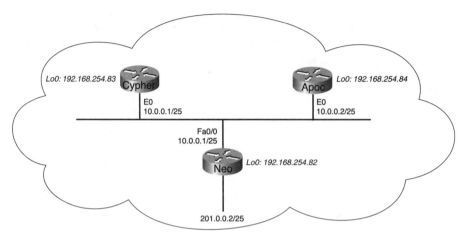

In this case study, you configure OSPF on three Cisco routers. First, you configure loopback interfaces to provide stable OSPF router IDs. Then, you configure the OSPF process and enable OSPF on the appropriate interfaces.

Configuring Loopback Interfaces

When a loopback interface is not configured, OSPF uses the highest active interface IP address as its router ID. In this network, a single Class C subnet contains all the network management addresses for the entire network. Because the loopback interfaces are immune to physical and data link problems, configuring them is an excellent method to set an RID. Example 2-8 shows the configuration of a loopback interface on Routers Neo, Cypher, and Apoc.

Example 2-8   *Configuring a Loopback Interface*

```
Neo(config)#interface lo0
Neo(config-if)#ip address 192.168. 254.82 255.255.255.0
Cypher(config)#interface lo0
Cypher(config-if)#ip address 192.168.254.83 255.255.255.0
Apoc(config)#interface lo0
Apoc config-if)#ip address 192.168.254.84 255.255.255.0
```

Enabling OSPF

Now that loopback interfaces are configured, you must configure OSPF. Use the commands in Example 2-9 to configure each router.

Example 2-9   *Configuring OSPF*

```
Neo(config)#router ospf 100
Neo(config-router)#network 192.168.254.0 0.0.0.255 area 0
Neo(config-router)#network 10.0.0.0 0.0.0.127 area 0
```

Verifying OSPF Operation

After you enable OSPF routing on each of the three routers, verify its operation using **show** commands, as demonstrated in Example 2-10.

Example 2-10   *Verifying OPSF Routing*

```
Neo#show ip protocols
Routing Protocol is "ospf 100"
  Sending updates every 0 seconds
  Invalid after 0 seconds, hold down 0, flushed after 0
  Outgoing update filter list for all interfaces is
  Incoming update filter list for all interfaces is
  Redistributing: ospf 100
  Routing for Networks:
    10.0.0.0/25
    192.168.254.0
    201.0.0.0/25
  Routing Information Sources:
    Gateway         Distance      Last Update
    192.168.254.84       110      03:09:43
    192.168.254.83       110      03:09:43
  Distance: (default is 110)
```

With this command output, you can gain some useful data regarding the operation of OSPF in your network. You can see the networks that OSPF is routing as well the RIDs of the other routers in the network that have sent routing information. The output from the **show ip ospf** command, as demonstrated in Example 2-11, displays more specific information regarding how OSPF is running on the router that the command is executed on.

Example 2-11   *Output from the **show ip ospf** Command*

```
Neo#show ip ospf
 Routing Process "ospf 100" with ID 192.168.254.82
 Supports only single TOS(TOS0) routes
 Supports opaque LSA
 It is an area border router
 SPF schedule delay 5 secs, Hold time between two SPFs 10 secs
 Minimum LSA interval 5 secs. Minimum LSA arrival 1 secs
 Number of external LSA 0. Checksum Sum 0x0
 Number of opaque AS LSA 0. Checksum Sum 0x0
 Number of DCbitless external and opaque AS LSA 0
 Number of DoNotAge external and opaque AS LSA 0
 Number of areas in this router is 2. 1 normal 1 stub 0 nssa
 External flood list length 0
    Area BACKBONE(0)
        Number of interfaces in this area is 2
        Area has no authentication
        SPF algorithm executed 15 times
        Area ranges are
        Number of LSA 4. Checksum Sum 0x158A8
        Number of opaque link LSA 0. Checksum Sum 0x0
        Number of DCbitless LSA 0
        Number of indication LSA 0
```

continues

Example 2-11 *Output from the* **show ip ospf** *Command (Continued)*

```
          Number of DoNotAge LSA 0
          Flood list length 0
     Area 201
          Number of interfaces in this area is 1
          It is a stub area
            generates stub default route with cost 1
          Area has no authentication
          SPF algorithm executed 7 times
          Area ranges are
              100.0.0.0/16 Passive Advertise
              201.0.0.0/16 Passive Advertise
          Number of LSA 6. Checksum Sum 0x42B44
          Number of opaque link LSA 0. Checksum Sum 0x0
          Number of DCbitless LSA 0
          Number of indication LSA 0
          Number of DoNotAge LSA 0
          Flood list length 0
```

This **show** command provides a wealth of OSPF information and how OSPF is operating on the router that it is executed on. Through this command, you see what the RID is for OSPF (192.168.254.82), which is the loopback interface's IP address that you configured earlier in Example 2-8. You can also see what kind of OSPF router it is (for example, an ABR). You can also see how many times the SPF algorithm has run per area (recall that OSPF calculates the LSDB on a per-area basis).

On the router you are evaluating, you want to find out what the router knows about OSPF on other routers and the network in general. The next set of commands reference the neighbors and what router (Neo) learned about them. Example 2-12 provides information about the neighboring routers using the **show ip ospf neighbor** command.

Example 2-12 *Displaying Neighboring Router OSPF Information*

```
Neo#show ip ospf neighbor

Neighbor ID     Pri   State         Dead Time   Address     Interface
192.168.254.83   1    FULL/DROTHER  00:00:38    10.0.0.1    FastEthernet0/0
192.168.254.84   1    FULL/BDR      00:00:37    10.0.0.2    FastEthernet0/0
Neo#
```

In this output, you can see the following:

- RIDs of Neo's neighboring routers
- State of communication each is in (more on that in Chapter 3)
- IP address on the neighbor router from which Neo received the OSPF communication
- Receiving interface

This is useful information when you are working with networks that have large numbers of neighbors. Now look at the State column. As previously mentioned, Neo is communicating to each neighbor, as represented by the FULL status. The other part of the State column indicates the role that router is playing. In other words, the 192.168.254.84 neighbor is the BDR for the network, and neighbor 192.168.254.83 says it is DROTHER (that is, DR other). Can you guess which of the three routers is the DR? The results of the **show ip ospf neighbor detail** command in Example 2-13 tells you if you guessed correctly.

Example 2-13 *Displaying Detailed Neighboring Router OSPF Information*

```
Neo#show ip ospf neighbor detail
 Neighbor 192.168.254.83, interface address 10.0.0.1
    In the area 0 via interface FastEthernet0/0
    Neighbor priority is 1, State is FULL, 6 state changes
    DR is 10.0.0.3 BDR is 10.0.0.2
    Options is 0x2
    Dead timer due in 00:00:33
    Index 2/2, retransmission queue length 0, number of retransmission 2
    First 0x0(0)/0x0(0) Next 0x0(0)/0x0(0)
    Last retransmission scan length is 1, maximum is 1
    Last retransmission scan time is 0 msec, maximum is 0 msec
 Neighbor 192.168.254.84, interface address 10.0.0.2
    In the area 0 via interface FastEthernet0/0
    Neighbor priority is 1, State is FULL, 6 state changes
    DR is 10.0.0.3 BDR is 10.0.0.2
    Options is 0x2
    Dead timer due in 00:00:39
    Index 1/1, retransmission queue length 0, number of retransmission 1
    First 0x0(0)/0x0(0) Next 0x0(0)/0x0(0)
    Last retransmission scan length is 1, maximum is 1
    Last retransmission scan time is 0 msec, maximum is 0 msec
Neo#
```

The **show ip ospf neighbor detail** command provides all the data needed to analyze the communication between OSPF neighbor routers. Notice that this command identifies the DR and BDR for the network and shows all the information regarding the various OSPF timers.

The **show ip ospf interface** command is one of the most descriptive regarding the status of the network. With this command, you can determine how OSPF is operating on the interface it is run on and what those operational parameters are. Because each interface on a given router is connected to a different network, some of the key OSPF information is interface-specific. Example 2-14 demonstrates sample output from this command.

Example 2-14 *Output from the* **show ip ospf interface** *Command*

```
Neo#show ip ospf interface fa0/0
FastEthernet0/0 is up, line protocol is up
  Internet Address 10.0.0.3/25, Area 0
  Process ID 100, Router ID 192.168.254.82, Network Type BROADCAST, Cost: 1
  Transmit Delay is 1 sec, State DR, Priority 1
  Designated Router (ID) 192.168.254.82, Interface address 10.0.0.3
  Backup Designated router (ID) 192.168.254.84, Interface address 10.0.0.2
  Timer intervals configured, Hello 10, Dead 40, Wait 40, Retransmit 5
    Hello due in 00:00:09
  Index 1/1, flood queue length 0
  Next 0x0(0)/0x0(0)
  Last flood scan length is 0, maximum is 3
  Last flood scan time is 0 msec, maximum is 0 msec
  Neighbor Count is 2, Adjacent neighbor count is 2
    Adjacent with neighbor 192.168.254.83
    Adjacent with neighbor 192.168.254.84  (Backup Designated Router)
  Suppress hello for 0 neighbor(s)
Neo#
```

The final command discussed in this chapter is the **show ip ospf database** command. You have seen how the LSDB is formed and the role that it plays in developing the routing table in an OSPF network. Example 2-15 demonstrates how the LSDB is represented in a Cisco router.

Example 2-15 *Output from the* **show ip ospf database** *Command*

```
Neo#show ip ospf database

        OSPF Router with ID (192.168.254.82) (Process ID 100)


                Router Link States (Area 0)

Link ID         ADV Router      Age        Seq#       Checksum Link count
192.168.254.82  192.168.254.82  1696       0x80000013 0x6A5A   2
192.168.254.83  192.168.254.83  1943       0x8000000D 0x4E71   2
192.168.254.84  192.168.254.84  1675       0x8000000D 0x5F5D   2

                Net Link States (Area 0)

Link ID         ADV Router      Age        Seq#       Checksum
10.0.0.3        192.168.254.82  1951       0x8000000B 0x2090

                Router Link States (Area 201)

Link ID         ADV Router      Age        Seq#       Checksum Link count
192.168.254.82  192.168.254.82  423        0x8000000F 0xD1EE    0
```

Example 2-15 *Output from the* **show ip ospf database** *Command (Continued)*

```
                    Summary Net Link States (Area 201)

Link ID           ADV Router       Age      Seq#        Checksum
0.0.0.0           192.168.254.82   1178     0x8000000C  0xA8CF
10.0.0.0          192.168.254.82   1953     0x80000011  0x1FC9
192.168.254.82    192.168.254.82   1698     0x8000000B  0xCCF1
192.168.254.83    192.168.254.82   1953     0x8000000B  0xCCEF
192.168.254.84    192.168.254.82   1698     0x8000000B  0xC2F8
```

This command presents which LSDB to use based on area and LSA type; more discussion is presented in Chapter 3. However, you can see that each link is represented.

Summary

This chapter discussed the fundamental concepts of routing protocols and analyzed the differences between the two most important link-state protocols, IS-IS and OSPF. One section was dedicated to objectively analyzing and supporting the choice of a network protocol. Hopefully though, the inherent benefits of OSPF are readily apparent to you! It is also important to understand that sometimes being able to make a business successful is almost as important as being able to implement and design a network.

The "OSPF Routing Hierarchy" section demonstrated how that protocol permits a variety of configurations and implementations. This capability requires many different levels or areas. OSPF's capability to perform as a hierarchical routing protocol allows it to be considered in networks of varying sizes. As a result of this, OSPF supports a variety of techniques and designations that make operation and design much smoother. Within this section, you learned about the types of OSPF routers and hierarchical design techniques. The latter included how OSPF separates the hierarchy through the use of areas and autonomous systems.

The "OSPF Operational Environment" section helped you understand the internetworking environment of the OSPF protocol so that you can design a network in which it operates properly. The functional environment is a key element in understanding OSPF. Within this section, several basics to the protocol are discussed: network types, router identification, adjacencies, designated routers, protocols within OSPF, and LSAs.

CHAPTER 3

OSPF Communication

Believe in yourself. You gain strength, courage, and confidence by every experience in which you stop to look fear in the face... You must do that which you think you cannot do.—Eleanor Roosevelt

This chapter introduces you to how OSPF communicates among routers running OSPF. Chapter 2, "Introduction to OSPF," introduced the components and roles that the routers play when using OSPF and how routes are calculated through the SPF algorithm. When discussing the SPF operations, you were presented with a case study that outlined entry processing in the OSPF link-state database and how routes were determined. This chapter covers how the link-state information is then entered into the link-state database through OSPF's use of link-state advertisements (LSAs). This chapter also covers the various internal OSPF protocols that define and allow OSPF routers to communicate.

Link-State Advertisements

A *link* is any type of connection between OSPF routers, such as a frame relay link or an Ethernet segment. The *state* is the condition of the link, that is, whether the link is available for use (for example, up or down). An *advertisement* is the method that OSPF uses to provide information to other OSPF routers. Therefore, LSAs are a special type of packet that OSPF uses to advertise changes in the state of a specific link to other OSPF routers.

Types of LSAs

Unlike distance vector protocols (RIP or IGRP), OSPF does not send its routing table to other routers. Instead, routing tables are derived from the LSA database, as discussed in Chapter 2. OSPF has a variety of router designations and area types. This complexity requires that OSPF communicates information as accurately as possible to achieve optimal routing. OSPF accomplishes this communication through the use of different types of LSAs. Table 3-1 describes the ten different types of LSA packets that can be generated by the source router and entered into the destination router's LSA database. However, note that Cisco has not implemented all the possible OSPF LSAs, specifically the Type 6 multicast LSA, as documented in RFC 1584.

Table 3-1   *Types of LSAs*

LSA Type Number	LSA Description
1	Router link advertisements
2	Network link advertisements
3	ABR summary link advertisements
4	ASBR summary link advertisements
5	Autonomous system external route advertisements
6	Multicast group LSA (not implemented by Cisco)
7	Not-so-stubby area (NSSAs) external
9	Opaque LSA: Link-local scope
10	Opaque LSA: Area-local Scope
11	Opaque LSA: autonomous system scope

The following section provides general descriptions, an operational overview, and the packet format of nine of the LSA packet types. (Type 6 is not discussed.)

Although several different types of LSAs exist and each has a unique structure to reflect the information it contains, they each share a common packet header, as shown in Figure 3-1. After the common header, the specific LSA packet information is then provided for router processing. You learn about the packet structure for each LSA type as it is discussed.

Figure 3-1   *Link-State Advertisement Common Header*

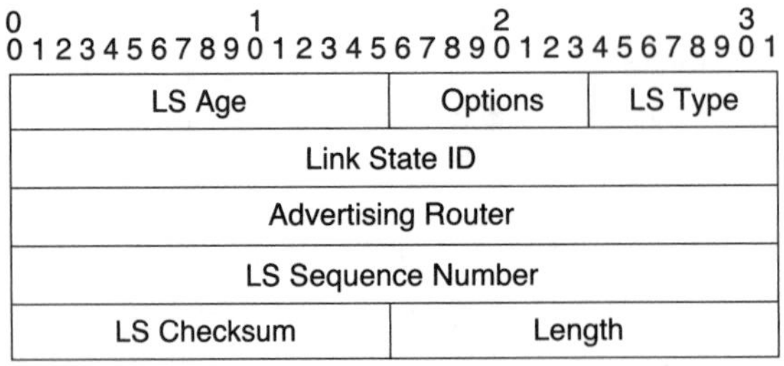

```
0                   1                   2                   3
0 1 2 3 4 5 6 7 8 9 0 1 2 3 4 5 6 7 8 9 0 1 2 3 4 5 6 7 8 9 0 1
```

LS Age	Options	LS Type
Link State ID		
Advertising Router		
LS Sequence Number		
LS Checksum	Length	

Type 1: Router LSAs

Router LSAs describe the states of the router's links within the area and are flooded only within an area for which that router is a member. The fact that Type 1 LSAs describe links in the area is a key differentiator between this LSA type and the others. For example, an OSPF ABR router is in two areas and sends router LSAs for the link that resides only in each area. (That is, cross-transmission is not allowed.)

When discussing OSPF LSAs, you need to understand that OSPF has two native types of routes:

- **Intra-area route**—A route found within an OSPF area
- **Inter-area route**—A route found in a different OSPF area

Figure 3-2 shows that Type 1 LSAs contain intra-area information.

Figure 3-2   *Type 1 LSA Operation: Router LSAs Describe the Current State of the Router's Links (Interfaces) to the OSPF Area (Intra-Area)*

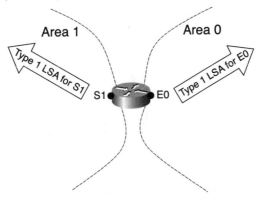

The link-state ID is the originating router's ID. Figure 3-3 shows the structure of each router LSA packet.

Figure 3-3   *Router LSA Packet Layout*

```
0                   1                   2                   3
0 1 2 3 4 5 6 7 8 9 0 1 2 3 4 5 6 7 8 9 0 1 2 3 4 5 6 7 8 9 0 1
```

0 V E B	0	Number of Links
Link ID		
Link Data		
Type	#TOS	TOS 0 Metric
TOS=x	0	TOS x Metric
TOS=y	0	TOS y Metric
---	---	---
TOS=z	0	TOS z Metric

Type 2: Network LSAs

Network LSAs are generated only by designated routers (DRs) and describe the set of routers attached to a particular nonbroadcast multiaccess (NBMA) or broadcast network.

The purpose of the network LSA is to ensure that only one LSA is generated for the NBMA or broadcast network (as opposed to one from each attached router). This is a form of internal OSPF summarization. Specifically, Type 2 LSAs describe all routers that are attached to a multiaccess network. This information is an indication of all routers that are connected to a particular multiaccess segment, such as Ethernet, Token Ring, FDDI, and Frame Relay (as well as NBMA). Figure 3-4 shows that Type 2 LSAs are flooded in the area that contains the network.

Figure 3-4   *Type 2 Network LSA Operation: Describing the OSPF Routers in a Network*

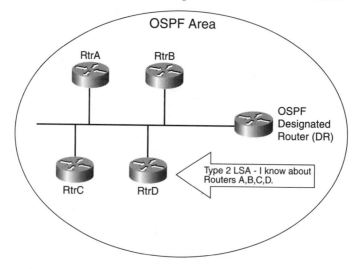

The link-state ID is the IP interface address of the DR. Figure 3-5 shows the structure of each network LSA packet.

Figure 3-5   *Network LSA Packet Format*

```
0                   1                   2                   3
0 1 2 3 4 5 6 7 8 9 0 1 2 3 4 5 6 7 8 9 0 1 2 3 4 5 6 7 8 9 0 1
```

LS Age	Options	2
Link State ID		
Advertising Router		
LS Sequence Number		
LS Checksum	Length	
Network Mask		
Attached Router		
...		

NOTE	Type of service (TOS) is no longer used in OSPF, so TOS fields remain for clarity in the packet structure.

Type 3: ABR Summary LSAs

Summary LSAs are generated only by area border routers (ABRs) and describe inter-area routes to various networks. Specifically, Type 3 LSAs describe networks that are within the OSPF autonomous system but outside of the particular OSPF area that is receiving the LSA. A Type 3 LSA has a *flooding scope* of being transmitted only into the area where the network or subnet is not found. For example, if an ABR is connected to area 1 and area 0 with a network that has subnet 172.16.1.0/24 in area 1, a Type 3 LSA is not flooded into area 1 for that subnet. The ABR generates a Type 3 LSA and floods it into area 0 but not into area 1. Figure 3-6 demonstrates this concept. These LSAs can also be used for aggregating routes.

Figure 3-6   *Type 3 LSA Operation: Type 3 LSAs Tell Other Areas About Other Inter-Area Routes*

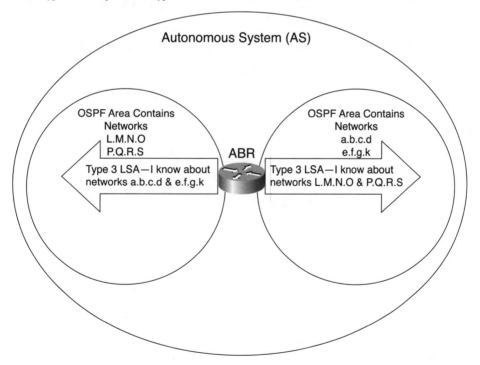

The link-state ID is the destination network number. Figure 3-7 shows the format of each summary LSA packet.

Figure 3-7   *Summary LSA Packet (Type 3 and 4) Format*

0	1	2	3
0 1 2 3 4 5 6 7 8 9	0 1 2 3 4 5 6 7 8 9	0 1 2 3 4 5 6 7 8 9	0 1

Network Mask		
TOS=0	0	TOS 0 Metric
TOS=x	0	TOS x Metric
- - -	- - -	- - -
TOS=z	0	TOS z Metric

Type 4: ASBR Summary LSAs

Type 4 LSAs are very similar in function to Type 3 LSAs, but the two must not be confused. Each summary LSA describes a route to a destination outside the OSPF area yet still inside the autonomous system (that is, an inter-area route). The Type 4 summary LSAs describe routes to autonomous system (AS) boundary routers (ASBRs) and are also generated by ABRs. Therefore, Type 4 LSAs enable other routers to find and reach the ASBR. Figure 3-8 shows the operation of Type 4 LSAs.

Figure 3-8   *Type 4 Summary LSAs: Type 4 LSAs Tell the Network How to Reach the ASBR*

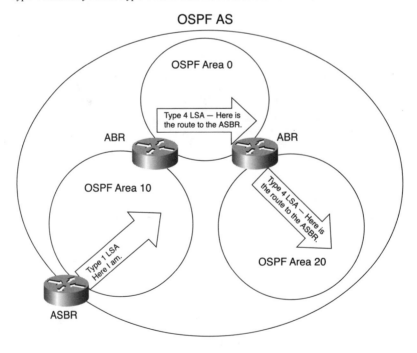

The link-state ID is the router ID of the described ASBR. Figure 3-7 (shown previously) illustrates the format of each packet.

Type 5: Autonomous System External LSAs

Type 5 LSAs are generated by the ASBRs. These LSAs describe routes to destinations that are external to the AS. Type 5 LSAs are flooded everywhere, with the exception of stub areas.

External links are an indication of networks outside of the OSPF routing process in the AS. These outside networks can be injected into OSPF via different sources, such as static and redistribution. The ASBR has the task of injecting these routes into an AS. Figure 3-9 illustrates the operation of Type 5 LSAs.

Figure 3-9   *Type 5 LSA Operation*

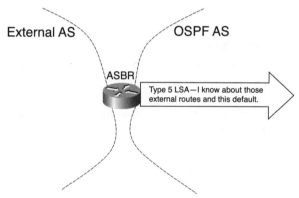

Consider a real-world example of how a Type 5 LSA might be used. In Figure 3-9, you see an AS that has a default route to the Internet. The ASBR knows about the default route, but in order for the rest of the network to know about it, the ASBR must inject the route into an advertisement. The advertisement that carries this default route information to the rest of the AS is the Type 5 LSA.

The link-state ID is the external network number. Type 5 LSAs also inform other routers about a default route if one is configured in your network. Figure 3-10 shows the format of Type 5 LSA packets.

Figure 3-10   *Type 5 LSA Packet Structure*

```
0                   1                   2                   3
0 1 2 3 4 5 6 7 8 9 0 1 2 3 4 5 6 7 8 9 0 1 2 3 4 5 6 7 8 9 0 1
```

Network Mask		
E	0	Metric
Forwarding Address		
External Route Tag		
E	TOS	TOS Metric
Forwarding Address		
External Route Tag		

Type 7: Not-So-Stubby Area LSAs

Type 7 LSAs are generated by ASBRs. These LSAs describe routes within a not-so-stubby-area (NSSA). Type 7 LSAs can be summarized and converted into Type 5 LSAs by the ABRs for transmission into other OSPF areas. After Type 7 LSAs are converted to Type 5 LSAs, they are distributed to areas that can support Type 5 LSAs. Figure 3-11 illustrates the operation of Type 7 LSAs, and Figure 3-12 illustrates the format of Type 7 LSA packets.

Figure 3-11   *Type 7 LSA Operation*

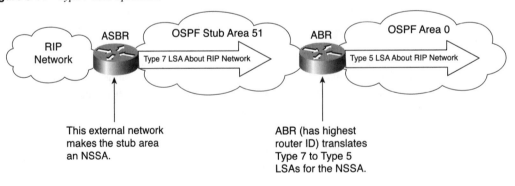

Figure 3-12 *Type 7 LSA Packet Format*

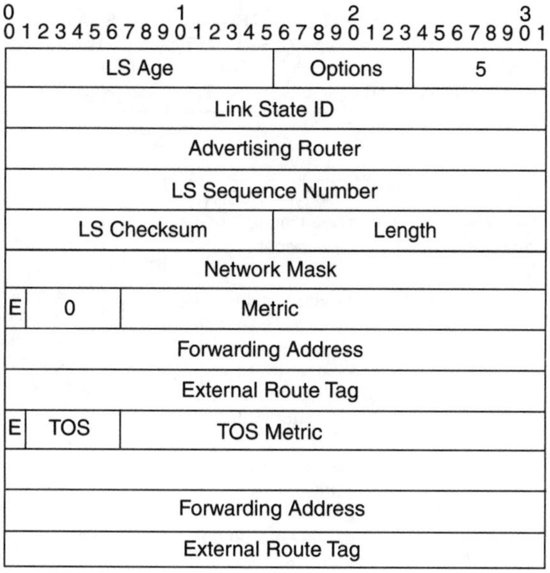

```
0                   1                   2                   3
0 1 2 3 4 5 6 7 8 9 0 1 2 3 4 5 6 7 8 9 0 1 2 3 4 5 6 7 8 9 0 1
```

LS Age	Options	5

Link State ID

Advertising Router

LS Sequence Number

LS Checksum	Length

Network Mask

E	0	Metric

Forwarding Address

External Route Tag

E	TOS	TOS Metric

Forwarding Address

External Route Tag

NOTE   When discussing NSSA operation and structure, be aware that NSSAs have their own RFC (1587). Refer to this RFC for more detailed information.

One of the most interesting features of NSSAs is how they convert Type 7 LSAs, which describe the external routes to all the routers in the NSSA, into the more commonly seen Type 5 LSAs so that all the rest of the OSPF autonomous systems know about the external routes. The RFC describes this process, but the flow chart in Figure 3-13 makes it easier to understand.

Figure 3-13 *NSSA Type 7-to-Type 5 LSA Translation Process*

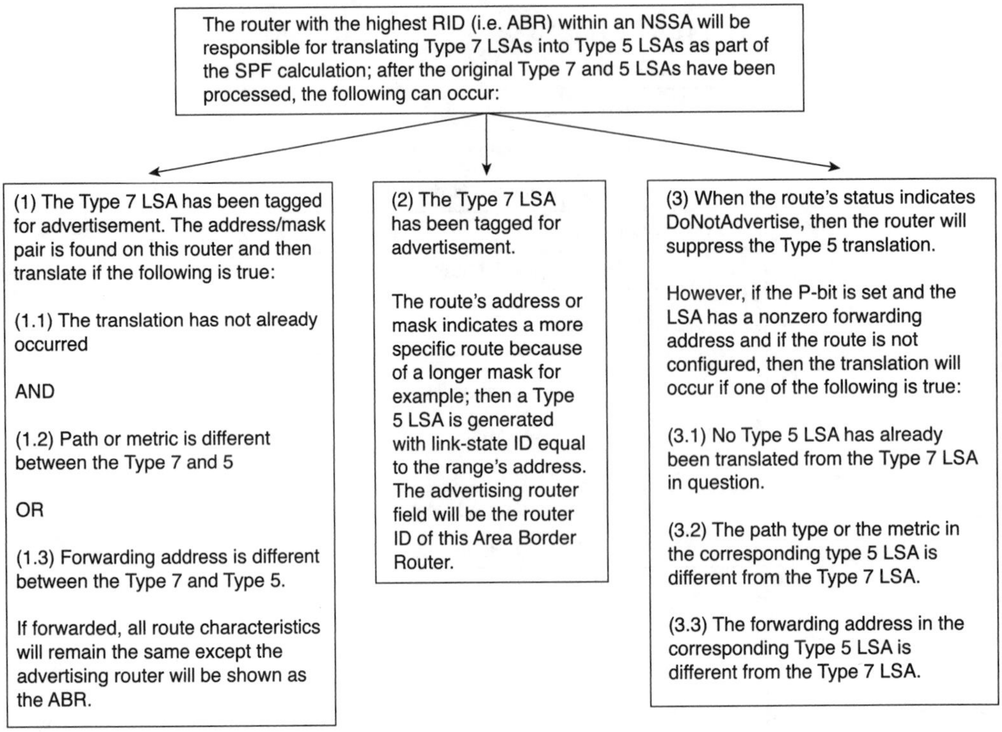

The router with the highest RID (i.e. ABR) within an NSSA will be responsible for translating Type 7 LSAs into Type 5 LSAs as part of the SPF calculation; after the original Type 7 and 5 LSAs have been processed, the following can occur:

(1) The Type 7 LSA has been tagged for advertisement. The address/mask pair is found on this router and then translate if the following is true:

(1.1) The translation has not already occurred

AND

(1.2) Path or metric is different between the Type 7 and 5

OR

(1.3) Forwarding address is different between the Type 7 and Type 5.

If forwarded, all route characteristics will remain the same except the advertising router will be shown as the ABR.

(2) The Type 7 LSA has been tagged for advertisement.

The route's address or mask indicates a more specific route because of a longer mask for example; then a Type 5 LSA is generated with link-state ID equal to the range's address. The advertising router field will be the router ID of this Area Border Router.

(3) When the route's status indicates DoNotAdvertise, then the router will suppress the Type 5 translation.

However, if the P-bit is set and the LSA has a nonzero forwarding address and if the route is not configured, then the translation will occur if one of the following is true:

(3.1) No Type 5 LSA has already been translated from the Type 7 LSA in question.

(3.2) The path type or the metric in the corresponding type 5 LSA is different from the Type 7 LSA.

(3.3) The forwarding address in the corresponding Type 5 LSA is different from the Type 7 LSA.

Type 9: Opaque LSA: Link-Local Scope

As the name of this LSA implies, its transmission scope is defined as being confined to a local network or subnet only.

NOTE Opaque LSAs are used for Multiprotocol Label Switching (MPLS) traffic engineering purposes. Specifically, opaque LSAs are used to distribute various MPLS traffic engineering attributes, such as capacity and topology of links, throughout a network. In addition to Cisco, other major vendors such as Juniper and Riverstone implement opaque LSAs; however, as indicated in RFC 2370, "The OSPF Opaque LSA Option," determining their use is vendor-specific. Therefore, some testing might be required to find the optimal use of opaque LSAs across different platforms.

Type 10: Opaque LSA: Area-Local Scope

As the name of this LSA implies, the transmission scope is defined as being confined to an OSPF area only.

Type 11: Opaque LSA: Autonomous System Scope

As the name of this LSA implies, the transmission scope is defined as being confined to an OSPF AS. Figure 3-14 illustrates the format of Type 9–11 LSA packets.

Figure 3-14   *Type 9, 10, and 11 LSA Packet Structure*

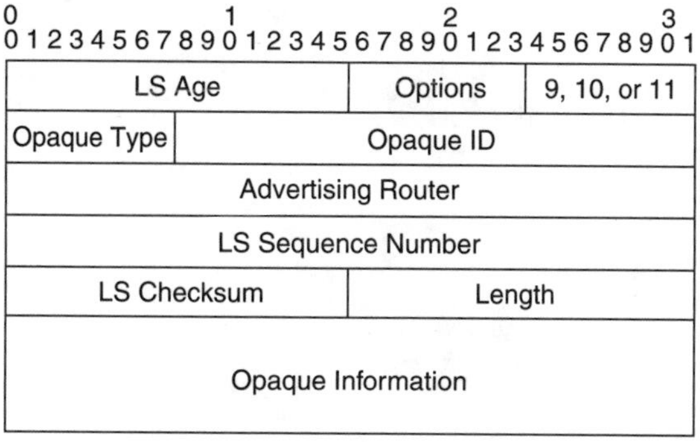

LSA Operation Example

Now that all nine implemented LSAs have been discussed and you understand how they operate within the OSPF functional environment, refer to Figure 3-15 for a visual representation of the operation and interaction among the various types of LSAs within an OSPF network.

Figure 3-15 *LSA Operation*

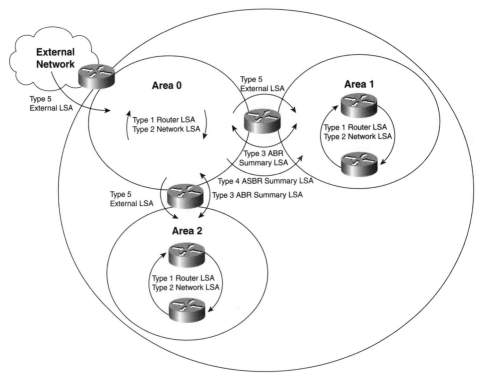

OSPF Autonomous System

Type 5 LSAs are flooded to all areas.

Type 4 ASBR Summary LSAs are sent to describe the ASBR by the ABRs.

Type 3 ABR Summary LSAs are sent describing the networks, but only to the area that does not know about the specific network.

Type 2 Network LSAs describe the OSPF routers in a network.

Type 1 Router LSAs describe the networks each router knows about.

As previously discussed, the router links are an indication of the state of the interfaces on a router belonging to a certain area. Each router generates a router link for all of its interfaces. Summary links are generated by ABRs; this is how network reachability information is disseminated among areas. Normally, all information is injected into the backbone (area 0), and the backbone, in turn, passes it on to other areas. ABRs also have the task of propagating the reachability of the ASBR. This is how routers know how to get to external routes in other autonomous systems.

Cisco's implementation of OSPF uses nine distinct LSAs, each of which is generated for a unique purpose that helps to keep the OSPF network routing table intact and accurate. When a router receives an LSA, it checks its link-state database. If the LSA is new, the router floods the LSA out to its neighbors. After the new LSA is added to the LSA database, the router reruns the SPF algorithm. This recalculation by the SPF algorithm is essential to preserving accurate routing tables. The SPF algorithm is responsible for calculating the routing table, and any LSA change might also cause a change in the routing table. Figure 3-16 demonstrates this transaction, where Router A loses a link and recalculates the shortest path first algorithm and then floods the LSA change out to the remaining interfaces. This new LSA is then immediately flooded to all other routers and then analyzed by Routers B and C, which recalculate and continue to flood the LSA out the other interfaces to Router D.

Figure 3-16   *Example of a Router Sending a New LSA and Flooding*

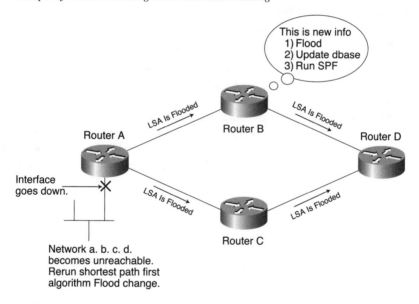

NOTE   If no link-state changes occur, LSAs are sent every 30 minutes to all neighboring routers to ensure that routers have the same link-state database.

OSPF routers in the same area all have the same link-state database and run the same SPF algorithm with themselves as the root, as discussed in Chapter 2. The SPF algorithm uses the records to determine the network topology and to compute the shortest path to a destination. The characteristics of the link-state database are as follows:

- All routers belonging to the same area have the identical link-state database.
- Calculating routes by using the SPF is performed separately by each router in the area.

- LSA flooding is contained within the area that experienced the change.

- The link-state database is comprised of LSA entries.

- A router has a separate link-state database for each area to which it belongs.

The SPF algorithm (aka Dijkstra's algorithm) computes the shortest path from the local OSPF router to each destination within the network. As these computations run and determine the shortest path, this information is placed into a routing table. From these computations, the router derives the next router (hop) that must be used to reach the destination. This information is used by the router to route packets on to their destination.

Many factors can affect the results of these calculations, such as TOS and externally derived routes.

Link-State Database Synchronization

Figure 3-17 illustrates the initial synchronization of the link-state database, which occurs in five steps, as detailed in the numbered sequence in the figure.

When an OSPF adjacency is formed, a router goes through several state changes before it becomes fully adjacent with its neighbor. Those states are defined in the OSPF RFC 2328, Section 10.1. See Figure 3-18 for a discussion of each state. Not every pair of neighboring routers becomes adjacent. Instead, adjacencies are established with some subset of the router's neighbors. Routers connected by point-to-point networks and virtual links always become adjacent. On multiaccess networks, all routers become adjacent to both the designated router and the backup designated router (defined later in this section).

Figure 3-17 *Link-State Database Synchronization*

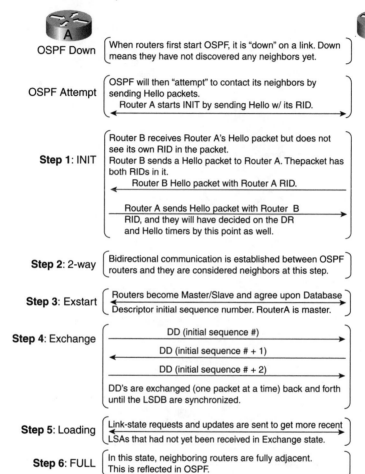

Figure 3-18 *OSPF States*

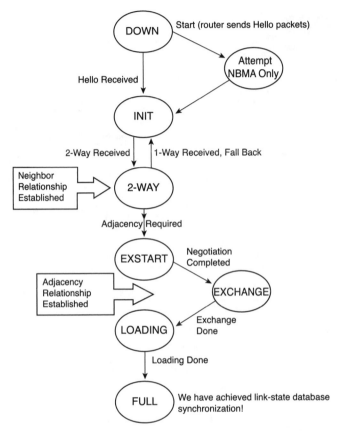

The states for link-state database synchronization, as illustrated in Figure 3-17, are described in the following list:

- **Down**—This is the first OSPF neighbor state. It means that no information has been received from this neighbor, but Hello packets can still be sent to the neighbor in this state.

- **Attempt**—This state is valid only for neighbors in an NBMA environment. Attempt means that the router is sending Hello packets to the neighbor but has not yet received any information.

  Alternatively in OSPF, if the routers had been neighbors (had successfully exchanged Hello packets) in the past but the neighbor relationship had been lost (possibly due to Hello timeout failure), the router restarts communication by attempting to reestablish the neighbor relationship by sending Hellos.

- **Init (Step 1 in Figure 3-17)**—This state specifies that the router has received a Hello packet from its neighbor, but the receiving router's ID was not included in the Hello packet. When a router receives a Hello packet from a neighbor, the router should list the sender's router ID in its Hello packet as an acknowledgment that it received a valid packet.

- **2-Way (Step 2 in Figure 3-17)**—After OSPF routers achieve this state, they are neighbors. This state designates that bidirectional communication has been established between two routers. Bidirectional means that each router has seen the other's Hello packet with its router ID in the other's Hello packet and that all Hello timers match. After the discovery of other OSPF routers and the election of a DR are complete, this state is achieved, and a router decides whether to increase the strength of its relationship by becoming adjacent with this neighbor. On broadcast media, a router becomes full only with the DR and the backup designated router (BDR); it stays in the 2-way state with all other neighbors. Database descriptor (DD) packets are sent between neighbors to synchronization their link-state databases during this step.

- **Exstart (Step 3 in Figure 3-17)**—This is the first state in forming an adjacency. Two neighbor routers form a master/slave relationship and agree on a starting sequence number that is incremented to ensure that LSAs are acknowledged properly and that no duplication occurs. The router with the higher router ID (RID) becomes the master and, as such, is the only router that can increment the sequence number. DD packets begin to be transmitted. The initial DD sequence number is agreed on here.

- **Exchange (Step 4 in Figure 3-17)**—DD packets continue to flow as the slave router acknowledges the master's packets and vice versa. The DD packets are sent back and forth one packet at a time until their respective link-state databases are completely synchronized. The master/slave relationship is negotiated in state Exstart.

- **Loading (Step 5 in Figure 3-17)**—Link-state requests are sent to neighbors asking for recent advertisements that have not yet been discovered. At this stage, the router builds several tables (see Chapter 2) to ensure that all links are up to date and have been acknowledged properly in the LSAs. Figure 3-19 shows the fields and information contained within the link-state request packet format.

Figure 3-19   *Link-State Request Packet Format*

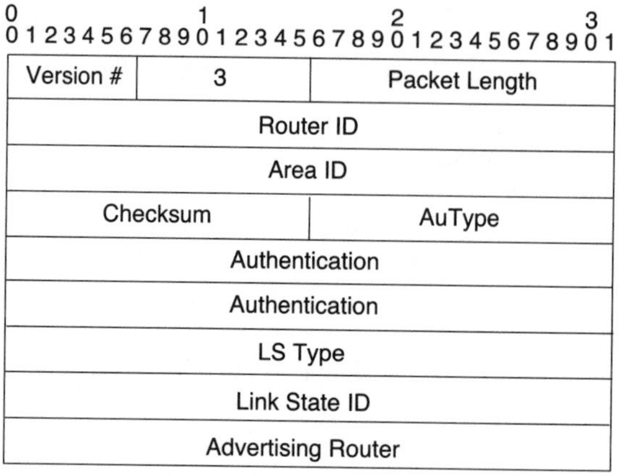

```
 0                   1                   2                   3
 0 1 2 3 4 5 6 7 8 9 0 1 2 3 4 5 6 7 8 9 0 1 2 3 4 5 6 7 8 9 0 1
```

Version #	3	Packet Length
Router ID		
Area ID		
Checksum		AuType
Authentication		
Authentication		
LS Type		
Link State ID		
Advertising Router		

- **Full (Step 6 in Figure 3-17)**—After OSPF routers achieve this state, they are adjacent. OSPF routers are now fully adjacent because their link-state databases are fully synchronized. Full is the normal state for DR and BDR or point-to-point links, but 2-Way is normal for non-DR or non-BDR routers.

NOTE   When a router is stuck in another state, this is an indication that there are problems in forming adjacencies. The only exception to this is the 2-way state, which is normal in a broadcast network. Routers achieve the full state with their DR and BDR only. Neighbors always see each other as 2-way. If a router does not receive a Hello packet from a neighbor within the *RouterDeadInterval* time (*RouterDeadInterval = 4 * HelloInterval* by default), the neighbor state changes from Full to Down.

During the beginning of the link-state database synchronization process, normal LSAs are not sent. Instead, the routers exchange DD packets; these are Type 2 packets that are used when an adjacency is being initialized and the two routers in question are exchanging and synchronizing their link-state databases. These DD packets contain the contents of the link-state database. Figure 3-20 shows the fields and information contained within each DD packet. The router first sends DDs and based on what it discovers, a router will send link-state requests. The receiving router will respond with LSAs, to which the first router sends link state acknowledgments.

Figure 3-20 *Database Descriptor Packet Format*

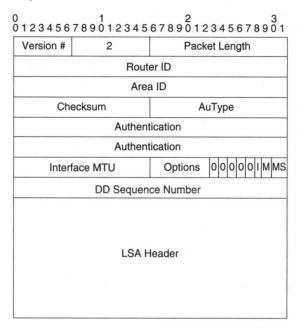

Multiple packets might be needed to complete the synchronization. In that case, a poll-response procedure is used, with one router becoming the master and the other the slave, as previously discussed.

Speaking OSPF

OSPF routers communicate with each other by using the various subprotocols with the OSPF protocol. OSPF runs on top of IP, although OSPF is composed of the following subprotocols:

- Hello
- Exchange
- Flooding

The following sections discuss these subprotocols in detail.

Types of OSPF Packets

OSPF uses five different packets in its protocols. Table 3-2 describes the different OSPF packet types. This section discusses each protocol and the role that the packets play.

Table 3-2 *Overview of OSPF Packet Types*

Packet Name	Type/Number	Function
Hello	1	Discovers and maintains neighbors.
Database description	2	Summarizes database contents.
Link state request	3	Requests LSAs that need to be downloaded to requesting router. Only sent during Exchange, Loading, or Full state.
Link state update	4	Contains a list of the LSAs that are to be updated. Often used in flooding, as discussed later in this chapter.
Link state acknowledgment	5	Acknowledges the packets sent out during flooding to ensure efficient use of floods.

All OSPF packets share a common header. Figure 3-21 illustrates a breakdown (by field) of the common header found at the beginning of each packet issued by an OSPF subprotocol (Hello, exchange, flooding). In OSPF, these packets are sent out to the multicast address (224.0.0.5) that is listened to only by OSPF routers.

Figure 3-21 *Common OSPF Packet Header*

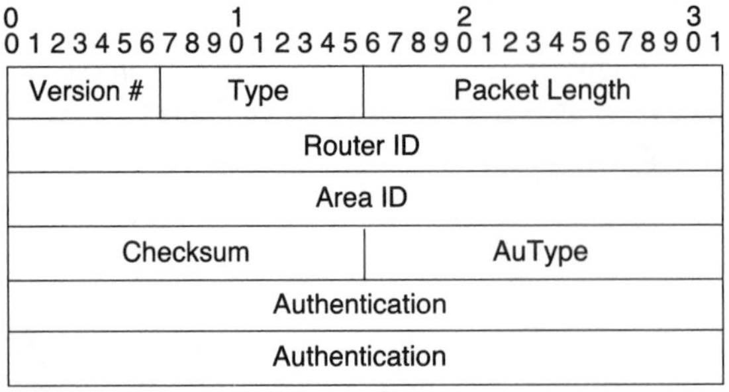

The OSPF version number is set in the header and it is currently at version 2. The type of packet allows OSPF to correctly interpret the packet when it is received (type shown in Table 3-2). The packet length is expressed in bytes and is the total size of the packet including the header.

Hello Process/Protocol

Although this is an OSPF book, many different protocols use a concept of *Hello* packets just like OSPF, for example EIGRP. Therefore, understanding the rationale behind the use and implementation of Hello is important. Specifically in OSPF, the Hello protocol is used for the following purposes:

- To ensure that communication between neighbors is bidirectional (two-way)
- To discover, establish, and maintain neighbor relationships
- To elect the DR and BDR on broadcast and NBMA networks
- To verify that neighboring OSPF routers are operational (that is, to act as a keepalive mechanism)

Figure 3-22 demonstrates how OSPF routers transmit Hello packets into the network to discover their neighbors.

Figure 3-22   *Hello Protocol Operation*

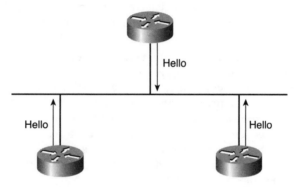

Unless otherwise configured, Hello packets default to a transmission time of once every 10 seconds or 30 seconds for nonbroadcast multiaccess (NBMA). When a new OSPF router is introduced, the operation of the Hello protocol is as follows:

1 The OSPF router sends out the Hello packet as a multicast.

2 The Hello packet is received by the new OSPF router.

3 All OSPF routers on that segment receive and process the Hello packet. Only the new OSPF router replies with its own multicast Hello packet.

Designating OSPF's Hello packets as multicast was a coherent protocol design decision by the OSPF Working Group. Multicasting provides the OSPF with the capability to forward a single packet, which is processed only by certain interfaces on the subnet or wire. Specifically, only those interfaces that have the OSPF routing process enabled are capable; therefore, those network interface cards (NICs) are "listening" for Hello packets with the OSPF multicast addresses in them. Interfaces that are not running OSPF ignore the multicast packet.

At the data link layer of the OSI reference model, the IP multicast address is mapped to a Layer 2 multicast address. For example, on Ethernet, the last 23 bits of the IP multicast address are added to the Ethernet multicast header of 0100.5e. Therefore, the AllSPFRouters multicast IP address maps to a MAC address of 0100.5e00.0005. In the event that a broadcast subnet does not support multicasting, the AllSPFRouters address is subsequently mapped into the Layer 2 broadcast address (ffff.ffff.ffff). The OSPF Hello protocol operates with some variation, depending on the type of network in use.

TIP

The Hello interval can be manipulated with the **ip ospf hello-interval** *seconds* interface configuration command, although there is rarely a good reason for changing this parameter. Also, the OSPF *dead interval = 4 x ospf hello interval* is good to know for the CCIE lab. Use care when changing the Hello interval because neighbor relationships might never come up. Two routers that cycle through various OSPF states frequently have mismatched Hello/dead intervals, as shown in the following example you can check timer values:

```
HAL9000#show ip ospf interface ethernet 0
Ethernet0 is up, line protocol is up
  Internet Address 192.168.254.253/24, Area 0
  Process ID 100, Router ID 10.10.10.10, Network Type BROADCAST, Cost: 10
  Transmit Delay is 1 sec, State DR, Priority 1
  Designated Router (ID) 10.10.10.10, Interface address 192.168.254.253
  No backup designated router on this network
  Timer intervals configured, Hello 10, Dead 40, Wait 40, Retransmit 5
    Hello due in 00:00:03
  Neighbor Count is 0, Adjacent neighbor count is 0
  Suppress hello for 0 neighbor(s)
HAL9000#
```

Hello Protocol Operational Variations

In broadcast networks (for example, Ethernet or Token Ring), each router advertises itself by periodically sending out multicast Hello packets, which allow neighbors to be discovered dynamically.

In NBMA networks (for example, frame relay, X.25, or ATM), the OSPF router can require some additional configuration information in order for the Hello protocol to operate correctly. This configuration is the protocol going out onto the network to find or elect the designated router, as previously discussed in the section "OSPF Network Types" in Chapter 2. In this case, the OSPF neighbor information must be manually configured, thereby allowing OSPF to send the Hello packets via unicast to the neighbor.

In point-to-point or point-to-multipoint networks (that is, Frame Relay topologies), the OSPF router sends out Hello multicast packets to every neighbor with which it can communicate directly. However, in point-to-multipoint networks, Hello packets can be sent as multicast if the data link layer replicated the packet. Neighbor information can be configured manually to indicate who to send a unicast Hello packet to if the data link replication does not work, such as in the ATM ARP server model.

Hello Protocol Packet Format

The OSPF Hello protocol packets are formatted in only one way. All OSPF packets start with a standardized 24-byte header, which contains information that determines whether processing is to take place on the rest of the packet. The packets contain the fields that are shown in Figure 3-23, always in the same order. All the fields in this format are 32-bit fields, except for the following fields:

- HelloInterval (16 bits)
- Options (8 bits)
- Priority (8 bits)

Figure 3-23 *Hello Packet Detail*

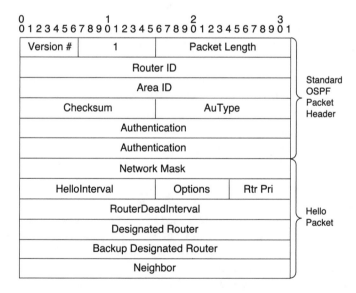

The following list describes what each of the packet fields represents:

- **Version #**—Identifies the OSPF version running on the router that is originating the Hello packet.
- **Packet length**—Provides the total length of the Hello packet in bytes.

- **Router ID**—Contains the originating router identification number as determined by OSPF (highest IP address or loopback). The RID must be unique, and if more than one loopback interface is figured, the loopback interface with the highest IP address is used.

- **Area ID**—Contains the area number to which the originating router is shown as a 32-bit number.

- **Checksum**—Ensure that the packet integrity has not been compromised during transmission. The same method is used in OSPF as is used in Ethernet and IP.

- **Network Mask**—Subnet mask that is associated with the interface. If subnetting is not used, this field is set to the number of bits in the network portion of the address.

- **HelloInterval**—Number of seconds between the Hello packets that the router transmits.

- **Rtr Pri**—If used, this is the where the router's priority would be annotated; otherwise, the default is 1. If the router priority value is set to 0, this indicates that this router is not eligible in the election of BDR or DR.

- **RouterDeadInterval**—Number of seconds since the last Hello packet was received before declaring a silent router as being no longer reachable.

- **Designated Router**—IP address of the network's designated router (if present). This field defaults to 0.0.0.0 when a designated router is not present, such as on point-to-point circuits.

- **Backup Designated Router**—IP address of the network's backup designated router (if present). This field defaults to 0.0.0.0 when a designated router is not present, like on-demand circuits.

- **Neighbor**—Contains the router IDs of each router that has sent a valid Hello packet. This field can have multiple entries.

Exchange Process/Protocol

When two OSPF routers have established bidirectional (two-way) communication, they synchronize their routing (link-state) databases. For point-to-point links, the two routers communicate this information directly between themselves. On network links (that is, multiaccess network—either broadcast or nonbroadcast), this synchronization takes place between the new OSPF router and the DR. The exchange protocol is first used to synchronize the routing (link-state) databases. After synchronization, any changes in the router's links use the flooding protocol to update all the OSPF routers.

Note that this protocol is asymmetric. The first step in the exchange process is to determine which is the master and which is the slave. After agreeing on these roles, the two routers begin to exchange the description of their respective link-state databases. This information is passed between the two routers via the exchange protocol packet layout, as shown in Figure 3-24.

Figure 3-24 *Exchange Protocol Packet Layout*

```
0                   1                   2                   3
0 1 2 3 4 5 6 7 8 9 0 1 2 3 4 5 6 7 8 9 0 1 2 3 4 5 6 7 8 9 0 1
```

OSPF Packet Header, Type = 2 (dd)			
0	0	Options	0 IMMs
DD Sequence Number			
Link State Type			
Link State ID			
Advertising Router			
Link State Sequence Number			
Link State Checksum		Link State Age	

As they receive and process these database description packets, the routers make a separate list that contains the records they need to exchange later. When the comparisons are complete, the routers then exchange the necessary updates that were put into the list so that their databases can be kept up to date.

Flooding Process/Protocol

Flooding in OSPF is responsible for validating and distributing link-state updates to the link-state database whenever a change or update occurs to a link. Changes or updates are key concepts regarding when flooding occurs. Flooding is part of the LSDB synchronization mechanism within OSPF. The goal of this mechanism is to keep the LSDBs of the routers in an OSPF domain synchronized within time in the presence of topological changes.

In the event of a link-state change (for example, from up to down), the router that experienced the change transmits a flooding packet (link-state update), which contains the state change. This update is flooded out all the routers' interfaces. The primary goal of flooding is to ensure that every router receives the changed or updated LSA within the flooding scope (area or domain).

Flooding occurs differently between neighbors in OSPF depending on a the following factors:

- Type 1 through 4 and 7 LSAs are flooded within an area; each LSA has a different flooding scope, as previously discussed.

- Type 5 LSAs are flooded throughout the OSPF domain, except for stub and NSSAs.

- When a DR is present, only non-DRs flood to the DR. The DR then floods to everyone as required.

- When two OSPF routers have not yet established an adjacency, they do not flood each other; that is, they are in the middle of LSDB synchronization.

OSPF expects an acknowledgment from each link-state update. To ensure that the flooded packet is received by all of its neighbors, OSPF continues to retransmit the link-state update packet until it receives an acknowledgment from each of its neighbors. OSPF can acknowledge an update in two ways:

- **When the destination router sends an acknowledgment directly to the source router**—In this case, there is no DR in use by OSPF if this is occurring.

- **When a DR is in use and it receives the update**—When this occurs, the DR immediately retransmits this update to all other routers. Therefore, when the sending router hears this retransmission, it is considered an acknowledgment, and no further action is taken.

Figure 3-25 shows the field names and packet layout for the flooding subprotocol.

Figure 3-25   *Flooding Protocol Packet Layout*

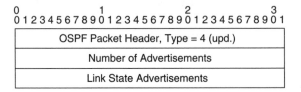

Manipulating LSAs

Cisco IOS Software Release 12.0 introduced several new features that allow you to alter the default behavior of the OSPF LSAs. These new features are Cisco proprietary in nature, so use them in a multivendor network with discretion.

You should first give a lot of thought to altering the OSPF default behaviors. With these precautions in mind, now it's time to discuss them and determine where they would fit in your network.

Understanding LSA Group Pacing

The OSPF LSA group pacing feature allows the router to group OSPF LSAs and pace the refreshing, checksumming, and aging functions. The group pacing results in more efficient use of the router.

NOTE   Cisco has made LSA group pacing the default behavior for OSPF in Cisco IOS Software Release 12.0 and later.

Each OSPF LSA is recorded and tracked with an age that indicates whether the LSA is still valid. When the LSA reaches the maximum age (60 minutes), the LSA is discarded from the link-state database. A router keeps track of LSAs that it generates and LSAs that it receives from other routers. The router refreshes LSAs that it generated; it ages the LSAs it received from other routers.

During normal OSPF operation, LSA refresh packets are sent to keep the LSA from expiring, regardless of whether a change has occurred in the network topology. The originating router sends a refresh packet every 30 minutes to refresh the LSA; this prevents the LSA age from ever reaching 60 minutes.

Sending an update every 30 minutes is not an ideal solution if that is the only method used. OSPF also performs checksumming on all LSAs, in the link-state database, every 10 minutes.

Prior to the LSA group pacing feature, Cisco IOS Software would perform LSA refreshing on a single timer, and checksumming and aging on another timer. For example, in the case of refreshing, the software would scan the entire database every 30 minutes, refreshing every LSA the router generated, no matter how old it was. Figure 3-26 illustrates all the LSAs being refreshed at once. This process wasted CPU resources because only a small portion of the database needed to be refreshed.

Figure 3-26   *OSPF LSAs on a Single Timer*

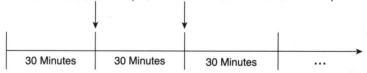

All LSAs refreshed, for example, 120 external LSAs on Ethernet need 3 packets.

| 30 Minutes | 30 Minutes | 30 Minutes | ... |

Prior to OSPF packet pacing, all LSAs refreshed at once.

A large OSPF database (several thousand LSAs) might have thousands of LSAs with different ages. Refreshing on a single timer resulted in the age of all LSAs becoming synchronized, which resulted in much CPU processing at once. Furthermore, a huge number of LSAs might cause a sudden increase of network traffic, consuming a large amount of network resources in a short period of time.

This problem is solved by each LSA having its own timer. Again using the example of refreshing, each LSA gets refreshed when it is 30 minutes old, independent of other LSAs. Therefore, the CPU is used only when necessary. However, LSAs being refreshed at frequent, random intervals would require many packets for the few refreshed LSAs that the router must send out. That would be inefficient use of bandwidth.

The router delays the LSA refresh function for an interval of time instead of performing it when the individual timers are reached. The accumulated LSAs constitute a group, which is then refreshed and sent out in one or more packets. Therefore, the refresh packets are paced, as are the checksumming and aging. Figure 3-27 illustrates the case of refresh packets. The first time line illustrates individual LSA timers; the second time line illustrates individual LSA timers with group pacing.

Figure 3-27   *OSPF LSAs on Individual Timers*

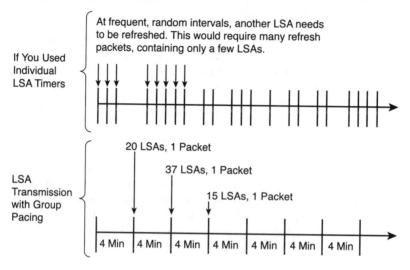

The router groups OSPF LSAs and paces the refreshing, checksumming, and aging functions so that sudden hits on CPU usage and network resources are avoided. This feature is most beneficial to large OSPF networks.

How to Configure LSA Group Pacing

OSPF LSA group pacing is enabled by default. For typical customers, the default group pacing interval for refreshing, checksumming, and aging is appropriate, and you do not need to configure this feature. The pacing interval is configurable; it defaults to 4 minutes, which is randomized to further avoid synchronization.

The group pacing interval is inversely proportional to the number of LSAs that the router is refreshing, checksumming, and aging. For example, if you have approximately 10,000 LSAs, decreasing the pacing interval would be beneficial. If you have a small database (40 to 100 LSAs), increasing the pacing interval to 10 to 20 minutes might benefit you slightly.

The default value of pacing between LSA groups is 240 seconds (4 minutes). The range is 10 seconds to 1800 seconds (half an hour). To configure the LSA group pacing interval, you would enter the following commands in router configuration mode:

```
router ospf 100
timers lsa-group-pacing 60
```

This configuration changes the OSPF pacing between LSA groups to 60 seconds.

Understanding OSPF Packet Pacing

Prior to this feature being added to Cisco IOS Software Release 12.0, some OSPF update packets were getting lost in cases where the link was slow—for example, when a neighbor could not receive the updates fast enough or the router was out of buffer space. As an example, packets might be dropped if either of these topologies existed:

- A fast router was connected to a slower router over a point-to-point link.

- During flooding, several neighbors dumped updates to a single router at the same time.

OSPF update packets are now automatically paced by a delay of 33 milliseconds. Pacing is also added between retransmissions to increase efficiency and minimize lost retransmissions.

Through the use of pacing, OSPF update and retransmission packets are sent more efficiently. In addition, you can display the LSAs waiting to be sent out an interface.

There are no configuration tasks for this new Cisco IOS Software feature; it occurs automatically. To observe OSPF packet pacing by displaying a list of LSAs waiting to be flooded over a specified interface, use the following command in EXEC mode:

```
show ip ospf flood-list
```

Blocking LSA Flooding

By default, OSPF floods new LSAs out all interfaces in the same area, except the interface on which the LSA arrives. OSPF floods based on the characteristics discussed earlier in this chapter. This is important because OSPF-specific behavior is to continue flooding until an acknowledgment on the link-state update packet is received.

Some redundancy is desirable because it ensures robust flooding and accurate routing; however, too much redundancy can waste bandwidth and might destabilize the network due to excessive link and CPU usage in certain topologies. For example, the bandwidth consumed by OSPF in a fully meshed topology might be considerable, and it might then be desirable to block flooding.

You can block OSPF flooding of LSAs two ways, depending on the type of networks:

- On broadcast, nonbroadcast, and point-to-point networks, you can block flooding over specified OSPF interfaces.

- On point-to-multipoint networks, you can block flooding to a specified neighbor.

On broadcast, nonbroadcast, and point-to-point networks, to prevent flooding of OSPF LSAs out of a specific interface, use the following command in interface configuration mode:

```
ospf database-filter all out
```

On point-to-multipoint networks, to prevent flooding of OSPF LSAs to a specific neighbor, use the following command in router configuration mode:

```
router ospf 109
neighbor ip-address database-filter all out
```

Ignoring MOSPF LSA Packets

Cisco routers do not support LSA Type 6 multicast OSPF (MOSPF), and they generate syslog messages if they receive such packets. If the router is receiving many MOSPF packets, you might want to configure the router to ignore the packets and thus prevent a large number of syslog messages. To do so, use the following command in router configuration mode:

```
router ospf 109
ignore lsa mospf
```

To configure the router to suppress the sending of syslog messages when it receives MOSPF packets, enter the following code:

```
router ospf 109
ignore lsa mospf
```

Altering LSA Retransmissions

Cisco routers have the capability to alter the timing in which they retransmit LSAs on a per-interface basis. When a router runs OSPF and when it transmits an LSA to a neighbor, the normal operation of OSPF is to hold that LSA until the router receives an acknowledgment that the LSA was received successfully. By default, a router waits 5 seconds for the acknowledgment and, if needed, the LSA is retransmitted. In certain instances, this waiting period is not long enough for the round trip when a slow serial link or perhaps a virtual link is involved. The need to adjust the waiting period prior to a retransmission has been addressed in the **ip ospf retransmit-interval** command, which is deployed on a per-interface basis, as shown in Example 3-1.

Example 3-1   *Adjusting the Waiting Period Prior to LSA Retransmission*

```
HAL9000(config)#int e0
HAL9000(config-if)#ip ospf ?
  authentication-key   Authentication password (key)
  cost                 Interface cost
  dead-interval        Interval after which a neighbor is declared dead
  demand-circuit       OSPF demand circuit
  hello-interval       Time between HELLO packets
  message-digest-key   Message digest authentication password (key)
  network              Network type
  priority             Router priority
  retransmit-interval  Time between retransmitting lost link state advertisements
  transmit-delay       Link state transmit delay

HAL9000(config-if)#ip ospf retransmit-interval ?
  <1-65535>  Seconds
```

If you decide to use this command, you need to alter the timer values on both ends of the link to ensure the smooth operation of OSPF.

Altering LSA Transmission Delay

The final option of altering the normal operation of OSPF LSAs also evolved from the need to have OSPF operate properly over slow links. Specifically, LSAs can take a longer time to be transmitted over a link. OSPF currently allows 1 second in the Cisco implementation. When this is not enough time, the **ip ospf transmit-delay** command should be used on the desired interface. This command allows a delay to be added prior to transmission, as demonstrated in Example 3-2.

Example 3-2   *Configuring a Delay Prior to LSA Transmission*

```
HAL9000#conf t
Enter configuration commands, one per line.  End with CNTL/Z.
HAL9000(config)#int e0
HAL9000(config-if)#ip ospf transmit-delay ?
  <1-65535>  Seconds
```

Detailed Neighbor Establishment

This section discusses some of the common issues that you can encounter in an OSPF network, including questions and issues related to neighbor and database initialization.

Typically, you see OSPF go from 2-way to full; however, when a full state is reached, this reflects that the LSDBs (that is, all the database exchanges) have been completely exchanged between the two routers in question. This process differs from the Hello protocol and is the subtle difference between the two.

The following sections cover Hello protocol state and database exchange state changes.

Hello Protocol State Changes

The following is a brief description of the possible OSPF neighbor state changes when the Hello protocol is being used:

- **Down**—This is the initial state of a neighbor conversation. This state means that no information has been sent from any neighbors. This state is usually seen when a router first begins speaking OSPF in a network or when there is a problem and the router dead interval timer (Hello interval * 4) has expired for some reason, resulting in OSPF.

- **Attempt**—This is valid only for neighbors that are attached to NBMA networks and reflects that the router has sent Hello packets to the neighbor but has not yet received a response; therefore, the router is attempting to form a neighbor relationship.

- **Init**—A Hello packet has been seen from the neighbor, but in that Hello packet, the receiving router's ID was not present. Therefore, communication is initialized; however; bidirectional communication has not yet been established with the neighbor.

- **2-Way**—In 2-way, the routers see their own ID in the neighbor's Hello packet. Communication between the two routers is bidirectional. At this point, the routers decide whether to proceed and become adjacent. If they choose to, they proceed.

Database Exchange State Changes

The following is a brief description of the possible OSPF neighbor state changes when the routers are exchanging DDs. These steps occur when two routers decide to form an adjacency. For example, on broadcast media, a router becomes full only with the DR and the BDR; it stays in the 2-way state with all other neighbors:

- **ExStart**—This state indicates the first step in creating an adjacency, the goal of which is to decide which router is the master and which is the slave. The master router is the router with the highest RID. It is the master router that controls the communication process by incrementing the initial DD sequence number.

- **Exchange**—In this state, the router is describing its entire LSDB by sending DD packets to the neighbor. Each DD packet has a sequence number that is explicitly acknowledged. Routers also send link-state request packets and link-state update packets (which contain the entire LSA) in this state.

- **Loading**—This state indicates that the transmission of the DD packets has been completed, and link-state request (LSR) packets are then sent to the neighbor asking for the more recent advertisements that are not yet received in the exchange state. As a result of these requests (that is, the LSR packets), LSAs are then transmitted to complete the exchange of routes.

- **Full**—This state indicates that the neighboring routers are fully adjacent and that all LSAs have been transmitted and acknowledged.

Full is the normal state for an OSPF router. If a router is stuck in another state, this is an indication that there are problems in forming adjacencies. The only exception to this is the 2-way state, which is normal in a broadcast network. Routers achieve the full state with their DR and BDR only. Neighbors always see each other as 2-way.

The console output sequence in Example 3-3 shows the distribution of the LSA packets and the building of the database. It also shows the building of the OSPF adjacency. The **debug ip ospf events** command is useful in discovering the problems that might be causing an OSPF adjacency problem on the network.

Remember that no DR/BDR election is on a point-to-multipoint interface and that you can confirm that with the appropriate **show** command.

If you do not see full adjacencies, you can pinpoint the packet negotiation sequence that occurs through the use of a **debug ip ospf events** command. This can be essential in identifying problems with the OSPF process by looking at the packets, as shown in Example 3-3.

Example 3-3   *Output from the* **debug ip ospf events** *Command*

```
HUB_ROUTER1#term monitor
HUB_ROUTER1#debug ip ospf events
%FR-5-DLCICHANGE: Interface Serial0 - DLCI 100 state changed to ACTIVE
OSPF: rcv. v:2 t:1 l:44 rid:10.0.1.2
Field definitions:
aid:0.0.0.0 chk:EE35 aut:0 auk: from Serial0
rcv - received packet
v:2 - OSPF v2
l:44
rid: - Router ID
aid: - Area ID
chk: -
aut: - Authentication
auk: - physical interface packet was received through
OSPF:    rcv. v:2 t:2 l:32 rid:10.0.1.2
    aid:0.0.0.0 chk:D363 aut:0 auk: from Serial0
OSPF: Receive dbd from 10.0.1.2 seq 0x1A6E --- begin of database exchange
OSPF: 2 Way Communication to neighbor 10.0.1.2 - building of adjacency
OSPF: send DBD packet to 10.0.1.2 seq 0x995
OSPF:    rcv. v:2 t:2 l:72 rid:10.0.1.2
    aid:0.0.0.0 chk:36C4 aut:0 auk: from Serial0
OSPF: Receive dbd from 10.0.1.2 seq 0x995
OSPF: NBR Negotiation Done We are the MASTER - neighbor negotiation
OSPF: send DBD packet to 10.0.1.2 seq 0x996
OSPF: Database request to 10.0.1.2
OSPF: sent LS REQ packet to 10.0.1.2, length 12 - we are sending a request to 10.0.1.2
    for link state data.
OSPF:    rcv. v:2 t:2 l:32 rid:10.0.1.2
    aid:0.0.0.0 chk:E442 aut:0 auk: from Serial0
OSPF: Receive dbd from 10.0.1.2 seq 0x996
OSPF: send DBD packet to 10.0.1.2 seq 0x997
OSPF:    rcv. v:2 t:3 l:48 rid:10.0.1.2
    aid:0.0.0.0 chk:5E71 aut:0 auk: from Serial0
OSPF:    rcv. v:2 t:4 l:64 rid:10.0.1.2
    aid:0.0.0.0 chk:98D8 aut:0 auk: from Serial0
OSPF:    rcv. v:2 t:2 l:32 rid:10.0.1.2
    aid:0.0.0.0 chk:E441 aut:0 auk: from Serial0
OSPF: Receive dbd from 10.0.1.2 seq 0x997
OSPF: Exchange Done with neighbor 10.0.1.2
OSPF: Synchronized with neighbor 10.0.1.2, state:FULL - completion of the adjacency
    process
```

Table 3-3 provides an explanation of the fields that are included with the first packet.

Table 3-3   *Fields in the* **debug ip ospf events** *Command*

Field	Description
V	ospf_version
T	ospf_type
1 Hello	To maintain neighbors

continues

Table 3-3 *Fields in the* **debug ip ospf events** *Command (Continued)*

Field	Description
2 Database Descriptor	Exchange to bring up adjacency
3 Link-State Request	Request data
4 Link-State Update	Receives data
5 Link-State Acknowledgment	Updates
l	ospf_length
Router ID (RID)	ospf_rtr_id
Aid	ospf_area_id
Chk	ospf_checksum
Authentication Type (Aut)	ospf_autype

The output from a **debug ip ospf events** command shows both the received and transmitted packets, the building of the OSPF adjacency, and the exchange of database information. If you have a problem building the OSPF adjacency or there are OSPF database problems, this **debug** command can help you identify whether the packets are being received or sent.

Example 3-4 illustrates a nonbroadcast point-to-multipoint network using the **frame-relay map** statement for clarification of the permanent virtual circuits (PVCs). This enables you to identify both ends of the PVC and to determine whether you need to define multiple data-link connection identifiers (DLCIs) for a split DLCI—one PVC for receiving and one PVC for transmitting. This enables you to work with your provider in setting the committed information rate (CIR) for each of the PVCs. As customers need to shape their user and application traffic across their frame relay circuits, the use of this kind of mapping is necessary.

Example 3-4 *Clarifying PVCs in a Point-to-Multipoint Network*

```
HUB_ROUTER1#
interface Serial0
ip address 10.0.1.1 255.255.255.0
ip ospf network point-to-multipoint non-broadcast
encapsulation frame-relay
frame-relay map ip 10.0.1.2 102
frame-relay map ip 10.0.1.3 103
frame-relay map ip 10.0.1.4 104
no shut
!
router ospf 1
network 10.0.1.0 0.0.0.255 area 0
neighbor 10.0.1.2
neighbor 10.0.1.3
neighbor 10.0.1.4
```

Example 3-4 also illustrates the use of the **neighbor** command to force the configured OSPF routers connecting to nonbroadcast networks. The **neighbor** statements are used to form OSPF adjacency. This also enables the user to dictate upon which connections the router attempts to form an OSPF adjacency. Note that in this type of network topology, the hub router is usually the DR as well.

Without the **neighbor** command, the OSPF adjacency would have problems being attained. The **frame-relay map** statements did not include the **broadcast** keyword, so multicast packets would not be forwarded and the normal OSPF Hellos would not discover the neighbors. With the **neighbor** command, you know which routers you should make an OSPF adjacency with, and therefore, you know what to look for if there are problems.

Because OSPF performs an election process for a DR and BDR, which acts as a central distribution point for routing information, the setting up of neighbors can be important. Also, OSPF routers form a full adjacency only to the DR and BDR. Therefore, OSPF can efficiently support a full mesh of neighboring routers per interface. This enables the point-to-multipoint feature to provide the connectivity that is needed for a non–fully meshed network.

Another command used to troubleshoot the connection is the **show frame-relay map** command, as demonstrated in Example 3-5. This command can be used to confirm the Layer 1 and 2 connectivity between the routers. This enables you to eliminate this as a problem before you begin concentrating on the Layer 3 issues.

Example 3-5   *Confirming Layer 1 and Layer 2 Connectivity Between Routers with the* **show frame-relay map** *Command*

```
HUB_ROUTER1#show frame map
Serial0 (up): point-to-point dlci, dlci 111(0x12,0x420), broadcast
Serial0 (up): point-to-point dlci, dlci 222(0x10,0x400), broadcast
Serial0 (up): point-to-point dlci, dlci 333(0x12,0x420), broadcast
```

The output in Example 3-5 shows the connection from Serial0 to three different DLCIs and shows that they are enabled for broadcast.

If there is no mapping to the other end, the PVC has not been fully constructed. Therefore, there is a problem with the frame relay circuit, and any associated problems with routing or with the OSPF process are not important until the physical layer problem has been taken care of.

Example 3-6 shows the output from the **show ip ospf interface serial 0** command.

Example 3-6   *Output from the* **show ip ospf interface serial 0** *Command Confirms Network Type and State as Well as OSPF Timer Settings*

```
Spoke_R2#show ip ospf interface serial 0
Serial0 is up, line protocol is up
Internet Address 10.0.1.2/24, Area 0
Process ID 1, Router ID 10.0.1.2, Network Type POINT_TO_MULTIPOINT, Cost: 64
Transmit Delay is 1 sec, State POINT_TO_MULTIPOINT,
```

continues

Example 3-6   *Output from the* **show ip ospf interface serial 0** *Command Confirms Network Type and State as Well as OSPF Timer Settings (Continued)*

```
Timer intervals configured, Hello 10, Dead 40, Wait 40, Retransmit 5
Hello due in 00:00:07
Neighbor Count is 1, Adjacent neighbor count is 1
Adjacent with neighbor 10.0.2.1
```

The output in Example 3-6 shows the network type and state. It also enables you to confirm the different timers that are set in OSPF. These should be identical between your routers. If they are not or if there is a problem with the subnet masks between the two routers, use the **debug ip ospf events** command; its output is shown in Example 3-7.

Example 3-7   *Output of the* **debug ip ospf events** *Command*

```
OSPF: Mismatched hello parameters from 200.1.3.2
Dead R 40 C 40, Hello R 10 C 10 Mask R 255.255.255.248 C 255.255.255.0
OSPF: Mismatched hello parameters from 200.1.3.2
Dead R 40 C 40, Hello R 10 C 10 Mask R 255.255.255.248 C 255.255.255.0
```

The following events occur in the output of Example 3-5:

- The mask is not matching.
- R indicates what you are receiving.
- C indicates what is configured.

One of the best commands that you can use to determine the state of the OSPF neighbor(s) is the **show ip ospf neighbor** command. The output of this command most likely reveals one of the following:

> nothing at all
> state = init
> state = exstart/exchange
> state = 2-way
> state = loading
> state = full

There are other OSPF states, but those listed are usually included in the **show ip ospf neighbor** command output. This command is used repeatedly in the scenarios that follow.

For further troubleshooting steps, see Chapter 9, "Troubleshooting OSPF."

Case Study: OSPF Initialization

This case study puts all the pieces together into a coherent overview of OSPF initialization and beginning operation. To do this, you take a pair of routers that are connected together via an Ethernet connection to form the OSPF backbone, Area 0. Each router is also connected to other OSPF areas, as shown in Figure 3-28. For brevity, only those packets that prove a concept or step are included.

Figure 3-28   *OSPF Network*

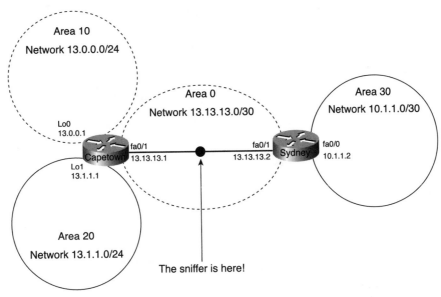

NOTE

To capture everything needed to demonstrate this case study, the routers were correctly configured and then a reboot was performed while a sniffer was running.

Capetown is the first router to initialize, and it immediately begins to transmit OSPF Hello packets out interface fa0/1. This first packet is shown in Figure 3-29, with a few aspects highlighted.

Figure 3-29 *Hello Packet from Capetown*

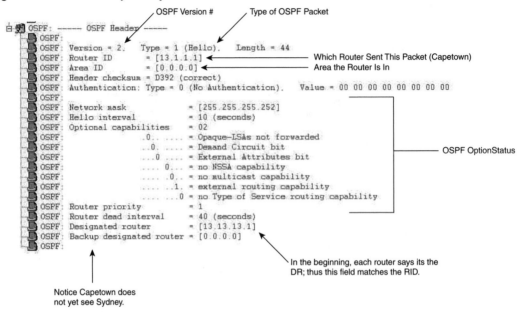

Sydney is to receive the Hello packet. When Sydney transmits its Hello packet, the RID of Capetown is present within, as illustrated by Figure 3-30.

Figure 3-30 *Hello Packet from Sydney*

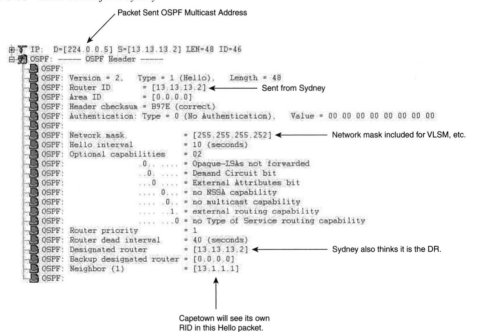

As the routers exchange Hello packets, it is clear that Capetown has the highest RID after two packets, and as a result, Sydney becomes the DR. The next information that needs to be exchanged between these two routers is link-state data. This is done via link-state update packets, as previously discussed. These specialized OSPF packets contain LSAs. Refer to Figure 3-31.

Figure 3-31 *Sydney's Link-State Update*

```
                                              / Identifies this packet as a link-state update
IP:  D=[224.0.0.5] S=[13.13.13.2] LEN=96 ID=53
OSPF: ------ OSPF Header ------
  OSPF:
  OSPF: Version = 2.    Type = 4 (Link State Update).    Length = 96
  OSPF: Router ID       = [13.13.13.2]
  OSPF: Area ID         = [0.0.0.0]
  OSPF: Header checksum = 6FFC (correct)
  OSPF: Authentication: Type = 0 (No Authentication).    Value = 00 00 00 00 00 00 00 00
  OSPF:
  OSPF: Number of Advertisements = 2  ◄────────── Tells us how many LSAs are in this packet
  OSPF: Link State Advertisement # 1
  OSPF: Link state age        = 1 (seconds)
  OSPF: Optional capabilities = 22
  OSPF:          .0.. .... = Opaque-LSAs not forwarded
  OSPF:          ..1. .... = Demand Circuit bit
  OSPF:          ...0 .... = External Attributes bit
  OSPF:          .... 0... = no NSSA capability
  OSPF:          .... .0.. = no multicast capability
  OSPF:          .... ..1. = external routing capability
  OSPF:          .... ...0 = no Type of Service routing capability
  OSPF: Link state type       = 1 (Router links) ◄────── Tells us type of LSA # and name
  OSPF: Link state ID         = [13.13.13.2]  ◄────── What the LSA is talking about
  OSPF: Advertising Router    = [13.13.13.2]
  OSPF: Sequence number       = 2147483650.   Checksum = 0387
  OSPF: Length                = 36
  OSPF: Router type flags     = 03
  OSPF:          .... 0... = Not a wild-card multicast receiver
  OSPF:          .... .0.. = Not endpoint of active virtual link
  OSPF:          .... ..1. = AS boundary router
  OSPF:          .... ...1 = Area border router
  OSPF: Reserved              = 0
  OSPF: Number of router links = 1
  OSPF:    Link ID            = [13.13.13.2] (IP address of Designated Router)
  OSPF:    Link Data          = [13.13.13.2]  ◄────── Network info/next hop
  OSPF:    Link type          = 2 (Connection to a transit network)
  OSPF:    Number of TOS metrics = 0.  TOS 0 metric = 1
  OSPF:
  OSPF: Link State Advertisement # 2
  OSPF: Link state age        = 1 (seconds)
  OSPF: Optional capabilities = 22
  OSPF:          .0.. .... = Opaque-LSAs not forwarded
  OSPF:          ..1. .... = Demand Circuit bit
  OSPF:          ...0 .... = External Attributes bit
  OSPF:          .... 0... = no NSSA capability
  OSPF:          .... .0.. = no multicast capability
  OSPF:          .... ..1. = external routing capability
  OSPF:          .... ...0 = no Type of Service routing capability
  OSPF: Link state type       = 2 (Network links)
  OSPF: Link state ID         = [13.13.13.2]  ◄────── LSA Type
  OSPF: Advertising Router    = [13.13.13.2]  ◄────── Information this LSA is conveying
  OSPF: Sequence number       = 2147483649.   Checksum = 624F
  OSPF: Length                = 32
  OSPF: Network mask          = [255.255.255.252] ◄────── network mask
  OSPF: Attached router (1)   = [13.13.13.2]  ◄────── Routers found
  OSPF: Attached router (2)   = [13.1.1.1]
  OSPF:
```

Type 1 LSA (1 of 2)

Type 1 LSA (2 of 2)

The information from the other areas needs to be propagated into Area 0 and shared between the two routers. For this to occur, Capetown transmits link-state updates to Sydney. You can see an example of this in Figure 3-32. Notice that in this packet, the RID has changed because Capetown's interface in Area 2 is also the RID for that area.

Figure 3-32 *Capetown's Link-State Update*

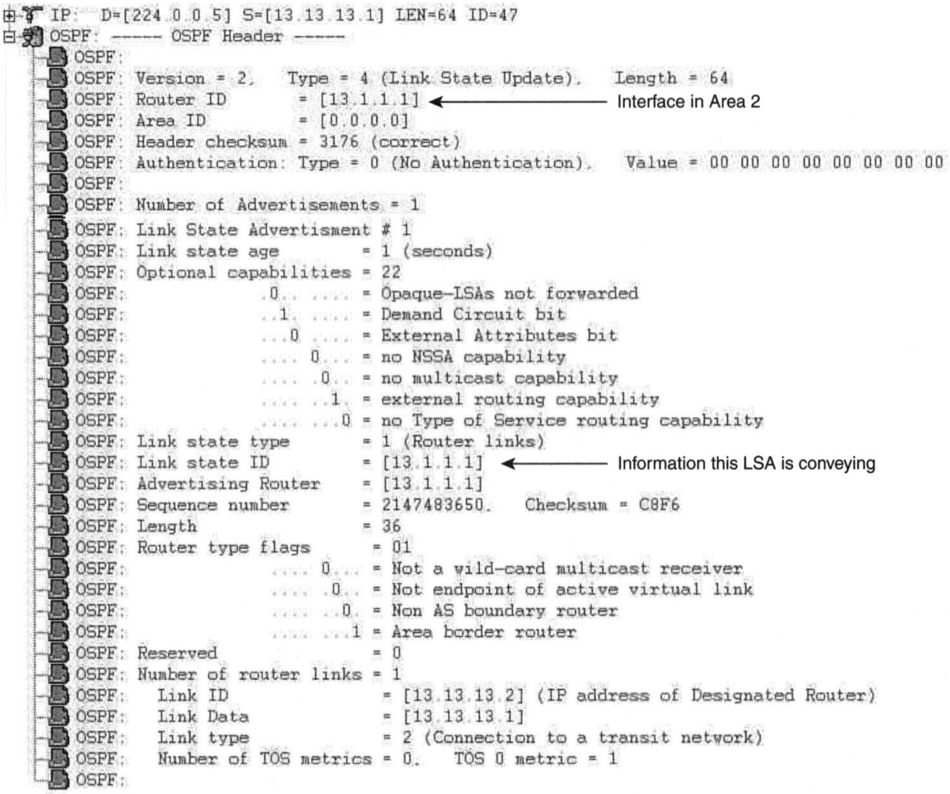

```
IP:   D=[224.0.0.5] S=[13.13.13.1] LEN=64 ID=47
OSPF: ----- OSPF Header -----
OSPF:
OSPF: Version = 2,   Type = 4 (Link State Update),   Length = 64
OSPF: Router ID      = [13.1.1.1]  <--------------- Interface in Area 2
OSPF: Area ID        = [0.0.0.0]
OSPF: Header checksum = 3176 (correct)
OSPF: Authentication: Type = 0 (No Authentication),   Value = 00 00 00 00 00 00 00 00
OSPF:
OSPF: Number of Advertisements = 1
OSPF: Link State Advertisment # 1
OSPF: Link state age          = 1 (seconds)
OSPF: Optional capabilities = 22
OSPF:                  .0.. .... = Opaque-LSAs not forwarded
OSPF:                  ..1. .... = Demand Circuit bit
OSPF:                  ...0 .... = External Attributes bit
OSPF:                  .... 0... = no NSSA capability
OSPF:                  .... .0.. = no multicast capability
OSPF:                  .... ..1. = external routing capability
OSPF:                  .... ...0 = no Type of Service routing capability
OSPF: Link state type        = 1 (Router links)
OSPF: Link state ID          = [13.1.1.1]  <------- Information this LSA is conveying
OSPF: Advertising Router     = [13.1.1.1]
OSPF: Sequence number        = 2147483650.   Checksum = C8F6
OSPF: Length                 = 36
OSPF: Router type flags      = 01
OSPF:                  .... 0... = Not a wild-card multicast receiver
OSPF:                  .... .0.. = Not endpoint of active virtual link
OSPF:                  .... ..0. = Non AS boundary router
OSPF:                  .... ...1 = Area border router
OSPF: Reserved               = 0
OSPF: Number of router links = 1
OSPF:    Link ID             = [13.13.13.2] (IP address of Designated Router)
OSPF:    Link Data           = [13.13.13.1]
OSPF:    Link type           = 2 (Connection to a transit network)
OSPF:    Number of TOS metrics = 0.   TOS 0 metric = 1
OSPF:
```

As Capetown and Sydney exchange their routes via the link-state update packets, they also acknowledge to assure the other router they were received. In Figure 3-33, Sydney is acknowledging one of the routes that it received from Capetown.

Figure 3-33 *Sydney Acknowledges*

```
IP: D=[224.0.0.5] S=[13.13.13.2] LEN=44 ID=60
OSPF: ------ OSPF Header ------
OSPF:
OSPF: Version = 2.    Type = 5 (Link State Acknowledgment).    Length = 44
OSPF: Router ID        = [13.13.13.2]
OSPF: Area ID          = [0.0.0.0]
OSPF: Header checksum = 5C98 (correct)
OSPF: Authentication: Type = 0 (No Authentication).    Value = 00 00 00 00 00 00 00 00
OSPF:
OSPF: Link State Advertisement Header # 1
OSPF: Link state age        = 5 (seconds)
OSPF: Optional capabilities = 22
OSPF:        .0.. .... = Opaque-LSAs not forwarded
OSPF:        ..1. .... = Demand Circuit bit
OSPF:        ...0 .... = External Attributes bit
OSPF:        .... 0... = no NSSA capability
OSPF:        .... .0.. = no multicast capability
OSPF:        .... ..1. = external routing capability
OSPF:        .... ...0 = no Type of Service routing capability
OSPF: Link state type    = 1 (Router links)
OSPF: Link state ID      = [13.1.1.1]
OSPF: Advertising Router = [13.1.1.1]
OSPF: Sequence number    = 2147483650.    Checksum = C8F6
OSPF: Length             = 36
OSPF:
```

When the packets are fully exchanged and the link-state databases are synchronized, the routers have become fully adjacent. You verify that this has occurred through the **show ip ospf neighbor** command, as shown in Example 3-8.

Example 3-8 *Verifying That the Routers Have Become Fully Adjacent*

```
CapeTown#show ip ospf neighbor

Neighbor ID     Pri   State      Dead Time   Address       Interface
13.13.13.2       1    FULL/DR    00:00:39    13.13.13.2    FastEthernet0/1
CapeTown#
```

Next, checking Sydney in Example 3-9, you can determine that Sydney is the DR.

Example 3-9 *Confirming That Sydney is the DR*

```
Sydney>show ip ospf neighbor

Neighbor ID     Pri   State      Dead Time   Address       Interface
13.1.1.1         1    FULL/BDR   00:00:30    13.13.13.1    FastEthernet0/1
Sydney>
```

Next, review the link-state database for each router. First, looking at Capetown in Example 3-10, you can see that as an ABR, it has the proper link data.

Example 3-10   *Looking at Capetown's Link-State Database*

```
Capetown#show ip ospf database

          OSPF Router with ID (13.1.1.1) (Process ID 100)


                Router Link States (Area 0)

Link ID        ADV Router       Age        Seq#        Checksum Link count
13.1.1.1       13.1.1.1         992        0x80000006 0xC0FA    1
13.13.13.2     13.13.13.2       1014       0x80000006 0xFA8B    1

                Net Link States (Area 0)

Link ID        ADV Router       Age        Seq#        Checksum
13.13.13.2     13.13.13.2       1014       0x80000005 0x5A53

                Summary Net Link States (Area 0)

Link ID        ADV Router       Age        Seq#        Checksum
10.1.1.0       13.13.13.2       1014       0x80000005 0x9A6B
13.0.0.1       13.1.1.1         993        0x80000005 0x4DCC
13.1.1.1       13.1.1.1         993        0x80000005 0x36E1

                Router Link States (Area 1)

Link ID        ADV Router       Age        Seq#        Checksum Link count
13.1.1.1       13.1.1.1         993        0x80000005 0x6F8     1

                Summary Net Link States (Area 1)

Link ID        ADV Router       Age        Seq#        Checksum
10.1.1.0       13.1.1.1         994        0x80000005 0x5FBE
13.1.1.1       13.1.1.1         994        0x80000005 0x36E1
13.13.13.0     13.1.1.1         994        0x80000007 0x15EC

                Summary ASB Link States (Area 1)

Link ID        ADV Router       Age        Seq#        Checksum
13.13.13.2     13.1.1.1         994        0x80000005 0x9F4

                Router Link States (Area 2)

Link ID        ADV Router       Age        Seq#        Checksum Link count
13.1.1.1       13.1.1.1         995        0x80000005 0x17E5    1

                Summary Net Link States (Area 2)

Link ID        ADV Router       Age        Seq#        Checksum
10.1.1.0       13.1.1.1         995        0x80000005 0x5FBE
13.0.0.1       13.1.1.1         999        0x80000005 0x4DCC
13.13.13.0     13.1.1.1         999        0x80000007 0x15EC
```

Example 3-10 *Looking at Capetown's Link-State Database (Continued)*

```
                   Summary ASB Link States (Area 2)

Link ID          ADV Router       Age         Seq#        Checksum
13.13.13.2       13.1.1.1         999         0x80000005 0x9F4
Capetown#
```

The entries in the link-state database are used to develop the routing table for Capetown, as shown in Example 3-11.

Example 3-11 *Capetown's Routing Table*

```
Capetown#show ip route
Codes: C - connected, S - static, I - IGRP, R - RIP, M - mobile, B - BGP
       D - EIGRP, EX - EIGRP external, O - OSPF, IA - OSPF inter area
       N1 - OSPF NSSA external type 1, N2 - OSPF NSSA external type 2
       E1 - OSPF external type 1, E2 - OSPF external type 2, E - EGP
       i - IS-IS, L1 - IS-IS level-1, L2 - IS-IS level-2, ia - IS-IS inter area
       * - candidate default, U - per-user static route, o - ODR
       P - periodic downloaded static route

Gateway of last resort is 13.13.13.2 to network 0.0.0.0

     10.0.0.0/30 is subnetted, 1 subnets
O IA    10.1.1.0 [110/2] via 13.13.13.2, 02:54:37, FastEthernet0/1
C    192.168.254.0/24 is directly connected, FastEthernet0/0
     13.0.0.0/8 is variably subnetted, 3 subnets, 2 masks
C       13.1.1.0/24 is directly connected, Loopback1
C       13.0.0.0/24 is directly connected, Loopback0
C       13.13.13.0/30 is directly connected, FastEthernet0/1
S*   0.0.0.0/0 [1/0] via 13.13.13.2
CapeTown#
```

The link-state database for Sydney is shown in Example 3-12.

Example 3-12 *Sydney's Link-State Database*

```
Sydney>show ip ospf database

       OSPF Router with ID (13.13.13.2) (Process ID 100)


             Router Link States (Area 0)

Link ID          ADV Router       Age         Seq#        Checksum Link count
13.1.1.1         13.1.1.1         1471        0x80000006 0xC0FA    1
13.13.13.2       13.13.13.2       1491        0x80000006 0xFA8B    1

             Net Link States (Area 0)

Link ID          ADV Router       Age         Seq#        Checksum
13.13.13.2       13.13.13.2       1491        0x80000005 0x5A53
```

continues

Example 3-12   *Sydney's Link-State Database (Continued)*

```
              Summary Net Link States (Area 0)

Link ID         ADV Router      Age        Seq#        Checksum
10.1.1.0        13.13.13.2      1491       0x80000005 0x9A6B
13.0.0.1        13.1.1.1        1471       0x80000005 0x4DCC
13.1.1.1        13.1.1.1        1471       0x80000005 0x36E1

              Router Link States (Area 5)

Link ID         ADV Router      Age        Seq#        Checksum Link count
13.13.13.2      13.13.13.2      1491       0x80000005 0xF9D5    1

              Summary Net Link States (Area 5)

Link ID         ADV Router      Age        Seq#        Checksum
13.0.0.1        13.13.13.2      449        0x80000006 0x9A64
13.1.1.1        13.13.13.2      449        0x80000006 0x8379
13.13.13.0      13.13.13.2      449        0x80000008 0x588F
Sydney>
```

Next, verify the routing table for Sydney, as shown in Example 3-13.

Example 3-13   *Verifying Sydney's Routing Table*

```
Sydney>show ip route
Codes: C - connected, S - static, I - IGRP, R - RIP, M - mobile, B - BGP
       D - EIGRP, EX - EIGRP external, O - OSPF, IA - OSPF inter area
       N1 - OSPF NSSA external type 1, N2 - OSPF NSSA external type 2
       E1 - OSPF external type 1, E2 - OSPF external type 2, E - EGP
       i - IS-IS, L1 - IS-IS level-1, L2 - IS-IS level-2, ia - IS-IS inter area
       * - candidate default, U - per-user static route, o - ODR
       P - periodic downloaded static route

Gateway of last resort is not set

     10.0.0.0/30 is subnetted, 1 subnets
C       10.1.1.0 is directly connected, FastEthernet0/0
     13.0.0.0/8 is variably subnetted, 3 subnets, 2 masks
O IA    13.1.1.1/32 [110/2] via 13.13.13.1, 02:54:59, FastEthernet0/1
O IA    13.0.0.1/32 [110/2] via 13.13.13.1, 02:54:59, FastEthernet0/1
C       13.13.13.0/30 is directly connected, FastEthernet0/1
Sydney>
```

Example 3-14 shows the configuration files for both routers.

Example 3-14 *Running Configuration Files for Capetown and Sydney*

```
Capetown#show running-config
Building configuration...

Current configuration:
!
version 12.0
service timestamps debug datetime msec localtime
service timestamps log datetime msec localtime
service password-encryption
!
hostname CapeTown
!
enable password 7 08274D5D1D0B0A02060E1E
!

ip subnet-zero
ip tcp synwait-time 5
no ip domain-lookup
!

voice-port 1/0/0
!
voice-port 1/0/1
!
interface Loopback0
 ip address 13.0.0.1 255.255.255.0
 no ip directed-broadcast
!
interface Loopback1
 ip address 13.1.1.1 255.255.255.0
 no ip directed-broadcast
!
interface FastEthernet0/0
 description CONNECTION TO CAT5K PORT 21
 ip address 192.168.254.100 255.255.255.0
 no ip directed-broadcast
 duplex auto
 speed auto
!
interface Serial0/0
 no ip address
 no ip directed-broadcast
 no ip mroute-cache
 shutdown
 no fair-queue
!
interface FastEthernet0/1
 description CONNECTION TO CAT5K - PORT 22
 ip address 13.13.13.1 255.255.255.252
 no ip directed-broadcast
 duplex auto
```

continues

Example 3-14 *Running Configuration Files for Capetown and Sydney (Continued)*

```
 speed auto
 !
 interface Serial0/1
  no ip address
  no ip directed-broadcast
  shutdown
 !
 router ospf 100
  network 13.0.0.0 0.0.0.255 area 1
  network 13.1.1.0 0.0.0.255 area 2
  network 13.13.13.0 0.0.0.255 area 0
 !
 ip classless
 ip route 0.0.0.0 0.0.0.0 13.13.13.2
 no ip http server
 !
 logging 192.168.254.69
 snmp-server location Raleigh, NC
 snmp-server contact Tom Thomas
 end

 Capetown#
```
```
Sydney#show running-config
Building configuration...

Current configuration:
!
version 12.0
service timestamps debug datetime msec localtime
service timestamps log datetime msec localtime
service password-encryption
!
hostname Sydney
!
enable password 7 094A4F1A0D1718071F0916
!
ip subnet-zero
ip tcp synwait-time 5
no ip domain-lookup
!
voice-port 1/0/0
!
voice-port 1/0/1
!
interface FastEthernet0/0
 description CONNECTION TO CAT5K - PORT 23
 ip address 10.1.1.2 255.255.255.252
 no ip directed-broadcast
 duplex auto
 speed auto
!
interface FastEthernet0/1
```

Example 3-14   *Running Configuration Files for Capetown and Sydney (Continued)*

```
 description CONNECTION TO CAT5K - PORT 24
 ip address 13.13.13.2 255.255.255.252
 no ip directed-broadcast
 duplex auto
 speed auto
!
router eigrp 65000
 network 13.13.13.0 0.0.0.3
 no auto-summary
!
router ospf 100
 redistribute eigrp 65000
 network 10.1.1.0 0.0.0.3 area 5
 network 13.13.13.0 0.0.0.255 area 0
!
ip classless
no ip http server
!
logging 192.168.254.69
snmp-server engineID local 00000009010000A1C0A8FE66
snmp-server location Raleigh, NC
snmp-server contact Tom Thomas
Sydney#
```

Case Study: Troubleshooting Neighbor Problems

When you execute a **show ip ospf neighbor** command and it reveals nothing or it shows nothing about the particular neighbor you are analyzing, it indicates that this router has seen no valid OSPF Hellos from that neighbor. Check the following items:

1 Is the local router or neighboring router's interface up, with line protocol up? Use the **show interface** command to find out.

2 Check for IP connectivity between the neighboring routers as follows:

   A Can you **ping** the neighbor?

   B Does the neighbor respond if you **ping 224.0.0.5**? (This is the address to which OSPF Hellos are sent.)

   C Check for any inbound access lists or other devices (such as a switch) that might prohibit sending/receipt of IP packets from one neighbor to the other.

3 Is OSPF enabled on the interfaces in question (that is, your router's interface and the neighboring router's interface)? Use the **show ip ospf interface** command to determine if OSPF is enabled.

4 Is OSPF configured as passive for the local router's or neighboring router's interface? (Use the **show running-config** command to check the configuration.)

— Verify that the following Hello parameters match on the neighboring interfaces of both routers:

— Same OSPF area (use the **show ip ospf interface** command to determine).

— Same type of OSPF area, such as stub or NSSA (use the **show ip ospf** command to check).

— Same subnet and subnet mask (use the **show interface** command to check).

— Same OSPF Hello and dead timer values (use the **show ip ospf interface** command to check).

TIP   OSPF adjacencies are formed only over primary networks and not secondary networks.

Neighbor Stuck in Init STATE

The init state indicates that a router sees Hello packets from the neighbor, but two-way communication has not been established. A Cisco router includes the router IDs of all neighbors in the init (or higher) state in the neighbor field of its Hello packets. Example 3-15 shows sample output of the **show ip ospf neighbor** command.

Example 3-15   *Output from the* **show ip ospf neighbor** *Command*

```
router2#show ip ospf neighbor

Neighbor ID    Pri  State     Dead Time   Address      Interface
10.10.5.1       1   INIT/-    00:00:34    10.10.1.1    Serial0
router2#
```

For two-way communication to be established with a neighbor, a router must also see its own router ID in the neighbor field of the neighbor's Hello packets. In other words, a router with a neighbor in the init state has received Hello packets from the neighbor but has not seen its own router ID in the neighbor's Hellos.

The most likely reason a local router is not listed in a neighbor's Hello packets is that the neighbor has not received Hello packets from the local router. Possible reasons for this are as follows:

● If any access lists are defined on the neighbor's interface, the destination IP of 224.0.0.5 must be permitted in the input access list. Remember that OSPF Hello packets have a destination address of 224.0.0.5 (the **all OSPF routers multicast** address).

- A Layer 2 or configuration problem might be keeping multicast packets from reaching the neighboring router. You can test this by pinging the multicast address 224.0.0.5 and confirming that responses are received from the neighboring router(s). In nonbroadcast media, such as frame relay, X.25, and ISDN, mapping is required between Layer 2 and the IP address. For example, in the case of static mapping, in the interface level command **frame-relay map ip 1.1.1.1 100 broadcast** or **dialer map ip 1.1.1.1 broadcast name router1 55346**, you must configure the keyword **broadcast** to avoid encapsulation failure every time OSPF tries to send the multicast Hello packet. The **debug ip packet detail** command used with the access list shows any encapsulation failures.

- OSPF authentication is not enabled on both sides or the passwords do not match. The router on which authentication is not enabled still processes Hello packets from the neighbor and sees the neighbor in the init state. To correct this problem, enable authentication on both sides.

- If you are running Cisco IOS Software Release 11.1.9 or earlier, check the output of the **show ip ospf interface** command for discrepancies such as the following:

  ```
  Neighbor Count is 0, Adjacent neighbor count is 1
  ```

  If the OSPF adjacent neighbor count is higher than the neighbor count, the neighbor list might be corrupted. This problem has the Cisco bug ID CSCdj01682. If you are a registered CCO user and you have logged in, you can view the bug details.

Neighbor Stuck in Exstart/Exchange State

OSPF neighbors that are in the exstart or exchange state are trying to exchange DD packets. The adjacency should continue past this state. If it does not, there is a problem with the DD exchange, such as a maximum transmission unit (MTU) mismatch or the receipt of an unexpected DD sequence number.

Although OSPF neighbors transition through the exstart/exchange states during the normal OSPF adjacency-building process, it is not normal for OSPF neighbors to be stuck in this state.

The problem occurs when the MTU settings for neighboring router interfaces do not match. The problem occurs most frequently when attempting to run OSPF between a Cisco router and another vendor's router. If the router with the higher MTU sends a packet larger than the MTU set on the neighboring router, the neighboring router ignores the packet. When this problem occurs, the **show ip ospf neighbor** command displays output similar to that shown in Figure 3-34.

Figure 3-34   *MTU Mismatch*

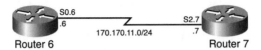

Routers 6 and 7 in the topology in Figure 3-34 are connected via frame relay, and Router 6 has been configured with 204 static routes redistributed into OSPF. The serial interface on Router 6 has the default MTU of 1500, while the serial interface on Router 7 has an MTU of 1450. Example 3-16 shows each router's configuration (only the necessary configuration information is shown):

Example 3-16   *Configurations for Routers 6 and 7 in Figure 3-34*

```
Router 6 Configuration              Router 7 Configuration
interface Serial2                   !
no ip address                       interface Serial0
no ip directed-broadcast            mtu 1450
encapsulation frame-relay           no ip address
no ip mroute-cache                  no ip directed-broadcast
frame-relay lmi-type ansi           encapsulation frame-relay
!                                    frame-relay lmi-type ANSI
interface Serial2.7 point-to-point
ip address 170.170.11.6 255.255.255.0
no ip directed-broadcast            !
frame-relay interface-dlci 101      interface Serial0.6 point-to-point
                                    ip address 170.170.11.7 255.255.255.0
                                    no ip directed-broadcast
router ospf 7                       frame-relay interface-dlci 110
redistribute static subnets
network 170.170.11.0 0.0.0.255 area 0    router ospf 7
                                    network 170.170.11.0 0.0.0.255 area 0
ip route 192.79.34.0 255.255.255.0 Null0
ip route 192.79.35.0 255.255.255.0 Null0
ip route 192.79.36.0 255.255.255.0 Null0
.
.
.
....204 total static routes
```

Example 3-17 shows the output of the **show ip ospf neighbor** command for each router.

Example 3-17   *Output of the* **show ip ospf neighbor** *Command for Routers 6 and 7*

```
router-6#show ip ospf neighbor

Neighbor ID     Pri   State        Dead Time   Address        Interface
170.170.11.7     1    EXCHANGE/  -   00:00:36    170.170.11.7   Serial2.7
router-7#show ip ospf neighbor

Neighbor ID     Pri   State        Dead Time   Address        Interface
170.170.11.6     1    EXSTART/   -   00:00:33    170.170.11.6   Serial0.6
```

The problem occurs when Router 6 sends an OSPF DD packet larger than 1450 bytes (Router 7's MTU) while in the exchange state. Using the **debug ip packet** and **debug ip ospf adjacency** commands on each router, you can see the OSPF adjacency process as it takes place. Table 3-4 documents the output following Routers 6 and 7 from Steps 1 through 14.

Table 3-4   *Output from the* **debug ip packet** *and* **debug ip ospf adjacency** *Command on Routers 6 and 7*

Router 6 Debug Output	Router 7 Debug Output
(1) *****ROUTER6 IS SENDING HELLOS BUT HEARS NOTHING, STATE OF NEIGHBOR IS DOWN** 00:03:53: OSPF: 170.170.11.7 address 170.170.11.7 on Serial2.7 is dead 00:03:53: OSPF: 170.170.11.7 address 170.170.11.7 on Serial2.7 is dead, state DOWN	**(2)** OSPF NOT ENABLED ON ROUTER7 YET
(3) *****ROUTER6 SENDING HELLOS** 00:03:53: IP: s=170.170.11.6 (local), d=224.0.0.5 (Serial2.7), len 64, sending broad/multicast, proto=89 00:04:03: IP: s=170.170.11.6 (local), d=224.0.0.5 (Serial2.7), Len 64, sending broad/multicast, proto=89	**(4)** OSPF NOT ENABLED ON ROUTER7 YET
(6) *****RECEIVE HELLO FROM ROUTER7** 00:04:04: IP: s=170.170.11.7 (Serial2.7), d=224.0.0.5, Len 64, rcvd 0, proto=89 00:04:04: OSPF: Rcv hello from 170.170.11.7 area 0 from Serial2.7 170.170.11.7 00:04:04: OSPF: End of hello processing	**(5)** *****OSPF ENABLED ON ROUTER7, BEGINS SENDING HELLOS AND BUILDING A ROUTER LSA** 00:17:44: IP: s=170.170.11.7 (local), d=224.0.0.5 (Serial0.6), Len 64, sending broad/multicast, proto=89 00:17:44: OSPF: Build router LSA for area 0, router ID 170.170.11.7, seq 0x80000001
(7) *****ROUTER6 SEND HELLO WITH ROUTER7 ROUTERID IN THE HELLO PACKET** 00:04:13: IP: s=170.170.11.6 (local), d=224.0.0.5 (Serial2.7), Len 68, sending broad/multicast, proto=89	**(8)** *****ROUTER7 RECEIVES HELLO FROM ROUTER6 CHANGES STATE TO 2WAY** 00:17:53: IP: s=170.170.11.6 (Serial0.6), d=224.0.0.5, Len 68, rcvd 0, proto=89 00:17:53: OSPF: Rcv hello from 170.170.11.6 area 0 from Serial0.6 170.170.11.6 00:17:53: OSPF: 2 Way Communication to 170.170.11.6 on Serial0.6, state 2WAY

Table 3-4   *Output from the* **debug ip packet** *and* **debug ip ospf adjacency** *Command on
Routers 6 and 7 (Continued)*

Router 6 Debug Output	Router 7 Debug Output
(10) ***ROUTER6 RECEIVES ROUTER7'S INITIAL DBD PACKET CHANGES STATE TO 2-WAY** 00:04:13: IP: s=170.170.11.7 (Serial2.7), d=224.0.0.5, Len 52, rcvd 0, proto=89 00:04:13: OSPF: Rcv DBD from 170.170.11.7 on Serial2.7 seq 0x13FD opt 0x2 flag 0x7 Len 32 mtu 1450 state INIT 00:04:13: OSPF: 2 Way Communication to 170.170.11.7 on Serial2.7, state 2WAY	**(9)** ***ROUTER7 SENDS INITIAL DBD PACKET WITH SEQ# 0x13FD** 00:17:53: OSPF: Send DBD to 170.170.11.6 on Serial0.6 seq 0x13FD opt 0x2 flag 0x7 Len 32 00:17:53: IP: s=170.170.11.7 (local), d=224.0.0.5 (Serial0.6), Len 52, sending broad/multicast, proto=89 00:17:53: OSPF: End of hello processing
(11) ***ROUTER6 SENDS DBD PACKET TO ROUTER7 (MASTER/SLAVE NEGOTIATION - ROUTER6 IS SLAVE)** 00:04:13: OSPF: Send DBD to 170.170.11.7 on Serial2.7 seq 0xE44 opt 0x2 flag 0x7 Len 32 00:04:13: IP: s=170.170.11.6 (local), d=224.0.0.5 (Serial2.7), Len 52, sending broad/multicast, proto=89 00:04:13: OSPF: NBR Negotiation Done. We are the SLAVE	**(12)** ***RECEIVE ROUTER6'S INITIAL DBD PACKET(MTU MISMATCH IS RECOGNIZED)** 00:17:53: IP: s=170.170.11.6 (Serial0.6), d=224.0.0.5, Len 52, rcvd 0, proto=89 00:17:53: OSPF: Rcv DBD from 170.170.11.6 on Serial0.6 seq 0xE44 opt 0x2 flag 0x7 Len 32 mtu 1500 state EXSTART 00:17:53: OSPF: Nbr 170.170.11.6 has larger interface MTU (MTU MISMATCH RECOGNIZED)
(13) ***SINCE ROUTER6 IS SLAVE SEND DBD PACKET WITH LSA HEADERS, SAME SEQ# (0x13FD) TO ACK ROUTER7'S DBD. (NOTE SIZE OF PKT)** 00:04:13: OSPF: Send DBD to 170.170.11.7 on Serial2.7 seq 0x13FD opt 0x2 flag 0x2 Len 1472 00:04:13: IP: s=170.170.11.6 (local), d=224.0.0.5 (Serial2.7), Len 1492, sending broad/multicast, proto=89	**(14)** ***NEVER RECEIVE ACK TO ROUTER7'S INITIAL DBD, RETRANSMIT** 00:17:54: IP: s=170.170.11.7 (local), d=224.0.0.5 (Serial0.6), Len 68, sending broad/multicast, proto=89 00:17:58: OSPF: Retransmitting DBD to 170.170.11.6 on Serial0.6 00:17:58: OSPF: Send DBD to 170.170.11.6 on Serial0.6 seq 0x13FD opt 0x2 flag 0x7 Len 32
AT THIS POINT ROUTER6 KEEPS TRYING TO ACK THE INITIAL DBD PACKET FROM ROUTER7	ROUTER7 NEVER GETS ACK FROM ROUTER6 BECAUSE DBD PACKET FROM ROUTER7 IS TOO BIG FOR ROUTER7'S MTU. ROUTER7 KEEPS RETRANSMITTING DBD PACKET.

Table 3-4   *Output from the* **debug ip packet** *and* **debug ip ospf adjacency** *Command on Routers 6 and 7 (Continued)*

Router 6 Debug Output	Router 7 Debug Output
00:04:13: IP: s=170.170.11.7 (Serial2.7), d=224.0.0.5, Len 68, rcvd 0, proto=89 00:04:13: OSPF: Rcv hello from 170.170.11.7 area 0 from Serial2.7 170.170.11.7 00:04:13: OSPF: End of hello processing 00:04:18: IP: s=170.170.11.7 (Serial2.7), d=224.0.0.5, Len 52, rcvd 0, proto=89 00:04:18: OSPF: Rcv DBD from 170.170.11.7 on Serial2.7 seq 0x13FD opt 0x2 flag 0x7 Len 32 mtu 1450 state EXCHANGE 00:04:18: OSPF: Send DBD to 170.170.11.7 on Serial2.7 seq 0x13FD opt 0x2 flag 0x2 Len 1472 00:04:18: IP: s=170.170.11.6 (local), d=224.0.0.5 (Serial2.7), Len 1492, sending broad/multicast, proto=89 00:04:23: IP: s=170.170.11.6 (local), d=224.0.0.5 (Serial2.7), Len 68, sending broad/multicast, proto=89 00:04:23: IP: s=170.170.11.7 (Serial2.7), d=224.0.0.5, Len 52, rcvd 0, proto=89 00:04:23: OSPF: Rcv DBD from 170.170.11.7 on Serial2.7 seq 0x13FD opt 0x2 flag 0x7 Len 32 mtu 1450 state EXCHANGE	0:17:58: IP: s=170.170.11.7 (local), d=224.0.0.5 (Serial0.6), Len 52, sending broad/multicast, proto=89 00:18:03: OSPF: Retransmitting DBD to 170.170.11.6 on Serial0.6 00:18:03: OSPF: Send DBD to 170.170.11.6 on Serial0.6 seq 0x13FD opt 0x2 flag 0x7 Len 32 00:18:03: IP: s=170.170.11.7 (local), d=224.0.0.5 (Serial0.6), Len 52, sending broad/multicast, proto=89 00:18:03: IP: s=170.170.11.6 (Serial0.6), d=224.0.0.5, Len 68, rcvd 0, proto=89 00:18:03: OSPF: Rcv hello from 170.170.11.6 area 0 from Serial0.6 170.170.11.6 00:18:03: OSPF: End of hello processing 00:18:04: IP: s=170.170.11.7 (local), d=224.0.0.5 (Serial0.6), Len 68, sending broad/multicast, proto=89 00:18:08: OSPF: Retransmitting DBD to 170.170.11.6 on Serial0.6 00:18:08: OSPF: Send DBD to 170.170.11.6 on Serial0.6 seq 0x13FD opt 0x2 flag 0x7 Len 32 00:18:08: IP: s=170.170.11.7 (local), d=224.0.0.5 (Serial0.6), Len 52, sending broad/multicast, proto=89 router-7#
ROUTERS REMAIN IN THIS RETRANSMIT SESSION INDEFINITELY	

In Step 9 of Table 3-4, Router 7 sends its first DBD packet with flag 0x7 set. This indicates that Router 7 is the master.

In Step 10, Router 6 receives Router 7's initial DBD packet and transitions its state to 2-way.

Step 11 shows Router 6 sending its initial DBD packet with flag 0x7 set, indicating that it is the master (this is part of the master—slave negotiation).

In Step 12, Router 7 receives Router 6's initial DBD packet and recognizes an MTU mismatch. (Router 7 can recognize an MTU mismatch because Router 6 includes its interface MTU in the interface MTU field of the DBD packet.) Router 6's initial DBD is rejected by Router 7. Router 7 retransmits the initial DBD packet.

Step 13 shows Router 6, as slave, adopting Router 7's sequence number and sending its second DBD packet containing the headers of its LSAs; this increases the size of the packet. However, Router 7 never receives this DBD packet because it is larger than Router 7's MTU.

After Step 13, Router 7 continues to retransmit the initial DBD packet to Router 6, while Router 6 continues to send DBD packets that follow the master sequence number. This loop continues indefinitely, preventing either router from making the transition out of the exstart/ exchange state.

What's the Solution?

Because the problem is caused by mismatched MTUs, the solution is to change either router's MTU to match the neighbor's MTU. When the problem occurs between a Cisco router and another vendor's router over LAN media, adjust the MTU carefully.

NOTE   Cisco IOS Software Release 12.0(3) introduced interface MTU mismatch detection. This detection involves OSPF advertising the interface MTU in the DBD packets, which is in accordance with the OSPF RFC 2178, Appendix G.9. When a router receives a DBD packet advertising an MTU larger than the router can receive, the router ignores the DBD packet and the neighbor state remains in exstart. This prevents an adjacency from forming. To fix this problem, make sure that the MTUs are the same on both ends of a link.

Cisco IOS Software Release 12.1(3) introduced the interface-level **ip ospf mtu-ignore** command to turn off the MTU mismatch detection.

Neighbor Stuck in 2-Way State

In the topology in Figure 3-35, all routers are running OSPF neighbors over the Ethernet network.

Figure 3-35   *Stuck in 2-Way State?*

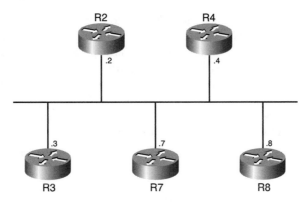

Example 3-18 provides sample output of the **show ip ospf neighbor** command on R7.

Example 3-18   *Output from the* **show ip ospf neighbor** *Command for Router 7*

```
router-7#show ip ospf neighbor

Neighbor ID    Pri    State          Dead Time    Address        Interface
170.170.3.2    1      FULL/BDR       00:00:37     170.170.3.2    Ethernet0
170.170.3.3    1      2WAY/DROTHER   00:00:30     170.170.3.3    Ethernet0
170.170.10.8   1      FULL/DR        00:00:39     170.170.3.8    Ethernet0
170.170.7.4    1      2WAY/DROTHER   00:00:39     170.170.3.4    Ethernet0
router-7#
```

R7 establishes full adjacency only with the DR and BDR. All other routers have a 2-way adjacency established. This is normal behavior for OSPF.

Whenever a router sees itself in a neighbor's Hello packet, it confirms bidirectional communication and transitions the neighbor state to 2-way. At this point, the routers perform DR and BDR election. A router attempts to form a full adjacency with a neighbor if one of the two routers is the DR or BDR. OSPF routers become fully adjacent with routers with which they have successfully completed the database synchronization process. This is the process by which OSPF routers exchange link-state information to populate their databases with the same information. Again, this database synchronization process is executed only between two routers if one of the two routers is the DR or BDR.

This was a trick question to remind you that not everything you see is wrong and to remember the unique aspects of the OSPF.

Summary

This chapter covered an important aspect of how OSPF communicates information within an OSPF routing domain. You learned about the nine types of OSPF LSAs and how an LSA begins the link-state database synchronization steps. You also learned about the formal processes and protocols that are used with OSPF—Hello, exchange, and flooding—each of which have different roles and responsibilities within OSPF. This chapter also covered manipulating LSAs as a new default behavior that Cisco implemented in OSPF. The chapter discussed LSA grouping and packet pacing, and it concluded with some troubleshooting and an exploration of some common problems.

PART II

OSPF Routing and Network Design

CHAPTER 4

Design Fundamentals

The Art of Strategy: "Those who are victorious plan effectively and change decisively. They are like a great river that maintains its course but adjusts its flow…they have form but are formless. They are skilled in both planning and adapting and need not fear the result of a thousand battles; for they win in advance, defeating those that have already lost."—Sun Tzu, Chinese warrior and philosopher, 100 B.C.

The chapter opening quote is clear evidence that thousands of years ago Sun-Tzu foresaw the Internet and the need to conduct effective network design. This chapter covers a variety of subjects relating to designing OSPF networks. The foundation of understanding the purpose for using OSPF and its operation as discussed in previous chapters is further expanded as the discussion of OSPF performance and design issues are expanded. Each design section presents a series of "golden design rules," which help you understand the constraints and recommendations of properly designing each area within an OSPF network. In many cases, you find examples that draw upon the presented material to further reinforce key topics and ideas:

- **OSPF design guidelines**—This section introduces designing OSPF networks and concentrates on two main points—network topology and scalability. This section examines the physical requirements and layout needed before the work begins.

- **Area design considerations**—The true fundamentals of any OSPF network are its areas. The proper design of these areas is essential for a successful OSPF design. The following areas are discussed: backbone, nonstub, and all the variations of the stub area.

- **Case studies**—The case studies provide some real-world OSPF design scenarios to apply the lessons that are learned throughout the chapter.

This chapter goes hand-in-hand with Chapter 5, "Routing Concepts and Configuration." When used together, these chapters allow your OSPF network to be the envy of all.

OSPF Design Guidelines

The OSPF protocol, as defined in RFC 2328, provides a high-functionality open protocol that enables multivendor networks to communicate using the TCP/IP protocol family. Some benefits of OSPF are as follows:

- Fast convergence
- Variable-length subnet masking (VLSM)
- Authentication
- Hierarchical segmentation
- Route summarization
- Aggregation

All these benefits are needed to handle large and complicated networks.

Whether you are building an OSPF internetwork from the ground up or converting your internetwork to OSPF, the design guidelines highlighted in the sections that follow provide a foundation from which you can construct a reliable, scalable OSPF-based environment.

Different people have different approaches to designing OSPF networks. The important thing to remember is that any protocol can fail under pressure. The idea is not to challenge the protocol but rather to work with it to get the best performance possible from your network.

The OSPF RFC 2328 specifies several important considerations that are essential to a properly designed OSPF network. However, because the operation of OSPF depends on how it is implemented, some guidance is available. Industry-referenced design techniques offer assistance in OSPF network design solutions.

NOTE   Two excellent books are available for assistance in designing Cisco-based networks. They are based on the Cisco Internetwork Design Course:

CID: Cisco Internetwork Design Course Companion

Cisco Internetwork Design

OSPF Design Goals

You identified all the resources you need to build a brilliant OSPF network, but what factors do you need to consider? What criteria do you need to keep in mind as you read the request for proposal (RFP)? The five basic network design goals for your OSPF network (or any network) are as follows:

- Functionality
- Scalability
- Adaptability

- Manageability
- Cost effectiveness

Functionality

"The network must work" is the bottom line. Because networks are an integral part of enabling entire businesses and individual users to do their jobs, this is the essential and only acceptable outcome. Here, you must use service level agreements (SLAs). You must know what is expected of the network to design it properly. You must also ensure that all the business needs have been defined. These needs are the goals by which you can later judge the success of your design. For example, if a business goal is to have a highly reliable network via redundant links between core devices and if you do not design the network to meet this business goal, the network design is flawed.

Scalability

As your organization grows, the network must be able to keep pace. Your network and its initial design must enable the organization to expand accordingly. Therefore, you must plan into a network the capability to further expand it. A network that cannot keep pace with the organization's business needs and growth is of little use.

For example, routing summarization is a major factor in the success of designing your network. To ensure that your network can scale properly, route summarization is the biggest factor against which to measure your success. Without summarization, you have a flat address design with specific route information for every subnet being transmitted across the network—a bad thing in large networks. In discussing summarization, remember that routers summarize at several levels, as shown in Figure 4-1.

Figure 4-1   *Route Summarization Affects Network Scalability*

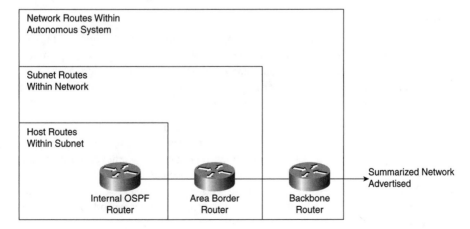

For example, hosts are grouped into subnetworks, subnetworks are then grouped into major networks, and major networks are then consolidated into OSPF areas. The overall OSPF network can then be grouped into an autonomous system (AS). Chapter 7, "Summarization," covers this topic in more detail.

NOTE   Many smaller networks can use a standard routing protocol such as OSPF. For example, these networks can have 100 or less routers with a relatively small IP space. In these situations, summarization might not be possible and might not gain much if it were implemented.

Adaptability

Adaptability refers to your network's capability to respond to changes. In most cases, adaptability refers to your network's capability to embrace new technologies in a timely and efficient manner. This becomes extremely important as the network ages because change within networking is occurring at breakneck speed.

Manageability

Providing proactive network management is the goal here. The network must have the proper tools and design to ensure that you are always aware of its operation and current status. It is always better to have your Network Operating Center (NOC) calling the customer before the customer calls you. I have always chuckled with the humorous cartoon that shows a NOC engineer in his doctor's office saying "every time the network goes down I get this ringing in my ears." That is a funny way to depict a situation you want to avoid.

Cost Effectiveness

Cost effectiveness is the true bottom line of network design. Budgets and resources are limited, and building or expanding the network while staying within the predetermined budget is always a benefit to your career and proper network design. Management is literally *always happy* when a project comes in under budget; consider this carefully and you know how they feel when it goes over budget.

Although the five basic goals of network design can be followed in any situation, there should also be a certain mind-set during the process regarding the technology you will be using. It is important to use state-of-the-art technologies whenever possible; although, this does not mean using unproven or inadequately tested technology. By spending extra money up front, you are investing for the future, knowing that the network you are building will be able to grow, from a technological standpoint, for a longer period of time than otherwise possible.

OSPF Network Design Methodology

Follow six common steps when designing your OSPF network. These steps are not absolute and do not guarantee the perfect network but provide you with realistic considerations for a well-designed OSPF network.

The six time-proven steps to designing a network are as follows:

Step 1 Analyze the requirements.

Step 2 Develop the network topology.

Step 3 Determine the addressing and naming conventions.

Step 4 Provision the hardware.

Step 5 Deploy protocol and Cisco IOS Software features.

Step 6 Implement, monitor, and maintain the network.

Although your network might not have the latest technology, it might not really need it if you objectively determine the needs of a network by following this design methodology (see Figure 4-2). A network does not always need to have routers with the latest technology; however, networks must have the capability to meet the business needs for which they were designed.

Figure 4-2   *Network Design Methodology*

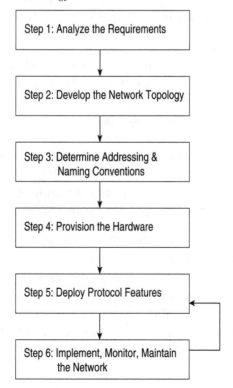

Step 1: Analyze the Requirements

This step details the process of determining expectations and then converting those expectations into a real network.

What Do You Know?

Going into Step 1, you know that an OSPF network is required, but you do not know what it will need to accomplish for your users or how you will physically design the network.

The needs of users are always changing. Nevertheless, as the engineer involved in the design of the network, you must still objectively listen and determine the users' needs. In the end, they are going to be the network's customers. You must also take into consideration what the future might hold for them. Therefore, always ask the users what needs they foresee. It is your responsibility to take their response and turn it into the requirements of the network.

A corporate vision is always important. For example, do the long-range corporate plans include having a website? If so, what will it be doing? Will the company be running voice over the network? Is videoconferencing going to be required?

Additional information that you should gather includes the current organization structure, organization locations, and flow of information within the organization as well as internal or external resources that are available to you. Armed with this information, your networks need analysis; you should then begin conducting a cost and benefit analysis. In many cases, you will not be able to get all the equipment or bandwidth that you think is necessary. Therefore, create a risk assessment that details the potential problems or areas of concern regarding the network design.

Consider the following issues when working through the network design process. I find that whenever I am called upon to design a network or respond to an Request for Proposal (RFP) that rereading this section benefits me greatly. Most of this information is common knowledge but a simple refresher will help you be more successful:

- **Reliability**—When designing networks, reliability is usually the most important goal, as the WAN is often the backbone of any network. There are several levels of redundancy, for example, physical redundancy via the presence of backup routers or logical redundancy via extra circuits between key sites. The resiliency and thus the reliability of a network is related, so plan according to your budget and customer expectations.

- **Latency**—At certain times, network access requests can take a long time to be granted. Users should be notified about a latency problem in the network whenever possible. When implementing your network, test its latency to ensure that this is not a problem.

  Investigate which applications are to be used. This information determines how much latency is acceptable and helps you design the network appropriately.

- **Cost of WAN resources**—WAN resources are expensive, and as such, frequently involve a trade-off between cost efficiency and full network redundancy. Cost efficiency is usually preferred when compared to price, so adjust the network design to reflect the most efficient solution.

- **Amount of traffic**—You must be able to accurately determine the amount of traffic that will be on the network to properly size its various components. As you implement the network, develop a baseline that can be used to project future growth. To do so, investigate the current network and determine the traffic levels and types.

- **Multiple protocols on the WAN**—The simplicity of IP is of great benefit to any network. For example, by allowing only IP-based protocols on the network, you avoid the unique addressing and configuration issues that are related to other protocols. Therefore, you should not allow multiple non-IP protocols in a network—especially in the backbone.

- **Compatibility with standards or legacy systems**—Compatibility will always be an issue with your network throughout its life. As a network designer, keep this in mind as you proceed. Business considerations are likely to force compatibility issues on you and the network.

- **Simplicity and ease of configuration**—You might be involved in only the design and implementation of the network and not the management of it. In that case, the knowledge that you develop must be passed on to those who will manage the network. Consider simplicity and ease of configuration while you develop your design documents for the network.

- **Support for remote offices and telecommuters**—In today's telecommunications environment, satellite offices are becoming commonplace and require network connectivity, so plan accordingly. Furthermore, the number of telecommuters is on the rise. Remember this as you determine the placement of network components to ensure that they can handle this requirement when it becomes a priority for your organization.

OSPF Deployment

As you determine the network requirements, some important questions exist regarding the requirements of OSPF. The answers to the following questions can help you further define the requirements of your OSPF network:

- How should the OSPF AS be delineated? How many areas should it have, and what should the boundaries be?

- Does your network and its data require built-in security? For example, is the encryption of data or authentication of routes required?

- What information from other autonomous systems should be imported into your network?

- Which sites will have links that should be preferred (lower cost)?

- Which sites will have links that should be avoided (higher cost)?

Load Balancing with OSPF

As you determine the network requirements, note the load-balancing feature of OSPF. In the Cisco implementation of OSPF, any router can, by default, support up to four equal-cost routes to a destination. When a failure to the destination is recognized, OSPF immediately switches to the remaining paths. OSPF can support a maximum of six equal-cost paths if it has been configured to do so.

OSPF automatically performs load balancing across or over equal-cost paths to a given destination. The cost associated is determined (by default) by the interface bandwidth statement, unless OSPF is configured to maximize multiple-path routing (that is, to use six paths instead of the default of four).

Cisco IOS Software calculates cost for OSPF by dividing 100 million by the configured bandwidth of the interface, as illustrated in Figure 4-3.

Figure 4-3 *OSPF Costs*

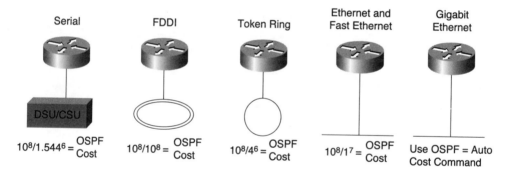

OSPF Cost is calculated as follows:
10^8 divided by bandwidth

Serial	FDDI	Token Ring	Ethernet and Fast Ethernet	Gigabit Ethernet
$10^8/1.544^6 = \dfrac{\text{OSPF}}{\text{Cost}}$	$10^8/10^8 = \dfrac{\text{OSPF}}{\text{Cost}}$	$10^8/4^6 = \dfrac{\text{OSPF}}{\text{Cost}}$	$10^8/1^7 = \dfrac{\text{OSPF}}{\text{Cost}}$	Use OSPF = Auto Cost Command

---

TIP

Cisco IOS Software Release 11.2 addressed this cost calculation issue with the introduction of the **ospf auto-cost reference bandwidth** command. This command alleviates the problem of how OSPF would calculate cost on a Gigabit Ethernet interface.

OSPF Convergence

When all routers know the current state of a network, OSPF convergence is extremely fast when compared to that of other protocols; this was one of the main features included in OSPF's initial design. To keep this desirable feature fully functional in your network, consider the following components, which determine how long it takes for OSPF to converge:

• The length of time it takes OSPF to detect a link or interface failure

- The length of time it takes the routers to exchange routing information via link-state advertisements (LSAs), rerun the shortest path first (SPF) algorithm, and build a new routing table

- A built-in SPF delay time of 5 seconds (the default value)

Therefore, the average time for OSPF to propagate LSAs and rerun the SPF algorithm is approximately 1 second. Then the SPF delay timer of 5 seconds must elapse. OSPF convergence can therefore be from 6 to 46 seconds, depending on the type of failure, SPF timer settings, size of the network, and size of the LSA database. The worst-case scenario is when a link fails but the destination is still reachable via an alternate route because the 40-second default dead timer needs to expire before the SPF is rerun.

Step 2: Develop the Network Topology

When designing an OSPF network, this step covers the process of determining the network's physical layout. Two common design topologies exist: meshed and hierarchical. The following sections discuss each topology and help you determine which is the most efficient design for today's networks.

What Do You Know?

Going into Step 2, you have developed a list of the requirements associated with the OSPF network. You have also begun to determine the financial costs associated with the network. These costs might include equipment, memory, and associated media.

Fully Meshed Topology

In a fully meshed structure, the topology is flat and all routers perform essentially the same function, so there is no clear definition of where specific functions are performed. Network expansion tends to proceed in a haphazard, arbitrary manner. This type of topology is not acceptable to the operation of OSPF. It does not correctly support the use of areas.

Hierarchical Topology

In a hierarchical topology, the network is organized in layers that have clearly defined functions. This type of network includes the following layers:

- **Core layer**—This is an excellent place for OSPF backbone routers that connect through area 0. All these routers would interconnect and without host connections. The primary purpose of the core layer is to provide connectivity between other areas.

  In modern network design, the core layer can also be Gigabit Ethernet switches rather than routers.

- **Distribution layer**—In this layer, you can locate other OSPF areas connected through Area Border Routers (ABRs) back to the core layer (area 0). This is also a good location to begin implementing various network policies, such as security, Domain Name System (DNS), and so on.

- **Access layer**—This layer includes the routers that provide connections to the users' LANs. This layer is where the majority of the hosts and servers need to connect to the network.

By using this type of logical layered design, you gain benefits that help you design the network, as shown in Figure 4-4.

Figure 4-4   *OSPF Hierarchical Topology*

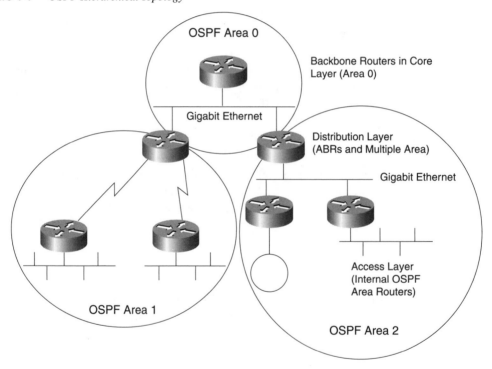

The benefits of the OSPF hierarchical topology as implemented in Figure 4-4 are as follows:

- **Scalability**—Networks can grow easily because functionality is localized, so additional sites can be added easily and quickly.

- **Ease of implementation**—This physical topology fits easily into OSPF's logical hierarchy, making network implementation easier.

- **Ease of troubleshooting**—Because functionality is localized, it is easier to recognize problem locations and isolate them.

- **Predictability**—Because of the layered approach, the functionality of each layer is more predictable. This makes capacity planning and modeling easier.

- **Protocol support**—An underlying physical architecture is already in place. If you want to incorporate additional protocols, such as BGP, or if your organization acquires a network running a different protocol, you can easily add the protocol. For example, being able to connect an external network at the appropriate place in your network is enhanced with a hierarchical design.

- **Manageability**—The physical layout of the network lends itself to logical areas that make network management easier.

At this point, you can see that the three-layered hierarchical model fits perfectly into OSPF's logical design, and it is this model on which you will be basing your network design. Before discussing how to implement and design this type of model, some basic OSPF backbone designs are reviewed.

OSPF Backbone Design in the Hierarchical Model

The process of designing the backbone area has been previously discussed, so it is only briefly reviewed here. Always keep the backbone area as simple as possible by avoiding a complex mesh. Consider using a LAN solution for the backbone. The transit across the backbone is always one hop, latency is minimized, and the backbone is a simple design that converges quickly. Figure 4-5 illustrates a simple OSPF backbone design.

Figure 4-5   *Simple OSPF Backbone Design*

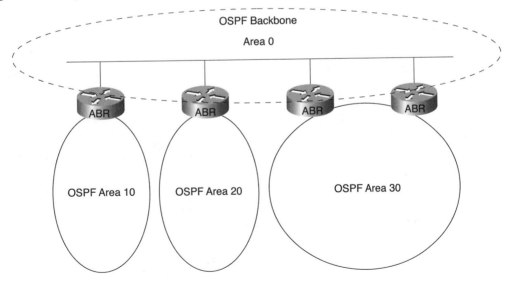

You need to keep users off the backbone because it is only a transit area. Because all other OSPF areas connect to the backbone, consider adding logical security. In OSPF, logical security can be in the form of route authentication. Furthermore, the entire network can be protected by using route authentication.

Also consider physically securing your backbone. As a network critical shared resource, the routers need to be physically secure. If you use the previously mentioned LAN backbone solution, securing your network is relatively easy; just place the backbone equipment in a secure closet or rack, as shown in Figure 4-6.

Figure 4-6 *Isolate and Secure the Backbone Physically and Logically*

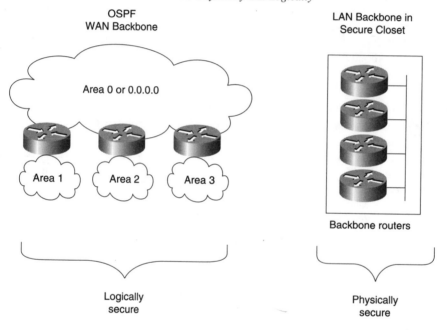

Area Design in the Hierarchical Model

Design your OSPF network with areas to make the network scalable and efficient. Areas have been discussed in previous chapters, but a brief review at this point is helpful. Keep areas simple and stubby, with less than 100 routers (optimally 40 to 50) and have maximum summarization for ease of routing. The network illustrated in Figure 4-7 demonstrates these suggestions.

Figure 4-7   *OSPF Network with Areas*

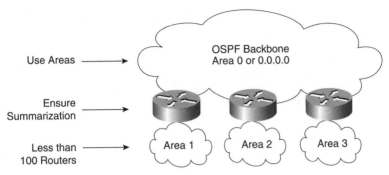

NOTE   Let me digress for a moment into the design debate surrounding the number of routers per area. Everyone has an opinion on this topic, and in actual implementation, you can go higher than the numbers I quote here. However, and I stress this point, you must take into consideration all the factors here to make this successful. You are now probably wondering if I will put a number on how far we can grow a single area and what I have experienced. Well, I am not going to do that, sorry. There are just too many variables to consider in a forum like this, but I will say that I have done a much higher number than Cisco recommends!

While I am also discussing highly opinionated topics, let me also mention that OSPF areas should also have a logical correlation to their placement, thus making the addressing and subnetting much easier to handle. One of the benefits here is that you can grow the areas much higher.

Using a Stub Area

What does your network gain by adding stub areas? Stub areas summarize all external LSAs into one default route, which provides a path to external routes for all traffic inside the stub area. The stub ABR forwards LSAs for inter-area routes but not external routes and floods them to other area 0 routers. The stub ABR keeps the LSA database for the stub area with this additional information and the default external route. Figure 4-8 illustrates the operations in a stub area. An ASBR cannot be part of a stub area, and redistribution of routes from other protocols cannot take place in this area.

Figure 4-8 *Stub Area Operation*

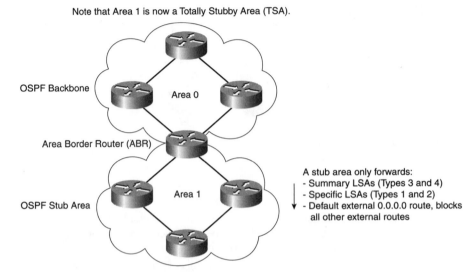

Note that Area 1 is now a Totally Stubby Area (TSA).

OSPF Backbone

Area 0

Area Border Router (ABR)

Area 1

OSPF Stub Area

A stub area only forwards:
- Summary LSAs (Types 3 and 4)
- Specific LSAs (Types 1 and 2)
- Default external 0.0.0.0 route, blocks all other external routes

You can also design totally stubby areas within your network. Totally stubby areas are a Cisco-specific feature that is available within its implementation of the OSPF standard.

If an area is configured as totally stubby, only the default summary link is propagated into the area by the ABR interarea, and external LSAs are blocked at the ABR of a totally stubby area. An ASBR cannot be part of a totally stubby area, and redistribution of routes from other protocols cannot take place in this area. Figure 4-9 shows the operations in a totally stubby area.

Figure 4-9 *Totally Stubby Area Operation*

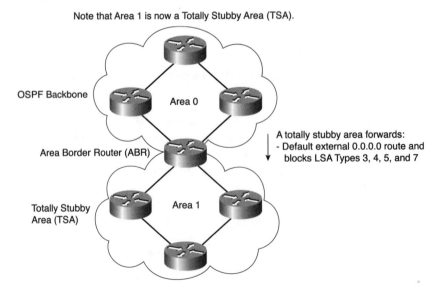

Note that Area 1 is now a Totally Stubby Area (TSA).

OSPF Backbone

Area 0

Area Border Router (ABR)

A totally stubby area forwards:
- Default external 0.0.0.0 route and blocks LSA Types 3, 4, 5, and 7

Totally Stubby Area (TSA)

Area 1

The main difference between a stub area and a not-so-stubby area (NSSA) is that the NSSA allows the import of a limited number of external routes. You can configure areas that redistribute routing information from another protocol to the NSSA. NSSAs are discussed later in the "Not-So-Stubby Areas" section.

Example of an OSPF Network with a Hierarchical Structure

To design this type of model network, gather a list of the different locations that require network connectivity within your organization. For purposes of this example and ease of understanding, consider that you have an international corporation and you have been asked to build its OSPF network within the United States. You have the following divisions (each having various business units within it). The following hierarchy groups the units by location and function:

- **Headquarters**: Washington, D.C. (all in the same building)
    - U.S. executives
    - Legal department
- **Human resources** (located at headquarters but in a different building)
    - Payroll
    - Benefits
    - Corporate recruiting
- **Sales and marketing**
    - Northern division (6 offices)
    - Southern division (6 offices)
    - Eastern division (5 offices)
    - Western division (7 offices)
- **Manufacturing**
    - Engineering located in western United States
    - Widgets division located in northern United States (4 factories)
    - Gidgets division located in southern United States (3 factories)
    - Tomgets division located in western United States (3 factories)

The listed units will become the basis of OSPF areas. Contained within the areas will be OSPF internal (intra-area) routers that connect to the various hosts.

Of these groupings, select essential locations at which to locate the backbone routers. For this example, the headquarters has a backbone router that is connected to area 0. You have been given the following requirements based on traffic flow and corporate guidelines:

- All divisions must be within the same area, regardless of geographic location.
- All divisions must be able to connect to headquarters.
- In this company, area 0 links all major continental locations throughout the globe.
- All regional clusters must have alternate routes.
- Internet connectivity is required for the entire company.
- If the backbone router fails, network operation within the U.S. divisions must continue.
- Engineering and manufacturing must be able to communicate quickly and easily.

Begin separating the sites into areas and picking one location within each area where the ABR is to reside. This results in a proposed set of OSPF routers deployed as follows:

- **Backbone router (area 0)**—Connects to global area 0
- **ABR (area 1)**—Executives and legal department
- **ABR (area 2)**—Human resources
- **ABR (area 3)**—Sales
- **ABR (area 4)**—Manufacturing and engineering
- **ASBR**—Internet connectivity

The remaining sites are each assigned an intra-area router to connect them to the network; this could be an ABR or internal OSPF area router. One main site within each geographical area is the hub site for that geographic area, thereby reducing bandwidth costs.

At this point, you should have your organization separated into areas or layers and an overall topology map laid out. Figure 4-10 illustrates the example network described so far.

Figure 4-10 *Proposed Network Design: Topology Map*

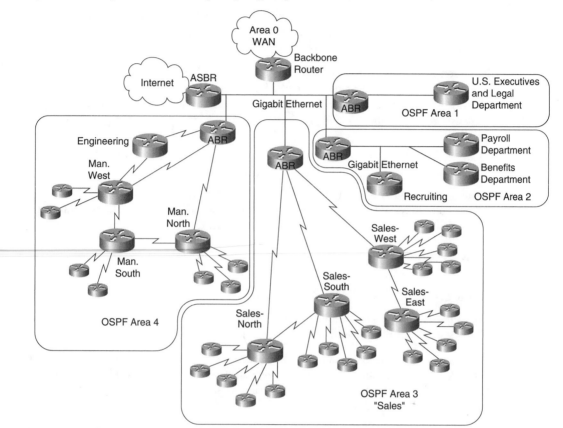

I want to throw out a couple of disclaimers here before people start tearing up my example:

- Remember requirement number 1. All divisions must be within the same area, regardless of geographic location.

- There are many ways of designing a network, and this is just one way and one person's opinion.

- Now that you think you have a solid network design, have someone else look at it and consider modeling it in a software package such as the ones found at www.wandl.com and www.opnet.com.

Step 3: Determine the Addressing and Naming Conventions

Step 3 covers the process of assigning the overall network-addressing scheme. By assigning blocks of addresses to portions of the network, you can simplify addressing, administration, and routing and increase scalability.

Because OSPF supports VLSM, you can develop a true hierarchical addressing scheme. This hierarchical addressing results in efficient summarization of routes throughout the network. VLSM and CIDR were discussed in Chapter 1, "Networking and Routing Fundamentals." You apply these techniques in this step of designing your OSPF network.

What Do You Know?

Coming into Step 3, you determined your network's requirements and developed a physical network topology. You continued to keep track of the costs—both one-time and recurring—while planning. In this step, you determine the addressing and naming conventions that you plan to use.

Public or Private Address Space

Your address scheme must be able to scale enough to support a larger network because your network will most likely continue to grow.

Now, you must determine what range of IP addresses you are going to deploy within your network. The first question you need to answer is, "Do I have public address space assigned to me by my Internet service provider (ISP), or am I going to be using private address space as specified in RFC 1918 and 1597?"

Either choice has its implications on the design of your network. By choosing to use private address space in connecting to the Internet, you must include the capability to do address translation as part of your network design.

To further complicate the issue, you might also have to deal with a preexisting addressing scheme and the need to support automatic address assignment through the use of Dynamic Host Configuration Protocol (DHCP) or DNS—This type of technology is beyond the scope of this book.

TIP   DHCP is a broadcast technique that obtains an IP address for an end station. DNS translates the names of network nodes into IP addresses.

Figure 4-11 shows an example of how to lay out the IP addresses and network names for the example network.

Figure 4-11 *Address and Naming Conventions*

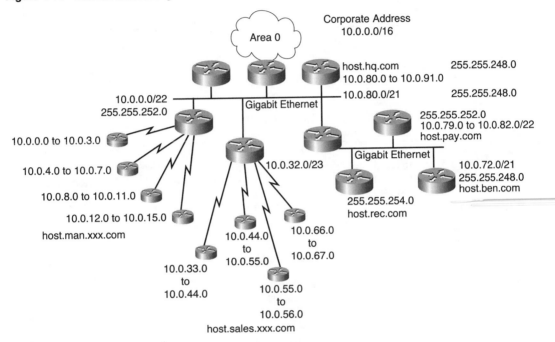

Plan Now for OSPF Summarization

The operation and benefits of route summarization have been discussed in previous chapters. At this point, you should realize the importance of proper summarization on your network. The OSPF network in Figure 4-12 does not have summarization turned on. Note that by not using summarization, LSAs are propagated into the OSPF backbone and beyond, causing unnecessary network traffic and router overhead.

Type 1 and Type 2 LSAs are translated into Type 3 LSAs at the ABR, even if summarization is not turned on. (That is one unfortunate aspect of the terminology used in the RFC that calls this a Type 3 summary LSA.) Whenever an LSA is sent, all affected OSPF routers might potentially have to recompute their LSA database and routes using the SPF algorithm.

Routers in a remote area receive a Type 3 LSA every time a subnet changes in an area, but they can handle that change without a new SPF calculation. That is a hidden benefit of multi-area OSPF: Routers in remote areas can process changes without a full SPF calculation.

Figure 4-12 *No Route Summarization Causes Network Problems*

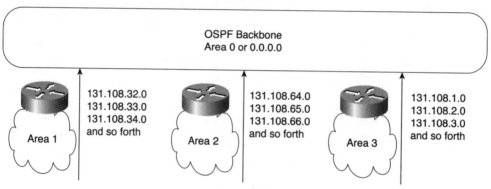

OSPF provides some added benefits if you design the network with summarization. For example, only summary-link LSAs propagate into the backbone (area 0). This is important because it prevents every router from having to rerun the SPF algorithm, helps increase the network's stability, and reduces unnecessary traffic. Figure 4-13 demonstrates this principle.

Although this section provides an overview of summarization, you learn more about the topic in Chapter 7.

IP addresses in an OSPF network should be grouped by area, and you can expect to see areas with some or all of the following characteristics:

- Major network number(s)
- Fixed subnet mask(s)
- Random combination of networks, subnets, and host addresses

Hosts, subnets, and networks must be allocated in a controlled manner during the design and implementation of your OSPF network. The allocation should be in the form of contiguous blocks that are adjacent so that OSPF LSAs can easily represent the address space. Figure 4-14 shows an example of this.

Figure 4-13   *Proper Route Summarization Improves OSPF Network Stability*

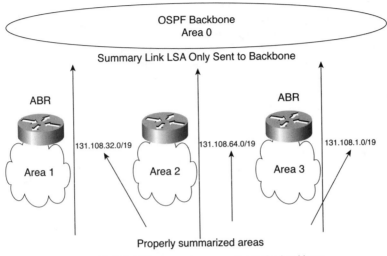

Figure 4-14   *Configuring OSPF for Summarization*

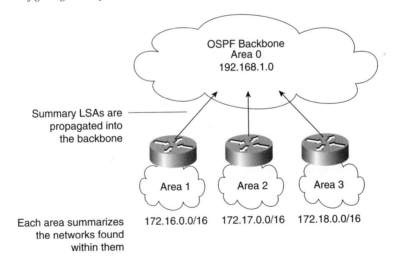

TIP	Allocation of IP addresses should be done in powers of 2 so that these "blocks" can be represented by a single summary link advertisement. Through the use of the **area range** command, you can summarize large contiguous blocks of addresses. To minimize the number of blocks, make them as large as possible. Furthermore, addresses should start on a bit boundary. Allocating addresses in blocks of 32, as illustrated in Figures 4-12 and 4-13, is good if the addresses start at 0, 32, and 64, but a block of 32 does not summarize well if the addresses start at 5, 37, and 69.

Bit Splitting (Borrowing Bits)

To differentiate two areas, split 1 bit. To differentiate 16 areas, split 4 bits. Figure 4-15 demonstrates this bit-splitting technique.

Figure 4-15   *Bit Splitting Address Space*

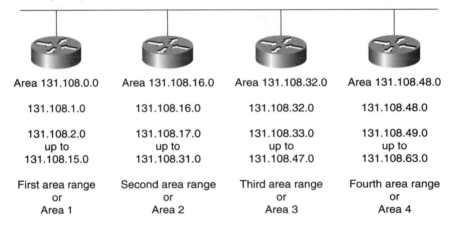

Area 131.108.0.0	Area 131.108.16.0	Area 131.108.32.0	Area 131.108.48.0
131.108.1.0	131.108.16.0	131.108.32.0	131.108.48.0
131.108.2.0 up to 131.108.15.0	131.108.17.0 up to 131.108.31.0	131.108.33.0 up to 131.108.47.0	131.108.49.0 up to 131.108.63.0
First area range or Area 1	Second area range or Area 2	Third area range or Area 3	Fourth area range or Area 4

The example uses 4 bits for the area and uses 32-bit numbers to represent 4 of the 16 possible areas. The area numbers appear in dotted decimal notation and look like subnet numbers. In fact, the 32-bit area numbers correspond to the summary advertisement that represents the area.

Map OSPF Addresses for VLSM

Variable-length subnet masking (VLSM) was discussed in Chapter 1, but the reasons behind VLSM are similar to bit splitting. Remember to keep small subnets in a contiguous block to increase the number of subnets for a serial meshed network. Figure 4-16 provides an example of VLSM OSPF mappings. Try to start at the beginning or end of a subnet because it's easier to manage. Because contiguous blocks do not always start at a logical beginning point for the sequence, this demonstration starts at the middle—you should try to figure out tough subnetting problems because you will most likely encounter the same scenarios when mapping OSPF addresses for VLSM!

Figure 4-16 *VLSM OSPF Mappings*

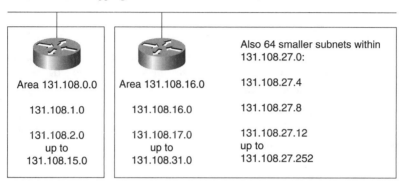

Discontiguous Subnets

Subnets become discontiguous when they are separated by one or more segments represented by a different major network number. Discontiguous subnets are supported by OSPF because subnets masks are part of the link-state database.

Consider the following example: The OSPF backbone area 0 might be a Class C address, while all the other areas might consist of address ranges from a Class B major network, as illustrated in Figure 4-17.

Figure 4-17 *OSPF Network with Discontiguous Subnets*

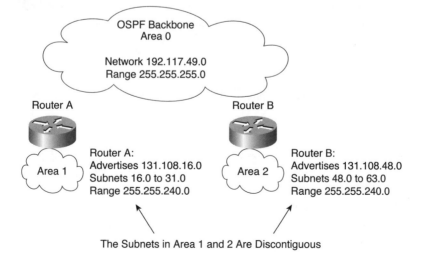

TIP	OSPF supports discontiguous subnets regardless of whether summarization is configured within the network. However, if you configure summarization, everything within your network routes more optimally, and you have a more stable design.

Naming Schemes

The naming scheme used in your network should also be designed in a systematic way. By using common prefixes for names within an organization, you make the network easier to manage and more scalable. All this is demonstrated in Figure 4-11.

It is also important to use a naming convention with your routers. This assists everyone who deals with your network because the router names hold some meaning, instead of having an abstract name, such as a purchase order number.

Step 4: Provision the Hardware

In Step 4, you must use vendor documentation, salespersons, and system engineers to determine the hardware that is required for your network. This holds for both LAN and WAN components.

For LANs, select and provision router models, switch models, cabling systems, and backbone connections. For WANs, select and provision router models, modems, CSUs/DSUs (channel service units/data service units), and remote access servers.

What Do You Know?

Coming into Step 4, you determined your network requirements, developed a physical network topology, and laid out your addressing and naming scheme. In this step, you select and provision the necessary network equipment to implement the design.

When selecting and provisioning routing or switching hardware, consider the following areas:

- Expected CPU usage
- Minimum RAM
- Bus budget
- Forwarding latency
- Required interface types and density

Step 5: Deploy Protocol and Cisco IOS Software Features

In Step 5, you deploy the more specific features made possible by the OSPF protocol and Cisco IOS Software running on your routers. It is not necessary to have a network with every option turned on, nor is this something you are likely to see. Some of the features that you need to consider implementing are covered in the two sections that follow.

What Do You Know?

Coming into Step 5, you determined your network requirements, developed a physical network topology, laid out your addressing and naming scheme, and began the provisioning of the network equipment. In this step, you deploy the OSPF and Cisco IOS Software features that you need to use within the network.

OSPF Features

This section covers authentication and route redistribution between protocols, two OSPF features that you should consider deploying within your network.

Protecting corporate resources, security, policing the network, ensuring correct usage of the network, authentication—these are different terms for a similar need within every network: network security. Network security should be built into the network from day one, not added as an afterthought. Mistakes have already happened in the networking environment you know today. Nevertheless, how could they not with the almost required Internet presence and "www" logo seen on almost every business card? The open unsecure protocols, such as Simple Mail Transfer Protocol (SMTP) or Simple Network Management Protocol (SNMP), are essential for business and network management; though, they are also vulnerable to exploitation. Hopefully, the respective working groups will move toward solving this problem. All is not doom and gloom though, as OSPF comes with built-in authentication—the way it should be!

OSPF's built-in authentication set is extremely useful and flexible. In the OSPF specification, MD5 is the only cryptographic algorithm that has been completely specified. The overall implementation of security within OSPF is rather straightforward. For example, you assign a key to OSPF. This key can either be the same throughout your network or different on each router's interface, or a combination of the two. However, each router that is directly connected to each other must have the same key for communication to take place. Further discussion of this OSPF feature is presented in Chapter 8, "Managing and Securing OSPF Networks."

Route redistribution is another useful Cisco IOS Software feature. Redistribution is the exchange of routing information between two different routing processes (protocols). This feature should be turned on in your routers if you have separate routing domains within your AS and you need to exchange routes between them. Chapter 6, "Redistribution," and Chapter 7 cover this feature in greater detail.

For example, the engineering department might be running OSPF and the accounting department might be running Enhanced Interior Gateway Protocol (EIGRP), as shown in Figure 4-18.

Figure 4-18 *Redistributing Routing Information Between Protocols*

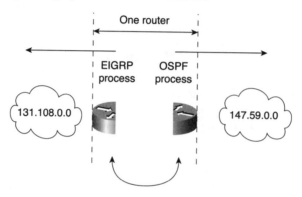

Figure 4-18 depicts one router connecting the two separate routing processes (protocols), which need to share routing information. This sharing process is called *redistribution.* The router shown in Figure 4-18 is configured to run both EIGRP and OSPF routing.

TIP   When routes are redistributed between major networks, no subnet information is required to be shared. Instead, summarization should be applied at major network boundaries.

Cisco IOS Software Features

Some of the features of Cisco IOS Software that you should consider deploying within your network are as follows:

- Access lists
- Queuing
- Route maps
- Limiting certain routes from being propagated
- Policy routing
- Quality of service (QoS)

Step 6: Implement, Monitor, and Manage the Network

The last step is also the first step to continually managing the growth of your network. Some time is spent on this subject later in the chapter, but Chapter 8 covers the network management arena in greater detail. In the context of this step, you should consider the following actions:

- Using network management tools for monitoring
- Performing proactive data gathering
- Knowing when to scale the network to meet new demands (install new hardware, upgrade circuit speeds, support new applications)

What Do You Know?

Coming into Step 6, you determined your network requirements, developed a physical network topology, laid out your addressing and naming scheme, provisioned your network equipment, and deployed the necessary OSPF and Cisco IOS Software features. In this step, you implement the network, institute monitoring, and engage in proactive network management.

OSPF Network Scalability

Your ability to scale an OSPF internetwork depends on your overall network structure and IP addressing scheme. Adopting a hierarchical network design with a structured address assignment (that is, using summarization whenever possible) is the most important factor in determining the overall scalability of your OSPF network. Network scalability is affected by both operational and technical considerations.

Operationally, OSPF networks should be designed so that areas do not need to be split to accommodate predicted and unpredicted growth. Networks will most likely not shrink in size, so plan accordingly. Specifically, reserve IP address space to permit the addition of new routers and areas.

Scalability should always be taken into consideration when designing your network. All routers keep a copy of the area's link-state database (LSDB). If a router is in more than one area, such as an ABR, the router has one LSDB for each area. As your network grows, its size eventually reaches a point where the database becomes too large, resulting in routing inefficiencies because the router does not have the resources to handle normal routing activities.

The larger the OSPF area, the more LSAs are flooded throughout the network whenever there is a topology change. This can result in network congestion. It is impossible to predict whether a congestion problem will result in normal LSA flooding. The factors involved are too extensive to accurately predict. In modern networks, congestion-causing LSAs are rare. However, too many LSAs causing slow SPF calculations is quite common–especially LSAs from external routes being flooded across the entire AS.

The capability of your OSPF network to scale properly is determined by a multitude of factors, including the following:

- OSPF functional requirements (that is, what a router needs to do)
- Router memory requirements
- CPU requirements
- Available bandwidth
- Security requirements

NOTE   In many cases, personnel who work directly with networks are not always in complete control of some of the factors discussed in this section. Of course, bigger routers are better; unfortunately, management does not always allow you to purchase the biggest routers. In the end, a compromise is usually required. Be sure to document the limitations and potential growth issues with the compromise solution that you implement.

OSPF Network Topology

OSPF works best in a hierarchical routing environment. When designing an OSPF network, the first and most important task is to determine which routers and links are to be included in the backbone (area 0) and which are to be included in each area. The following are three important characteristics to OSPF to ensure that your OSPF network has a hierarchical routing structure:

- The hierarchical routing structure must exist or be created to effectively use OSPF. The benefits of having a single area include simplicity, ease of troubleshooting, and so on.
- A contiguous backbone area must be present, and all areas must have a connection to the backbone.
- Explicit topology (shortest path) has precedence over any IP addressing schemes that might have been applied; that is, your physical topology takes precedence over a summarized route.

When designing the topology for an OSPF network, consider the following important items:

- Number of routers in an area
- Number of areas connected to an ABR
- Number of neighbors for a router
- Number of areas supported by a router
- Selection of the designated router (DR)
- Size and development of the OSPF LSDB

These topics are covered in the following sections.

Area Sizing

Determining the number of routers to deploy within each OSPF area is extremely important and should be done with flexibility in mind. Factors that are hard to know during design (such as which links will flap) can be compensated for with flexibility in your design and implementation.

During initial network convergence, OSPF uses the CPU-intensive SPF algorithm. Experience has shown that 40 to 50 routers per area is the optimal upper limit for OSPF in the majority of networks.

This is not to say that there are not larger and smaller areas running just fine. The point here is that 40 to 50 routers per area is the proper size for most networks and routers. Of course, a network full of 12000s can do things differently than a network composed of 2500s.

The number of calculations that must be performed by the router, given that n is the number of link-state packets (LSPs), is proportional to $n \log n$. As a result, the larger the area, the greater the likelihood for performance problems associated with OSPF routing recalculation, and the more unstable the area becomes.

Generally speaking, an area should have less than 100 routers. That does not mean that networks with 100 or more routers in an area won't function, but why experiment with stability if you don't need to? Areas with unstable links should be even smaller to reduce the impact of those links.

NOTE   If you have a stable network infrastructure, you can most likely run many more routers per area—assuming that the router specifications (for example, LSDB processing capacity) allow it. Additionally, a well-designed OSPF structure is essential in making areas with larger numbers of routers more viable. This chapter is designed to enable you to make your OSPF implementation scalable, allowing you to surpass the limit set by the less-than-100-router rule.

One of the main problems with OSPF areas is that network administrators let their backbone area grow too large. Some administrators erroneously believe that most routes should belong in area 0. Use the following guidelines for the best results:

- Outline the logical view of the network from the beginning.
- Focus on which routes, routers, or networks belong in what area.
- Start creating nonrequired areas before they are needed.

A good rule of thumb is to plan for maximum growth coupled with long-term planning at the beginning of the network design process. Has this point been stressed enough yet? This has the added benefit of ensuring your network can handle rapid growth. In this case, planning for too much is not a bad thing to do.

The OSPF network sizing recommendations shown in Table 4-1 are made in accordance with Cisco recommendations regarding OSPF networks. As stated earlier, studies and real world implementations have gone further. For example, the statistics in Table 4-1 came from the old "IETF OSPF Standard Report." Although, that report is many years old now and does not take into account today's carrier class routers and thus has been adjusted. These are not hard and fast numbers but are good indicators for you so you can plan accordingly and understand when you might be stretching things a bit.

Table 4-1   *OSPF Network Size Recommendations*

Parameter	Minimum	Mean	Maximum
Routers per domain	1	500	1000
Routers per area	1	100	350
Areas per domain	1	25	75
Neighbors per router	1	50	100
Areas per router	1	3	5

OSPF has been thoroughly tested and can withstand substantial scaling.

Determining the Number of Areas per ABR

ABRs keep a copy of the database for all areas that they service. For example, if a router is connected to five areas, it must keep five different databases. It is better not to overload an ABR; rather, you should spread the areas over other routers. The ideal design is to have each ABR connected to two areas only—the backbone and another area—with three to five areas being the upper limit. Figure 4-19 shows the difference between one ABR holding five different databases, including area 0 (part a), and two ABRs holding three databases each (part b).

These are just guidelines; the more areas you attach per ABR, the lower the performance you get from that router. This is a simple case of resource management. In some cases, network administrators will accept the lower performance; but usually, end users won't see it that way. As you do this, remember to check your routers' memory and CPU utilization, as there is a point in which every router ceases to function properly if asked to do too much.

Figure 4-19   *How Many Areas Should Be Connected per ABR?*

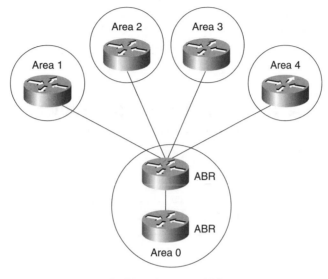

Too Many Areas per ABR
(a)

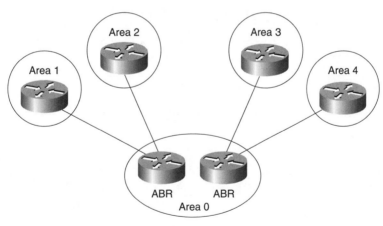

Two Areas per ABR Is Optimal
(b)

Determining the Number of Areas per Router

A router must run the link-state algorithm for each link-state change that occurs for every area in which the router resides. Every ABR is in at least two areas (the backbone and another area). To maximize stability, one router should generally not be in more than three areas. For more information, refer to Table 4-1.

Determining the Number of Neighbors per Router

OSPF floods all link-state changes to all routers in an area. Routers with many neighbors have the most work to do when link-state changes occur. In general, a router should have no more than 60 to 100 neighbors.

TIP   Chapter 2, "Introduction to OSPF," discussed the differences between neighbors and adjacencies. Refer to that chapter as necessary.

An example of the 60 to 100 neighbor rule is the case of a number of routers connected on the same LAN. Each LAN has a DR and BDR that build adjacencies with all other routers. The fewer the neighbors on the LAN, the smaller the number of adjacencies a DR or BDR has to build. Figure 4-20 shows that more neighbors result in more work for the DR and BDR. (This is also the case in NBMA networks.) To improve performance, avoid having a single router be the DR on more than one segment.

Figure 4-20   *More Neighbors Equal More Work for the DR and BDR*

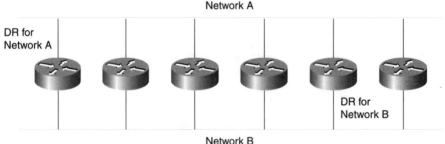

Network A

DR for
Network A

DR for
Network B

Network B
More neighbors = more work for the DR & BDR

This, of course, depends on how much processing power your router has. You can always change the OSPF priority to select your DR, but more on that later. Also, if possible, try to *avoid having the same router from being the DR on more than one segment.*

If OSPF defaults to the DR selection based on the highest router ID (loopback interface or highest active IP address on an interface), one router might accidentally become a DR over all segments to which it connects. In this example, consider the additional load that a single router would incur if it accidentally became the DR for two large segments, as shown in Figure 4-20. This router might become overloaded while other routers are idle. Then, consider the impact on network convergence if this router fails. The key points here are

- Do not allow a router to "accidentally" become the DR.

- Plan which router is to be the DR in an area.

Selecting the Designated Router

The DR and BDR on a LAN generally have the most OSPF work to do. Select routers to be the DR and BDR that are not already heavily loaded with CPU-intensive activities. This can be accomplished by using the **ip ospf priority** *priority* command, which enables you to organize the DRs as needed. In review, some of the characteristics and behavior of Cisco routers when using priority are as follows:

- By default, all Cisco routers have a priority of 1, thus forcing the use of the router ID (RID) as the deciding factor. However, this does not assure you that the best choice is made, so the outcome can be altered with the **priority** command.

- When two routers attached to a network both attempt to become the DR, the one with the higher router priority takes precedence. If there is a tie, the router with the higher RID takes precedence. Adding a router with a high priority to a segment does not cause a new election.

- A router with a router priority set to 0 is ineligible to become the DR or BDR. You can set the priority to 0 and remove small (SOHO) routers from consideration. Also, it's a good idea to set OSPF priority to zero on firewalls that happen to speak OSPF, or your DR might become a firewall that is routing packets in software, rather than ASICs.

- Router priority is configured only for interfaces to multiaccess (Ethernet, Frame Relay, ATM, and so on) networks (that is, not point-to-point networks). This priority value is used to determine the DR when you configure OSPF for nonbroadcast networks using the **neighbor** router configuration command for OSPF.

In addition, it is generally not a good idea to select the same router to be the DR on more than one LAN simultaneously. These guidelines help ensure that no single broadcast link has too many neighbors with excessive Hello traffic. From an NBMA network perspective, this is also something to consider because you would not want your expensive WAN links full of unnecessary overhead.

Plan which router is to be the DR in each OSPF segment as appropriate. To make the right choice, check the current router utilization and available memory with the **show process cpu** and **memory** commands, respectively.

Fully Meshed Versus Partially Meshed Network Topology

Nonbroadcast multiaccess (NBMA) clouds, such as Frame Relay or X.25, are always a challenge in OSPF. The combination of low bandwidth and too many LSAs can cause problems. A partially meshed topology has been proven to behave much better than a fully meshed network topology. Figure 4-21 shows the benefits and differences between the two topologies.

In some cases, a carefully laid out point-to-point or point-to-multipoint network can work better than multipoint networks, which must deal with LSA and DR issues.

Figure 4-21   *Examples of Fully and Partially Meshed Networks*

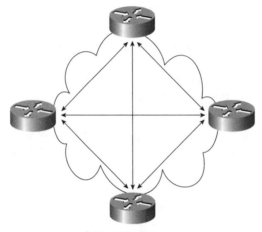

fully meshed network
(not recommended)

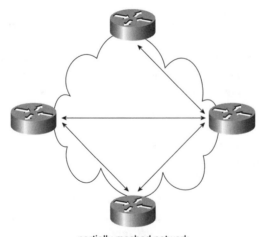

partially meshed network
(recommended)

Link-State Database Size Considerations

Issues relating to the size of the LSDB are important and deal directly with the LSDB operation in relation to the topology of the network. The LSDB is everywhere within an OSPF network, and the LSDB has the following functional characteristics, which do not change:

- A router has a separate LSDB for each area to which it belongs.

- All routers belonging to the same area have an identical LSDB.

- A router performs separate SPF calculations on associated LSDBs for each area.

- LSA flooding occurs only within the area that is sending the advertisement (that is, experiencing the topology change). Remember that Type 1–4 and Type 7 LSAs are flooded within an area, and Type 5 LSAs are flooded throughout the OSPF domain, except for stub and NSSA areas. This is covered in Chapter 3, "OSPF Communication."

When encountered in an area, the LSDB is identical in each router within the area. The LSDB also contains the following different LSAs:

- Router link advertisements

- Network link advertisements

- Summary link advertisements (IP network and ASBR)

- Autonomous system (AS) external advertisements (nonstub areas only)

- Opaque LSAs, if implemented

These factors show you how the LSDB uses the routers' memory when running OSPF. This makes determining the minimum memory requirement to run OSPF crucial in creating an effective OSPF design. The sections that follow examine this sizing process in more detail.

Determining Router Memory Requirements

An OSPF router stores all the link states for all the areas that it is in. As described in the case study in Chapter 3, this is a complex process, and if enough memory is not provided in the router, serious OSPF routing problems might result. Ensuring an effectively designed OSPF network can also conserve router memory.

In addition to storing the state of each link within an area, the LSDB stores summary and external routes. Careful use of route summarization techniques and the creation of stub areas can substantially reduce router memory use. Therefore, if memory issues become a concern, consider using stub areas because doing so reduces the amount of routes.

It is not easy to determine the amount of memory needed for a particular OSPF configuration. From a design perspective, the best you can do is to *approximate* the memory requirements. Memory issues usually arise when too many external routes are injected into the OSPF domain. Consider the following two scenarios:

- An OSPF backbone area with 40 routers and a default route to the Internet
- An OSPF backbone area with 4 routers and 33,000 external routes being injected into OSPF

The first network would be less likely to have memory issues on routers than the network described in the second example. Summarization at the ABRs and the use of stub areas might further minimize the number of routes exchanged.

The total memory used by OSPF is the sum of the memory used by the routing table (verified by the **show ip route summary** command) and the memory used by the LSDB. The following numbers provide a rule-of-thumb estimate:

- Each entry in the routing table consumes 200 to 280 bytes plus 44 bytes per link.
- Each LSA consumes 100 bytes worth of overhead plus the size of the actual LSA, possibly another 60 to 100 bytes. (For router links, this depends on the number of interfaces on the router.) These amounts should be added to memory already used by other processes and by the Cisco IOS Software.

A routing table using less than 500 KB might normally be accommodated with 2–16 MB of RAM; large networks that have routing tables greater than 500 KB might need 16–64 MB. Furthermore, large networks might require 512 MB or more if full routes are injected from the Internet.

NOTE   As Cisco IOS Software continues to grows, the memory needed to hold and run that software will also increase.

To determine the exact amount of memory used by OSPF, you can execute the **show memory** command with and without OSPF being turned on. The difference in the processor memory used indicates how much memory OSPF is using.

CAUTION   Do not do this **show memory** test in the middle of the business day. You might also want to make a backup copy of the router configuration before beginning this process.

Router CPU Requirements

An OSPF router uses CPU cycles whenever a link-state change occurs. This is because Cisco IOS Software is run in the router's flash memory, and every time a decision is required, the CPU must process it. Thus, keeping the OSPF areas small and using route summarization dramatically reduce usage of the router's CPU and create a more stable environment within which OSPF can operate.

Bandwidth Usage

OSPF sends partial LSA updates when a link-state change occurs. The updates are flooded to all routers in the area. In a network with substantial topology changes, OSPF LSA frequency and size increase, reducing the bandwidth available for customer usage.

OSPF Security

The two kinds of security mechanisms applicable to routing protocols are as follows:

- The routers that participate in an OSPF network are controlled.
- OSPF contains an optional authentication field.

You might think it is possible to control the routing information within an OSPF area. However, for OSPF to operate properly, all routers within an area must have the same database. As a result, it is not possible to use route filters in an OSPF network to provide security because OSPF exchanges route information through the use of LSAs, not routes. OSPF then calculates the route to a destination based on the LSA. This is different than route maps and redistribution, as discussed in later chapters.

However, you can ensure that an OSPF area is secured via authenticated route exchanges. To do this, OSPF has an optional authentication field. Using this optional feature also requires additional router resources. All routers within an area must agree on the value of the authentication field (that is, the password). Because OSPF is a standard protocol, which can be implemented on many platforms, including some hosts, using the authentication field prevents the inadvertent startup of OSPF in an uncontrolled platform on your network and reduces the potential for instability. Chapter 8 discusses the use of OSPF authentication features. Just be aware that it exists and will cost you resources if you implement it. So, plan for it during the design stage (definitely stressing that point) if you think you will use it.

Area Design Considerations

Area Design Overview

When creating large-scale OSPF internetworks, the definition of areas and assignment of resources within areas must be done with a pragmatic view of your OSPF internetwork. This assignment of resources includes both physical and logical networking components so that optimal performance results. This section discusses some of the items that are applicable to designing any type of OSPF area. Specific considerations are discussed after each area type.

Areas are essentially small networks contained within the larger OSPF routing domain or AS, and as such, areas route only necessary traffic within themselves, thereby reducing overall network traffic. The capability of OSPF to create areas is key to its successful operation. These areas allow for hierarchical design and implementation because all areas are required to connect to area 0.

Many reasons justify the use of OSPF's capability to create areas. The use of areas is necessary so that OSPF's required hierarchical structure can be put into place. The topology of the network within an area is invisible to anything outside of that area, as demonstrated in Figure 4-22.

Figure 4-22   *Areas Serve as Small Networks, Subsequently Resulting in Reduced Network Traffic*

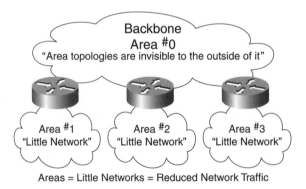

The two most critical aspects of designing an area are as follows:

- Determining how the area is addressed
- Determining how the area is connected to the backbone

Areas should have a contiguous set of network and subnet addresses whenever possible. You can have an area with any combination of networks and subnets, but this is strongly discouraged. Whenever possible, you should have an area that consists of grouped networks and subnets so that route summarization can be easily accomplished. Without a contiguous address space, the implementation of route summarization is impossible. Chapter 7 discusses the practical application of summarization in greater detail.

The routers that connect an area to the backbone area are called Area Border Routers (ABRs). Areas can have a single ABR or they can have multiple ABRs. In general, you should have more than one ABR per area to minimize the chance of the area becoming disconnected from the backbone because it is a single point of failure.

Considering Physical Proximity

If a particular location within your network is densely connected, create an area specifically for the routers at that location. This enables OSPF to better handle a large, dense cluster of routers, and it enables more efficient management and routing.

Reducing the Area Size if Links Are Unstable

If your internetwork includes unstable links, consider implementing smaller areas to reduce the effects of route flapping. Whenever a route is lost or comes online, each affected area must converge on the new topology upon receiving the LSA that describes the change. The shortest path first (SPF) algorithm is again run on all the affected routers that received the LSA. By segmenting your network into smaller or multiple areas, you can isolate unstable links and deliver more reliable overall service. This is always of benefit to everyone concerned.

Ensuring Contiguous Areas

A contiguous OSPF area (see Figure 4-23) is one in which a continuous path can be traced from any router in an area to any other router in the same area. Basically, all routers in the backbone should be directly connected to other backbone routers. This does not mean that all routers must share a common network media (such as Ethernet).

Figure 4-23 *Contiguous Areas Within an OSPF Network*

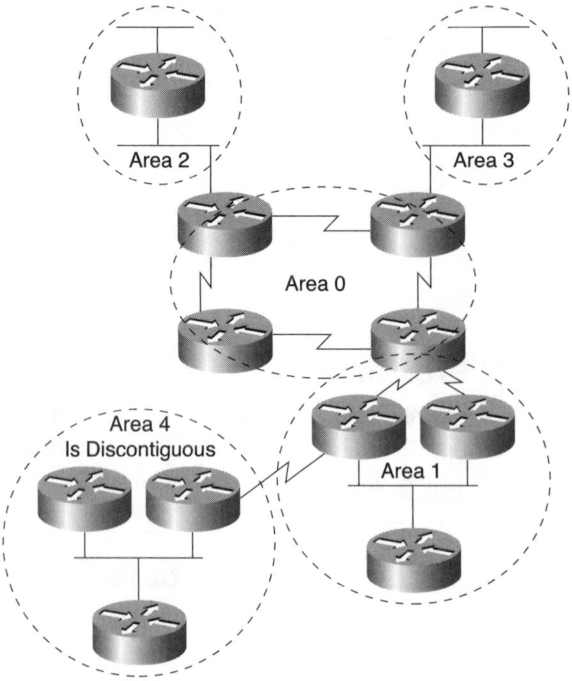

Ideally, areas should have multiple redundant internal and external links to prevent partitioning.

Using Tunable OSPF Parameters

A group of tunable OSPF parameters can help you design an area to more readily meet your network's specific needs. All of these commands and their associated values generally default to good values. If you are considering changing these defaults, it is good practice to change them in all routers in an area, or your routers might have trouble communicating. Make sure you take precautionary measures *before* you change the default values.

TIP   Cisco routers do not show default values in their configuration files. For example, IP routing being enabled is never shown because that is the default, but it is shown if disabled.

The tunable OSPF parameters are as follows:

- **ip ospf hello-interval {default = 10 seconds}**—This command defaults to a value of 10 seconds. By modifying this value, you can specify the transmission interval between Hello packets sent out an interface. The smaller the Hello interval, the faster the topological changes are detected, but more routing traffic ensues. This value must be the same for all routers and access servers on a specific subnet. The following example sets the interval between Hello packets to 15 seconds:

```
interface ethernet 1
ip ospf hello-interval 15
```

- **ip ospf dead interval {default = hello interval * 4}**—This command defaults to a value four times the Hello interval; normally, this is 40 seconds. This command specifies how long a router's Hello packets must not have been seen before its neighbors declare the router down. If you alter this value on one router on a subnet, you must change the value on all routers. The following example sets the OSPF dead interval to 60 seconds:

```
interface ethernet 1
ip ospf dead-interval 60
```

- **ip ospf retransmission-interval {default = 5 seconds}**—This command defaults to a value of 5 seconds. By modifying this value, you can specify the number of seconds between LSA retransmissions. An LSA retransmission automatically occurs while the transmitting router is waiting for an acknowledgment from the receiving router. Remember if you alter this to allow for round-trip time and delays between routers. The following example sets the retransmit interval value to 8 seconds:

```
interface ethernet 2
ip ospf retransmit-interval 8
```

- **ip ospf transmit-delay {default = 1 second}**—Now, at first glance, this seems like a very odd command; I mean, why place a built-in delay in updates? Consider if the delay is not added before transmission over a slow speed link; the time in which the LSA propagates over the link is not considered. This setting has more significance on very low speed links.

  Link-state advertisements in the update packet must have their ages incremented by the amount specified in the *seconds* argument before transmission. The value assigned should take into account the transmission and propagation delays for the interface. In other words, to increase the amount of time between LSA transmissions, use this command.

  This command defaults to a value of 1 second. By modifying this value, you can set the time to delay before transmitting a link-state update from an interface. The following example sets the retransmit delay value to 3 seconds:

```
interface ethernet 0
ip ospf transmit-delay 3
```

- **ip ospf cost**—This command enables you to explicitly specify the cost of sending a packet out an interface. The cost that you set on an interface via this command is retransmitted in the router LSA (Type 1).

  To reset the path cost to the default value, use the **no** form of this command.

  To change the default, you can set the metric manually using this command. Using the **bandwidth** command changes the link cost as long as **ip ospf cost** is not used.

  In general, the path cost is calculated using the following formula:

  10^8 / Bandwidth

  Using this formula, the default path costs were calculated as noted in the following list. If the following values do not suit your network, you can use your own method of calculating path costs:

  — 56-kbps serial link default cost is 1785.

  — 64-kbps serial link default cost is 1562.

  — T1 (1.544-Mbps serial link) default cost is 65.

  — E1 (2.048-Mbps serial link) default cost is 48.

  — 4-Mbps Token Ring default cost is 25.

  — 10-Mbps Ethernet default cost is 10.

  — 100-Mbps Fast Ethernet default cost is 1.

  — 16-Mbps Token Ring default cost is 6.

  The following example sets the interface cost value to 65:

  ```
  interface ethernet 0
  ip ospf cost 65
  ip ospf mtu-ignore
  ```

Naming an Area

This is an important task because everyone will be using the convention and name that you choose. OSPF uses an area ID (AID) to uniquely identify each area. In OSPF, the AID is a 32-bit number, which can be expressed either in dotted decimal format, like an IP address, or as a decimal number. Cisco routers understand either, and the formats can be used interchangeably, for example:

AID 0.0.0.1 and AID 1 are the same.
AID 192.168.5.0 and AID 3232236800 are the same.

In the first example, AID 1 is easier to write than AID 0.0.0.1, whereas in the second case, the dotted decimal format is easier to write than the decimal format. In the second case, the 32-bit number in binary form is as follows:

11000000101010000000010100000000

Standard Area Design

Standard, or nonstub, OSPF areas carry a default route, static routes, intra-area routes, and external routes. The use of standard areas is more resource intensive within an OSPF network. However, standard areas are also the most common, and they carry inter-area routes. Characteristics of standard areas are as follows:

- An area must be a standard area when it contains a router that uses both OSPF and any other protocol, such as the Routing Information Protocol (RIP). Such a router is known as an Autonomous System Boundary Router (ASBR).

- An area must also be a standard area when a virtual link is configured across the area. This is because the various types of stub areas are not allowed to have virtual links in them. See "OSPF Virtual Links: Bane or Benefit?" later in the chapter for more information on virtual links.

Golden Rules of Standard Area Design

When you design your OSPF network, you must start with area 0, the backbone area of every OSPF network. The following rules help get you started properly:

- A contiguous backbone area must be present.
- All OSPF areas must have a connection to the backbone (area 0). This includes standard areas.

The following are more general rules and OSPF capabilities that help ensure that your OSPF network remains flexible and provides the kind of performance needed to deliver reliable service to all of its users:

- A standard area has an ABR in it; if possible, consider having two ABRs for redundancy.
- Summarize whenever and as often as possible.
- Do not redistribute Border Gateway Protocol (BGP) into OSPF.

Backbone Area Design

The OSPF backbone (also known as area 0) is extremely important. If more than one area is configured in an OSPF network, one of these areas must be area 0. When designing networks, it is good practice to start with area 0 and then later expand into other areas. To summarize, the OSPF backbone is the part of the OSPF network that acts as the primary path for traffic that is destined to other areas or networks.

Accepted network design theory recommends a three-tiered approach (see Figure 4-24). This theory states that there should never be more than three tiers with a maximum of six router hops across the farthest points of the network. This type of design suits OSPF well because of its area concepts and need for hierarchical routing. This design also reduces convergence time and facilitates route summarization.

Figure 4-24   *Three-Tiered Network Design Model*

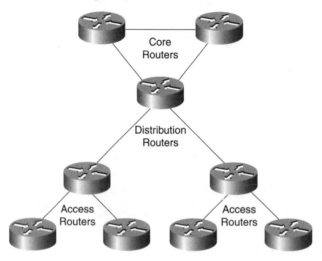

Backbone Design Golden Rules

Use the following guidelines when designing an OSPF backbone (area 0):

- Understand that area 0 is a transit area, not a destination for traffic.
- Ensure that the stability of the backbone area is maintained and monitored.
- Ensure that redundancy is built into the design whenever possible.
- Ensure that OSPF backbones are contiguous.
- Keep this area simple. Fewer routers are better.
- Keep the bandwidth symmetrical so that OSPF can maintain load balancing.
- Ensure that all other areas connect directly to area 0.
- Restrict all end-user (host) resources from area 0.

The backbone must be at the center of all other areas, that is, all areas must be connected to the backbone. This is because OSPF expects all areas to inject routing information into the backbone, and in turn, the backbone disseminates that routing information into other areas. Figure 4-25 illustrates the flow of routing information in an OSPF network.

Figure 4-25   *Flow of Information in an OSPF Network, in Which the Backbone Is the Key*

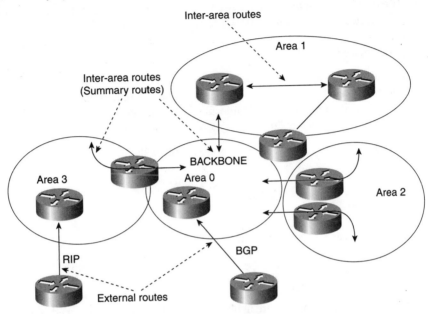

In Figure 4-25, all areas are directly connected to the backbone. Stability and redundancy are the most important criteria for the backbone. Keeping the size of the backbone reasonable results in stability. This is desirable because every router in the backbone needs to recompute its routes after every link-state change. Keeping the backbone small reduces the likelihood of a change and reduces the amount of CPU cycles required to recompute routes.

Redundancy is important in the backbone to prevent partition when a link fails. Good backbones are designed so that no single link failure can cause a partition (that is, the backbone becomes isolated). OSPF backbones must be contiguous. All routers in the backbone should be directly connected to other backbone routers. Avoid placing hosts (such as workstations, file servers, or other shared resources) in the backbone area. Keeping hosts out of the backbone area simplifies internetwork expansion and creates a more stable environment because a host's normal operation (morning or evening, power up or down) causes unnecessary LSA traffic.

Stub Area Design

A stub area is a powerful network design technique. In OSPF, this area carries a default route and inter-area routes but does not carry external routes. Placing sections of the network in stub areas reduces network overhead because stub areas are essentially dead end areas. This reduces the routes being advertised across the network.

For example, consider that you were redistributing 10,000 routes into area 0 of your OSPF network. Standard areas receive all sent routes; however, stub area do not receive all sent routes. Instead, a default route 0.0.0.0/0 is advertised into the stub area, saving the routers inside from the entire added load. Therefore, stub areas allow for a reduction in LSA traffic and can make OSPF more stable.

Because default routing is used, the LSDB is reduced in size. This, in turn, also reduces the load being placed on the router's CPU and memory. Routing updates are also reduced because specific link flaps are not injected across the network; instead, they are confined to the area or they do not enter the area, depending on where they occurred.

The three different types of stub areas are as follows:

- Normal stub areas
- Totally stubby areas (TSAs)
- Not-so-stubby areas (NSSAs)

Each stub area and the corresponding characteristics are discussed in the sections that follow.

Stub Area Design Golden Rules

Many stub area design rules are in place because a stub area is designed and configured not to carry external routers. If a situation occurred within a stub area that caused external links to be injected into the area, the stub area's usefulness is ruined. The following are the stub area design golden rules:

- A single ABR is needed for a stub area, but if there is more than one ABR, accept nonoptimal routing paths.
- No ASBRs can be within a stub area.
- No virtual links are allowed to transit the area.
- All routers within any type of stub area must be configured to recognize their location (that is, what area they are in and any specific OSPF settings for that area). If the routers do not all agree on their location, they do not become neighbors and routing does not take effect.
- The backbone area cannot be configured as a stub area.

Stub Area Configuration

The configuration command **area** *area-id* **stub** turns on stub area routing by converting a standard area into a stub area and must be applied to all routers in the area being designated as a stub.

Normal stub areas block only external routes; however, they do allow summary routes. For example, LSA Types 1 through 4 are allowed and 5 through 7 are blocked. This is the difference between normal stub areas and the other types of stub areas.

The command that configures an area as stub is as follows:

area *area-id* **stub**

The command that configures a default cost into an area is as follows:

area *area-id* **default-cost** *cost*

If the cost is not set using the **area** *area-id* **default-cost** *cost* command, a cost of 1 is advertised by the ABR. Figure 4-26 shows an example of stub areas. Examples 4-3 through 4-6 present the router configuration files based on the setup in Figure 4-26.

Figure 4-26   *Configuring an OSPF Area as a Stub Area*

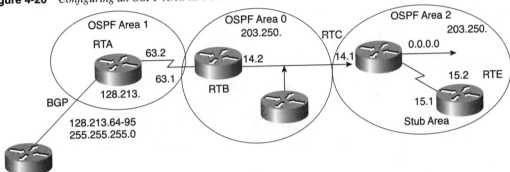

Assume that area 2 is to be configured as a stub area. Example 4-1 shows the routing table of RTE before configuring area 2 as a stub area, and Example 4-3 shows the routing table after configuring area 2 as a stub area.

Example 4-1   *Before Becoming a Stub Area*

```
RTC#
interface Ethernet 0
ip address 203.250.14.1 255.255.255.0
interface Serial1
ip address 203.250.15.1 255.255.255.252
router ospf 10
network 203.250.15.0 0.0.0.255 area 2
network 203.250.14.0 0.0.0.255 area 0
RTE#show ip route
Codes: C - connected, S - static, I - IGRP, R - RIP, M - mobile, B - BGP
       D - EIGRP, EX - EIGRP external, O - OSPF, IA - OSPF inter area
       E1 - OSPF external type 1, E2 - OSPF external type 2, E - EGP
       i - IS-IS, L1 - IS-IS level-1, L2 - IS-IS level-2, * - candidate
       default
Gateway of last resort is not set
     203.250.15.0 255.255.255.252 is subnetted, 1 subnets
C       203.250.15.0 is directly connected, Serial0
O IA    203.250.14.0 [110/74] via 203.250.15.1, 00:06:31, Serial0
     128.213.0.0 is variably subnetted, 2 subnets, 2 masks
O E2    128.213.64.0 255.255.192.0
```

continues

Example 4-1   *Before Becoming a Stub Area (Continued)*

```
[110/10] via 203.250.15.1, 00:00:29, Serial0
O IA 128.213.63.0 255.255.255.252
[110/84] via 203.250.15.1, 00:03:57, Serial0
131.108.0.0 255.255.255.240 is subnetted, 1 subnets
O 131.108.79.208 [110/74] via 203.250.15.1, 00:00:10, Serial0
```

RTE has learned the inter-area routes (O IA) 203.250.14.0 and 128.213.63.0, and it has learned the intra-area route (O) 131.108.79.208 and the external route (O E2) 128.213.64.0. If you configure area 2 as stub, you need to configure RTC and RTE as shown in Example 4-2.

Example 4-2   *After Becoming a Stub Area*

```
RTC#
interface Ethernet 0
ip address 203.250.14.1 255.255.255.0
interface Serial1
ip address 203.250.15.1 255.255.255.252
router ospf 10
network 203.250.15.0 0.0.0.255 area 2
network 203.250.14.0 0.0.0.255 area 0
area 2 stub
```
```
RTE#
interface Ethernet0
ip address 203.250.14.2 255.255.255.0
interface Ethernet1
ip address 131.108.79.209 255.255.255.240
interface Serial1
ip address 203.250.15.1 255.255.255.252
router ospf 10
network 203.250.15.0 0.0.0.255 area 2
network 203.250.14.0 0.0.0.255 area 0
network 131.108.0.0 0.0.255.255 area 2
area 2 stub
```

NOTE   The **stub** command is configured on RTE also; otherwise, RTE never becomes a neighbor to RTC. The default cost was not set, so RTC advertises 0.0.0.0 to RTE with a metric of 1.

Example 4-3   *Routing Table After Configuring Area 2 as Stub*

```
RTE#show ip route
Codes: C - connected, S - static, I - IGRP, R - RIP, M - mobile, B - BGP
D - EIGRP, EX - EIGRP external, O - OSPF, IA - OSPF inter area
E1 - OSPF external type 1, E2 - OSPF external type 2, E - EGP
i - IS-IS, L1 - IS-IS level-1, L2 - IS-IS level-2, * - candidate default
Gateway of last resort is 203.250.15.1 to network 0.0.0.0
203.250.15.0 255.255.255.252 is subnetted, 1 subnets
C 203.250.15.0 is directly connected, Serial0
O IA 203.250.14.0 [110/74] via 203.250.15.1, 00:26:58, Serial0
128.213.0.0 255.255.255.252 is subnetted, 1 subnets
O IA 128.213.63.0 [110/84] via 203.250.15.1, 00:26:59, Serial0
131.108.0.0 255.255.255.240 is subnetted, 1 subnets
O 131.108.79.208 [110/74] via 203.250.15.1, 00:26:59, Serial0
O*IA 0.0.0.0 0.0.0.0 [110/65] via 203.250.15.1, 00:26:59, Serial0
```

All the routes show up except the external routes that were replaced by a default route of
0.0.0.0. The cost of the route happened to be 65 (64 for a T1 line + 1 advertised by RTC).
In Example 4-4, you now configure area 2 to be totally stubby and change the default cost
of 0.0.0.0 to 10.

Example 4-4   *Configuring Area 2 to Be Totally Stubby*

```
RTC#
interface Ethernet 0
ip address 203.250.14.1 255.255.255.0
interface Serial1
ip address 203.250.15.1 255.255.255.252
router ospf 10
network 203.250.15.0 0.0.0.255 area 2
network 203.250.14.0 0.0.0.255 area 0
area 2 stub no-summary
```
```
RTE#show ip route
Codes: C - connected, S - static, I - IGRP, R - RIP, M - mobile, B - BGP
D - EIGRP, EX - EIGRP external, O - OSPF, IA - OSPF inter area
E1 - OSPF external type 1, E2 - OSPF external type 2, E - EGP
i - IS-IS, L1 - IS-IS level-1, L2 - IS-IS level-2, * - candidate default
Gateway of last resort is not set
203.250.15.0 255.255.255.252 is subnetted, 1 subnets
C 203.250.15.0 is directly connected, Serial0
131.108.0.0 255.255.255.240 is subnetted, 1 subnets
O 131.108.79.208 [110/74] via 203.250.15.1, 00:31:27, Serial0
O*IA 0.0.0.0 0.0.0.0 [110/74] via 203.250.15.1, 00:00:00, Serial0
```

The only routes that appear are the intra-area routes (O) and the default route 0.0.0.0. The
external and inter-area routes have been blocked. The cost of the default route is now 74
(64 for a T1 line + 10 advertised by RTC). No configuration is needed on RTE in this case.
The area is already stub, and the **no-summary** command does not affect the Hello packet
as the **stub** command does.

Totally Stubby Areas

The totally stubby area (TSA) feature is Cisco proprietary and not supported in the official OSPF standard. But as long as the ABR connected to the TSA is a Cisco router, the rest of the routers in the TSA are not affected.

The key to this type of area is to add the **no-summary** keyword, as is done in the command sequence that follows. When this occurs, the ABR(s) advertise only a default route into the rest of the stub area. This results in an even further reduction in the size of the OSPF database and routing table.

A TSA blocks external routes and summary routes from entering the area. This leaves the default route and intra-area routes (routes in the TSA) as the only types being advertised throughout the area. This is most complete summarization technique possible in OSPF and results in extremely small routing tables that are made up of only networks found within the area.

You can also add the **default-cost** command, which sets the cost of the default route that is advertised into the TSA. An example of the configuration commands needed is as follows:

```
router ospf 1
area 1 stub no-summary
area 1 default-cost 10000
```

Not-So-Stubby Areas

As mentioned in Chapter 2, NSSAs have their own RFC and are an interesting concept to the normal operation of OSPF. The advent of this new type of hybrid stub area also introduced a new LSA, Type 7, which is responsible for carrying external route information. NSSAs are similar to regular OSPF stub areas; except that an NSSA does not flood Type 5 external LSAs from the core into the NSSA, but as a hybrid stub area, an NSSA has the capability to import AS external routes in a limited fashion within the area, which is what makes it an NSSA.

LSA behavior for an NSSA is altered from what you have seen in other OSPF areas. In general, an NSSA acts similarly to a stub area and is based on the stub area's design with a special caveat to handle the connection to an external network in the form of a Type 7 LSA, which can exist only in an NSSA.

TIP   NSSAs are supported in Cisco IOS Software Release 11.2 and later.

Prior to NSSA, the connection between the corporate site border router and the remote router might not be run as an OSPF stub area because routes for the remote site cannot be redistributed into the stub area. A simple protocol like RIP is usually run to handle the redistribution. This has meant maintaining two routing protocols. With NSSA, you can extend

OSPF to cover the remote connection by defining the area between the corporate router and the remote router as an NSSA. Figure 4-27 illustrates the overall operation of an OSPF NSSA.

Figure 4-27   *OSPF NSSA Overview*

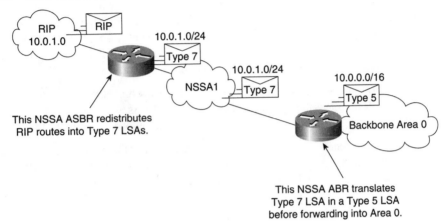

The operation of an NSSA is rather straightforward. For example, consider an ASBR connected to a network running RIP. This router is also configured as part of an NSSA. The router redistributes the routes learned from RIP into an OSPF Type 7 LSA for transmission into the NSSA. The NSSA ABR sees these advertisements and wants to forward them onto area 0 for distribution throughout the network. The ABR then redistributes the Type 7 LSAs into Type 5 LSAs.

If you are an ISP or a network administrator who needs to connect a central site using OSPF to a remote site that is using a different protocol, such as RIP or EIGRP, you can use NSSA to simplify the administration of this kind of topology. Before NSSA, the connection between the corporate site ABR and the remote router used RIP or EIGRP. This meant maintaining two routing protocols. Now, with NSSAs, you can extend OSPF to cover the remote connection by defining the area between the corporate router and the remote router as an NSSA, as shown in Figure 4-28. You cannot expand the normal OSPF area to the remote site because the Type 5 external overwhelms both the slow link and the remote router.

Figure 4-28   *Reasons to Use the OSPF NSSA Option*

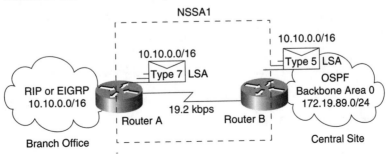

The key advantage of using NSSAs in this situation is that the routers do not have to be purchased with the memory and CPU needed to handle the entire OSPF LSDB, yet the router can accept external routes as part of an NSSA.

This allows a uniform network architecture and hardware specifications for your core router nodes, even if they have to redistribute RIP at a few sites. You can have stub areas everywhere and not have to size your routers larger for the entire LSDB, except for a couple of sites. This also means that overall network convergence time is lower, as you do not have weaker leaf-node routers struggling through the entire database.

NSSA allows importing of Type 7 AS external routes within NSSA areas by redistribution. NSSA ABR translates these Type 7 LSAs into Type 5 LSAs, which are flooded throughout the entire routing domain. Summarization and filtering are supported during the translation.

The two main benefits of the Type 7 LSA are that it can be filtered and flexibly summarized. Generally speaking, use an NSSA when the area lies between an ASBR and ABR, and where the ASBR connects to a different routing protocol and the ABR connects to OSPF's area 0.

NOTE   In Appendix A, under RFC 1587, you find a detailed description of the reasons to use an NSSA. You should also read the RFC for detailed information.

NSSA Implementation Considerations

Consider the following items before implementing NSSA:

- You can set a Type 7 default route that can be used to reach external destinations. When configured, the router generates a Type 7 default into the NSSA by the NSSA ABR.
- Every router within the same area must agree that the area is NSSA; otherwise, the routers cannot communicate with each other.

If possible, avoid using explicit redistribution on NSSA ABRs because confusion can result over which packets are being translated by which router.

In router configuration mode, specify the following area parameters as needed to configure and define the OSPF NSSA:

```
area area-id nssa [no-redistribution] [default-information-originate]
```

In router configuration mode on the ABR, specify the following command to control summarization and filtering of a Type 7 LSA into a Type 5 LSA during the translation process:

```
summary address prefix mask [not advertise] [tag tag]
```

OSPF Virtual Links: Bane or Benefit?

OSPF includes the concept of virtual links. *Virtual links* mend the OSPF backbone area (area 0). The backbone should never be intentionally partitioned, but if partitioning occurs, consider using a virtual link to temporarily repair the backbone area. Virtual links are logical connections that are vaguely analogous to a tunnel. Virtual links are not a true tunnel in the sense that one protocol is encapsulated by another. You can use a virtual link in the following cases:

- Area 0 becomes partitioned
- A nonbackbone area does not have a physical connection to area 0

Accepted network design theory considers the use of virtual links a result of a poorly designed backbone or network.

Mending a Partitioned Area 0

OSPF does not actively attempt to repair area 0 partitions. When an area becomes partitioned, the new sections simply become separate areas. As long as the backbone can reach both of these areas, it continues to route information to them.

A virtual link functions as if it were a point-to-point link. Physically, however, the link is composed of the two backbone routers, each of which is connected to area 0.

The two backbone routers establish a virtual adjacency so that LSAs and other OSPF packets are exchanged as if no other internal OSPF router were involved.

Even though partitioning your OSPF backbone is considered bad practice, at times it might be beneficial, so OSPF allows it. An example is a company that is trying to merge two separate OSPF networks into one network with a common area 0. In other instances, virtual links are added for logical redundancy in case a router failure causes the backbone to be split into two. For whatever reason, a virtual link can be configured between separate ABRs that touch area 0 from each side and have a common area (see Figure 4-29).

In Figure 4-29, two area 0s are linked via a virtual link. If a common area does not exist, an additional area, such as area 3, could be created to become the transit area. If any area that is different than the backbone becomes partitioned, the backbone takes care of the partitioning without using virtual links. One part of the partitioned area is known to the other part via inter-area routes rather than intra-area routes.

A virtual link can connect an ABR to the backbone (area 0), even though the virtual link is not directly connected (see Figure 4-30 in the next section). You can accomplish this through the use of a virtual link.

Figure 4-29 *Repairing Area 0 with a Virtual Link*

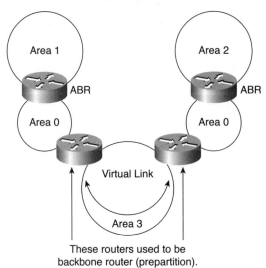

These routers used to be
backbone router (prepartition).

Ensuring a Connection to Area 0

In the rare situation that a new area, which cannot have a direct physical access to the
backbone, is introduced, you need to configure a virtual link. A virtual link creates a path
between two ABRs that are not directly connected. Refer to Figure 4-30 for an example of
this concept. Here, area 4 does not have a physical connection to area 0, so it uses a virtual
link (through area 1) to connect to area 0 using Routers A and B, respectively.

Figure 4-30 *Connecting to Area 0 with a Virtual Link*

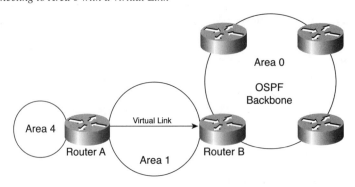

Golden Rules of Virtual Link Design

Some of the characteristics and suggested uses for virtual links are as follows:

- Virtual link stability is determined by the stability of the area that the virtual links transit.
- Virtual links can only be configured on ABRs.
- Virtual links cannot run across stub areas.
- Virtual links assist in solving short-term network connectivity problems.
- Virtual links can assist in providing logical redundancy.
- OSPF treats two routers joined by a virtual link as if they were connected by an unnumbered point-to-point network.
- Virtual links cannot be configured on unnumbered links.

To maintain forwarding, an IP address range should not be spread across the split area. This assumes that some destinations now require inter-area routing as a result. If this does occur, some destinations become unreachable and routing loops might occur. In an outage condition, this information is not helpful, but when designing areas, assign IP address ranges accordingly so that growth can be handled more easily in the future should a new area be needed.

Virtual Link Configuration Example

Previous sections discussed the characteristics of OSPF virtual links and provided an example. You now learn how to configure a virtual link in a real network. You are also going to see some packet captures of the virtual link in operation as well as understand the operation of a virtual link. This can help you understand how the packets flow throughout the network. The network you are to configure is shown in Figure 4-31. Note that a new area exists that cannot be physically connected to area 0, so as a temporary solution, a virtual link is configured while waiting for the delivery of the physical circuit that is on order.

Figure 4-31 *Virtual Link Example*

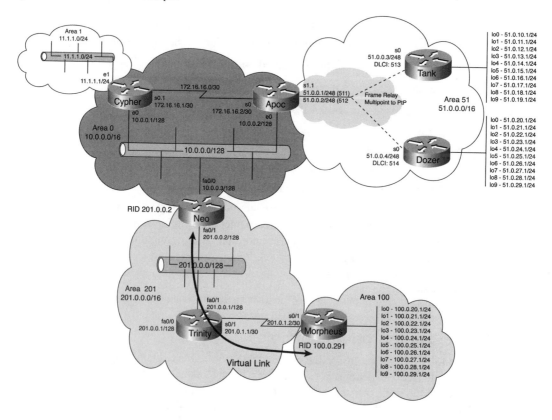

Notice the OSPF RIDs of the Morpheus and Neo routers and the loopback interfaces (networks 100.0.x.x) that are found in area 100. In Example 4-5, you see that these networks are missing from Cypher.

Example 4-5 *Missing Routes*

```
Cypher#show ip route
Codes: C - connected, S - static, I - IGRP, R - RIP, M - mobile, B - BGP
       D - EIGRP, EX - EIGRP external, O - OSPF, IA - OSPF inter area
       N1 - OSPF NSSA external type 1, N2 - OSPF NSSA external type 2
       E1 - OSPF external type 1, E2 - OSPF external type 2, E - EGP
       i - IS-IS, L1 - IS-IS level-1, L2 - IS-IS level-2, * - candidate default
       U - per-user static route, o - ODR

Gateway of last resort is not set

     51.0.0.0/32 is subnetted, 23 subnets
O IA    51.0.18.1 [110/129] via 172.16.16.2, 00:37:14, Serial0.1
O IA    51.0.19.1 [110/129] via 172.16.16.2, 00:37:15, Serial0.1
```

Example 4-5 *Missing Routes (Continued)*

```
O IA    51.0.16.1 [110/129] via 172.16.16.2, 00:37:15, Serial0.1
O IA    51.0.17.1 [110/129] via 172.16.16.2, 00:37:15, Serial0.1
O IA    51.0.22.1 [110/129] via 172.16.16.2, 00:37:15, Serial0.1
O IA    51.0.23.1 [110/129] via 172.16.16.2, 00:37:15, Serial0.1
O IA    51.0.20.1 [110/129] via 172.16.16.2, 00:37:15, Serial0.1
O IA    51.0.21.1 [110/129] via 172.16.16.2, 00:37:15, Serial0.1
O IA    51.0.26.1 [110/129] via 172.16.16.2, 00:37:15, Serial0.1
O IA    51.0.27.1 [110/129] via 172.16.16.2, 00:37:15, Serial0.1
O IA    51.0.24.1 [110/129] via 172.16.16.2, 00:37:15, Serial0.1
O IA    51.0.25.1 [110/129] via 172.16.16.2, 00:37:15, Serial0.1
O IA    51.0.28.1 [110/129] via 172.16.16.2, 00:37:16, Serial0.1
O IA    51.0.29.1 [110/129] via 172.16.16.2, 00:37:16, Serial0.1
O IA    51.0.0.3 [110/128] via 172.16.16.2, 00:37:16, Serial0.1
O IA    51.0.0.1 [110/64] via 172.16.16.2, 00:37:16, Serial0.1
O IA    51.0.0.4 [110/128] via 172.16.16.2, 00:37:16, Serial0.1
O IA    51.0.10.1 [110/129] via 172.16.16.2, 00:37:16, Serial0.1
O IA    51.0.11.1 [110/129] via 172.16.16.2, 00:37:16, Serial0.1
O IA    51.0.14.1 [110/129] via 172.16.16.2, 00:37:16, Serial0.1
O IA    51.0.15.1 [110/129] via 172.16.16.2, 00:37:16, Serial0.1
O IA    51.0.12.1 [110/129] via 172.16.16.2, 00:37:17, Serial0.1
O IA    51.0.13.1 [110/129] via 172.16.16.2, 00:37:17, Serial0.1
        201.0.0.0/25 is subnetted, 1 subnets
O IA    201.0.0.0 [110/75] via 172.16.16.2, 00:00:38, Serial0.1
        172.16.0.0/30 is subnetted, 1 subnets
C       172.16.16.0 is directly connected, Serial0.1
        10.0.0.0/25 is subnetted, 1 subnets
C       10.0.0.0 is directly connected, Ethernet0
        11.0.0.0/24 is subnetted, 1 subnets
C       11.1.1.0 is directly connected, Ethernet1
```

As you can see, the networks are not present in the routing tables, so the first step in configuring a virtual link is to complete the following command on each end. In this case, the ABRs are Neo and Morpheus:

area *area-id* **virtual-link** *router-id*

Here, *area-id* is the OSPF area that the virtual link transits through to connect to area 0 and the other area. This other area could be either another area 0 if the backbone is partitioned or a nonbackbone area. (This is what you are doing.) Example 4-6 shows this configuration on Neo.

Example 4-6 *Configuring a Virtual Link*

```
Neo(config)#router ospf 100
Neo(config-router)#area 201 virtual-link 100.0.29.1

Morpheus(config-router)#area 201 virtual-link 201.0.0.2
```

Here, *router-id* is the OSPF RID and can be found for each router by using the **show ip ospf** command, as demonstrated in Example 4-7.

Example 4-7   *Determining the OSPF RID for Each Router*

```
Morpheus#show ip ospf
 Routing Process "ospf 100" with ID 100.0.29.1
 Supports only single TOS(TOS0) routes
 Supports opaque LSA
 It is an area border router
 SPF schedule delay 5 secs, Hold time between two SPFs 10 secs
 Minimum LSA interval 5 secs. Minimum LSA arrival 1 secs
 Number of external LSA 0. Checksum Sum 0x0
 Number of opaque AS LSA 0. Checksum Sum 0x0
 Number of DCbitless external and opaque AS LSA 0
 Number of DoNotAge external and opaque AS LSA 0
 Number of areas in this router is 3. 3 normal 0 stub 0 nssa
 External flood list length 0
    Area BACKBONE(0)
        Number of interfaces in this area is 1
        Area has no authentication
        SPF algorithm executed 3 times
        Area ranges are
        Number of LSA 43. Checksum Sum 0x1441C8
        Number of opaque link LSA 0. Checksum Sum 0x0
        Number of DCbitless LSA 0
        Number of indication LSA 0
        Number of DoNotAge LSA 30
        Flood list length 0
    Area 100
        Number of interfaces in this area is 10
        Area has no authentication
        SPF algorithm executed 3 times
        Area ranges are
        Number of LSA 29. Checksum Sum 0xF019F
        Number of opaque link LSA 0. Checksum Sum 0x0
        Number of DCbitless LSA 0
        Number of indication LSA 0
        Number of DoNotAge LSA 0
        Flood list length 0
    Area 201
        Number of interfaces in this area is 1
        Area has no authentication
        SPF algorithm executed 4 times
        Area ranges are
        Number of LSA 76. Checksum Sum 0x287C6F
        Number of opaque link LSA 0. Checksum Sum 0x0
        Number of DCbitless LSA 0
        Number of indication LSA 0
        Number of DoNotAge LSA 0
        Flood list length 0

Morpheus#
```

After the virtual links are configured on both routers, the OSPF Hellos begin to flow as they develop the proper relationship. Several items must be checked when these first Hellos arrive. The receiving router must do the following:

- **Match the area ID of the receiving interface**—This means that the receiving interface must be in the OSPF area that was configured as transit in the virtual link command.

- **Be an ABR**—The RID in the packet must match that which was configured in the virtual link command.

If all these checks succeed, the packet is accepted and from now on is associated with the virtual link. In Figure 4-32, you see the Hello packet that is sent from Routers Morpheus to Neo (via Trinity). Notice that this packet is a normal OSPF IP packet with the correct Time-To-Live (TTL), source address (SA), and destination address (DA). Furthermore, the RID is Morpheus, and via this virtual link, you can see that Morpheus now believes it has a link to area 0 (see the packet's area ID).

Figure 4-32 *Hello Packet via a Virtual Link*

```
⊟ 🖳 DLC:  ------ DLC Header ------
   🗋 DLC:
   🗋 DLC:  Frame 1 arrived at  16:06:05.8186; frame size is 78 (004E hex) bytes.
   🗋 DLC:  Destination = Station 0004DD81FCA1
   🗋 DLC:  Source      = Station 0004DD81FE01
   🗋 DLC:  Ethertype   = 0800 (IP)
   🗋 DLC:
⊟ 🗂 IP:  ------ IP Header ------
   🗋 IP:
   🗋 IP:  Version = 4, header length = 20 bytes
   🗋 IP:  Type of service = C0
   🗋 IP:      110. ....  = internetwork control
   🗋 IP:      ...0 ....  = normal delay
   🗋 IP:      .... 0...  = normal throughput
   🗋 IP:      .... .0..  = normal reliability
   🗋 IP:      .... ..0.  = ECT bit - transport protocol will ignore the CE bit
   🗋 IP:      .... ...0  = CE bit - no congestion
   🗋 IP:  Total length   = 64 bytes
   🗋 IP:  Identification = 64
   🗋 IP:  Flags          = 0X
   🗋 IP:      .0.. ....  = may fragment
   🗋 IP:      ..0. ....  = last fragment
   🗋 IP:  Fragment offset = 0 bytes
   🗋 IP:  Time to live    = 254 seconds/hops
   🗋 IP:  [Protocol       = 89] (OSPFIGP)
   🗋 IP:  Header checksum = 2860 (correct)
   🗋 IP:  [Source address      = [201.0.1.2]]
   🗋 IP:  [Destination address = [201.0.0.2]]
   🗋 IP:  No options
   🗋 IP:
⊟ 📨 OSPF:  ------ OSPF Header ------
   📨 OSPF:
   📨 OSPF:  Version = 2,  Type = 1 (Hello),   Length = 44
   📨 OSPF:  [Router ID        = [100.0.29.1]]
   📨 OSPF:  [Area ID          = [0.0.0.0]]
   📨 OSPF:  Header checksum = 5A9E (correct)
   📨 OSPF:  Authentication: Type = 0 (No Authentication),   Value = 00 00 00 00 00 00 00 00
   📨 OSPF:
   📨 OSPF:  Network mask            = [0.0.0.0]
   📨 OSPF:  Hello interval          = 10 (seconds)
   📨 OSPF:  Optional capabilities   = 22
   📨 OSPF:             .0.. ....   = Opaque-LSAs not forwarded
   📨 OSPF:             ..1. ....   = Demand Circuit bit
   📨 OSPF:             ...0 ....   = External Attributes bit
   📨 OSPF:             .... 0...   = no NSSA capability
   📨 OSPF:             .... .0..   = no multicast capability
   📨 OSPF:             .... ..1.   = external routing capability
   📨 OSPF:             .... ...0   = no Type of Service routing capability
   📨 OSPF:  Router priority         = 1
   📨 OSPF:  Router dead interval    = 40 (seconds)
   📨 OSPF:  Designated router       = [0.0.0.0]
   📨 OSPF:  Backup designated router = [0.0.0.0]
   📨 OSPF:
```

After communication is established, the next packets you would expect to see would be the database descriptor packets. Figure 4-33 includes the full capture of the largest database descriptor packet. There are other smaller packets, but this one best describes the data that is flowing from Router Morpheus across the virtual link.

Figure 4-33   *Database Descriptor Packet*

```
⊟━ DLC:  ───── DLC Header ─────
    ─ DLC:
    ─ DLC:  Frame 3 arrived at  16:06:06.4098; frame size is 326 (0146 hex) bytes.
    ─ DLC:  Destination = Station 0004DD81FCA1
    ─ DLC:  Source      = Station 0004DD81FE01
    ─ DLC:  Ethertype   = 0800 (IP)
    ─ DLC:
⊟━ IP:   ───── IP Header ─────
    ─ IP:
    ─ IP:  Version = 4, header length = 20 bytes
    ─ IP:  Type of service = C0
    ─ IP:       110. ....  = internetwork control
    ─ IP:       ...0 ....  = normal delay
    ─ IP:       .... 0...  = normal throughput
    ─ IP:       .... .0..  = normal reliability
    ─ IP:       .... ..0.  = ECT bit – transport protocol will ignore the CE bit
    ─ IP:       .... ...0  = CE bit – no congestion
    ─ IP:  Total length   = 312 bytes
    ─ IP:  Identification = 68
    ─ IP:  Flags          = 0X
    ─ IP:       .0.. ....  = may fragment
    ─ IP:       ..0. ....  = last fragment
    ─ IP:  Fragment offset = 0 bytes
    ─ IP:  Time to live    = 254 seconds/hops
    ─ IP:  Protocol        = 89 (OSPFIGP)
    ─ IP:  Header checksum = 2764 (correct)
    ─ IP:  Source address      = [201.0.1.2]
    ─ IP:  Destination address = [201.0.0.2]
    ─ IP:  No options
    ─ IP:
⊟━ OSPF:  ───── OSPF Header ─────
    ─ OSPF:
    ─ OSPF:  Version = 2,  Type = 2 (Database Description),  Length = 292
    ─ OSPF:  Router ID    = [100.0.29.1]
    ─ OSPF:  Area ID      = [0.0.0.0]
    ─ OSPF:  Header checksum = 2E35 (correct)
    ─ OSPF:  Authentication: Type = 0 (No Authentication),  Value = 00 00 00 00 00 00 00 00
    ─ OSPF:
    ─ OSPF:  Reserved            = 0
    ─ OSPF:  Optional capabilities  = 62
    ─ OSPF:                  .1.. ....  = Opaque–LSAs forworded
    ─ OSPF:                  ..1. ....  = Demand Circuit bit
    ─ OSPF:                  ...0 ....  = External Attributes bit
    ─ OSPF:                  .... 0...  = no NSSA capability
    ─ OSPF:                  .... .0..  = no multicast capability
    ─ OSPF:                  .... ..1.  = external routing capability
    ─ OSPF:                  .... ...0  = no Type of Service routing capability
    ─ OSPF:  Flags = 02
    ─ OSPF:       .... .0..  = Not init
    ─ OSPF:       .... ..1.  = More
    ─ OSPF:       .... ...0  = Slave
    ─ OSPF:  Sequence number = 9330
    ─ OSPF:
    ─ OSPF:  Link State Advertisement Header # 1,
    ─ OSPF:  Link state age    = 0 (seconds)
    ─ OSPF:  Optional capabilities = 22
    ─ OSPF:                  .0.. ....  = Opaque–LSAs not forwarded
    ─ OSPF:                  ..1. ....  = Demand Circuit bit
    ─ OSPF:                  ...0 ....  = External Attributes bit
    ─ OSPF:                  .... 0...  = no NSSA capability
    ─ OSPF:                  .... .0..  = no multicast capability
    ─ OSPF:                  .... ..1.  = external routing capability
    ─ OSPF:                  .... ...0  = no Type of Service routing capability
    ─ OSPF:  Link state type  = 1 (Router links)
    ─ OSPF:  Link state ID    = [100.0.29.1]
    ─ OSPF:  Advertising Router = [100.0.29.1]
    ─ OSPF:  Sequence number    = 2147483649,  Checksum = E359
```

continues

Figure 4-33 *Database Descriptor Packet (Continued)*

```
OSPF: Length              = 24
OSPF:
OSPF: Link State Advertisement Header # 2,
OSPF: Link state age      = 0 (seconds)
OSPF: Optional capabilities = 22
OSPF:          .0.. .... = Opaque-LSAs not forwarded
OSPF:          ..1. .... = Demand Circuit bit
OSPF:          ...0 .... = External Attributes bit
OSPF:          .... 0... = no NSSA capability
OSPF:          .... .0.. = no multicast capability
OSPF:          .... ..1. = external routing capability
OSPF:          .... ...0 = no Type of Service routing capability
OSPF: Link state type     = 3 (Summary link (IP network))
OSPF: Link state ID       = [100.0.20.1]
OSPF: Advertising Router   = [100.0.29.1]
OSPF: Sequence number     = 2147483649,  Checksum = 3A06
OSPF: Length              = 28
OSPF:
OSPF: Link State Advertisement Header # 3,
OSPF: Link state age      = 0 (seconds)
OSPF: Optional capabilities = 22
OSPF:          .0.. .... = Opaque-LSAs not forwarded
OSPF:          ..1. .... = Demand Circuit bit
OSPF:          ...0 .... = External Attributes bit
OSPF:          .... 0... = no NSSA capability
OSPF:          .... .0.. = no multicast capability
OSPF:          .... ..1. = external routing capability
OSPF:          .... ...0 = no Type of Service routing capability
OSPF: Link state type     = 3 (Summary link (IP network))
OSPF: Link state ID       = [100.0.21.1]
OSPF: Advertising Router   = [100.0.29.1]
OSPF: Sequence number     = 2147483649,  Checksum = 2F10
OSPF: Length              = 28
OSPF:
OSPF: Link State Advertisement Header # 4,
OSPF: Link state age      = 0 (seconds)
OSPF: Optional capabilities = 22
OSPF:          .0.. .... = Opaque-LSAs not forwarded
OSPF:          ..1. .... = Demand Circuit bit
OSPF:          ...0 .... = External Attributes bit
OSPF:          .... 0... = no NSSA capability
OSPF:          .... .0.. = no multicast capability
OSPF:          .... ..1. = external routing capability
OSPF:          .... ...0 = no Type of Service routing capability
OSPF: Link state type     = 3 (Summary link (IP network))
OSPF: Link state ID       = [100.0.22.1]
OSPF: Advertising Router   = [100.0.29.1]
OSPF: Sequence number     = 2147483649,  Checksum = 241A
OSPF: Length              = 28
OSPF:
OSPF: Link State Advertisement Header # 5,
OSPF: Link state age      = 0 (seconds)
OSPF: Optional capabilities = 22
OSPF:          .0.. .... = Opaque-LSAs not forwarded
OSPF:          ..1. .... = Demand Circuit bit
OSPF:          ...0 .... = External Attributes bit
OSPF:          .... 0... = no NSSA capability
OSPF:          .... .0.. = no multicast capability
OSPF:          .... ..1. = external routing capability
OSPF:          .... ...0 = no Type of Service routing capability
OSPF: Link state type     = 3 (Summary link (IP network))
OSPF: Link state ID       = [100.0.23.1]
OSPF: Advertising Router   = [100.0.29.1]
OSPF: Sequence number     = 2147483649,  Checksum = 1924
OSPF: Length              = 28
OSPF:
OSPF: Link State Advertisement Header # 6,
OSPF: Link state age      = 0 (seconds)
OSPF: Optional capabilities = 22
OSPF:          .0.. .... = Opaque-LSAs not forwarded
OSPF:          ..1. .... = Demand Circuit bit
OSPF:          ...0 .... = External Attributes bit
OSPF:          .... 0... = no NSSA capability
```

Figure 4-33 *Database Descriptor Packet (Continued)*

```
OSPF:                    .... .0.. = no multicast capability
OSPF:                    .... ..1. = external routing capability
OSPF:                    .... ...0 = no Type of Service routing capability
OSPF: Link state type       = 3 (Summary link (IP network))
OSPF: Link state ID         = [100.0.24.1]
OSPF: Advertising Router    = [100.0.29.1]
OSPF: Sequence number       = 2147483649.   Checksum = 0E2E
OSPF: Length                = 28
OSPF:
OSPF: Link State Advertisement Header # 7.
OSPF: Link state age        = 0 (seconds)
OSPF: Optional capabilities = 22
OSPF:                    .0.. .... = Opaque-LSAs not forwarded
OSPF:                    ..1. .... = Demand Circuit bit
OSPF:                    ...0 .... = External Attributes bit
OSPF:                    .... 0... = no NSSA capability
OSPF:                    .... .0.. = no multicast capability
OSPF:                    .... ..1. = external routing capability
OSPF:                    .... ...0 = no Type of Service routing capability
OSPF: Link state type       = 3 (Summary link (IP network))
OSPF: Link state ID         = [100.0.25.1]
OSPF: Advertising Router    = [100.0.29.1]
OSPF: Sequence number       = 2147483649.   Checksum = 0338
OSPF: Length                = 28
OSPF:
OSPF: Link State Advertisement Header # 8.
OSPF: Link state age        = 0 (seconds)
OSPF: Optional capabilities = 22
OSPF:                    .0.. .... = Opaque-LSAs not forwarded
OSPF:                    ..1. .... = Demand Circuit bit
OSPF:                    ...0 .... = External Attributes bit
OSPF:                    .... 0... = no NSSA capability
OSPF:                    .... .0.. = no multicast capability
OSPF:                    .... ..1. = external routing capability
OSPF:                    .... ...0 = no Type of Service routing capability
OSPF: Link state type       = 3 (Summary link (IP network))
OSPF: Link state ID         = [100.0.26.1]
OSPF: Advertising Router    = [100.0.29.1]
OSPF: Sequence number       = 2147483649.   Checksum = F742
OSPF: Length                = 28
OSPF:
OSPF: Link State Advertisement Header # 9.
OSPF: Link state age        = 0 (seconds)
OSPF: Optional capabilities = 22
OSPF:                    .0.. .... = Opaque-LSAs not forwarded
OSPF:                    ..1. .... = Demand Circuit bit
OSPF:                    ...0 .... = External Attributes bit
OSPF:                    .... 0... = no NSSA capability
OSPF:                    .... .0.. = no multicast capability
OSPF:                    .... ..1. = external routing capability
OSPF:                    .... ...0 = no Type of Service routing capability
OSPF: Link state type       = 3 (Summary link (IP network))
OSPF: Link state ID         = [100.0.27.1]
OSPF: Advertising Router    = [100.0.29.1]
OSPF: Sequence number       = 2147483649.   Checksum = EC4C
OSPF: Length                = 28
OSPF:
OSPF: Link State Advertisement Header # 10.
OSPF: Link state age        = 0 (seconds)
OSPF: Optional capabilities = 22
OSPF:                    .0.. .... = Opaque-LSAs not forwarded
```

The next series of packets are the link-state requests transmitted from Morpheus to Neo, requesting that information be provided on Morpheus' links. This one packet of several shows many of the networks that Neo is aware of being mentioned. Figure 4-34 shows this link-state request.

Figure 4-34 *Link-State Request Packet*

```
⊟-🖳 DLC:  ------ DLC Header ------
   -📄 DLC:
   -📄 DLC:  Frame 5 arrived at  16:06:06.5715; frame size is 454 (01C6 hex) bytes.
   -📄 DLC:  Destination = Station 0004DD81FCA1
   -📄 DLC:  Source      = Station 0004DD81FE01
   -📄 DLC:  Ethertype   = 0800 (IP)
   -📄 DLC:
⊟-🍹 IP:  ------ IP Header ------
   -📄 IP:
   -📄 IP:  Version = 4, header length = 20 bytes
   -📄 IP:  Type of service = C0
   -📄 IP:       110. ....  = internetwork control
   -📄 IP:       ...0 ....  = normal delay
   -📄 IP:       .... 0...  = normal throughput
   -📄 IP:       .... .0..  = normal reliability
   -📄 IP:       .... ..0.  = ECT bit - transport protocol will ignore the CE bit
   -📄 IP:       .... ...0  = CE bit - no congestion
   -📄 IP:  Total length   = 440 bytes
   -📄 IP:  Identification = 70
   -📄 IP:  Flags          = 0X
   -📄 IP:       .0.. ....  = may fragment
   -📄 IP:       ..0. ....  = last fragment
   -📄 IP:  Fragment offset = 0 bytes
   -📄 IP:  Time to live   = 254 seconds/hops
   -📄 IP:  Protocol       = 89 (OSPFIGP)
   -📄 IP:  Header checksum = 26E2 (correct)
   -📄 IP:  Source address     = [201.0.1.2]
   -📄 IP:  Destination address = [201.0.0.2]
   -📄 IP:  No options
   -📄 IP:
⊟-🕸 OSPF:  ------ OSPF Header ------
   -📄 OSPF:
   -📄 OSPF:  Version = 2,   Type = 3 (Link State Request),   Length = 420
   -📄 OSPF:  Router ID       = [100.0.29.1]
   -📄 OSPF:  Area ID         = [0.0.0.0]
   -📄 OSPF:  Header checksum = DF6B (correct)
   -📄 OSPF:  Authentication: Type = 0 (No Authentication),   Value = 00 00 00 00 00 00 00 00
   -📄 OSPF:
   -📄 OSPF:  Link State Advertisement # 1
   -📄 OSPF:  Link State type    = 1 (Router links)
   -📄 OSPF:  Link State ID      = [201.0.1.1]
   -📄 OSPF:  Advertising Router = [201.0.1.1]
   -📄 OSPF:
   -📄 OSPF:  Link State Advertisement # 2
   -📄 OSPF:  Link State type    = 1 (Router links)
   -📄 OSPF:  Link State ID      = [201.0.0.2]
   -📄 OSPF:  Advertising Router = [201.0.0.2]
   -📄 OSPF:
   -📄 OSPF:  Link State Advertisement # 3
   -📄 OSPF:  Link State type    = 1 (Router links)
   -📄 OSPF:  Link State ID      = [172.16.16.1]
   -📄 OSPF:  Advertising Router = [172.16.16.1]
   -📄 OSPF:
   -📄 OSPF:  Link State Advertisement # 4
   -📄 OSPF:  Link State type    = 1 (Router links)
   -📄 OSPF:  Link State ID      = [51.0.0.1]
   -📄 OSPF:  Advertising Router = [51.0.0.1]
   -📄 OSPF:
   -📄 OSPF:  Link State Advertisement # 5
   -📄 OSPF:  Link State type    = 2 (Network links)
   -📄 OSPF:  Link State ID      = [10.0.0.3]
   -📄 OSPF:  Advertising Router = [201.0.0.2]
   -📄 OSPF:
   -📄 OSPF:  Link State Advertisement # 6
   -📄 OSPF:  Link State type    = 3 (Summary link (IP network))
   -📄 OSPF:  Link State ID      = [201.0.1.0]
   -📄 OSPF:  Advertising Router = [201.0.1.1]
   -📄 OSPF:
   -📄 OSPF:  Link State Advertisement # 7
   -📄 OSPF:  Link State type    = 3 (Summary link (IP network))
   -📄 OSPF:  Link State ID      = [201.0.1.0]
   -📄 OSPF:  Advertising Router = [201.0.0.2]
   └-📄 OSPF:
```

Figure 4-34 *Link-State Request Packet (Continued)*

```
OSPF: Link State Advertisement # 8
OSPF: Link State type    = 3 (Summary link (IP network))
OSPF: Link State ID      = [201.0.0.0]
OSPF: Advertising Router = [201.0.1.1]
OSPF:
OSPF: Link State Advertisement # 9
OSPF: Link State type    = 3 (Summary link (IP network))
OSPF: Link State ID      = [201.0.0.0]
OSPF: Advertising Router = [201.0.0.2]
OSPF:
OSPF: Link State Advertisement # 10
OSPF: Link State type    = 3 (Summary link (IP network))
OSPF: Link State ID      = [51.0.29.1]
OSPF: Advertising Router = [51.0.0.1]
OSPF:
OSPF: Link State Advertisement # 11
OSPF: Link State type    = 3 (Summary link (IP network))
OSPF: Link State ID      = [51.0.28.1]
OSPF: Advertising Router = [51.0.0.1]
OSPF:
OSPF: Link State Advertisement # 12
OSPF: Link State type    = 3 (Summary link (IP network))
OSPF: Link State ID      = [51.0.27.1]
OSPF: Advertising Router = [51.0.0.1]
OSPF:
OSPF: Link State Advertisement # 13
OSPF: Link State type    = 3 (Summary link (IP network))
OSPF: Link State ID      = [51.0.26.1]
OSPF: Advertising Router = [51.0.0.1]
OSPF:
OSPF: Link State Advertisement # 14
OSPF: Link State type    = 3 (Summary link (IP network))
OSPF: Link State ID      = [51.0.25.1]
OSPF: Advertising Router = [51.0.0.1]
OSPF:
OSPF: Link State Advertisement # 15
OSPF: Link State type    = 3 (Summary link (IP network))
OSPF: Link State ID      = [51.0.24.1]
OSPF: Advertising Router = [51.0.0.1]
OSPF:
OSPF: Link State Advertisement # 16
OSPF: Link State type    = 3 (Summary link (IP network))
OSPF: Link State ID      = [51.0.23.1]
OSPF: Advertising Router = [51.0.0.1]
OSPF:
OSPF: Link State Advertisement # 17
OSPF: Link State type    = 3 (Summary link (IP network))
OSPF: Link State ID      = [51.0.22.1]
OSPF: Advertising Router = [51.0.0.1]
OSPF:
OSPF: Link State Advertisement # 18
OSPF: Link State type    = 3 (Summary link (IP network))
OSPF: Link State ID      = [51.0.21.1]
OSPF: Advertising Router = [51.0.0.1]
OSPF:
OSPF: Link State Advertisement # 19
OSPF: Link State type    = 3 (Summary link (IP network))
OSPF: Link State ID      = [51.0.20.1]
OSPF: Advertising Router = [51.0.0.1]
OSPF:
OSPF: Link State Advertisement # 20
OSPF: Link State type    = 3 (Summary link (IP network))
OSPF: Link State ID      = [51.0.19.1]
OSPF: Advertising Router = [51.0.0.1]
OSPF:
OSPF: Link State Advertisement # 21
OSPF: Link State type    = 3 (Summary link (IP network))
OSPF: Link State ID      = [51.0.18.1]
OSPF: Advertising Router = [51.0.0.1]
```

continues

Figure 4-34 *Link-State Request Packet (Continued)*

```
OSPF:
OSPF: Link State Advertisement # 22
OSPF: Link State type    = 3 (Summary link (IP network))
OSPF: Link State ID      = [51.0.17.1]
OSPF: Advertising Router = [51.0.0.1]
OSPF:
OSPF: Link State type    = 3 (Summary link (IP network))
OSPF: Link State ID      = [51.0.16.1]
OSPF: Advertising Router = [51.0.0.1]
OSPF:
OSPF: Link State Advertisement # 24
OSPF: Link State type    = 3 (Summary link (IP network))
OSPF: Link State ID      = [51.0.15.1]
OSPF: Advertising Router = [51.0.0.1]
OSPF:
OSPF: Link State Advertisement # 25
OSPF: Link State type    = 3 (Summary link (IP network))
OSPF: Link State ID      = [51.0.14.1]
OSPF: Advertising Router = [51.0.0.1]
OSPF:
OSPF: Link State Advertisement # 26
OSPF: Link State type    = 3 (Summary link (IP network))
OSPF: Link State ID      = [51.0.13.1]
OSPF: Advertising Router = [51.0.0.1]
OSPF:
OSPF: Link State Advertisement # 27
OSPF: Link State type    = 3 (Summary link (IP network))
OSPF: Link State ID      = [51.0.12.1]
OSPF: Advertising Router = [51.0.0.1]
OSPF:
OSPF: Link State Advertisement # 28
OSPF: Link State type    = 3 (Summary link (IP network))
OSPF: Link State ID      = [51.0.11.1]
OSPF: Advertising Router = [51.0.0.1]
OSPF:
OSPF: Link State Advertisement # 29
OSPF: Link State type    = 3 (Summary link (IP network))
OSPF: Link State ID      = [51.0.10.1]
OSPF: Advertising Router = [51.0.0.1]
OSPF:
OSPF: Link State Advertisement # 30
OSPF: Link State type    = 3 (Summary link (IP network))
OSPF: Link State ID      = [51.0.0.4]
OSPF: Advertising Router = [51.0.0.1]
OSPF:
OSPF: Link State Advertisement # 31
OSPF: Link State type    = 3 (Summary link (IP network))
OSPF: Link State ID      = [51.0.0.3]
OSPF: Advertising Router = [51.0.0.1]
OSPF:
OSPF: Link State Advertisement # 32
OSPF: Link State type    = 3 (Summary link (IP network))
OSPF: Link State ID      = [51.0.0.1]
OSPF: Advertising Router = [51.0.0.1]
OSPF:
OSPF: Link State Advertisement # 33
OSPF: Link State type    = 3 (Summary link (IP network))
OSPF: Link State ID      = [11.1.1.0]
```

This is the behavior that you want to take place when you have a virtual link configured. The acknowledgment packets are not shown, but they have occurred. As you can see in Example 4-8, Router Cypher has all the networks that Morpheus knows about.

Example 4-8 *Verifying That Router Cypher Acknowledges the Virtual Link*

```
Cypher#show ip route
Codes: C - connected, S - static, I - IGRP, R - RIP, M - mobile, B - BGP
       D - EIGRP, EX - EIGRP external, O - OSPF, IA - OSPF inter area
       N1 - OSPF NSSA external type 1, N2 - OSPF NSSA external type 2
       E1 - OSPF external type 1, E2 - OSPF external type 2, E - EGP
       i - IS-IS, L1 - IS-IS level-1, L2 - IS-IS level-2, * - candidate default
       U - per-user static route, o - ODR

Gateway of last resort is not set

     51.0.0.0/32 is subnetted, 23 subnets
O IA    51.0.18.1 [110/75] via 10.0.0.2, 03:35:11, Ethernet0
O IA    51.0.19.1 [110/75] via 10.0.0.2, 03:35:11, Ethernet0
O IA    51.0.16.1 [110/75] via 10.0.0.2, 03:35:11, Ethernet0
O IA    51.0.17.1 [110/75] via 10.0.0.2, 03:35:11, Ethernet0
O IA    51.0.22.1 [110/75] via 10.0.0.2, 03:35:11, Ethernet0
O IA    51.0.23.1 [110/75] via 10.0.0.2, 03:35:11, Ethernet0
O IA    51.0.20.1 [110/75] via 10.0.0.2, 03:35:11, Ethernet0
O IA    51.0.21.1 [110/75] via 10.0.0.2, 03:35:11, Ethernet0
O IA    51.0.26.1 [110/75] via 10.0.0.2, 03:35:11, Ethernet0
O IA    51.0.27.1 [110/75] via 10.0.0.2, 03:35:11, Ethernet0
O IA    51.0.24.1 [110/75] via 10.0.0.2, 03:35:11, Ethernet0
O IA    51.0.25.1 [110/75] via 10.0.0.2, 03:35:11, Ethernet0
O IA    51.0.28.1 [110/75] via 10.0.0.2, 03:35:11, Ethernet0
O IA    51.0.29.1 [110/75] via 10.0.0.2, 03:35:13, Ethernet0
O IA    51.0.0.3 [110/74] via 10.0.0.2, 03:35:13, Ethernet0
O IA    51.0.0.1 [110/10] via 10.0.0.2, 03:35:13, Ethernet0
O IA    51.0.0.4 [110/74] via 10.0.0.2, 03:35:13, Ethernet0
O IA    51.0.10.1 [110/75] via 10.0.0.2, 03:35:13, Ethernet0
O IA    51.0.11.1 [110/75] via 10.0.0.2, 03:35:13, Ethernet0
O IA    51.0.14.1 [110/75] via 10.0.0.2, 03:35:13, Ethernet0
O IA    51.0.15.1 [110/75] via 10.0.0.2, 03:35:13, Ethernet0
O IA    51.0.12.1 [110/75] via 10.0.0.2, 03:35:13, Ethernet0
O IA    51.0.13.1 [110/75] via 10.0.0.2, 03:35:13, Ethernet0
     100.0.0.0/32 is subnetted, 10 subnets
O IA    100.0.21.1 [110/76] via 10.0.0.3, 03:35:13, Ethernet0
O IA    100.0.20.1 [110/76] via 10.0.0.3, 03:35:13, Ethernet0
O IA    100.0.23.1 [110/76] via 10.0.0.3, 03:35:13, Ethernet0
O IA    100.0.22.1 [110/76] via 10.0.0.3, 03:35:13, Ethernet0
O IA    100.0.29.1 [110/76] via 10.0.0.3, 03:35:13, Ethernet0
O IA    100.0.28.1 [110/76] via 10.0.0.3, 03:35:13, Ethernet0
O IA    100.0.25.1 [110/76] via 10.0.0.3, 03:35:13, Ethernet0
O IA    100.0.24.1 [110/76] via 10.0.0.3, 03:35:13, Ethernet0
O IA    100.0.27.1 [110/76] via 10.0.0.3, 03:35:13, Ethernet0
O IA    100.0.26.1 [110/76] via 10.0.0.3, 03:35:13, Ethernet0
     201.0.1.0/30 is subnetted, 1 subnets
O IA    201.0.1.0 [110/75] via 10.0.0.3, 03:35:13, Ethernet0
     201.0.0.0/25 is subnetted, 1 subnets
O IA    201.0.0.0 [110/11] via 10.0.0.3, 03:35:15, Ethernet0
     172.16.0.0/30 is subnetted, 1 subnets
C       172.16.16.0 is directly connected, Serial0.1
     10.0.0.0/25 is subnetted, 1 subnets
C       10.0.0.0 is directly connected, Ethernet0
     11.0.0.0/24 is subnetted, 1 subnets
C       11.1.1.0 is directly connected, Ethernet1
Cypher#
```

With the routes in Cypher, this indicates that the virtual link is functioning properly.
Example 4-9 checks the status of the virtual link on Router Neo.

Example 4-9   *Verifying That Router Neo Acknowledges the Virtual Link*

```
Neo#show ip ospf virtual-links
Virtual Link OSPF_VL1 to router 100.0.29.1 is up
  Run as demand circuit
  DoNotAge LSA allowed.
  Transit area 201, via interface FastEthernet0/1, Cost of using 65
  Transmit Delay is 1 sec, State POINT_TO_POINT,
  Timer intervals configured, Hello 10, Dead 40, Wait 40, Retransmit 5
    Hello due in 00:00:01
    Adjacency State FULL (Hello suppressed)
    Index 2/3, retransmission queue length 0, number of retransmission 1
    First 0x0(0)/0x0(0) Next 0x0(0)/0x0(0)
    Last retransmission scan length is 1, maximum is 1
    Last retransmission scan time is 0 msec, maximum is 0 msec
Neo#
```

OSPF Design Tools

This section reviews some useful network design tools that are available in OSPF.

Altering Neighbor Cost

In your network, you want to prioritize or alter traffic flow based on the cost of a link.
Suppose that you want to alter (increase or decrease) the default cost that is associated with
a link to a neighbor. You can change this cost by assigning a cost associated with that
neighbor as follows:

- On point-to-multipoint broadcast networks, there is no need to specify neighbors.
  However, you can specify neighbors with the **neighbor** command; in which case; you
  should specify a cost to that neighbor.

- On point-to-multipoint nonbroadcast networks, you now use the **neighbor** command
  to identify neighbors. Assigning a cost to a neighbor is optional.

Before the option of altering the neighbor cost was available, some OSPF point-to-multipoint protocol traffic was treated as multicast traffic. Therefore, the **neighbor** command
was not needed for point-to-multipoint interfaces because multicast took care of the traffic.
Hellos, updates, and acknowledgments were sent using multicast. In particular, multicast
hellos discovered all neighbors dynamically.

However, some customers were using point-to-multipoint on nonbroadcast media (such as
classic IP over ATM), so their routers could not dynamically discover their neighbors. This
feature allows the **neighbor** command to be used on point-to-multipoint interfaces.

On any point-to-multipoint interface (broadcast or not), Cisco IOS Software assumed
that the cost to each neighbor was equal. The cost was configured with the **ip ospf cost**
command. In reality, the bandwidth to each neighbor is different, so the cost should be

different. With this feature, you can configure a separate cost to each neighbor. This feature applies to point-to-multipoint interfaces only.

To configure OSPF routers interconnecting to nonbroadcast networks, use the following form of the neighbor router configuration command (to remove a configuration, use the **no** form of this command):

```
neighbor ip-address [priority number] [poll-interval seconds] [cost number]
```

Neighbors with no specific cost configured assume the cost of the interface, based on the **ip ospf cost** command. On point-to-multipoint interfaces, this is the only keyword and argument that make sense. This keyword does not apply to NBMA networks.

Configuring a Neighbor's Cost on Point-to-Multipoint Broadcast Networks

To treat an interface as point-to-multipoint broadcast and assign a cost to each neighbor, perform the tasks in Table 4-2, beginning in interface configuration mode.

Table 4-2   *Steps to Assigning a Cost to Each Neighbor in Point-to-Multipoint Broadcast Networks*

Action	Command
Configure an interface as point-to-multipoint for broadcast media.	**ip ospf network point-to-multipoint**
Configure an OSPF routing process and enter router configuration mode.	**router ospf** *process-id*
Specify a neighbor and assign a cost to the neighbor.	**neighbor** *ip-address* **cost** *number*

Repeat these steps for each neighbor to specify a cost. Otherwise, neighbors assume the cost of the interface, based on the **ip ospf cost** command.

Configuring an Interface as Point-to-Multipoint Nonbroadcast

To treat the interface as point-to-multipoint nonbroadcast when the media does not support broadcast, perform the tasks in Table 4-3 in interface configuration mode.

Table 4-3   *Steps to Assigning a Cost to Each Neighbor in Point-to-Multipoint Nonbroadcast Networks*

Action	Command
Configure an interface as point-to-multipoint for nonbroadcast media. This is the only difference from Table 4-2.	**ip ospf network point-to-multipoint non-broadcast**
Configure an OSPF routing process and enter router configuration mode.	**router ospf** *process-id*
Specify a neighbor and assign a cost to the neighbor.	**neighbor** *ip-address* **cost** *number*

Repeat these steps for each neighbor to specify a cost. Otherwise, neighbors assume the cost of the interface, based on the **ip ospf cost** command.

You can find additional information about all these commands at the following website:

www.cisco.com/univercd/cc/td/doc/product/software/ios120/12cgcr/cbkixol.htm

Configuring Route Calculation Timers

You can configure the delay time between when OSPF receives a topology change and when it starts an SPF calculation. You can also configure the hold time between two consecutive SPF calculations. To do this, use the following command in router configuration mode:

```
timers spf spf-delay spf-holdtime
```

Suppressing OSPF Updates

Because simplex interfaces between two devices on an Ethernet represent only one network segment, for OSPF you must configure the transmitting interface to be a passive interface. Additionally, you might not want to advertise OSPF to a customer's router. This prevents (suppresses) OSPF from sending Hello packets out of the transmitting interface that is specified in the following command. Both devices can see each other via the Hello packet that is generated for the receiving interface. To configure OSPF on simplex Ethernet interfaces, use the following command in router configuration mode:

```
passive-interface type number
```

Summary

This chapter covers the fundamentals of designing the various types of OSPF areas. The discussion began by looking at the issues surrounding the scalability and topology of OSPF, with a focus on the factors that you need to consider when designing a network. You then learned about the general items to consider that are common to designing all areas.

The "golden rules of design" were provided for all the essential portions of an OSPF network. Included within those discussions were the ability of OSPF to summarize routes and the benefits of using such a strong feature of the protocol.

Case Studies

Case Study: Understanding Subinterfaces

One of the most difficult concepts to understand is the difference between point-to-point and multipoint interfaces on a router. This section briefly discusses the different scenarios regarding the use of each.

A router has two different types of serial subinterfaces that provide a flexible solution for routing various protocols over partially meshed networks. A single, physical interface can be logically divided into multiple, virtual subinterfaces. The serial subinterface can be defined as either a point-to-point connection or a multipoint connection.

The concept of subinterfaces was originally created to better handle issues caused by split horizon over NBMA networks (such as Frame Relay and X.25) and distance-vector–based routing protocols (such as IPX [Internetwork Packet Exchange], RIP/SAP, and AppleTalk).

Split horizon dictates that a routing update received on an interface cannot be retransmitted out onto the same interface. This rule holds even if the routing update was received on one Frame Relay permanent virtual circuit (PVC) and was destined to retransmit out onto another Frame Relay PVC. Assuming a Frame Relay setup of sites A, B, and C, this would mean that sites B and C can exchange routing information with site A, but would not be able to exchange routing information with each other. Split horizon does not allow site A to send routing updates received from site B on to site C, and vice versa.

TIP   For TCP/IP, Cisco routers can disable split horizon limitations on all Frame Relay interfaces and multipoint subinterfaces and can do this by default. However, split horizon cannot be disabled for other protocols, such as IPX and AppleTalk. These other protocols must use subinterfaces if dynamic routing is desired.

Point-to-Point Subinterfaces

By dividing the partially meshed Frame Relay network into a number of virtual, point-to-point networks using subinterfaces, you can overcome the split horizon problem. Each new point-to-point subnetwork is assigned its own network number. To the routed protocol, each subnetwork now appears to be located on separate interfaces. Routing updates received from site B on one logical point-to-point subinterface can be forwarded to site C on a separate logical interface without violating split horizon.

Multipoint Subinterfaces

Cisco serial interfaces are multipoint interfaces by default, unless specified as a point-to-point subinterface. However, it is possible to divide the interface into separate virtual multipoint subinterfaces.

Multipoint interfaces or subinterfaces are still subject to the split horizon limitations, as previously discussed. All nodes attached to a multipoint subinterface belong to the same network number. Typically, multipoint subinterfaces are used in conjunction with point-to-point interfaces in cases in which an existing multipoint Frame Relay cloud is migrating to a subinterfaced point-to-point network design. A multipoint subinterface is used to keep remote sites on a single network number while slowly migrating remote sites to their own point-to-point subinterface network. Eventually, all remote sites can be moved to their own point-to-point subinterface networks, and the multipoint subinterface is not necessary.

OSPF does not form adjacencies if Hello and dead timers do not match. The Hello and dead timers vary for different network types as follows:

Network Type	Hello Value	Dead Value
broadcast	H 10	D 40
non-broadcast	H 30	D 120
point-to-point	H 10	D 40
point-to-multipoint	H 10	D 40

The output from the **debug ip ospf events** command should result in a mismatched parameters message (as shown in Example 4-10), stemming from an omitted **ospf network type** command under an interface when doing the virtual link configuration. When looking at the error messages, remember that R is Received and C is Configured; notice the correction and remember from previous chapters why it worked.

Example 4-10 *Output from the* **debug ip ospf events** *Command on Router Apoc*

```
Apoc#debug ip OSPF events
*Mar  1 01:38:54.259: OSPF: Rcv hello from 172.16.16.1 area 2 from Serial0
172.16.16.1
*Mar  1 01:38:54.263: OSPF: Mismatched hello parameters from 172.16.16.1
*Mar  1 01:38:54.263: Dead R 40 C 120, Hello R 10 C 30  Mask R 255.255.255.252 C
255.255.255.252
*Mar  1 01:39:01.991: OSPF: Rcv hello from 51.0.19.1 area 51 from Serial1.1 51.0.0.3
*Mar  1 01:39:01.991: OSPF: End of hello processing
*Mar  1 01:39:04.183: OSPF: Rcv hello from 172.16.16.1 area 2 from Serial0
172.16.16.1
*Mar  1 01:39:04.187: OSPF: Mismatched hello parameters from 172.16.16.1
*Mar  1 01:39:04.191: Dead R 40 C 120, Hello R 10 C 30  Mask R 255.255.255.252 C
255.255.255.252
*Mar  1 01:39:05.327: OSPF: Rcv hello from 51.0.29.1 area 51 from Serial1.1 51.0.0.4
*Mar  1 01:39:05.331: OSPF: End of hello processing
*Mar  1 01:39:14.199: OSPF: Rcv hello from 172.16.16.1 area 2 from Serial0
172.16.16.1
*Mar  1 01:39:14.203: OSPF: Mismatched hello parameters from 172.16.16.1
*Mar  1 01:39:14.207: Dead R 40 C 120, Hello R 10 C 30  Mask R 255.255.255.252 C
255.255.255.252
*Mar  1 01:39:24.199: OSPF: Rcv hello from 172.16.16.1 area 2 from Serial0
172.16.16.1
```

Example 4-10 *Output from the* **debug ip ospf events** *Command on Router Apoc (Continued)*

```
*Mar  1 01:39:24.203: OSPF: Mismatched hello parameters from 172.16.16.1
*Mar  1 01:39:24.207: Dead R 40 C 120, Hello R 10 C 30  Mask R 255.255.255.252 C
255.255.255.252
Apoc#u all
All possible debugging has been turned off
Apoc#conf t
Enter configuration commands, one per line.  End with CNTL/Z.
Apoc(config)#int s0
Apoc(config-if)#ip ospf network ?
  broadcast         Specify OSPF broadcast multi-access network
  non-broadcast     Specify OSPF NBMA network
  point-to-multipoint  Specify OSPF point-to-multipoint network
  point-to-point    Specify OSPF point-to-point network
Apoc(config-if)#ip ospf network point-to-point
Apoc(config-if)#^Z
Apoc#
*Mar  1 01:43:46.831: %SYS-5-CONFIG_I: Configured from console by console
Apoc#debug ip ospf events
OSPF events debugging is on
*Mar  1 01:44:02.047: OSPF: Rcv hello from 51.0.19.1 area 51 from Serial1.1 51.0.0.3
*Mar  1 01:44:02.051: OSPF: End of hello processing
*Mar  1 01:44:04.687: OSPF: Rcv hello from 172.16.16.1 area 2 from Serial0
172.16.16.1
*Mar  1 01:44:04.691: OSPF: End of hello processing
*Mar  1 01:44:05.287: OSPF: Rcv hello from 51.0.29.1 area 51 from Serial1.1 51.0.0.4
*Mar  1 01:44:05.291: OSPF: End of hello processing
*Mar  1 01:44:10.095: OSPF: Rcv hello from 172.16.16.1 area 0 from OSPF_VL0
172.16.16.1
*Mar  1 01:44:10.387: OSPF: Interface OSPF_VL0 going Up
*Mar  1 01:44:14.691: OSPF: Rcv hello from 172.16.16.1 area 2 from Serial0
172.16.16.1
*Mar  1 01:44:14.695: OSPF: End of hello processing
```

Case Study: Point-to-Multipoint Link Networks

The objective of this case study is to demonstrate how to design, configure, and trouble-shoot an OSPF point-to-multipoint link network.

This feature's importance is linked with the increased use of Frame Relay and ATM due to reduced cost for the service. As customers used point-to-multipoint on nonbroadcast media (Frame Relay), they found that their routers could not dynamically discover their neighbors. The OSPF point-to-multipoint link feature allows the **neighbor** command to be used on point-to-multipoint interfaces. Point-to-multipoint can minimize the number of IP addresses that are used and basically enable the user to configure a nonbroadcast media similarly to a LAN.

Before the OSPF point-to-multipoint link feature, some OSPF point-to-multipoint protocol traffic was treated as multicast traffic. This meant that the **neighbor** command was not needed for point-to-multipoint interfaces because multicast took care of the traffic. In particular, multicast hellos discovered all neighbors dynamically.

Also, on any point-to-multipoint interface (broadcast or not), Cisco IOS Software assumed that the cost to each neighbor was equal. In reality, the bandwidth to each neighbor can be different; therefore, the cost should be different because the OSPF point-to-multipoint link enables you to configure a separate cost for each neighbor.

How many data-link connection identifiers (DLCIs) can you configure per physical interface? How many DLCIs can you configure in a specific router? The answer is, "It depends" as you can see from the following conditions:

- **DLCI address space**—Approximately 1000 DLCIs can be configured on a single physical link, given a 10-bit address. Because certain DLCIs are reserved (vendor implementation dependent), the maximum is approximately 1000.

- **Local Management Interface (LMI) status update**—The LMI protocol (ANSI Annex D and ITU-T standards) requires that all PVC status reports fit into a single packet and generally limits the number of DLCIs to 800, depending on the maximum transmission unit (MTU) size. This limit does not apply to Cisco LMI (also known as the Gang of Four LMI), which allows fragmentation of the PVC status report.

Configuring NBMA networks as either broadcast or nonbroadcast assumes that there are virtual circuits (VCs) from every router to every other router. This is often not the case because of real-world cost constraints. In these cases, you can configure the OSPF network type as point-to-multipoint. This enables routing between two routers that are not directly connected to go through the router that has the VCs to each.

Figure 4-35 illustrates the network topology considered in this case study.

Figure 4-35 *Network Topology*

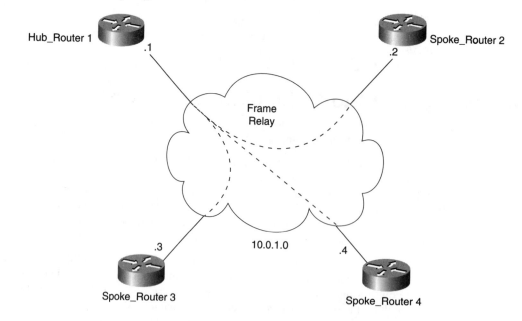

As illustrated in Figure 4-35, Hub_Router R1 has virtual circuits to Spoke_Routers R2, R3, and R4, but the other three routers do not have direct circuits to each other. This will be configured as a single subnet and point-to-multipoint links rather than multiple subnets and point-to-point links.

To configure an interface as point-to-multipoint broadcast and assign a cost to each neighbor, perform the following tasks on each interface while in configuration mode:

Step 1   Configure an interface as point-to-multipoint for broadcast media using the **ip ospf network point-to-multipoint** command.

Step 2   Configure an OSPF routing process and enter router configuration mode with **router ospf process-id**.

Step 3   Specify a neighbor and assign a cost to the neighbor using **neighbor** *ip-address* **cost** *number*.

Step 4   Repeat Step 3 for each neighbor to specify a cost. Otherwise, neighbors assume the cost of the interface, based on the **ip ospf cost** command.

Router Configuration Examples

Example 4-11 shows the configurations contained within the routers shown in Figure 4-35. These configurations were built with Cisco IOS Software Release 11.3. They do not work with older releases of Cisco IOS Software. For older releases, add the **frame-relay map ip** *address dlci* **broadcast** command.

Example 4-11   *Case Study: Router Configuration for the Network Topology Shown in Figure 4-35*

```
Hub_Router1#
interface Serial 0
ip address 10.0.1.1 255.255.255.0
encapsulation frame-relay
ip ospf network point-to-multipoint non-broadcast
frame-relay local-dlci 100
!
router ospf 1
network 10.0.1.0 0.0.0.255 area 0
neighbor 10.0.1.2 10
neighbor 10.0.1.3 10
neighbor 10.0.1.4 10
Spoke_Router2#
interface Serial 0
ip address 10.0.1.2 255.255.255.0
encapsulation frame-relay
ip ospf network point-to-multipoint non-broadcast
frame-relay local dlci 101
!
router ospf 1
network 10.0.1.0 0.0.0.255 area 0
network 10.2.0.0 0.0.255.255 area 2
neighbor 10.0.1.1 10
```

continues

Example 4-11 *Case Study: Router Configuration for the Network Topology Shown in Figure 4-35 (Continued)*

```
Spoke_Router3#
interface Serial 0
ip address 10.0.1.3 255.255.255.0
encapsulation frame-relay
ip ospf network point-to-multipoint non-broadcast
frame-relay local-dlci 103
!
router ospf 1
network 10.0.1.0 0.0.0.255 area 0
network 10.3.0.0 0.0.255.255 area 3
neighbor 10.0.1.1 10
Spoke_Router4#
interface Serial 0
ip address 10.0.1.4 255.255.255.0
encapsulation frame-relay
ip ospf network point-to-multipoint non-broadcast
frame-relay local-dlci 104
!
router ospf 1
network 10.0.1.0 0.0.0.255 area 0
network 10.4.0.0 0.0.255.255 area 4
neighbor 10.0.1.1 10
```

NOTE   No **static frame-relay map** statements were configured because Inverse ARP (Address Resolution Protocol) takes care of the DLCI-to-IP resolution and mapping.

You cannot ping your own IP address on a multipoint Frame Relay interface because Frame Relay multipoint (sub)interfaces are nonbroadcast (unlike Ethernet and point-to-point interfaces [HDLC] and Frame Relay point-to-point sub-interfaces). Furthermore, you cannot ping from one spoke router to another spoke router in a hub-and-spoke configuration because there is no mapping for your own IP address (and none was learned via Inverse ARP). However, if you configure a static map (**frame-relay map**) for your own IP address (or one for the remote spoke) to use the local DLCI, you can ping yourself.

Example 4-12 shows the output from the **show ip ospf interface** command on Router Hub_Router1 before the circuit went active. Check the state. This example highlights the important fields that you would use in troubleshooting an OSPF link-state problem.

Example 4-12 *Displaying OSPF-Related Interface Information Prior to the Circuit Going Active*

```
Hub_Router1#show ip ospf interface serial 0
Serial0 is up, line protocol is up
Internet Address 10.0.1.1/24, Area 0
Process ID 10, Router ID 10.0.1.1, Network Type POINT_TO_MULTIPOINT, Cost: 64
DoNotAge LSA allowed.
Transmit Delay is 1 sec, State DOWN,
Timer intervals configured, Hello 10, Dead 40, Wait 40, Retransmit 5
```

Example 4-13 shows the output from the **show ip ospf interface** command on Router Hub_Router1 after the OSPF state goes active.

Example 4-13 *Displaying OSPF-Related Interface Information After the OSPF State Goes Active*

```
Hub_Router1#show ip ospf interface serial 0
Serial0 is up, line protocol is up
Internet Address 10.0.1.1/24, Area 0
Process ID 10, Router ID 10.0.1.1, Network Type POINT_TO_MULTIPOINT, Cost: 64
DoNotAge LSA allowed.
Transmit Delay is 1 sec, State POINT_TO_MULTIPOINT,
Timer intervals configured, Hello 10, Dead 40, Wait 40, Retransmit 5
Hello due in 00:00:01
Neighbor Count is 1, Adjacent neighbor count is 1
Adjacent with neighbor 10.0.1.2
Suppress hello for 0 neighbor(s)
```

Example 4-14 shows the output from the **show ip ospf neighbor** command for each of the routers.

Example 4-14 *Displaying OSPF Neighbor Information*

```
Hub_Router1#show ip ospf neighbor
Neighbor ID      Pri      State      Dead Time      Address      Interface
10.0.1.2          1       FULL/ -    00:01:30       10.0.1.1     Serial0
10.0.1.3          1       FULL/ -    00:01:30       10.0.1.1     Serial0
10.0.1.4          1       FULL/ -    00:01:30       10.0.1.1     Serial0
```

The preceding command shows that the state is a full adjacency. There is no DR or BDR, which is normal and expected behavior for an NBMA media. If the state is anything but full, the adjacencies have not been completely built, and there might be a problem with the multicast LSA packets being passed through the interface. To check the state, use the **show ip ospf neighbor** command, as demonstrated in Example 4-15.

Example 4-15 *Checking the OSPF Neighbor State*

```
Spoke_Router2#show ip ospf neighbor
Neighbor ID      Pri      State      Dead Time      Address      Interface
10.0.1.1          1       FULL/ -    00:01:52       10.0.1.2     Serial0
Spoke_Router3#show ip ospf neighbor
Neighbor ID      Pri      State      Dead Time      Address      Interface
10.0.1.1          1       FULL/ -    00:01:52       10.0.1.3     Serial0
Spoke_Router4#show ip ospf neighbor
Neighbor ID      Pri      State      Dead Time      Address      Interface
10.0.1.1          1       FULL/ -    00:01:52       10.0.1.4     Serial0
```

Case Study Conclusion

The objective of this case study was to demonstrate how to use, configure, and troubleshoot an OSPF point-to-multipoint link. You have seen an example and explanation for the configuration, which should help you in both design considerations and implementation. The different **show** and **debug** commands reviewed can assist you in troubleshooting the point-to-multipoint configuration and, by demonstrating the data, should be helpful in troubleshooting more general OSPF problems as well. A summary of the appropriate **show** and **debug** commands for OSPF point-to-multipoint use, configuration, and trouble-shooting is as follows:

- **show ip ospf neighbor**
- **show ip ospf interface**
- **show ip ospf virtual**
- **debug ip ospf packet**
- **debug ip ospf events**
- **show frame-relay map**
- **show frame-relay PVC**

Note that while this case study presents a viable technique for some situations, the commonly accepted optimum solution for OSPF over Frame Relay or other NBMA network is point-to-point subinterfaces.

Case Study: Designing an OSPF Network

This case study uses the technical aspects discussed in the previous two case studies and then follows the design tenets and procedures that were presented in this chapter. Every network is different, having unique requirements and business considerations. Keep in mind that this fictional case study is not designed to be the ultimate answer or the only possible solution; instead, consider it an outline on how to successfully meet design needs.

Terrapin Pharmaceuticals has 25 regional sales offices dispersed throughout the eastern United States. The main corporate headquarters and the data center for Terrapin Pharmaceuticals is located in the Research Triangle Park (RTP) area of North Carolina, adjacent to the Cisco Systems campus. The following list details some of the attributes of the current Terrapin Pharmaceuticals network setup:

- Network connections to these sales offices primarily consist of IBM Systems Network Architecture (SNA) mainframe access over dedicated 56-KB leased lines.
- IBM 3174 cluster controllers connect directly to the 56-kbps modems using Synchronous Data Link Control (SDLC) modules.
- Each branch office also has small Novell NetWare 4.0 networks installed on a stand-alone Ethernet LAN for local file sharing and printing.

- All PCs have Ethernet cards for LAN connectivity and 3270-type coaxial (dumb terminal) cards for IBM host connectivity. This allows employees to access the Ethernet LAN resources and SNA mainframe at the Terrapin Headquarters in North Carolina.

The current network is ready to evolve as Terrapin begins plans to roll out expanded services, and thus a network upgrade is needed. The existing Terrapin Pharmaceuticals network connectivity is shown in Figure 4-36.

Figure 4-36 *Existing Terrapin Pharmaceuticals Network*

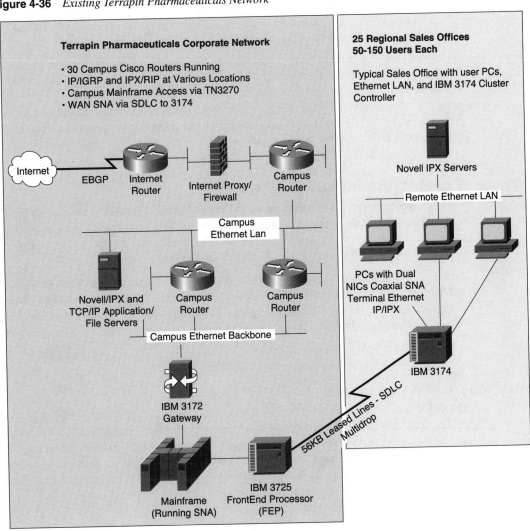

New WAN Requirements

Terrapin wants to remove the leased lines and 3174 cluster controllers and to network its sales offices using Frame Relay. The new WAN must seamlessly integrate into the existing corporate internetwork. Be aware of the following items from a WAN design perspective:

- The existing corporate campus network infrastructure is 10-Mbps Ethernet, with an established router base of 30 Cisco routers of various models.

- The current network protocols in use are IPX/RIP and TCP/IP with Interior Gateway Routing Protocol (IGRP) as the routing protocol.

- The new WAN must implement OSPF as the routing protocol, because that is the future direction of the campus network and TCP/IP elsewhere.

As the network design engineer, you are responsible for the OSPF design and implementation, TCP/IP addressing scheme, and router configuration or implementation of this new Frame Relay network. To construct a scalable OSPF network capable of meeting both the present and future requirements, you must gather the necessary information from the appropriate company decision-makers. This information consists of determining the customer's requirements as discussed in the following section.

Determining the Frame Relay PVC Architecture

The Terrapin corporate engineering group has control of all circuit and transmission architectural decisions, such as the planning and ordering of all data and voice lines, as well as equipment procurement and installation. You are told that the new Frame Relay topology is to be a hub-and-spoke design. Figure 4-37 illustrates this new topology.

Each remote sales office (spoke) is to have a 56-kbps local circuit installed into the Frame Relay Point-of-Presence (POP) with a single 32-kbps committed information rate (CIR) permanent virtual circuit (PVC) provisioned to a T1 circuit. The T1 circuit will be installed on a central hub router at the corporate headquarters and data center facility in the Research Triangle Park, NC. The CIR on the T1 circuit will be 384 kbps.

Determining Multiprotocol Support

The WAN network must support Novell IPX in addition to TCP/IP because Novell IPX is on the customer's LANs. The corporate information services (IS) manager indicates that no native SNA needs to be supported on this network because all the IBM 3174 controllers will be removed after conversion to Frame Relay. Mainframe access is to be accomplished using TCP/IP directly from terminal emulation software running TN3270 (Telnet) at the regional sales offices.

Figure 4-37   *Partially Meshed Hub-and-Spoke PVC Topology*

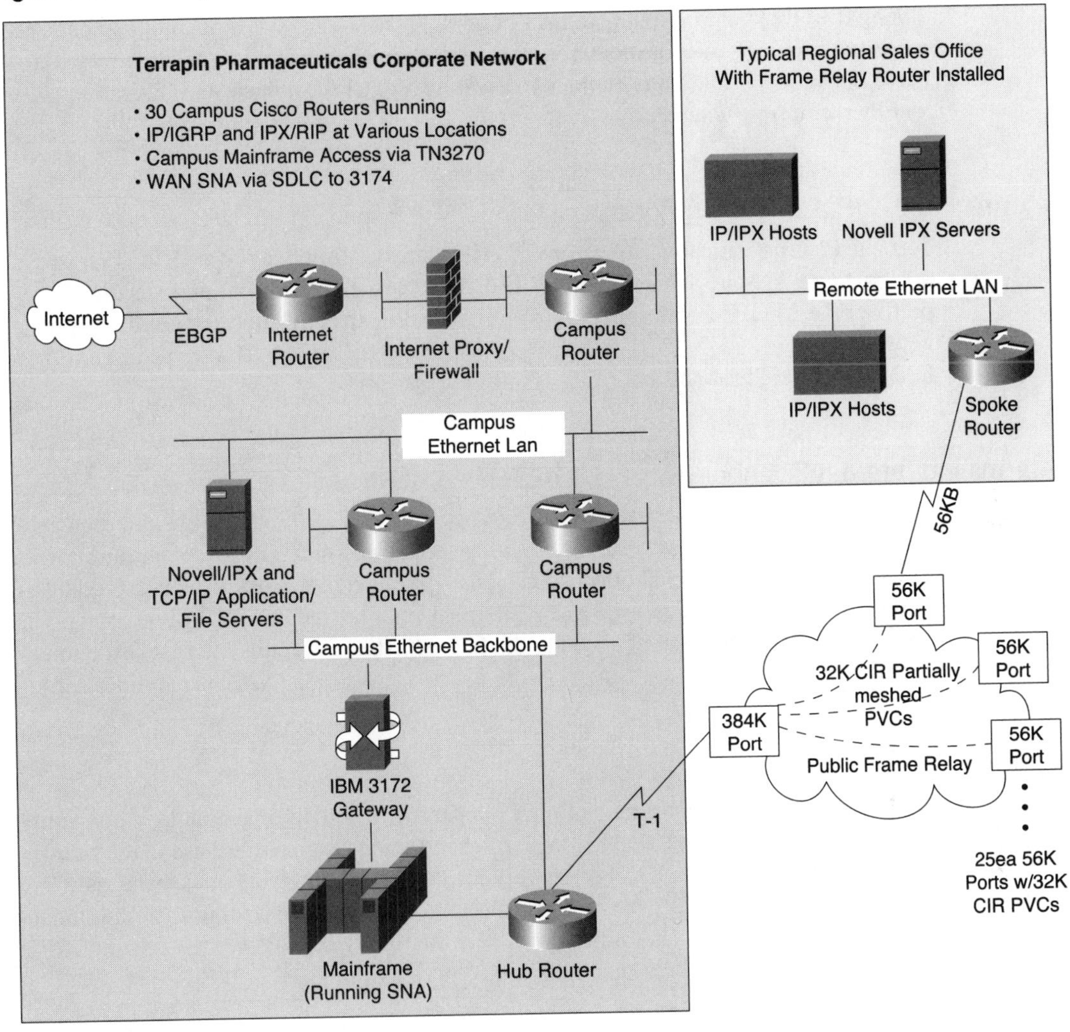

Determining the Traffic Flow

The IS manager tells you that the majority of traffic on this Frame Relay network is to flow from individual branches to corporate headquarters, in the form of PC-to-mainframe communications. Certain sales offices must be able to share and print files on remote Novell servers and printers. All remote sales offices are located in the northeastern and southeastern United States.

Determining the Number of Routers

Twenty-five routers need to be on this Frame Relay network, with a potential 10 percent increase (3 routers) over the next 3 years (one location per year). The existing corporate network has 30 Cisco routers deployed, servicing 50 TCP/IP subnets and IPX networks on an Ethernet infrastructure.

Determining the IP Addressing Scheme

Terrapin Pharmaceuticals is allocating TCP/IP addresses from the private RFC 1918 space. All existing LANs are subnetted out of 172.17.0.0 space using 24-bit prefixes (the /24 prefix or the 255.255.255.0 subnet mask). IP subnets currently allocated on the corporate network are 172.17.1.0–172.17.55.0. You must support 50 to 150 IP hosts per remote sales LAN from unused subnets out of this same address space.

Determining Internet Connectivity

Terrapin Pharmaceuticals currently has Internet connectivity through a firewall segment. The default route or "gateway of last resort" is propagated into IGRP from a central router on the internal network to all other IGRP-speaking routers. A registered Class C address has been obtained and is deployed as the Internet Demilitarized Zone (DMZ) segment. This is the only address that is announced to the Internet from Terrapin's Internet Cisco router because the firewall has proxy and network address translation (NAT) capabilities.

Determining Enterprise Routing Policies

After speaking with the managers of the IS department, you discover that they intend to migrate the network from IGRP to OSPF on the existing Cisco router base in the near future. Therefore, the Frame Relay network must run OSPF and integrate seamlessly into the eventual corporate OSPF network architecture. Because no time frame for the campus OSPF conversion can be determined, your network must integrate into the existing IGRP network upon installation for an undetermined period of time.

Establishing Security Concerns

The company plans to use OSPF password authentication when the network is converted to OSPF from IGRP. The security manager indicates that a single password will be sufficient across all OSPF-speaking router links.

After evaluating all of Terrapin's requirements, Figure 4-38 illustrates the proposed OSPF network design.

Figure 4-38 *Proposed Terrapin Pharmaceuticals OSPF Frame Relay Network*

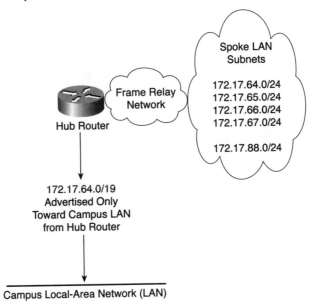

Implementing Your Design

This section discusses some of the design topics to consider within this case study and how to implement them in the network given the preceding discussion. These can be both OSPF-specific topics and other all-encompassing network issues, such as IP addressing.

IP Addressing

You are able to obtain a contiguous block of 32 Class C (/24 or 255.255.255.0 mask) subnets for this network from the IP address manager. The address block is 172.17.64.0/19, which allows clean summarization into the backbone area after the corporate network converts to OSPF. This occurs because all the Frame Relay network LAN and WAN addresses are to be summarized as one route (172.17.64.0/19) after the backbone routers are converted to OSPF, as shown in Figure 4-39.

Figure 4-39 *IP Addressing Scheme*

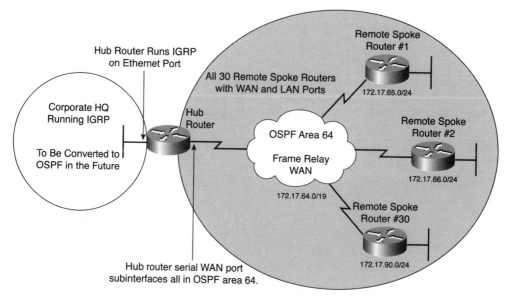

Sales Office LAN Addressing

Given the host requirements of 50–150 nodes per remote LAN and the existing subnetting scheme of /24 (Class C mask) on the corporate network, you should assign /24 subnets of the 172.17.64.0/19 space to each of the 25 spoke LANs. Every LAN is to have addressing space for up to 254 nodes with this subnetting scheme to facilitate future growth requirements at each site. This fulfills the earlier requirement concerning network growth and planning. This masking scheme will be easily understood by the desktop support staff and will work with existing routers running IGRP, which does not carry subnet information in routing updates. Routers require a uniform masking scheme enterprise-wide.

The spoke router LAN subnets on this network are assigned the range 172.17.65.0 to 172.17.90.255.

The hub router attaches to an existing corporate backbone Ethernet segment. The router is assigned an IP address from that subnet, which does not fall within the 172.17.64.0/19 range. You are given 172.17.10.240/24 for the hub router Ethernet IP address.

WAN Addressing

Before the WAN IP address plan can be devised for the routers on this network, you must decide whether to treat the Frame Relay PVCs as a single multipoint subnet or a collection of point-to-point links on the Cisco routers. Remember, multipoint makes the Frame Relay cloud behave as a large LAN subnet, whereas the point-to-point mode models each PVC as a separate WAN point-to-point link in terms of addressing and routing.

Given the additional requirements to support the IPX protocol in an any-to-any fashion, the point-to-point model is the only option. IPX RIP is a distance-vector routing protocol. The protocol has the split-horizon behavior limitation of not sending routing updates out an interface on which they were received. The multipoint model would not facilitate IPX any-to-any because the router would not send IPX routing updates out to any of the remote routers.

To support the point-to-point model, you must define individual router serial port logical interfaces or subinterfaces, each of which represent a discrete IP subnet and IPX network. TCP/IP addressing can accommodate this model most efficiently by assigning each of the subinterfaces with a /30 subnet. IP address space for these WAN links is derived from further subnetting of a single /24 bit subnet (172.17.95.0). The hub router configuration in Example 4-16 provides more details.

Example 4-16 *Hub Router Configuration*

```
RTP_HQ#
interface serial 0
encapsulation frame-relay ietf
frame-relay lmi-type ansi
no ip address
interface serial 0.1 point-to-point
description PVC to Cumberland router
ip address 172.17.95.1 255.255.255.252
ipx network 179500
frame-relay interface-dlci 401 broadcast
interface serial 0.2 point-to-point
description PVC to west LA router
ip address 172.17.95.5 255.255.255.252
ipx network 179504
frame-relay interface-dlci 402 broadcast
```

OSPF Area Organization

Given the relatively small size of this network (less than 50 routers), it is practical to include all routers into one OSPF area. This creates a "portable" OSPF network that can be easily integrated into the enterprise corporate OSPF network after it is converted from IGRP. Because you do not know the future location of the OSPF backbone, you decide to be safe and put all routers in this network into a nonzero area. Putting this network into a nonzero area allows you to avoid a future mass router reconfiguration after the corporate network is converted to OSPF. You assign this nonzero OSPF area an identifier of 64 because this is the base number of the /19 CIDR block, which is a logical representation of the addressing. You decide to use the company's registered BGP AS number of 5775 as the OSPF process ID number for this network, as follows:

```
Router(config)#router ospf 5775
```

The hub router at Terrapin corporate headquarters in RTP, NC is to be the sole ASBR in this network because it must run OSPF and IGRP to support mutual redistribution of routes between the campus and WAN networks.

Because all routers in the Frame Relay network are to be in area 64, no backbone area (area 0) is created; and subsequently, no routers are configured as ABRs or backbone routers at this point. Figure 4-40 shows the OSPF area architecture established for Terrapin.

Figure 4-40 *New OSPF Network Design*

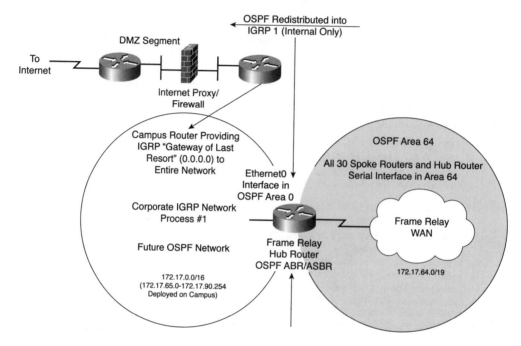

Specifying the OSPF Network Type

Use the default OSPF network type of point-to-point because you are modeling the router Frame Relay cloud as individual point-to-point subinterfaces. The initial step of DR/BDR election is not required because only two routers exist on point-to-point networks, resulting in quick adjacency formation upon startup.

Implementing Authentication

The IS security manager insists that you use OSPF authentication to provide a level of security on this network. You implement simple password authentication by assigning a key of WhatIsTheMatrix to your OSPF area 64. All OSPF routers added to this Frame Relay network need this key configured to form an OSPF adjacency with the hub router. This authentication must be entered under the OSPF process ID and on each serial interface, as shown in Example 4-17.

Example 4-17   *Configuring OSPF Authentication*

```
interface serial 0.1 point-to-point
description PVC to Cumberland router
ip address 172.17.95.1 255.255.255.252
ip ospf authentication-key WhatIsTheMatrix
ipx network 179500
frame-relay interface-dlci 401 broadcast
!
router ospf 5775
area 64 authentication
```

NOTE   If you are planning on implementing OSPF authentication, you should also enable the Cisco password encryption option through the use of the **service password-encryption** command.

Configuring Link Cost

Because all spoke routers have only one PVC provisioned to the hub router, there is no need to configure specific OSPF costs to links in order to engineer traffic patterns in a particular matter. Use the defaults by not assigning costs in router configurations.

Tuning OSPF Timers

Because all routers are Cisco routers and all run the same version of code, you do not need to tune individual Hello, dead, or retransmit timers. Cisco's default WAN values of 10, 40, and 120, respectively, provide fast convergence times and ensure consistency across all routers (see Example 4-18).

Example 4-18   *Relevant Configuration of the Terrapin Headquarters Router*

```
RTP_HQ#
interface Ethernet 0
description LAN connection to campus backbone
ip address 172.17.10.240 255.255.255.0
!
interface serial 0.1 point-to-point
description PVC to Cumberland router
ip address 172.17.95.1 255.255.255.252
ip ospf authentication-key WhatIsTheMatrix
ipx network 179500
frame-relay interface-dlci 401 broadcast
!
interface serial 0.2 point-to-point
description PVC to west LA router
ip address 172.17.95.5 255.255.255.252
ip ospf authentication-key WhatIsTheMatrix
```

continues

Example 4-18 *Relevant Configuration of the Terrapin Headquarters Router (Continued)*

```
ipx network 179504
frame-relay interface-dlci 401 broadcast
!
router ospf 5775
network 172.17.95.0 0.0.0.255 area 64
area 64 authentication
```

Strategizing Route Redistribution

Redistribution of routes between the OSPF and IGRP domains are to be done at the Frame Relay hub router (ASBR) at RTP, NC. To learn of routes from both domains, the hub router must run both an OSPF and an IGRP routing process. Redistribution of routes must address all the issues detailed in the sections that follow.

Campus Routing to Frame Relay WAN

This section discusses how the existing campus routers dynamically learn about the new Frame Relay networks, specifically examining the following issues:

- OSPF route redistribution into IGRP
- Static route aggregation and redistribution into IGRP
- OSPF route aggregation and redistribution into IGRP
- Testing of OSPF route redistribution into IGRP

Redistribution of OSPF routes into the IGRP process causes the hub router to send IGRP advertisements of all /24 subnets known to OSPF. This allows all spoke router LAN subnets to be learned by IGRP routers. This topic is covered in Chapter 6.

Use the **internal** keyword when performing this redistribution on the hub Cisco router to allow only OSPF internal routes to be redistributed into IGRP. This prevents a possible router loop in the future if more routers are installed and are running two-way OSPF/IGRP redistribution. (All the Frame Relay LAN or WAN networks are known as OSPF internal routes because the networks originated from this same domain.)

However, the WAN subnets cannot be redistributed into IGRP this easily because of the classless IP subnetting scheme of /30. IGRP supports only classful subnetting, and routers would ignore all /30 subnets when redistributing. Although this would not affect host-to-host IP connectivity, it might potentially cause a problem with network management tools, subsequently causing routing holes when accessing the router's WAN IP address directly to or from Frame Relay.

Two possible strategies for handling the WAN link advertisements into IGRP are as follows:

- Static route aggregation redistribution into IGRP
- OSPF route aggregation and redistribution into IGRP

With static route aggregation and redistribution into IGRP, you must represent all /30 WAN subnets into an aggregate 24-bit summary and then redistribute them because only /24 prefixed routes are announced into IGRP. Configure a static route on the hub router for 172.17.95.0255.255.255.0, with the next hop as the Null 0 interface (aka the hub router). Now, redistribute static routes into IGRP, and all IGRP routers can route traffic to these WAN links. Control redistribution of routes to just the 172.17.95.0/24 network by defining an access list that allows only redistribution of this route. Defining an access list can prevent future routing problems if additional static routes are added to the hub router, which the campus need not know about through IGRP. The configuration in Example 4-19 demonstrates how to control redistribution of routes.

Example 4-19 *Configuring Route Redistribution*

```
RTP_HQ#
router igrp 10
network 172.17.0.0
passive-interface serial0.1:0.30
default-metric 10000 100 255 1 1500
redistribute ospf 5774 match internal
redistribute static
distribute-list 3 out static

ip route 172.17.95.0 255.255.255.0 null0
access-list 3 permit 172.17.95.0
```

The **passive-interface** command stops IGRP updates from being broadcasted unnecessarily across all WAN PVCs.

The **default-metric** command assigns IGRP metrics to routes known from all other route sources (in this case, static routes) that need redistribution into IGRP.

NOTE	IGRP uses bandwidth, delay, reliability, load, and MTU components to calculate route metrics across specific interfaces. The values 1000010025511500 are defaults for 10-MB Ethernet.

An alternative to static route aggregation of the WAN subnets would be to use OSPF route aggregation and redistribution into IGRP to accomplish this task. This is the preferred solution and the one chosen for this case study because OSPF is already currently being redistributed into the IGRP process to propagate the LAN subnets.

To accomplish OSPF route summarization, the hub router must be configured as an ABR or ASBR because OSPF inter-area summarization can occur only at area boundaries toward the backbone. You can accomplish this by adding the Ethernet interface into OSPF area 0. Now that the hub router (RTP_HQ) is an ABR, you can summarize the WAN subnets as one

/24 network (172.17.95.0/24). This network falls on the established 24-bit boundary and is redistributed into IGRP, understood by all interior IGRP-speaking routers, as shown in Example 4-20.

Example 4-20 *Configuring OSPF Route Summarization*

```
RTP_HQ#
router igrp 10
network 172.17.0.0
passive-interface serial0.1:0.30
default-metric 10000 100 255 1 1500
redistribute ospf 5775 match internal

router ospf 5775
network 172.17.64.0 0.0.0.255 area 64
network 172.17.10.240 0.0.0.0 area 0
area 64 range 172.17.64.0 255.255.255.0
area 64 authentication
```

To test the OSPF route redistribution into IGRP, you can display the routing table of any IGRP internal router, which indicates the success or failure of the redistribution of OSPF routes into IGRP. If problems arise, debugging IGRP transactions on the ASBR (hub) router can provide the necessary troubleshooting information.

CAMPUS-to-WAN Routing

Now that all WAN routes are available on the campus IGRP backbone, it is necessary to advertise routing information to the WAN routers so that all campus subnets can be reached. This can be accomplished in the following ways:

- Redistributing IGRP routes into OSPF
- Generating a default route into OSPF

All known IGRP subnets can be redistributed into OSPF at the hub router with the configuration shown in Example 4-21.

Example 4-21 *Configuring IGRP Subnets to Be Redistributed into OSPF at the Hub Router*

```
RTP_HQ#
router ospf 5775
redistribute igrp 10 metric 100 metric-type 1 subnets
```

The keyword **metric 100** is an arbitrary default metric that is attached to IGRP routes redistributed into OSPF.

The keyword **metric-type 1** makes redistributed IGRP routes external Type 1. This allows the OSPF spoke routers to add individual link costs to calculate OSPF metrics.

The **subnets** keyword is necessary to allow subnets of natural Class B address 172.17.0.0 to be redistributed into OSPF.

When generating a default route into OSPF, because all spoke routers have only a single path (one PVC) out to the WAN, all destinations that are not locally connected would need to traverse that path. A default route (0.0.0.0 0.0.0.0) can be sent from the ASBR hub router in lieu of specific subnet routes. This is the preferred method in this case because the routing tables on remote routers become smaller, and potential routing loops that can result from two-way redistribution can be avoided. Example 4-22 demonstrates this procedure.

Example 4-22 *Changing the Metric*

```
RTP_HQ#
router ospf 5775
default information originate metric 100 metric-type 1
```

Refer to Figure 4-40 to see the implementation of the techniques covered in this section for campus-to-WAN routing. Although the Terrapin OSPF network design was fairly straight-forward in terms of IP addressing and OSPF architecture, the integration into the existing IGRP network presented a number of challenges. Adding OSPF into existing networks running other routing protocols is often a difficult task and must be carefully planned out; otherwise, suboptimal routing or even loops can occur.

CHAPTER 5

Routing Concepts and Configuration

"The ultimate measure of a man is not where he stands in moments of comfort and convenience, but where he stands at times of challenge and controversy."—Martin Luther King, Jr.

This chapter discusses various OSPF features, knobs, and functionality. Many examples in the chapter allow you to later use the material as a reference.

This chapter covers the following topics:

- **OSPF routing concepts**—This section covers the issues surrounding configuration techniques that affect the overall routing of OSPF. Consider how routing can be affected by altering OSPF cost, or the various OSPF timers. Also consider the external routes OSPF uses?

- **Configuring OSPF**—Proper configuration is the essence of every successful use of a routing protocol. This section includes many examples and discussions on how these examples can impact your network. Three configuration steps are shown in the examples: Before, During, and After. These steps take you through the process of configuring OSPF.

OSPF Routing Concepts

OSPF is a dynamic link-state routing protocol that uses a link-state database (LSDB) to build and calculate the shortest path to all known destinations. It is through the use of Dijkstra's SPF algorithm that the information contained within the LSDB is calculated into routes.

The shortest path algorithm by itself is quite complicated, and its inner workings were covered in depth in Chapter 3, "OSPF Communication." It is important to have a good understanding of Dijkstra's SPF algorithm to achieve the maximum benefit of this chapter. The following is a high-level, simplified way of looking at the various steps used by the algorithm. The full SPF recalculation is as follows:

1 Upon initialization or due to a change in routing information, a router generates a link-state advertisement (LSA). This advertisement represents the collection of all link states on that router or information regarding what had changed.

2 All OSPF routers exchange LSAs by means of the OSPF flooding protocol. Each router that receives a link-state update stores the update in its LSDB and then floods the update to other routers.

3 After the link-state database of each router is updated, each router recalculates a shortest-path tree to all destinations. The router uses the shortest path first (Dijkstra) algorithm to calculate the shortest-path tree based on the LSDB. The destinations, their associated costs, and the next hop to reach those destinations form the IP routing table.

4 The shortest path through the network to each destination is calculated using the Dijkstra algorithm. The algorithm places each router at the root of a tree and calculates the shortest path to each destination based on the cumulative cost required to reach that destination. Each router has its own view of the network's topology, even though all the routers build a shortest-path tree using the same LSDB. This view consists of what paths and their associated costs are available to reach destinations throughout the network.

The following sections discuss what is involved in building a shortest-path tree. This root concept is repeated from the perspective of every router in the network.

OSPF Cost

The default value for OSPF metrics (cost) is based on bandwidth. The following characteristics show how OSPF metrics are generated:

- Each link is given a metric value based on its bandwidth.
- The metric for a specific link is the inverse of the bandwidth for that link.
- Link metrics are normalized to give Fast Ethernet a metric of 1.
- The metric for a route is the sum of the metrics for all the links in the route.

OSPF uses cost as the routing metric to determine which paths to a destination are the shortest. The cost is assigned to an interface/link, so consider this value the "toll" to cross that link to get to a destination. Before presenting an example of cost in action, you need to understand how cost is calculated in OSPF. The cost of an interface is inversely proportional to the bandwidth of that interface. In OSPF terminology, the formula for calculating cost is expressed as follows:

Cost = reference bandwidth / interface bandwidth

Reference bandwidth has a default (per RFC) value of 100,000,000 or 10^8, and interface bandwidth varies by interface.

Therefore a higher bandwidth (link speed) indicates a lower OSPF cost. For example, it costs $10^8/10^7 = 10$ to cross a 10-Mbps Ethernet line, and it costs $10^8/1,544,000 = 64$ to cross a T1 line. The formula used by OSPF to calculate the cost is as follows:

Cost = 100,000,000/bandwith (in bps)

Table 5-1 lists the OSPF costs based on link type and speed.

Table 5-1   *OSPF Cost Based on Link Type and Speed*

Link Type	Speed (divide by 10^8)	OSPF Cost
Serial	56,000	1785
DS0	64,000	1562
T1	1,544,000	65
E1	2,048,000	48
Token Ring	4,000,000	25
Ethernet	10,000,000	10
Token Ring	16,000,000	6
T3	44,736,000	3
Fast Ethernet	100,000,000	1
Gigabit Ethernet	1,000,000,000	1
OC-3	155,520,000	1
OC-12	622,080,000	1

Cost in OSPF also has a minimum value of 1. You can see this in the cost associated with Gigabit Ethernet, OC-3, or higher speeds, for example. This introduces a problem in that OSPF cannot differentiate between high-speed links, so suboptimal routing might result; however, there is a solution—but more on that in a minute. First, here's an example of OSPF costs in action.

As previously discussed, the cost or metric associated with an interface in OSPF is an indication of the routing overhead required to send packets across that interface. For example, in Figure 5-1, Headquarters can reach 192.213.11.0 via the Manufacturing router with a cost of 20 (10+10). Headquarters can also reach 222.211.10.0 via the Sales router with a cost of 15 (10+5) or via the Manufacturing router with a cost of 15 (10+5).

Figure 5-1 *Shortest-Path Cost Calculation: How the Network Looks from the Headquarters Router Perspective*

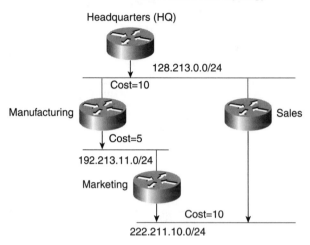

View A: Network Topology

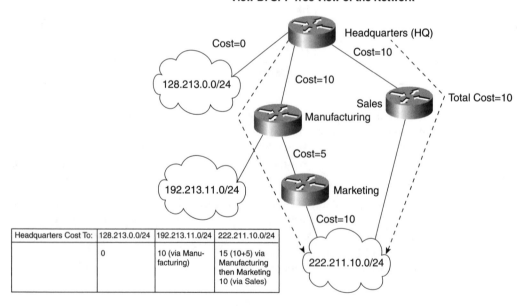

View B: SPF Tree View of the Network

Headquarters Cost To:	128.213.0.0/24	192.213.11.0/24	222.211.10.0/24
	0	10 (via Manufacturing)	15 (10+5) via Manufacturing then Marketing 10 (via Sales)

When route summarization is enabled, OSPF uses the metric of the best route in the summary advertisement.

ip cost Interface Command

In Cisco IOS Software Release 10.2 and earlier, Cisco's implementation of OSPF assigned default costs to a router's interface, regardless of the bandwidth attached to the interface. For example, Cisco IOS Software would give a 64-kbps line and a T1 link the same OSPF cost—clearly a problem. This required the user to override the default value to take advantage of the faster link. Cisco IOS Software gave both the 64-kbps line and the T1 link the same cost because they were both on serial interfaces. Therefore, it is interface type that defined cost, not the actual bandwidth.

This overriding was accomplished through the use of the **ip ospf cost** *value* command, which would be placed on each interface as desired. By default, the cost of an interface is calculated based on the interface's bandwidth, but you can also place a cost on an interface through the use of the **ip ospf cost** *value* interface command. When setting a specific cost on an interface, that cost overrides all other OSPF cost considerations, specifically altering the reference bandwidth.

```
Trinity(config)#int fastethernet0/0
Trinity(config-if)#ip ospf cost ?
  <1-65535>  Cost
Trinity(config-if)#ip ospf cost 10
```

NOTE   Another way to change the OSPF metric is to simply change the interface bandwidth.

Changing the Reference Bandwidth

Another way of altering the way that Cisco IOS Software calculates OSPF cost is by altering the reference bandwidth value used by OSPF in calculating cost. The **auto-cost reference-bandwidth** *ref-bw* command is set under the OSPF routing process. The default reference bandwidth is 100, but this value is in Mbps, so in this case, 100 is really 100,000,000 bps. Keep this in mind when setting the value.

The following configuration caveats are associated with this command:

- The command is applied in OSPF configuration mode and thus globally alters the operation of that OSPF process.

- This command should be deployed throughout each area to keep the costs similar.

Earlier you saw how the current OSPF metric calculations have trouble dealing with high-speed links before the use of the **reference-bandwidth** command. Table 5-2 shows the default interface costs.

Table 5-2   *OSPF Cost Without Reference Bandwidth*

Link Type	Speed (divide by 10^8)	OSPF Cost
Ethernet	10,000,000	10
Fast Ethernet	100,000,000	1
Gigabit Ethernet	1,000,000,000	1

By altering the reference bandwidth for OSPF, you can have the costs adjusted to more clearly differentiate between link speeds.

```
Trinity(config)#router ospf 100
Trinity(config-router)#auto-cost reference-bandwidth ?
  <1-4294967>  The reference bandwidth in terms of Mbits per second
```

The new reference bandwidth, with a value of 100,000,000,000, allows OSPF to more accurately adjust cost, as shown in Table 5-3.

Table 5-3 *OSPF Cost After Changing the Reference*

Link Type	Speed (divide by 10^{10})	OSPF Cost
Ethernet	10,000,000	10000
Fast Ethernet	100,000,000	1000
Gigabit Ethernet	1,000,000,000	100

When using Cisco IOS Software Release 12.0 and later, the **auto-cost reference-bandwidth** is set as shown in the preceding syntax; however, in earlier versions of Cisco IOS Software, the command must be entered with the term **ospf** in the beginning, as follows:

ospf auto-cost reference-bandwidth *ref-bw*

You can see the interface metric through the use of the **show ip ospf interface** command, as demonstrated in Example 5-1.

Example 5-1 *Displaying the Interface Metric*

```
Trinity#show ip ospf interface
FastEthernet0/0 is up, line protocol is up
  Internet Address 192.168.254.71/24, Area 201
  Process ID 100, Router ID 201.0.1.1, Network Type BROADCAST, Cost: 1
  Transmit Delay is 1 sec, State UP, Priority 1
  No designated router on this network
  No backup designated router on this network
  Timer intervals configured, Hello 10, Dead 40, Wait 40, Retransmit 5
FastEthernet0/1 is up, line protocol is up
  Internet Address 201.0.0.1/25, Area 201
  Process ID 100, Router ID 201.0.1.1, Network Type BROADCAST, Cost: 1
  Transmit Delay is 1 sec, State UP, Priority 1
  No designated router on this network
  No backup designated router on this network
  Timer intervals configured, Hello 10, Dead 40, Wait 40, Retransmit 5
Serial0/1.1 is up, line protocol is up
  Internet Address 201.0.1.1/30, Area 201
  Process ID 100, Router ID 201.0.1.1, Network Type POINT_TO_POINT, Cost: 64
  Transmit Delay is 1 sec, State UP,
  Timer intervals configured, Hello 10, Dead 40, Wait 40, Retransmit 5
Trinity#
```

Altering OSPF Convergence

One of the most attractive features of OSPF is its capability to quickly adapt to topology changes. The two essential components to routing convergence are as follows:

- Detecting changes to the network topology
- Rapid recalculation of routes

OSPF uses the following mechanisms to detect topology changes:

- Interface status changes (such as carrier failure on a serial link).
- The failure of OSPF to receive a Hello packet from its neighbor within a specified timing window, called a dead timer. Both of these timers (dead and Hello) in OSPF can be altered from the default if needed.

To summarize, fault detection by OSPF can differ slightly depending on the media type. In general, the failure of a Hello packet can supersede the failure of keepalive packets. The media type affects how OSPF detects a failure as shown in the following list:

- Serial interface faults are detected in one of two ways:
  - Immediate detection of carrier Local Management Interface (LMI) loss, if you are using Frame Relay
  - No keepalives received in three times the time of the keepalive limit (default limit is 10 seconds)
- Token Ring and FDDI are detected immediately.
- Ethernet is detected after the keepalive packet fails three times.

CAUTION   Altering the defaults of OSPF should be done only after careful consideration and testing to ensure that the changes do not adversely affect your network. Also, anytime that the timers are altered on a link, ensure that they are changed on *all* OSPF routers connected to that link for the changes to work properly.

Hello Timers

As discussed in Chapter 3, Hello packets provide the means for OSPF to build adjacencies and monitor (keepalive) adjacent OSPF routers. The Hello packet transmission defaults to being sent every 10 seconds on broadcast networks (Ethernet) and every 30 seconds on nonbroadcast networks (Frame Relay).

You might encounter circumstances that require altering the frequency of OSPF Hello packet transmission. Typically this command is rarely implemented.

```
Trinity(config)#int faastethernet0/0
Trinity(config-if)#ip ospf hello-interval ?
  <1-65535>   Seconds
```

The smaller the Hello interval, the faster the topological changes are detected, but more routing traffic ensues. This value must be the same for all routers and access servers on a specific network.

Dead Timers

After the dead timer expires, the router assumes that the neighbor is down. The dead timer is configured using the **ip ospf dead-interval interface configuration** command; its syntax is as follows:

```
Trinity(config)#int fa0/0
Trinity(config-if)#ip ospf dead-interval ?
  <1-65535>  Seconds
```

The default value of the dead timer is four times the value of the Hello interval, which results in a dead timer default of 40 seconds for broadcast networks and 120 seconds for nonbroadcast networks.

The setting of the dead timer overrides the default value for the dead timer. This value must be the same for all routers and access servers on a specific network.

SPF Timers

You can configure the delay time between when OSPF receives a topology change and when it starts an SPF calculation. You can also configure the hold time between two consecutive SPF calculations. The **timers spf** command was added to prevent routers from computing new routing tables. This is important if you are running OSPF in a very active network that experiences a lot of interface changes or other occurrences that would cause an LSA to be sent, such as a rapidly flapping serial line.

After a failure has been detected in a network, the router that detected the failure floods an LSA packet with the topology change information to all routers to which it is directly connected. The detecting router continues to flood this information until each router to which it is directly connected acknowledges its receipt.

All the routers recalculate their routes using the Dijkstra (or SPF) algorithm. Remember that each router builds its routing table based on the LSDB, and this change alters the contents of that database. Therefore, the router rebuilds its routing tables with itself as the base of the route tree. The time required to run the algorithm depends on a combination of the size of the area and the number of routes in the database.

Cisco IOS Software has the capability to alter the frequency of running the SPF algorithm. Through this alteration, the direct impact on the routing ability of OSPF is affected. Specifically, this command alters the time from when an OSPF router receives a topology change (LSA) and when it starts the SPF calculation process that was discussed in earlier chapters.

By default, OSPF waits 5 seconds after receiving a topology change before the change is processed. This command is configured in router configuration mode as follows:

```
Trinity(config)#router ospf 100
Trinity(config-router)#timers spf ?
  <0-4294967295>  Delay between receiving a change to SPF calculation
Trinity(config-router)#timers spf 5 ?
  <0-4294967295>  Hold time between consecutive SPF calculations
```

In the example, there is a delay time and a hold time. You already know about the delay time. The hold time (second value) allows you to set the amount of time (default value of 10 seconds) that the router waits between SPF calculations. Therefore, when using the default value, if two updates arrive at a Router 7 seconds apart, the router will wait an additional 3 seconds to allow for 10 seconds to pass between SPF consecutive calculations.

Changing these values can allow routing to an alternate route/path more quickly; however, these commands alter the performance of OSPF and can increase the drain on a router's resources.

TIP   OSPF load balances along equal-cost paths; this, in turn, allows for almost immediate convergence. OSPF can also load share across four equal-cost paths by default; however, this can be altered.

This section provided several examples of how to alter the operation of OSPF routing functionality on a Cisco router. Cisco's OSPF implementation enables you to alter certain interface-specific OSPF parameters as needed. You are not required to alter any of these parameters, but some interface parameters must be consistent across all routers in an attached network. Therefore, if you configure any of these parameters, the configurations for all routers on your network must have compatible values. Table 5-4 provides many of the tunable parameters that are covered in this and other chapters.

Table 5-4   *Summary of Tunable OSPF Parameters*

OSPF Command	Function
ip ospf cost *cost*	Explicitly specifies the cost of sending a packet on an OSPF interface
ip ospf hello-interval *seconds*	Specifies the length of time, in seconds, between Hello packets the Cisco IOS Software sends on an OSPF interface
ip ospf dead-interval *seconds*	Sets the number of seconds that a device's Hello packets must not have been seen before its neighbors declare the OSPF router down
timers spf *seconds seconds*	Allows for the altering of when the SPF algorithm is executed and how frequently it is executed

continues

Table 5-4   *Summary of Tunable OSPF Parameters (Continued)*

OSPF Command	Function
ip ospf priority *number*	Sets the priority to help determine the OSPF-designated router for a network (see Chapter 2 "Introduction to OSPF")
ip ospf retransmit-interval *seconds*	Specifies the number of seconds between LSA retransmissions for adjacencies belonging to an OSPF interface (see Chapter 3)
ip ospf transmit-delay *seconds*	Sets the estimated number of seconds it takes to transmit a link-state update packet on an OSPF interface (see Chapter 3)

Setting the Router ID

Chapter 2 discussed the purpose and function of the OSPF router ID (RID) and how it is randomly determined. In certain circumstances, you might not want to use a loopback address or you might want to statically assign the RID in a different way. Fortunately, Cisco IOS Software Release 12.0(1)T or later provides this capability with the **router-id** command, as follows:

```
Trinity(config)#router ospf 100
Trinity(config-router)#router-id ?
  A.B.C.D  OSPF router-id in IP address format
Trinity(config-router)#router-id
```

Remember that each RID must be unique. If you apply a RID, via this command, to a router already running OSPF, the OSPF process or the router must be restarted. You can do this either with a **clear ip ospf process** command or a **reload** command.

```
Trinity#clear ip ospf ?
  <1-4294967295>  Process ID number
  counters        OSPF counters
  process         Reset OSPF process
  redistribution  Clear OSPF route redistribution

Trinity#clear ip ospf process
Reset ALL OSPF processes? [no]: yes
```

NOTE	Another way to restart OSPF is to cut and paste **no router ospf** *xx* followed by **router ospf** ......etc... to restart the process without a reload of the router.

Loopback Interfaces

OSPF uses the highest IP address configured on an active interface as its RID. If the interface associated with this IP address is ever unavailable, or if the address is removed, the OSPF process must recalculate a new RID and flood all its routing information out its interfaces.

The highest IP address on a router would be the largest numerical IP address assigned to an active interface.

If a loopback interface is configured with an IP address, OSPF defaults to using this IP address as its RID, even if other interfaces have higher IP addresses. Because loopback interfaces never go down, greater stability throughout your OSPF network is achieved.

TIP   You cannot tell OSPF to use a particular interface as its RID. It has built-in defaults that force it to accept a loopback interface first and then accept the highest IP address on any interface.

Configuring a Loopback Interface

As previously discussed, the use of a loopback interface forces the selection by OSPF of its RID. The default method to determine the OSPF RID for Cisco routers is loopback interface and then the highest IP address assigned to an interface. The use of a loopback interface enables you to assign the RID. This can be very beneficial. Because a loopback interface is not a physical interface, like Ethernet, you must create it.

You can configure a loopback interface by executing the **interface loopback 0** command in the router configuration mode. Example 5-2 demonstrates the process.

Example 5-2   *Configuring a Loopback Interface*

```
Trinity# config terminal
Enter configuration commands, one per line. End with CNTL/Z.
Trinity(config)# interface loopback 0
Trinity(config-if)# ip address 10.251.11.1 255.255.255.255
Trinity(config-if)# description Configured to be OSPF Router ID
```

Routing Loopback Interfaces

Loopback interfaces have a unique characteristic about them when used in OSPF. In accordance with RFC 2328 (page 129, third bullet), loopback interfaces are advertised as /32 host routes. This is an interesting aspect of what you find in a routing table. Consider the routing table in Example 5-3, where the /32 is preserved throughout the network, regardless of the mask that is assigned to the loopback interfaces.

Example 5-3   *Loopback Advertised in a Routing Table as a /32*

```
HAL9000#show ip route
Codes: C - connected, S - static, I - IGRP, R - RIP, M - mobile, B - BGP
       D - EIGRP, EX - EIGRP external, O - OSPF, IA - OSPF inter area
       N1 - OSPF NSSA external type 1, N2 - OSPF NSSA external type 2
       E1 - OSPF external type 1, E2 - OSPF external type 2, E - EGP
       i - IS-IS, L1 - IS-IS level-1, L2 - IS-IS level-2, * - candidate default
       U - per-user static route, o - ODR

Gateway of last resort is 192.168.254.1 to network 0.0.0.0
```

continues

Example 5-3   *Loopback Advertised in a Routing Table as a /32 (Continued)*

```
      51.0.0.0/32 is subnetted, 5 subnets
O IA    51.0.16.1 [110/77] via 192.168.254.71, 00:00:09, Ethernet0
O IA    51.0.17.1 [110/77] via 192.168.254.71, 00:00:09, Ethernet0
O IA    51.0.18.1 [110/77] via 192.168.254.71, 00:00:09, Ethernet0
O IA    51.0.19.1 [110/77] via 192.168.254.71, 00:00:09, Ethernet0
O IA    51.0.20.1 [110/77] via 192.168.254.71, 00:00:09, Ethernet0
      1.0.0.0/32 is subnetted, 1 subnets
O        1.1.1.1 [110/11] via 192.168.254.71, 00:00:10, Ethernet0
      100.0.0.0/32 is subnetted, 5 subnets
O        100.0.20.1 [110/75] via 192.168.254.71, 00:00:10, Ethernet0
O        100.0.21.1 [110/75] via 192.168.254.71, 00:00:10, Ethernet0
O        100.0.22.1 [110/75] via 192.168.254.71, 00:00:10, Ethernet0
O        100.0.23.1 [110/75] via 192.168.254.71, 00:00:10, Ethernet0
O        100.0.24.1 [110/75] via 192.168.254.71, 00:00:10, Ethernet0
```

Configuring the Designated Router

As discussed in Chapter 4, "Design Fundamentals," some definite benefits are to be gained by selecting the router within the network that should be the designated router (DR) as well as the backup designated router (BDR). Here, you want to choose a specific router to be the DR by manually assigning the priority of a router and thus affecting the DR election process. Recall that the election process first compares priority (default of 1), where the highest value wins (in the case of a tie, the highest RID wins). If the priority is set to 0, the router is ineligible to become the DR:

```
interface ethernet 0
 ip ospf priority 4
```

Route Types

As discussed in Chapter 2, OSPF has four types of routes that it can handle and report to you. This section looks at these route types in depth so that you can understand the role they play in an OSPF routed network. The four types of OSPF routes are as follows:

- **Intra-area**—Routes to networks within an area, cost based on link.

- **Inter-area**—Routes to networks in another area, cost based on link.

- **E1**—Routes to networks outside an OSPF AS that have total cost to them calculated as follows: cost = external + internal metrics per link.

- **E2**—Routes to networks outside the OSPF AS that have their cost set to the external metric. This cost never changes. E2 routes are also the default type for external OSPF routes.

Knowing the route type has an obvious importance; however, it is equally important to know how route types are identified in an IP routing table. Every routing table has some header information, as demonstrated in Example 5-4, and in this header information are the codes used in the routing table to identify route types.

Example 5-4   *Using Routing Table Header Information to Identify Route Type*

```
HAL9000#show ip route
Codes: C - connected, S - static, I - IGRP, R - RIP, M - mobile, B - BGP
       D - EIGRP, EX - EIGRP external, O - OSPF, IA - OSPF inter area
       N1 - OSPF NSSA external type 1, N2 - OSPF NSSA external type 2
       E1 - OSPF external type 1, E2 - OSPF external type 2, E - EGP
       i - IS-IS, L1 - IS-IS level-1, L2 - IS-IS level-2, * - candidate default
       U - per-user static route, o - ODR
```

Routes that originate from other routing protocols (or different OSPF processes) and that are injected into OSPF via redistribution are called *external routes*. There are two forms of external metrics: Type 1 (E1) and Type 2 (E2). These routes are represented by O E1 or O E2 in the IP routing table. They are examined after the router is done building its internal routing table. After the routes are examined, they are flooded throughout the autonomous system (AS), unaltered. External information can come from a variety of sources, such as another routing protocol.

Figure 5-2 demonstrates the concepts of cost for the external routes.

When OSPF has multiple routes to the same destination network, OSPF uses the following order of preference to route to the destination network:

1 Intra-area

2 Inter-area

3 E1

4 E2

E1 metrics result in routes adding the internal OSPF metric to the external route metric; they are also expressed in the same terms as an OSPF link-state metric. The internal OSPF metric is the total cost of reaching the external destination, including whatever internal OSPF network costs are incurred to get there. These costs are calculated by the router that wants to reach the external route.

E2 metrics do not add the internal OSPF metric to the cost of external routes; they are also the default type used by OSPF. The E1 metric is generally preferred. The use of E2 metrics assumes that you are routing between autonomous systems; therefore, the cost is considered greater than any internal metrics. This eliminates the need to add the internal OSPF metrics. Figure 5-2 shows a comparison of the two metrics.

Figure 5-2 *External Route Cost Calculation*

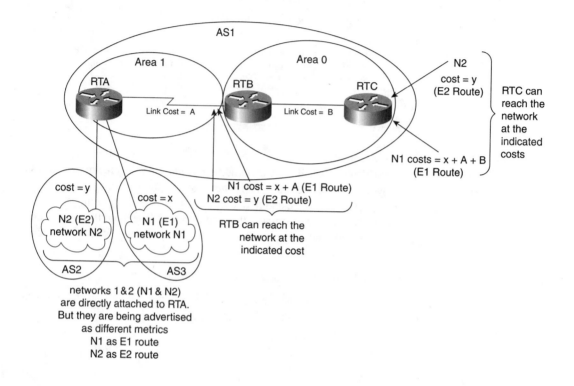

Which Is Better—E1 or E2 Routes?

This section provides some guidelines on what type of OSPF external route is best used in a given set of circumstances. This information is crucial; however, it is also controversial because the "depends factor" is strong in these discussions because although a statement might be the rule for Network A, it depends if that will hold true for Network B.

NOTE   I polled many people when writing this section to get different viewpoints about external routes, and it is amazing the strong positions people have on this issue. Keep this in mind as you read on and as you consider what you want to accomplish in your network.

When to Use E1 Routes

Even though an external Type 1 route, commonly referred to as E1 in OSPF, is not the default, it is in fact usually preferred. This preference comes from the root belief that OSPF as a routing protocol, which uses cost as it metric, should never disregard cost from making routing decisions. Therefore, E1 routes are preferred by many because they take into account the cost of the links to the external network wherever you are in the OSPF AS. As a result, many people configure OSPF to alter all external routes by changing them all to E1s, thereby ensuring that cost is always considered. In addition to this blanket belief, consider using E1 routes under the following circumstances:

- Your network has multiple exit points from your OSPF AS to the same external network (for example, multiple connections to the Internet). The use of E1 routes would allow routers to choose the shortest path to the Internet for them.

- Your network has multiple paths to a single external network from many destinations, for example, a large and extremely meshed network. Again, the E1 route type allows routers to determine the shortest path to the destination.

When to Use E2 Routes

Some defining characteristics and needs of E2 routes are as follows:

- The default route generated by a stub Area Broder Router (ABR) is an E2 route into the stub area because a stub network is usually simple in its topology—there is just one way out.

- Your network is not very large, and thus you do not need E1 routes (yet).

The conversion of the default E2 route types into E1 routes requires redistribution to occur (a concept covered in Chapter 6, "Redistribution"). However, it is important to discuss these network types here because you will see them more frequently as you progress through more advanced OSPF topics.

Controlling Inter-Area Traffic

When an area has only a single ABR (a simple stub area), all traffic that does not belong in the area is sent to the ABR. In areas that have multiple ABRs, the following choices are available for traffic that needs to leave the area:

- Use the ABR closest to the originator of the traffic. This results in traffic leaving the area as soon as possible.

- Use the ABR closest to the destination of the traffic. This results in traffic leaving the area as late as possible. However, if the ABRs are only injecting a default route, the traffic goes to the ABR that is closest to the source of the traffic.

Generally, the former behavior is more desirable because the backbone typically has higher bandwidth lines available. Also, the faster packets get there, the quicker they can be routed to their destination.

However, if you want the traffic to use the ABR that is nearest the destination (so that traffic leaves the area as late as possible), the ABRs should inject route summaries into the area instead of just injecting the default route.

Most network designers prefer to avoid asymmetric routing (that is, using a different path for packets that are going from A to B than for those packets that are going from B to A). It is important to understand how routing occurs between areas so that you can avoid asymmetric routing if possible. Ideally, you want symmetric routing, which occurs when traffic that exits a network from a given point returns via that same point, as demonstrated in Figure 5-3.

Figure 5-3   *Symmetric Routing*

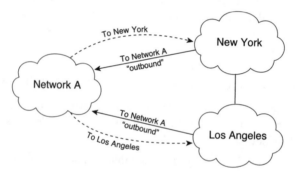

Outbound and inbound routing paths are identical.

Routes that are generated from within an area (the destination belongs to the area) are called *intra-area routes*. The letter O in the IP routing table represents these routes. Routes that originate from other areas are called *inter-area routes* or *summary routes*. The notation for these routes is **O IA** in the IP routing table.

Configuring OSPF

OSPF is a straightforward protocol to get running at a basic level in Cisco routers. This section covers the process needed to activate OSPF and then examines how some of OSPF's advanced features can be configured and properly deployed on the different types of OSPF functional routers.

OSPF typically requires coordination among many internal routers, ABRs (routers connected to multiple areas), and Autonomous System Boundary Routers (ASBRs). At a minimum, OSPF-based routers, or access servers, can be configured with all default parameter values, no authentication, and interfaces assigned to areas. If you intend to customize your environment, you must ensure coordinated configurations of all routers.

To configure OSPF, complete the tasks in the following sections. Activating OSPF is mandatory. The other tasks are optional, but they might be required for your network.

Activating OSPF

As with other routing protocols, the enabling of OSPF on Cisco routers requires taking the following preliminary steps before the process begins:

1   Determine the process ID under which OSPF is to run within your network. This process ID must be different from any other OSPF network to which you might be connecting. The possible range for an OSPF process ID is 1–65535.

2   Specify the range of addresses that are to be associated with the OSPF routing process. This is part of one command that must also include the area with which this range of addresses is to be associated.

Now that you have determined how the OSPF process should be configured, you need to start configuring the router. Perform the following tasks, starting in global configuration mode:

Step 1   Enable OSPF routing, which places you in router configuration mode. You do this with the following command:

```
HAL9000(config)#router ospf ?
  <1-65535>  Process ID
```

Step 2   Define the interface or interfaces (via the **network** command) on which you want to OSPF run, and define the area ID for that interface. You do this with the following command:

```
HAL9000(config)#router ospf 100
HAL9000(config-router)#network ?
  A.B.C.D  Network number

HAL9000(config-router)#network 10.10.10.0 0.0.0.255 area 10
```

In this example, using the **network** command with a 24-bit inverse mask places all interfaces within that range assigned to the router in area 10. The following section discusses the **network** command in more detail. If this were an internal OSPF router, the process for configuring it for OSPF would now be complete. There are a few subtle differences when configuring the different types of OSPF routers, as described in the next few sections.

network Command

The **network** command activates OSPF per interface; however, you can define this as a network entry or as a host address—the choice is yours. Specifically, that means a mask of 255.255.255.0 (/24), expressed in the OSPF **network** command as 0.0.0.255, activates all interfaces within that range for OSPF to use. With this command, the mask entry uses the wildcard (inverse) style mask.

Some people prefer to keep configuration as simple, as follows:

```
network 10.10.10.1 0.0.0.0 area 0
```

This command tells the router that only the interface address 10.10.10.1 is in area 0. That is simpler because it keeps the mask 0.0.0.0, and you just specify each interface address. Of course, this involves a lot more typing on a router with many interfaces. To avoid repetitive typing and configure smarter rather that harder, consider the following example.

Suppose that you have a large router with many interfaces in OSPF. This might be a core router, and you want to place all the interfaces into OSPF area 0 with one command. All router interfaces fall within the range 10.10.31.0 to 10.10.95.0, so you want to place the entire range into OSPF. Use the following commands:

```
HAL9000(config)#router ospf 100
HAL9000(config-router)#network 10.10.0.0 0.0.31.255 area 0
```

This syntax accomplishes the result you need; however, to understand why, review the binary form to see how this command is interpreted by the router:

```
10.10.  0.  0        10.10.  64.  0
 0.  0. 31.255        0.  0. 31.255
---------------       ---------------
10.10. 31.255        10.10. 95.255
```

In this example, all router interfaces in the range 131.108.64.0 to 131.108.95.255 should be in area 0.

When you experiment with OSPF, there can be order sensitivity to the commands. The problem seems to be that if you configure network..., then no network ..., then network <something else>, the router might not re-initialize OSPF on the relevant interfaces—so it doesn't send Hellos and doesn't form adjacencies. The solution is to either save your configuration and reboot the router (drastic) or to use a Windows PC cut-and-paste operation to copy the **router ospf** part of the config, do **no router ospf 1** to stop OSPF, and then paste the correct config back in. Who said Windows had no redeeming value!

NOTE   **shut/no shut** on an interface fixes this as well but remember to let it be shut down long enough for all the OSPF timers to expire.

OSPF Router Considerations

The process for activating OSPF on any type of router begins with the **network** command. However, a variety of OSPF router types exist that have some unique configuration considerations. The sections that follow discuss these considerations. Before starting the OSPF routing process, consider a few general items about how OSPF is going to be configured to operate in your network. These considerations are as follows:

1   Decide what OSPF routing process ID number you want to assign within your network. One method is to use the AS number that you have been given (if you do not have one, pick a number that is easy to type quickly).

2   Decide if you want OSPF to determine which router becomes the DR and BDR or whether you should use the **priority** command and make that determination. A router should not be a DR for more than one network.

3   Are you going to use a loopback interface?

4   Turn on the OSPF routing process with the **router ospf process-id** command, as described in the previous section.

5   Assign the appropriate network statements to the OSPF routing process with the correct area ID, for example:

```
router ospf 109
network 130.10.8.0 0.0.0.255 area 0
network 172.25.64.0 0.0.0.255 area 1
```

ABR Considerations

Configuring an ABR for OSPF is essentially the same as described in the preceding section with a few minor considerations that reflect the role this type of OSPF router plays within a network. These considerations are as follows:

1   Is one of the areas that the ABR will connect to a stub area? If so, execute the **area** *area-id* **stub** command, which defines an OSPF area as stub area.

2   You might need to enter the **area** *area-id* *default-cost* command, which assigns a specific cost. You review this command and its effects later in this chapter.

3   Add the **area range** command so that the networks within each area can be properly summarized, for example:

```
router ospf 109
network 130.10.8.0 0.0.0.255 area 0
```

```
network 172.25.64.0 0.0.0.255 area 1
area 1 range 130.10.8.0 255.255.255.0
```

4 Determine if you are going to use optional OSPF parameters. You do not need to decide now to use any of these options, but be aware that they can help your OSPF network. Although many of these options have not yet been discussed, the following list highlights the more significant optional parameters in command syntax:

```
area area-id authentication
area area-id authentication message-digest
ip ospf authentication-key
ip ospf hello-interval
ip ospf dead-interval
timers spf spf-delay spf-holdtime
```

You can use the **show ip ospf border-routers** command to see the ABRs within your network. This command is explained in more detail in Chapter 8, "Managing and Securing OSPF Networks."

ASBR Considerations

The process of configuring an Autonomous System Boundary Router (ASBR) for OSPF is similar to how you would configure an ABR. Use the following steps:

Step 1 You should already know what the OSPF process ID is, whether you need a loopback interface, and which optional OSPF parameters you are going to be using.

Step 2 Turn on the OSPF routing process, as previously described in the "Activating OSPF." Again, use the **router ospf** *process-id* command.

Step 3 Assign the appropriate network statements to the OSPF routing process with the correct area ID, for example:

```
router ospf 109
  network 130.10.8.0 0.0.0.255 area 0
  network 172.25.64.0 0.0.0.255 area 1
```

Step 4 Add the **area range** command so that the networks within each area can be properly summarized. This only works if the ASBR is also an ABR. The use of **summary-address** statements would be appropriate here, as they are placed on ASBRs, for example:

```
router ospf 109
  network 130.10.2.0 0.0.0.255 area 0
  network 130.10.3.0 0.0.0.255 area 0
  network 130.10.4.0 0.0.0.255 area 0
  network 172.25.64.0 0.0.0.255 area 1
  area 1 range 130.10.1.0 255.255.252.0
```

The **area range** command is covered later in this chapter, but notice that the network mask is normal as opposed to being an inverse mask. (Inverse masks are more commonly used in OSPF.)

Step 5   Configure the redistribution process between your OSPF AS and the external AS to which the ASBR is providing connectivity, for example:

```
router ospf 109
redistribute rip subnets metric-type 1 metric 12
network 130.10.8.0 0.0.0.255 area 0
network 172.25.64.0 0.0.0.255 area 1
area 1 range 130.10.8.0 255.255.255.0
router rip
network 128.130.0.0
passive interface s 0
default-metric 5
```

You can use the **show ip ospf border-routers** command to see the area border routers within your network. This command is explained in more detail in Chapter 8.

Backbone Router Considerations

The process of configuring an OSPF backbone router for OSPF is similar to how you would configure an ABR. Use the following steps:

Step 1   You should already know what the OSPF process ID, whether you need a loopback interface, and which optional OSPF parameters you are going to use.

Step 2   Turn on the OSPF routing process, as previously described in "Activating OSPF." Again, you use the **router ospf process-id** command.

Step 3   Assign the appropriate network statements to the OSPF routing process with the correct area ID, for example:

```
router ospf 109
network 130.10.8.0 0.0.0.255 area 0
network 172.25.64.0 0.0.0.255 area 0
```

   5   Add the **area range** command if the backbone router is also acting as an ABR so that the networks within each area can be properly summarized, for example:

```
router ospf 109
 network 130.10.2.0 0.0.0.255 area 0
 network 130.10.3.0 0.0.0.255 area 0
 network 130.10.4.0 0.0.0.255 area 0
 network 172.25.64.0 0.0.0.255 area 0
 area 1 range 130.10.1.0 255.255.252.0
```

Different Network Types and OSPF

There are three distinct classifications of physical network media that OSPF can differentiate between. Each of these network types requires a slightly different configuration to optimize the performance of OSPF. Configuring your OSPF network type is one of the most prominent features of OSPF. The strength of OSPF lies in its flexibility to meet certain network design requirements. The following sections show you how to customize OSPF to your network's design.

Cisco IOS Software allows five main network types to be configured, as displayed in Table 5-5. Each network type has predefined *n* timers, such as Hello/dead.

Table 5-5   *OSPF over NBMA Using Cisco IOS Software*

Method	Description
Point-to-point nonbroadcast	Typically used for Frame Relay interfaces
Point-to-point	Default mode for subinterfaces
Point-to-multipoint	Used for multiple destinations
Nonbroadcast	NBMA mode
Broadcast	Used in Ethernet and broadcast environments where the election of DR/BDR takes place

This section covers the methods and procedures needed to configure OSPF over different physical networks. In this case, consider the following four network types:

- Broadcast networks (Ethernet, Token Ring, FDDI)
- Nonbroadcast multiaccess networks (Switched Multimegabit Data Service [SMDS], Frame Relay, X.25, ATM)
- Point-to-multipoint networks (ATM and Frame Relay)
- Point-to-point networks (HDLC, PPP)

Configuring the Network Type

OSPF is highly adaptable. Consider its capability to accommodate either broadcast or nonbroadcast multiaccess (NBMA) network types. OSPF responds accordingly by altering its operation to reflect the configuration that you have given it.

OSPF attempts to sense the physical media and defaults to the appropriate behavior for that media. In the event that you do not want this default behavior, you can change it by using the following command:

```
HAL9000(config-if)#ip ospf network ?
  broadcast            Specify OSPF broadcast multi-access network
  non-broadcast        Specify OSPF NBMA network
  point-to-multipoint  Specify OSPF point-to-multipoint network
  point-to-point       Specify OSPF point-to-point network
```

This command alters the behavior of OSPF and how adjacencies are built because the underlying requirement is based on the network type.

Using this feature, you can configure broadcast networks as NBMA networks when, for example, you have routers in your network that do not support multicast addressing. You also can configure NBMA networks to simulate a broadcast network. This feature saves you from having to configure neighbors.

Why would it be beneficial not to have a neighbor? Assume, for example, that you have a point-to-point network. By not using neighbors, you can reduce router memory and processor usage because there is only one other router to talk with. Having a simple adjacency in this scenario works well.

Keep in mind that this is a book on OSPF that details the granular level of control that OSPF affords you and how OSPF's adaptability lends itself to disparate media types. Specifically consider the following as examples:

- You have a pair of directly connected routers via their physical interfaces (with no subinterfaces). Using the **frame-relay map** commands you could make the link broadcast-capable; however, use the **ip ospf network point-to-point** command in this case. OSPF would view this as an NBMA network and form an adjacency with the opposite router.

- You can use a point-to-point subinterface and configure Frame Relay via the **interface dlci** command. OSPF understands this is a point-to-point link because of the subinterface type and forms an adjacency with the opposite router.

The value of having this capability becomes clear when you examine the relationship made between configuring OSPF in a myriad of environments and how those configuration choices affect OSPF's behavior as well as its capability to function when forming adjacencies. The **ip ospf network** *type* command allows you to force OSPF to behave in a manner that ignores all other concerns.

Broadcast Networks

Set an interface to operate in broadcast network mode when the network is a fully meshed. For this command to be properly applied, all routers must have virtual circuits (links) to all other routers in the network. When this command is applied to an interface, OSPF elects a DR/BDR, builds an adjacency with the DR, and builds neighbor relationships with all other OSPF routers in the network. Ethernet interfaces are considered to be broadcast-mode network interfaces by OSPF's default operation. Consider the network example shown in Figure 5-4.

Figure 5-4 *Broadcast Network Type*

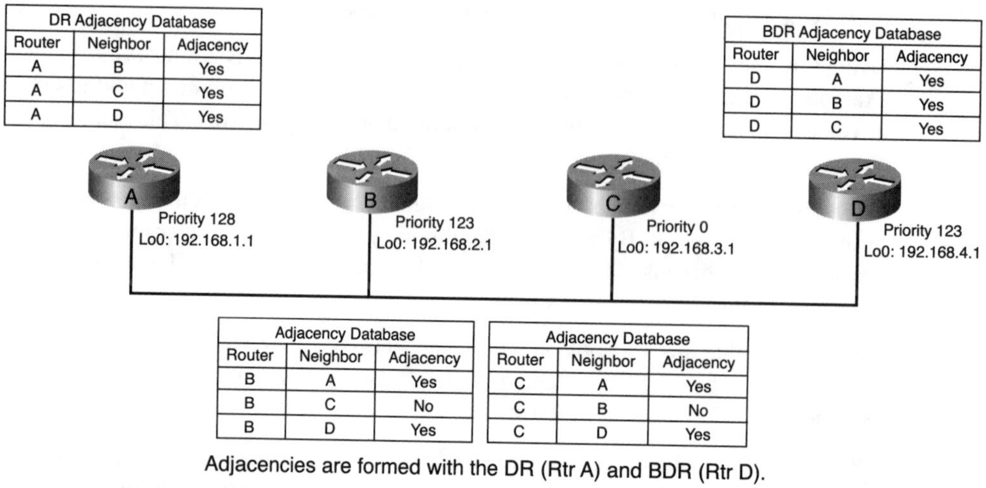

DR Adjacency Database		
Router	Neighbor	Adjacency
A	B	Yes
A	C	Yes
A	D	Yes

BDR Adjacency Database		
Router	Neighbor	Adjacency
D	A	Yes
D	B	Yes
D	C	Yes

A — Priority 128 / Lo0: 192.168.1.1

B — Priority 123 / Lo0: 192.168.2.1

C — Priority 0 / Lo0: 192.168.3.1

D — Priority 123 / Lo0: 192.168.4.1

Adjacency Database		
Router	Neighbor	Adjacency
B	A	Yes
B	C	No
B	D	Yes

Adjacency Database		
Router	Neighbor	Adjacency
C	A	Yes
C	B	No
C	D	Yes

Adjacencies are formed with the DR (Rtr A) and BDR (Rtr D).

The charts in this figure show how the adjacencies are formed and developed within the broadcast network shown.

Nonbroadcast Networks

When configuring an interface as nonbroadcast, OSPF cannot perform multicasting on that link. Lack of multicast functionality impacts OSPF's operation because OSPF Hellos cannot be properly transmitted. Hellos are "multicasted" to different well-known OSPF multicast addresses. If OSPF cannot send these multicast Hello packets, other OSPF routers do not receive the Hello packets, causing communication problems.

Point-to-point Frame Relay interfaces and multipoint subinterfaces are recognized as nonbroadcast by default. The following alternatives allow you to make OSPF operate when a nonbroadcast type network is encountered:

- Change the network type of OSPF. This is the easiest change but is not possible in every instance.

- Manually define the neighbors. This forces adjacencies that are created by sending unicast Hello packets.

- Alter the behavior of the Layer 2 protocol.

Frame Relay Layer 2 connectivity is provided via Inverse Address Resolution Protocol (IARP) or by the use of the **frame-relay map** command. Cisco IOS Software-specific Frame Relay commands are outside of the scope of this book. Consider the example shown in Figure 5-5.

Figure 5-5   *Nonbroadcast Network Type*

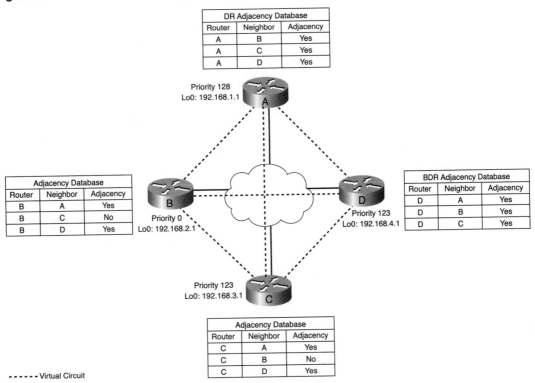

In this network type, the routers are fully meshed by virtual circuits;
adjacencies are formed with DR & BDR (Routers A & D).

The charts in this figure show how the adjacencies are formed and developed within the
nonbroadcast network shown.

Point-to-Multipoint Networks

OSPF point-to-multipoint interfaces are defined as numbered point-to-point subinterfaces,
with the router having one or more OSPF neighbors. Configuring an interface as a point-to-
multipoint OSPF assumes a fully meshed network (virtual circuits from every router to
every router). OSPF creates multiple host routes, and broadcasts must be manually enabled.
This concept is demonstrated later in this section through examples.

An OSPF point-to-multipoint network has the following benefits compared to nonbroadcast
multiaccess and point-to-point networks:

- Point-to-multipoint is easier to configure because it requires no configuration of neighbor commands. Point-to-multipoint connections consume only one IP subnet and require no designated router election process.

- Point-to-multipoint has a fully or partial meshed topology.

- Point-to-multipoint can be more reliable in fully meshed networks because it maintains connectivity in case of virtual circuit failure.

- When you configure the OSPF network type as point-to-multipoint, routing between two routers not directly connected goes through the router (hub) that has virtual circuits to both routers (spokes).

The value of this capability is made clear when you examine the relationship made between configuring OSPF in a myriad of environments and how those configuration choices affect OSPF's behavior as well as its capability to function when forming adjacencies.

When adjacencies are formed, LSAs are used to keep the LSDBs synchronized, and each router is responsible for ensuring this occurs because no DR is present. Consider the example shown in Figure 5-6.

Figure 5-6   *Point-to-Multipoint Network Type*

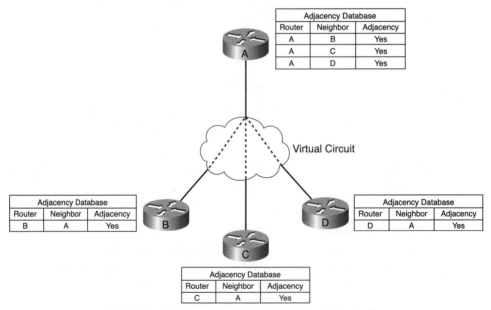

Each virtual circuit and associated subinterface is treated as a
point-to-point link but all on same subnet. No DR or BDR needed.

The charts in this figure show how the adjacencies are formed and developed within the point-to-multipoint network shown.

Point-to-Multipoint Configuration Example

Figure 5-7 shows an example of OSPF configuration in a point-to-multipoint networking environment.

Figure 5-7   *Point-to-Multipoint Configuration Example*

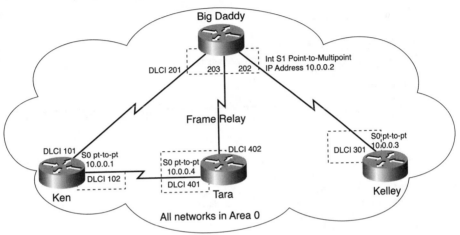

TIP   No DRs or BDRs are on a point-to-multipoint subnet. The OSPF Hello protocol finds other OSPF routers and builds neighbor relationships.

Referring to the setup in Figure 5-7 and for demonstration purposes, assume the following scenario:

- Router BigDaddy uses DLCI 201 to communicate with Router Ken, DLCI 202 to Router Kelley, and DLCI 203 to Router Tara.
- Router Ken uses DLCI 101 to communicate with BigDaddy and DLCI 102 to communicate with Tara.
- Router Tara communicates with Ken using DLCI 401 and BigDaddy using DLCI 402.
- Router Kelley communicates with BigDaddy using DLCI 301.

In this example, all interfaces are point-to-multipoint, and Frame Relay map statements are used with the **broadcast** keyword. Given this setup, Example 5-5 shows the configurations for Routers BigDaddy, Ken, Tara, and Kelley.

Example 5-5 *Router Configuration in a Point-to-Multipoint Network*

```
! BigDaddy's Configuration
hostname BigDaddy
!
interface serial 1
ip address 10.0.0.2 255.0.0.0
ip ospf network point-to-multipoint
encapsulation frame-relay
frame-relay map ip 10.0.0.1 201 broadcast
frame-relay map ip 10.0.0.3 202 broadcast
frame-relay map ip 10.0.0.4 203 broadcast
!
router ospf 1
network 10.0.0.0 0.0.0.255 area 0
! Ken's Configuration
hostname Ken
!
interface serial 0
ip address 10.0.0.1 255.0.0.0
ip ospf network point-to-multipoint
encapsulation frame-relay
frame-relay map ip 10.0.0.2 101 broadcast
frame-relay map ip 10.0.0.4 102 broadcast
!
router ospf 1
network 10.0.0.0 0.0.0.255 area 0
! Tara's Configuration
hostname Tara
!
interface serial 3
ip address 10.0.0.4 255.0.0.0
ip ospf network point-to-multipoint
encapsulation frame-relay
clockrate 1000000
frame-relay map ip 10.0.0.1 401 broadcast
frame-relay map ip 10.0.0.2 402 broadcast
!
router ospf 1
network 10.0.0.0 0.0.0.255 area 0
! Kelley's Configuration
hostname Kelley
!
interface serial 2
ip address 10.0.0.3 255.0.0.0
ip ospf network point-to-multipoint
encapsulation frame-relay
clockrate 2000000
frame-relay map ip 10.0.0.2 301 broadcast
!
router ospf 1
network 10.0.0.0 0.0.0.255 area 0
```

Point-to-Point Networks

When you configure an interface as an OSPF point-to-point network type, this command understands that the only other OSPF-speaking router on that interface is directly connected. Therefore, there is no need to configure neighbors or alter cost as discussed with previous network types. Consider the example shown in Figure 5-8, which presents a network that is fully meshed but via individual point-to-point interfaces. Therefore, Router A forms individual adjacencies with Routers B, C, and D. Recall that this occurs because, when using point-to-point, the routers view the other routers as only directly connected to them so adjacencies are formed with each.

Figure 5-8   *Point-to-Point Network Type*

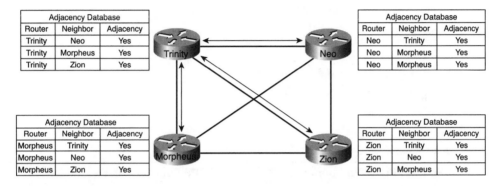

Adjacency Database

Router	Neighbor	Adjacency
Trinity	Neo	Yes
Trinity	Morpheus	Yes
Trinity	Zion	Yes

Adjacency Database

Router	Neighbor	Adjacency
Neo	Trinity	Yes
Neo	Morpheus	Yes
Neo	Morpheus	Yes

Adjacency Database

Router	Neighbor	Adjacency
Morpheus	Trinity	Yes
Morpheus	Neo	Yes
Morpheus	Zion	Yes

Adjacency Database

Router	Neighbor	Adjacency
Zion	Trinity	Yes
Zion	Neo	Yes
Zion	Morpheus	Yes

All routers viewed as directly connected, no logical mesh, no DR/BDR.

When adjacencies are formed, LSAs are used to keep the LSDBs synchronized, and each router is responsible for ensuring that this occurs because no DR is present. Tables 5-6 and 5-7 document how to configure this type of OSPF network. In this example, you have two routers (Trinity and Morpheus), and they are directly connected via interfaces serial 0/1, in a classic point-to-point configuration. As previously mentioned, the following methods can be used to get OSPF to operate in such a configuration:

- Use point-to-point subinterfaces
- Use a physical interface and an OSPF point-to-point network type

Either way, the OSPF adjacency forms and proper operation results. If you do not want to use point-to-point subinterfaces, use the OSPF **network** command.

Table 5-6 *Router Trinity Configuration*

Point-to-Point Subinterfaces	OSPF Point-to-Point
```!interface Serial0/1 description CONNECTION TO MORPHEUS (s0/1) no ip address no ip directed-broadcast encapsulation frame-relay clockrate 64000 frame-relay intf-type dce ! interface Serial0/1.1 point-to-point ip address 201.0.1.1 255.255.255.252 no ip directed-broadcast frame-relay interface-dlci 201 ! router ospf 100 network 192.168.254.0 0.0.0.255 area 201 network 201.0.0.0 0.0.0.127 area 201 network 201.0.1.0 0.0.0.3 area 201 !```	```interface Serial0/1 description CONNECTION TO MORPHEUS (s0/1) ip address 201.0.1.1 255.255.255.252 no ip directed-broadcast encapsulation frame-relay ip ospf network point-to-point clockrate 64000 frame-relay map ip 201.0.1.2 201 broadcast frame-relay intf-type dce ! ! router ospf 100 network 192.168.254.0 0.0.0.255 area 201 network 201.0.0.0 0.0.0.127 area 201 network 201.0.1.0 0.0.0.3 area 201 !```

Table 5-7 *Router Morpheus Configuration*

Point-to-Point Subinterfaces	OSPF Point-to-Point
```!interface Serial0/1 description CONNECTION TO TRINITY no ip address no ip directed-broadcast encapsulation frame-relay ! interface Serial0/1.1 point-to-point ip address 201.0.1.2 255.255.255.252 no ip directed-broadcast frame-relay interface-dlci 201 ! router ospf 100 network 100.0.0.0 0.0.255.255 area 201 network 201.0.1.0 0.0.0.3 area 201 !```	```!interface Serial0/1 description CONNECTION TO TRINITY ip address 201.0.1.2 255.255.255.252 no ip directed-broadcast encapsulation frame-relay ip ospf network point-to-point frame-relay map ip 201.0.1.1 201 broadcast ! router ospf 100 network 100.0.0.0 0.0.255.255 area 201 network 201.0.1.0 0.0.0.3 area 201 !```

Area Configuration

Areas have additional roles and functions similar in scope and purpose to OSPF route types. This section discusses OSPF areas and how to configure them within OSPF. You should review "OSPF Areas" in Chapter 2 and "Area Design" in Chapter 4. You should know how to activate a basic OSPF area by using the **network** command, as described earlier in this chapter.

Normal Area Configuration

To configure a normal OSPF area, the **network** command is used when in OSPF router configuration mode. Example 5-6 initializes OSPF routing process 109 and defines four OSPF areas: 10.9.50.0, 2, 3, and 0, respectively.

Areas 10.9.50.0 and 2 have masks covering specific address ranges; whereas area 3 activates OSPF on a specific interface, and area 0 enables OSPF for all other networks (note the address/mask).

Example 5-6   *Normal Area Configuration*

```
interface ethernet 0
 ip address 131.108.20.1 255.255.255.0
interface ethernet 1
 ip address 131.108.30.1 255.255.255.0
interface ethernet 2
 ip address 222.209.20.1 255.255.255.0
<more interfaces - omitted for brevity>
router ospf 109
 network 131.108.20.0  0.0.0.255 area 10.9.50.0
 network 131.108.0.0  0.0.255.255 area 2
 network 222.209.20.1  0.0.0.0 area 3
 network 0.0.0.0  255.255.255.255 area 0
```

LSA behavior in a regular OSPF area is straightforward because LSAs are transmitted freely. Table 5-8 shows which LSAs are active in a regular area.

Table 5-8   *LSA Operation in Regular Areas*

LSA Type	Description	Allowed
1	Router link connected intra-area routes	Yes
2	Network links area route via DR	Yes
3	ABR summary links inter-area via ABR	Yes
4	ASBR summary links route to ASBR	Yes
5	AS external links external routes via ASBR	Yes
7	Not-so-stubby areas NSSA routes via ABR	No

Figure 5-9 reviews the flow of LSA packets.

In this example, each OSPF area has its own unique network interface card (NIC)-assigned IP address range. This can be as grand as a Class A address for the entire network, with multiple Class Bs assigned to each area, or more realistically, you can use a group of Class C addresses. This example is demonstrated in an exaggerated fashion in Figure 5-10. The benefits of this method are as follows:

- Address assignment is easy.

- Configuration of the routers is easy, and mistakes are unlikely.

- Network operations are streamlined because each area has a simple unique address prefix.

Figure 5-9 *LSAs in a Regular Area*

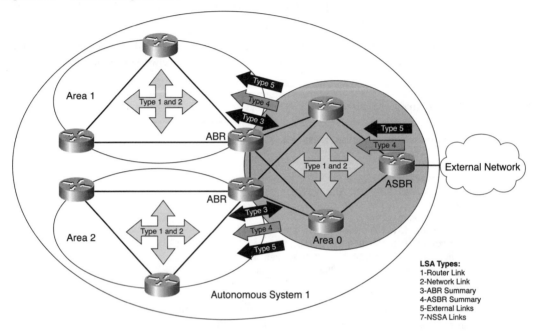

Figure 5-10 *Assigning Unique Network Numbers to an OSPF Area*

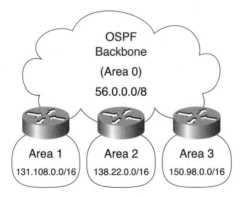

The following steps create such a network:

Step 1 Define your structure (identify areas and allocate nodes to areas).

Step 2 Assign addresses to networks, subnets, and end stations, as demonstrated in Figure 5-10.

The main drawback of this approach is that it can waste important IP address space. Of course, this space might also be difficult to obtain, at least until IPv6.

As an example, the route summarization configuration at the ABRs is greatly simplified. Routes from area 3 injected into the backbone would be summarized as "all routes starting with 150.98 are found in area 3." This can be accomplished on a Cisco router with the following command:

```
area 4 range 150.98.0.0 255.255.0.0
```

This section provides detailed coverage of the **area range** command and how it provides automatic route summarization for an area. The section takes a network and configures it with regular areas, as shown in Figure 5-11.

Figure 5-11 *Area Configuration*

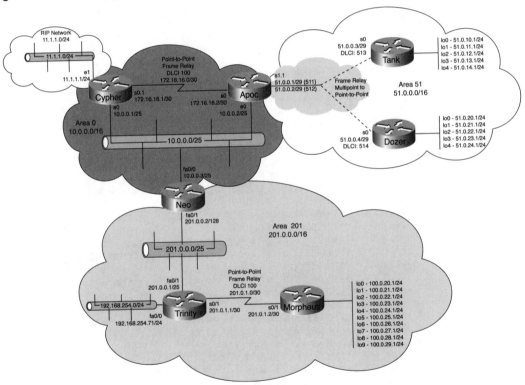

One of the benefits/functions of the different types of areas is that they stop certain LSAs that are used in an area from spilling over into other areas. LSAs, as discussed in Chapters 2 and 3, are the source of the routing table. In this chapter, you manipulate area 201, as shown in Figure 5-11, and because router Neo is the ABR, you review its routing table in Example 5-7 before changing area types.

Example 5-7 *Neo's Routing Table Prior to Changing Area Types*

```
Neo# show ip route
Codes: C - connected, S - static, I - IGRP, R - RIP, M - mobile, B - BGP
       D - EIGRP, EX - EIGRP external, O - OSPF, IA - OSPF inter area
       N1 - OSPF NSSA external type 1, N2 - OSPF NSSA external type 2
       E1 - OSPF external type 1, E2 - OSPF external type 2, E - EGP
       i - IS-IS, L1 - IS-IS level-1, L2 - IS-IS level-2, ia - IS-IS inter area
       * - candidate default, U - per-user static route, o - ODR
       P - periodic downloaded static route

Gateway of last resort is not set

      51.0.0.0/32 is subnetted, 18 subnets
O IA    51.0.18.1 [110/66] via 10.0.0.2, 00:21:32, FastEthernet0/0
O IA    51.0.19.1 [110/66] via 10.0.0.2, 00:21:32, FastEthernet0/0
O IA    51.0.16.1 [110/66] via 10.0.0.2, 00:21:32, FastEthernet0/0
O IA    51.0.17.1 [110/66] via 10.0.0.2, 00:21:32, FastEthernet0/0
O IA    51.0.22.1 [110/66] via 10.0.0.2, 00:21:32, FastEthernet0/0
O IA    51.0.23.1 [110/66] via 10.0.0.2, 00:21:32, FastEthernet0/0
O IA    51.0.20.1 [110/66] via 10.0.0.2, 00:21:32, FastEthernet0/0
O IA    51.0.21.1 [110/66] via 10.0.0.2, 00:21:32, FastEthernet0/0
O IA    51.0.24.1 [110/66] via 10.0.0.2, 00:21:32, FastEthernet0/0
O IA    51.0.0.3 [110/65] via 10.0.0.2, 00:21:32, FastEthernet0/0
O IA    51.0.0.1 [110/1] via 10.0.0.2, 00:22:02, FastEthernet0/0
O IA    51.0.0.4 [110/65] via 10.0.0.2, 00:21:32, FastEthernet0/0
O IA    51.0.10.1 [110/66] via 10.0.0.2, 00:21:34, FastEthernet0/0
O IA    51.0.11.1 [110/66] via 10.0.0.2, 00:21:34, FastEthernet0/0
O IA    51.0.14.1 [110/66] via 10.0.0.2, 00:21:34, FastEthernet0/0
O IA    51.0.15.1 [110/66] via 10.0.0.2, 00:21:34, FastEthernet0/0
O IA    51.0.12.1 [110/66] via 10.0.0.2, 00:21:34, FastEthernet0/0
O IA    51.0.13.1 [110/66] via 10.0.0.2, 00:21:34, FastEthernet0/0
      100.0.0.0/32 is subnetted, 10 subnets
O       100.0.21.1 [110/66] via 201.0.0.1, 00:23:23, FastEthernet0/1
O       100.0.20.1 [110/66] via 201.0.0.1, 00:23:24, FastEthernet0/1
O       100.0.23.1 [110/66] via 201.0.0.1, 00:23:24, FastEthernet0/1
O       100.0.22.1 [110/66] via 201.0.0.1, 00:23:24, FastEthernet0/1
O       100.0.29.1 [110/66] via 201.0.0.1, 00:23:24, FastEthernet0/1
O       100.0.28.1 [110/66] via 201.0.0.1, 00:23:24, FastEthernet0/1
O       100.0.25.1 [110/66] via 201.0.0.1, 00:23:24, FastEthernet0/1
O       100.0.24.1 [110/66] via 201.0.0.1, 00:23:24, FastEthernet0/1
O       100.0.27.1 [110/66] via 201.0.0.1, 00:23:24, FastEthernet0/1
O       100.0.26.1 [110/66] via 201.0.0.1, 00:23:24, FastEthernet0/1
      201.0.1.0/30 is subnetted, 1 subnets
O       201.0.1.0 [110/65] via 201.0.0.1, 00:23:24, FastEthernet0/1
      201.0.0.0/25 is subnetted, 1 subnets
C       201.0.0.0 is directly connected, FastEthernet0/1
      172.16.0.0/30 is subnetted, 1 subnets
O       172.16.16.0 [110/65] via 10.0.0.2, 00:22:04, FastEthernet0/0
                    [110/65] via 10.0.0.1, 00:22:04, FastEthernet0/0
      10.0.0.0/25 is subnetted, 1 subnets
C       10.0.0.0 is directly connected, FastEthernet0/0
      11.0.0.0/24 is subnetted, 1 subnets
O IA    11.1.1.0 [110/11] via 10.0.0.1, 00:22:05, FastEthernet0/0
O     192.168.254.0/24 [110/2] via 201.0.0.1, 00:23:26, FastEthernet0/1
Neo#
```

Stub Area Configuration

Stub areas are special OSPF areas into which information on external routes within an OSPF AS is not sent. Instead, a default external route is generated by the area border router into the stub area for destinations outside the area.

LSA behavior for a stub area is altered from what you have seen in regular areas. Table 5-9 provides shows which LSAs are active in a stub area.

Table 5-9   *LSA Operation in Stub Areas*

LSA Type	Description	Allowed
1	Router link connected intra-area routes	Yes
2	Network links area route via DR	Yes
3	ABR summary links inter-area via ABR	Yes
4	ASBR summary links route to ASBR	Yes
5	AS external links external routes via ASBR	No
7	Not-so-stubby areas NSSA routes via ABR	No

In Figure 5-12, you can see how and where the LSAs are transmitted within a stub area. Remember that a default route is also automatically injected by the ABR.

Figure 5-12   *LSAs in a Stub Area*

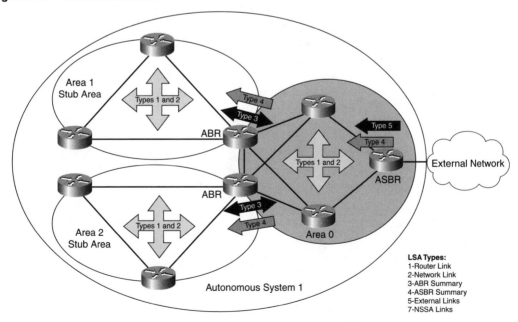

To configure an area as a stub, all routers within the area must use the **area stub** configuration command, as demonstrated in the before, during, and after of Example 5-8.

Example 5-8 *Stub Area Configuration*

```
Before
!
router ospf 100
 network 192.168.254.0 0.0.0.255 area 201
 network 201.0.0.0 0.0.0.127 area 201
 network 201.0.1.0 0.0.0.3 area 201
 !
During
Trinity#conf t
Enter configuration commands, one per line.  End with CNTL/Z.
Trinity(config)#router ospf 100
Trinity(config-router)#area 201 stub
After
 !
router ospf 100
 area 201 stub
 network 192.168.254.0 0.0.0.255 area 201
 network 201.0.0.0 0.0.0.127 area 201
 network 201.0.1.0 0.0.0.3 area 201
 !
```

In this configuration example, you configure the entire area and every network assigned to that area as stub. Recall the discussion of the effect of LSAs on the routing table and with Routers Neo, Trinity, and Morpheus all configured to have OSPF area 201 as a stub area. The network in this section shows that area 201 has become a stub area, as shown in Figure 5-13.

Figure 5-13 *Area 201 Stub Area Configuration*

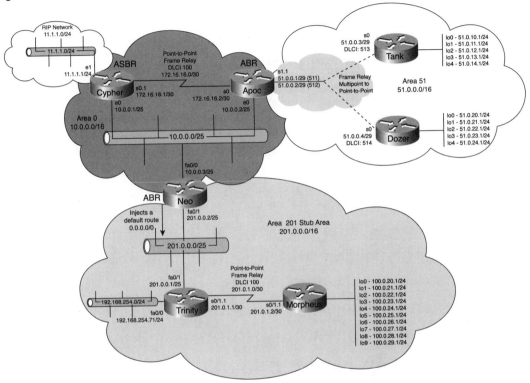

Router Trinity Routing Table Before Area 201 Stub

When reviewing the command output in Example 5-9, remember that the Type 5 LSAs are present on Router Trinity and in area 201 via the RIP network shown as an OSPF E2 route, as highlighted.

Before

Example 5-9 *Router Trinity's Routing Table Before Configuring Area 201 as a Stub Area*

```
Trinity#show ip route
Codes: C - connected, S - static, I - IGRP, R - RIP, M - mobile, B - BGP
       D - EIGRP, EX - EIGRP external, O - OSPF, IA - OSPF inter area
       N1 - OSPF NSSA external type 1, N2 - OSPF NSSA external type 2
       E1 - OSPF external type 1, E2 - OSPF external type 2, E - EGP
       i - IS-IS, L1 - IS-IS level-1, L2 - IS-IS level-2, ia - IS-IS inter area
       * - candidate default, U - per-user static route, o - ODR
       P - periodic downloaded static route
```

Example 5-9   *Router Trinity's Routing Table Before Configuring Area 201 as a Stub Area (Continued)*

```
Gateway of last resort is not set

     51.0.0.0/32 is subnetted, 18 subnets
O IA    51.0.18.1 [110/67] via 201.0.0.2, 00:02:54, FastEthernet0/1
O IA    51.0.19.1 [110/67] via 201.0.0.2, 00:02:54, FastEthernet0/1
O IA    51.0.16.1 [110/67] via 201.0.0.2, 00:02:54, FastEthernet0/1
O IA    51.0.17.1 [110/67] via 201.0.0.2, 00:02:54, FastEthernet0/1
O IA    51.0.22.1 [110/67] via 201.0.0.2, 00:02:54, FastEthernet0/1
O IA    51.0.23.1 [110/67] via 201.0.0.2, 00:02:54, FastEthernet0/1
O IA    51.0.20.1 [110/67] via 201.0.0.2, 00:02:54, FastEthernet0/1
O IA    51.0.21.1 [110/67] via 201.0.0.2, 00:02:54, FastEthernet0/1
O IA    51.0.24.1 [110/67] via 201.0.0.2, 00:02:54, FastEthernet0/1
O IA    51.0.0.3 [110/66] via 201.0.0.2, 00:02:54, FastEthernet0/1
O IA    51.0.0.1 [110/2] via 201.0.0.2, 00:02:54, FastEthernet0/1
O IA    51.0.0.4 [110/66] via 201.0.0.2, 00:02:54, FastEthernet0/1
O IA    51.0.10.1 [110/67] via 201.0.0.2, 00:02:56, FastEthernet0/1
O IA    51.0.11.1 [110/67] via 201.0.0.2, 00:02:56, FastEthernet0/1
O IA    51.0.14.1 [110/67] via 201.0.0.2, 00:02:56, FastEthernet0/1
O IA    51.0.15.1 [110/67] via 201.0.0.2, 00:02:56, FastEthernet0/1
O IA    51.0.12.1 [110/67] via 201.0.0.2, 00:02:56, FastEthernet0/1
O IA    51.0.13.1 [110/67] via 201.0.0.2, 00:02:56, FastEthernet0/1
     100.0.0.0/32 is subnetted, 10 subnets
O       100.0.21.1 [110/65] via 201.0.1.2, 00:02:56, Serial0/1.1
O       100.0.20.1 [110/65] via 201.0.1.2, 00:02:56, Serial0/1.1
O       100.0.23.1 [110/65] via 201.0.1.2, 00:02:56, Serial0/1.1
O       100.0.22.1 [110/65] via 201.0.1.2, 00:02:56, Serial0/1.1
O       100.0.29.1 [110/65] via 201.0.1.2, 00:02:56, Serial0/1.1
O       100.0.28.1 [110/65] via 201.0.1.2, 00:02:56, Serial0/1.1
O       100.0.25.1 [110/65] via 201.0.1.2, 00:02:56, Serial0/1.1
O       100.0.24.1 [110/65] via 201.0.1.2, 00:02:56, Serial0/1.1
O       100.0.27.1 [110/65] via 201.0.1.2, 00:02:57, Serial0/1.1
O       100.0.26.1 [110/65] via 201.0.1.2, 00:02:57, Serial0/1.1
     201.0.1.0/30 is subnetted, 1 subnets
C       201.0.1.0 is directly connected, Serial0/1.1
     201.0.0.0/25 is subnetted, 1 subnets
C       201.0.0.0 is directly connected, FastEthernet0/1
     172.16.0.0/30 is subnetted, 1 subnets
O IA    172.16.16.0 [110/66] via 201.0.0.2, 00:02:57, FastEthernet0/1
     10.0.0.0/25 is subnetted, 1 subnets
O IA    10.0.0.0 [110/2] via 201.0.0.2, 00:02:58, FastEthernet0/1
     11.0.0.0/24 is subnetted, 1 subnets
O E2    11.1.1.0 [110/20] via 10.0.0.1, 00:00:07, FastEthernet0/0
     192.168.254.0/24 is directly connected, FastEthernet0/0
Trinity#
```

Router Trinity Routing Table After Area 201 Stub

In the command output in Example 5-10, area 201 is not a stub area; therefore, you can expect to see the external route disappear from the routing table. However, Router Neo (area 201 ABR) is advertising the default route to the entire area. You can see this by executing a **show ip ospf database** command and noting the advertising router for the 0.0.0.0 route.

After

Example 5-10 *Verifying the 0.0.0.0 Route*

```
Trinity#show ip route
Codes: C - connected, S - static, I - IGRP, R - RIP, M - mobile, B - BGP
       D - EIGRP, EX - EIGRP external, O - OSPF, IA - OSPF inter area
       N1 - OSPF NSSA external type 1, N2 - OSPF NSSA external type 2
       E1 - OSPF external type 1, E2 - OSPF external type 2, E - EGP
       i - IS-IS, L1 - IS-IS level-1, L2 - IS-IS level-2, ia - IS-IS inter area
       * - candidate default, U - per-user static route, o - ODR
       P - periodic downloaded static route

Gateway of last resort is 201.0.0.2 to network 0.0.0.0

     51.0.0.0/32 is subnetted, 18 subnets
O IA    51.0.18.1 [110/67] via 201.0.0.2, 00:16:48, FastEthernet0/1
O IA    51.0.19.1 [110/67] via 201.0.0.2, 00:16:48, FastEthernet0/1
O IA    51.0.16.1 [110/67] via 201.0.0.2, 00:16:48, FastEthernet0/1
O IA    51.0.17.1 [110/67] via 201.0.0.2, 00:16:48, FastEthernet0/1
O IA    51.0.22.1 [110/67] via 201.0.0.2, 00:16:48, FastEthernet0/1
O IA    51.0.23.1 [110/67] via 201.0.0.2, 00:16:48, FastEthernet0/1
O IA    51.0.20.1 [110/67] via 201.0.0.2, 00:16:48, FastEthernet0/1
O IA    51.0.21.1 [110/67] via 201.0.0.2, 00:16:49, FastEthernet0/1
O IA    51.0.24.1 [110/67] via 201.0.0.2, 00:16:49, FastEthernet0/1
O IA    51.0.0.3 [110/66] via 201.0.0.2, 00:16:49, FastEthernet0/1
O IA    51.0.0.1 [110/2] via 201.0.0.2, 00:16:49, FastEthernet0/1
O IA    51.0.0.4 [110/66] via 201.0.0.2, 00:16:49, FastEthernet0/1
O IA    51.0.10.1 [110/67] via 201.0.0.2, 00:16:50, FastEthernet0/1
O IA    51.0.11.1 [110/67] via 201.0.0.2, 00:16:50, FastEthernet0/1
O IA    51.0.14.1 [110/67] via 201.0.0.2, 00:16:50, FastEthernet0/1
O IA    51.0.15.1 [110/67] via 201.0.0.2, 00:16:50, FastEthernet0/1
O IA    51.0.12.1 [110/67] via 201.0.0.2, 00:16:50, FastEthernet0/1
O IA    51.0.13.1 [110/67] via 201.0.0.2, 00:16:50, FastEthernet0/1
     100.0.0.0/32 is subnetted, 10 subnets
O       100.0.21.1 [110/65] via 201.0.1.2, 00:16:50, Serial0/1.1
O       100.0.20.1 [110/65] via 201.0.1.2, 00:16:50, Serial0/1.1
O       100.0.23.1 [110/65] via 201.0.1.2, 00:16:50, Serial0/1.1
O       100.0.22.1 [110/65] via 201.0.1.2, 00:16:50, Serial0/1.1
O       100.0.29.1 [110/65] via 201.0.1.2, 00:16:50, Serial0/1.1
O       100.0.28.1 [110/65] via 201.0.1.2, 00:16:50, Serial0/1.1
O       100.0.25.1 [110/65] via 201.0.1.2, 00:16:50, Serial0/1.1
O       100.0.24.1 [110/65] via 201.0.1.2, 00:16:50, Serial0/1.1
O       100.0.27.1 [110/65] via 201.0.1.2, 00:16:51, Serial0/1.1
O       100.0.26.1 [110/65] via 201.0.1.2, 00:16:51, Serial0/1.1
     201.0.1.0/30 is subnetted, 1 subnets
C       201.0.1.0 is directly connected, Serial0/1.1
     201.0.0.0/25 is subnetted, 1 subnets
C       201.0.0.0 is directly connected, FastEthernet0/1
     172.16.0.0/30 is subnetted, 1 subnets
O IA    172.16.16.0 [110/66] via 201.0.0.2, 00:16:51, FastEthernet0/1
     10.0.0.0/25 is subnetted, 1 subnets
O IA    10.0.0.0 [110/2] via 201.0.0.2, 00:16:52, FastEthernet0/1
C    192.168.254.0/24 is directly connected, FastEthernet0/0
O*IA 0.0.0.0/0 [110/2] via 201.0.0.2, 00:16:52, FastEthernet0/1
Trinity#
```

Totally Stubby Area Configuration

To further reduce the number of link-state advertisements sent into a stub area, you configure **no-summary** on the ABR to prevent it from sending a summary link advertisement (LSA Type 3) into the stub area. By altering the behavior of the ABR, you automatically convert the entire stub area into a totally stubby area.

LSA behavior for a stub area is altered from what you have seen in regular areas. Table 5-10 shows which LSAs are active in a stub area.

Table 5-10 *LSA Operation in Stub Areas*

LSA Type	Description	Allowed
1	Router link connected intra-area routes	Yes
2	Network links area route via DR	Yes
3	ABR summary links inter-area via ABR	No
4	ASBR summary links route to ASBR	No
5	AS external links external routes via ASBR	No
7	Not-so-stubby areas NSSA routes via ABR	No

In Figure 5-14, you can see how and where the LSAs are transmitted within a stub area. Remember that a default route is also automatically injected by the ABR.

Figure 5-14 *LSAs in a Totally Stubby Area*

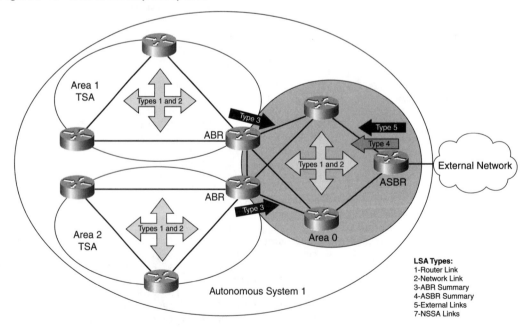

To configure an OSPF area as a totally stubby area, the ABR router for the area only must use the **area stub no-summary** configuration command, as demonstrated in Example 5-11.

Example 5-11   *Configuring an OSPF Area as Totally Stubby—Before, During, and After*

```
Before
!
router ospf 100
 area 201 stub
 network 10.0.0.0 0.0.0.127 area 0
 network 201.0.0.0 0.0.0.127 area 201
!
```
```
During
Neo#conf t
Enter configuration commands, one per line.  End with CNTL/Z.
Neo(config)#router ospf 100
Neo(config-router)#area 201 stub no-summary
Neo(config-router)#^Z
Neo#
!
```
```
After
router ospf 100
 area 201 stub no-summary
 network 10.0.0.0 0.0.0.127 area 0
 network 201.0.0.0 0.0.0.127 area 201
!
```

In this configuration example shows only the ABR configured with the **no-summary** keyword. This directs the ABR to not forward any LSAs into the totally stubby area. The NDS network in this section shows that area 201 has become a stub area, as shown in Figure 5-15.

The ABR continues to advertise a default route to the entire area, as you will see in the command output of Example 5-12. However, the drastic change in the routing table size is because the only routes Router Trinity is aware of are those inside area 201 and the default route. This default route says "If the destination network cannot be found in my routing table, I will send the packets to the ABR and they will know what to do." This makes sense when you remember that every OSPF area must be connected to the OSPF backbone area (area 0).

Figure 5-15 *Area 201 Totally Stubby Area Configuration*

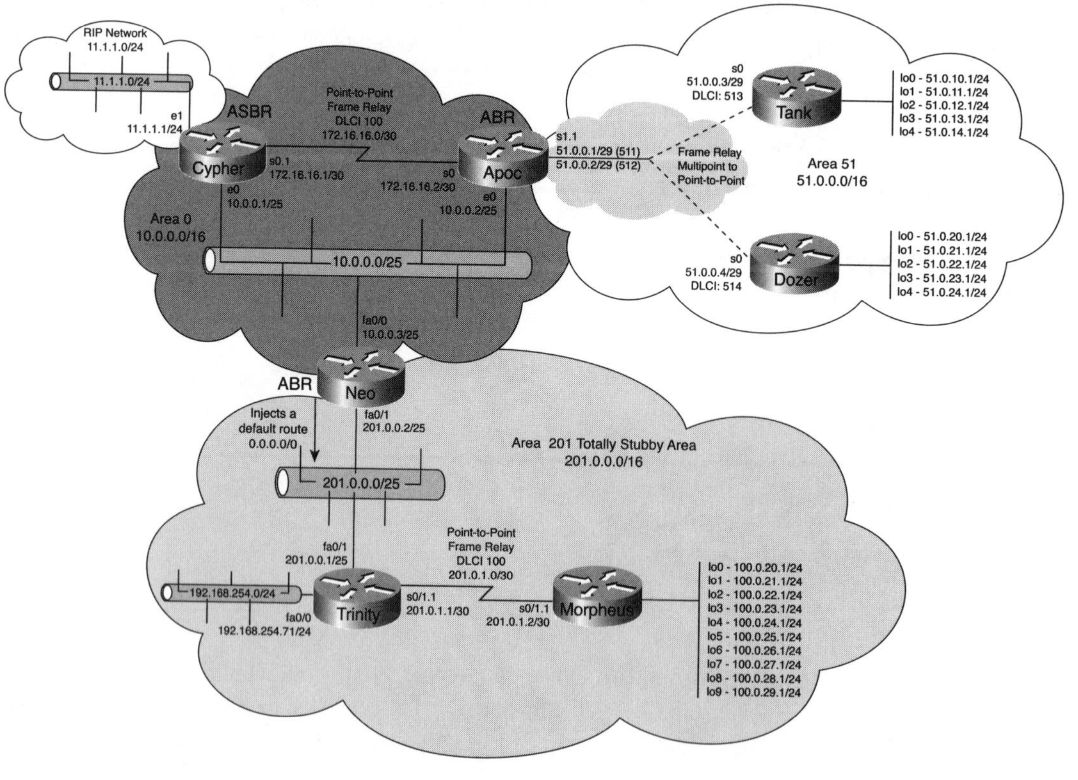

Example 5-12 *Routing Table with the Default Route*

```
Trinity#show ip route
Codes: C - connected, S - static, I - IGRP, R - RIP, M - mobile, B - BGP
       D - EIGRP, EX - EIGRP external, O - OSPF, IA - OSPF inter area
       N1 - OSPF NSSA external type 1, N2 - OSPF NSSA external type 2
       E1 - OSPF external type 1, E2 - OSPF external type 2, E - EGP
       i - IS-IS, L1 - IS-IS level-1, L2 - IS-IS level-2, ia - IS-IS inter area
       * - candidate default, U - per-user static route, o - ODR
       P - periodic downloaded static route

Gateway of last resort is 201.0.0.2 to network 0.0.0.0

     100.0.0.0/32 is subnetted, 10 subnets
O       100.0.21.1 [110/65] via 201.0.1.2, 00:05:32, Serial0/1.1
O       100.0.20.1 [110/65] via 201.0.1.2, 00:05:32, Serial0/1.1
O       100.0.23.1 [110/65] via 201.0.1.2, 00:05:32, Serial0/1.1
O       100.0.22.1 [110/65] via 201.0.1.2, 00:05:32, Serial0/1.1
O       100.0.29.1 [110/65] via 201.0.1.2, 00:05:32, Serial0/1.1
O       100.0.28.1 [110/65] via 201.0.1.2, 00:05:32, Serial0/1.1
O       100.0.25.1 [110/65] via 201.0.1.2, 00:05:32, Serial0/1.1
```

Example 5-12 *Routing Table with the Default Route (Continued)*

```
O       100.0.24.1 [110/65] via 201.0.1.2, 00:05:33, Serial0/1.1
O       100.0.27.1 [110/65] via 201.0.1.2, 00:05:33, Serial0/1.1
O       100.0.26.1 [110/65] via 201.0.1.2, 00:05:33, Serial0/1.1
        201.0.1.0/30 is subnetted, 1 subnets
C          201.0.1.0 is directly connected, Serial0/1.1
        201.0.0.0/25 is subnetted, 1 subnets
C          201.0.0.0 is directly connected, FastEthernet0/1
C       192.168.254.0/24 is directly connected, FastEthernet0/0
O*IA 0.0.0.0/0 [110/2] via 201.0.0.2, 00:05:50, FastEthernet0/1
Trinity#
```

Not-So-Stubby-Area (NSSA) Configuration

Networking makes for interesting situations. The OSPF NSSA and the unique requirement of having this type of OSPF area to connect to an external network represent two of these situations. Specifically, an NSSA allows you to attach an external network to an area that is not the backbone and yet still allow access to that external network within the OSPF domain. Granted, this is not the most common way of designing an OSPF network; however, business factors can dictate such a configuration when, for example, it is not cost effective to buy a new connection to the backbone.

In this situation, you would have an ASBR in an OSPF; this is the point of having an NSSA. NSSAs allow ASBRs to be in stub areas. You can have ASBRs in normal, nonbackbone areas with no special configuration.

You can make an NSSA behave in several unique ways, so take a moment to review the manner in which they operate as defined in the RFC, prior to altering this behavior with some of the options Cisco provides in Cisco IOS Software.

Redistributing external networks into an NSSA is at the heart of an NSSA. Specifically, an NSSA is a stub area, and yet you are connecting an external network to this specialized stub area. You are presented with the problem that Type 5 LSAs are not allowed within a stub area because, as previously discussed, external networks are advertised normally via the Type 5 LSA. The NSSA RFC has defined a new LSA, the Type 7, to provide a means to propagate the external networks to rest of the OSPF domain.

The primary advantage of an NSSA is that it allows only that area's external routes and not the rest of the autonomous system's externals. This reduces memory and CPU usage and is typically used for redistributing other routing protocols into stub areas (like RIP from dial-up access servers).

Types of NSSAs

You can implement an NSSA in two ways: normally (as described in the RFC) and as a totally stubby NSSA. A totally stubby NSSA allows only summary default routes and filters out all other LSAs.

In an NSSA, a default summary route is not automatically generated. Specifically, in a normal NSSA, there is no generated default route; however, as in stub and totally stub areas, the totally stubby NSSA generates a default route.

Normal NSSA Operation and Configuration

Table 5-11 presents shows which LSAs are active in a normal NSSA.

Table 5-11 *LSA Operation in a Normal NSSA*

LSA Type	Description	Allowed
1	Router link connected intra-area routes	Yes
2	Network links area route via DR	Yes
3	ABR summary links inter-area via ABR	Yes
4	ASBR summary links route to ASBR	Yes
5	AS external links external routes via ASBR	No
7	Not-so-stubby areas NSSA routes via ABR	Yes

In Figure 5-16, you can see how and where the LSAs are transmitted within a stub area.

Figure 5-16 *LSAs in a Normal NSSA*

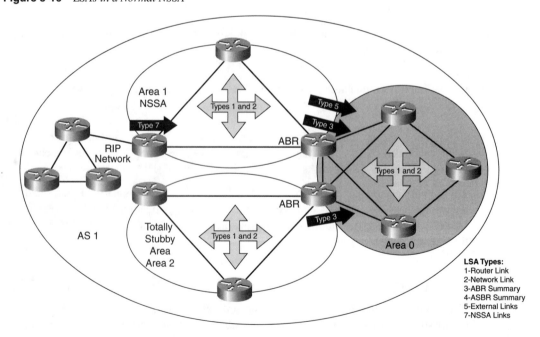

When configuring an area as an NSSA, all routers in the area must be configured to identify the area as an NSSA. In Example 5-13, you change area 201 from a stub area to an NSSA.

Example 5-13 *Configuring a Router as an NSSA*

```
Before
!
router ospf 100
 area 201 stub
 network 192.168.254.0 0.0.0.255 area 201
 network 201.0.0.0 0.0.0.127 area 201
 network 201.0.1.0 0.0.0.3 area 201
 !
```
```
During
Trinity#conf t
Enter configuration commands, one per line.  End with CNTL/Z.
Trinity(config)#router ospf 100
Trinity(config-router)#no  network 192.168.254.0 0.0.0.255 area 201
Trinity(config-router)#exit
Trinity(config)#router rip
Trinity(config-router)#network 192.168.254.0
Trinity(config-router)#router ospf 100
Trinity(config-router)#no area 201 stub
Trinity(config-router)#area 201 nssa
Trinity(config-router)#redistribute rip subnets
Trinity(config-router)#^Z
Trinity#
```
```
After
!
router ospf 100
 area 201 nssa
 redistribute rip subnets
 network 201.0.0.0 0.0.0.127 area 201
 network 201.0.1.0 0.0.0.3 area 201
 !
router rip
 network 192.168.254.0
 !
```

Figure 5-17 shows the resulting topology, now that you have converted area 201 to an NSSA. Notice the introduction of another external RIP network connected to Router Trinity.

When looking at how the routing table changes as a result of area 201 becoming an NSSA, the first change is the disappearance of a default route, and the second change is the inclusion of the new external RIP network (N2); however, the other external RIP network is still present. Example 5-14 demonstrates the routing table changes.

Figure 5-17 *Normal Not-So-Stubby-Area Configuration*

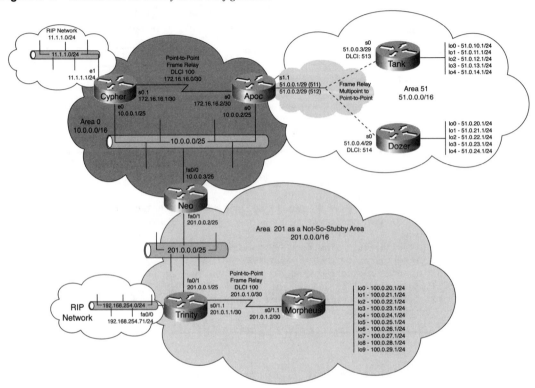

Example 5-14 *Identifying NSSA Routes*

```
Neo#show ip route
Codes: C - connected, S - static, I - IGRP, R - RIP, M - mobile, B - BGP
       D - EIGRP, EX - EIGRP external, O - OSPF, IA - OSPF inter area
       N1 - OSPF NSSA external type 1, N2 - OSPF NSSA external type 2
       E1 - OSPF external type 1, E2 - OSPF external type 2, E - EGP
       i - IS-IS, L1 - IS-IS level-1, L2 - IS-IS level-2, ia - IS-IS inter area
       * - candidate default, U - per-user static route, o - ODR
       P - periodic downloaded static route

Gateway of last resort is not set

     51.0.0.0/32 is subnetted, 18 subnets
O IA    51.0.18.1 [110/66] via 10.0.0.2, 00:23:48, FastEthernet0/0
O IA    51.0.19.1 [110/66] via 10.0.0.2, 00:23:48, FastEthernet0/0
O IA    51.0.16.1 [110/66] via 10.0.0.2, 00:23:48, FastEthernet0/0
O IA    51.0.17.1 [110/66] via 10.0.0.2, 00:23:48, FastEthernet0/0
O IA    51.0.22.1 [110/66] via 10.0.0.2, 00:23:48, FastEthernet0/0
O IA    51.0.23.1 [110/66] via 10.0.0.2, 00:23:48, FastEthernet0/0
O IA    51.0.20.1 [110/66] via 10.0.0.2, 00:23:48, FastEthernet0/0
O IA    51.0.21.1 [110/66] via 10.0.0.2, 00:23:49, FastEthernet0/0
```

Example 5-14 *Identifying NSSA Routes (Continued)*

```
O IA    51.0.24.1 [110/66] via 10.0.0.2, 00:23:49, FastEthernet0/0
O IA    51.0.0.3 [110/65] via 10.0.0.2, 00:23:49, FastEthernet0/0
O IA    51.0.0.1 [110/1] via 10.0.0.2, 00:23:49, FastEthernet0/0
O IA    51.0.0.4 [110/65] via 10.0.0.2, 00:23:49, FastEthernet0/0
O IA    51.0.10.1 [110/66] via 10.0.0.2, 00:23:50, FastEthernet0/0
O IA    51.0.11.1 [110/66] via 10.0.0.2, 00:23:50, FastEthernet0/0
O IA    51.0.14.1 [110/66] via 10.0.0.2, 00:23:50, FastEthernet0/0
O IA    51.0.15.1 [110/66] via 10.0.0.2, 00:23:50, FastEthernet0/0
O IA    51.0.12.1 [110/66] via 10.0.0.2, 00:23:50, FastEthernet0/0
O IA    51.0.13.1 [110/66] via 10.0.0.2, 00:23:50, FastEthernet0/0
        100.0.0.0/32 is subnetted, 10 subnets
O          100.0.21.1 [110/66] via 201.0.0.1, 00:23:50, FastEthernet0/1
O          100.0.20.1 [110/66] via 201.0.0.1, 00:23:51, FastEthernet0/1
O          100.0.23.1 [110/66] via 201.0.0.1, 00:23:51, FastEthernet0/1
O          100.0.22.1 [110/66] via 201.0.0.1, 00:23:51, FastEthernet0/1
O          100.0.29.1 [110/66] via 201.0.0.1, 00:23:51, FastEthernet0/1
O          100.0.28.1 [110/66] via 201.0.0.1, 00:23:51, FastEthernet0/1
O          100.0.25.1 [110/66] via 201.0.0.1, 00:23:51, FastEthernet0/1
O          100.0.24.1 [110/66] via 201.0.0.1, 00:23:51, FastEthernet0/1
O          100.0.27.1 [110/66] via 201.0.0.1, 00:23:51, FastEthernet0/1
O          100.0.26.1 [110/66] via 201.0.0.1, 00:23:51, FastEthernet0/1
        201.0.1.0/30 is subnetted, 1 subnets
O          201.0.1.0 [110/65] via 201.0.0.1, 00:23:51, FastEthernet0/1
        201.0.0.0/25 is subnetted, 1 subnets
C          201.0.0.0 is directly connected, FastEthernet0/1
        172.16.0.0/30 is subnetted, 1 subnets
O          172.16.16.0 [110/65] via 10.0.0.2, 00:23:51, FastEthernet0/0
                       [110/65] via 10.0.0.1, 00:23:51, FastEthernet0/0
        10.0.0.0/25 is subnetted, 1 subnets
C          10.0.0.0 is directly connected, FastEthernet0/0
        11.0.0.0/24 is subnetted, 1 subnets
O E2    11.1.1.0 [110/20] via 10.0.0.1, 00:23:53, FastEthernet0/0
O N2 192.168.254.0/24 [110/20] via 201.0.0.1, 00:23:53, FastEthernet0/1
Neo#
```

The routing table has increased in size, and one of the challenges that you face when creating an NSSA is the need for a default route. Optional keywords for use on the NSSA ABR are as follows:

```
Neo(config-router)#area 201 nssa ?
  default-information-originate  Originate Type 7 default into NSSA area
  no-redistribution              No redistribution into this NSSA area
  no-summary                     Do not send summary LSA into NSSA
  <cr>
```

Totally Stubby NSSA Operation and Configuration

In Table 5-10, you can see how and where the LSAs are transmitted within this type of area. Remember that a default route is also automatically injected by the ABR.

Table 5-12 *1LSA Operation in a Totally Stubby NSSA*

LSA Type	Description	Allowed
1	Router link connected intra-area routes	Yes
2	Network links area route via DR	Yes
3	ABR summary links inter-area via ABR	No
4	ASBR summary links route to ASBR	No
5	AS external links external routes via ASBR	No
7	Not-so-stubby areas NSSA routes via ABR	Yes

To configure an NSSA as totally stubby, you use the **area** *number* **nssa no-summary** command. The **no-summary** keyword, when also used on the ABR, creates a totally stubby NSSA. The way to clearly see the result of this keyword is on Router Morpheus. In Example 5-15, you can see that the ABR (Router Neo) is now announcing a default route, and the external network (192.168.254.0) connected to Router Trinity is advertised as a Type 7 LSA; this is reflected in the fact that the default route is an N2 route.

Example 5-15 *NSSA Routes When Totally Stubby*

```
Morpheus#show ip route
Codes: C - connected, S - static, I - IGRP, R - RIP, M - mobile, B - BGP
       D - EIGRP, EX - EIGRP external, O - OSPF, IA - OSPF inter area
       N1 - OSPF NSSA external type 1, N2 - OSPF NSSA external type 2
       E1 - OSPF external type 1, E2 - OSPF external type 2, E - EGP
       i - IS-IS, L1 - IS-IS level-1, L2 - IS-IS level-2, ia - IS-IS inter area
       * - candidate default, U - per-user static route, o - ODR
       P - periodic downloaded static route

Gateway of last resort is 201.0.1.1 to network 0.0.0.0

     100.0.0.0/24 is subnetted, 10 subnets
C       100.0.20.0 is directly connected, Loopback0
C       100.0.21.0 is directly connected, Loopback1
C       100.0.22.0 is directly connected, Loopback2
C       100.0.23.0 is directly connected, Loopback3
C       100.0.28.0 is directly connected, Loopback8
C       100.0.29.0 is directly connected, Loopback9
C       100.0.24.0 is directly connected, Loopback4
C       100.0.25.0 is directly connected, Loopback5
C       100.0.26.0 is directly connected, Loopback6
C       100.0.27.0 is directly connected, Loopback7
     201.0.1.0/30 is subnetted, 1 subnets
C       201.0.1.0 is directly connected, Serial0/1.1
     201.0.0.0/25 is subnetted, 1 subnets
O       201.0.0.0 [110/65] via 201.0.1.1, 00:09:03, Serial0/1.1
O N2 192.168.254.0/24 [110/20] via 201.0.1.1, 00:09:03, Serial0/1.1
O*IA 0.0.0.0/0 [110/66] via 201.0.1.1, 00:09:03, Serial0/1.1
Morpheus#
```

NSSA default-information-originate

Used on the NSSA ABR (Router Neo) and in addition to the normal NSSA behavior that you would expect to see (inter- and intra-area routes), with this keyword option you also force the ABR to inject a default route (0.0.0.0/0) into the NSSA. Be aware of the following rules in this regard:

- An NSSA ABSR can generate a default route but only when it has a default route in its routing table; therefore, if it does not know about a default route, it cannot be expected to tell the NSSA about it.

- AN NSSA ABR can generate a default route regardless of the presence of a default route in its own routing table.

This default route is shown as an N2 route in the routing table, as the snippet of an output in Example 5-16.

Example 5-16 *Default Route in an NSSA*

```
<<<output omitted for brevity>>>
O       201.0.0.0 [110/65] via 201.0.1.1, 00:04:16, Serial0/1.1
        172.16.0.0/30 is subnetted, 1 subnets
O IA    172.16.16.0 [110/130] via 201.0.1.1, 00:04:16, Serial0/1.1
        10.0.0.0/25 is subnetted, 1 subnets
O IA    10.0.0.0 [110/66] via 201.0.1.1, 00:04:17, Serial0/1.1
O N2 192.168.254.0/24 [110/20] via 201.0.1.1, 00:04:17, Serial0/1.1
O*N2 0.0.0.0/0 [110/1] via 201.0.1.1, 00:04:17, Serial0/1.1
```

NSSA **no-redistribution**

Sometimes, an ABR router must also become an ASBR. This can happen for a number of reasons. For example, you might need to make a new connection and the only place you have an available interface to do so is on the router that is already an ABR. Perhaps budgetary restrictions are in place and you plan on making a change in the future. In addition, the ABR can handle the capacity of the new connection...as mentioned, this might occur for any number of things. You can see this situation evolve in Figure 5-18.

Figure 5-18 *NSSA with No-Redistribution*

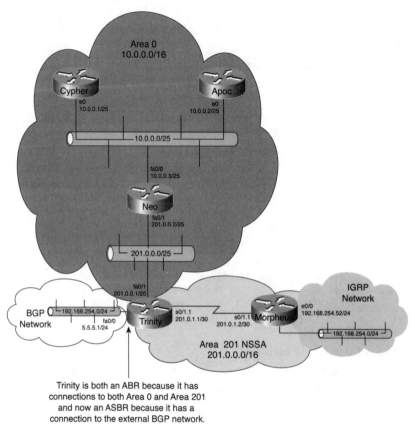

Trinity is both an ABR because it has
connections to both Area 0 and Area 201
and now an ASBR because it has a
connection to the external BGP network.

When this situation occurs, into which area does Router Trinity send the LSAs? By default, they are generated and sent into area 0 (as Type 5) and area 201 (as Type 7). This automatic redistribution might not be the most appropriate behavior, and to correct it, Cisco's implementation of OSPF has a new keyword that you can apply to the resulting ABR/ASBR (Router Trinity). This keyword takes effect only on an NSSA ABR/ASBR and prevents Type 7 LSAs entering into the NSSA by default. You can prevent the router from creating Type 7 LSAs for this external network by using the following keyword as part of the NSSA command:

```
router ospf 100
 area 201 nssa no-redistribution
```

In Example 5-17, Router Morpheus sees the BGP network as a Type 7 route in its routing table.

Before

Example 5-17 *Before the* **no-redistribute** *Command*

```
Morpheus#show ip route
Codes: C - connected, S - static, I - IGRP, R - RIP, M - mobile, B - BGP
       D - EIGRP, EX - EIGRP external, O - OSPF, IA - OSPF inter area
       N1 - OSPF NSSA external type 1, N2 - OSPF NSSA external type 2
       E1 - OSPF external type 1, E2 - OSPF external type 2, E - EGP
       i - IS-IS, L1 - IS-IS level-1, L2 - IS-IS level-2, * - candidate default
       U - per-user static route, o - ODR

Gateway of last resort is not set

     201.0.1.0/30 is subnetted, 1 subnets
C       201.0.1.0 is directly connected, Serial0/1.1
     5.0.0.0/24 is subnetted, 1 subnets
O N2    5.5.5.0 [110/20] via 201.0.1.1, 00:07:25, Serial0/1.1
     201.0.0.0/25 is subnetted, 1 subnets
O IA    201.0.0.0 [110/65] via 201.0.1.1, 00:42:38, Serial0/1.1
     10.0.0.0/25 is subnetted, 1 subnets
O IA    10.0.0.0 [110/66] via 201.0.1.1, 00:42:38, Serial0/1.1
C    192.168.254.0/24 is directly connected, Ethernet0/0
```

During

At this point, you implement the **no-redistribution** keyword on Router Trinity, as shown in Example 5-18.

Example 5-18 *During the* **no-redistribution** *Configuration*

```
Trinity(config)#router ospf 100
Trinity(config-router)#area 201 nssa ?
  default-information-originate  Originate Type 7 default into NSSA area
  no-redistribution             No redistribution into this NSSA area
  no-summary                    Do not send summary LSA into NSSA
  <cr>

Trinity(config-router)#area 201 nssa no-redistribution
```

After

The result is that the BGP network is removed as an N2 route, as verified in Example 5-19.

Example 5-19 *After Configuring* **no-redistribution**

```
Morpheus#show ip route
Codes: C - connected, S - static, I - IGRP, R - RIP, M - mobile, B - BGP
       D - EIGRP, EX - EIGRP external, O - OSPF, IA - OSPF inter area
       N1 - OSPF NSSA external type 1, N2 - OSPF NSSA external type 2
       E1 - OSPF external type 1, E2 - OSPF external type 2, E - EGP
       i - IS-IS, L1 - IS-IS level-1, L2 - IS-IS level-2, * - candidate default
       U - per-user static route, o - ODR
```

continues

Example 5-19 *After Configuring* **no-redistribution** *(Continued)*

```
Gateway of last resort is 201.0.1.1 to network 0.0.0.0

     201.0.1.0/30 is subnetted, 1 subnets
C       201.0.1.0 is directly connected, Serial0/1.1
     201.0.0.0/25 is subnetted, 1 subnets
O IA    201.0.0.0 [110/65] via 201.0.1.1, 00:00:30, Serial0/1.1
     10.0.0.0/25 is subnetted, 1 subnets
O IA    10.0.0.0 [110/66] via 201.0.1.1, 00:00:30, Serial0/1.1
C    192.168.254.0/24 is directly connected, Ethernet0/0
S*   0.0.0.0/0 [1/0] via 201.0.1.1
Morpheus#
```

NSSA Type 7 LSA Filtering

Review the network that was just discussed, and consider how you can accomplish stopping the network 192.168.254.0/24 from being propagated to the rest of the OSPF domain. Because OSPF is a flexible protocol, it has a built-in way of filtering out routes. This is a way to control which Type 7 LSAs are translated and forwarded outside the NSSA. Use the following configuration on either the NSSA ASBR or the NSSA ABR to selectively block the translation of LSAs:

```
router ospf 100
  summary-address 192.168.254.0 255.255.255.0 not-advertise
```

This configuration generates a Type 7 LSA that is not translated into a Type 5 by the NSSA ABR.

area default-cost Command

In a stub area, you have learned how a default route is injected into the area by the ABR. In the examples so far, you have only had one ABR for the stub area. However, that represents a single point of failure, and if the ABR loses connectivity to the stub area, it would severely impact network operation.

An easy way to fix this is to introduce a second ABR, right? Yes it is and you know there is a "but" coming don't you? When you introduce a second ABR you will have two default routes being injected into the area—which do you use? For example, consider that the original default route is preferred because the connection has greater bandwidth. Enter the **area default-cost** command, and use its ability to assign a cost to the default route.

In Figure 5-19, Router Oracle has been introduced to the network as a second ABR between the backbone area and area 201, our stub area.

Figure 5-19   *Default Cost Example*

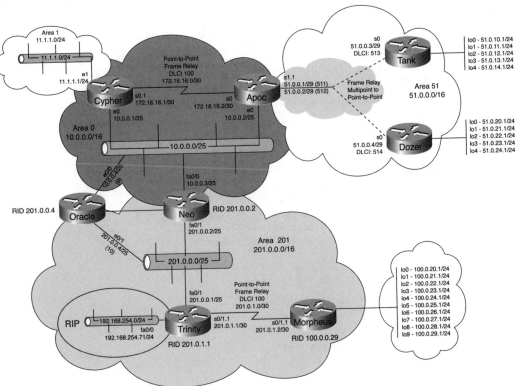

In addition to Router Neo, Router Oracle also injects a default route into the stub area. Example 5-20 shows the results on Router Trinity of two default routes being injected.

Example 5-20   *Resulting Route Table Before Default Cost*

```
<<<output omitted for brevity>>>
     172.16.0.0/30 is subnetted, 1 subnets
O IA   172.16.16.0 [110/66] via 201.0.0.2, 00:00:30, FastEthernet0/1
     10.0.0.0/25
C    192.168.254.0/24 is directly connected, FastEthernet0/0
O*IA 0.0.0.0/0 [110/2] via 201.0.0.4, 00:00:32, FastEthernet0/1
              [110/2] via 201.0.0.2, 00:00:32, FastEthernet0/1
```

In reviewing the network topology, you can see that Router Oracle has access only to area 0 via Ethernet. However, Router Neo has access via Fast Ethernet, so increase the cost associated with Router Oracle's default route to make that the preferred route. Examples 5-21, 5-22, and 5-23 show the before, during, and after results of doing this.

Before

Example 5-21 *1OSPF Area Default Cost: Before*

```
!
router ospf 100
 network 10.0.0.4 0.0.0.0 area 0
 network 201.0.0.4 0.0.0.0 area 201
 area 201 stub
!
```

During

Example 5-22 *2OSPF Area Default Cost: During*

```
Oracle#conf t
Enter configuration commands, one per line.  End with CNTL/Z.
Oracle(config)#router ospf 100
Oracle(config-router)#area 201 default-cost ?
  <0-16777215>  Stub's advertised external route metric
Oracle(config-router)#area 201 default-cost 55
```

After

Example 5-23 *OSPF Area Default Cost: After*

```
!
router ospf 100
 network 10.0.0.4 0.0.0.0 area 0
 network 201.0.0.4 0.0.0.0 area 201
 area 201 stub
 area 201 default-cost 55
!
```

The output from the **show ip route** command on Router Trinity in Example 5-24 shows that now only the lower-cost route from Router Neo appears.

Example 5-24 *Routing Table After the* **area default-cost** *Command*

```
<<<output omitted for brevity>>>
     172.16.0.0/30 is subnetted, 1 subnets
O IA    172.16.16.0 [110/66] via 201.0.0.2, 00:01:51, FastEthernet0/1
     10.0.0.0/25 is subnetted, 1 subnets
O IA    10.0.0.0 [110/2] via 201.0.0.2, 00:01:17, FastEthernet0/1
C    192.168.254.0/24 is directly connected, FastEthernet0/0
O*IA 0.0.0.0/0 [110/2] via 201.0.0.2, 00:00:09, FastEthernet0/1
```

As you can see in Example 5-25, Router Trinity has both default routes in its LSDB, but it prefers the route with the lower cost.

Example 5-25 *LSDB with the* **area default-cost** *Command Applied*

```
Trinity#show ip ospf database

        OSPF Router with ID (201.0.1.1) (Process ID 100)

<<<output omitted for brevity>>>

Link ID          ADV Router       Age       Seq#        Checksum
0.0.0.0          201.0.0.2        372       0x80000001 0x8DE4
0.0.0.0          201.0.0.4        246       0x80000004 0x999D
10.0.0.0         201.0.0.2        314       0x80000008 0xFFE0
10.0.0.0         201.0.0.4        320       0x80000007 0x5086
```

The link from Router Neo to the backbone goes down so Router Trinity now checks its LSDB and discovers that it has another default route from Router Oracle. Now, Router Trinity prefers Router Oracle's default route. The changed cost of 56 is now visible in Example 5-26.

Example 5-26 *Routing Table Changes Default Routes with the* **default auto-cost** *Command*

```
<<<output omitted for brevity>>>
O IA    172.16.16.0 [110/75] via 201.0.0.4, 00:00:09, FastEthernet0/1
        10.0.0.0/25 is subnetted, 1 subnets
O IA    10.0.0.0 [110/11] via 201.0.0.4, 00:00:01, FastEthernet0/1
C       192.168.254.0/24 is directly connected, FastEthernet0/0
O*IA 0.0.0.0/0 [110/56] via 201.0.0.4, 00:00:01, FastEthernet0/1
```

Area Range

There are several key considerations when setting up your OSPF areas for proper summarization. OSPF route summarization occurs in the ABRs. OSPF supports variable-length subnet masks (VLSMs), so it is possible to summarize on any bit boundary in a network or subnet address. OSPF requires manual summarization. As you design the areas, you need to determine summarization at each ABR.

Four potential types of routing information exist in an area and are listed in Table 5-13. This table shows the different types of areas according to the routing information that they use.

Table 5-13 *OSPF Area Route Types*

Area Type	Default	Intra-Area	Inter-Area	External
Nonstub	Yes	Yes	Yes	Yes
Stub	Yes	Yes	Yes	No
Totally stub	Yes	Yes	No	No
NSSA	Yes	Yes	Yes	Yes

The types of routes defined in Table 5-13 for OSPF areas are as follows:

- **Default routes**—If an explicit route cannot be found for a given IP network or subnetwork, the router forwards the packet to the destination specified in the default route.

- **Intra-area routes**—Explicit network or subnet routes must be carried for all networks or subnets inside an area.

- **Inter-area routes**—Areas can carry explicit network, subnet, or summary routes for networks or subnets that are in the OSPF AS but not in the area.

- **External routes**—When different autonomous systems exchange routing information, the routes they exchange are referred to as *external routes*. These external routes can either be explicit subnet or network routes, or even a summarized version.

Certainly, you noticed these large routing tables coming from the loopback interfaces of the routers used in this section of the book. Rather annoying isn't it?

Some sort of summarization is definitely needed, especially in area 51, where the IP address administrator for this entire network generously supplied area 51 with an entire Class B. Although only a fraction of that space is in use, the entire range is there, so any packet destined to 51.0.0.0/16 can go there. The administrator supplied area 201 with a Class B range as well. Note the **show ip route** command output from Router Cypher and the entries under 51.0.0.0/16 and 201.0.0.0/16 in Example 5-27.

Example 5-27 *Routing Table Before the* **area-range** *Command*

```
Cypher#show ip route
Codes: C - connected, S - static, I - IGRP, R - RIP, M - mobile, B - BGP
       D - EIGRP, EX - EIGRP external, O - OSPF, IA - OSPF inter area
       N1 - OSPF NSSA external type 1, N2 - OSPF NSSA external type 2
       E1 - OSPF external type 1, E2 - OSPF external type 2, E - EGP
       i - IS-IS, L1 - IS-IS level-1, L2 - IS-IS level-2, * - candidate default
       U - per-user static route, o - ODR

Gateway of last resort is not set

     51.0.0.0/32 is subnetted, 18 subnets
O IA    51.0.18.1 [110/75] via 10.0.0.2, 00:00:05, Ethernet0
O IA    51.0.19.1 [110/75] via 10.0.0.2, 00:00:05, Ethernet0
O IA    51.0.16.1 [110/75] via 10.0.0.2, 00:00:05, Ethernet0
O IA    51.0.17.1 [110/75] via 10.0.0.2, 00:00:05, Ethernet0
O IA    51.0.22.1 [110/75] via 10.0.0.2, 00:00:05, Ethernet0
O IA    51.0.23.1 [110/75] via 10.0.0.2, 00:00:05, Ethernet0
O IA    51.0.20.1 [110/75] via 10.0.0.2, 00:00:05, Ethernet0
O IA    51.0.21.1 [110/75] via 10.0.0.2, 00:00:05, Ethernet0
O IA    51.0.24.1 [110/75] via 10.0.0.2, 00:00:05, Ethernet0
O IA    51.0.0.3 [110/74] via 10.0.0.2, 00:00:05, Ethernet0
O IA    51.0.0.1 [110/10] via 10.0.0.2, 00:00:05, Ethernet0
O IA    51.0.0.4 [110/74] via 10.0.0.2, 00:00:05, Ethernet0
O IA    51.0.10.1 [110/75] via 10.0.0.2, 00:00:05, Ethernet0
O IA    51.0.11.1 [110/75] via 10.0.0.2, 00:00:07, Ethernet0
```

Example 5-27 *Routing Table Before the* **area-range** *Command (Continued)*

```
O IA    51.0.14.1 [110/75] via 10.0.0.2, 00:00:07, Ethernet0
O IA    51.0.15.1 [110/75] via 10.0.0.2, 00:00:07, Ethernet0
O IA    51.0.12.1 [110/75] via 10.0.0.2, 00:00:07, Ethernet0
O IA    51.0.13.1 [110/75] via 10.0.0.2, 00:00:07, Ethernet0
        100.0.0.0/32 is subnetted, 10 subnets
O IA    100.0.21.1 [110/85] via 10.0.0.4, 00:39:46, Ethernet0
O IA    100.0.20.1 [110/85] via 10.0.0.4, 00:39:46, Ethernet0
O IA    100.0.23.1 [110/85] via 10.0.0.4, 00:39:46, Ethernet0
O IA    100.0.22.1 [110/85] via 10.0.0.4, 00:39:46, Ethernet0
O IA    100.0.29.1 [110/85] via 10.0.0.4, 00:39:46, Ethernet0
O IA    100.0.28.1 [110/85] via 10.0.0.4, 00:39:46, Ethernet0
O IA    100.0.25.1 [110/85] via 10.0.0.4, 00:39:46, Ethernet0
O IA    100.0.24.1 [110/85] via 10.0.0.4, 00:39:46, Ethernet0
O IA    100.0.27.1 [110/85] via 10.0.0.4, 00:39:46, Ethernet0
O IA    100.0.26.1 [110/85] via 10.0.0.4, 00:39:46, Ethernet0
        201.0.1.0/30 is subnetted, 1 subnets
O IA    201.0.1.0 [110/84] via 10.0.0.4, 00:39:46, Ethernet0
        201.0.0.0/25 is subnetted, 1 subnets
O IA    201.0.0.0 [110/20] via 10.0.0.4, 00:39:46, Ethernet0
        172.16.0.0/30 is subnetted, 1 subnets
C       172.16.16.0 is directly connected, Serial0.1
        10.0.0.0/25 is subnetted, 1 subnets
C       10.0.0.0 is directly connected, Ethernet0
        11.0.0.0/24 is subnetted, 1 subnets
C       11.1.1.0 is directly connected, Ethernet1
O IA 192.168.254.0/24 [110/21] via 10.0.0.4, 00:39:48, Ethernet0
Cypher#
```

In OSPF, an ABR advertises addresses that describe how to reach networks (routes) from one area into another area. Route summarization is the consolidation of these advertised addresses. This feature causes a single summary route to be advertised to other areas by an ABR, thereby representing multiple routes in a single statement. This has several benefits, but the primary one is a reduction in the size of routing tables.

If the network numbers in an area are assigned so that they are contiguous, you can configure the ABR to advertise a summary route that covers all the individual networks within the area that fall into the range specified by the summary route.

Examples 5-28, 5-29, and 5-30 use Router Cypher to demonstrate what this command can do as a router in area 0, where it receives all the routes from areas 51 and 201. Some summarization of these ranges of addresses is definitely needed, and this is accomplished with the **area-range** command. Because you are looking at all the networks from a specific area, this configuration command is applied to the area ABR, in this case Router Apoc.

Before

Example 5-28 *The* **area-range** *Command Configuration: Before*

```
!
router ospf 100
 network 10.0.0.0 0.0.255.255 area 0
 network 51.0.0.0 0.0.255.255 area 51
 network 172.16.16.0 0.0.0.3 area 0
 !
```

During

Example 5-29 *The* **area-range** *Command Configuration: During*

```
Apoc#conf t
Enter configuration commands, one per line.  End with CNTL/Z.
Apoc(config)#router ospf 100
Apoc(config-router)#area 51 range 51.0.0.0 255.255.0.0 ?
  advertise       Advertise this range (default)
  not-advertise   DoNotAdvertise this range
  <cr>

Apoc(config-router)#area 51 range 51.0.0.0 255.255.0.0 advertise
Apoc(config-router)#^Z
Apoc#
```

After

Example 5-30 *The* **area-range** *Command Configuration: After*

```
!
router ospf 100
 area 51 range 51.0.0.0 255.255.0.0
 network 10.0.0.0 0.0.255.255 area 0
 network 51.0.0.0 0.0.255.255 area 51
 network 172.16.16.0 0.0.0.3 area 0
 !
```

See the **not-advertise** keyword used in the **area-range** command. By using this keyword, all the networks included in the **area-range** command are not advertised out of the area. However, this command was not used, so the **range** command should have summarized all the 51.0.0.0/16 networks as configured. You can see the result of summarizing all the areas in Example 5-31 in the much smaller routing table. This is also known as a *summary-only aggregate route.*

Example 5-31 *Cypher's Routing Table After Route Summarization*

```
Cypher#show ip route
Codes: C - connected, S - static, I - IGRP, R - RIP, M - mobile, B - BGP
       D - EIGRP, EX - EIGRP external, O - OSPF, IA - OSPF inter area
       N1 - OSPF NSSA external type 1, N2 - OSPF NSSA external type 2
       E1 - OSPF external type 1, E2 - OSPF external type 2, E - EGP
       i - IS-IS, L1 - IS-IS level-1, L2 - IS-IS level-2, * - candidate default
       U - per-user static route, o - ODR

Gateway of last resort is not set

     51.0.0.0/16 is subnetted, 1 subnets
O IA    51.0.0.0 [110/10] via 10.0.0.2, 00:00:03, Ethernet0
     100.0.0.0/16 is subnetted, 1 subnets
O IA    100.0.0.0 [110/85] via 10.0.0.4, 00:00:33, Ethernet0
     172.16.0.0/30 is subnetted, 1 subnets
C       172.16.16.0 is directly connected, Serial0.1
     10.0.0.0/25 is subnetted, 1 subnets
C       10.0.0.0 is directly connected, Ethernet0
     11.0.0.0/24 is subnetted, 1 subnets
C       11.1.1.0 is directly connected, Ethernet1
O IA 192.168.254.0/24 [110/21] via 10.0.0.4, 00:45:45, Ethernet0
O IA 201.0.0.0/16 [110/20] via 10.0.0.4, 00:00:28, Ethernet0
Cypher#
```

Tuning OSPF Operation

The previous sections covered the common aspects of OSPF configuration commands. At this point, some additional commands are presented that allow you to tune OSPF.

Altering OSPF Administrative Distance

An *administrative distance* is a rating of the priority (that is, trustworthiness) of a routing information source, such as an individual router or a group of routers. Numerically, an administrative distance is an integer from 0 to 255. Specifically, the higher the numerical value of administrative distance, the lower the trust rating. An administrative distance of 255 means that the routing information source cannot be trusted and should be ignored. Table 5-14 shows administrative distance values.

Table 5-14 *Default Administrative Distances*

Route Source/Type	Default Administrative Distance
Connected interface	0
Static route pointing at an interface	0
Static route to a next-hop interface	1
EIGRP summary route	5
External BGP	20
EIGRP	90

Table 5-14 *Default Administrative Distances (Continued)*

IGRP	100
OSPF	110
IS-IS	115
RIP-1 and RIP-2	120
EGP	140
External EIGRP	170
Internal BGP	200
Unknown route or Unreachable	255

As previously discussed, OSPF uses three different types of routes: intra-area, inter-area, and external. Routes within an area are intra-area; routes to another area are inter-area; and routes from another routing domain learned via redistribution are external. The default distance for each type of route is 110. Use the **distance ospf** command when you have multiple OSPF routing processes doing mutual redistribution and you want to prefer internal routes over all external routes. You can accomplish this by setting all the external routes to a distance of 200, for example.

To change any of the OSPF distance values, use the following command in router configuration mode:

```
distance  ospf {[intra-area dist1] [inter-area dist2] [external dist3]}
```

When using this command, you must use at least one of the keywords.

CAUTION   Use care when changing the defaults here because problems such as a routing loop might result.

Load Balancing

As part of your design, you must consider the traffic flow across the network and whether to use load balancing. This OSPF feature can be helpful in your network's overall design. This section discusses how to best utilize the OSPF load-balancing feature with a network.

In routing, *load balancing* is the capability of a router to distribute traffic over all its network ports that are the same distance from the destination address. Good load-balancing algorithms use both line speed and reliability information. Load balancing increases the utilization of network segments, thus increasing effective use of network bandwidth.

Internetwork topologies are typically designed to provide redundant routes in order to prevent a partitioned network. Redundancy is also useful for providing additional bandwidth for high-traffic areas. If equal-cost paths between nodes exist, Cisco routers automatically load balance in an OSPF environment. By default, when OSPF has equal-cost multiple paths (ECMPs) to a given destination, load balancing occurs.

Cisco routers can use up to four equal-cost paths for a given destination by default. Packets might be distributed either on a per-destination basis (when fast-switching) or on a per-packet basis. Per-destination load balancing is the default behavior. Per-packet load balancing can be enabled by turning off fast-switching using the **no ip route-cache** interface configuration command.

Even More ECMP

OSPF performs ECMP per destination over up to four paths to a destination, but what happens when you have five or even six equal-cost paths—do they go unused? Absolutely not! The **maximum-path** command, when applied to OSPF, allows you increase from four to six the maximum number of paths supported. The example that follows shows this in action with OSPF.

In Example 5-32, eight ECMPs route to network 192.168.1.0 from Router 1 to Router 2 have been configured. By default, OSPF places four ECMP route entries into the routing table. When using the **maximum-paths** command, OSPF includes six equal-cost paths.

Example 5-32   *Eight ECMP Routes*

```
R2#show ip route
Codes: C - connected, S - static, I - IGRP, R - RIP, M - mobile, B - BGP
       D - EIGRP, EX - EIGRP external, O - OSPF, IA - OSPF inter area
       N1 - OSPF NSSA external type 1, N2 - OSPF NSSA external type 2
       E1 - OSPF external type 1, E2 - OSPF external type 2, E - EGP
       i - IS-IS, L1 - IS-IS level-1, L2 - IS-IS level-2, * - candidate
default
       U - per-user static route, o - ODR

Gateway of last resort is not set

     172.16.0.0/24 is subnetted, 8 subnets
C       172.16.8.0 is directly connected, Serial0.8
C       172.16.4.0 is directly connected, Serial0.4
C       172.16.5.0 is directly connected, Serial0.5
C       172.16.6.0 is directly connected, Serial0.6
C       172.16.7.0 is directly connected, Serial0.7
C       172.16.1.0 is directly connected, Serial0.1
C       172.16.2.0 is directly connected, Serial0.2
C       172.16.3.0 is directly connected, Serial0.3
O IA 192.168.1.0/24 [110/65] via 172.16.8.1, 00:02:34, Serial0.8
                    [110/65] via 172.16.7.1, 00:02:34, Serial0.7
                    [110/65] via 172.16.6.1, 00:02:34, Serial0.6
                    [110/65] via 172.16.5.1, 00:02:34, Serial0.5
                    [110/65] via 172.16.4.1, 00:02:34, Serial0.4
                    [110/65] via 172.16.3.1, 00:02:34, Serial0.3
C    192.168.2.0/24 is directly connected, Loopback0
R2#
```

Example 5-33 shows the configuration for Router 2 in this example.

Example 5-33 *ECMP Router 2 Configuration*

```
R2#show running-config
Building configuration...
!
hostname R2
!
logging buffered 32768 debugging
enable password cisco
!
interface Loopback0
 ip address 192.168.2.2 255.255.255.0
 ip ospf network point-to-point
!
interface Serial0
 no ip address
 encapsulation frame-relay
!
interface Serial0.1 point-to-point
 ip address 172.16.1.2 255.255.255.0
 ip ospf network point-to-point
 frame-relay interface-dlci 211
!
interface Serial0.2 point-to-point
 ip address 172.16.2.2 255.255.255.0
 ip ospf network point-to-point
 frame-relay interface-dlci 221
!
interface Serial0.3 point-to-point
 ip address 172.16.3.2 255.255.255.0
 ip ospf network point-to-point
 frame-relay interface-dlci 231
!
interface Serial0.4 point-to-point
 ip address 172.16.4.2 255.255.255.0
 ip ospf network point-to-point
 frame-relay interface-dlci 241
!
interface Serial0.5 point-to-point
 ip address 172.16.5.2 255.255.255.0
 ip ospf network point-to-point
 frame-relay interface-dlci 251
!
interface Serial0.6 point-to-point
 ip address 172.16.6.2 255.255.255.0
 ip ospf network point-to-point
 frame-relay interface-dlci 261
!
interface Serial0.7 point-to-point
 ip address 172.16.7.2 255.255.255.0
 ip ospf network point-to-point
 frame-relay interface-dlci 271
!
```

Example 5-33 *ECMP Router 2 Configuration (Continued)*

```
interface Serial0.8 point-to-point
 ip address 172.16.8.2 255.255.255.0
 ip ospf network point-to-point
 frame-relay interface-dlci 281
!
router ospf 1
 network 172.16.0.0 0.0.255.255 area 0
 network 192.168.2.0 0.0.0.255 area 2
 maximum-paths 6
!
ip classless
!
line con 0
 password cisco
```

Example 5-34 shows the configuration for Router 1, which is the other router and is the source of the routing updates.

Example 5-34 *ECMP Router 1 Configuration*

```
R1#show running-config
!
hostname R1
!
logging buffered 32768 debugging
enable password cisco
!
interface Loopback0
 ip address 192.168.1.1 255.255.255.0
 ip ospf network point-to-point
!
interface Serial0
 no ip address
 encapsulation frame-relay
!
interface Serial0.1 point-to-point
 ip address 172.16.1.1 255.255.255.0
 ip ospf network point-to-point
 frame-relay interface-dlci 112
!
interface Serial0.2 point-to-point
 ip address 172.16.2.1 255.255.255.0
 ip ospf network point-to-point
 frame-relay interface-dlci 122
!
interface Serial0.3 point-to-point
 ip address 172.16.3.1 255.255.255.0
 ip ospf network point-to-point
 frame-relay interface-dlci 132
!
```

continues

Example 5-34 *ECMP Router 1 Configuration (Continued)*

```
interface Serial0.4 point-to-point
 ip address 172.16.4.1 255.255.255.0
 ip ospf network point-to-point
 frame-relay interface-dlci 142
 !
interface Serial0.5 point-to-point
 ip address 172.16.5.1 255.255.255.0
 ip ospf network point-to-point
 frame-relay interface-dlci 152
 !
interface Serial0.6 point-to-point
 ip address 172.16.6.1 255.255.255.0
 ip ospf network point-to-point
 frame-relay interface-dlci 162
 !
interface Serial0.7 point-to-point
 ip address 172.16.7.1 255.255.255.0
 ip ospf network point-to-point
 frame-relay interface-dlci 172
 !
interface Serial0.8 point-to-point
 ip address 172.16.8.1 255.255.255.0
 ip ospf network point-to-point
 frame-relay interface-dlci 182
 !
router ospf 1
 network 172.16.0.0 0.0.255.255 area 0
 network 192.168.1.0 0.0.0.255 area 1
 maximum-paths 6
 !
ip classless
 !
line con 0
 password cisco
```

Default Routes

The capability to generate and redistribute default routes is of extreme importance within any large network. The most common method of generating a default route is through the use of a static route statement within the router. An ASBR can be forced to generate a default route into an OSPF network (domain). Whenever you configure the **redistribute** command or the **default information originate** command into OSPF, the router becomes an ASBR. An ASBR in OSPF does not by default distribute a default route nor does it automatically generate one. You can force an ASBR to generate a default route into an OSPF routing domain, as illustrated in Figure 5-20.

Figure 5-20 *ASBRs Consolidate Routes*

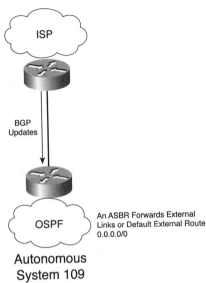

To force the ASBR to generate a default route, execute the following command in router configuration mode:

```
default-information originate [always] [metric metricvalue] [metric-type type-
value] [route-map map-name]
```

In OSPF, the **default-information originate** command allows the OSPF routing process to propagate a default route that is originated from the router that has the default route configured. With this command, a default route must be configured on the router that has received the **default-information originate** command.

This unique command also has an **always** keyword that can be added to the original command. With the **always** keyword, the router advertises a default route into OSPF, regardless of whether the router knows of or has a default route configured. This is how the keyword alters router operation. However, this might result in a black hole, so use this keyword with caution.

You must use the **default-information originate** command to redistribute a static default route. If you want the router to create and redistribute a default route whether you have one configured or not, use the **default-information originate always** command.

Figure 5-21 shows a sample network, and an example demonstrates how a default route is determined.

Figure 5-21 *Injecting a Default Route*

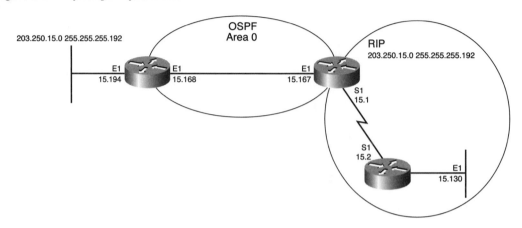

Referring to Figure 5-21, assuming that Router E is injecting a default route of 0.0.0.0 into the RIP network, and knowing that Router C has a gateway of last resort of 203.250.15.2, the following is true of Routers A, C, and E:

- Router A knows only what Router C tells it about the default route.

- Router C sees the default route but does not share the information with other routers until told to by the **default-information originate** command.

- Router E knows a default route of 0.0.0.0.

The output in Example 5-35 shows that Router C knows about the default route, but it does not tell other routers until told to do so with the **default-information originate** command.

Example 5-35 *Router C Has a Default Route*

```
Router C#show ip route
Codes: C - connected, S - static, I - IGRP, R - RIP, M - mobile, B - BGP
D - EIGRP, EX - EIGRP external, O - OSPF, IA - OSPF inter area
E1 - OSPF external type 1, E2 - OSPF external type 2, E - EGP
i - IS-IS, L1 - IS-IS level-1, L2 - IS-IS level-2, * - candidate
default
Gateway of last resort is 203.250.15.2 to network 0.0.0.0
203.250.15.0 255.255.255.192 is subnetted, 4 subnets
C 203.250.15.0 is directly connected, Serial1
C 203.250.15.64 is directly connected, Ethernet0
R 203.250.15.128 [120/1] via 203.250.15.2, 00:00:17, Serial1
O 203.250.15.192 [110/20] via 203.250.15.68, 2d23, Ethernet0
R* 0.0.0.0 0.0.0.0 [120/1] via 203.250.15.2, 00:00:17, Serial1
[120/1] via 203.250.15.68, 00:00:32, Ethernet0
interface Ethernet0
ip address 203.250.15.67 255.255.255.192
```

Example 5-35   *Router C Has a Default Route (Continued)*

```
interface Serial1
ip address 203.250.15.1 255.255.255.192

router ospf 10
redistribute rip metric 10 subnets
network 203.250.15.0 0.0.0.255 area 0
default-information originate metric 10

router rip
redistribute ospf 10 metric 2
passive-interface Ethernet0
network 203.250.15.0
```

Now that Router C has been configured to tell Router A about the default route, you can check Router A's routing table. You can quickly see in Example 5-36 that the default route is known by the router.

Example 5-36   *Router A's Routing Table Confirms Router A's Knowledge of the Default Route*

```
Router A#show ip route
Codes: C - connected, S - static, I - IGRP, R - RIP, M - mobile, B - BGP
       D - EIGRP, EX - EIGRP external, O - OSPF, IA - OSPF inter area
       E1 - OSPF external type 1, E2 - OSPF external type 2, E - EGP
       i - IS-IS, L1 - IS-IS level-1, L2 - IS-IS level-2, * - candidate
       default
Gateway of last resort is 203.250.15.67 to network 0.0.0.0
       203.250.15.0 255.255.255.192 is subnetted, 4 subnets
O      203.250.15.0 [110/74] via 203.250.15.67, 2d23, Ethernet0
C      203.250.15.64 is directly connected, Ethernet0
O E2   203.250.15.128 [110/10] via 203.250.15.67, 2d23, Ethernet0
C      203.250.15.192 is directly connected, Ethernet1
O*E2   0.0.0.0 0.0.0.0 [110/10] via 203.250.15.67, 00:00:17, Ethernet0
```

Router A has learned about 0.0.0.0 as an external route with a metric of 10. The gateway of last resort is set to 203.250.15.67, as expected. Therefore, Router A's default route is the E0 interface of Router C that has a default route in Router E.

Passive Interfaces

You can encounter a situation where you want an interface advertised via a routing protocol, but you do not want to have the routing protocol sending updates out that interface. This is made possible through the use of the **passive-interface** command, which is entered in router configuration mode for OSPF, as demonstrated in Example 5-37. This example shows the configuration in three stages: before configuring the passive interface, while configuring the passive interface, and after configuring the passive interface.

Example 5-37 *Configuring a Passive Interface: Before, During, and After*

```
Before
!
router ospf 100
 area 201 stub
 network 192.168.254.0 0.0.0.255 area 201
 network 201.0.0.0 0.0.0.127 area 201
 network 201.0.1.0 0.0.0.3 area 201
!
During
Trinity# conf t
Enter configuration commands, one per line.  End with CNTL/Z.
Trinity(config)#router ospf 100
Trinity(config-router)#passive-interface ?
  BRI          ISDN Basic Rate Interface
  FastEthernet FastEthernet IEEE 802.3
  Null         Null interface
  Serial       Serial
  default      Suppress routing updates on all interfaces
  <cr>
Trinity(config-router)#passive-interface fastEthernet 0/0
After
!
router ospf 100
 area 201 stub
 passive-interface FastEthernet0/0
 network 192.168.254.0 0.0.0.255 area 201
 network 201.0.0.0 0.0.0.127 area 201
 network 201.0.1.0 0.0.0.3 area 201
!
```

OSPF routing information is neither sent nor received through the specified router interface. The specified interface address appears as a stub network in the OSPF domain.

On-Demand Circuits

The OSPF on-demand circuit operational capability is an enhancement to the OSPF protocol that allows efficient operation over on-demand circuits such as ISDN, X.25, switched virtual circuits (SVCs), and dial-up lines. This feature set is fully supported by Cisco (in certain Cisco IOS Software versions) and follows the standard as described in RFC 1793, "Extending OSPF to Support Demand Circuits." This RFC is worth consulting if you plan to configure OSPF to operate within this type of networking environment.

Prior to this RFC, periodic OSPF Hellos and LSAs would be exchanged between routers that connected on the demand link, even when no changes were reported in the Hello or LSA information. This caused the costs involved with these types of connectivity to skyrocket.

However, with this enhancement to OSPF, periodic Hellos are suppressed, and the periodic refreshes of LSAs are not flooded over the demand circuit. These packets bring up the link only under the following tightly controlled circumstances:

- When they are exchanged for the first time
- When a change occurs in the information they contain

This operation allows the underlying data link layer to be closed when the network topology is stable, thus saving unnecessary costs. This is useful because if your company is paying ISDN costs every time a call is placed, you want to ensure that the call is necessary.

This feature is also useful when you want to connect telecommuters or branch offices to an OSPF backbone at a central site. In this case, OSPF for on-demand circuits allows the benefits of OSPF over the entire domain, without excess connection costs. Periodic refreshes of Hello updates, LSA updates, and other protocol overhead are prevented in this configuration from enabling the on-demand circuit when there is no real data to transmit. Figure 5-21 illustrates this type of OSPF setup.

Figure 5-22   *OSPF On-Demand Circuit Operation*

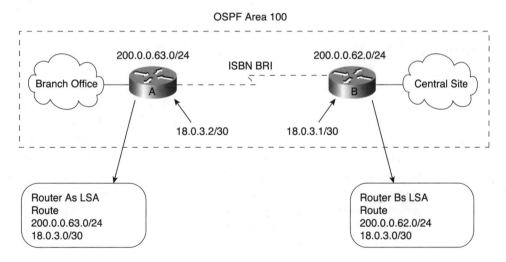

Overhead protocols within OSPF, such as Hellos and LSAs, are transferred over the on-demand circuit only upon initial setup and when they are required to reflect a change in the network topology. This means that critical changes to the topology that require new SPF calculations are transmitted to maintain network topology integrity. However, periodic refreshes that do not include changes are not transmitted across the link.

To configure OSPF for on-demand circuits, enter the following command in interface configuration mode:

```
ip ospf demand-circuit
```

Example 5-38 demonstrates how to configure this command.

Example 5-38   *Configuring OSPF for On-Demand Circuits*

```
OSPF_Router(config)#router ospf 100
OSPF_Router(config-router)#network 18.0.3.0 0.0.0.3 area 100
OSPF_Router(config-router)#network 200.0.62.0 0.0.0.255 area 100
OSPF_Router(config-router)#network 200.0.63.0 0.0.0.255 area 100
OSPF_Router(config-router)#interface bri0
OSPF_Router(config-if)#ip ospf demand-circuit
```

TIP   If the router is part of a point-to-point topology, only one end of the demand circuit must be configured with this command. However, both routers must have this Cisco IOS Software feature set loaded. If the router is part of a point-to-multipoint topology, only the multipoint end must be configured with this command. You can also try the hidden **no neighbor peer** command, which keeps OSPF neighbor down over bri.

Implementation Considerations

Consider the following items before implementing on-demand circuits on a Cisco router in an OSPF network:

- Because LSAs that include topology changes are flooded over an on-demand circuit, you need to put demand circuits within OSPF stub areas or within NSSAs to isolate the demand circuits from as many topology changes as possible. If these circuits are constantly being activated, high costs result, defeating the purpose of their design.

- To take advantage of the on-demand circuit functionality within a stub area or NSSA, every router in the area must have the correct IOS feature set loaded. If this feature set is deployed within a regular area, all other regular areas must also support this feature before the demand circuit functionality can take effect. This is because Type 5 external LSAs are flooded throughout all areas.

- Do not implement this OSPF feature on a broadcast-based network topology because the overhead protocols (such as Hellos and LSAs) cannot be successfully suppressed; this means that the link remains activated.

On-Demand Configuration Examples

A number of scenarios can be encountered if you are planning to use this feature of OSPF. The first two examples, described in the following sections, are incorrect ways to implement OSPF. In the following scenarios, site Router A is the router equipped with on-demand dialing.

Example 1: Remote Router Is in Two Areas (Neither Is Area 0)

This approach does not work because the LAN interface cannot be in more than one area, as shown in Figure 5-23. There is no exchange of link-state information between areas 1 and 2.

As shown in Figure 5-23, the site router is located in two different OSPF areas, and neither of them is in area 0. However, if the site LAN is not included in the OSPF routing, and its routing information is injected with a static route either at the site router or at the ABR for area 1, this approach can be made to work, although it is not the most optimal OSPF network design.

Figure 5-23 *Remote Site Router Is in Two areas (Neither Area is Area 0)*

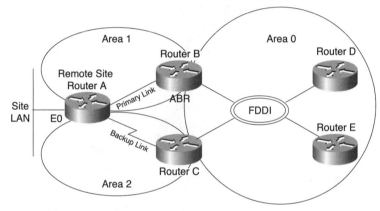

Example 2: Site Router Is in Two Areas (One Is Area 0)

This approach makes the site router (Router A) an ABR under failure. It does work; however, it is not considered an acceptable design because it would make the site router part of area 0 if it were ever disconnected from Router B. This design would require more resources than would be cost-effective in all but the smallest networks (see Figure 5-24).

Figure 5-24 *Site Router Is in Two Areas (One Is Area 0)*

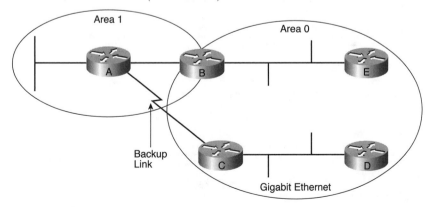

Example 3: Remote Site Router Is in One Area

This approach is the most suitable and works even if the backup router (Router C in Figure 5-25) is located elsewhere. The secret is that Router C does not summarize for its attached areas; therefore, Router C originates more specific prefixes for the networks in failure. The disadvantage is that dedicated backup interfaces are required for each area.

Figure 5-25 *Site Router Is in One Area*

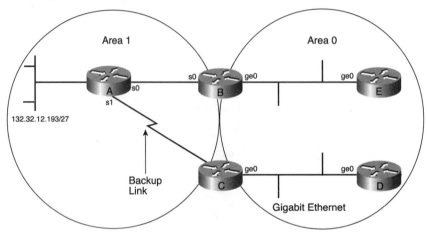

Example 5-39 shows some sample configurations for this design scenario.

Example 5-39 *Configuring OSPF for On-Demand Circuits: Remote Site Router Is in One Area*

```
! Site Router A Configuration
interface ethernet 0
ip address 132.32.12.193 255.255.255.224
interface serial 0
ip address 132.32.12.254 255.255.255.252
backup interface serial 1
backup delay 0 5
interface serial 1
ip address 132.32.12.250 255.255.255.252
router ospf 1
network 132.32.0.0 0.0.255.255 area 1
! Site Router B Configuration
interface ge 0
ip address 132.32.1.1 255.255.255.248
interface serial 0
ip address 132.32.12.253 255.255.255.252
router ospf 1
network 132.32.12.0 0.0.3.255 area 1
area 1 range 132.32.12.0 255.255.252.0
network 132.32.0.0 0.0.255.255 area 0
! Site Router C Configuration
interface ge 0
ip address 132.32.1.2 255.255.255.248
```

Example 5-39 *Configuring OSPF for On-Demand Circuits: Remote Site Router Is in One Area (Continued)*

```
interface serial 0
ip address 132.32.12.249 255.255.255.252
router ospf 1
network 132.32.12.0 0.0.3.255 area 1
network 132.32.0.0 0.0.255.255 area 0
```

Example 4: Remote Site Router Is in Two Routing Domains

This approach relies on one-way redistribution of multiple instances of a separate routing protocol into OSPF, as shown in Figure 5-26. Auto-summarization must also be disabled in this scenario. Administrative distances should be tweaked to ensure that OSPF is the favored routing protocol. This approach has the advantage that interfaces can be shared among areas, that is, a dedicated set of interfaces for each area is not required.

Figure 5-26 *Remote Site Router in Two Routing Domains*

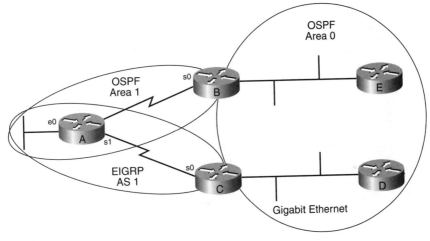

Example 5-40 shows some sample configurations for this scenario.

Example 5-40 *Configuring OSPF for On-Demand Circuits: Remote Site Router Is in Two Routing Domains*

```
! Router A Configuration
interface ethernet 0
ip address 132.132.132.193 255.255.255.224
interface serial 0
ip address 132.132.132.254 255.255.255.252
backup interface serial 1
backup delay 0 5
interface serial 1
ip address 132.132.132.250 255.255.255.252
router ospf 1
```

continues

Example 5-40 *Configuring OSPF for On-Demand Circuits: Remote Site Router Is in Two Routing Domains (Continued)*

```
network 132.132.132.192 0.0.0.31 area 1
network 132.132.132.252 0.0.0.3 area 1
router eigrp 1
network 132.132.0.0 distance 200 0.0.0.0 255.255.255.255
! Router B Configuration
interface fddi 0
ip address 132.132.1.1 255.255.255.248
interface serial 0
ip address 132.132.132.253 255.255.255.252
router ospf 1
network 132.132.132.0 0.0.3.255 area 1
area 1 range 132.132.132.0 255.255.252.0
network 132.132.0.0 0.0.255.255 area 0
! Router C Configuration
interface fddi 0
ip address 132.132.1.2 255.255.255.248
interface serial 0
ip address 132.132.132.249 255.255.255.252
router ospf 1
network 132.132.1.0 0.0.0.7 area 0
redistribute eigrp 1 subnets metric 32000
router eigrp 1
network 132.132.0.0
passive-interface fddi 0
distance 200 0.0.0.0 255.255.255.255
```

On-Demand Circuits Summary

The preceding examples work with dial-on-demand routing as well as dial-backup. Set the metric on the backup interface to be less favorable than that on the primary. Also, set the administrative distance on the backup routing protocol to be greater than that of the primary. (Set both the metric and administrative distance to allow the idle timer to work.) The redistribution of a static route for the backed-up site is mandatory. Not only does it speed convergence, but it also is the controlling factor in directing traffic at the upstream dial-on-demand interface to trigger dialing. After the primary interface goes down, all knowledge of the site LAN is lost. If the backup server is originating routes for the site LANs at a much higher cost, these now come into effect.

Summary

This chapter provided considerable OSPF information and samples for your use. The discussion began with altering the costs, working with loopback interfaces, and discussing everything you need to know to get OSPF working.

The primary topics of this chapter were how OSPF creates routes as well as how OSPF configuration. Reviewing the different area configurations and options provided a detailed look into the different area types and the ways to fine-tune each to effect routing in an OSPF network.

The remainder of the chapter provides case studies that can help you review these concepts and introduce a few more to prepare you for the topics of summarization and redistribution in Chapter 6 .

Case Study: Assigning Unique Network Numbers to Each OSPF Area

In this scenario, each OSPF area has its own unique NIC-assigned IP address range. This can be as grand as a Class A address for the entire network, with multiple Class Bs assigned to each area, or more realistically, it can be a group of Class C addresses. This example is demonstrated in Figure 5-27. The benefits of this method are as follows:

- Address assignment is simple because each area has its own unique network.

- Configuration of the routers is easy, reducing the likelihood of errors.

- Network operations are streamlined because each area has a simple unique address prefix.

Figure 5-27 *Assigning Unique Network Numbers to Each OSPF Area*

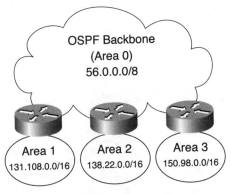

The following basic steps allow you to create such a network:

Step 1   Define your structure (identify areas and allocate nodes to areas).

Step 2   Assign addresses to networks, subnets, and end stations, as demonstrated in Figure 5-27.

As an example, the route summarization configuration at the ABRs is greatly simplified. Routes from area 3 injected into the backbone would be summarized as "all routes starting with 150.98 are found in area 3." You can accomplish this on a Cisco router with the following command:

```
area 3 range 150.98.0.0 255.255.0.0
```

The main drawback of this approach is that it can waste important and scarce IP address space. As an alternative, you can use private addressing throughout all areas except area 0, as follows:

> Area 0: 56.0.0.0/8
> Area 1: 10.1.0.0/16
> Area 2: 10.2.0.0/16
> Area 3: 10.3.0.0/16

The main point of this case study is that when assigning IP address ranges to areas, put some thought into it and try to make the assignments make sense to people outside the networking arena.

Case Study: OSPF with Multiple Areas

In this case study and throughout the next several case studies, you review a series of network scenarios that implement and build on the OSPF technologies discussed in the previous several chapters. This case study evaluates the configuration of OSPF and three routers into a multi-area OSPF network design solution, as shown in Figure 5-28.

Figure 5-28   *OSPF Multi-Area Design*

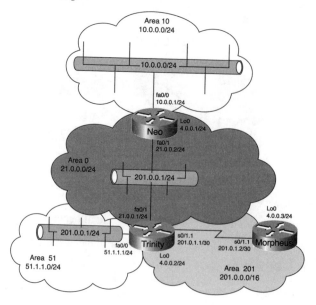

First, configure IP to get the network running and assign interfaces as well as loopback interfaces. In this scenario, subnets have been chosen that stand out to facilitate referencing their purpose. For example, all the loopback addresses in this network are from the 4.0.0.x/ 24 subnet.

The deployment of loopback interfaces prior to the activation of OSPF ensures that the loopback interfaces become the preferred RID. Activate OSPF to see how OSPF begins forming its relationships through the use of Hello packets. To do this properly, you configure Routers Neo and Morpheus and then configure Trinity last, as shown in Example 5-41.

Example 5-41 *Configuring Router Trinity*

```
Trinity#conf t
Enter configuration commands, one per line.  End with CNTL/Z.
Trinity(config)#router ospf 100
Trinity(config-router)#network 51.1.1.0 0.0.0.255 area 51
Trinity(config-router)#network 201.0.0.0 0.0.255.255 area 201
Trinity(config-router)#network 21.0.0.0 0.0.0.255 area 0
Trinity(config-router)#^Z
Trinity#
```

At the same, execute the **debug ip ospf events** command on Neo (see Example 5-42) to see the development of the OSPF relationship between Neo and Trinity.

Example 5-42 *Debugging IP OSPF Events*

```
Neo#debug ip ospf events
*Mar  1 01:36:18.587: OSPF: Rcv hello from 4.0.0.2 area 0 from FastEthernet0/1
21.0.0.1
*Mar  1 01:36:18.587: OSPF: End of hello processing
*Mar  1 01:36:27.479: OSPF: Rcv DBD from 4.0.0.2 on FastEthernet0/1 seq 0x232D opt
0x42 flag 0x7 len 32   mtu 1500 state INIT
*Mar  1 01:36:27.479: OSPF: 2 Way Communication to 4.0.0.2 on FastEthernet0/1, state
2WAY
!The routers have achieved the 2Way state as described in Chapter 4
!and because they are on a broadcast media they must next elect a DR & BDR as
!the following output demonstrates.
*Mar  1 01:36:27.479: OSPF: Neighbor change Event on interface FastEthernet0/1
*Mar  1 01:36:27.479: OSPF: DR/BDR election on FastEthernet0/1
*Mar  1 01:36:27.479: OSPF: Elect BDR 4.0.0.2
*Mar  1 01:36:27.479: OSPF: Elect DR 4.0.0.1
*Mar  1 01:36:27.483:         DR: 4.0.0.1 (Id)    BDR: 4.0.0.2 (Id)
!At this point the election process is complete and the DR has the RID of 4.0.0.1
!however this not what would be expected is it? Trinity has the higher RID, recall
!that I mentioned Neo was activated first and as the first OSPF router it claimed
!the DR position for the 201.0.0.0/24 Ethernet segment since it was first. The next
!step we would expect to see on this is the routers becoming adjacent and
!exchanging Database Descriptor and Link State Request packets.
*Mar  1 01:36:27.483: OSPF: Send DBD to 4.0.0.2 on FastEthernet0/1 seq 0x7A3
  opt 0x42 flag 0x7 len 32?
*Mar  1 01:36:27.483: OSPF: NBR Negotiation Done. We are the SLAVE
*Mar  1 01:36:27.483: OSPF: Send DBD to 4.0.0.2 on FastEthernet0/1 seq 0x232D
  opt 0x42 flag 0x2 len 72
```

Example 5-42   *Debugging IP OSPF Events (Continued)*

```
*Mar  1 01:36:27.487: OSPF: Rcv DBD from 4.0.0.2 on FastEthernet0/1 seq 0x232E
   opt 0x42 flag 0x3 len 72  mtu 1500 state EXCHANGE
*Mar  1 01:36:27.487: OSPF: Send DBD to 4.0.0.2 on FastEthernet0/1 seq 0x232E
   opt 0x42 flag 0x0 len 32
*Mar  1 01:36:27.491: OSPF: Database request to 4.0.0.2
*Mar  1 01:36:27.491: OSPF: sent LS REQ packet to 21.0.0.1, length 24
*Mar  1 01:36:27.491: OSPF: Rcv DBD from 4.0.0.2 on FastEthernet0/1 seq 0x232F
   opt 0x42 flag 0x1 len 32  mtu 1500 state EXCHANGE
*Mar  1 01:36:27.495: OSPF: Exchange Done with 4.0.0.2 on FastEthernet0/1
*Mar  1 01:36:27.495: OSPF: Send DBD to 4.0.0.2 on FastEthernet0/1 seq 0x232F
   opt 0x42 flag 0x0 len 32
*Mar  1 01:36:27.495: OSPF: Synchronized with 4.0.0.2 on FastEthernet0/1, state FULL
!At this point the routers are completely adjacent with their
!Link State Databases fully synchronized as well. From this point forward
!we will see the hello packets sent every 10 seconds to ensure the adjacent router
!is present and operational as shown below.
*Mar  1 01:36:38.583: OSPF: Rcv hello from 4.0.0.2 area 0 from FastEthernet0/1
   21.0.0.1
*Mar  1 01:36:38.583: OSPF: End of hello processing
*Mar  1 01:36:48.583: OSPF: Rcv hello from 4.0.0.2 area 0 from FastEthernet0/1
   21.0.0.1
*Mar  1 01:36:48.583: OSPF: End of hello processing
*Mar  1 01:36:58.583: OSPF: Rcv hello from 4.0.0.2 area 0 from FastEthernet0/1
   21.0.0.1
*Mar  1 01:36:58.583: OSPF: End of hello processing
```

One of the fastest ways to determine the status of OSPF communication between routers is to use the **show ip ospf neighbor** command. Example 5-43 shows the results of running this command on Router Trinity.

Example 5-43   *Determining OSPF Communication Status Between Routers*

```
Trinity#show ip ospf neighbor

Neighbor ID     Pri   State         Dead Time   Address     Interface
4.0.0.1          1    FULL/DR       00:00:34    21.0.0.2    FastEthernet0/1
4.0.0.3          1    FULL/  -      00:00:37    201.0.1.2   Serial0/1.1
Trinity#
```

The output of this command shows that Trinity formed a full adjacency with Routers Neo (4.0.0.1) and Morpheus (4.0.0.3); however, there is a difference between the two. Specifically, the media type used with Neo indicates the need for a DR, while that used with Morpheus does not. More detailed information can be found by adding the keyword **detail** to this command, as demonstrated in Example 5-44.

Example 5-44 *Displaying More Detailed OSPF Communication Status Between Routers*

```
Trinity#show ip ospf neighbor detail
 Neighbor 4.0.0.1, interface address 21.0.0.2
    In the area 0 via interface FastEthernet0/1
    Neighbor priority is 1, State is FULL, 6 state changes
    DR is 21.0.0.2 BDR is 21.0.0.1
    Options is 0x42
    Dead timer due in 00:00:33
    Index 1/2, retransmission queue length 0, number of retransmission 1
    First 0x0(0)/0x0(0) Next 0x0(0)/0x0(0)
    Last retransmission scan length is 1, maximum is 1
    Last retransmission scan time is 0 msec, maximum is 0 msec
 Neighbor 4.0.0.3, interface address 201.0.1.2
    In the area 201 via interface Serial0/1.1
    Neighbor priority is 1, State is FULL, 6 state changes
    DR is 0.0.0.0 BDR is 0.0.0.0
    Options is 0x2
    Dead timer due in 00:00:36
    Index 1/1, retransmission queue length 0, number of retransmission 0
    First 0x0(0)/0x0(0) Next 0x0(0)/0x0(0)
    Last retransmission scan length is 0, maximum is 0
    Last retransmission scan time is 0 msec, maximum is 0 msec
 Trinity#
```

Remember that OSPF operates differently over different types of networks. In this case study, an area 0 core was created over Ethernet, which is designated as a BROADCAST. This is shown in the command output of Example 5-45 from the **show ip ospf interface** command. Contrast the behavior on the broadcast media with the behavior you saw over the POINT_TO_POINT link. On a point-to-point link, there is no need to elect a DR/BDR (this is required on a broadcast network). In a point-to-point network, no other routers can join; however, on a broadcast network, you can add new routers, so a DR/BDR is needed.

Example 5-45 *Determining OSPF Network Type*

```
Trinity#show ip ospf interface
FastEthernet0/0 is up, line protocol is up
  Internet Address 51.1.1.1/24, Area 51
  Process ID 100, Router ID 4.0.0.2, Network Type BROADCAST, Cost: 1
  Transmit Delay is 1 sec, State DR, Priority 1
  Designated Router (ID) 4.0.0.2, Interface address 51.1.1.1
  No backup designated router on this network
  Timer intervals configured, Hello 10, Dead 40, Wait 40, Retransmit 5
    Hello due in 00:00:06
  Index 1/2, flood queue length 0
  Next 0x0(0)/0x0(0)
  Last flood scan length is 0, maximum is 0
  Last flood scan time is 0 msec, maximum is 0 msec
  Neighbor Count is 0, Adjacent neighbor count is 0
  Suppress hello for 0 neighbor(s)
FastEthernet0/1 is up, line protocol is up
  Internet Address 21.0.0.1/24, Area 0
```

continues

Example 5-45   *Determining OSPF Network Type (Continued)*

```
    Process ID 100, Router ID 4.0.0.2, Network Type BROADCAST, Cost: 1
    Transmit Delay is 1 sec, State BDR, Priority 1
    Designated Router (ID) 21.0.0.2, Interface address 21.0.0.2
    Backup Designated router (ID) 4.0.0.2, Interface address 21.0.0.1
    Timer intervals configured, Hello 10, Dead 40, Wait 40, Retransmit 5
      Hello due in 00:00:04
    Index 1/1, flood queue length 0
    Next 0x0(0)/0x0(0)
    Last flood scan length is 1, maximum is 1
    Last flood scan time is 0 msec, maximum is 0 msec
    Neighbor Count is 1, Adjacent neighbor count is 1
      Adjacent with neighbor 21.0.0.2  (Designated Router)
    Suppress hello for 0 neighbor(s)
Serial0/1.1 is up, line protocol is up
    Internet Address 201.0.1.1/30, Area 201
    Process ID 100, Router ID 4.0.0.2, Network Type POINT_TO_POINT, Cost: 64
    Transmit Delay is 1 sec, State POINT_TO_POINT,
    Timer intervals configured, Hello 10, Dead 40, Wait 40, Retransmit 5
      Hello due in 00:00:02
    Index 1/3, flood queue length 0
    Next 0x0(0)/0x0(0)
    Last flood scan length is 1, maximum is 1
    Last flood scan time is 0 msec, maximum is 0 msec
    Neighbor Count is 1, Adjacent neighbor count is 1
      Adjacent with neighbor 4.0.0.3
    Suppress hello for 0 neighbor(s)
```

Finally, you want to determine whether the routing table is correct and that OSPF
exchanged all the routes properly for your network. Look for the five different networks in
use by using a **show ip route** command (see Example 5-46). This command is executed
from Morpheus; in it, you can see all the configured networks. Three networks show up as
O IA, which are OSPF inter-area routes. In other words, Morpheus learned that the
networks are part of the OSPF AS, but they are not in an area that Morpheus is connected
to, which means they are inter-area.

Example 5-46   *Verifying Networks in the Routing Table*

```
Morpheus#show ip route
Codes: C - connected, S - static, I - IGRP, R - RIP, M - mobile, B - BGP
       D - EIGRP, EX - EIGRP external, O - OSPF, IA - OSPF inter area
       N1 - OSPF NSSA external type 1, N2 - OSPF NSSA external type 2
       E1 - OSPF external type 1, E2 - OSPF external type 2, E - EGP
       i - IS-IS, L1 - IS-IS level-1, L2 - IS-IS level-2, * - candidate default
       U - per-user static route, o - ODR

Gateway of last resort is not set

     51.0.0.0/24 is subnetted, 1 subnets
O IA    51.1.1.0 [110/65] via 201.0.1.1, 01:04:41, Serial0/1.1
     4.0.0.0/24 is subnetted, 1 subnets
```

Example 5-46   *Verifying Networks in the Routing Table (Continued)*

```
C       4.0.0.0 is directly connected, Loopback0
        21.0.0.0/24 is subnetted, 1 subnets
O IA    21.0.0.0 [110/65] via 201.0.1.1, 01:12:06, Serial0/1.1
        201.0.1.0/30 is subnetted, 1 subnets
C       201.0.1.0 is directly connected, Serial0/1.1
        10.0.0.0/24 is subnetted, 1 subnets
O IA    10.0.0.0 [110/66] via 201.0.1.1, 01:11:56, Serial0/1.1
Morpheus#
```

Case Study: OSPF with Stub and Totally Stubby Areas

In this case study, you have determined that Morpheus is having performance problems. If you convert area 201 into an OSPF stub area, some of the problems are alleviated. These problems might be related to low memory, a slow processor, or a general load. Altering the configuration of the network is a way to solve these problems without spending money.

Start this change by telling Morpheus and Trinity that area 201 should now be treated as a stub area, as shown in Example 5-47.

Example 5-47   *Configuring an OSPF Stub Area: Before, During, and After*

```
Before
!
router ospf 100
 network 201.0.0.0 0.0.255.255 area 201
!
During
Morpheus#conf t
Enter configuration commands, one per line.  End with CNTL/Z.
Morpheus(config)#router ospf 100
Morpheus(config-router)#area 201 stub
Morpheus(config-router)#^Z
Morpheus#
After
!
router ospf 100
 area 201 stub
 network 201.0.0.0 0.0.255.255 area 201
!
```

Both routers are now configured to recognize and treat area 201 as a stub. Now, look at the resulting change in the routing table in Example 5-48, and see if this had the desired effect.

Example 5-48 *Routing Table After Configuring Area 201 as a Stub*

```
Morpheus#show ip route
Codes: C - connected, S - static, I - IGRP, R - RIP, M - mobile, B - BGP
       D - EIGRP, EX - EIGRP external, O - OSPF, IA - OSPF inter area
       N1 - OSPF NSSA external type 1, N2 - OSPF NSSA external type 2
       E1 - OSPF external type 1, E2 - OSPF external type 2, E - EGP
       i - IS-IS, L1 - IS-IS level-1, L2 - IS-IS level-2, * - candidate default
       U - per-user static route, o - ODR

Gateway of last resort is 201.0.1.1 to network 0.0.0.0

     51.0.0.0/24 is subnetted, 1 subnets
O IA    51.1.1.0 [110/65] via 201.0.1.1, 00:04:01, Serial0/1.1
     4.0.0.0/24 is subnetted, 1 subnets
C       4.0.0.0 is directly connected, Loopback0
     21.0.0.0/24 is subnetted, 1 subnets
O IA    21.0.0.0 [110/65] via 201.0.1.1, 00:04:01, Serial0/1.1
     201.0.1.0/30 is subnetted, 1 subnets
C       201.0.1.0 is directly connected, Serial0/1.1
     10.0.0.0/24 is subnetted, 1 subnets
O IA    10.0.0.0 [110/66] via 201.0.1.1, 00:04:01, Serial0/1.1
O*IA 0.0.0.0/0 [110/65] via 201.0.1.1, 00:04:01, Serial0/1.1
Morpheus#
```

You see the expected default route, but the routing table has not decreased in size; in fact, it has increased through the inclusion of the default route. Perhaps making area 201 a totally stubby area is the solution. The configuration is simple—just add the **no-summary** keyword to the end of the **area stub** statement, as shown in Example 5-49. This example shows the resulting routing table.

Example 5-49 *Results of a Totally Stubby Area*

```
!
router ospf 100
 area 201 stub no-summary
 network  201.0.0.0 0.0.255.255  area 201
!

Morpheus#show ip route
Codes: C - connected, S - static, I - IGRP, R - RIP, M - mobile, B - BGP
       D - EIGRP, EX - EIGRP external, O - OSPF, IA - OSPF inter area
       N1 - OSPF NSSA external type 1, N2 - OSPF NSSA external type 2
       E1 - OSPF external type 1, E2 - OSPF external type 2, E - EGP
       i - IS-IS, L1 - IS-IS level-1, L2 - IS-IS level-2, * - candidate default
       U - per-user static route, o - ODR

Gateway of last resort is 201.0.1.1 to network 0.0.0.0

     4.0.0.0/24 is subnetted, 1 subnets
C       4.0.0.0 is directly connected, Loopback0
     201.0.1.0/30 is subnetted, 1 subnets
C       201.0.1.0 is directly connected, Serial0/1.1
O*IA 0.0.0.0/0 [110/65] via 201.0.1.1, 00:00:10, Serial0/1.1
Morpheus#
```

This is the desired result: The routing table is substantially smaller, and Morpheus knows that if it needs to go outside the 201 network, it uses its default route to Trinity. In Example 5-50, you can see that complete connectivity is still in place for the entire OSPF AS.

Example 5-50 *Confirming Connectivity*

```
Morpheus#ping 10.0.0.1

Type escape sequence to abort.
Sending 5, 100-byte ICMP Echos to 10.0.0.1, timeout is 2 seconds:
!!!!!
Success rate is 100 percent (5/5), round-trip min/avg/max = 28/32/40 ms
Morpheus#ping 51.1.1.1

Type escape sequence to abort.
Sending 5, 100-byte ICMP Echos to 51.1.1.1, timeout is 2 seconds:
!!!!!
Success rate is 100 percent (5/5), round-trip min/avg/max = 28/28/32 ms
Morpheus#
```

CHAPTER 6

Redistribution

> The highest courage is to dare to be yourself in the face of adversity. Choosing right over wrong, ethics over convenience, and truth over popularity...these are the choices that measure your life. Travel the path of integrity without looking back, for there is never a wrong time to do the right thing.
> —Author unknown

By now, you have discovered that minimizing routing tables and choosing the next-hop destination path are critical for a well-tuned IP network. When routing information from one routing protocol, such as OSPF, is redistributed into IGRP, you must be mindful of possible routing loops.

A *routing loop* is a path to a remote network that alternates between two routers that assume the path is reachable via each other. Hence, the time to live that is present in every IP packet expires, and the packet or user data is dropped, resulting in loss of network connectivity.

Routing that uses a single routing algorithm is usually more desirable than running multiple IP and non-IP routing protocols, especially from a configuration and troubleshooting perspective.

However, in today's changing networks and with mergers, department politics, and acquisitions, more than one IP routing protocol is likely in use.

Before "diving in," you first need a definition of *redistribution* and *summarization* to clarify your understanding of these concepts. These are potentially confusing topics. Hopefully, they will be clearer to you after reading this chapter and Chapter 7, "Summarization."

- **Redistribution** is when a router takes routing information it has discovered in one routing protocol and distributes it into a different routing protocol, thus allowing the redistribution of the first protocol's networks into the second routing protocol. For example, a router running RIP and OSPF has a need for those in the OSPF section of the network to know the routes in the RIP network. Redistribution is used to accomplish this feat of routing magic! Sometimes, redistribution is referred to more specifically as *route redistribution*—both terms mean the same thing.

- **Summarization** is the taking of multiple route entries and representing them by a smaller number of routes.

  This smaller representation is known as *summarizing your routes*. For example, this technique is used to minimize the routing table size, which is useful when connecting to the Internet, conserving router resources, or simplifying the next hop. For example, routing table entries represent blocks of addresses and use the subnet mask to determine the size of the block. Through summarization, the router can tell the difference between 10.20.30.0 /24 and 10.20.30.0 /22. The former is a Class C–sized block of addresses, 256 addresses. The latter is four Class C–sized blocks, or 1024 addresses.

In many books and in most chapters of this book, the case studies are found at the end of each chapter. I am going to alter that in this chapter because redistribution and summarization go well together. To build on these concepts logically, I include several configuration examples within the chapter as built-in case studies and then add to them in each section as you proceed through the chapter.

Redistribution and summarization are interesting concepts. This chapter attempts to decipher and demystify the challenges that you face when one routing algorithm is redistributed into another, when one of those protocols is OSPF (of course), or when the OSPF routing table is optimized through summarization.

OSPF Redistribution

Given the brief overview of redistribution, take a moment and consider when you might encounter redistribution or have a need to implement it. Many people have given lists of when you would use redistribution, but in reality, you need to know just four categories:

- **Politics**—A decision-maker has forced the running of another protocol besides OSPF. Work on this person—who needs to see the benefits of OSPF; however, until the decision is changed, you must use redistribution.

- **Profit**—Perhaps, there has been a merger of two companies with different protocols, or different needs exist within different divisions of the same company and network and the network cannot afford to be without connectivity, so you are called upon to "make it happen."

- **Certification**—You are studying for a networking certification and you need to practice, practice, practice all aspects of protocol operation and interaction.

- **Hardware support**—You might have legacy hardware that does not run OSPF or does not run it reliably. This is the number one reason to redistribute RIP into OSPF.

In defining the concept and outlining the process of redistribution, I have presented the proper information on what is happening according to today's accepted terminology and usage. The word *redistribution* does not accurately describe what is going on, and it is rather counterintuitive. When you say, "I am redistributing RIP into OSPF," this sounds like RIP is being told to export route information to OSPF. However, the truth is that the OSPF routing process is being told to *import* routes from the RIP routing process.

Therefore, conceptually, it makes more sense to think of it as *exporting* or *importing* routes from one routing process to another. These terms are common when using BGP and more accurately reflect what is actually going on. For example, if you configured redistribution from RIP to OSPF, the configuration might look as follows on the router:

```
router ospf 200
  network x.x.x.x
  redistribute rip  metric 100
  default-metric 100
```

In reality, you can rephrase this router configuration to make a bit more sense, as follows:

```
router ospf 1
  import routes from RIP,
  throw away the RIP metrics
  replace them with OSPF metric 100
```

Administrative Distance and Metrics

Regardless of the reason that you have encountered redistribution, there are some charac-teristics of how it operates within OSPF and on Cisco routers. When redistributing from one routing protocol to another, keep in mind the following items:

- Administrative distances
- Routing metrics

Previous chapters have discussed the metrics used by OSPF and how to manipulate them. Administrative distances help with route selection among different routing protocols, but they can cause problems for redistribution. These problems can be in the form of routing loops, convergence, or inefficient routing.

The key point here is that Cisco routers always make a forwarding decision based on the administrative distance of a route over any metric that it might have. For example, a router might learn about two routes to the same destination, and each route has a different metric. Which route should the router believe and use?

Administrative distance is the deciding factor in this regard because the routing protocol with the lowest administrative distance has its route believed and thus preferred. The various default administrative distances used by Cisco routers and associated with the method of sourcing are shown in Table 6-1.

Table 6-1   *Administrative Distances by Source*

Source of the Route	Default Administrative Distance
Connected interface	0
Static route	1
Enhanced IGRP summary route	5
External BGP	20

continues

Table 6-1   *Administrative Distances by Source (Continued)*

Source of the Route	Default Administrative Distance
Internal Enhanced IGRP	90
IGRP	100
OSPF	110
IS-IS	115
RIP	120
EGP	140
External Enhanced IGRP	170
Internal BGP	200
Unknown	255

NOTE   As soon as a route has been redistributed, the route is then "present" in two routing protocols, and thus the routing protocol with the better (that is, lower) administrative distance is preferred for that route.

The next section looks at the various rules that should be considered when redistribution is in place.

Redistribution Golden Rules

The parameters surrounding the use of redistribution have a set of rules that if used when designing, implementing, and troubleshooting can make the use of redistribution in your network a much more trouble-free process. These rules can be summarized as follows:

1 **Whenever possible, redistribute from a less powerful routing protocol to a more powerful routing protocol**—This rule can be implemented easily by giving two examples; the first is that you would always want to redistribute RIP into OSPF, and the second is that you would always want to redistribute OSPF into BGP. You would never want to do the opposite. Redistributing BGP into OSPF, for example, is a bad design for obvious reasons.

NOTE   This section discusses the golden rule regarding redistribution into a more powerful routing protocol. The most accepted method of ranking protocols from most to least powerful is as follows: BGP, OSPF, IS-IS, EIGRP, IGRP, and RIP.

2   **Whenever possible, redistribute at only a single point**—While this is sometimes hard to accomplish when a network requires a high degree of redundancy, the presence of just one redistribution point between the same routing domain greatly reduces the burden on your networking staff and smoothes the operation of the network.

3   **Filter routes**—The use of filters is important when redistributing because they help ensure that you have a split-horizon mechanism in place to reduce the chance of a routing loop. A subset of this rule is to never redistribute unfiltered, unverified routes into another routing domain. So when in doubt—filter!

4   **Redistribute only what is needed, not what is possible**—When redistributing, do so with this rule in mind because this allows you to know what routes need to be redistributed and how to construct your filters. Ask yourself, "What information does each routing domain need to know?"

5   **Adjust administrative distances and routing metrics**—This rule refers to the earlier part of this section, where these concepts and their relevance to redistribution were discussed. In many cases, metrics vary so much between routing protocols that it is advisable to set them when redistributing to ensure that the routes are operating as you want them to.

6   **Always set a metric**—In Cisco IOS Software, you can enter the **redistribute** command without a metric into the router's configuration. However, you should always include the metric or default metric commands (see the following); if you do not, redistribution does not work, although it appears to be correctly configured.

If you follow these rules, you can effectively design how you need to summarize routes within your OSPF network.

NOTE   Cisco IOS Software automatically redistributes between Interior Gateway Routing Protocol (IGRP) and Extended Internet Gateway Routing Protocol (EIGRP) when the same autonomous system (AS) is defined. This is the only form of automatic redistribution that Cisco IOS Software performs. All other methods must be manually configured.

Redistribution Configuration

This section reviews the command that is used to configure redistribution on a Cisco router. Note that the **redistribute** command can be used in any routing protocol, not just OSPF.

Redistributing routes into OSPF from other routing protocols or from static routes causes these redistributed routes to be labeled in the routing tables as OSPF external routes. This makes sense if you recall the external route discussion in Chapter 5, "Routing Concepts and Configuration." Because these routes are from outside the OSPF process, they are considered to be external.

To redistribute routes into OSPF, use the following command syntax in router configuration mode:

```
redistribute routing-process [process-id] [metric ospf-metric-value] [metric-type
ospf-metric-type-value] [route-map map-tag-value] [subnets]
```

This syntax is an abbreviated example of the full **redistribution** command, which is much more complex, as you will see at the end of this section.

Ensure that you consider the golden rules and read this section prior to activating redistribution. Of the following command options, only *routing-process* is required. Each of the following fields, shown in italics, requires a decision and input from you when configuring redistribution:

- *routing-process*—Identifies the routing process to redistribute into OSPF. The routing process can be BGP, Connected, EGP, EIGRP, IGRP, ISIS, ISO-IGRP, Mobile, ODR, OSPF, RIP, or Static.

- *process-id*—The process ID of the routing process (if applicable). For example, if you were redistributing EIGRP into OSPF, the autonomous system number used by EIGRP would be used as its process ID when redistributing.

- *ospf-metric-value*—The metric or cost to assign to the redistributed routes when they are placed into OSPF. If this option is not used, a default metric of 1 is used for redistributed BGP routes and a default metric of 20 is used for all other protocols. The range of values is 0 to 16,777,214. You should set the metric value here that is applicable to your network. For example, a network based on 10-Mbps Ethernet would need a different metric for routes than a network based on Frame Relay.

- *ospf-metric-type-value*—Routes are redistributed into OSPF as either an OSPF external Type 1 or Type 2 route. The default is Type 2; if you want to change the type of redistributed routes, you can do that here. However, changing the metric type here affects all routes.

- *map-tag-value*—A numerical value that is attached to the redistributed routes. The route tag is not specifically used by OSPF. However, the presence of a route tag can be used as a basis for making policy decisions as defined in a route map. For example, one use is to base the decision to redistribute a route based on the value present in the *route-tag* field. The default tag value is 0. The range of values for the tag is 0 to 4,294,967,295 (32 bits).

- **subnets**—If this command is not used when redistributing, only classful networks are redistributed into OSPF. With OSPF, the keyword **subnets** is typically used when redistributing more then one network into OSPF. When redistributing routes into OSPF, only routes that are not subnetted are redistributed if the **subnets** keyword is not specified.

A route map is a method used to control the redistribution of routes between routing domains. The format of the command to configure a route map is as follows:

```
route-map map-tag [[permit | deny] | [sequence-number]]
```

The next section discusses the various methods of filtering routing information between different routing algorithms.

To configure redistribution between routing protocols, use the following command under the routing process configuration:

```
redistribute protocol [process-id] {level-1 | level-1-2 | level-2} [as-number] [metric
metric-value] [metric-type type-value] [match {internal | external 1 | external 2}]
[tag tag-value] [route-map map-tag] [weight number-value] [subnets]
```

Table 6-2 explains the **redistribution** command syntax in further detail.

Table 6-2   *Command Syntax for Redistribution*

Command	Description
protocol	Source protocol from which routes are being redistributed. It can be one of the following keywords: **bgp**, **connected**, **egp**, **igrp**, **isis**, **mobile**, **ospf**, **static** [**ip**], or **rip**.
	The **static** [**ip**] keyword is used to redistribute IP static routes. The optional **ip** keyword is used when redistributing into the Intermediate System-to-Intermediate System (IS-IS) Protocol.
	The **connected** keyword refers to routes that are established automatically by virtue of having enabled IP on an interface. For routing protocols such as Open Shortest Path First (OSPF) and IS-IS, these routes are redistributed as external to the autonomous system.
process-id	(Optional) For the **bgp**, **egp**, or **igrp** keyword, this is an autonomous system number, which is a 16-bit decimal number.
	For the **ospf** keyword, this is an appropriate OSPF process ID from which routes are to be redistributed.
level-1	Specifies that for IS-IS Level 1, routes are redistributed into other IP routing protocols independently.
level-1-2	Specifies that for IS-IS both Level 1 and Level 2, routes are redistributed into other IP routing protocols.
level-2	Specifies that for IS-IS Level 2, routes are redistributed into other IP routing protocols independently.
as-number	Autonomous system number for the redistributed route.
metric *metric-value*	(Optional) Metric used for the redistributed route. If a value is not specified for this option and no value is specified using the **default-metric** command, the default metric value is 0. Use a value consistent with the destination protocol.

continues

Table 6-2 *Command Syntax for Redistribution (Continued)*

Command	Description
metric-type *type-value*	(Optional) For OSPF, the external link type associated with the default route advertised into the OSPF routing domain. It can be either a Type 1 or Type 2 external route. If a metric type is not specified, the Cisco IOS Software adopts a Type 2 external route. For IS-IS, it can be one of two values: • internal: IS-IS metric that is less than 63 • external: IS-IS metric that is between 64 and 128 The default is internal.
match {**internal** | **external 1** | **external 2**}	(Optional) The criteria by which OSPF routes are redistributed into other routing domains. It can be one of the following: • **internal**—Routes that are internal to a specific autonomous system. • **external 1**—Routes that are external to the autonomous system but are imported into OSPF as Type 1 external routes. • **external 2**—Routes that are external to the autonomous system but are imported into OSPF as Type 2 external routes.
tag *tag-value*	(Optional) A 32-bit decimal value attached to each external route. This is not used by OSPF itself. It can be used to communicate information between Autonomous System Boundary Routers (ASBRs). If none is specified, the remote autonomous system number is used for routes from Border Gateway Protocol (BGP) and Exterior Gateway Protocol (EGP); for other protocols, 0 is used.
route-map	(Optional) Route map that should be interrogated to filter the importation of routes from this source routing protocol to the current routing protocol. If not specified, all routes are redistributed. If this keyword is specified but no route map tags are listed, no routes are imported.
map-tag	(Optional) Identifier of a configured route map.
weight *number-value*	(Optional) Network weight when redistributing into BGP. The value is an integer from 0 to 65,535.
subnets	(Optional) For redistributing routes into OSPF, the scope of redistribution for the specified protocol.

External Routes

In OSPF, external routes are classified either as Type E1 or Type E2; the difference is the calculation of the metric (cost) associated with each route. Specifically, a Type E2 route has a metric that is equal to the external cost, whereas a Type E1 route has a metric of the external cost plus the internal cost to that route. Remember the following points when performing redistribution:

- By default, all redistributed routes are automatically categorized as Type E2 by OSPF.

- You can alter the type of external routes during redistribution if you want.

You can select the type of external route that you want the new routes to be through the use of the **metric-type** keyword when using the **redistribute** command, as follows:

```
Trinity(config)#router OSPF 100
Trinity(config-router)#redistribute rip metric-type ?
  1  Set OSPF External Type 1 metrics
  2  Set OSPF External Type 2 metrics
Trinity(config-router)#
```

The next section discusses the use of default routes in OSPF and as part of redistribution.

Default Routes

The ability to generate and propagate a default route in a network is important. Chapter 4, "Design Fundamentals," discussed the methods of default routes in OSPF areas. This chapter covers the redistribution of an existing default route into OSPF.

You can create a default route using one of the following two methods:

- Advertise 0.0.0.0 inside the domain, but only if the ASBR itself already has a default route.

- Advertise 0.0.0.0 regardless of whether the ASBR has a default route.

The latter method can be set by adding the **always** keyword to the end of the command; this in essence forces the route to always be present in the routing table. Be careful when using the **always** keyword. If your router advertises a default route (0.0.0.0) inside your OSPF domain and there is no default route present or a path to reach the destinations, routing is broken. Complete one of the following tasks to prevent this:

- Identify the default route in the configuration; this is accomplished in one of two ways:
    - Create a static default route (for example, **ip route 0.0.0.0 0.0.0.0** *next hop ip_address*)
    - Create a default network (for example, **ip default-network** *ip_address*)
- Configure OSPF to propagate the default network that was just configured. To propagate the default network, use the **default-information originate always** command.

This section provided an overview of default routes, and as such, it built on knowledge that you should have regarding default routes. The next section takes a closer look at the **default-information originate** command and its use in OSPF.

default-information originate Command

Chapter 4 discussed that, by default, normal OSPF area routers do not generate default routes. To have an OSPF router generate a default route, use the following command:

```
default-information originate [always] [metric metric-value] [metric-type type-
value] [route-map map-name]
```

This command generates an external Type 2 link with link-state ID 0.0.0.0 and network mask 0.0.0.0. This makes the router an ASBR.

In a scenario where the default route for your network is via another routing process, you must be able to advertise this default route throughout the entire OSPF domain. Figure 6-1 shows that Router Trinity is receiving the default route from the RIP network.

Figure 6-1 *Default Route*

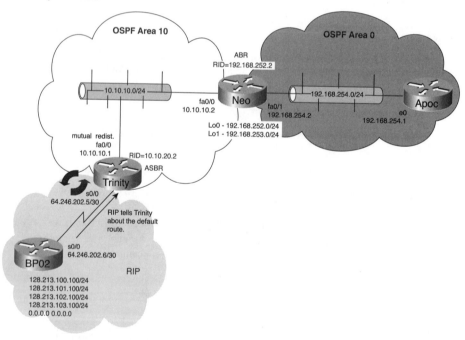

Router Trinity thus places this default route into its routing table; however, it does not tell the rest of the network of its presence. Because this is the default route for the entire network, Router Trinity needs to advertise this route. To accomplish this objective, you must use the **default-information originate** command on the OSPF ASBR, Router Trinity, as shown in the following examples.

Before

In this state, the default route is present in the routing table of Router Trinity. However, Router Neo does not yet have know about this default route, as shown in Example 6-1.

Example 6-1 *Router Neo's Routing Table Before the Advertisement of the Default Route on Router Trinity*

```
Neo>show ip route
Codes: C - connected, S - static, I - IGRP, R - RIP, M - mobile, B - BGP
       D - EIGRP, EX - EIGRP external, O - OSPF, IA - OSPF inter area
       N1 - OSPF NSSA external type 1, N2 - OSPF NSSA external type 2
       E1 - OSPF external type 1, E2 - OSPF external type 2, E - EGP
       i - IS-IS, L1 - IS-IS level-1, L2 - IS-IS level-2, ia - IS-IS inter area
       * - candidate default, U - per-user static route, o - ODR
       P - periodic downloaded static route

Gateway of last resort is not set

     64.0.0.0/8 is variably subnetted, 2 subnets, 2 masks
O E2    64.246.202.4/30 [110/200] via 10.10.10.1, 00:09:52, FastEthernet0/0
O E2    64.246.202.6/32 [110/200] via 10.10.10.1, 00:09:52, FastEthernet0/0
     128.213.0.0/22 is subnetted, 1 subnets
O E2    128.213.100.0 [110/200] via 10.10.10.1, 00:09:52, FastEthernet0/0
     10.0.0.0/24 is subnetted, 2 subnets
C       10.10.10.0 is directly connected, FastEthernet0/0
O       10.10.20.0 [110/2] via 10.10.10.1, 00:09:52, FastEthernet0/0
C    192.168.254.0/24 is directly connected, FastEthernet0/1
C    192.168.253.0/24 is directly connected, Loopback1
C    192.168.252.0/24 is directly connected, Loopback0
Neo>
```

During

To "redistribute" the default route that Trinity knows about, use the **default-information originate** command in OSPF, as shown in Example 6-2.

Example 6-2 *Router Trinity Advertises a Default Route*

```
Trinity#config terminal
Enter configuration commands, one per line.  End with CNTL/Z.
Trinity(config)#router ospf 100
Trinity(config-router)#default-information originate ?
  always       Always advertise default route
  metric       OSPF default metric
  metric-type  OSPF metric type for default routes
  route-map    Route-map reference
  <cr>

Trinity(config-router)#default-information originate
Trinity(config-router)#
```

After

After entering the command into Router Trinity's configuration, the default route is now present in the routing table of Router Neo, as shown in Example 6-3.

Example 6-3   *Router Neo's Routing Table After the Advertisement of the Default Route on Router Trinity*

```
Neo>show ip route
Codes: C - connected, S - static, I - IGRP, R - RIP, M - mobile, B - BGP
       D - EIGRP, EX - EIGRP external, O - OSPF, IA - OSPF inter area
       N1 - OSPF NSSA external type 1, N2 - OSPF NSSA external type 2
       E1 - OSPF external type 1, E2 - OSPF external type 2, E - EGP
       i - IS-IS, L1 - IS-IS level-1, L2 - IS-IS level-2, ia - IS-IS inter area
       * - candidate default, U - per-user static route, o - ODR
       P - periodic downloaded static route

Gateway of last resort is 10.10.10.1 to network 0.0.0.0

     64.0.0.0/8 is variably subnetted, 2 subnets, 2 masks
O E2    64.246.202.4/30 [110/200] via 10.10.10.1, 00:12:51, FastEthernet0/0
O E2    64.246.202.6/32 [110/200] via 10.10.10.1, 00:12:51, FastEthernet0/0
     128.213.0.0/22 is subnetted, 1 subnets
O E2    128.213.100.0 [110/200] via 10.10.10.1, 00:12:51, FastEthernet0/0
     10.0.0.0/24 is subnetted, 2 subnets
C       10.10.10.0 is directly connected, FastEthernet0/0
O       10.10.20.0 [110/2] via 10.10.10.1, 00:12:51, FastEthernet0/0
C    192.168.254.0/24 is directly connected, FastEthernet0/1
C    192.168.253.0/24 is directly connected, Loopback1
C    192.168.252.0/24 is directly connected, Loopback0
O*E2 0.0.0.0/0 [110/1] via 10.10.10.1, 00:01:34, FastEthernet0/0
Neo>
```

Notice in the routing table of Example 6-3 that the default route is a Type 2 external route, which as discussed is the default route type for redistributed routes. Also note that the metric has a value of 1. This is not the metric that you should be seeing.

NOTE   The default metric for OSPF routes according to Cisco documentation is 10; however, you can clearly see in the routing table that this is not true. Even adding the **default-metric** command to OSPF on Trinity has no effect in changing the value. I have tested this erroneous behavior on Cisco IOS Software versions ranging from 11.2(18) to 12.0(7), so be aware of it.

The question now becomes "How do you deal with this undocumented feature (that is, bug) and allow a more realistic metric to be given to a default route?" You can do this by adding the **metric** keyword to the **default-information originate** command in OSPF. Also, you can change the route from a Type 2 to a Type 1 route at the same time.

Before

In Example 6-4, Router Trinity has the correct commands in its OSPF configuration; you should be seeing the default route with a metric of 50 (or at the very least 10!).

Example 6-4   *Router Trinity Configuration Before Altering the Default Metric*

```
!
router ospf 100
 log-adjacency-changes
 summary-address 128.213.100.0 255.255.252.0
 redistribute rip metric 200 subnets tag 200
 network 10.10.10.0 0.0.0.255 area 10
 network 10.10.20.0 0.0.0.255 area 10
 default-information originate
 default-metric 50
!
```

Regardless, those metric values are not appearing as they should on Router Neo in Example 6-5, so you need to alter them and convert the default route to a Type 1 route.

Example 6-5   *Router Neo's Routing Table with the Original Default Route and Its Cost*

```
Neo>show ip route
Codes: C - connected, S - static, I - IGRP, R - RIP, M - mobile, B - BGP
       D - EIGRP, EX - EIGRP external, O - OSPF, IA - OSPF inter area
       N1 - OSPF NSSA external type 1, N2 - OSPF NSSA external type 2
       E1 - OSPF external type 1, E2 - OSPF external type 2, E - EGP
       i - IS-IS, L1 - IS-IS level-1, L2 - IS-IS level-2, ia - IS-IS inter area
       * - candidate default, U - per-user static route, o - ODR
       P - periodic downloaded static route

Gateway of last resort is 10.10.10.1 to network 0.0.0.0

     64.0.0.0/8 is variably subnetted, 2 subnets, 2 masks
O E2    64.246.202.4/30 [110/200] via 10.10.10.1, 00:25:17, FastEthernet0/0
O E2    64.246.202.6/32 [110/200] via 10.10.10.1, 00:25:17, FastEthernet0/0
     128.213.0.0/22 is subnetted, 1 subnets
O E2    128.213.100.0 [110/200] via 10.10.10.1, 00:25:17, FastEthernet0/0
     10.0.0.0/24 is subnetted, 2 subnets
C       10.10.10.0 is directly connected, FastEthernet0/0
O       10.10.20.0 [110/2] via 10.10.10.1, 00:25:17, FastEthernet0/0
C       192.168.254.0/24 is directly connected, FastEthernet0/1
C       192.168.253.0/24 is directly connected, Loopback1
C       192.168.252.0/24 is directly connected, Loopback0
O*E2 0.0.0.0/0 [110/1] via 10.10.10.1, 00:13:59, FastEthernet0/0
Neo>
```

During

Example 6-6 shows the changes that you want to apply to router Trinity because it is the ASBR that is receiving and then redistributing the default route throughout our OSPF domain.

Example 6-6   *Changing the Default Route Cost on Router Trinity*

```
Trinity#conf t
Enter configuration commands, one per line.  End with CNTL/Z.
Trinity(config)#router ospf 100
Trinity(config-router)#default-information originate metric 50 metric-type 1
Trinity(config-router)#^Z
Trinity#
```

After

After adding the commands to Router Trinity, you can check the routing table on Neo to see if the changes were successful in getting the results desired for the network (see Example 6-7).

Example 6-7   *Router Neo's Routing Table with the Altered Default Route Metric*

```
Neo>show ip route
Codes: C - connected, S - static, I - IGRP, R - RIP, M - mobile, B - BGP
       D - EIGRP, EX - EIGRP external, O - OSPF, IA - OSPF inter area
       N1 - OSPF NSSA external type 1, N2 - OSPF NSSA external type 2
       E1 - OSPF external type 1, E2 - OSPF external type 2, E - EGP
       i - IS-IS, L1 - IS-IS level-1, L2 - IS-IS level-2, ia - IS-IS inter area
       * - candidate default, U - per-user static route, o - ODR
       P - periodic downloaded static route

Gateway of last resort is 10.10.10.1 to network 0.0.0.0

     64.0.0.0/8 is variably subnetted, 2 subnets, 2 masks
O E2    64.246.202.4/30 [110/200] via 10.10.10.1, 00:29:15, FastEthernet0/0
O E2    64.246.202.6/32 [110/200] via 10.10.10.1, 00:29:15, FastEthernet0/0
     128.213.0.0/22 is subnetted, 1 subnets
O E2    128.213.100.0 [110/200] via 10.10.10.1, 00:29:15, FastEthernet0/0
     10.0.0.0/24 is subnetted, 2 subnets
C       10.10.10.0 is directly connected, FastEthernet0/0
O       10.10.20.0 [110/2] via 10.10.10.1, 00:29:15, FastEthernet0/0
C    192.168.254.0/24 is directly connected, FastEthernet0/1
C    192.168.253.0/24 is directly connected, Loopback1
C    192.168.252.0/24 is directly connected, Loopback0
O*E1 0.0.0.0/0 [110/51] via 10.10.10.1, 00:01:08, FastEthernet0/0
Neo>
```

The results at this point are mixed. You have the default route now being advertised as a Type E1 route; however, the metric has increased to 51, not 50 as configured. This is another issue with Cisco IOS Software, so be aware that in this case the metrics are cumulative, not set, as you would expect.

However, you are not done. There is a problem in the network where links are unstable. As a result of this, the default route is constantly being withdrawn and then added to the routing tables. This can have a negative impact on the network's operation and performance. The solution with OSPF is to add another keyword to the **default-information originate** command. If you apply the **always** keyword to the configuration for Router Trinity, Trinity always advertises the default route regardless of the status of its links. Example 6-8 demonstrates the configuration.

Example 6-8   *Configuring Router Trinity to Always Advertise a Default Route*

```
Trinity#config terminal
Enter configuration commands, one per line.  End with CNTL/Z.
Trinity(config)#router ospf 100
Trinity(config-router)#default-information originate metric 50 metric-type 1 always
Trinity(config-router)#exit
Trinity#
```

CAUTION   Use care in applying the **always** keyword. If more than one default route exists in your network, the **always** keyword should not be used because it would cause some traffic to be discarded when another valid route that it could use was present.

There is no obvious effect on the route; however, if you were to shut down the serial link to the RIP domain, you would expect to see all RIP routes be removed from Router Neo's routing table, but the default route remains as a result of the **always** keyword. Check Example 6-9 to see if this is indeed the case.

Example 6-9   *Router Neo's Routing Table After the* **always** *Keyword*

```
Neo>show ip route
Codes: C - connected, S - static, I - IGRP, R - RIP, M - mobile, B - BGP
       D - EIGRP, EX - EIGRP external, O - OSPF, IA - OSPF inter area
       N1 - OSPF NSSA external type 1, N2 - OSPF NSSA external type 2
       E1 - OSPF external type 1, E2 - OSPF external type 2, E - EGP
       i - IS-IS, L1 - IS-IS level-1, L2 - IS-IS level-2, ia - IS-IS inter area
       * - candidate default, U - per-user static route, o - ODR
       P - periodic downloaded static route

Gateway of last resort is 10.10.10.1 to network 0.0.0.0

     10.0.0.0/24 is subnetted, 2 subnets
C       10.10.10.0 is directly connected, FastEthernet0/0
O       10.10.20.0 [110/2] via 10.10.10.1, 00:39:56, FastEthernet0/0
C     192.168.254.0/24 is directly connected, FastEthernet0/1
C     192.168.253.0/24 is directly connected, Loopback1
C     192.168.252.0/24 is directly connected, Loopback0
O*E1 0.0.0.0/0 [110/51] via 10.10.10.1, 00:11:49, FastEthernet0/0
```

Yes, the RIP routes are all gone, but the default route remains, so this worked as intended. In reviewing the concepts of external and default routes, this has reinforced some concepts with redistribution. Specifically, redistributed routes into OSPF are considered external routes, and a default route can also be redistributed. These characteristics might not be what you intended, so caution is warranted! Remember to go slowly with a plan and check the results at each step. The next section discusses how to assign routing metrics to a routing protocol as it is redistributed into OSPF.

Assigning Metrics for Redistributed Protocols

The **redistribution** command enables you to assign a metric for the routes that are being redistributed into OSPF. On Cisco routers using OSPF, if you have not assigned a metric when redistributing, OSPF assigns a default value of 20 to each route. This metric might have unexpected consequences in your network. However, do not worry; Cisco has also provided a couple of "nerd knobs," as covered in the following sections.

Using the **redistribute** Command to Assign a Metric

You can set the metric of routes redistributed into OSPF on a per-protocol basis. Specifically, this means that when you are configuring redistribution into OSPF from EIGRP, you can have all EIGRP routes use an assigned metric. If having all routes with the same metric is acceptable to your network's operation, review the configuration in Example 6-10.

Example 6-10 *Configuring a Routing Metric When Redistributing*

```
Tank#config terminal
Enter configuration commands, one per line.  End with CNTL/Z.
Tank(config)#router ospf 100
Tank(config-router)#redistribute EIGRP 100 metric ?
  <0-4294967295>  Default metric

Tank(config-router)#redistribute EIGRP 100 metric 110
```

Therefore, the metric for all EIGRP routes in the OSPF network would have been set to 110 through this configuration.

Using the **default-metric** Command to Assign a Metric

When you decide not to assign a metric using the **redistribute** command, you can use the **default-metric** *value* command in OSPF configuration mode. This command allows you to set the metric on all routes that are redistributed into OSPF without an assigned metric.

However, should you set the metric using the **redistribute** command, the **default-metric** *value* command does not alter what has been previously configured.

In the command output of Example 6-11, you can see that the range of metrics available to be assigned through this command is 1 to 4,294,967,295, thus giving you a metric for every conceivable need!

Example 6-11 *Range of the* **default-metric** *Command*

```
Trinity(config)#router ospf 100
Trinity (config-router)#default-metric ?
  <1-4294967295>  Default metric

Trinity (config-router)
```

The **default-metric** command can be useful when redistributing OSPF. The next section presents some configuration examples that demonstrate how to implement and configure a router using this command.

Configuration Example 1: Setting the Default Metric for Redistributed Routes

In Figure 6-2, Router Trinity is receiving the routes 212.54.190.0/24 and 10.1.1.4/30 from Router Neo via EIGRP. These EIGRP routes are initially redistributed into OSPF using the default metric of 20.

Figure 6-2 *Default Metric Configuration*

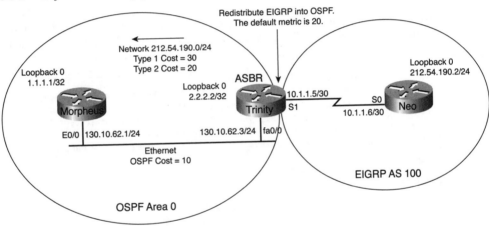

Once the network begins routing OSPF, the first thing that you need to verify is that Routers Morpheus and Trinity have established an OSPF neighbor relationship. Use the **show ip ospf neighbor** command on both routers to check the state of their communication, as shown in Example 6-12.

Example 6-12 *Verifying OSPF Neighbor Relationship*

```
Morpheus#show ip ospf neighbor

Neighbor ID     Pri   State         Dead Time   Address        Interface
2.2.2.2          1    FULL/BDR      00:00:30    130.10.62.1 Ethernet0/0
Trinity#show ip ospf neighbor

Neighbor ID     Pri   State         Dead Time   Address        Interface
1.1.1.1          1    FULL/DR       00:00:38    130.10.62.3    Ethernet0
```

Now that OSPF is working well, check the operation of EIGRP between Routers Trinity and Neo, as shown in Example 6-13.

Example 6-13 *Verifying EIGRP's Operation*

```
Trinity#show ip eigrp neighbors
IP-EIGRP neighbors for process 100
H   Address                 Interface   Hold Uptime    SRTT   RTO  Q  Seq
                                        (sec)          (ms)        Cnt Num
0   10.1.1.6                Se1         10 00:13:27    399    2394 0  4
Neo#show ip eigrp neighbors
IP-EIGRP neighbors for process 100
H   Address                 Interface   Hold Uptime    SRTT   RTO  Q  Seq
                                        (sec)          (ms)        Cnt Num
0   10.1.1.5                Se0         11 00:13:53    28     2280 0  6
```

After confirming that routing is working well for the network, verify that Router Trinity is receiving the 212.54.190.0/24 network from Router Neo, as shown in Example 6-14.

Example 6-14 *Identifying the Routing for EIGRP*

```
Trinity#show ip route
Codes: C - connected, S - static, I - IGRP, R - RIP, M - mobile, B - BGP
       D - EIGRP, EX - EIGRP external, O - OSPF, IA - OSPF inter area
       N1 - OSPF NSSA external type 1, N2 - OSPF NSSA external type 2
       E1 - OSPF external type 1, E2 - OSPF external type 2, E - EGP
       i - IS-IS, L1 - IS-IS level-1, L2 - IS-IS level-2, * - candidate default
       U - per-user static route, o - ODR

Gateway of last resort is not set

     1.0.0.0/32 is subnetted, 1 subnets
O       1.1.1.1 [110/11] via 172.16.1.1, 00:13:37, FastEthernet0/0
     2.0.0.0/32 is subnetted, 1 subnets
C       2.2.2.2 is directly connected, Loopback0
     212.54.190.0/24 is subnetted, 1 subnets
D       212.54.190.0 [90/40640000] via 10.1.1.6, 00:13:38, Serial1
     130.10.62.0/24 is subnetted, 1 subnets
C       130.10.62.0 is directly connected, FastEthernet0/0
     10.0.0.0/30 is subnetted, 1 subnets
C       10.1.1.4 is directly connected, Serial1
```

Inspect the routing table in Example 6-15 for Router Morpheus to verify that the default cost of the redistributed route is in fact present, as you would expect.

Example 6-15 *Verifying the Redistributed Default Route*

```
Morpheus#show ip route
Codes: C - connected, S - static, I - IGRP, R - RIP, M - mobile, B - BGP
       D - EIGRP, EX - EIGRP external, O - OSPF, IA - OSPF inter area
       N1 - OSPF NSSA external type 1, N2 - OSPF NSSA external type 2
       E1 - OSPF external type 1, E2 - OSPF external type 2, E - EGP
       i - IS-IS, L1 - IS-IS level-1, L2 - IS-IS level-2, * - candidate default
       U - per-user static route, o - ODR
```

Example 6-15 *Verifying the Redistributed Default Route (Continued)*

```
Gateway of last resort is not set

     1.0.0.0/32 is subnetted, 1 subnets
C       1.1.1.1 is directly connected, Loopback0
     2.0.0.0/32 is subnetted, 1 subnets
O       2.2.2.2 [110/11] via 130.10.62.3, 00:27:10, Ethernet0/0
     212.54.190.0/24 is subnetted, 1 subnets
O E2    212.54.190.0 [110/20] via 130.10.62.3, 00:01:58, Ethernet0/0
     130.10.62.0/24 is subnetted, 1 subnets
C       130.10.62.0 is directly connected, Ethernet0/0
     10.0.0.0/30 is subnetted, 1 subnets
O E2    10.1.1.4 [110/20] via 130.10.62.3, 00:01:58, Ethernet0/0
```

As you can see, the redistributed EIGRP routes have a cost, or metric, of 20 by default. These routes were redistributed as OSPF external Type 2 routes, so the cost of crossing the Ethernet network is not included. For this network, the default metric for all redistributed routes should be 100 unless specified differently. Therefore, you should configure Router Trinity so that all redistributed routes, including EIGRP routes, are assigned a metric of 100, as shown in Example 6-16.

Example 6-16 *Configuring the Default Metric for Redistribution*

```
Trinity#
router ospf 100
 redistribute eigrp 100 subnets
 network 2.2.2.2 0.0.0.0 area 0
 network 130.10.62.0 0.0.0.255 area 0
 default-metric 100
```

Next, in Example 6-17, verify that the redistributed EIGRP routes have now been assigned a metric of 100 per the configuration in Example 6-16.

Example 6-17 *Verifying the New Default Metric*

```
Morpheus#show ip route
Codes: C - connected, S - static, I - IGRP, R - RIP, M - mobile, B - BGP
       D - EIGRP, EX - EIGRP external, O - OSPF, IA - OSPF inter area
       N1 - OSPF NSSA external type 1, N2 - OSPF NSSA external type 2
       E1 - OSPF external type 1, E2 - OSPF external type 2, E - EGP
       i - IS-IS, L1 - IS-IS level-1, L2 - IS-IS level-2, * - candidate default
       U - per-user static route, o - ODR

Gateway of last resort is not set

     1.0.0.0/32 is subnetted, 1 subnets
C       1.1.1.1 is directly connected, Loopback0
     2.0.0.0/32 is subnetted, 1 subnets
O       2.2.2.2 [110/11] via 130.10.62.3, 00:27:10, Ethernet0/0
     212.54.190.0/24 is subnetted, 1 subnets
O E2    212.54.190.0 [110/100] via 130.10.62.3, 00:01:58, Ethernet0/0
     130.10.62.0/24 is subnetted, 1 subnets
```

continues

Example 6-17   *Verifying the New Default Metric (Continued)*

```
C       130.10.62.0 is directly connected, Ethernet0/0
        10.0.0.0/30 is subnetted, 1 subnets
O E2    10.1.1.4 [110/100] via 130.10.62.3, 00:01:58, Ethernet0/0
```

As expected, the metric of the routes is now appearing with a value of 100. Example 6-18 shows the relevant portions of the router configuration files that are used for this configuration example.

Example 6-18   *Relevant Configurations*

```
Morpheus#
interface Loopback0
 ip address 1.1.1.1 255.255.255.255
!
interface Ethernet0/0
 ip address 130.10.62.0 255.255.255.0
!
router ospf 1
 network 1.1.1.1 0.0.0.0 area 0
 network 172.16.1.0 0.0.0.255 area 0
Trinity#
interface Loopback0
 ip address 2.2.2.2 255.255.255.255
!
interface FastEthernet0/0
 ip address 130.10.62.0 255.255.255.0
!
interface Serial1
 bandwidth 64
 ip address 10.1.1.5 255.255.255.252
 clockrate 64000
!
router eigrp 100
 network 10.0.0.0

router ospf 100
 redistribute eigrp 100 subnets
 network 2.2.2.2 0.0.0.0 area 0
 network 172.16.1.0 0.0.0.255 area 0
 default-metric 100
Neo#
interface Loopback0
 description Simulate the network 3.3.3.0/24
 ip address 3.3.3.3 255.255.255.0
!
interface Serial0
 bandwidth 64
 ip address 10.1.1.6 255.255.255.252
!
router eigrp 100
 network 212.54.190.0
 network 10.0.0.0
 no auto-summary
```

The next section discusses the concept of mutual redistribution and describes how mutual redistribution allows redistribution of routes between routing protocols at the same time. This is all accomplished through a concept known as *route tagging*.

Route Tagging

Route tagging is one of the neatest possible ways of manipulating routes. Having learned how to manipulate routes the long way with access control lists, you are now ready for the more efficient manner of manipulation using route tagging. While many network engineers use route tagging as a way to filter routes (which is certainly a good use), there are many other uses. Although this is not a book on route filtering, I have included tagging in this redistribution chapter because it is of value in OSPF. A route tag is a number that is placed into each routing update and carried by that route until altered. A route tag allows that route to be identified, and the presence of a tag in no way alters the validity or integrity of the route. All the major IP-based routing protocols support route tagging.

Consider the simple network shown in Figure 6-3 and see how the network consists of an OSPF core surrounded by other routing protocols. This kind of situation typically occurs during business changes involving acquisitions or a major redesign of an existing network, but you can use it whenever the situation warrants.

Figure 6-3   *When to Tag*

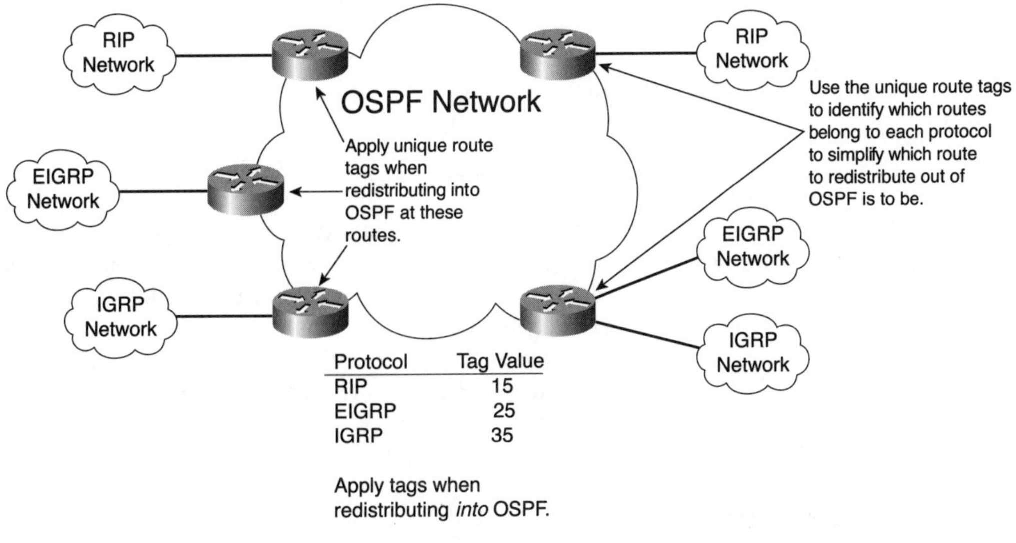

Protocol	Tag Value
RIP	15
EIGRP	25
IGRP	35

Apply tags when redistributing *into* OSPF.

NOTE	A route tag is similar in concept to a BGP community.

As shown in Figure 6-3, route tags are applied to keep the appropriate routes for each protocol together when redistributing into or out of OSPF. Another use for a route tag is to identify and filter routes. Figure 6-4 presents several different autonomous systems (routing domains) that are sharing routes. It is the routing policy of AS 2 to share the routes of AS 1 to AS 4. However, AS 2 also knows about the routes from AS 3, but those routes are not shared with AS 4. One of the easiest ways to configure your routers to follow this policy is through the use of route tags.

Figure 6-4   *Tagging and Filtering Routes*

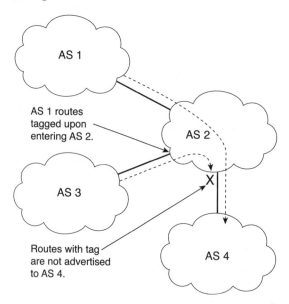

The challenge is to always tag the routes coming into AS 2 from AS 3 without having to manually change router configurations every time that AS 3 gets a new subnet or has an internal change. Therefore, when the routes from AS 3 are redistributed into AS 2, you tag them all. The routes are then shared throughout AS 2. On the router that is sending routes to AS 4, you have a route map that says "Do not advertise any routes that have this tag on them to AS 4"—very elegant and simple. This chapter looks at how to apply tags when redistributing during the configuration examples.

Mutual Redistribution

So far, you have learned about redistribution, how to generate default routes, and how external routes represent routes that are redistributed into OSPF, but there is still a bit more to redistribution. Enter the last concept before getting into more configuration examples. This concept is known as *mutual redistribution*. As you should know by now, redistribution is the process of importing route information from one routing protocol into another. The concept is further expanded through mutual redistribution, where routing protocol information is both imported and exported (kind of like "I tell you my routes and you tell me yours"). When beginning a mutual redistribution project, go through the following checks:

1 Deploy mutual redistribution between routing protocols carefully and in a controlled manner.

2 Use filters to ensure that unthrottled redistribution does not allow route information learned from a protocol to be injected back into the same protocol.

NOTE   Because OSPF is a link-state protocol and not a distance-vector protocol, you should be concerned about unthrottled routing information as opposed to split horizon. In other words, be careful not to inject a routing loop!

---

3 Deploy passive interfaces whenever possible to prevent routing loops or suboptimal routing.

4 Use route maps, not distribute lists, to filter OSPF routes because distribute lists have no effect in OSPF.

Distribute List Concerns

This is an important point to note regarding the operation of OSPF. Recall that redistribution occurs on an OSPF ASBR because in OSPF an ASBR connects to other routing domains. This concept will become important shortly. There are two ways to apply a distribute list on a router:

- To affect routing updates coming inbound
- Applied outbound to affect the routing updates be sent by the router.

Use the following commands to achieve applying a distribute list:

- **distribute-list out**—When applying a distribute list outbound to filter OSPF routes on an ASBR into another protocol, you can expect this to work normally.

- **distribute-list in**—When applying a distribute list inbound to filter routes, the list prevents the routes from being placed into the routing table. However, the list does not prevent link-state packets with that routing information from being sent to connected routers, who then have the routes present in their routing table.

Overall, you should perform route filtering in other protocols before the routes enter the OSPF routing domain.

Refer to Figure 6-5, which shows a sample network that has Routers Neo, Trinity, and
Oracle, all of which are running RIP. Notice that in this sample network, Routers Trinity and
Neo are also running OSPF in the core of the network. (By the way, this network should not be
considered a template for the real world; it is a bad design used to illustrate a concept.) Both
Routers Trinity and Neo are doing mutual redistribution between RIP and OSPF.

Figure 6-5   *OSPF and Distribute Lists*

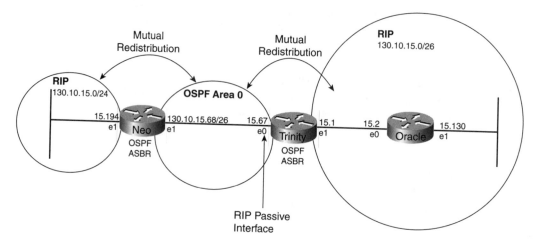

Assume that you do not want the RIP routes coming from Router Oracle to be injected into
the OSPF core (area 0), so you put a passive interface for RIP on interface E0 of Router
Trinity. This prevents RIP from being sent out E0 into the OSPF area 0. However, you have
still allowed the RIP routes coming from Router Neo to be injected into the OSPF core.
Example 6-19 shows the configurations and the resulting routing table.

Example 6-19   *Configurations Using Distribute Lists*

```
Oracle#
interface Ethernet0
  ip address 130.10.15.130 255.255.255.192
interface Serial0
  ip address 130.10.15.2 255.255.255.192
router rip
  network 130.10.15.0
Trinity#
interface Ethernet0
  ip address 130.10.15.67 255.255.255.192
interface Serial1
  ip address 130.10.15.1 255.255.255.192
router ospf 10
  redistribute rip metric 10 subnets
  network 130.10.15.0 0.0.0.255 area 0
router rip
```

Example 6-19   *Configurations Using Distribute Lists (Continued)*

```
 redistribute ospf 10 metric 2
 passive-interface Ethernet0
 network 130.10.15.0
Neo#
interface Ethernet0
 ip address 130.10.15.68 255.255.255.192
router ospf 10
 redistribute rip metric 10 subnets
 network 130.10.15.0 0.0.0.255 area 0
router rip
 redistribute ospf 10 metric 1
 network 130.10.15.0
```

Notice that in the routing table of Example 6-20, Router Trinity has two routes to reach the 130.10.15.128 subnet: Ethernet 1 and Ethernet 0 (E0 is obviously the wrong path).

Example 6-20   *Sample Routing Table with Erroneous Entry*

```
Trinity#show ip route
Codes: C - connected, S - static, I - IGRP, R - RIP, M - mobile, B - BGP
D - EIGRP, EX - EIGRP external, O - OSPF, IA - OSPF inter area
E1 - OSPF external type 1, E2 - OSPF external type 2, E - EGP
i - IS-IS, L1 - IS-IS level-1, L2 - IS-IS level-2, * - candidate default
Gateway of last resort is not set
130.10.15.0 255.255.255.192 is subnetted, 4 subnets
C 130.10.15.0 is directly connected, Ethernet1
C 130.10.15.64 is directly connected, Ethernet0
R 130.10.15.128 [120/1] via 130.10.15.68, 00:01:08, Ethernet0
                [120/1] via 130.10.15.2, 00:00:11, Ethernet1
O 130.10.15.192 [110/20] via 130.10.15.68, 00:21:41, Ethernet0
```

This routing loop happened because Router Trinity gave that route entry to Router Neo via OSPF, and Router Neo gave it back via RIP because Router Neo did not learn about it via RIP. This example is a small scale of the routing loops that can occur because of an incorrect configuration. In large networks, this situation is even more pronounced and harder to isolate. This can also lead to route oscillation, where routes are quickly asserted and withdrawn, causing high CPU usage and overall poor router performance.

To fix the routing loop in this example, you could stop RIP routing updates from being sent on Router Neo's Ethernet 0 by making it a passive interface in RIP. This might not be suitable in case some routers in the OSPF Ethernet core are RIP-only routers. In this case, you could allow Router Trinity to send RIP on its Ethernet 0 interface; this way, Router Neo does not send it back on the wire because of split horizon. (This might not work on NBMA media if split horizon is off.) Split horizon does not allow updates to be sent back on the same interface that they were learned from (via the same protocol). Another good method is to apply distribute lists on Router Neo to deny subnets that are learned via OSPF from being put back into RIP on the Ethernet, as demonstrated in Example 6-21.

Example 6-21 *Configuration Using Distribute Lists*

```
Neo#
interface Ethernet0
  ip address 130.10.15.68 255.255.255.192
router ospf 10
  redistribute rip metric 10 subnets
  network 130.10.15.0 0.0.0.255 area 0
router rip
  redistribute ospf 10 metric 1
  network 130.10.15.0
  distribute-list 1 out ospf 10
```

As previously discussed, the distribute list is applied outbound on the ASBR. Example 6-22 shows Trinity's resulting routing table.

Example 6-22 *Corrected Routing Table After Application of Distribute List*

```
Trinity#show ip route
Codes: C - connected, S - static, I - IGRP, R - RIP, M - mobile, B - BGP
  D - EIGRP, EX - EIGRP external, O - OSPF, IA - OSPF inter area
  E1 - OSPF external type 1, E2 - OSPF external type 2, E - EGP
  i - IS-IS, L1 - IS-IS level-1, L2 - IS-IS level-2, * - candidate default
Gateway of last resort is not set
130.10.15.0 255.255.255.192 is subnetted, 4 subnets
C 130.10.15.0 is directly connected, Ethernet1
C 130.10.15.64 is directly connected, Ethernet0
R 130.10.15.128 [120/1] via 130.10.15.2, 00:00:19, Ethernet1
O 130.10.15.192 [110/20] via 130.10.15.68, 00:21:41, Ethernet0
```

Avoiding Redistribution Loops

Even though trying to avoid redistribution loops is a golden rule for route redistribution, these loops do occur. To summarize what is occurring, realize that Router A is distributing network 230.250.15.0 into the RIP network. Router B then sees this network advertised by RIP as a valid destination, so Router B tells the OSPF network that it can reach network 230.250.15.0. This results in a nasty routing loop, as illustrated in Figure 6-6.

Figure 6-6 *Example of a Redistribution Loop*

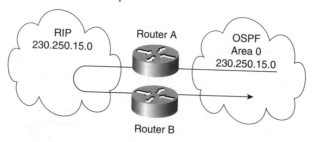

Example 6-23 shows the initial configuration of Router A.

Example 6-23 *Initial Configuration*

```
Router A (config)#
router ospf 10
redistribute rip subnets
network 230.250.0.0 0.0.255.255 area 0
```

As previously mentioned, this configuration would result in a routing loop caused by the uncontrolled redistribution. To prevent this, Example 6-24 shows modifications that must be made, this time to router B.

Example 6-24 *Updated Router Configuration*

```
Router B (config)#
router ospf 10
redistribute rip subnets
network 230.250.0.0 0.0.255.255 area 0
distribute-list 1 out rip
access-list 1 deny 230.250.0.0
access-list 1 permit any
```

The **distribute-list** commands were designed specifically to filter routing updates based on an access list, in this case access-list 1.

But what did these commands do? Simply put, the **distribute-list 1** command is invoked under the OSPF process, and it applies access-list 1 to the outbound updates from OSPF and RIP. This configuration is applied if the redistribution source is the RIP network. In summary, this filter (access list) prevents the network 230.250.0.0 from being advertised back into the OSPF network. You should apply this solution to all routers advertising this network.

Route Maps

Use route maps when you want detailed control over how routes are redistributed between routing processes. The destination routing protocol is the one that you specify with the **router** global configuration command. The source routing protocol is the one that you specify with the **redistribute** router configuration command. The route map is a method used to control the redistribution of routes between routing domains. The command syntax of a route map is as follows:

```
route-map map-tag [[permit | deny] | [sequence-number]]
```

When you are passing routes through a route map, a route map can have several parts. Any route that does not match at least one match clause relating to a **route-map** command is ignored; that is, the route is not advertised for outbound route maps and is not accepted for inbound route maps. To modify only some data, you must configure a second route map section with an explicit match specified or you can use a permit, depending upon your requirements.

When redistributing routes into OSPF, only routes that are not subnetted are redistributed if the **subnets** keyword is not specified.

Configuration Example 2: RIP and OSPF

This case study is a classic for those making the transition from RIP to OSPF. It has become extremely popular within networking circles after it was published in the first edition of this book, and it has been updated.

This case study addresses the issue of integrating RIP networks with OSPF networks. Most OSPF networks also use RIP to communicate with hosts or to communicate with portions of the internetwork that do not use OSPF, such as older legacy areas or small business partners.

Cisco routers support both RIP and OSPF routing protocols and provide a way to exchange routing information between RIP and OSPF networks through redistribution. This case study provides examples of how to complete the following phases in redistributing information between RIP and OSPF networks:

- Configuring a RIP network
- Adding OSPF to the center of a RIP network
- Adding OSPF areas
- Setting up mutual redistribution

Configuring the RIP Network

Figure 6-7 illustrates a RIP network. Three sites are connected with serial lines. The RIP network uses a Class B address and an 8-bit subnet mask. Each site has a contiguous set of network numbers assigned to it. The creators must have read the first edition of this book when designing the network because they clearly planned for future growth in the OSPF direction!

Table 6-2 lists the network address assignments for the RIP v2 network, including the network number, subnet range, and subnet masks. All interfaces indicate network 130.10.0.0; however, the specific address includes the subnet and subnet mask. For example, serial interface 0 on router C has an IP address of 130.10.63.3 with a subnet mask of 255.255.255.0.

Table 6-3   *RIP Network Assignments*

Network Number	Subnets	Subnet Masks
130.10.0.0	Site A: 8–15	255.255.255.0
130.10.0.0	Site B: 16–23	255.255.255.0
130.10.0.0	Site C: 24–31	255.255.255.0
130.10.0.0	Core: 62–64	255.255.255.0

Figure 6-7   *Typical RIP Network*

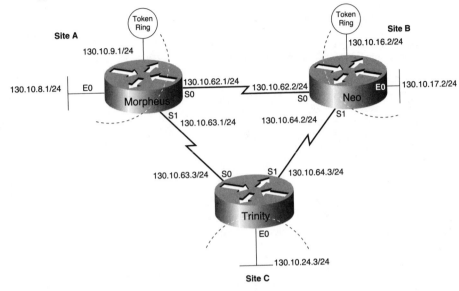

Configuration File Examples

Example 6-25 shows the commands in the configuration file for Router Morpheus that determine the IP address for each interface and enable RIP on those interfaces.

Example 6-25   *Morpheus Configuration*

```
interface serial 0
  ip address 130.10.62.1 255.255.255.0

interface serial 1
  ip address 130.10.63.1 255.255.255.0

interface ethernet 0
  ip address 130.10.8.1 255.255.255.0

interface tokenring 0
  ip address 130.10.9.1 255.255.255.0

router rip
  network 130.10.0.0
```

Example 6-26 shows the commands in the configuration file for Router Neo to determine the IP address for each interface and enable RIP on those interfaces.

Example 6-26   *Neo Configuration*

```
interface serial 0
  ip address 130.10.62.2 255.255.255.0

interface serial 1
  ip address 130.10.64.2 255.255.255.0

interface ethernet 0
  ip address 130.10.17.2 255.255.255.0

interface tokenring 0
  ip address 130.10.16.2 255.255.255.0

router rip
  network 130.10.0.0
```

Example 6-27 shows the commands in the configuration file for router Trinity to determine the IP address for each interface and enable RIP on those interfaces.

Example 6-27   *Trinity Configuration*

```
interface serial 0
  ip address 130.10.63.3 255.255.255.0

interface serial 1
  ip address 130.10.64.3 255.255.255.0

interface ethernet 0
  ip address 130.10.24.3 255.255.255.0

router rip
  network 130.10.0.0
```

Adding OSPF to the Center of a RIP Network

A common first step in converting a RIP network to an OSPF network is to convert backbone routers into running both RIP and OSPF, while the remaining network edge devices run RIP. These backbone routers automatically become OSPF ASBRs (redistributing RIP into OSPF).

Each ASBR controls the flow of routing information between OSPF and RIP. In Figure 6-8, Routers Morpheus, Neo, and Trinity are configured as ASBRs when redistributing RIP into OSPF.

Figure 6-8   *RIP with an OSPF Center*

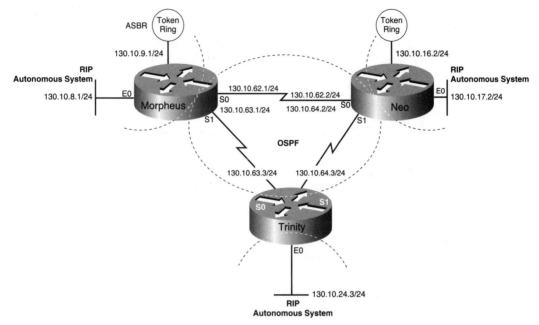

RIP does not need to run between the backbone routers; therefore, RIP is suppressed on all three routers with the following commands applied to each:

```
router rip
  passive-interface serial 0
  passive-interface serial 1
```

The RIP routes are redistributed into OSPF by all three routers with the following commands:

```
router ospf 109
  redistribute rip subnets
  network 130.10.0.0 255.255.0.0 area 0
```

The **subnets** keyword tells OSPF to redistribute all subnet routes. Without the **subnets** keyword, only networks that are not subnetted are redistributed by OSPF. Redistributed routes appear as external Type 2 routes in OSPF. For more detail on route types, see the *Cisco IOS Software Command Reference*.

Each RIP domain receives information about networks in other RIP domains and in the OSPF backbone area from the following commands, which redistribute OSPF routes into RIP:

```
router rip
  redistribute ospf 109 match internal external 1 external 2
  default-metric 10
```

The **redistribute** command uses the **ospf** keyword to specify that OSPF routes are redistributed into RIP. The **internal** keyword indicates the OSPF intra-area and inter-area routes: **external 1** is the external route Type 1, and **external 2** is the external route Type 2. Because the command in the example uses the default behavior, these keywords might not appear when you use the **show running-config** command. This is important because the routes being sent to the other OSPF routers contain E2 routes, the other RIP networks, so this is a crucial aspect to consider so that convergence occurs.

Because metrics for different protocols cannot be directly compared, you must specify the default metric to designate the cost of the redistributed route used in RIP updates. All routes that are redistributed use the default metric.

As illustrated in Figure 6-8, no paths are directly connecting the RIP clouds. However, in typical networks, these paths, or "back doors," frequently exist, allowing the potential for routing loops to occur. You can use access lists to determine the routes that are advertised and accepted by each router.

For example, access list 11 in the configuration file for router Morpheus allows OSPF to redistribute information learned from RIP only for networks 130.10.8.0 through 130.10.15.0, as follows:

```
router ospf 109
  redistribute rip subnet
  distribute-list 11 out rip

  access-list 11 permit 130.10.8.0 0.0.7.255
  access-list 11 deny 0.0.0.0 255.255.255.255
```

These commands prevent router Morpheus from advertising networks in other RIP domains onto the OSPF backbone, thereby preventing other boundary routers from using false information and forming a loop.

Configuration File Examples

Compare the partial configuration options in Examples 6-25, 6-26, and 6-27 with the full configuration files in Examples 6-28, 6-29, and 6-30 for the routers in question.

Example 6-28   *Full Configuration for Router Morpheus*

```
interface serial 0
ip address 130.10.62.1 255.255.255.0
interface serial 1
ip address 130.10.63.1 255.255.255.0
interface ethernet 0
ip address 130.10.8.1 255.255.255.0
interface tokenring 0
ip address 130.10.9.1 255.255.255.0
!
router rip
default-metric 10
network 130.10.0.0
```

Example 6-28   *Full Configuration for Router Morpheus (Continued)*

```
passive-interface serial 0
passive-interface serial 1
redistribute ospf 109 match internal external 1 external 2
!
router ospf 109
network 130.10.62.0 0.0.0.255 area 0
network 130.10.63.0 0.0.0.255 area 0
redistribute rip subnets
distribute-list 11 out rip
!
access-list 11 permit 130.10.8.0 0.0.7.255
access-list 11 deny 0.0.0.0 255.255.255.255
```

Example 6-29   *Full Configuration for Router Neo*

```
interface serial 0
ip address 130.10.62.2 255.255.255.0
interface serial 1
ip address 130.10.64.2 255.255.255.0
interface ethernet 0
ip address 130.10.17.2 255.255.255.0
interface tokenring 0
ip address 130.10.16.2 255.255.255.0
!
router rip
default-metric 10
network 130.10.0.0
passive-interface serial 0
passive-interface serial 1
redistribute ospf 109 match internal external 1 external 2
!
router ospf 109
network 130.10.62.0 0.0.0.255 area 0
network 130.10.64.0 0.0.0.255 area 0
redistribute rip subnets
distribute-list 11 out rip
access-list 11 permit 130.10.16.0 0.0.7.255
access-list 11 deny 0.0.0.0 255.255.255.255
```

Example 6-30   *Full Configuration for Router Trinity*

```
interface serial 0
ip address 130.10.63.3 255.255.255.0
interface serial 1
ip address 130.10.64.3 255.255.255.0
interface ethernet 0
ip address 130.10.24.3 255.255.255.0
!
router rip
default-metric 10
!
```

continues

Example 6-30 *Full Configuration for Router Trinity (Continued)*

```
network 130.10.0.0
passive-interface serial 0
passive-interface serial 1
redistribute ospf 109 match internal external 1 external 2
!
router ospf 109
network 130.10.63.0 0.0.0.255 area 0
network 130.10.64.0 0.0.0.255 area 0
redistribute rip subnets
distribute-list 11 out rip
access-list 11 permit 130.10.24.0 0.0.7.255
access-list 11 deny 0.0.0.0 255.255.255.255
```

Adding OSPF Areas

Figure 6-9 illustrates how each of the RIP clouds can be converted into an OSPF area. All three routers then become ABRs, which control network information distribution between OSPF areas and the OSPF backbone. Each router keeps a detailed record of the topology of its area and receives summarized information from the other ABRs on their respective areas.

Figure 6-9 also illustrates VLSM addressing. VLSM uses different size network masks in different parts of the network for the same network number. VLSM conserves address space by using a longer mask in portions of the network that have fewer hosts.

Table 6-3 lists the network address assignments for the network, including the network number, subnet range, and subnet masks. All interfaces indicate network 130.10.0.0.

Table 6-4 *OSPF Area Address Assignments*

Network Number	Subnets	Subnet Masks
130.10.0.0	Area 0: 62–64	255.255.255.248
130.10.0.0	Area 1: 8–15	255.255.255.0
130.10.0.0	Area 2: 16–23	255.255.255.0
130.10.0.0	Area 3: 24–31	255.255.255.0

To conserve address space, a mask of 255.255.255.248 is used for all the serial lines in area 0. If an area contains a contiguous range of network numbers, an ABR uses the **range** keyword with the **area** command to summarize the routes that are injected into the backbone, as follows:

```
router ospf 109
network 130.10.8.0 0.0.7.255 area 1
area 1 range 130.10.8.0 255.255.248.0
```

Figure 6-9   *Configuring Route Summarization Between OSPF Areas*

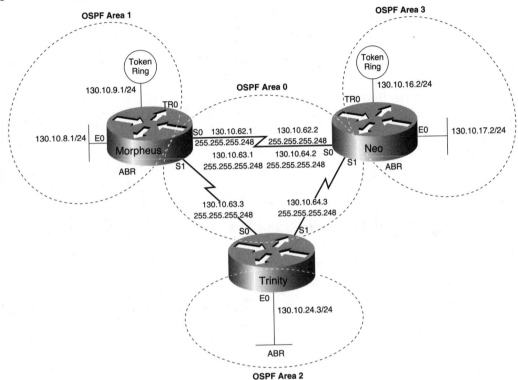

These commands allow router Morpheus to advertise one route, 130.10.8.0255.255.248.0, which covers all subnets in area 1 into area 0. Without the **range** keyword in the **area** command, Morpheus would advertise each subnet individually, for example, one route for 130.10.8.0255.255.255.0, one route for 130.10.9.0255.255.255.0, and so on.

Because Morpheus no longer needs to redistribute RIP routes (all of them actually), the **router rip** command can now be removed from the configuration file.

Configuration File Examples

The following configuration files in Examples 6-31, 6-32, and 6-33 reflect the presence of OSPF within the network and on the routers.

Example 6-31   *Full Configuration for Morpheus*

```
interface serial 0
ip address 130.10.62.1 255.255.255.248

interface serial 1
ip address 130.10.63.1 255.255.255.248

interface ethernet 0
ip address 130.10.8.1 255.255.255.0
ip irdp

interface tokenring 0
ip address 130.10.9.1 255.255.255.0
ip irdp
router ospf 109
network 130.10.62.0 0.0.0.255 area 0
network 130.10.63.0 0.0.0.255 area 0
network 130.10.8.0 0.0.7.255 area 1
area 1 range 130.10.8.0 255.255.248.0
```

Example 6-32   *Full Configuration for Router Neo*

```
interface serial 0
ip address 130.10.62.2 255.255.255.248

interface serial 1
ip address 130.10.64.2 255.255.255.248

interface ethernet 0
ip address 130.10.17.2 255.255.255.0
ip irdp

interface tokenring 0
ip address 130.10.16.2 255.255.255.0
ip irdp

router ospf 109
network 130.10.62.0 0.0.0.255 area 0
network 130.10.64.0 0.0.0.255 area 0
network 130.10.16.0 0.0.7.255 area 2
area 2 range 130.10.16.0 255.255.248.0
```

Example 6-33   *Full Configuration for Router Trinity*

```
interface serial 0
ip address 130.10.63.2 255.255.255.248

interface serial 1
ip address 130.10.64.2 255.255.255.248

interface ethernet 0
ip address 130.10.24.3 255.255.255.0
```

Example 6-33 *Full Configuration for Router Trinity (Continued)*

```
ip irdp

router ospf 109
network 130.10.63.0 0.0.0.255 area 0
network 130.10.64.0 0.0.0.255 area 0
network 130.10.24.0 0.0.0.255 area 3
area 3 range 130.10.24.0 255.255.248.0
```

What If Mutual Redistribution Were Required?

It is sometimes necessary to accommodate more complex network topologies, such as independent RIP and OSPF clouds, that must perform mutual redistribution. In this what-if scenario, it is important to prevent potential routing loops by filtering routes. The router in Figure 6-10 is running both OSPF and RIP.

Figure 6-10 *Mutual Redistribution and OSPF Networks*

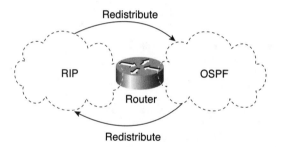

With the following commands, OSPF routes are redistributed into RIP. You must specify the default metric to designate the cost of the redistributed route in RIP updates. All routes that are redistributed into RIP have the following default metric:

```
! passive interface subcommand from previous example is left out for clarity!
router rip
default-metric 10
network 130.10.0.0
redistribute ospf 109
```

It is a good practice to strictly control which routes are advertised when redistribution is configured. In Example 6-34, a **distribute-list out** command causes RIP to ignore routes coming from the OSPF process that originated from the RIP domain.

Example 6-34 *Distribute List to Ignore Routes*

```
router rip
distribute-list 10 out ospf 109
!
access-list 10 deny 130.10.8.0 0.0.7.255
access-list 10 permit 0.0.0.0 255.255.255.255
!Full Configuration for Router Morpheus
```

continues

Example 6-34 *Distribute List to Ignore Routes (Continued)*

```
interface serial 0
ip add 130.10.62.1 255.255.255.0
!
interface serial 1
ip add 130.10.63.1 255.255.255.0
!
interface ethernet 0
ip add 130.10.8.1 255.255.255.0
!
interface tokenring 0
ip add 130.10.9.1 255.255.255.0
!
router rip
default-metric 10
network 130.10.0.0
passive-interface serial 0
passive-interface serial 1
redistribute ospf 109
distribute-list 10 out ospf 109
!
router ospf 109
network 130.10.62.0 0.0.0.255 area 0
network 130.10.63.0 0.0.0.255 area 0
redistribute rip subnets
distribute-list 11 out rip
!
access-list 10 deny 130.10.8.0 0.0.7.255
access-list 10 permit 0.0.0.0 255.255.255.255
access-list 11 permit 130.10.8.0 0.0.7.255
access-list 11 deny 0.0.0.0 255.255.255.255
```

Because it is common for OSPF and RIP to be used together, it is important to use the practices described here to provide functionality for both protocols on an internetwork. You can configure ASBRs that run both RIP and OSPF and redistribute RIP routes into the OSPF, and vice versa. You can also create OSPF areas using ABRs that provide route summarizations. Use VLSM to conserve address space.

Configuration Example 3: Redistributing Connected and Loopback Interfaces

This example looks at redistributing connected networks into OSPF, the results of this, and alternative ways of handling connected networks.

In cases where you must redistribute connected networks into OSPF instead of configuring OSPF to recognize them via the **network** command, all the connected networks show up as external routes in OSPF.

In this example, Router Neo is configured with a loopback interface, which is assigned the network 192.168.253.0/24. Figure 6-11 shows the overall network for this example. The configuration steps are described in the text that follows.

Figure 6-11 *Network Topology for Connected and Loopback Interface Redistribution*

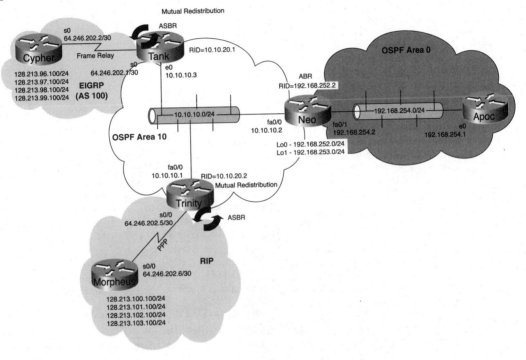

Example 6-35 shows how to assign a determined network to the loopback interface and then configure OSPF to redistribute connected networks.

Example 6-35 *Configuration to Redistribute Connected Routes*

```
Neo(config)#int lo1
Neo(config-if)#ip address 192.168.253.1 255.255.255.0
Neo(config-if)#router ospf 100
Neo(config-router)#redistribute connected
```

The result of this configuration is the introduction of the network 192.168.253.0/24 into the routing table. Example 6-36 shows the results by viewing the routing table on Router Tank. Other methods can accomplish the same result (such as including changing the default network type on a loopback interface). These methods are much easier than redistributing connected networks because you might have connected interfaces as part of another routing domain.

Example 6-36 *Redistribution Example*

```
Tank#show ip route
Codes: C - connected, S - static, I - IGRP, R - RIP, M - mobile, B - BGP
       D - EIGRP, EX - EIGRP external, O - OSPF, IA - OSPF inter area
       N1 - OSPF NSSA external type 1, N2 - OSPF NSSA external type 2
       E1 - OSPF external type 1, E2 - OSPF external type 2, E - EGP
       i - IS-IS, L1 - IS-IS level-1, L2 - IS-IS level-2, * - candidate default
       U - per-user static route, o - ODR

Gateway of last resort is not set

     10.0.0.0/24 is subnetted, 2 subnets
C       10.10.10.0 is directly connected, Ethernet0
C       10.10.20.0 is directly connected, Loopback0
     64.0.0.0/30 is subnetted, 1 subnets
C       64.246.202.0 is directly connected, Serial0
     128.213.0.0/24 is subnetted, 4 subnets
D       128.213.97.0 [90/2297856] via 64.246.202.2, 01:02:35, Serial0
D       128.213.96.0 [90/2297856] via 64.246.202.2, 01:02:35, Serial0
D       128.213.99.0 [90/2297856] via 64.246.202.2, 01:02:35, Serial0
D       128.213.98.0 [90/2297856] via 64.246.202.2, 01:02:35, Serial0
O IA 192.168.252.0/24 [110/11] via 10.10.10.2, 00:00:06, Ethernet0
O E2 192.168.253.0/24 [110/20] via 10.10.10.2, 00:00:07, Ethernet0
O IA 192.168.254.0/24 [110/11] via 10.10.10.2, 00:00:07, Ethernet0
```

The redistributed network is treated as an external network. Notice how the route is now present as an OSPF external Type 2 route, which is the default type of external route.

You can use another way to get this network into OSPF. This method is important to know if you are studying for certification or do not want to redistribute. To accomplish this, place the network assigned to the loopback interface into OSPF via the **network** command, as shown in Example 6-37.

Example 6-37 *Advertising Without Redistributing*

```
Neo(config)#router ospf 100
Neo(config-router)#no redistribute connected
Neo(config-router)#network 192.168.253.0 0.0.0.255 area 0
Neo(config-router)#
```

This changes the OSPF route type for this network from external to inter-area (O IA in the routing table) from Router Tank's perspective because this router is area 10, as shown in Example 6-38.

Example 6-38 *Changes to the OSPF Route Type*

```
Tank#show ip route
Codes: C - connected, S - static, I - IGRP, R - RIP, M - mobile, B - BGP
       D - EIGRP, EX - EIGRP external, O - OSPF, IA - OSPF inter area
       N1 - OSPF NSSA external type 1, N2 - OSPF NSSA external type 2
       E1 - OSPF external type 1, E2 - OSPF external type 2, E - EGP
```

Example 6-38 *Changes to the OSPF Route Type (Continued)*

```
                i - IS-IS, L1 - IS-IS level-1, L2 - IS-IS level-2, * - candidate default
                U - per-user static route, o - ODR

Gateway of last resort is not set

       10.0.0.0/24 is subnetted, 2 subnets
C         10.10.10.0 is directly connected, Ethernet0
C         10.10.20.0 is directly connected, Loopback0
       64.0.0.0/30 is subnetted, 1 subnets
C         64.246.202.0 is directly connected, Serial0
       128.213.0.0/24 is subnetted, 4 subnets
D         128.213.97.0 [90/2297856] via 64.246.202.2, 01:04:02, Serial0
D         128.213.96.0 [90/2297856] via 64.246.202.2, 01:04:02, Serial0
D         128.213.99.0 [90/2297856] via 64.246.202.2, 01:04:02, Serial0
D         128.213.98.0 [90/2297856] via 64.246.202.2, 01:04:02, Serial0
O IA 192.168.252.0/24 [110/11] via 10.10.10.2, 00:00:30, Ethernet0
       192.168.253.0/32 is subnetted, 1 subnets
O IA     192.168.253.1 [110/11] via 10.10.10.2, 00:00:11, Ethernet0
O IA 192.168.254.0/24 [110/11] via 10.10.10.2, 00:00:30, Ethernet0
```

However, notice that the network is now represented as a /32 host entry in the routing table. This is not the desired result. What you want to see is a network entry (that is, /24). To correct this, use the OSPF **network** *type* command on the loopback interface to configure OSPF to recognize that interface as a different network type and thus alter its advertisement of the network, as demonstrated in Example 6-39.

Example 6-39 *Setting the OSPF Network Type*

```
Neo(config-router)#int lo1
Neo(config-if)#ip ospf network ?
  broadcast           Specify OSPF broadcast multi-access network
  non-broadcast       Specify OSPF NBMA network
  point-to-multipoint Specify OSPF point-to-multipoint network
  point-to-point      Specify OSPF point-to-point network

Neo(config-if)#ip ospf network point-to-point
Neo(config-if)#
```

The result of this configuration can now be seen in the routing table of Router Tank in Example 6-40.

Example 6-40 *How OSPF Network Type Affects Route Entries*

```
Tank#show ip route
Codes: C - connected, S - static, I - IGRP, R - RIP, M - mobile, B - BGP
       D - EIGRP, EX - EIGRP external, O - OSPF, IA - OSPF inter area
       N1 - OSPF NSSA external type 1, N2 - OSPF NSSA external type 2
       E1 - OSPF external type 1, E2 - OSPF external type 2, E - EGP
       i - IS-IS, L1 - IS-IS level-1, L2 - IS-IS level-2, * - candidate default
       U - per-user static route, o - ODR
```

continues

Example 6-40   *How OSPF Network Type Affects Route Entries (Continued)*

```
Gateway of last resort is not set

     10.0.0.0/24 is subnetted, 2 subnets
C       10.10.10.0 is directly connected, Ethernet0
C       10.10.20.0 is directly connected, Loopback0
     64.0.0.0/30 is subnetted, 1 subnets
C       64.246.202.0 is directly connected, Serial0
     128.213.0.0/24 is subnetted, 4 subnets
D       128.213.97.0 [90/2297856] via 64.246.202.2, 01:05:38, Serial0
D       128.213.96.0 [90/2297856] via 64.246.202.2, 01:05:38, Serial0
D       128.213.99.0 [90/2297856] via 64.246.202.2, 01:05:38, Serial0
D       128.213.98.0 [90/2297856] via 64.246.202.2, 01:05:38, Serial0
O IA 192.168.252.0/24 [110/11] via 10.10.10.2, 00:02:06, Ethernet0
O IA 192.168.253.0/24 [110/11] via 10.10.10.2, 00:01:03, Ethernet0
O IA 192.168.254.0/24 [110/11] via 10.10.10.2, 00:02:07, Ethernet0
Tank#
```

That is perfect. The network in question now appears as an intra-area OSPF route and a /24. Example 6-41 shows the final configuration for this on Router Neo.

Example 6-41   *OSPF Network Type Configuration Example*

```
!
interface Loopback1
 ip address 192.168.253.1 255.255.255.0
 no ip directed-broadcast
 ip ospf network point-to-point
!
router ospf 100
 network 10.10.10.0 0.0.0.255 area 10
 network 192.168.252.0 0.0.0.255 area 0
 network 192.168.253.0 0.0.0.255 area 0
 network 192.168.254.0 0.0.0.255 area 0
```

The next section discusses how to redistribute EIGRP into OSPF.

Configuration Example 4: Redistributing OSPF and EIGRP

EIGRP is a popular routing protocol for those wishing to deploy a single-vendor network (and obviously that vendor is Cisco). Is that a smart move? That is a Layer 8—political discussion. Having options and flexibility does not mean that you only look at buying one vendor's product. I like Cisco equipment and Cisco's routing protocol EIGRP, but having both together puts too many constraints on the business of running a network. The use of EIGRP is solid, and it is useful to understand how to get routes from EIGRP into OSPF via redistribution; just remember that OSPF is number one. Figure 6-12 shows the sample network used for this configuration example.

NOTE   For more information on EIGRP, consult the Cisco Press book *EIGRP Network Design Solutions* by Ivan Pepelnjak.

Figure 6-12 *Redistributing OSPF and EIGRP*

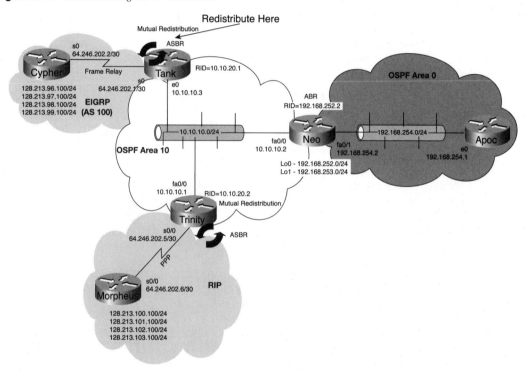

In this network, Router Tank is connected to OSPF area 10 and EIGRP AS 100. The entire OSPF network needs to know about the following networks:

> 64.246.202.0/30
> 128.213.96.0/24
> 128.213.97.0/24
> 128.213.98.0/24
> 128.213.99.0/24

These networks are found on Router Tank and are part of the EIGRP routing domain. Because the objective is for the entire OSPF network to learn about these networks, the following examples monitor the routing table of Router Apoc to see when it learns of these routes.

Before

At this time, Router Apoc has no idea that those routes are present; however, that will change when OSPF learns of them.

Example 6-42 *Before OSPF Learns About the EIGRP Routes*

```
Apoc>show ip route
Codes: C - connected, S - static, I - IGRP, R - RIP, M - mobile, B - BGP
       D - EIGRP, EX - EIGRP external, O - OSPF, IA - OSPF inter area
       N1 - OSPF NSSA external type 1, N2 - OSPF NSSA external type 2
       E1 - OSPF external type 1, E2 - OSPF external type 2, E - EGP
       i - IS-IS, L1 - IS-IS level-1, L2 - IS-IS level-2, * - candidate default
       U - per-user static route, o - ODR

Gateway of last resort is not set

     10.0.0.0/8 is variably subnetted, 3 subnets, 2 masks
O IA    10.10.10.0/24 [110/11] via 192.168.254.2, 00:23:12, Ethernet0
O IA    10.10.20.0/24 [110/12] via 192.168.254.2, 00:23:12, Ethernet0
O IA    10.10.20.1/32 [110/12] via 192.168.254.2, 00:23:12, Ethernet0
O       192.168.252.0/24 [110/11] via 192.168.254.2, 01:11:52, Ethernet0
O       192.168.253.0/24 [110/11] via 192.168.254.2, 01:11:52, Ethernet0
C       192.168.254.0/24 is directly connected, Ethernet0
Apoc>
```

During

Router Tank, as the router with interfaces in both OSPF and EIGRP, is responsible for required to redistribution the EIGRP routes into OSPF. Example 6-43 shows the current configuration of Router Tank.

Example 6-43 *Configuring OSPF to Redistribute EIGRP*

```
!
router eigrp 100
 network 64.0.0.0
 no auto-summary
!
router ospf 100
 redistribute eigrp 100
 network 10.10.10.0 0.0.0.255 area 10
 network 10.10.20.0 0.0.0.255 area 10
!
```

As you prepare for redistribution, you need to understand the various methods of assigning metrics to the redistributed networks. In this case, you assign the metric via the **redistribute** command. Also, the **subnets** keyword is used because this is always a good design rule in today's world of many subnets! Example 6-44 shows the configuration tasks.

Example 6-44   *Configuring the Metric and Using the* **subnets** *Keyword*

```
Tank#conf t
Enter configuration commands, one per line.  End with CNTL/Z.
Tank(config)#router ospf 100
Tank(config-router)#redistribute eigrp 100 metric 100 ?
  metric      Metric for redistributed routes
  metric-type OSPF/IS-IS exterior metric type for redistributed routes
  route-map   Route map reference
  subnets     Consider subnets for redistribution into OSPF
  tag         Set tag for routes redistributed into OSPF
  <cr>

Tank(config-router)#redistribute eigrp 100 metric 100 subnets
Tank(config-router)#
```

After

With the configuration completed on Router Tank, you would expect the routes to be sent as external routes via type LSAs through OSPF area 10 and then into area 0 to Router Apoc. Example 6-45 confirms this.

Example 6-45   *Routing Table with EIGRP Routes Redistributed into OSPF*

```
Apoc>show ip route
Codes: C - connected, S - static, I - IGRP, R - RIP, M - mobile, B - BGP
       D - EIGRP, EX - EIGRP external, O - OSPF, IA - OSPF inter area
       N1 - OSPF NSSA external type 1, N2 - OSPF NSSA external type 2
       E1 - OSPF external type 1, E2 - OSPF external type 2, E - EGP
       i - IS-IS, L1 - IS-IS level-1, L2 - IS-IS level-2, * - candidate default
       U - per-user static route, o - ODR

Gateway of last resort is not set

     10.0.0.0/8 is variably subnetted, 3 subnets, 2 masks
O IA    10.10.10.0/24 [110/11] via 192.168.254.2, 00:01:39, Ethernet0
O IA    10.10.20.0/24 [110/12] via 192.168.254.2, 00:01:39, Ethernet0
O IA    10.10.20.1/32 [110/12] via 192.168.254.2, 00:01:39, Ethernet0
     64.0.0.0/30 is subnetted, 1 subnets
O E2    64.246.202.0 [110/100] via 192.168.254.2, 00:01:39, Ethernet0
     128.213.0.0/24 is subnetted, 4 subnets
O E2    128.213.97.0 [110/100] via 192.168.254.2, 00:01:39, Ethernet0
O E2    128.213.96.0 [110/100] via 192.168.254.2, 00:01:39, Ethernet0
O E2    128.213.99.0 [110/100] via 192.168.254.2, 00:01:39, Ethernet0
O E2    128.213.98.0 [110/100] via 192.168.254.2, 00:01:40, Ethernet0
O    192.168.252.0/24 [110/11] via 192.168.254.2, 01:40:59, Ethernet0
O    192.168.253.0/24 [110/11] via 192.168.254.2, 01:40:59, Ethernet0
C    192.168.254.0/24 is directly connected, Ethernet0
Apoc>
```

OSPF and EIGRP Mutual Redistribution

Referring to the network in Figure 6-12, you can see in Example 6-46 that Router Cypher
has no idea if any of the OSPF routes are possible via its connection to Router Tank.

Before

Example 6-46 *Routing Table Before Mutual Redistribution*

```
Cypher#show ip route
Codes: C - connected, S - static, I - IGRP, R - RIP, M - mobile, B - BGP
       D - EIGRP, EX - EIGRP external, O - OSPF, IA - OSPF inter area
       N1 - OSPF NSSA external type 1, N2 - OSPF NSSA external type 2
       E1 - OSPF external type 1, E2 - OSPF external type 2, E - EGP
       i - IS-IS, L1 - IS-IS level-1, L2 - IS-IS level-2, * - candidate default
       U - per-user static route, o - ODR

Gateway of last resort is not set

     64.0.0.0/30 is subnetted, 1 subnets
C       64.246.202.0 is directly connected, Serial0
     128.213.0.0/24 is subnetted, 4 subnets
C       128.213.97.0 is directly connected, Loopback1
C       128.213.96.0 is directly connected, Loopback0
C       128.213.99.0 is directly connected, Loopback3
C       128.213.98.0 is directly connected, Loopback2
Cypher#
```

During

Example 6-47 shows how to configure redistribution on Router Tank. When this is combined
with currently configured redistribution, you have achieved a state of mutual redistribution.

Example 6-47 *Configuring Mutual Redistribution*

```
Tank(config)#router eigrp 100

Tank(config-router)#redistribute ospf 100 metric ?
  <1-4294967295>  Bandwidth metric in Kbits per second

Tank(config-router)#redistribute ospf 100 metric 1500 ?
  <0-4294967295>  IGRP delay metric, in 10 microsecond units

Tank(config-router)#redistribute ospf 100 metric 1500 10 ?
  <0-255>  IGRP reliability metric where 255 is 100% reliable

Tank(config-router)#redistribute ospf 100 metric 1500 10 255 ?
  <1-255>  IGRP Effective bandwidth metric (Loading) where 255 is 100% loaded

Tank(config-router)#redistribute ospf 100 metric 1500 10 255 1 ?
  <1-4294967295>  IGRP MTU of the path

Tank(config-router)#redistribute ospf 100 metric 1500 10 255 1 1500
Tank(config-router)#
```

Having configured the metrics of the OSPF routes to equal the defaults of a serial line, you are ready to check if Router Cypher now knows about the OSPF routes.

After

The configuration was successful, and you can see in Example 6-48 that the routes are appearing as external EIGRP routes.

Example 6-48   *Verifying That Redistribution Occurred*

```
Cypher#show ip route
Codes: C - connected, S - static, I - IGRP, R - RIP, M - mobile, B - BGP
       D - EIGRP, EX - EIGRP external, O - OSPF, IA - OSPF inter area
       N1 - OSPF NSSA external type 1, N2 - OSPF NSSA external type 2
       E1 - OSPF external type 1, E2 - OSPF external type 2, E - EGP
       i - IS-IS, L1 - IS-IS level-1, L2 - IS-IS level-2, * - candidate default
       U - per-user static route, o - ODR

Gateway of last resort is not set

     10.0.0.0/24 is subnetted, 2 subnets
D EX    10.10.10.0 [170/2221056] via 64.246.202.1, 00:00:10, Serial0
D EX    10.10.20.0 [170/2221056] via 64.246.202.1, 00:00:11, Serial0
     64.0.0.0/30 is subnetted, 1 subnets
C       64.246.202.0 is directly connected, Serial0
     128.213.0.0/24 is subnetted, 4 subnets
C       128.213.97.0 is directly connected, Loopback1
C       128.213.96.0 is directly connected, Loopback0
C       128.213.99.0 is directly connected, Loopback3
C       128.213.98.0 is directly connected, Loopback2
D EX 192.168.252.0/24 [170/2221056] via 64.246.202.1, 00:00:11, Serial0
D EX 192.168.253.0/24 [170/2221056] via 64.246.202.1, 00:00:11, Serial0
D EX 192.168.254.0/24 [170/2221056] via 64.246.202.1, 00:00:11, Serial0
Cypher#
```

So far in this example, you have not encountered a routing loop because the networks used are all different and because there are not many routes. However, in practice, such a problem is more likely to occur, and you should always use route maps to protect against routing loops. The next section discusses how to configure the route maps.

Using Route Maps to Protect Against Routing Loops

This section shows you the configuration steps used to deploy route maps to stop routing loops from occurring.

Before

At first, you have the same basic redistribution configuration as shown in Example 6-49. You build the route map from this base configuration.

Example 6-49   *Beginning Basic Redistribution Configuration*

```
!
router eigrp 100
 redistribute ospf 100 metric 1500 10 255 1 1500
 network 64.0.0.0
 no auto-summary
!
router ospf 100
 redistribute eigrp 100 metric 100 subnets
 network 10.10.10.0 0.0.0.255 area 10
 network 10.10.20.0 0.0.0.255 area 10
!
```

During

To configure the route map to protect the networks from route feedback and thus the creation of a routing loop, take the following steps:

Step 1   List all the networks to be permitted through the use of access lists in both directions.

Step 2   Create the route maps.

Step 3   Assign the route map to the redistribution action for each protocol.

For Step 1, in Example 6-50, **access-list 66** is used to identify the routes allowed from OSPF into EIGRP.

Example 6-50   *Using Access Lists to Identify the Routes to Redistribute from OSPF into EIGRP*

```
Tank(config)#access-list 66 permit 128.213.100.0 0.0.3.255
Tank(config)#access-list 66 permit 64.246.202.4 0.0.0.3
Tank(config)#access-list 66 permit 10.10.10.0 0.0.0.255
Tank(config)#access-list 66 permit 10.10.20.0 0.0.0.255
Tank(config)#access-list 66 permit 192.168.254.0 0.0.0.255
Tank(config)#access-list 66 permit 192.168.252.0 0.0.0.255
Tank(config)#access-list 66 permit 192.168.253.0 0.0.0.255
```

In Example 6-51, **access-list 97** identifies the routes allowed from EIGRP into OSPF. Recall the implicit deny all at the end of every access list.

Example 6-51   *Using Access Lists to Identify the Routes to Redistribute from OSPF into EIGRP*

```
Tank(config)#access-list 97 permit 128.213.96.0 0.0.3.255
Tank(config)#access-list 97 permit 64.246.202.0 0.0.0.3
```

For Step 2 (creating the route maps), give the route maps names that describe their function and then map the right access list to the route map, as demonstrated in Example 6-52.

Example 6-52 *Assigning the Access Lists to the Route Map*

```
Tank(config)#route-map OSPF-to-EIGRP permit 10
Tank(config-route-map)#match ip address 66

Tank(config)#route-map EIGRP-to-OSPF permit 10
Tank(config-route-map)#match ip address 97
```

For Step 3 (assigning the route map to the redistribution action for each protocol), in the case of Example 6-53, the route maps were created to allow only the identified routes into the other protocol upon redistribution.

Example 6-53 *Applying the Route Map to the* **redistribution** *Command*

```
Tank(config)#router ospf 100
Tank(config-router)#redistribute eigrp 100 route-map EIGRP-to-OSPF

Tank(config-router)#router eigrp 100
Tank(config-router)#redistribute ospf 100 route-map OSPF-to-EIGRP
```

After

Example 6-54 shows the final configuration of the route maps. Always check your routing table after a route map is applied to ensure that it gave you the desired results.

Example 6-54 *Final Configuration*

```
!
router eigrp 100
 redistribute ospf 100 metric 1500 10 255 1 1500 route-map OSPF-to-EIGRP
 network 64.0.0.0
 no auto-summary
!
router ospf 100
 redistribute eigrp 100 metric 100 subnets route-map EIGRP-to-OSPF
 network 10.10.10.0 0.0.0.255 area 10
 network 10.10.20.0 0.0.0.255 area 10
!
no ip classless
access-list 66 permit 128.213.100.0 0.0.3.255
access-list 66 permit 64.246.202.4 0.0.0.3
access-list 66 permit 10.10.10.0 0.0.0.255
access-list 66 permit 10.10.20.0 0.0.0.255
access-list 66 permit 192.168.254.0 0.0.0.255
access-list 66 permit 192.168.252.0 0.0.0.255
access-list 66 permit 192.168.253.0 0.0.0.255
access-list 97 permit 128.213.96.0 0.0.3.255
access-list 97 permit 64.246.202.0 0.0.0.3
route-map OSPF-to-EIGRP permit 10
 match ip address 66
!
route-map OSPF-to-EIGRP deny 65535
!
```

continues

Example 6-54   *Final Configuration (Continued)*

```
route-map EIGRP-to-OSPF permit 10
 match ip address 97
!
route-map EIGRP-to-OSPF deny 65535
!
```

Although not required, creating route maps in OSPF like this is strongly recommended, and doing so is considered best practice and appropriate whenever possible.

Using Route Tagging to Protect Against Routing Loops

This section shows you the configuration steps used to identify routes via a route tag during mutual redistribution to prevent loops.

Before

At first, you have the same basic redistribution configuration that was used in the previous example. From the base configuration in Example 6-55, you build the route tag configuration.

Example 6-55   *Basic Redistribution Configuration*

```
!
router eigrp 100
 redistribute ospf 100 metric 1500 10 255 1 1500
 network 64.0.0.0
 no auto-summary
!
router ospf 100
 redistribute eigrp 100 metric 100 subnets
 network 10.10.10.0 0.0.0.255 area 10
 network 10.10.20.0 0.0.0.255 area 10
!
```

During

During the steps to configure and assign a route tag, you are first going to create a route map that tags each route. One route map is created for EIGRP and another for OSPF. You then permit the correct routes to be redistributed and deny the others, as shown in the configuration steps that follow.

You first create the route maps for OSPF; these route maps identify the routes to be denied when they are redistributed. The route maps become part of the **redistribution** commands, so when you say "deny routes that have a route tag of 3," the routes will have already been redistributed and thus tagged through the other route map. This provides protection of OSPF. The same concept applies in reverse as you set the route tag of 4 because it is denied as part of the EIGRP redistribution route map. Example 6-56 shows the configuration tasks necessary to configure the router to use tags.

Example 6-56   *Assigning Route Tags to Route Maps*

```
Tank(config)#route-map DEN3-PERM4 deny 10
Tank(config-route-map)#match tag 3
Tank(config-route-map)#route-map DEN3-PERM4 permit 20
Tank(config-route-map)#set tag 4

Tank(config-route-map)#route-map DEN4-PERM3 den 10
Tank(config-route-map)#match tag 4
Tank(config-route-map)#route-map DEN4-PERM3 perm 20
Tank(config-route-map)#set tag 3
```

Now that the route maps and tags are assigned and the permit/deny statements are in sync with the primary goal, it is time to add the route maps to the **redistribution** statements in OSPF and EIGRP, as shown in Example 6-57.

Example 6-57   *Configuring the Route Maps to Work with Redistribution*

```
Tank(config-route-map)#router ospf 100
Tank(config-router)#redistribute eigrp 100 route-map DEN3-PERM4
Tank(config-router)#router eigrp 100
Tank(config-router)#redi
Tank(config-router)#redistribute ospf 100 rout
Tank(config-router)#redistribute ospf 100 route-map DEN4-PERM3
```

Example 6-58 shows the final configurations of the routers from this section.

After

Example 6-58   *Final Route Tag Configurations*

```
router eigrp 100
 redistribute ospf 100 metric 1500 10 255 1 1500 route-map DEN4-PERM3
 network 64.0.0.0
 no auto-summary
!
router ospf 100
 redistribute eigrp 100 metric 100 subnets route-map DEN3-PERM4
 network 10.10.10.0 0.0.0.255 area 10
 network 10.10.20.0 0.0.0.255 area 10
!
no ip classless
access-list 66 permit 128.213.100.0 0.0.3.255
access-list 66 permit 64.246.202.4 0.0.0.3
access-list 66 permit 10.10.10.0 0.0.0.255
access-list 66 permit 192.168.254.0 0.0.0.255
access-list 66 permit 192.168.252.0 0.0.0.255
access-list 66 permit 192.168.253.0 0.0.0.255
access-list 97 permit 128.213.96.0 0.0.3.255
access-list 97 permit 64.246.202.0 0.0.0.3
!
route-map DEN3-PERM4 deny 10
 match tag 3
```

continues

Example 6-58 *Final Route Tag Configurations (Continued)*

```
!
route-map DEN3-PERM4 permit 20
 set tag 4
!
route-map DEN4-PERM3 deny 10
 match tag 4
!
route-map DEN4-PERM3 permit 20
 set tag 3
!
```

One of the useful features of tagging routes like this is that after you have identified them, they are easy to manipulate based on the presence of that tag. The next configuration example examines how the tagging of a route is accomplished.

Configuration Example 5: Redistributing OSPF and RIP and Tagging Routes

In your network, you have connected Router Trinity to OSPF area 10 and a RIP network as well. The entire OSPF network needs to know about the following networks:

64.246.202.4/30
128.213.100.0/24
128.213.101.0/24
128.213.102.0/24
128.213.103.0/24

These networks are found on Router Trinity and are part of the RIP routing domain. Because the objective is for the entire OSPF network to learn about them, you are going to be monitoring the routing table of Router Apoc to see when it learns of these routes.

Before

As you would expect, in the routing table in Example 6-59, Router Apoc has no knowledge of any of the routes in the RIP network attached to Router Trinity.

Example 6-59 *Configuration Before Redistributing RIP with Route Tags*

```
Apoc>show ip route
Codes: C - connected, S - static, I - IGRP, R - RIP, M - mobile, B - BGP
       D - EIGRP, EX - EIGRP external, O - OSPF, IA - OSPF inter area
       N1 - OSPF NSSA external type 1, N2 - OSPF NSSA external type 2
       E1 - OSPF external type 1, E2 - OSPF external type 2, E - EGP
       i - IS-IS, L1 - IS-IS level-1, L2 - IS-IS level-2, * - candidate default
       U - per-user static route, o - ODR

Gateway of last resort is not set
```

Example 6-59 *Configuration Before Redistributing RIP with Route Tags (Continued)*

```
         10.0.0.0/8 is variably subnetted, 3 subnets, 2 masks
O IA    10.10.10.0/24 [110/11] via 192.168.254.2, 00:01:39, Ethernet0
O IA    10.10.20.0/24 [110/12] via 192.168.254.2, 00:01:39, Ethernet0
O IA    10.10.20.1/32 [110/12] via 192.168.254.2, 00:01:39, Ethernet0
         64.0.0.0/30 is subnetted, 1 subnets
O E2    64.246.202.0 [110/100] via 192.168.254.2, 00:01:39, Ethernet0
         128.213.0.0/24 is subnetted, 4 subnets
O E2    128.213.97.0 [110/100] via 192.168.254.2, 00:01:39, Ethernet0
O E2    128.213.96.0 [110/100] via 192.168.254.2, 00:01:39, Ethernet0
O E2    128.213.99.0 [110/100] via 192.168.254.2, 00:01:39, Ethernet0
O E2    128.213.98.0 [110/100] via 192.168.254.2, 00:01:40, Ethernet0
O       192.168.252.0/24 [110/11] via 192.168.254.2, 01:40:59, Ethernet0
O       192.168.253.0/24 [110/11] via 192.168.254.2, 01:40:59, Ethernet0
C       192.168.254.0/24 is directly connected, Ethernet0
Apoc>
```

During

In Example 6-60, you alter the metric to a value of 200 to allow a more visual distinction between the routes from RIP and those from EIGRP.

Example 6-60 *Altering the Metric for RIP Routes*

```
Trinity(config)#router ospf 100
Trinity(config-router)#redistribute rip metric 200 subnets
Trinity(config)#
```

After

With the redistribution of RIP into OSPF complete, review the routing table on Router Apoc in Example 6-61. You would expect to see the routes from the RIP domain (as identified in Example 6-60) with a metric of 200.

Example 6-61 *Verifying Redistribution*

```
Apoc>show ip route
Codes: C - connected, S - static, I - IGRP, R - RIP, M - mobile, B - BGP
       D - EIGRP, EX - EIGRP external, O - OSPF, IA - OSPF inter area
       N1 - OSPF NSSA external type 1, N2 - OSPF NSSA external type 2
       E1 - OSPF external type 1, E2 - OSPF external type 2, E - EGP
       i - IS-IS, L1 - IS-IS level-1, L2 - IS-IS level-2, * - candidate default
       U - per-user static route, o - ODR

Gateway of last resort is not set

         10.0.0.0/8 is variably subnetted, 3 subnets, 2 masks
O IA    10.10.10.0/24 [110/11] via 192.168.254.2, 00:00:27, Ethernet0
O IA    10.10.20.0/24 [110/12] via 192.168.254.2, 00:00:27, Ethernet0
O IA    10.10.20.1/32 [110/12] via 192.168.254.2, 00:00:27, Ethernet0
         64.0.0.0/8 is variably subnetted, 3 subnets, 2 masks
O E2    64.246.202.4/30 [110/200] via 192.168.254.2, 00:00:27, Ethernet0
```

continues

Example 6-61 *Verifying Redistribution (Continued)*

```
O E2    64.246.202.6/32 [110/200] via 192.168.254.2, 00:00:27, Ethernet0
O E2    64.246.202.0/30 [110/100] via 192.168.254.2, 00:00:27, Ethernet0
        128.213.0.0/24 is subnetted, 8 subnets
O E2    128.213.101.0 [110/200] via 192.168.254.2, 00:00:27, Ethernet0
O E2    128.213.100.0 [110/200] via 192.168.254.2, 00:00:28, Ethernet0
O E2    128.213.103.0 [110/200] via 192.168.254.2, 00:00:28, Ethernet0
O E2    128.213.102.0 [110/200] via 192.168.254.2, 00:00:28, Ethernet0
O E2    128.213.97.0 [110/100] via 192.168.254.2, 00:00:28, Ethernet0
O E2    128.213.96.0 [110/100] via 192.168.254.2, 00:00:29, Ethernet0
O E2    128.213.99.0 [110/100] via 192.168.254.2, 00:00:29, Ethernet0
O E2    128.213.98.0 [110/100] via 192.168.254.2, 00:00:30, Ethernet0
O    192.168.252.0/24 [110/11] via 192.168.254.2, 02:08:41, Ethernet0
O    192.168.253.0/24 [110/11] via 192.168.254.2, 02:08:41, Ethernet0
C    192.168.254.0/24 is directly connected, Ethernet0
Apoc>
```

The redistribution was successful. Now you can move on to activating redistribution in the other direction (OSPF to RIP) to establish a running mutual redistribution scenario.

OSPF and RIP Mutual Redistribution

The next step is to make the necessary configuration to get the OSPF routes into RIP, as shown in Example 6-62.

Example 6-62 *Beginning RIP Configuration with Basic Redistribution*

```
!
router rip
 version 2
 redistribute ospf 100 metric 5
 network 64.0.0.0
!
```

Looking at Router Morpheus's routing table in Example 6-63, you can see that all the routes are available and that they have a metric of 5. You would expect this according to the redistribution configuration.

Example 6-63 *Verifying the Operation*

```
Morpheus#show ip route
Codes: C - connected, S - static, I - IGRP, R - RIP, M - mobile, B - BGP
       D - EIGRP, EX - EIGRP external, O - OSPF, IA - OSPF inter area
       N1 - OSPF NSSA external type 1, N2 - OSPF NSSA external type 2
       E1 - OSPF external type 1, E2 - OSPF external type 2, E - EGP
       i - IS-IS, L1 - IS-IS level-1, L2 - IS-IS level-2, * - candidate default
       U - per-user static route, o - ODR

Gateway of last resort is not set
```

Example 6-63   *Verifying the Operation (Continued)*

```
        64.0.0.0/8 is variably subnetted, 3 subnets, 2 masks
C          64.246.202.4/30 is directly connected, Serial0/0
C          64.246.202.5/32 is directly connected, Serial0/0
R          64.246.202.0/30 [120/5] via 64.246.202.5, 00:00:07, Serial0/0
        128.213.0.0/16 is variably subnetted, 5 subnets, 2 masks
C          128.213.101.0/24 is directly connected, Loopback1
C          128.213.100.0/24 is directly connected, Loopback0
C          128.213.103.0/24 is directly connected, Loopback3
C          128.213.102.0/24 is directly connected, Loopback2
R          128.213.0.0/16 [120/5] via 64.246.202.5, 00:00:07, Serial0/0
R       10.0.0.0/8 [120/5] via 64.246.202.5, 00:00:07, Serial0/0
R       192.168.254.0/24 [120/5] via 64.246.202.5, 00:00:07, Serial0/0
R       192.168.253.0/24 [120/5] via 64.246.202.5, 00:00:07, Serial0/0
R       192.168.252.0/24 [120/5] via 64.246.202.5, 00:00:07, Serial0/0
Morpheus#
```

Redistributing into OSPF with Route Tagging

There are many reasons to tag routes, some of which have already been covered. Some others reflect the desire of network engineers to manipulate routes based on tags. This is a nice way to quickly identify which routes you need. Consider that you want to know which routes are from RIP, say on Router Apoc. You could create an access list and a route map, but what if you tagged all the routes during the redistribution on Router Trinity, thus allowing a more flexible and faster identification of routes? This is possible with route tagging, and applying a route tag while redistributing is shown in Example 6-64.

Before

Example 6-64   *Basic OSPF Redistribution Configuration*

```
!
router ospf 100
 log-adjacency-changes
 redistribute rip metric 200 subnets
 network 10.10.10.0 0.0.0.255 area 10
 network 10.10.20.0 0.0.0.255 area 10
!
```

In OSPF, you can see the route tags in the OSPF link-state database. Therefore, by checking the database before you add the tag, the database has all the tag values as 0 (default), as expected for the RIP routes. Now tag the routes, release them, and see what happens in Example 6-65.

Example 6-65 *No Route Tags in the OSPF Link-State Database*

```
Apoc#show ip ospf database

          OSPF Router with ID (192.168.254.1) (Process ID 100)


               Router Link States (Area 0)

Link ID         ADV Router      Age       Seq#        Checksum Link count
192.168.252.2   192.168.252.2   735       0x80000011 0xD7B4    3
192.168.254.1   192.168.254.1   345       0x8000000A 0x87F2    1

               Net Link States (Area 0)

Link ID         ADV Router      Age       Seq#        Checksum
192.168.254.2   192.168.252.2   1226      0x80000006 0x8C04

               Summary Net Link States (Area 0)

Link ID         ADV Router      Age       Seq#        Checksum
10.10.10.0      192.168.252.2   479       0x8000000B 0x1398
10.10.20.0      192.168.252.2   479       0x80000009 0xB2EF
10.10.20.1      192.168.252.2   479       0x80000009 0xA8F8

               Summary ASB Link States (Area 0)

Link ID         ADV Router      Age       Seq#        Checksum
10.10.20.1      192.168.252.2   983       0x80000003 0x9C0B
10.10.20.2      192.168.252.2   1228      0x80000002 0x9413

               Type-5 AS External Link States

Link ID         ADV Router      Age       Seq#        Checksum Tag
64.246.202.0    10.10.20.1      1242      0x80000003 0x2AFB    0
64.246.202.4    10.10.20.2      1201      0x80000003 0x6ED     0
64.246.202.6    10.10.20.2      1201      0x80000003 0x4EA     0
128.213.96.0    10.10.20.1      1242      0x80000003 0x1955    0
128.213.97.0    10.10.20.1      1242      0x80000003 0xE5F     0
128.213.98.0    10.10.20.1      1242      0x80000003 0x369     0
128.213.99.0    10.10.20.1      1242      0x80000003 0xF773    0
128.213.100.0   10.10.20.2      1201      0x80000003 0xF04B    0
128.213.101.0   10.10.20.2      1201      0x80000003 0xE555    0
128.213.102.0   10.10.20.2      1201      0x80000003 0xDA5F    0
128.213.103.0   10.10.20.2      1201      0x80000003 0xCF69    0
Apoc#
```

During

Through the use of an additional keyword, **tag 200**, in the redistribution statement, you can easily create a route tag with a value of 200 and assign it to all routes coming into OSPF from RIP, as shown in Example 6-66.

Example 6-66 *Configuring Redistribution via Route Tagging*

```
Trinity(config)#router ospf 100
Trinity(config-router)#redistribute rip metric 200 subnets ?
  metric     Metric for redistributed routes
  metric-type OSPF/IS-IS exterior metric type for redistributed routes
  route-map  Route map reference
  subnets    Consider subnets for redistribution into OSPF
  tag        Set tag for routes redistributed into OSPF
  <cr>

Trinity(config-router)#redistribute rip metric 200 subnets tag ?
  <0-4294967295>  32-bit tag value

Trinity(config-router)#redistribute rip metric 200 subnets tag 200
Trinity(config-router)#
```

After

In Example 6-67, you determine whether the external RIP routes are now tagged with a value of 200 per the configuration.

Example 6-67 *Verifying the Presence of the Tagged Routes in the OSPF Link-State Database*

```
Apoc#show ip ospf database

        OSPF Router with ID (192.168.254.1) (Process ID 100)

<<<Some output omitted for brevity>>>>

                Type-5 AS External Link States

Link ID         ADV Router      Age      Seq#        Checksum Tag
64.246.202.0    10.10.20.1      1242     0x80000003 0x2AFB   0
64.246.202.4    10.10.20.2      1201     0x80000003 0x6ED    200
64.246.202.6    10.10.20.2      1201     0x80000003 0x4EA    200
128.213.96.0    10.10.20.1      1242     0x80000003 0x1955   0
128.213.97.0    10.10.20.1      1242     0x80000003 0xE5F    0
128.213.98.0    10.10.20.1      1242     0x80000003 0x369    0
128.213.99.0    10.10.20.1      1242     0x80000003 0xF773   0
128.213.100.0   10.10.20.2      1201     0x80000003 0xF04B   200
128.213.101.0   10.10.20.2      1201     0x80000003 0xE555   200
128.213.102.0   10.10.20.2      1201     0x80000003 0xDA5F   200
128.213.103.0   10.10.20.2      1201     0x80000003 0xCF69   200
Apoc#
```

Having the router display the OSPF link-state database can result in some very long output, and at times you might just want to check the presence of a tag on a single route. You can accomplish this using the **show ip route** *network number* command, as shown in Example 6-68.

Example 6-68   *Viewing the Route Tag*

```
Apoc#show ip route 64.246.202.4
Routing entry for 64.246.202.4/30
  Known via "ospf 100", distance 110, metric 200
  Tag 200, type extern 2, forward metric 11
  Redistributing via ospf 100
  Last update from 192.168.254.2 on Ethernet0, 00:07:53 ago
  Routing Descriptor Blocks:
  * 192.168.254.2, from 10.10.20.2, 00:07:53 ago, via Ethernet0
      Route metric is 200, traffic share count is 1

Apoc#
```

With the presence of the routes tagged with a value of 200, you can now more easily identify these external RIP routes at a later time. The next section looks at other methods of controlling the redistribution of routes within OSPF.

Configuration Example 6: Controlling Redistribution

To this point, the concepts of redistribution have been presented and examples were given to show how to make redistribution operate effectively. The following configuration example was placed later in the chapter for a specific reason. This example is a good review of the routing and redistribution concepts that were covered up to this point. By placing the concepts together, you can see some interesting OSPF effects. The following sections offer a review of the concepts previously presented.

Altering Link Cost

Recall that OSPF calculates its cost (metric) to a destination based on the bandwidth of the link(s) to that destination. Therefore, to influence OSPF's routing decisions, you can either change the bandwidth on the interface, which in turn affects the cost of the link, or you can directly change the OSPF cost of the interface. You can apply the following commands on a per-interface basis:

- Router(config-if)**ip ospf cost** *1-65355*—Allows you to configure the cost of an interface in OSPF, thus overriding the process of OSPF calculating interface cost. This command is used only by OSPF. It does not affect traffic on the link, but it does affect route calculation and selection.

- Router(config-if)**bandwidth** *1-10000000*—Allows you to configure the bandwidth of an interface in kilobits per second. This command is used by routing protocols as the basis to calculate the cost for the interface. Many people forget to set this in their routers, so be careful. Changing this value does not affect traffic on the link, but it does affect route calculation and selection.

- **auto reference bandwidth**—Allows you to easily alter the link cost.

Therefore, you have a couple of ways to alter the calculation of the OSPF cost (metric) and thereby affect how OSPF calculates its route selection.

Altering Routes

OSPF also allows the altering of routes, as discussed in Chapter 5. Specifically, OSPF also supports the direct changing of the administrative distance associated with OSPF routes, through the use of the **distance** command. OSPF can also uses the **passive** interface command to prevent Hello packets and LSAs from being sent on the specified link. The list that follows shows the general syntax and descriptions for these commands that allow you to alter routes:

- Router(config-router)**distance ospf** *1-255*—Use this command to change the administrative distance of all OSPF routes from the default of 110 to a value you define. Alternatively, a more granular control is possible, as shown in the next command.

- Router(config-router)**distance ospf** {[**intra-area** *[1-255]*] [**inter-area** *[1-255]*] [**external** *[1-255]*]}—Use this command to change the administrative distance of specific types of OSPF routes. OSPF uses three different routes: intra-area, inter-area, and external. Routes within an area are intra-area, routes from another area are inter-area, and routes injected via redistribution are external. This command allows you to change the default administrative distance of 110 to the designated value.

CAUTION   Use the **distance ospf** command with care because it can easily cause routing loops.

- Router(config-router)**default-metric cost** *1-4294967295*—Use this command to set the default cost of all routes redistributed into OSPF. You should always supply a default metric whenever redistributing into OSPF. Recall that a metric must always be assigned for redistribution to work.

- Router(config-router)**passive-interface** *interface_name*—Use this command to prevent the sending of OSPF Hello packets and LSAs on the specified interface. Because Hellos are suppressed, neighbor relationships are not formed; therefore, no routing updates are sent or received.

Filtering Routes

Two methods are used to filter routes with OSPF, distribute lists and route maps. The command syntax for configuring each is as follows:

- Router(config-router)**redistribute** *protocol-name* **route-map** *route-map-name*—A route map is a powerful tool that allows easy altering of routing information. Route maps should be used in place of distribute lists whenever possible in OSPF because route maps do not have the limitations of distribute lists, as previously discussed.

- Router(config-router)**distribute-list** *[1-99]* **[in]** **[interface]**—Use this command to call a standard access list to filter inbound routing updates. The **in** option is applied from the view of the router. In other words, to prevent a routing update from entering into the router's routing table, use the **in** option. Recall that in OSPF, this command only filters the route, not the LSA, so the network being filtered is still placed into the LSDB. Route maps should be used instead.

The next section demonstrates the correct manner in which to use a distribute list in OSPF.

Distribute Lists and OSPF

This chapter has already mentioned many of the difficulties with distribute lists and how Cisco has designed them to interact incorrectly with OSPF. While the recommended practice is to use route maps instead of distribute lists whenever possible, distribute lists still have their place. This section discusses how to configure them correctly to perform route filtering. You are going to use this "gotcha" with OSPF and distribute lists to accomplish the mission at hand and in the process find out about what actually happens:

> Your mission is to not allow routing on Router Neo to route network 128.213.102.0/24, but Router Apoc must have a route to it.

Configuring a distribute list has steps that are similar to those needed to configure a route map. In this example, you apply the distribute list to Router Trinity, as shown in Figure 6-13.

Figure 6-13 *Network Topology for Distribute List Example*

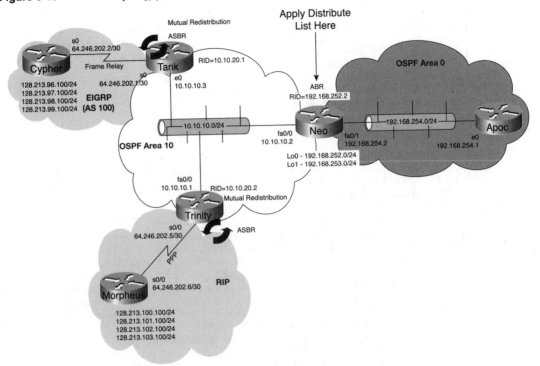

The following configuration steps are necessary to stop network 128.213.102.0/24 from being known by Router Apoc. Example 6-69 shows a basic OSPF configuration to which you apply a distribute list.

Before

Example 6-69 *OSPF Configuration Before Distribution Lists*

```
!
router ospf 100
 network 10.10.10.0 0.0.0.255 area 10
 network 192.168.252.0 0.0.0.255 area 0
 network 192.168.253.0 0.0.0.255 area 0
 network 192.168.254.0 0.0.0.255 area 0
!
```

As you can see in Example 6-70, the route to the network in question is present in the routing table of Router Neo, and it must be removed.

Example 6-70 *Unwanted Route Is in Neo's Routing Table*

```
Neo>show ip route
Codes: C - connected, S - static, I - IGRP, R - RIP, M - mobile, B - BGP
       D - EIGRP, EX - EIGRP external, O - OSPF, IA - OSPF inter area
       N1 - OSPF NSSA external type 1, N2 - OSPF NSSA external type 2
       E1 - OSPF external type 1, E2 - OSPF external type 2, E - EGP
       i - IS-IS, L1 - IS-IS level-1, L2 - IS-IS level-2, ia - IS-IS inter area
       * - candidate default, U - per-user static route, o - ODR
       P - periodic downloaded static route

Gateway of last resort is not set

     64.0.0.0/8 is variably subnetted, 3 subnets, 2 masks
O E2    64.246.202.4/30 [110/200] via 10.10.10.1, 00:00:57, FastEthernet0/0
O E2    64.246.202.6/32 [110/200] via 10.10.10.1, 00:00:57, FastEthernet0/0
O E2    64.246.202.0/30 [110/100] via 10.10.10.3, 00:00:57, FastEthernet0/0
     128.213.0.0/24 is subnetted, 7 subnets
O E2    128.213.101.0 [110/200] via 10.10.10.1, 00:00:57, FastEthernet0/0
O E2    128.213.100.0 [110/200] via 10.10.10.1, 00:00:57, FastEthernet0/0
O E2    128.213.103.0 [110/200] via 10.10.10.1, 00:00:57, FastEthernet0/0
O E2    128.213.102.0 [110/200] via 10.10.10.1, 00:00:57, FastEthernet0/0
O E2    128.213.97.0 [110/100] via 10.10.10.3, 00:00:57, FastEthernet0/0
O E2    128.213.96.0 [110/100] via 10.10.10.3, 00:00:57, FastEthernet0/0
O E2    128.213.99.0 [110/100] via 10.10.10.3, 00:00:57, FastEthernet0/0
O E2    128.213.98.0 [110/100] via 10.10.10.3, 00:00:57, FastEthernet0/0
     10.0.0.0/8 is variably subnetted, 3 subnets, 2 masks
C       10.10.10.0/24 is directly connected, FastEthernet0/0
O       10.10.20.0/24 [110/2] via 10.10.10.1, 00:00:59, FastEthernet0/0
O       10.10.20.1/32 [110/2] via 10.10.10.3, 00:00:59, FastEthernet0/0
C    192.168.254.0/24 is directly connected, FastEthernet0/1
C    192.168.253.0/24 is directly connected, Loopback1
C    192.168.252.0/24 is directly connected, Loopback0
Neo>
```

During

The first steps in configuring a distribute list are to identify the network that you want to deny (or permit) and to configure an access list accordingly. The next steps are to assign the access list to OSPF and to specify the direction and interface name. Example 6-71 shows the resulting configuration.

Example 6-71 *Configuration of the Distribute List*

```
!
router ospf 100
 network 10.10.10.0 0.0.0.255 area 10
 network 192.168.252.0 0.0.0.255 area 0
 network 192.168.253.0 0.0.0.255 area 0
 network 192.168.254.0 0.0.0.255 area 0
 distribute-list 50 in FastEthernet0/0
!
ip classless
```

Example 6-71 *Configuration of the Distribute List (Continued)*

```
no ip http server
!
access-list 50 deny    128.213.102.0 0.0.0.255
access-list 50 permit any
!
```

Make sure that you do not forget the **permit any** keywords, or all routes will disappear. This is a problem if you are configuring the router via Telnet for this example. Also, for practice, consider reversing the solution given and permit only the networks you want while denying all other routes.

After

To verify that you have accomplished your goal, check the routing table on Router Neo and ensure that network 128.213.102.0/24 is missing. As the output in Example 6-72 confirms, it is in fact missing.

Example 6-72 *Verifying That the Route Has Been Removed*

```
Neo#show ip route
Codes: C - connected, S - static, I - IGRP, R - RIP, M - mobile, B - BGP
       D - EIGRP, EX - EIGRP external, O - OSPF, IA - OSPF inter area
       N1 - OSPF NSSA external type 1, N2 - OSPF NSSA external type 2
       E1 - OSPF external type 1, E2 - OSPF external type 2, E - EGP
       i - IS-IS, L1 - IS-IS level-1, L2 - IS-IS level-2, ia - IS-IS inter area
       * - candidate default, U - per-user static route, o - ODR
       P - periodic downloaded static route

Gateway of last resort is not set

     64.0.0.0/8 is variably subnetted, 3 subnets, 2 masks
O E2    64.246.202.4/30 [110/200] via 10.10.10.1, 00:02:38, FastEthernet0/0
O E2    64.246.202.6/32 [110/200] via 10.10.10.1, 00:02:38, FastEthernet0/0
O E2    64.246.202.0/30 [110/100] via 10.10.10.3, 00:02:38, FastEthernet0/0
     128.213.0.0/24 is subnetted, 7 subnets
O E2    128.213.101.0 [110/200] via 10.10.10.1, 00:02:38, FastEthernet0/0
O E2    128.213.100.0 [110/200] via 10.10.10.1, 00:02:38, FastEthernet0/0
O E2    128.213.103.0 [110/200] via 10.10.10.1, 00:02:39, FastEthernet0/0
O E2    .128.213.97.0 [110/100] via 10.10.10.3, 00:02:39, FastEthernet0/0
O E2    128.213.96.0 [110/100] via 10.10.10.3, 00:02:39, FastEthernet0/0
O E2    128.213.99.0 [110/100] via 10.10.10.3, 00:02:39, FastEthernet0/0
O E2    128.213.98.0 [110/100] via 10.10.10.3, 00:02:39, FastEthernet0/0
     10.0.0.0/8 is variably subnetted, 3 subnets, 2 masks
C       10.10.10.0/24 is directly connected, FastEthernet0/0
O       10.10.20.0/24 [110/2] via 10.10.10.1, 00:02:39, FastEthernet0/0
O       10.10.20.1/32 [110/2] via 10.10.10.3, 00:02:39, FastEthernet0/0
C    192.168.254.0/24 is directly connected, FastEthernet0/1
C    192.168.253.0/24 is directly connected, Loopback1
C    192.168.252.0/24 is directly connected, Loopback0
Neo#
```

Now verify the routes that the router still knows about and that the network is still present in its OSPF link-state database, as shown in Example 6-73. Some irrelevant bits are omitted to save space.

Example 6-73 *Verifying the Route Presence in the OSPF LSDB*

```
Neo#show ip ospf database

        OSPF Router with ID (192.168.253.1) (Process ID 100)
! some output omitted for brevity


            Type-5 AS External Link States

Link ID          ADV Router       Age        Seq#        Checksum Tag
64.246.202.0     10.10.20.1       1329       0x8000000C 0x1805   0
64.246.202.4     10.10.20.2       1515       0x8000000B 0xF5F5   200
64.246.202.6     10.10.20.2       1515       0x8000000B 0xF3F2   200
128.213.96.0     10.10.20.1       1329       0x8000000C 0x75E    0
128.213.97.0     10.10.20.1       1329       0x8000000C 0xFB68   0
128.213.98.0     10.10.20.1       1329       0x8000000C 0xF072   0
128.213.99.0     10.10.20.1       1329       0x8000000C 0xE57C   0
128.213.100.0    10.10.20.2       1515       0x8000000B 0xE053   200
128.213.101.0    10.10.20.2       1515       0x8000000B 0xD55D   200
128.213.102.0    10.10.20.2       1516       0x8000000B 0xCA67   200
128.213.103.0    10.10.20.2       1516       0x8000000B 0xBF71   200
Neo#
```

The final check, shown in Example 6-74, is to determine if the route is still in Router Apoc's routing table and to make sure that you are going to clear the routing table prior to executing the command.

Example 6-74 *Clearing the Routing Table*

```
Apoc#clear ip route *
Apoc#show ip route
Codes: C - connected, S - static, I - IGRP, R - RIP, M - mobile, B - BGP
       D - EIGRP, EX - EIGRP external, O - OSPF, IA - OSPF inter area
       N1 - OSPF NSSA external type 1, N2 - OSPF NSSA external type 2
       E1 - OSPF external type 1, E2 - OSPF external type 2, E - EGP
       i - IS-IS, L1 - IS-IS level-1, L2 - IS-IS level-2, * - candidate default
       U - per-user static route, o - ODR

Gateway of last resort is not set

     10.0.0.0/8 is variably subnetted, 3 subnets, 2 masks
O IA    10.10.10.0/24 [110/11] via 192.168.254.2, 00:00:03, Ethernet0
O IA    10.10.20.0/24 [110/12] via 192.168.254.2, 00:00:03, Ethernet0
O IA    10.10.20.1/32 [110/12] via 192.168.254.2, 00:00:03, Ethernet0
     64.0.0.0/8 is variably subnetted, 3 subnets, 2 masks
O E2    64.246.202.4/30 [110/200] via 192.168.254.2, 00:00:03, Ethernet0
O E2    64.246.202.6/32 [110/200] via 192.168.254.2, 00:00:03, Ethernet0
O E2    64.246.202.0/30 [110/100] via 192.168.254.2, 00:00:03, Ethernet0
     128.213.0.0/24 is subnetted, 8 subnets
```

Example 6-74   *Clearing the Routing Table (Continued)*

```
O E2    128.213.101.0 [110/200] via 192.168.254.2, 00:00:03, Ethernet0
O E2    128.213.100.0 [110/200] via 192.168.254.2, 00:00:03, Ethernet0
O E2    128.213.103.0 [110/200] via 192.168.254.2, 00:00:03, Ethernet0
O E2    128.213.102.0 [110/200] via 192.168.254.2, 00:00:03, Ethernet0
O E2    128.213.97.0 [110/100] via 192.168.254.2, 00:00:03, Ethernet0
O E2    128.213.96.0 [110/100] via 192.168.254.2, 00:00:05, Ethernet0
O E2    128.213.99.0 [110/100] via 192.168.254.2, 00:00:05, Ethernet0
O E2    128.213.98.0 [110/100] via 192.168.254.2, 00:00:05, Ethernet0
O      192.168.252.0/24 [110/11] via 192.168.254.2, 00:00:05, Ethernet0
O      192.168.253.0/24 [110/11] via 192.168.254.2, 00:00:05, Ethernet0
C      192.168.254.0/24 is directly connected, Ethernet0
Apoc#
```

This was a strange scenario, but it demonstrates the use and issues that are associated with distribute lists. This section covered redistribution with many examples and with an emphasis on the redistribution of default routes and described how external routes are used. In addition several redistribution examples were presented to include samples of mutual redistribution. The next section discusses summarization—a technique that is used to properly represent a block of IP addresses within a routing table in the fewest possible entries.

Chapter Summary

This chapter covered route redistribution and how it operates within OSPF. You have just begun to scratch the surface of the potential for redistributing routes; you will find that from the topics presented, you are ready to solve redistribution scenarios or design them. A variety of golden rules were covered as they relate to redistribution. These rules form the basis of understanding how to design redistribution scenarios in OSPF. When you have trouble with redistribution, these golden rules are also an excellent troubleshooting tool.

A variety of different configuration examples and caveats were covered as well. It is important to understand that redistribution in OSPF can be highly dependent on what type of route you are trying to redistribute, as discussed. The discussion concluded with route tags and distribute lists. In Chapter 7, you begin to explore the complex topic of summarization.

Summarization with OSPF

Eternal vigilance is the price of liberty.—Thomas Jefferson, 1801

Originally, the concepts of redistribution and summarization were envisioned to be covered in one chapter. However, during the research and outline development for that one big chapter, I learned the following things:

1 There is a lot of material to cover on each topic.

2 No one has really explained these concepts in such a way that people referred others to that source.

I was determined then to create a chapter that would be good enough for you to recommend to others, and as I started writing it, I learned quickly that I needed two chapters. This chapter details the concepts of summarization, when to use it, how to use it, and more importantly, where to use it in an OSPF network. These concepts are closely intertwined with the concepts of redistribution, which you learned in Chapter 6, "Redistribution."

Redistribution is when a router takes routing information it has discovered in one routing protocol and shares it with a different routing protocol, thus allowing the redistribution of the first protocol's networks into the second routing protocol. For example, a router running RIP and OSPF has a need for those users in the OSPF section of the network to know the routes in the RIP network. Redistribution accomplishes this feat of routing magic! Sometimes, redistribution is referred to more specifically as *route redistribution;* however, either term means the same thing.

Summarization is the taking of multiple route entries and representing them by a smaller number of entries. This smaller representation is known as *summarizing your routes*. For example, this technique minimizes the routing table size, which is useful when connecting to the Internet, by allowing the conservation of router resources. It allows for simplification of the next hop and is useful in helping you conserve router resources (that is, memory, CPU time, and so on).

For example, routing table entries represent blocks of addresses and use the subnet mask to determine the size of the block. Through summarization, the router can tell the difference between 10.20.30.0 /24 and 10.20.30.0 /22. The former is a Class C–sized block of addresses, 256 addresses. The latter is four Class C–sized blocks, or 1024 addresses.

This chapter focuses on the concept of summarization and builds on the theory and examples that were covered in Chapter 6.

Summarization with OSPF

IP address assignment and route summarization are inextricably linked when designing OSPF networks. To create a scalable OSPF network, you should implement route summarization, thus allowing you to reduce the memory requirements on a router. You must exercise caution and consider the impact of a large number of route entries if you are not going to use summarization. To create an environment capable of supporting route summarization, you must implement an effective hierarchical addressing scheme. The addressing structure that you implement can have a profound impact on the performance and scalability of your OSPF network. The ultimate goal is to put as few routes as possible into the routing tables and reduce the number of updates.

Figure 7-1 illustrates the benefits of route summarization on a routing table. Without summarization, only three entries exist in the routing table, and with summarization, only one entry exists in the routing table.

Figure 7-1   *Benefits of IP Address Conservation with Route Summarization*

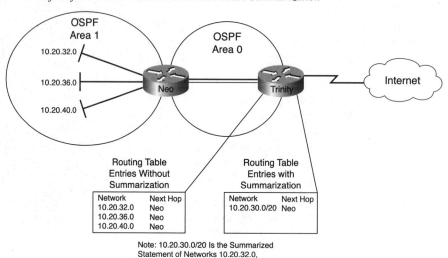

The concept of summarization and how to configure it within OSPF is similar to that of other routing protocols. Conceptually, you can think of summarization as blocks of IP addresses. In this analogy, the subnet mask defines the size of each block. This is an important point because a router typically selects the summarized route that most specifically defines the destination network of the host you are trying to reach. The following analogy and example illustrate this more clearly.

Driving directions are a commonly used analogy for how summarization works. Assume you are driving to New York City. Now as you know, there is New York State and New York City.

Assume you begin your trip in North Carolina, which is south of New York City and New York State. You initially see road signs in the beginning of your trip that direct you to go north to New York; that is enough information to continue driving. However, when you reach New Jersey (which connects to New York), you must begin following signs for New York City, as those are the most specific directions to your destination. This analogy can be demonstrated with a real-world example.

Suppose your packets are trying to reach host 10.20.30.40, and the first router they enter has a summarized route entry of 10.20.30.0/22 (New York State), of which your destination 10.20.30.40 (New York City) is a part. Your packets continue along until a more specific routing table entry of 10.20.30.0/24 is found. The summary route of 10.20.30.0/20 is also present; however, this is where the router chooses the most specific routing table entry to use.

The other concept that is important to understand when using summarization is *longest prefix match*. Returning to the New York analogy, consider that a city the size of New York has many streets, and to route the packets accordingly, you need to find the correct street. You have street signs, a map, or an atlas, and the atlas contains a list of every street, highway, city, and so on. Now, suppose you have all this information and you need to find the one street (subnet) that holds your final destination. It would not be good if you (the router) had to pause and read through each entry. Fortunately, route table lookups are not linear because you have all sorts of algorithms written by folks who think in numbers. Without getting into the details, focus on the use of the longest prefix match, which is concerned not with the sending of packets but rather how the router looks up the next-hop address. For example, if a packet has a destination IP address of 10.20.30.40, the router begins with the first octet (10) and searches its routing tables for it. When a match is found, the router goes on to the next octet (20) and so on, until enough information is learned so that the packet can be routed to its next destination. This behavior of the router matching each octet until a match is found is known as the *longest prefix match rule* in routing.

If you have ever driven in a large city, you are aware of the never-ending road maintenance that is constantly taking place. This has an analogy in networking as well. In networking, remember that it is always someone's maintenance window somewhere in the world, and if a subnet were down, it would not be listed in the routing table. Although this might seem like a digression from the running analogy, this is an important point on the operation of OSPF.

Routes (subnets) are listed in the routing table when they are up, denoting that the advertised router can reach that subnet. If the interface is down, the route to that subnet is not advertised to the neighboring routers. Specifically, OSPF requires the link to be up. If that link is not up, the route is withdrawn from the routing table. The point is if you are not using summarization, your network routing is based on the up/down status of every interface in your network. If your network is then connected to the Internet, advertisements reflecting this propagate through the Internet; this completes the point and analogy about it always being someone's maintenance window. Summarizations of the routes within your network allow better control of routing updates.

NOTE

The preceding example should not be taken as the way to design a network that connects to the Internet. Best practices dictate using floating static routes to advertise to the Internet. The example was only for illustrative purposes.

Benefits of Summarization

Summarization, in general, provides many benefits to your network and its operation; some of these benefits are apparent and others have a smaller impact on the health of network. There are four primary reasons to implement proper summarization:

- **Shrink the routing table**—This benefit should be clear to you after the preceding discussion. The use of summarization allows a smaller number of route entries in your table, with the added benefits of decreasing the amount of memory used. Specifically, it is much faster for a router to look up a summarized single route to find a match than it is to look up smaller /24 routes, for example.

- **Improve router operation**—Using summarization means fewer routes in the routing table and thus fewer times that the router needs to run the SPF algorithm. Additionally, summarization of routes gives you a smaller link-state database, which also speeds things considerably.

- **Reduce routing updates**—In this case, when you are advertising a summary, say /22, and a /24 within that, /22 begins to flap. Other routers do not see the routing updates because the summary route, in essence, hides these changes in your network, thus reducing routing updates.

  This benefit assumes that flapping is not a normal occurrence in a network; in general, that is true. Enter the *depends* rule! Dial-up interfaces, where users are accessing the network through modems, flap as part of their operation, with calls connecting and disconnecting constantly. By summarizing the networks, you in effect isolate all the flapping, whether it is as a result of an issue or by design. The disadvantage here is that the network might be down, and the other routers keep sending data to the router that is advertising the summarized network.

- **Provide troubleshooting**—Troubleshooting is a benefit of summarization. For example, if you summarize parts of your network either based on geography (for example, England) or perhaps on function (for example, dial-up), when a routing problem occurs or is suspected, you can easily track down the issue instead of dealing with many smaller subnets.

Are you now convinced that summarization is an excellent solution and something you cannot live without? Well, not so fast—there is a hidden cost to summarization that you must be aware of. Consider for a moment that you are summarizing based on geographical location. Therefore, you choose to summarize England. This is handy to do because it is an island, and links to it from any continent can get pricey; you definitely want the benefit of summarization. This results in a simplified routing table; however, the subnet that is associated with everyone in Scotland goes down, and that change does not leave the England network. There are two ways to get into England's network. One way is shorter to Scotland, the other longer. If you summarize, you might take the less-optimal entry point into England's network, which means that it takes longer to get to Scotland. This is a weakness of summarization and aggregation—loss of routing information. If both routes were still advertised, there would be a difference in OSPF metric, so the shortest path would be followed.

Therefore, you experience *suboptimal routing* because your packets had to go all the way to the destination to discover that it was down. Suboptimal routing is taking a longer-than-necessary path to a reachable destination. So, like many things in networking, a trade-off exists with regard to summarization. Being aware of this trade-off upfront allows you to understand and better deploy summarization effectively.

Summarization Golden Rules

When planning any type of network, consider the following golden rules of design for IP addressing and implementing route summarization. The key in deploying summarization and having it be successful is a well-thought-out IP addressing scheme and deployment plan. To narrow that some, you need to have a clear understanding of the following specifics in a series of golden rules:

- Thoroughly define and deploy your network's addressing structure on paper. This enables you to allocate and plan more effectively and to keep your IP addressing scheme structured and simple. You should also definitely keep records!

- Design and configure the network's IP addressing scheme so that the range of subnets assigned within each OSPF area is contiguous. This allows for summarization and easy subnetting for and within an area. Summarizing many networks into a single advertisement decreases the route table and improves the overall performance and scalability of OSPF.

- Allocate your IP address space within each area so that it permits you to easily split areas as your network grows. Planning for future growth before it happens makes sense by enabling your network to be prepared for the future.

- Whenever possible, assign subnets according to simple octet or bit boundaries to make addressing and summarization easier to accomplish. If you also have a classful routing protocol in your network, such as RIP or IGRP, you must summarize on bit boundaries that the classful routing protocol can receive.

CAUTION   When summarizing classful protocols, the size of summarization must be the same throughout the network. Therefore, if you summarize as a /20 at one place, you must do so throughout; failure to do so causes routing problems.

- Determine the correct locations of each type of router, area, backbone, and so on. This assists you in determining which router should summarize.

- Optimize summarization by placing subnets in blocks that are a power of 2 (2, 4, 8, 16, and so on). The first subnet starts on the bit boundary for that power of 2.

Of course, no matter what happens, things will not work quite as planned when summarizing, so there are a few steps that you follow to help you.

Troubleshooting Summarization

This section could also be called *verifying summarization*. Whether you are troubleshooting a summarization problem or verifying that a summarization is functioning properly, use the following steps:

Step 1   Verify that the IP address and subnet mask you used in the **summary address** command is correct.

Step 2   Verify that the summarization is applied properly. Remember that summarization is effective only on an OSPF Autonomous System Boundary Router (ASBR) and ABRs.

Step 3   Verify that OSPF is communicating properly with its neighbors. You might have done everything correctly, but if OSPF is not capable of forming a neighbor relationship to tell the other OSPF routers about the new summary, all your work is in vain. Here you can use the **show ip ospf neighbor** command.

Refer to Chapters 2, "Introduction to OSPF," and 3, "OSPF Communication," for more information about the way OSPF communicates and the role of routers in OSPF. The next section discusses the specific methods within OSPF that are used to perform summarization.

Types of OSPF Summarization

Route summarization is particularly important in an OSPF environment because it increases the stability and efficiency of the network. Summarization, as you just learned, is useful in representing networks as a block of addresses. When this representation is used, it allows for a smaller routing table, reduced routing updates, and troubleshooting.

Summarizing is the consolidation of multiple routes into a single route advertisement. This is normally done at the boundaries of the OSPF autonomous system on the ABRs or ASBRs. Although summarization could be configured between any two areas, it is better to summarize in the direction of the backbone. This way the OSPF backbone receives all the aggregate addresses and, in turn, injects them, already summarized, into other areas. When OSPF is used as the routing protocol in your network, summarization can be configured in the following ways:

- **Summarize area routes**—Routes within an OSPF area are known as *intra-area routes* in OSPF. When you summarize the routes within an area, this allows more optimal routing and reduced SPF calculations. When summarization is used, OSPF generates a Type 5 Summary LSA to represent these routes.

- **Summarize external routes**—To make redistribution easier or to control what is advertised, you can summarize the networks that are redistributed into OSPF. This can be useful when receiving several contiguous networks from another autonomous system because summarization allows these networks to be represented by one route entry in your autonomous system. When summarization is used for redistributed routes, OSPF generates a Type 4 Summary LSA to represent these routes. These Type 4 LSAs replace the normal Type 5 or 7 LSAs that you would typically see.

With both forms of summarization, summary LSAs are created and flooded toward area 0, the backbone area. The backbone area, in turn, floods the LSAs out to the other OSPF areas. The next section looks at some design and configuration issues that you face when performing each type of summarization and provides some examples.

Summarize Area Routes

To allow for a more specific understanding of the category of routes within OSPF that you are going to summarize, review the two types of routes:

- **Intra-area**—Routes to networks within an area, where cost is based on the link type (see Table 5-1). Intra-area routes usually do not need to be summarized because all routers in the area must know about every network within that area. Summarization of an area can be possible or required due to excessive subnetting or improper planning of IP address usage.

- **Inter-area**—Routes to networks in another area, where the cost is based on link type. Summarizing how OSPF advertises the routes that are part of an area and thus how to get to them is the most common use of summarization. The techniques for these types of routes can be used throughout your network.

Inter-area route summarization is done on ABRs, and it applies to the act of summarizing routes from within the OSPF autonomous system, specifically routes within an OSPF area. This technique does not apply to external routes injected into OSPF via redistribution.

Configuration Example 1: Area Summarization

To take advantage of summarization, network numbers in areas should be assigned contiguously so that you can lump these addresses into one range or block when summarizing them. Figure 7-2 illustrates an example of summarization. Review the figure, and then read the explanation of what is happening.

Figure 7-2   *Summarizing an OSPF Area*

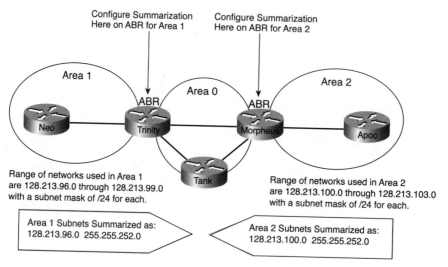

In Figure 7-2, the ABR for area 1 Router Trinity is configured to summarize the range of subnets found within area 1 of 128.213.96.0/22 through 128.213.99.0/22 into one range: 128.213.64.0 with a mask of 255.255.252.0 into the OSPF backbone. The area 1 networks are summarized as follows:

> 128.213.96.0 255.255.252.0

In the same way, the ABR for area 2 Router Morpheus is configured to summarize the range of subnets found within area 2 of 128.213.100.0/22 through 128.213.103.0/2 into the OSPF backbone. The area 2 networks are summarized as follows:

> 128.213.100.0 255.255.252.0

Note that this summarization was successful because you have the following distinct and contiguous ranges of subnets:

- x.x.96.x to x.x.99.x in area 1
- x.x.100.x to x.x.103.x in area 2

Keep this in mind as you learn what to do if you need to summarize and your networks are not contiguous, as shown later in the chapter. The configuration tasks needed to accomplish this summarization are as follows for Router Trinity. (Router Morpheus is similar but with different subnets.) The **area range** configuration command summarizes this type of network; the command syntax is as follows:

```
Trinity(config-router)#area area-id range ip-address mask [advertise ¦ not-advertise]
```

This command requires you to define the area that contains the routes you are summarizing into a range and then define the range. The IP address and mask specify the range of addresses to be summarized in one range. Optionally, you can add the keyword **not-advertise**. Use this command when you want the ABR to not advertise a particular subnet out of a summarized range; the default is to advertise. Examples 7-1 through 7-3 show the configuration for Router Trinity before, during, and after defining the IP addresses in area 1 for summarization.

Before

Example 7-1   *Trinity Configuration Before Summarization*

```
!
router ospf 100
 network 128.213.96.0 0.0.3.255 area 1
 network 192.168.254.0 0.0.0.255 area 0
 !
```

During

Example 7-2   *Trinity Configuration During Summarization*

```
Trinity#conf t
Enter configuration commands, one per line.  End with CNTL/Z.
Trinity(config)#router ospf 100
Trinity(config-router)#
Trinity(config-router)#area 1 range 123.213.96.255.255.252.0
  advertise      Advertise this range (default)
  not-advertise  DoNotAdvertise this range
  <cr>
Trinity(config-router)#area 1 range 128.213.96.0 255.255.252.0
Trinity(config-router)#
```

After

Example 7-3   *Trinity Configuration After Summarization*

```
!
router ospf 100
 network 128.213.96.0 0.0.3.255 area 1
 network 192.168.254.0 0.0.0.255 area 0
 area 1 range 128.213.96.0 255.255.252.0
 !
```

It would be hard to summarize if the subnets between area 1 and area 2 were overlapping. The backbone area would receive summary ranges that overlap, and routers in the middle would not know where to send the traffic based on the summary address. The preceding is the relative configuration of Router Trinity, and you can extrapolate the Router Morpheus configuration as well.

Summarize External Routes

When redistributing routes from other protocols into OSPF, each route is advertised individually in an external link-state advertisement (LSA). External route summarization is specific to external routes that are injected into OSPF via redistribution done by ASBRs. When configuring external route summarization, make sure that external ranges being summarized are contiguous. Summarization that overlaps ranges from two different routers could cause packets to be sent to the wrong destination.

You can configure OSPF to advertise a single route for all the redistributed routes that are covered by a specified network address and mask. Doing so helps decrease the size of the OSPF link-state databases and, in turn, the routing table. The same benefits discussed when configuring route summarization between areas are applicable here; only now, the routes are coming from an external source.

Configuration Example 2: External Route Summarization

Configuring external route summarization has the same result as area summarization. The difference is between the type of summarization you are trying to accomplish (that is, area versus external).

To have OSPF advertise one summary route for all redistributed routes covered by a single network address and mask, perform the following task in router configuration mode. Summarization is done via the following router OSPF subcommand:

```
summary-address summary-ip-address subnet-mask [not-advertise] [tag tag]
```

This command is effective only on ASBRs doing redistribution of routes into the OSPF routing process. One key aspect of this command is the **not-advertise** keyword, which allows you to not advertise routes that match the command with this keyword. The **tag** keyword allows for the matching of values that are referenced in a route map; that is, you set the tag here and the route map sees that tag and takes action.

NOTE   The OSPF documentation on cisco.com is incorrect regarding this command in all versions of Cisco IOS Software. Specifically, the Cisco documentation states that in OSPF, command entries of *prefix* and *mask* are required. This is not the case.

In Figure 7-3, Router BP01 and Router BP02 are external business partners and have subnets associated with them as shown. Router BP01 is advertising subnets in the range 128.213.96–99.0, and Router BP02 is advertising subnets in the range 128.213.100–103.0. In the OSPF network, Routers Tank and Trinity (both OSPF ASBRs) are configured with redistribution of the business partner networks into OSPF, and the **summary-address** command needs to be applied, thus allowing the business partners' networks to be summarized and advertised throughout the OSPF network.

This **summary-address** command causes the routers to generate one external summary route each, for example, 128.213.96.0 with a mask of 255.255.252.0 by Router Tank; this causes Router Trinity to generate an external summary route of 128.213.100.0 with a mask of 255.255.252.0. Note that the **summary-address** command has no effect if used on Router Neo because Router Neo is not doing the redistribution into OSPF; it is also not an ASBR.

Figure 7-3   *Summarizing External Routes*

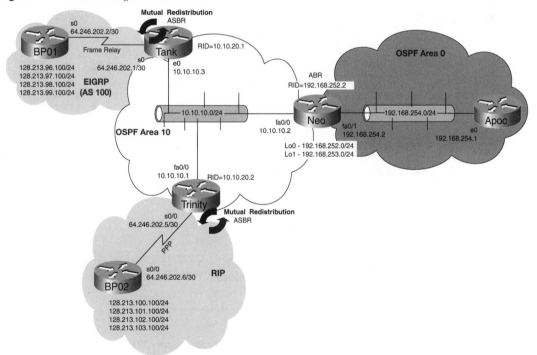

To properly summarize the subnets into one range on each router, you can configure the routers, as shown in Examples 7-4 through 7-6. Looking at the routing table on Router Neo in Example 7-4, you can see that none of the routes are summarized at this point—but they will be soon.

Before

Example 7-4   *Router Neo Routing Table Before Summarizing BP01 and BP02 Subnets*

```
Neo#show ip route
Codes: C - connected, S - static, I - IGRP, R - RIP, M - mobile, B - BGP
       D - EIGRP, EX - EIGRP external, O - OSPF, IA - OSPF inter area
       N1 - OSPF NSSA external type 1, N2 - OSPF NSSA external type 2
       E1 - OSPF external type 1, E2 - OSPF external type 2, E - EGP
       i - IS-IS, L1 - IS-IS level-1, L2 - IS-IS level-2, ia - IS-IS inter area
       * - candidate default, U - per-user static route, o - ODR
       P - periodic downloaded static route

Gateway of last resort is not set

     64.0.0.0/8 is variably subnetted, 3 subnets, 2 masks
O E2    64.246.202.4/30 [110/200] via 10.10.10.1, 00:54:29, FastEthernet0/0
O E2    64.246.202.6/32 [110/200] via 10.10.10.1, 00:54:29, FastEthernet0/0
O E2    64.246.202.0/30 [110/100] via 10.10.10.3, 00:54:29, FastEthernet0/0
     128.213.0.0/24 is subnetted, 8 subnets
O E2    128.213.101.0 [110/200] via 10.10.10.1, 00:54:29, FastEthernet0/0
O E2    128.213.100.0 [110/200] via 10.10.10.1, 00:54:29, FastEthernet0/0
O E2    128.213.103.0 [110/200] via 10.10.10.1, 00:54:30, FastEthernet0/0
O E2    128.213.102.0 [110/200] via 10.10.10.1, 00:54:30, FastEthernet0/0
O E2    128.213.97.0 [110/100] via 10.10.10.3, 00:54:30, FastEthernet0/0
O E2    128.213.96.0 [110/100] via 10.10.10.3, 00:54:30, FastEthernet0/0
O E2    128.213.99.0 [110/100] via 10.10.10.3, 00:54:30, FastEthernet0/0
O E2    128.213.98.0 [110/100] via 10.10.10.3, 00:54:30, FastEthernet0/0
     10.0.0.0/8 is variably subnetted, 3 subnets, 2 masks
C       10.10.10.0/24 is directly connected, FastEthernet0/0
O       10.10.20.0/24 [110/2] via 10.10.10.1, 00:54:35, FastEthernet0/0
O       10.10.20.1/32 [110/2] via 10.10.10.3, 00:54:35, FastEthernet0/0
C    192.168.254.0/24 is directly connected, FastEthernet0/1
C    192.168.253.0/24 is directly connected, Loopback1
C    192.168.252.0/24 is directly connected, Loopback0
Neo#
```

During

Moving into configuration mode, you apply the **summary-address** command on both Tank and Trinity, as shown in Example 7-5.

Example 7-5   *Summarizing BP01 and BP02 Subnets*

```
Trinity#conf t
Enter configuration commands, one per line.  End with CNTL/Z.
Trinity(config)#router ospf 100
Trinity(config-router)#summary-address 128.213.100.0 255.255.252.0
Trinity(config-router)#^Z
Trinity#
```

Example 7-5   *Summarizing BP01 and BP02 Subnets (Continued)*

```
Tank#conf t
Enter configuration commands, one per line.  End with CNTL/Z.
Tank(config)#router ospf 100
Tank(config-router)#summary-address 128.213.96.0 255.255.252.0
Tank(config-router)#^Z
Tank#
```

After

That is an easy command, isn't it? One command on each router and the routing table should be reduced from eight entries to the two summarized entries. As you can see in Example 7-6, Router Neo is now seeing the summary routes instead of the eight.

Example 7-6   *Router Neo Routing Table After Summarizing BP01 and BP02 Subnets*

```
Neo#show ip route
Codes: C - connected, S - static, I - IGRP, R - RIP, M - mobile, B - BGP
       D - EIGRP, EX - EIGRP external, O - OSPF, IA - OSPF inter area
       N1 - OSPF NSSA external type 1, N2 - OSPF NSSA external type 2
       E1 - OSPF external type 1, E2 - OSPF external type 2, E - EGP
       i - IS-IS, L1 - IS-IS level-1, L2 - IS-IS level-2, ia - IS-IS inter area
       * - candidate default, U - per-user static route, o - ODR
       P - periodic downloaded static route

Gateway of last resort is not set

     64.0.0.0/8 is variably subnetted, 3 subnets, 2 masks
O E2    64.246.202.4/30 [110/200] via 10.10.10.1, 01:02:23, FastEthernet0/0
O E2    64.246.202.6/32 [110/200] via 10.10.10.1, 01:02:23, FastEthernet0/0
O E2    64.246.202.0/30 [110/100] via 10.10.10.3, 01:02:23, FastEthernet0/0
     128.213.0.0/22 is subnetted, 2 subnets
O E2    128.213.100.0 [110/200] via 10.10.10.1, 00:02:00, FastEthernet0/0
O E2    128.213.96.0 [110/100] via 10.10.10.3, 00:00:18, FastEthernet0/0
     10.0.0.0/8 is variably subnetted, 3 subnets, 2 masks
C       10.10.10.0/24 is directly connected, FastEthernet0/0
O       10.10.20.0/24 [110/2] via 10.10.10.3, 01:02:23, FastEthernet0/0
O       10.10.20.1/32 [110/2] via 10.10.10.3, 01:02:23, FastEthernet0/0
C    192.168.254.0/24 is directly connected, FastEthernet0/1
C    192.168.253.0/24 is directly connected, Loopback1
C    192.168.252.0/24 is directly connected, Loopback0
```

It is a good idea to randomly ping networks that should be reachable via the summary entries, as shown in Example 7-7.

Example 7-7 *Pinging Networks Reachable via Summary Entries*

```
Neo#ping 128.213.97.100
Type escape sequence to abort.
Sending 5, 100-byte ICMP Echos to 128.213.97.100, timeout is 2 seconds:
!!!!!
Success rate is 100 percent (5/5), round-trip min/avg/max = 32/32/36 ms

Neo#ping 128.213.102.100
Type escape sequence to abort.
Sending 5, 100-byte ICMP Echos to 128.213.102.100, timeout is 2 seconds:
!!!!!
Success rate is 100 percent (5/5), round-trip min/avg/max = 28/28/32 ms
Neo#
```

Summarizations Effect on the Routing Table

Chapter 6 discussed several techniques used to avoid routing loops when dealing with redistribution. Summarization has these issues as well, and there is a unique way to prevent them in summarization. Refer to Figure 7-4 for another view of the network you are summarizing.

Figure 7-4 *Summarization Sample Network*

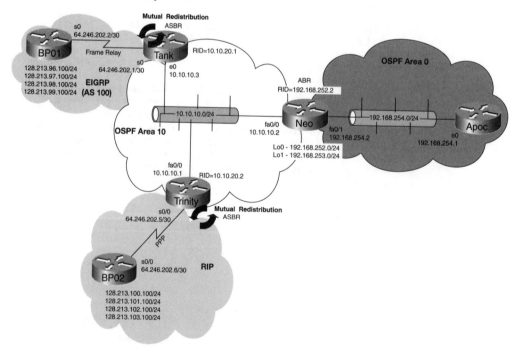

Because Routers Trinity and Tank performed the summarization when a router is trying to reach one of the summarized networks, they go to the router that is advertising the summary. Notice the highlighted entry in Trinity's routing table in Example 7-8.

Example 7-8   *Trinity's Routing Table*

```
Trinity#show ip route
Codes: C - connected, S - static, I - IGRP, R - RIP, M - mobile, B - BGP
       D - EIGRP, EX - EIGRP external, O - OSPF, IA - OSPF inter area
       N1 - OSPF NSSA external type 1, N2 - OSPF NSSA external type 2
       E1 - OSPF external type 1, E2 - OSPF external type 2, E - EGP
       i - IS-IS, L1 - IS-IS level-1, L2 - IS-IS level-2, ia - IS-IS inter area
       * - candidate default, U - per-user static route, o - ODR
       P - periodic downloaded static route

Gateway of last resort is not set

     64.0.0.0/8 is variably subnetted, 3 subnets, 2 masks
C       64.246.202.4/30 is directly connected, Serial0/0
C       64.246.202.6/32 is directly connected, Serial0/0
O E2    64.246.202.0/30 [110/100] via 10.10.10.3, 01:03:06, FastEthernet0/0
     128.213.0.0/16 is variably subnetted, 6 subnets, 2 masks
R       128.213.101.0/24 [120/1] via 64.246.202.6, 00:00:23, Serial0/0
O       128.213.100.0/22 is a summary, 01:10:18, Null0
R       128.213.100.0/24 [120/1] via 64.246.202.6, 00:00:23, Serial0/0
R       128.213.103.0/24 [120/1] via 64.246.202.6, 00:00:24, Serial0/0
R       128.213.102.0/24 [120/1] via 64.246.202.6, 00:00:24, Serial0/0
O E2    128.213.96.0/22 [110/100] via 10.10.10.3, 00:00:19, FastEthernet0/0
     10.0.0.0/8 is variably subnetted, 3 subnets, 2 masks
C       10.10.10.0/24 is directly connected, FastEthernet0/0
C       10.10.20.0/24 is directly connected, Loopback0
O       10.10.20.1/32 [110/2] via 10.10.10.3, 01:03:10, FastEthernet0/0
O IA 192.168.254.0/24 [110/2] via 10.10.10.2, 01:03:10, FastEthernet0/0
O IA 192.168.253.0/24 [110/2] via 10.10.10.2, 01:03:10, FastEthernet0/0
O IA 192.168.252.0/24 [110/2] via 10.10.10.2, 01:03:10, FastEthernet0/0
Trinity#
```

Rather curious to see the entire summary routed to null0? Null0 is a fictitious interface that causes the router to drop into the bit bucket any information that is destined to it. This begs the question: Why is it present in Trinity's routing table? In addition, the following entry is also present in Router Tank's routing table for the summary it is advertising:

```
O       128.213.96.0/22 is a summary, 00:02:30, Null0
```

These entries are placed into the routing table to prevent routing loops. To understand how this could happen, consider that this route entry is not present in the routing table and a failure occurs, making network 128.216.101.0/24 unreachable. Other OSPF routers do not know and do not care. Because this route entry has the summary, it continues to advertise that summary, thus making it appear that the route to the network is still valid. Add the presence of a default route in area 10, which points to Router Neo.

NOTE   These null routes are automatically entered only in Cisco IOS Software Release 12.1(6) and later. Previously, you would have had to enter a static discard route manually in configuring a router.

Now, try and reach network 128.216.101.0/24 from Router Apoc. The packets are going to go to Router Neo, which on checking its routing table, sees the summary route and forwards the packets to Router Trinity, the ASBR advertising the summary. When Router Trinity receives these packets, it knows that this network is down, so it uses the default route and sends the packets back to Router Neo, which sends them back to Trinity. The result is one big routing loop.

However, when summarizing in OSPF, you have the summary route to Null0 which, regardless of the up/down status of a network that is part of the summary, is always active. When out packets come from Router Neo destined to 128.216.101.0/24, they are routed to Null0, not back to Router Neo, thus avoiding a routing loop.

The next section looks at a real-world example of how you can take a network and subnet it effectively while ensuring that each summarization is possible.

Configuration Example 3: Subnetting with Summarization

Summarization is a wonderful concept in networking that can give networks a variety of benefits, as discussed earlier in this chapter. It is important to provide a template that demonstrates how you might go about designing or redesigning an OSPF network with summarization in place from the beginning. This latter case is the more likely scenario, and you might have already been involved in projects to renumber and readdress networks that needed a new and improved *logical look*. These situations develop for a variety of reasons, some within your control but many not in your control. This example looks at taking a single public network and, through the use of subnetting with variable-length subnet masking (VLSM), allows clean summarization at the various area boundaries. Use this example as a template to follow when you are faced with such a situation.

NOTE   Route summarization is desirable for a reliable and scalable OSPF internetwork. The effectiveness of route summarization, and your OSPF implementation in general, hinges on the addressing scheme that you adopt. Summarization in an OSPF internetwork occurs between each area and the backbone area. Summarization must be configured manually in OSPF.

There might be a situation where you have only one public address (a single Class B, for example) to allocate for all areas of your multi-area OSPF network. You might also want to save some address space by using VLSM so that the point-to-point serial links in each area have a subnet mask that allows two hosts per subnet, which is perfect for point-to-point networks. You have also learned that summarizing on area boundaries is very useful.

This example uses part of the address space 150.100.0.0/16. It is meant to illustrate both the concept of area masks and the breakdown of large subnets into smaller ones through the use VLSM. The following points list the assumptions that are made and describe the process used to allocate addresses:

- Determine how many areas you will have in your OSPF network. While you are considering this, evaluate the business factors that are facing your company. For example, is your company likely to expand or contract in a given area? What effect will this have on your network? This kind of business thinking is crucial. While you are a network engineer, you must also be aware of the business factors that affect your network. A value of 500 areas has been chosen for this example. This is a large number, and a 500-area OSPF network is not realistic, but it can help to illustrate the methodology used in a large fashion to make the point.

- Create an "area mask boundary" in your address space through the use of subnetting. This boundary will be where the subnets found within each area will be *summarized*. You have a Class B, so you must subnet how to get 500 areas, thus using the formula of $2^{N-2} = X$ where N is the number of bits to be used for extending the subnet mask and X is the number of usable subnets. Note that $2^9-2 = 510$ meets the requirement of 500 areas and you have ten more reserved for future use; you know just in case the unexpected happens, which is good planning! In Figure 7-5, you can see where 9 bits of subnetting have been applied to the class B address, which results in the number of subnets required for each area.

- Determine the number of subnets required in each area and the maximum number of hosts required per subnet. In this example, you require a minimum of 100 subnets with 50 hosts each and 100 subnets with 2 hosts each (the serial lines) for each area. Perhaps, this is a design for a large chain of coffee shops that needs only a few host addresses per location but has many locations. Perhaps, this is a fast-food restaurant chain, retail shops, or an auto maintenance shop. All these possibilities have the requirement of multiple clustered locations in a given area with a small number of hosts needed at each location, perhaps all in a city or single geographical area.

- Now that you understand the requirements of how many subnets you need in each area, proceed with additional subnetting. Note that you have only 7 host bits left to use because of the creation of the area summarization. In fact, the 9 bits of the area mask are part of the subnet portion of the address, but you have restricted their flexibility so that you can summarize all the subnets of an area with one range command. In taking the first subnet from the previous figure, the subnet mask has been extended to get the minimum requirements, and expansion is planned for. You can see this in Figure 7-6.

Figure 7-5 *Subnetting to Get Areas Properly Summarized*

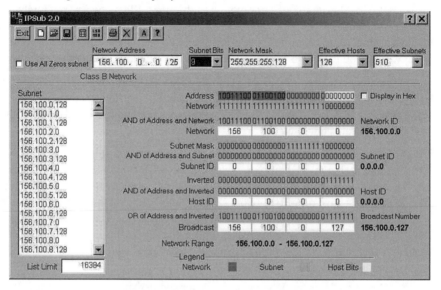

Figure 7-6 *Subnetting to Get Each Location*

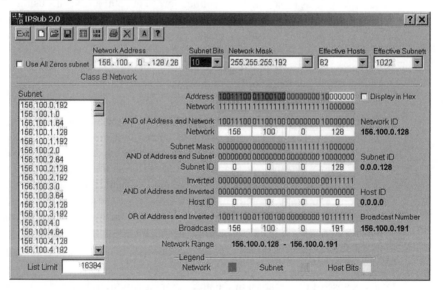

- Choose the portion of the address space that has the 2-bit host field (subnet mask of 255.255.255.252) for the serial lines arbitrarily from one of the larger subnet fields. This method of assigning addresses for the VLSM portion of the address space is done to guarantee no address overlap. Alternatively, if the requirement had been different, you could have chosen any number of the larger subnets (with mask 255.255.255.240) and broken them up into smaller ranges with fewer hosts, or combined several of them to create subnets with more hosts.

In this example, the addresses and mask boundaries were chosen simply to demonstrate the concept of summarization and the process of subnetting. Hopefully, you have noticed how intertwined they are! An alternative and possibly more realistic design could include the following items:

- Approximately 20–30 areas (maximum) for the entire OSPF AS
- Approximately 20–30 routers per OSPF area
- One or more Class B addresses, with several Class C networks to allocate for the AS

Alternative Area Summarization Example

Now that you know about segmenting the IP address space for 500 areas, consider the situation with an approach focused on address conservation. Assume that you have the following design criteria and IP addresses to work with:

- 18 OSPF areas, including the backbone area
- The following assigned network addresses:
  - Class B: 150.100.0.0/16
  - Class C: 198.22.33.0/24 and 198.22.34.0/24

Area Address Assignment

Here, each Class C network is used entirely in its own area, which leaves you needing 16 more, so the Class B address is subdivided using an area subnet mask so that its addresses are distributed equally among the 16 areas. The Class B network, 150.100.0.0/16, could be subnetted as follows. The letters x, y, and z represent bits of the last two octets of Class B:

```
150.100. x x x x y y y y . y z z z z z z z
area mask boundary
```

Note the following points about this command:

- The 4 x bits are used to identify 16 areas.
- The 5 y bits represent up to 32 subnets per area.
- The 7 z bits allow 126 (128–2) hosts per subnet.

All the previously shown principles used for area summarization and subnetting using VLSM also apply for this more realistic example. Because of the careful assignment of addresses, each area can be summarized with a single **area range** command. This is a requirement to be able to scale an OSPF network. The first set of addresses starting with 150.100.2.0xxxxxxx (the last octet is represented in binary) can be summarized into the backbone with the following command:

```
area 8 range 150.100.2.0 255.255.255.128
```

This means that all addresses starting with 150.100.2.0xxxxxxx can be found in area 8.

Similarly, with the second area shown, the range of addresses starting with 150.100.2.1xxxxxxx can be summarized as follows:

```
area 17 range 150.100.2.128 255.255.255.128
```

This design methodology is extensible such that the area mask boundary and the subnet masks can be drawn at any point in the address space. This might be required if you had originally planned for 32 areas in your network but then later decided that you needed more. Here, you might decide to have a variable-length subnet mask (VLSM) boundary. This becomes much more complex to manage and is beyond the scope of this book. The strategy here was meant to show one approach that tries to simplify something—a concept that is inherently complicated and often difficult to understand.

Using Private Addressing to Summarize?

Private addressing is another option often cited as being simpler than developing an area scheme using bit-wise subnetting from a network range assigned to you by your ISP. However, in many cases, you do not get what is optimal for your needs.

Therefore, your business might need to develop its network address plan using solid business reasons to ensure success. Recall that networks are designed to meet a business need. This is especially true when making the decision on whether to use private addressing. Although private address schemes provide an excellent level of flexibility and do not limit the growth of your OSPF internetwork, they have certain disadvantages.

For example, developing a large-scale internetwork of privately addressed IP nodes limits total access to the Internet and mandates the implementation of a *demilitarized zone (DMZ)*. All nodes (hosts, servers, and routers) on the network in the DMZ must have assigned public IP addresses. Your ISP might, for example, assign a single Class C network number to you.

If you need to connect to the Internet, Figure 7-7 illustrates the way in which a DMZ provides a buffer of valid public IP addressing on nodes between a privately addressed network and the Internet.

Figure 7-7   *Connecting to the Internet from a Privately Addressed Network*

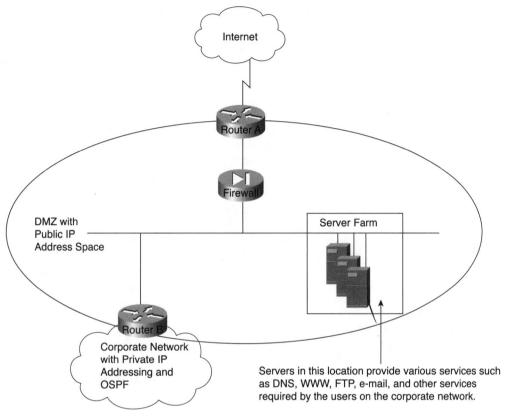

Router A provides the interface between the DMZ and the Internet, and Router B provides the firewall between the DMZ and the private address environment. All applications that need to run over the Internet must access the Internet through the DMZ.

NOTE   Firewalls can take many forms. They can be a router that is specially configured through the use of the Cisco firewall feature set or can be a dedicated machine specifically designed to perform firewall duties, such as a Cisco PIX Firewall or CheckPoints Firewall-1.

In the next configuration example, you look at the use of VLSM and summarization in more depth.

Configuration Example 4: Using VLSM with Summarization

IP networks are divided into Class A, B, and C addresses. You can define a mask that specifies which bits in the address define the subnet and which define the host. OSPF supports a concept called variable-length subnet masking (VLSM), which enables an administrator to use different masks for the same network number on different interfaces.

VLSM Functionality

A customer who has many hosts on some subnets and few hosts on others does not implement VLSM and thus must implement a consistent mask on all subnets. This results in wasted host addresses on subnets with few hosts. You might want to use VLSM if you are concerned about running out of IP address space because the subnet mask used with VLSM can be chosen to match the number of hosts required. VLSM enables you to get more use out of your available space. VLSM offers the flexibility to handle subnets with different numbers of hosts. For example, a customer who has not implemented VLSM and who has some interfaces with only a few hosts and other interfaces with many hosts can choose to use a long mask on the first interface and a short mask on the second interface. This address space must be assigned VERY carefully. It is likely that existing networks must be renumbered to be able to take advantage of this feature.

With VLSM, you do not have to waste network numbers on serial interfaces because you can support unnumbered IP interfaces. Also, VLSM supports discontinuous subnets. An example of a discontinuous subnet application is where a customer has two Class B addresses: One is used in the backbone, and one is used by sites. The site network number is discontiguous if more than one site has the same network number. The existing solution is to use secondary IP addresses on the same interface. In this way, you can provide a set of network numbers across the backbone and, thus, connect the discontinuous subnets.

VLSM Pitfalls

Some of the disadvantages of VLSM are as follows:

- It is easy to make mistakes in address assignment, so double-check your calculations before deploying them.
- It is more confusing and difficult to monitor your network with all the new subnets.
- There are more routing entries, and it is difficult to configure summarization.
- There is an increased possibility of assigning overlapping subnets.

When using VLSM, be careful about assigning addresses, for example, with a Class B network number of 131.108.0.0.

Table 7-3 shows some common masks and then manipulates this network with VLSM.

Table 7-1   *Common Subnet Masks and Possible Hosts*

Common Subnet Masks	Number of Hosts
255.255.255.252	2
255.255.255.248	6
255.255.255.240	14
255.255.255.224	30
255.255.255.192	62
255.255.255.128	126
255.255.255.0	254

Suppose that you had two offices to which you want to assign subnet numbers. The first office is very small and will never have more than six hosts. The second office is large and might need to support up to 126 hosts. The obvious thing to do is to assign the masks appropriately. However, it is easy to make mistakes when doing this; see Table 7-4.

Table 7-2   *Mask Assignments*

IDs	Network Number	Mask	Legal Host
Office A	131.108.13.248	255.255.255.248	249–254
Office B	131.108.13.128	255.255.255.128	129–254

This is an illegal configuration because one of the network/mask pairs is a bit-wise subset of the other. The owners of those offices are allowed to assign their IP addresses within the offices themselves. Suppose that the owner of office A assigns a host the IP address of 131.108.13.250—this is host 2 in network 131.108.13.248. Meanwhile, the owner of office B assigns a host the IP address 131.108.13.250—this is host 122 in network 131.108.13.128. Both of these are legal addresses.

However, it is impossible for a router to tell which host should get packets that are sent to that IP address. Worse yet, neither office owner realizes that he has created a problem. To make this even harder to keep straight, the configuration in Table 7-5 shows other legal possibilities.

Table 7-3   *IP Configurations*

IDs	Network Number	Mask	Legal Host
Office A	131.108.13.248	255.255.255.248	249–254
Office B	131.108.13.0	255.255.255.128	1–127

A final pitfall to consider is the use of subnet 0, which, until Cisco IOS Software Release 11.3, was off by default. Remember this if you are using an older version of Cisco IOS Software. OSPF is extremely sophisticated in its use of classless addressing, and now that subnet 0 is used by default, things are getting much more interesting.

If you use subnet masks that do not fall on 8-bit boundaries, you can end up creating a nonobvious subnet 0.

For example, network 192.111.108.0 mask 255.255.255.0 has 254 hosts on it (192.111.108.[1–254]). You can try to expand the number of networks by stretching the mask: network 192.111.108.0 mask 255.255.255.240 (16 nets with 14 hosts each).

However, this leaves 14 of the existing hosts in subnet 0, which does not work. The hosts need to be renumbered (17–24, for example). This problem exists even when VLSMs are not used. However, VLSM makes this more likely to occur.

TIP

The only illegal number is subnet 0. The all-1s subnet is fair game. In fact, the **ip subnet zero** command gets around the first restriction.

Proper Implementation of VLSM

The best way to use VLSM is to keep the existing numbering plan and to gradually migrate some networks to recover address space. In Cisco's network, the Class B address is 131.108.0.0. You use a mask of 255.255.255.0. You could take one address and decide to use it for all serial lines, as shown in the following example:

Existing addressing: network number: 131.108.0.0, mask: 255.255.255.0
Reserve one existing subnet for all serial lines: network number: 131.108.254.0, mask: 255.255.255.252

The use of VLSM allows 6 bits or 64 subnets for serial lines. These subnets would be as follows:

131.108.254.1 and 131.108.254.2
131.108.254.5 and 131.108.254.6
131.108.254.9 and 131.108.254.10
and so on

Note that host numbers with all 0s or all 1s are not supported. This achieves a 64:1 improvement in address space allocation on serial lines. It also assumes that you are including subnet 0, network and the broadcast.

Interoperability Issues with VLSM

Routers in a single segment must agree on the network mask. For example, if every router does not agree on the same mask for an Ethernet segment or a Frame Relay link, a breakdown in communication will occur.

Consider that IGRP does not support VLSM, so when information is redistributed from OSPF to IGRP or RIP version 1 (RIP-1), only a single mask is used. The best way to make redistribution work is to hide all VLSMs from IGRP. OSPF should summarize the networks to achieve one mask per network number.

The idea behind VLSMs is to offer more flexibility in dealing with dividing a major network into multiple subnets and still being able to maintain an adequate number of hosts in each subnet. Without VLSM, one subnet mask can be applied only to a major network. This would restrict the number of hosts given the number of subnets required. If you pick the mask such that you have enough subnets, you would not be able to allocate enough hosts in each subnet. The same is true for the hosts: A mask that allows enough hosts might not provide enough subnet space.

For example, suppose you were assigned a Class C network 192.214.11.0, and you need to divide that network into three subnets with 100 hosts in one subnet and 50 hosts for each of the remaining subnets. Ignoring the two end limits, 0 and 255, you theoretically have 254 usable addresses (192.214.11.0–192.214.11.255) available. This cannot be done without VLSM. Figure 7-8 shows an example of how you can use VLSM to segment a Class C address.

Figure 7-8   *VLSM Example*

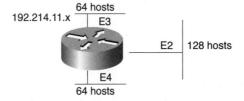

A handful of subnet masks can be used; remember that a mask should have a contiguous number of 1s starting from the left with the rest of the bits being all 0s. As an example, some common VLSM configurations are as follows:

- For ...252 (1111 1100), the address space is divided into 64.
- For ...248 (1111 1000), the address space is divided into 32.
- For ...240 (1111 0000), the address space is divided into 16.

- For ... 224 (1110 0000), the address space is divided into 8.
- For ... 192 (1100 0000), the address space is divided into 4.
- For ... 128 (1000 0000), the address space is divided into 2.

Without VLSM, you have the choice of using mask 255.255.255.128 and dividing the addresses into 2 subnets with 128 hosts each, or using 255.255.255.192 and dividing the space into 4 subnets with 64 hosts each.

This would not meet the requirement. By using multiple masks, you can use mask 128 and further subnet the second chunk of addresses with mask 192. Figure 7-9 shows the proper division of address space.

Figure 7-9 *Figure 7-9VLSM Address Distribution*

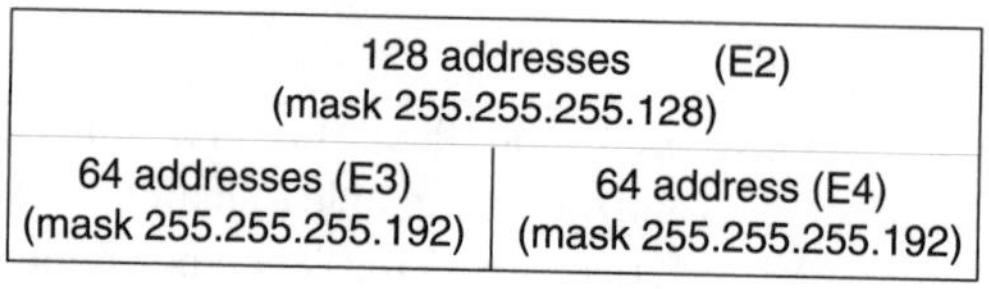

128 addresses (E2) (mask 255.255.255.128)	
64 addresses (E3) (mask 255.255.255.192)	64 address (E4) (mask 255.255.255.192)

Be careful in allocating the IP addresses to each mask. After you assign an IP address to the router or to a host, you have used up the entire subnet for that segment. For example, if you assign 192.214.11.10255.255.255.128 to E2, the entire range of addresses between 192.214.11.0 and 192.214.11.127 is consumed by E2. In the same way, if you assign 192.214.11.160255.255.255.128 to E2, the entire range of addresses between 192.214.11.128 and 192.214.11.255 is consumed by the E2 segment.

Example 7-9 shows an illustration of how the router interprets these addresses.

Example 7-9 *How a Router Interprets IP Addresses in a Network Using VLSM*

```
RTA#
ip subnet-zero
interface Ethernet2
ip address 192.214.11.10 255.255.255.128
interface Ethernet3
ip address 192.214.11.160 255.255.255.192
interface Ethernet4
ip address 192.214.11.226 255.255.255.192

RTA# show ip route connected
192.214.11.0 is variably subnetted, 3 subnets, 2 masks
C 192.214.11.0 255.255.255.128 is directly connected, Ethernet2
C 192.214.11.128 255.255.255.192 is directly connected, Ethernet3
C 192.214.11.192 255.255.255.192 is directly connected, Ethernet4
```

Summary

This chapter introduced some of the golden rules that you should follow when considering and deploying summarization with OSPF, looked at the ways in which you can summarize external routes, and then considered private versus public addressing with examples of how VLSM can also be used to summarize various network routes and subnets. Provided throughout this chapter are several configuration examples that demonstrate the concepts by showing them in real network scenarios.

Final Router Example Configurations

This section contains the final router configurations used in the many configuration examples in this chapter and in Chapter 7. Some valuable alias commands are included in these examples.

Example 7-10 *Cypher's Configuration*

```
!
interface Loopback0
 ip address 128.213.96.100 255.255.255.0
!
interface Loopback1
 ip address 128.213.97.100 255.255.255.0
!
interface Loopback2
 ip address 128.213.98.100 255.255.255.0
!
interface Loopback3
 ip address 128.213.99.100 255.255.255.0
!
interface Ethernet0
 no ip address
 shutdown
!
interface Ethernet1
 no ip address
 shutdown
!
interface Serial0
 ip address 64.246.202.2 255.255.255.252
 encapsulation frame-relay
 no ip split-horizon eigrp 100
 frame-relay map ip 64.246.202.1 702 broadcast
 frame-relay map ip 64.246.202.2 702 broadcast
 frame-relay lmi-type ansi
!
interface Serial1
 no ip address
 shutdown
!
router eigrp 100
```

continues

Example 7-10 *Cypher's Configuration (Continued)*

```
 redistribute connected
 network 64.0.0.0
 network 128.213.0.0
 no auto-summary
 !
```

Example 7-11 *Tank's Configuration*

```
hostname Tank
!
enable password 7 00021215104904131B245E
!
no ip domain-lookup
!
interface Loopback0
 description USED FOR OSPF RID
 ip address 10.10.20.1 255.255.255.0
!
interface Ethernet0
 description OSPF AREA 10
 ip address 10.10.10.3 255.255.255.0
!
interface Ethernet1
 no ip address
 shutdown
!
interface Serial0
 ip address 64.246.202.1 255.255.255.252
 encapsulation frame-relay
 no ip split-horizon eigrp 100
 frame-relay map ip 64.246.202.1 701 broadcast
 frame-relay map ip 64.246.202.2 701 broadcast
 frame-relay lmi-type ansi
!
interface Serial1
 no ip address
 shutdown
!
router eigrp 100
 redistribute ospf 100 metric 1500 10 255 1 1500 route-map DEN4-PERM3
 network 64.0.0.0
 no auto-summary
!
router ospf 100
 summary-address 128.213.96.0 255.255.252.0
 redistribute eigrp 100 metric 100 subnets route-map DEN3-PERM4
 network 10.10.10.0 0.0.0.255 area 10
 network 10.10.20.0 0.0.0.255 area 10
!
no ip classless
access-list 66 permit 128.213.100.0 0.0.3.255
```

Example 7-11   *Tank's Configuration (Continued)*

```
access-list 66 permit 64.246.202.4 0.0.0.3
access-list 66 permit 10.10.10.0 0.0.0.255
access-list 66 permit 192.168.254.0 0.0.0.255
access-list 66 permit 192.168.252.0 0.0.0.255
access-list 66 permit 192.168.253.0 0.0.0.255
access-list 97 permit 128.213.96.0 0.0.3.255
access-list 97 permit 64.246.202.0 0.0.0.3
route-map OSPF-to-EIGRP permit 10
 match ip address 66
!
route-map OSPF-to-EIGRP deny 65535
!
route-map EIGRP-to-OSPF permit 10
 match ip address 97
!
route-map EIGRP-to-OSPF deny 65535
!
route-map DEN3-PERM4 deny 10
 match tag 3
!
route-map DEN3-PERM4 permit 20
 set tag 4
!
route-map DEN4-PERM3 deny 10
 match tag 4
!
route-map DEN4-PERM3 permit 20
 set tag 3
!
```

Example 7-12   *Apoc's Configuration*

```
interface Ethernet0
 description OSPF AREA ZERO
 ip address 192.168.254.1 255.255.255.0
!
interface Serial0
 no ip address
shutdown
!
interface Serial1
 no ip address
 shutdown
!
router ospf 100
 network 192.168.254.0 0.0.0.255 area 0
 network 192.168.252.0 0.0.0.255 area 0
```

Example 7-13 *Neo's Configuration*

```
!
interface Loopback0
 description USED FOR OSPF RID
 ip address 192.168.252.2 255.255.255.0
 no ip directed-broadcast
 ip ospf network point-to-point
!
interface Loopback1
 ip address 192.168.253.1 255.255.255.0
 no ip directed-broadcast
 ip ospf network point-to-point
!
interface FastEthernet0/0
 description OSPF AREA 10
 ip address 10.10.10.2 255.255.255.0
 no ip directed-broadcast
 duplex auto
 speed auto
!
interface FastEthernet0/1
 description OSPF AREA 0
 ip address 192.168.254.2 255.255.255.0
 no ip directed-broadcast
 duplex auto
 speed auto
!
router ospf 100
 network 10.10.10.0 0.0.0.255 area 10
 network 192.168.252.0 0.0.0.255 area 0
 network 192.168.253.0 0.0.0.255 area 0
 network 192.168.254.0 0.0.0.255 area 0
!
ip classless
!
access-list 50 deny    128.213.102.0 0.0.0.255
access-list 50 permit any
!
```

Example 7-14 *Morpheus's Configuration*

```
!
interface Loopback0
 ip address 128.213.100.100 255.255.255.0
 no ip directed-broadcast
!
interface Loopback1
 ip address 128.213.101.100 255.255.255.0
 no ip directed-broadcast
!
interface Loopback2
 ip address 128.213.102.100 255.255.255.0
```

Example 7-14 *Morpheus's Configuration*

```
 no ip directed-broadcast
!
interface Loopback3
 ip address 128.213.103.100 255.255.255.0
 no ip directed-broadcast
!
interface Ethernet0/0
 no ip address
 no ip directed-broadcast
!
interface Serial0/0
 ip address 64.246.202.6 255.255.255.252
 no ip directed-broadcast
 encapsulation ppp
 no ip mroute-cache
!
interface Serial0/1
 no ip address
 no ip directed-broadcast
shutdown
!
interface Serial0/2
 no ip address
 no ip directed-broadcast
 shutdown
!
router rip
 version 2
 redistribute connected
 network 64.0.0.0
 no auto-summary
!
ip classless
```

Example 7-15 *Trinity's Configuration*

```
!
interface Loopback0
 description USED FOR OSPF RID
 ip address 10.10.20.2 255.255.255.0
 ip ospf network point-to-point
!
interface FastEthernet0/0
 description OSPF AREA 10
 ip address 10.10.10.1 255.255.255.0
 duplex auto
 speed auto
!
interface Serial0/0
 ip address 64.246.202.5 255.255.255.252
 encapsulation ppp
```

continues

Example 7-15 *Trinity's Configuration (Continued)*

```
 no fair-queue
 clock rate 64000
!
interface FastEthernet0/1
 no ip address
 shutdown
 duplex auto
 speed auto
!
interface Serial0/1
 ip address 51.51.51.1 255.255.255.252
 encapsulation ppp
!
router ospf 100
 log-adjacency-changes
 summary-address 128.213.100.0 255.255.252.0
 redistribute rip metric 200 subnets tag 200
 network 10.10.10.0 0.0.0.255 area 10
 network 10.10.20.0 0.0.0.255 area 10
 default-information originate always metric 50 metric-type 1
 default-metric 50
!
router rip
 version 2
 redistribute ospf 100 metric 5
 network 64.0.0.0
!
ip classless
no ip http server
!
```

PART III

OSPF Implementation, Troubleshooting, and Management

CHAPTER 8

Managing and Securing OSPF Networks

No poor bastard ever won a war by dying for his country. He won it by making the other poor bastard die for his.—General S. Patton

The management of your OSPF network is just as important as the security. In fact, a case could be made that proper network management is the most important aspect of having your network operate smoothly. In many cases this a true statement; this is because organizations and users now depend on the network to perform their daily activities. The success of a well-designed and seamlessly implemented OSPF network is lost in the user's cry of "My network is down and no one is doing anything about it."

This OSPF network management section of this chapter is comprised of the following sections:

- **Network management**—This section discusses what network management is and why it is so important in today's complex networks. This section also covers the accepted model of network management as designed by the Internet Engineering Task Force (IETF) through its publications of RFCs. In addition, you see some examples of common network management systems and enhancements that make the basic function of managing a network easier.

- **Simple Network Management Protocol (SNMP)**—SNMP is the de facto standard of network management. This section discusses the components and operation of SNMPv1, with some references to SNMPv2 and SNMPv3 This section also covers some of the particulars surrounding the hows and whys of Cisco's SNMP implementation within its network equipment.

- **Management Information Base (MIB)**—MIBs are probably the least understood and yet the most powerful features available to network engineers and managers. This section discusses the overall operation of MIBs under the SNMP umbrella of network management. This section also focuses on the OSPF-specific MIBs and briefly discusses the power that they can bring if properly used.

Security has become extremely important, not only in our networks but in our lives as well. This is quickly becoming the norm for most of the world. This chapter discusses reviewing and analyzing your needs for a secure network infrastructure.

The chapter covers a broad range of security topics, from very basic security techniques to the more advanced forms of encryption and filtering. The network security section consists of three major parts:

- **Network security**—This section introduces you to a variety of security threats and concerns that demonstrate the need for a coordinated network security plan. Some of the more recent attacks against the Cisco IOS Software and how it has responded are discussed. This section is not all doom and gloom, because it also covers a variety of defensive techniques that have been developed to repel the attacks described.

- **Golden rules of designing a secure network**—This section covers the golden rules that you must follow to develop a comprehensive network security plan. Many of the golden rules are common sense–oriented topics that network designers might forget in their rush to design the network. This chapter also briefly discusses the need to include a comprehensive security plan in the initial stages of the network's design.

- **Securing your OSPF network**—This section contains the meat of how to secure your network. Covered is the entire range of security implementations that you can use in your network—from simple configuration commands that should be deployed within your routers to how OSPF can protect the integrity of your routing structure.

- **Configuring traffic filters**—Do you have users who are traveling inside or outside your network? Is it possible that someone is trying to get into your network? Then this section is for you! This section covers the various types of filters—also known as access lists—and describes how to deploy them within your network to enable you to sleep better at night by getting very granular with their place in your security design.

Network Management

As network deployment and use increase, network management is increasingly becoming the focus of many organizations. These organizations range from those using a network to support their core business to those using networks as sales tools to those outsourcing or selling network management solutions.

The goal of everyone involved in network management is to proactively find and fix all network problems before users know that a problem exists. Many obstacles must be tackled—ranging from the sheer scope of the project to many different possible management techniques—before you can achieve this goal. This chapter covers the more tested and accepted common techniques such as SNMP and MIBs.

In its simplest form, network management can be described as the monitoring and tracking of network equipment and the resources that link them. The goal is to ensure that the network is always available for use by all appropriate users, all the time.

Network management, especially outsourced network management, brings to mind opportunities that allow today's network engineers and managers to reach toward a "bold new frontier." At one time, corporations of all sizes had a dedicated staff of IT professionals responsible for every aspect of the corporate network. Some of these aspects are as follows:

- Implementing security
- Changing management
- Contacting management
- Tracking inventory
- Analyzing performance
- Documenting the network
- Managing configuration
- Backing up and recovering data
- Designing the LANs and WANs
- Monitoring proactively and reactively
- Analyzing and planning for future growth
- Ordering the equipment and services
- Determining standardization requirements
- Upgrading licenses, equipment, and services
- Implementing the required equipment and service

All of these functions and responsibilities can be applied to both LANs and WANs. This is a daunting and exhaustive task for any organization, but it becomes even more so when it falls outside what a company would consider its core business. This is when the use of outsourced network management can become a real benefit to a company. Through outsourcing, a company can move many of these functions and responsibilities to companies that have the capability to leverage the expertise needed to fulfill these needs. Companies should not completely remove their internal IT staffs, but rather increase their use of outsourcing in areas in which their staff might not have expertise, for example, network security, VoIP, or perhaps Multiprotocol Label Switching (MPLS). This enables companies to focus on the business that made them successful in the first place.

To summarize, network management is a mission-critical aspect of any network. You can take one of two approaches to network management—you can be proactive or reactive. The former is more desirable. The differences in a customer's perception of the network can be profound. In a proactive environment, you can make sure everything is fixed before a network problem occurs (with the potential of causing many negative repercussions). In a reactive environment, the negative repercussions have already occurred, and you must get the network up and running as soon as possible.

A variety of tools and technologies can assist you in managing your network. The remainder of this chapter covers some of the tools and technologies that are available to manage your network and discusses methods to increase the security of your network.

Network Management Tools

Literally hundreds of solutions, tools, and technologies exist in the market today to make the job of managing networks better, easier, and more efficient.

Many different sources provide information regarding network management systems (NMSs). Therefore, you do not see coverage of specific systems, but rather details on some overall general characteristics that should be present in every enterprise-capable NMS.

Cisco has developed the following tools to streamline network management:

- CiscoView
- CiscoWorks
- ConfigMaker

CiscoView

CiscoView is a GUI-based device management software application that provides dynamic status, statistics, and comprehensive configuration information for Cisco Systems' internetworking products (switches, routers, concentrators, and adapters). CiscoView graphically displays a real-time physical view of Cisco devices. Additionally, this SNMP-based network management tool provides monitoring functions and offers basic troubleshooting capabilities. Figure 8-1 shows a typical view of a router (4700) using CiscoView. When shown in color, you can easily see the interface status (that is, green is up and red is down, and so on).

Figure 8-1 *Viewing Router Status with CiscoView*

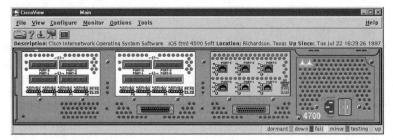

Using CiscoView, users can more easily understand the tremendous volume of management data available for internetworking devices. CiscoView organizes the data into graphical device representations that are presented in a clear, consistent format, as shown in Figure 8-2. This figure shows a sample of the interface statistics from a 4700 Series router.

CiscoView software can be integrated with several of the leading SNMP-based network management platforms, providing a seamless, powerful network view. It is also included within CiscoWorks, CiscoWorks for Switched Internetworks, and CiscoWorks for Windows. CiscoView software can also be run on UNIX workstations as a fully functional, independent management application.

Figure 8-2   *Viewing Router Interface Statistics in CiscoView*

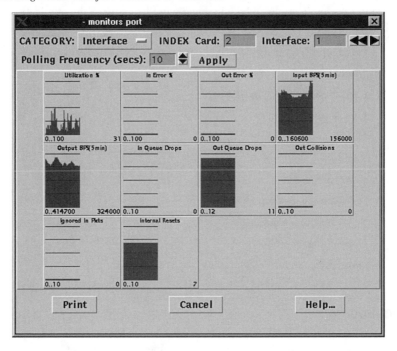

As previously mentioned, a variety of network management features are incorporated within CiscoView, including the following:

- Graphical display of Cisco products from a centralized network management location, giving network managers a complete view of Cisco products without physically checking each device at remote sites

- An exception-reporting design that enables network managers to quickly grasp essential inquiry information

- A GUI interface that continuously shows an updated physical picture of routers, hubs, and switches or access servers

- Can be invoked several times in the same session to simultaneously support multiple switches, routers, hubs, or access servers

CiscoWorks

CiscoWorks network management software enables you to monitor complex internetworks that use Cisco routing devices, and it helps you plan, troubleshoot, and analyze your network. CiscoWorks uses SNMP to monitor and control any SNMP-enabled device on the network.

CiscoWorks works directly with your SNMP network management platform, allowing CiscoWorks applications to be integrated with the features and applications of your platform. The following is a brief list of the features found in CiscoWorks:

- Configuration management
- CiscoView
- Configuration Snap-In Manager
- Device management
- Device monitor
- Path tool
- Security manager
- Software inventory manager
- Software library manager
- Contact management
- **show** commands

Cisco ConfigMaker

Cisco ConfigMaker is a freely available, easy-to-use Microsoft Windows application that is used to configure a small network of Cisco routers. It can run on Windows 98, Me, NT4, or 2000, offering a GUI alternative to the existing Cisco command-line interface (CLI). ConfigMaker enables Cisco resellers or end users to configure one or a network of Cisco routers, Cisco access servers, Cisco Micro Hubs, Cisco Micro Switches, or Cisco Micro Webservers. You can download ConfigMaker from the following website:

www.cisco.com/cgi-bin/tablebuild.pl/configmaker

A Cisco Connection Online (CCO) login is required to download ConfigMaker from this location.

Simple Network Management Protocol

As TCP/IP developed through the U.S. Department of Defense (DoD) Advanced Research Projects Agency (ARPA) in the late 1960s and early 1970s, it was accepted as a USDoD networking standard. The further development of ARPA, or rather the ARPA network (ARPAnet), allowed the continued development of a global set of networks based on the TCP/IP protocol. This global set of networks evolved into the Internet. The Internet quickly outgrew the capability of network engineers to manually monitor and maintain, and another solution was needed.

As the Internet developed, so did the desire and need to monitor the performance of the various network components that comprised the Internet. This desire manifested itself in the development of the Simple Gateway Monitoring Protocol (SGMP). The Internet Activities Board (IAB)—renamed in 1992 to the Internet Architecture Board—was involved with the evolutionary changes to SGMP and recommended the development of an expanded Internet network management standard.

The IAB handed off this new project to the Internet Engineering Task Force (IETF), which began designing, testing, and implementing a new Internet management standard. The task force's efforts resulted in three new RFCs: 1065, 1066, and 1067. These three documents formed the basis of SNMPv1.

NOTE   SNMP is part of a larger architecture called the Network Management Framework (NMF), which is defined in RFCs. The SNMPv1 NMF is defined in RFCs 1155, 1157, 1212, and 1902 through 1908. The SNMPv2 NMF is defined by RFCs 1441 through 1452. Note that while SNMPv1 was approved as a standard, SNMPv2 was not, and thus SNMPv2 is not well implemented.

The network management solution that has come to dominate the arena is known as the SNMP. As specified in Internet RFCs and other documents, a network management system is comprised of the following items:

- **Managed devices**—Sometimes called network elements, managed devices are hardware devices such as computers, servers, routers, bridges, switches, and terminal servers that are connected to networks.

- **Agents**—Agents are SNMP software modules that reside in managed devices. They collect and store management information, such as the number of error packets received by a network element, and they make that information available via SNMP.

- **Managed object**—A managed object is a characteristic of something that can be managed, for example, a list of currently active interfaces or the number of routes in a routing table. Managed objects differ from variables, which are particular object instances, in the sense that objects are a definitive value and can be scalar (defining a single object instance, such as interface up) or tabular (defining multiple, related instances, such as number of routes).

- **MIB**—A MIB is a collection of managed objects that reside in a virtual information store. Collections of related managed objects are defined in specific MIB modules. These modules are databases that store information in the format defined by the standards.

- **Abstract syntax notation**—Abstract syntax notation is a language used to describe a MIB's managed objects in a machine-independent format. Consistent use of a syntax notation enables different types of computers to share information. Internet management systems use a subset of the International Organization for Standardization's (ISO's) Open System Interconnection (OSI) Abstract Syntax Notation 1 (ASN.1) to define both the packets exchanged by the management protocol and the objects that are to be managed. Syntax notation is the standard-based method of storing and addressing data for use by the MIBs. The rules are based on SMI (see the following).

- **Structure of Management Information (SMI)**—SMI defines the rules for describing management information. The SMI is defined using ASN.1.

- **NMSs**—Sometimes called consoles, these devices execute management applications that monitor and control network elements. Physically, NMSs are usually engineering workstation–caliber computers with fast CPUs, megapixel color displays, substantial memory, and abundant disk space. At least one NMS must be present in each managed environment. NMS might be better defined as Servers, which reflects the computing power needed to accurately process and present network management information.

- **Parties**—Newly defined in SNMPv2, a party is a logical SNMPv2 entity that can initiate or receive SNMPv2 communication. Each SNMPv2 party comprises a single, unique party identity, a logical network location, a single authentication protocol, and a single privacy protocol. SNMPv2 messages are communicated between two parties. An SNMPv2 entity can define multiple parties, each with different parameters. For example, different parties can use different authentication and/or privacy protocols and their associated restricted subset of operations.

- **Management protocol**—A management protocol is used to convey management information between agents and NMSs. SNMP is the networking community's de facto standard management protocol.

NOTE   You can find all RFCs online at the following website:

www.isi.edu/in-notes/rfc*xxxx*.txt

where *xxxx* is the number of the RFC. If you do not know the number of the RFC, you can try searching by topic at the following website:

www.rfc-editor.org/cgi-bin/rfcsearch.pl

Figure 8-3 graphically represents the most basic and common elements of the Internet management model. The previous section covered the general network management model. The following section, presents more specific details regarding the tools needed for SNMP.

Figure 8-3 *A Detailed Network Management Model*

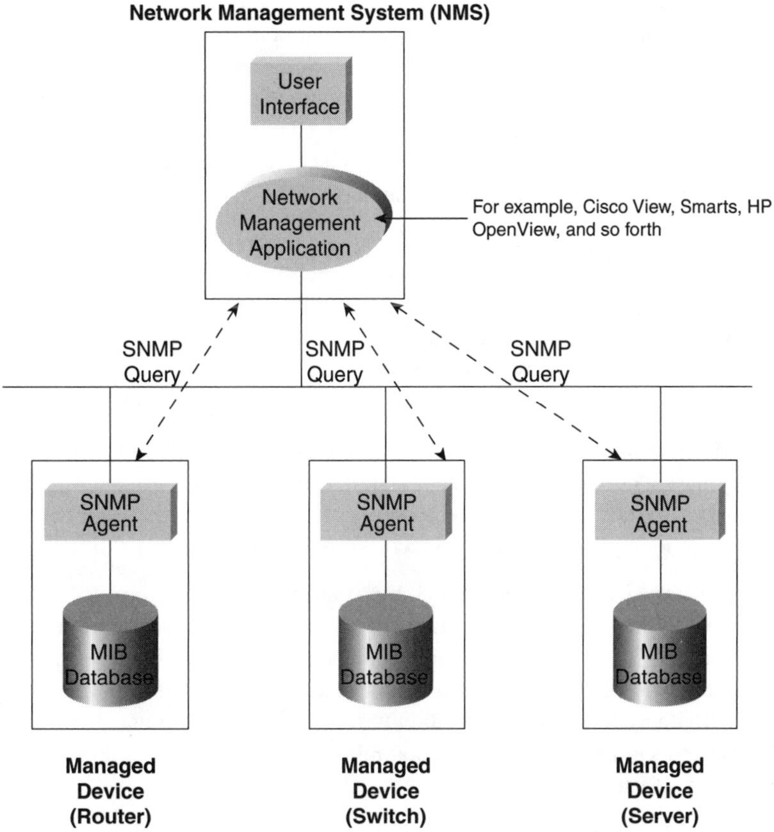

NOTE To avoid confusion in this chapter, Simple Network Management Protocol version 1 is referred to as SNMPv1, version 2 as SNMPv2, version 3 as SNMPv3, and general comments that cross versions as just SNMP. Although this can be tedious, it preserves the accuracy of the text.

Like the Transmission Control Protocol (TCP), SNMP is an IP-based protocol. SNMP is an application-layer protocol that is designed to facilitate the exchange of management information between network devices. By using SNMP-recorded data (such as packets per second and network error rates per interface), network engineers and managers can more easily manage network performance, find and solve network problems, and assist in planning for network growth.

Introduction to SNMP

Until the early to mid-1990s, the network management method used for these devices depended on SNMP-compatible management platforms offered by the hardware vendors. The vendors provided remote configuration of the devices, capabilities for minor and major alarms, and network mapping. All of these items provided benefits to network managers, who no longer had to configure a device on site or look at the LEDs for alarms. Network management could now be controlled via a centrally located administration package that was compatible with the industry-standard SNMP.

There are three versions of SNMP: version 1, version 2, and version 3. Most of the changes introduced in version 2 increase SNMP's security capabilities. Other changes increase interoperability by more rigorously defining the specifications for SNMP implementation. SNMP's creators believe that after a relatively brief period of coexistence, SNMP version 3 (SNMPv3) will largely replace SNMP version 1 (SNMPv1) and the few parts of SNMP v2 that have been approved due to SNMPv3's security support.

SNMP, in both agents and clients, is based on MIBs. MIBs can be standards-based or propi-etary-based, complying with those standards written for particular applications to collect statistics or track information on a variety of networking activities. These MIBs are publicly available to any manufacturer to incorporate into its products.

Proprietary MIBs are those written by a particular manufacturer to track either specific network anomalies, such as bandwidth utilization, or to track particular device activity, such as packet discards. For example, standards do not define how to gather operation characteristics that are unique to Cisco routers (for example, Hot Standby Router Protocol [HSRP] data), but Cisco has written the MIBs necessary to make your NMS capable to retrieve this information. A good example of this is the Cisco BGP MIB, where you can find a variety of useful information.

These MIBs are the sole property of the manufacturer and might not be made available to other companies. Vendor-specific MIBs are typically created to make a company's own devices or network management software product more valuable to the end users.

SNMP does have drawbacks, however. Most SNMP capability is embedded in network devices such as hubs, routers, Frame Relay Access Devices (FRADs), digital service units/ channel service units (DSU/CSUs), and switches. These devices primarily pass or route data, although they can provide snapshots of the network at intervals ranging from 5 to 30 minutes via SNMP through a **get request** command. They have neither the processing power nor the memory capacity to store real-time data for any length of time. This does not enable you to see what is going on in your network 100 percent of the time; instead, you must piece together snapshots. If you want to see everything that is going on, you need to consider adding a device (that is, a specialized server or poller) specifically designed to fulfill this requirement. Another way of achieving this it through your NMS, which is discussed in the next section.

Network Management System

The network management system (NMS) (also known as the manager) is software that has the capability of operating on one or more workstations. This software can be configured to manage different portions of a network, or multiple managers can manage the same network. The manager's requests are transmitted to one or more managed devices on the desired network. These requests are sent via TCP/IP. SNMP does not depend on TCP/IP for transport across a network. SNMP has the capability to be transported via numerous other transport mechanisms such as Novell's NetWare IPX and various other transport protocols. However, as previously mentioned, this book concentrates on the TCP/IP implementation. You can define the operation of an NMS as follows:

- An NMS executes applications that monitor and control managed devices. An NMS provides the bulk of the processing and memory resources required for network management. One or more NMSs must exist on any managed network.

- The network manager has a few commands at his/her fingertips to get information from a managed device. These commands are **GETREQUEST**, **GETNEXTREQUEST**, and **SETREQUEST**. Fortunately, most personnel engaged in network management do not realize that these are the SNMP commands they are executing, because the NMS presents the terms in more user-friendly ways or generally refers to the process as *polling*. Because SNMP is based on the utilization of the TCP/IP transport protocol, to issue any SNMP command, the manager must have the IP address of the destination agent.

- Therefore, for example, the NMS issues the **GETREQUEST** command to an SNMP agent in a managed device. This command can be used in one of two ways: It can be used to view a single MIB variable or to view a list of MIB variables from the destination agent.

- The **GETNEXTREQUEST** command is similar to the **GETREQUEST** command. However, when the agent receives the particular request, it attempts to retrieve the next entry in the MIB for the identified managed object. For example, if the manager were to issue a sequence of the **GETNEXTREQUEST** commands to a managed object, the manager has the ability to browse through that managed object's MIB. Therefore, a series of **GETNEXTREQUEST** commands can be used to read through a MIB that has multiple entries, for example, all the interfaces on a router and the transmission rates of these interfaces.

- The final manager-based command is the **SETREQUEST** command. This command is similar to the previous two in one way: The network manager issues it to a defined agent. The **SETREQUEST** command requests that the agent set the value of an individual instance of a managed object—these are variables stored at a device—or instances contained in the command. The **SETREQUEST** command is successful only if the network manager can write to the managed object. If the managed object is read-only, the command fails because the value of the managed object instance could not be amended.

Agents

An agent is a network management software module that resides in a managed device. It has local knowledge of management information and translates that information into a form that is compatible with SNMP by storing operational data in the MIB database for retrieval by the NMS.

To be a managed device, each device must have firmware in the form of code. This firmware translates the requests from the SNMP manager and responds to these requests. The software, or firmware (not the device itself), is referred to as an *agent*. It is possible to manage a non-SNMP compatible device, but it must support a proprietary management protocol.

TIP   To support a non-SNMP compatible device, you must first obtain a proxy agent. This proxy agent acts as an interpreter because it translates the SNMP requests into the proprietary protocol on the non-SNMP device.

SNMP agents have two commands, **GETRESPONSE** and **TRAP,** which function as follows:

- **GETRESPONSE**—This command flows from the agent to the NMS to confirm that the received command was processed and, if successfully received and processed, it returns a listing of occurrences of the managed objects polled and the current values for each of those managed objects.

- **TRAP**—This command is not generated as a response to a manager-generated command. Rather, it is an unsolicited response. This response occurs when an alarm condition occurs, for example, a router or switch interface going down.

Traps are very important to the smooth operation of network management because they allow a network event to be noticed and reported on.

Managed Devices

A *managed device* is a network node that contains an SNMP agent and resides on a managed network. Managed devices collect and store management information and make this information available to NMSs using SNMP.

Managed devices, sometimes called network elements, can be routers and access servers, switches and bridges, hubs, computer hosts, or printers. Figure 8-4 shows the relationship between an NMS and agents and how SNMP ties them together.

Figure 8-4   *Network Management Model*

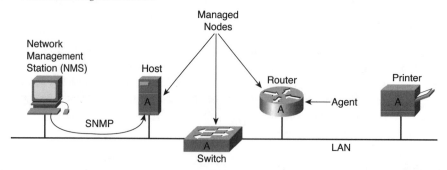

Management Information Base Overview

The MIB is an established database of the hardware settings, variables, memory tables, or records stored within files. These records are called *data elements.*

Data elements contain the information concerning the status, configuration, and statistical information base used to define the functionality and operational capacity of each managed device. This information is referred to as a MIB. Each data element is referred to as a *managed object.* These managed objects are comprised of a name, one or more attributes, and a set of operations that can be performed on the managed object.

MIBs and Object Identifiers

A MIB can be depicted as an abstract tree with an unnamed root. Individual data items make up the leaves of the tree. Object Identifiers (OIDs) uniquely identify or name MIB objects in the tree. OIDs are like telephone numbers; they are organized hierarchically with specific digits assigned by different organizations.

The OID structure of an SNMP MIB defines three main branches:

- Consultative Committee for International Telegraph and Telephone (CCITT)
- ISO
- Joint ISO/CCITT

Much of the current MIB activity occurs in the portion of the ISO branch defined by OID 1.3.6.1 and dedicated to the Internet community.

The current Internet-standard MIB, MIB-II, is defined in RFC 1213 and contains 171 objects. These objects are grouped by protocol (including TCP, IP, User Datagram Protocol [UDP], SNMP, and others) and other categories, including "system" and "interfaces."

The MIB tree is extensible by virtue of experimental and private branches. Vendors can define their own private branches to include instances of their own products. For example, Cisco's private MIB is represented by the object identifier 1.3.6.1.4.1.9, as shown in Figure 8-5. The OID is the address in the tree to the specific MIB that you are looking for. Follow the numbers in the circles from the top starting with ISO, which equals 1, until you get to where the data that you need is stored.

Figure 8-5 *Basic MIB Structure*

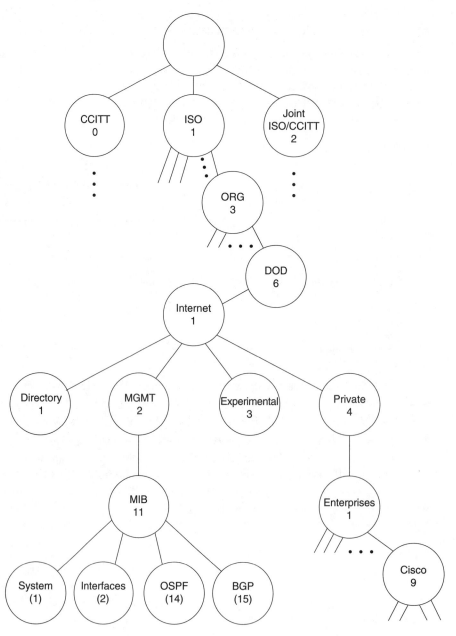

SNMP Operation

The information previously discussed on network management systems detailed how they use SNMP to accomplish their goals. This section discusses in more detail actual SNMP commands, their purpose, and their functionality. SNMP itself is a simple request/response protocol. Network management systems can send multiple requests without receiving a response when using UDP, which is also connectionless. Therefore, data is sent/received with no guarantee that it is delivered to SNMP.

SNMP Operation Definitions

The five most commonly used SNMP operations are as follows:

- **GET**—This command allows the network management system to retrieve an individual nontabled manageable object instance from the agent via SNMP. This operation is further defined in Figure 8-6.

- **GETNEXT**—This command allows the network management system to retrieve the next object instance from a table or list within an agent. In SNMPv1, when an NMS wants to retrieve all elements of a table from an agent, it initiates a **GET** operation, followed by a series of **GETNEXT** operations.

- **GETBULK**—This command is new for SNMPv2 and only works on MIB2 MIBs. The **GETBULK** operation was added to make it easier to acquire large amounts of related information without initiating repeated **GETNEXT** operations. **GETBULK** was designed to virtually eliminate the need for **GETNEXT** operations.

- **SET**—This command allows the network management system to set values in read-writable object instances within an agent.

- **INFORM (also known as Trap)**—This command is used by the agent to asynchronously inform the network management system of some event. The SNMPv2 inform message is designed to replace the SNMPv1 trap message.

As you can see in Figure 8-6, when you place all the network management pieces together, you can see a more coherent picture of how the system operates.

Figure 8-6   *Network Management Overview*

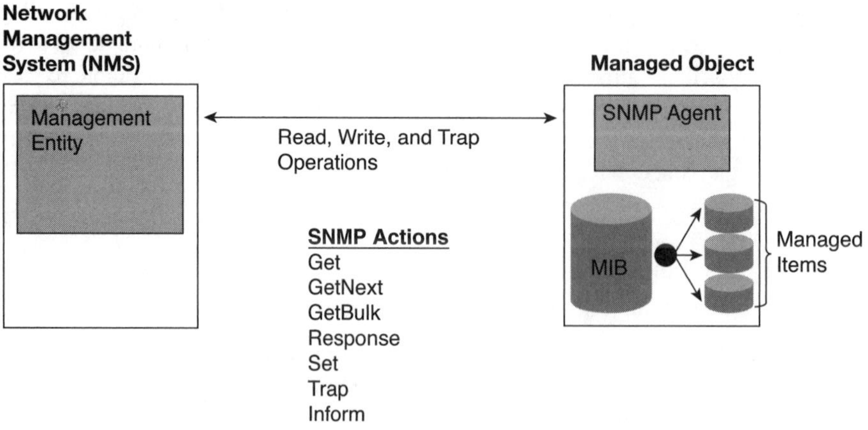

Network Management System (NMS) · Managed Object · Management Entity · SNMP Agent · Read, Write, and Trap Operations · MIB · Managed Items · SNMP Actions · Get · GetNext · GetBulk · Response · Set · Trap · Inform

Network Management System Operation

The flow chart presented in Figure 8-7 enables you to better understand the sequence of events that happens when an NMS requests information through the use of SNMP. This flow of events is presented in a generic format from a high-level perspective. As with any complex network operation, many events also occur that allow the operation to take place.

The sequence of events that occurs during an NMS request can be described more fully as follows:

1   The network manager or engineer decides he needs information from a managed device. He then selects the device and information required within the NMS. This information corresponds to an OID with a MIB as previously discussed, and the device is identified by an IP address.

2   The NMS reads the MIB database to select the correct OID that represents the information requested.

3   The NMS then selects the correct Protocol Data Unit (PDU) format (that is, type of PDU) for the type of data being requested.

4   The NMS then combines the selected MIB OID and local SNMP data (that is, version, community string) into the PDU.

5   The completed PDU is then compiled using Abstract Syntax Notation 1 (ASN.1) and the Basic Encoding Rules (BERs). When completed, the PDU is sent down the UDP/IP stack to the network layer and sent out onto the network for transmission to the managed device.

Figure 8-7 *Network Management System Request Events*

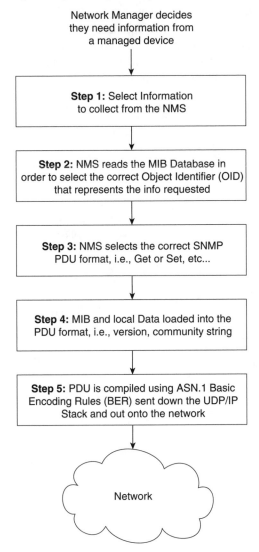

Network Manager decides
they need information from
a managed device

Step 1: Select Information
to collect from the NMS

Step 2: NMS reads the MIB Database in
order to select the correct Object Identifier (OID)
that represents the info requested

Step 3: NMS selects the correct SNMP
PDU format, i.e., Get or Set, etc...

Step 4: MIB and local Data loaded into the
PDU format, i.e., version, community string

Step 5: PDU is compiled using ASN.1 Basic
Encoding Rules (BER) sent down the UDP/IP
Stack and out onto the network

Network

This is only the first part of the process (that is, the request for information); the second part
of the process is where the managed device receives the request. The managed device then
passes the request on to the SNMP agent, which then processes and replies to the request.
This sequence of events is covered in the next section.

Agent Response to NMS Request

The flow chart presented in Figure 8-8 describes the second part of the SNMP operation in which the SNMP request is received by the managed device, which passes it on to the agent who processes and answers the request. This flow of events is presented in a generic format from a high-level perspective. As with any complex network operation, many events also occur that allow the operation to take place.

Figure 8-8   *Agent Response Flow Chart to NMS Request*

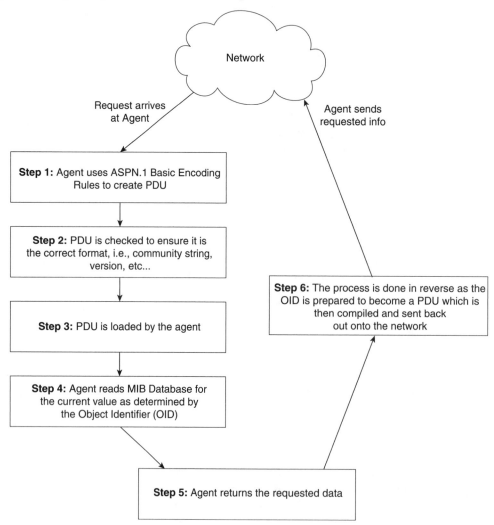

The sequence of events that occurs during an agent response to an NMS request can be more fully describe as follows:

1   The request arrives via the network and is given to the agent. The agent then uses ASN.1 and the BERs to translate them into a locally readable PDU.

2   The PDU is separated into MIB information and SNMP data. The SNMP data is then checked to ensure that it is correct (that is, version and community string). If the SNMP data is correct, the agent proceeds to Step 3; if the SNMP data is not correct, the agent issues an authentication trap that the NMS receives and processes, letting the network manager know an unauthorized security breach has occurred.

3   The agent loads the PDU MIB information and then separates the PDU data field into individual MIB OID requests.

4   The agent processes each MIB OID by reading its database for the current value, as determined by the OID.

5   The agent builds a response that is similar to the process described in the previous section on NMS operation (that is, this process in reverse). The response is built with the values as requested by the NMS and SNMP data.

6   The entire transmission is also done in reverse. The agent compiles the PDU and sends it back down the UDP/IP stack for transmission back out onto the network to be returned to the NMS.

Cisco's MIB Extensions+

With several hundred unique objects, Cisco's private MIB extensions provide network managers with broad, powerful monitoring and control facilities. Cisco's private MIB supports DECnet (including DECnet routing and host tables), XNS, AppleTalk, Banyan VINES, Novell NetWare, and additional system variables that highlight information such as average CPU utilization over selectable intervals. Furthermore, Cisco developers can add private extensions to the MIB as required. This capability gives managers the flexibility to mold Cisco's SNMP products to their own networks, optimizing management capabilities. Figure 8-9 illustrates Cisco's private MIB tree. This figure expands on the lower-right section of the diagram shown in Figure 8-5.

Figure 8-9   *Cisco's Private MIB Structure*

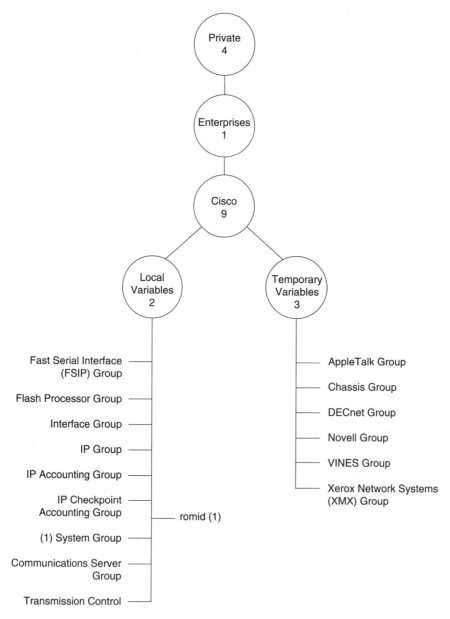

Cisco also supports other MIBs that are relevant to router operation. For example, support for some chassis MIB objects enables users to retrieve information about router chassis and installed cards. Card types, card serial numbers, the number of cards in a particular router, the ROM version of those cards, and many other useful variables can be retrieved. Support for the chassis MIB eases network administration. Those responsible for network maintenance can remotely query Cisco routers to quickly discover a router's hardware configuration, thereby saving time and money. This capability is provided through the use of Cisco's private MIB, as shown in Figure 8-10.

Figure 8-10   *Detailed Cisco Private MIB Hierarchy*

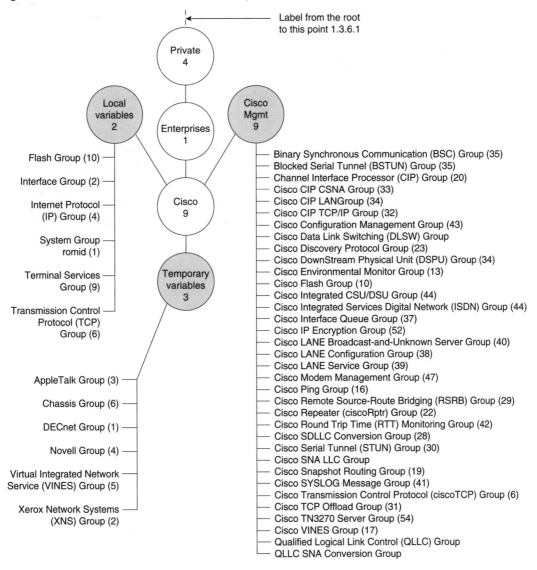

Access Lists for SNMP

Access lists can be used to prevent SNMP-enabled devices from responding to an SNMP request from someone who is not allowed to have it. For example, this feature can be used to prevent other NMSs from altering the configuration of a given router or router group; if they are not permitted in the access list, they are denied. Access lists are extremely useful in complex internetworks and are implemented across the majority of Cisco's supported protocols. This use of access lists is similar to an access class on vty ports in that it does not evaluate *all* traffic (as an interface based access list does) but only is applied to SNMP packets for which the local router is the destination so it is more efficient. Also it works without being tied to a specific interface which could be important if there are multiple paths from the NMS to the managed device.

Multiple Community Strings

For SNMPv1 operation, Cisco permits multiple community strings so that a router can belong to multiple communities. An SNMP community string is simply a password in the sense that if you know the community string, you can access SNMP data.

Furthermore, community strings can be either read-only or read/write. This feature provides further security by restricting the capability to alter the configuration of Cisco devices to those that have the community string assigned the read/write capability.

OSPF MIBs

OSPF has a large selection of MIBs, which provides you with a powerful resource to monitor and configure the protocol. Figure 8-11 details where OSPF is located in the MIB tree and shows some of the areas in which you can find information.

As defined in the following RFCs, the OSPF MIBs have some descriptive names that help you determine what kind of information is included within them:

* RFC 1248
* RFC 1252
* RFC 1253
* RFC 1850

The OSPF MIB as described in RFC 1850 has the following impressive list of characteristics:

* 12 distinct tables
* 110 management variables
* 65 of the management variables are read-only OSPF values
* 45 configurable management variables

Figure 8-11   *OSPF MIB Tree Location*

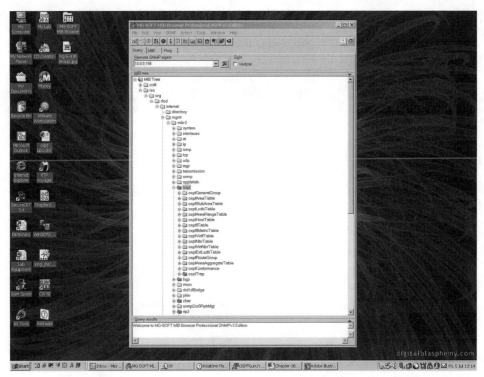

You may be wondering how you can keep track of the 110 management variables for OSPF
(and why you would want to). This is a valid question because the amount of information
made available to you through MIBs is impressive. However, most implementations of
OSPF are not concerned with every management variable. Figure 8-12 shows the more
commonly used variables.

Figure 8-12 *Detailed OSPF MIB Tree*

Figure 8-12 *Detailed OSPF MIB Tree (continued)*

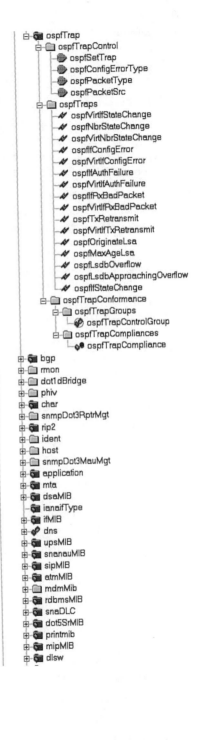

Refer to RFC 1850 for additional information regarding the other tables not commonly used in OSPF implementations.

Network Security

Network security has probably been one of the least considered aspects of network operation and design. As enterprise networks evolve, it has become an increasingly larger concern. Is this concern justified? The answer is a resounding yes—and the concerns are probably late in coming.

The Computer Security Institute conducts an annual Computer Crime and Security Survey. In 2002, the Institute reported that 90% of the companies polled detected computer security breaches within the last 12 months, and 80% acknowledged financial losses due to these breaches.

These are some staggering statistics. For example, most companies do not acknowledge such breaches unless they have to; it makes stockholders and employees nervous. Furthermore, not all attempts were detected, and for 80% of companies to have incurred some financial loss, the breaches were successful!

Financial losses are now being reported in the tens of billions of dollars, which is larger than the gross national product of many nations. When considered this way, you can easily see why people have dedicated their lives to computer theft. Network security must be an integral part of the design of every aspect of your network from the beginning and always.

When most people talk about network security, they mean ensuring that users can only perform tasks they are authorized to do, can only obtain information they are authorized to have, and cannot cause damage to the data, applications, or operating environment of a system.

The word *security* connotes protection against malicious attack by outsiders. Security also involves controlling the effects of errors and equipment failures. Anything that can protect against a deliberate, intelligent, calculated attack would probably prevent random misfortune as well. While many people do have a sort of instinctive reaction that security is oriented to keeping out "the bad guys" from outside, there have been several studies that have identified the greater risk as being inside (and probably more often the result of innocent mistakes than malicious actions).

The question that is applicable to this chapter is "Are security breaches occurring in the wide-area portion of your network as well?"

This is possible and becoming more widely publicized. When this book was going to press, you could not download any versions of Cisco IOS Software without seeing a warning about security issues. Visit the following website to see the extensive list of security issues for Cisco equipment as documented by the Cisco Product Security Incident Response Team advisories:

www.cisco.com/warp/public/707/advisory.html

Every networking equipment manufacturer, network protocol, user, and service provider has security problems. Consider the following two examples.

First, with today's technologies, a cyber-thief could put a PC running sniffer software with a cellular telephone and modem on a circuit. This is easier than you think if you consider the miles of accessible physical cabling (copper, fiber, and so on) that stretch across the United States. However, given the upsurge in wireless technology, access can also be gained through wireless connections.

The second most obvious network protocol example is SNMP. If you had the SNMP community string, every SNMP-manageable device would allow the cyber-thief read/write access. You should deal with a reputable vendor, such as Cisco, that has an open disclosure policy of identified and corrected security breaches so that you can react accordingly. The alternative is to use a vendor that does not share the holes in its equipment. You are only protected until a cyber-thief decides that he wants access.

Because network security is such a broad topic, this chapter does not delve too deeply into any single area. Everyone concerned with this subject must be aware of how security must be stretched across every network.

Assessing the Need for Security

As more users access the Internet, and as companies expand their networks, the challenge to provide security for internal networks becomes increasingly difficult. Companies must determine which areas of their internal networks they must protect, learn how to restrict user access to these areas, and determine which types of network services they should filter to prevent potential security breaches.

It should now be obvious that security must be a consideration at all levels of your network. It cannot be stressed enough that part of every network design should consider the security of the network; considering security after the fact is often too late. Complacency is also something to avoid when considering security. The rapidly advancing sophistication of technology means that your security measures are limited in the length of time that they are effective. This means that you must always be watching your security measures to ensure that they are doing their job.

Golden Rules for Designing a Secure Network

Security measures keep people honest in the same way that locks do. Cyber-thieves by nature go after the least-defended part of a network. Consider this analogy. In a neighborhood where 25 percent of the homes have home security systems, thieves target the least-defended homes (those without security systems) first. This analogy fits well with networking. When a hacker is doing reconnaissance (for example, port scanning, nmap, and so on) against potential targets, a percentage of these hackers are going to go after the easy-to-target networks. Another small percentage has an "issue" with a potential target and goes after that target regardless of the perceived issue.

Because hackers often have issues that drive their attacks, people need to understand that these issues are usually a result of strong beliefs and feelings, for example, differing political beliefs, differing religious ideologies, differing social beliefs, the desire for attention, the desire for achievement, and financial gain. To back this up, consider the following reports, all within a week of each other in June 2002:

PRO-ISLAMIC GROUPS ENGAGE IN 'HACKTIVISM'

UK security firm mi2g says there's mounting evidence that individual hacker groups with a pro-Islamic agenda are working together to disrupt Web sites in India, Israel and other target countries. (BBC News 19 Jun 2002)

news.bbc.co.uk/hi/english/sci/tech/newsid_2052000/2052320.stm

LEGISLATION WOULD SANCTION STUDIO HACK ATTACKS

Included in the legislation is that a copyright holder would be allowed to take certain actions to protect on-line music. Specifically they are: interdiction, in which the copyright holder swamps a P2P file server with false requests so that downloads can't get through; redirection, in which would-be file swappers are pointed to a site that doesn't contain the files they're seeking; and spoofing, in which a corrupt or otherwise undesirable file masquerades as the song or movie file being sought by a file swapper. File-swapping companies criticized the bill, saying it opens the door for copyright holders to conduct "cyber warfare" against consumers. (CNet News.com 25 Jun 2002)

news.com.com/2100-1023-939333.html?tag=fd_top

RUSSIAN MOB TARGETS SOME U.S. COLLEGE COMPUTER SYSTEMS

A Russian-born man at Pasadena City College has been arrested as he tried to install keystroke-recording software to capture student credit card information, and Arizona State University officials found that a program had been surreptitiously installed to steal student credit card numbers, passwords, and e-mail. Linking these and other activities to Russian organized crime, the Secret Service and the Education Department have joined in issuing a general alert to American college computer centers. (AP/USA Today 26 Jun 2002)

www.usatoday.com/life/cyber/tech/2002/06/26/college-computers.htm

These examples demonstrate that literally everyday, there are reports of people and groups conducting attacks, and the reasons for the attacks run the entire range of human emotions. Also consider that many other attacks occur that are never documented. This section provides specific ideals to consider to improve the security of your network, whether you already have network security in place or you are designing a new network.

Document Your Security Plan

This does not mean that you should write down all your network passwords! Instead, as you go through the process of identifying and designing your network security needs and actions, you should document your findings and the resulting security actions. Having a written "living" security document is vital to proper implementation of your overall network security strategy. This also helps those that succeed you understand why the network security was implemented and designed in such a way. It can also be a learning tool for future network engineers. This document should not be publicly accessible because of its sensitive nature.

This document is also the basis of your security policy. Assume that you do not have a security policy or that you do not believe in using one. You need to start one! These policies are crucial to the protection of your network, your company, and yourself. This document defines the who, what, where, when, why, and how of security for your network. From this document, you have a clear directive and support of corporate management to protect your network.

Security policies and baseline security standards underpin the security of your information and your organization. However, having a security policy document in itself is not enough. The contents must be deployed and implemented to be effective. This is often easier said than done, and the following online resources can help you:

www.sans.org/newlook/resources/policies/policies.htm
www.information-security-policies-and-standards.com/
www.information-security-policies.com/

Know Your Enemy

Know who might want to cause harm to your network and, if possible, know why! This statement refers specifically to cyber-thieves, hackers, crackers, and script kiddies. They all have the same intentions against your network; they are either attackers or intruders and must be defended against. Consider who might want to circumvent your security measures, and identify their motivations to give you an edge. Determine what they might want to do and the damage that they could cause to your network. Once you understand these things, you know your enemy.

Just as important as knowing your enemy is knowing the threats that they can bring against you as well as the targets they would go after.

Security measures can never make it impossible for a trusted user to perform unauthorized tasks with a computer system. These measures can only make performing unauthorized tasks harder. The goal is to make sure that the network security controls are beyond the attacker's ability or motivation. In simpler terms, you want to make the hacker go down the street to the house that does not have a security system, a dog, or lights on in the evening and who does not participate in the neighborhood watch.

Count the Cost

Security measures usually reduce convenience, especially for sophisticated users. Security can delay work and create expensive administrative and educational overhead. Security can use significant computing resources and require dedicated hardware. Just as with anything in life, nothing that is worth having is free; you must work for the results that you want to receive and understand that you must pay a price for security in convenience. The trick is to attain effective security without placing excessive restrictions on your users. There are costs to implementing security and it is crucial that we recognized them. For example there are direct hard dollar costs such as hardware and then there are indirect costs such as training and inconvenience when using the network, perhaps through several levels of security.

When designing your security measures, understand their costs and weigh those costs against the potential benefits. To do that, you must understand the costs of the measures themselves and the likelihood of security breaches. If you incur security costs that are out of proportion to the actual dangers, you have done yourself a disservice. For example, few organizations can justify having the extreme security measures found within and protecting the government and large financial networks. Yes, they are effective, but at what cost?

Identify Your Assumptions

Every security system has underlying assumptions. For example, you might assume that your network has not been compromised, that attackers know less than you do, that hackers are using standard software, or that a locked room is safe. All of these assumptions are most likely incorrect and could cause holes in your security policy. Be sure to examine and justify your assumptions. Any hidden assumption is a potential security hole. Consider the assumptions made in the following example, where a major telecommunications firm said that its network had never been compromised. Then along came Kevin Mitnick with proof that he had access to every telephone switch in Las Vegas!

MITNICK TESTIFIES AGAINST SPRINT IN VICE HACK CASE

The ex-hacker details his past control of Las Vegas' telecom network, and raids his old storage locker to produce the evidence.

online.securityfocus.com/news/497

A nice rule of thumb is to be painfully honest concerning your network security require-ments. Remember, when assumptions are incomplete or not duly considered, they can cause disastrous consequences. Sometimes when you are identifying your assumptions, you might find an area of concern within your network that has nothing to do with security, so this is truly a double-edged sword. Never trust an assumption; test it repeatedly as you know the hackers will.

Control and Limit Your Secrets

Most security is based on information that is required to be secret. Passwords, SSH or PGP encryption keys, and SNMP community strings, for example, should be kept secret. Too often, though, the secrets are not all that secret. The most important part of keeping secrets is in knowing the areas that you need to protect through secrecy.

For example, what knowledge would enable someone to circumvent your system? You should jealously guard that knowledge and assume that your adversaries know everything else. The more secrets that you have, the harder it is to keep them all. Security systems should be designed so that only a limited number of secrets need to be kept.

Remember Human Factors

Many security procedures fail because their designers do not consider how users are going to react to them. For example, because they can be difficult to remember, automatically generated "nonsense" passwords are often found written on the undersides of keyboards. For convenience, a secure door that leads to the system's only tape drive is sometimes propped open. For expediency, unauthorized modems are often connected to a PC, which is in turn connected to the corporate network to avoid onerous dial-in security measures.

If your security measures interfere too much with the essential use of the system or network, those measures are resisted and perhaps circumvented by resourceful users. To get compliance, you must make sure that users can get their work done, and you must sell your security measures to users. Users must understand and accept the need for security while acknowledging that some inconvenience results in the benefit of all. Communication with users is essential because if users understand the business reasons behind your security measures, they are more open to accepting them. If your users understand security issues, and if they understand the reasons for your security measures, they are less likely to make an intruder's job easier.

Any user can compromise system security to some degree. Simply calling legitimate users on the telephone, claiming to be a system administrator, can often trick them into revealing passwords. No matter how hard you try, some users still try to get around your security. These are the users you need to watch!

At a minimum, users should be taught never to release passwords or other secrets over unsecured telephone lines (especially cellular telephones) or through e-mail. Users should be wary of questions asked by people who call them on the telephone.

Some companies have implemented formalized network security training for their employees. These employees are not allowed access to the corporate network or Internet until they have completed a formal security-training program. This is helpful in raising awareness in a user community, and the training should be reinforced with a written security policy for your organization that is accessible to every user. One last point to make is that you should never violate your own security procedures, no matter how tempting it is to do so!

Know Your Weaknesses

Every security system has vulnerabilities, and identifying them is no place for egos but rather honesty and directness. It is sometimes helpful to have another set of eyes assist you in reviewing the network for weaknesses. This review should be done regularly.

You should be able to understand your system's weak points and know how they could be exploited. You should also know the areas that present the largest danger and prevent access to these areas immediately. Understanding the weak points in your network is the first step toward turning them into secure areas.

Limit the Scope of Access

You should create appropriate barriers inside your network so that if intruders access one part of the network, they do not automatically have access to the rest of the network.

As with many things, the security of a network is only as good as the weakest security level of any single device in the system. Having a layered approach to security can slow an intruder and allow detection of him or her. Having a big lock is good, but if that lock is your only line of defense, you might want to consider adding motion sensors, a dog, outside lights, a home security system, and nosy neighbors! This is a simplistic analogy, but it is always harder to be a criminal when many barriers must be overcome.

Understand Your Environment

Understanding how your system normally functions, knowing what is expected and what is unexpected, and being familiar with how devices are usually used can help you detect security problems. Noticing unusual events can help you catch intruders before they can damage the system. Auditing tools can help you detect those unusual events.

Auditing tools are useful, but you must also ensure that there are methods by which you can receive alarms when there is an attempt to violate or bypass your security measures. It is better to know it is happening before you lose something than to have to go back and audit the crime; it's an ounce of prevention!

Limit Your Trust

You should know exactly which software or hardware you rely on, and your security system should not have to rely on the assumption that all software is bug-free. Learn from history by not reliving it, and remember to question everything! In the security arena, it is not wise to trust every source of data that is coming into your network.

Remember Physical Security

Physical access to a workstation, server, switch, or router usually gives a sufficiently sophisticated user total control over that device through the console port. Physical access to a network link usually enables a person to tap that link, jam it, or inject traffic into it. It makes no sense to install complicated software security measures when access to the hardware is not controlled.

Security Is Pervasive

Almost any change you make in your system can have security effects. This is especially true when new services are created. Network engineers, system administrators, programmers, and users should consider the security implications of every change they make. Understanding the security implications of a change is something that takes practice. It requires lateral thinking and a willingness to explore every way in which a service could potentially be manipulated. Intelligent changes are good and can be judged accordingly; however, quick or ill-considered changes can often result in severe security problems.

Additional Resources on Network Security

Now that you know that security should be a serious part of your network at all levels, and you know some of the golden rules of designing a secure network, you can visit the following websites for additional information on cyber-thieves:

> www.iss.net
> www.sans.org/
> www.cert.org/
> www.itprc.com/security.htm

This section covered many of the questions that you should be asking yourself when considering how to secure your network.

Securing Your OSPF Network

There are many ways to secure your network. The sections that follow discuss the easiest and most basic ways to do this with OSPF. Controlling access to network equipment is the simplest and perhaps the most important. A hacker can inflict substantial damage to your network if he gains access to your routers or switches. There are many levels of security, although you should also understand how to encrypt data and use OSPF authentication within your network. These concepts are important to know for a variety of reasons: for securing your network, for ensuring valid routing, and when you are interested in pursuing a certification, because these tasks are testable!

OSPF and Network Devices

A variety of discussions and network design considerations usually need to be addressed when dealing with network security issues—the use of OSPF or more accurately the *use of OSPF* with security appliances such as Firewalls or VPN Concentrators. Some of the more commonly asked questions with regards to these design considerations are:

> "I think I need to run OSPF or a dynamic protocol on or in my DMZ for my Firewall?"
> "Should my firewall run OSPF natively or should it be tunneled through the firewall?"

Of course these are weighty questions that are not easily answered as every network will have its own unique considerations and needs to effectively meet the business requires behind it. In general there are a few items that we can discuss, which every network will have to ensure are met.

- The symmetry of the routing within the network must be preserved while monitoring the *state* caching on a firewall
- Routing integrity must be maintained
- Ensure erroneous black holing of traffic does occur

I believe that network devices should be allowed to do what they do best. Thus firewalls should be responsible for filtering traffic and routers should route. I understand that is not always easily which is why we discussed ways to design an effective OSPF network design in Chapter 5, "Routing Concepts and Configuration."

This means that your network should not run routing protocols through a firewall if at all possible. Should you have to do this try to schedule a network design meeting very soon and be cautious!

Cisco IOS Password Encryption

A non-Cisco source has released a new program to decrypt user passwords (and other passwords) in Cisco configuration files. The program does not decrypt passwords that are set with the **enable secret** command. Why not? Because MD5 triple DES (3DES) is used. Triple DES is too hard to crack; DES is not. A 56-bit key is only used for the enable password if the **service encryption** command is enabled globally.

The unexpected concern that this program has caused among Cisco customers indicates that many of them are relying on Cisco password encryption for more security than it was designed to provide. The sections that follow explain the security model behind Cisco password encryption and the security limitations of that encryption.

Network Impact: User Passwords (vty and Enable)

User passwords and most other passwords (not **enable secret**–encrypted commands) in Cisco IOS Software configuration files are encrypted using a scheme that is weak by modern cryptographic standards.

Although Cisco does not distribute a decryption program, at least two different decryption programs for Cisco IOS Software passwords are available to the public on the Internet. The first public release of such a program (to Cisco's knowledge) was in early 1995. Any amateur cryptographer would be expected to be able to create a new program with only a few hours of work.

The scheme used by Cisco IOS Software for user passwords was never intended to resist a determined, intelligent attack; it was designed to avoid casual "over-the-shoulder" password theft. The threat model was someone reading a password from an administrator's screen or from a printed configuration. The scheme was never supposed to protect against someone conducting a determined analysis of the configuration file. Cisco implemented the **service password-encryption** command to deal with this "casual" threat.

Because of the weak encryption algorithm, it has always been Cisco's position that customers should treat any configuration file containing passwords as sensitive information, the same way they would treat a clear-text list of passwords.

Enable Secret Passwords

The **enable secret**–encrypted passwords are hashed (that is, encrypted) using the MD5 algorithm. As far as anyone at Cisco knows, it is impossible to recover an enable secret password based on the contents of a configuration file (other than by obvious dictionary attacks), which would allow the password to be guessed if you were to use a word and not a random string of different characters. Please note that impossible means that many people cannot gather the resources needed to crack MD5, as you all know there is no algorithm that cannot be cracked given sufficient time and resources.

This applies only to passwords that are set with **enable secret**, not to passwords set with **enable password**. Indeed, the strength of the encryption used is the only significant difference between the two commands. Whenever possible, use **enable secret**, which is far more secure and better protects your network devices.

Other Passwords

Almost all passwords and other authentication strings in Cisco IOS Software configuration files are encrypted using the weak, reversible scheme used for user passwords. To determine which scheme has been used to encrypt a specific password, check the digit preceding the encrypted string in the configuration file. If that digit is a 7, the password has been encrypted using the weak algorithm. If the digit is a 5, the password has been hashed using the stronger MD5 algorithm. For example, in the following configuration, the **enable secret**–encrypted password has been hashed with MD5:

```
enable secret 5 $1$iUjJ$cDZ03KKGh7mHfX2RSbDqP
```

However, in the following command, the password has been encrypted using the weak, reversible algorithm and is easily decrypted using one of the many free and publicly available applications available, as shown in Figure 8-13:

username cisco password 7 0822455D0A16

Figure 8-13 *Password Decryption*

Backup Configuration Files   If a router regularly downloads configuration files from or to a Trivial File Transfer Protocol (TFTP) server, anyone with access to the server can modify the router configuration files that are stored on the server.

This can be a serious security breach if this server is not also protected in your security plan. In today's enterprise networks, you must at least back up your router configuration files. Therefore, because this function is so essential to the safe and continued operation of a network, it must also be protected.

Using Banners to Set Up Unauthorized Use Notifications   It is also wise to use the **motd banner** EXEC global configuration command to provide messages and unauthorized use notifications, which are displayed on all new connections. For example, on any network equipment, you could enter the following message:

```
### #    # ######  #####  ###
 # ##   # #     # #     #  # #
 # # #  # #       # #        #
 #  # # # ######  #  ####    #
 #  # ### # #    #  #      # #
 #  #  ## #  #   # #       # #
### #    # #    #  #####  ###

      Authorized Access Only!

This system is owned and operated by the
International Network Resource Group Inc.

Unauthorized use will be prosecuted, you
are advised to disconnect IMMEDIATELY if
you are not an authorized user! Access to
this device and any attempts are logged
for misuse and reporting. For assistance
contact: noc@inrgi.net
```

A message-of-the-day banner like this in your network equipment is effective. It covers all the possible consequences and states that consequences are based on users' actions.

Increasing SNMP Security

In the networking arena, it is generally understood that SNMP is not as secure as it can be. However, SNMP is widely used throughout most networks as a management and trending tool. In networks where security is extremely important, you should implement an access list on SNMP to limit who can access the device in question via SNMP. This is considered a best practice and can be accomplished as shown in the example that follows.

This example permits the host IP addresses of 10.1.3.5 and 10.5.2.53 to access SNMP on the device; these happen to be our Network Management servers. You do this by adding the access list number to the **snmp-server community** command.

```
access-list 1 permit 10.1.3.5
access-list 1 permit 10.5.2.53
snmp-server community cisco 1
```

On Cisco routers, all other devices in the network that try to contact the router with this configuration are denied due to the implicit deny all at the end of every access list.

SNMP Access

SNMP is a method you can use to access your network equipment. With SNMP, you can gather statistics or configure the router. In fact, you could even configure the router to start an OSPF routing process! SNMP is also useful in helping you to gather statistics with **GETREQUEST** and **GETNEXTREQUEST** messages and to configure routers with

SETREQUEST messages. Each of these SNMP messages has a community string. This string is a clear-text password that is sent in every packet between a management station and the router (which contains an SNMP agent). The SNMP community string is used to authenticate messages that are sent between the manager and agent. Only when the manager sends a message with the correct community string does the agent respond.

The SNMP agent on the router allows you to configure different community strings for read-only and read-write access. You configure community strings on the router via the following configuration command:

```
snmp-server community <string> [RO | RW] [access-list]
```

Unfortunately, SNMP community strings are sent on the network in clear-text ASCII. Therefore, anyone with the ability to capture a packet on the network can discover the community string. This can allow unauthorized users to query or modify routers via SNMP. For this reason, using the **no snmp-server trap-authentication** command can prevent intruders from using trap messages (sent between SNMP managers and agents) to discover community strings.

The Internet community, recognizing this problem, greatly enhanced the security of SNMP version 2 (SNMPv2), as described in RFC 1446. SNMPv2 uses the MD5 algorithm to authenticate communications between an SNMP server and agent. SNMP verifies the integrity of the communications, authenticates the origin, and checks for timeliness when communication is protected by an MD5 hash. Furthermore, SNMPv2 can use the Data Encryption Standard (DES) for encrypting information. However, because that aspect of SNMPv2 is not a standard, it was never implemented.

Network Data Encryption

To safeguard your network data, Cisco provides network data encryption and route authentication services in Cisco IOS Software. This section briefly discusses how route authentication in OSPF is done and how it can benefit your network.

Network data encryption is provided at the IP packet level. IP packet encryption prevents eavesdroppers from reading the data that is being transmitted. When IP packet encryption is used, IP packets can be seen during transmission, but the IP packet contents (payload) cannot be read. Specifically, the IP header and upper-layer protocol (TCP or UDP) headers are not encrypted, but all payload data within the TCP or UDP packet is encrypted and therefore is not readable during transmission.

The actual encryption and decryption of IP packets occurs only at routers that you configure for network data Intermediate routers do not participate in encryption/decryption.

Typically, when an IP packet is initially generated at a host, it is unencrypted (cleartext). This occurs on a secured (internal) portion of your network. Then when the transmitted IP packet passes through an encrypting router, the router determines if the packet should be encrypted. If the packet is encrypted, the encrypted packet travels through the unsecured network portion (usually an external network such as the Internet) until it reaches the remote peer-encrypting router. At this point, the encrypted IP packet is decrypted and forwarded to the destination host as cleartext. Further discussion on the proper techniques and process involved in deploying data encryption in your network is beyond the scope of this book.

NOTE   By requiring the routers to encrypt data, you are adding overhead to the routers' processing load. You should first test this to ensure that the routers in your network can handle the added load.

Router authentication enables peer-encrypting routers to positively identify the source of incoming encrypted data. This means that attackers cannot forge transmitted data or tamper with transmitted data without detection. Router authentication occurs between peer routers each time a new encrypted session is established. An encrypted session is established each time an encrypting router receives an IP packet that should be encrypted (unless an encrypted session is already occurring at that time).

TIP   Encryption is applied to your data only after it leaves the router because that is the device that applies the encryption. This is important because the data travels from the host to the router in an unsecured format. Of course the depends rule hits again here as it certainly is possible in today's processing environment that the host will do its own encryption.

To provide IP packet encryption with router authentication, Cisco implements the following standards: the Digital Signature Standard (DSS), the Diffie-Hellman (DH) public key algorithm, and the DES. DSS is used in router authentication. The DH algorithm and DES are used to initiate and conduct encrypted communication sessions between participating routers.

OSPF Authentication

OSPF incorporates a minimal amount of security within its design. That sounds contradictory. How can a protocol be designed with security, yet be minimal? OSPF is not responsible for transmitting data, OSPF is responsible for transmitting routing updates and building a routing table. The authentication capacity provided is sufficient to protect its design goals. When OSPF was designed, the necessary fields required for security were included in the design of OSPF's packets. Nevertheless, the security that is included within OSPF only protects its link-state avertisements (LSAs), thus protecting and maintaining the integrity of your network's routing tables, but nothing else.

OSPF security is minimal. It does not protect the data flowing across the network but only protects how OSPF routers (that is, the LSAs) know to route it. This security was designed to protect only the integrity of the routing information within an OSPF routing domain. You can prevent any OSPF router from receiving fraudulent route updates by configuring this type of security, known as *neighbor router authentication*. The following characteristics define how OSPF authentication operates:

- OSPF authentication is activated for an entire area.

- The authentication key must match for routers on the same link between neighbors.

This section describes OSPF authentication as part of a total security plan and explains what neighbor router authentication is, how it works, and why you should use it to increase your overall network security. Several topics are important regarding this issue:

- Benefits of neighbor authentication

- Conditions for deploying OSPF neighbor authentication

- How neighbor authentication works

- Configuring neighbor authentication

You can deploy this type of security in several different ways within your OSPF network. The first way is by assigning the same OSPF authentication key throughout the entire OSPF area. The second is to assign a different key for every link within the network. Regardless of which technique you decide to use, the passwords used between neighboring routers must match.

NOTE This section refers to neighbor router authentication as *neighbor authentication*. Neighbor router authentication is also sometimes called *route authentication*.

Benefits of OSPF Neighbor Authentication

When configured, neighbor authentication occurs whenever routing updates are exchanged between neighboring OSPF routers within the OSPF area that has authentication activated. This authentication ensures that a router receives reliable routing information from a trusted source (that is, an OSPF neighbor).

Without OSPF authentication, unauthorized or deliberately malicious routing updates could compromise the integrity of your network traffic. A security compromise could occur if an unfriendly party diverts or analyzes your network traffic. The compromising might not be the result of malicious action—a clueless desktop administrator who installs a server running gateD and defines a local default route will also compromise the integrity of your routing table but it was not intentional.

For example, an unauthorized or compromised device could send a fictitious routing update to convince your router to send traffic to an incorrect destination. This diverted traffic could be analyzed to learn confidential information of your organization, or it could merely be used to disrupt your organization's ability to effectively communicate using the network. OSPF authentication prevents any such fraudulent route updates from being received by your router.

When to Deploy OSPF Neighbor Authentication

You should consider configuring a router for OSPF authentication if that router meets any or all of the following conditions:

- If the router might receive a false route update.
- If the router were to receive a false route update, your network might be compromised.
- You deem it necessary as part of your network security plan.

Remember that if you configure a router for OSPF authentication, you also need to configure the neighbor router for authentication as well *and* when OSPF authentication is activated for the entire OSPF area!

How OSPF Authentication Works

When OSPF authentication has been configured on a router, the router authenticates the source of each routing update packet that it receives. This is accomplished by the exchange of an authenticating key (sometimes referred to as a password) that is known to both the sending and the receiving router. The following types of OSPF neighbor authentication are used:

- Plaintext authentication
- Message Digest Algorithm Version 5 (MD5) authentication

Both forms work in essentially the same way, with the exception that MD5 sends a "message digest" instead of the authenticating key itself. The message digest is created using the key and a message, but the key itself is not sent, preventing it from being read while it is being transmitted. Plaintext authentication sends the authenticating key itself over the wire.

NOTE	Plaintext authentication is not recommended for use as part of your security strategy against malicious attacks. The primary use of plaintext authentication is to avoid accidental changes to the routing infrastructure. Using MD5 authentication, however, is a recommended security practice. I think there are two kinds of threats we might want to protect against: the unintentional (clueless) mistake; and the intentional (malicious) attack. If we decide that we need to protect against the malicious attack and MD5 is the recommended approach. But if we need protection from the unintentional action then we do not need the overhead of calculating the hash for every routing protocol packet and plaintext authentication will provide sufficient protection.

As with all keys, passwords, and other security secrets, it is imperative that you closely guard the authenticating keys used in neighbor authentication. The security benefits of this feature rely on your keeping all authenticating keys confident. Also, when performing router management tasks via SNMP, do not ignore the risk that is associated with sending keys using nonencrypted SNMP.

Plaintext Authentication

Each participating neighbor router must share an authenticating key. This key is specified at each router during configuration. Multiple keys can be specified with OSPF. For example, you can have a different key for each WAN interface on a router running OSPF. The caveat is that the neighbor router off each interface must have a matching key configured on the receiving interface, as shown in Figure 8-14.

Figure 8-14 *OSPF Plaintext Authentication*

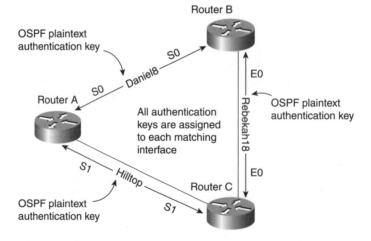

In general, when a routing update is sent, the following authentication sequence occurs:

1   A router sends a routing update with a plaintext authentication key (that is, password) within an LSA.

2   The receiving (neighbor) router checks the received authentication key against the same key stored in its own memory.

3   If the two keys match, the receiving router accepts the routing update packet. If the two keys do not match, the routing update packet is rejected.

MD5 Authentication

MD5 authentication works similarly to plaintext authentication, except that the key is never sent over the wire. Instead, the router uses the MD5 algorithm to produce a message digest of the key (also called a *hash*). The message digest is then sent instead of the key itself. This ensures that no one can eavesdrop and learn keys during transmission.

One difference between plaintext and MD5 authentication is that MD5 does support defining more than one key per interface (and uses the key number to differentiate the keys). One implication of potentially having more than one key defined is that key management and especially changing keys can be more graceful with MD5 (define a new key on one router (they become out-of sync but continue using the old key); define the new key on the other router (they become in-sync and use the new key); remove the old key from both routers. In contrast with plaintext when you define a new key on one router they become out-of-sync and terminate the neighbor relationship until the new key is defined on the second router.

Configuring OSPF Authentication in an Area

Review for a moment why you would want to configure OSPF authentication. You want to protect and preserve the routing updates that flow between our routers, but why? Someone might spoof routing updates, which leads you to the conclusion that if someone could gain access to spoof your routing updates, protecting him/her with a plain text password is useless. A nice side benefit of this configuring section is that if you understand MD5 you should have no difficulty with plaintext which is less complex.

No discussion or demonstration of configuring plain text authentication is presented here, because there is no good reason to use it. MD5 is the only way to go! In the example that follows, the network is configured as shown in the "Network Management" section of this chapter. Review this network, and concentrate on the link between routers Dozer and Oracle because that is where you are going to first configure OSPF MD5 authentication.

Figure 8-15 *OSPF Authentication*

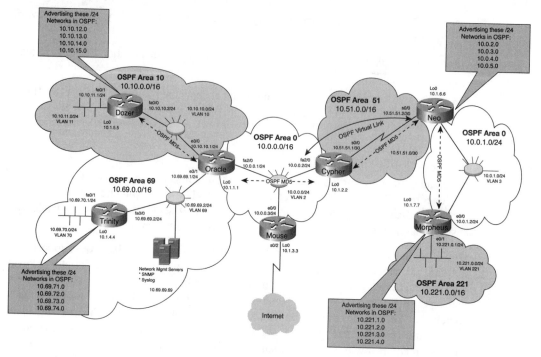

The first step is to decide on a password which will need to be configured on both routers. You will configure the password in both places because the password is a *shared secret* and is used to generate the MD5, resulting in it never being sent across the network. For a book about OSPF there can only be one password to start out with, OSPF-rocks! Now that you have that part worked out, it's configuration time.

Before

In Example 8-1, you activate OSPF MD5 authentication in area 10 between routers Dozer and Oracle starting from having a functional OSPF network without authentication.

Example 8-1 *Activating OSPF MD5 Authentication in Area 10 Between Dozer and Oracle*

```
!
interface FastEthernet0/0
 description VLAN 10 TO ORACLE
 ip address 10.10.10.2 255.255.255.0
 no ip directed-broadcast
!


!
router ospf 100
 network 10.10.0.0 0.0.255.255 area 10
!
```

The OSPF configuration was unremarkable, and OSPF is operating as you would expect as well, with router Dozer having all the routes in the network and one OSPF neighbor, router Oracle. Example 8-2 shows the IP routing table for router Dozer.

Example 8-2   *Dozer's IP Routing Table*

```
Dozer#show ip route
Codes: C - connected, S - static, I - IGRP, R - RIP, M - mobile, B - BGP
       D - EIGRP, EX - EIGRP external, O - OSPF, IA - OSPF inter area
       N1 - OSPF NSSA external type 1, N2 - OSPF NSSA external type 2
       E1 - OSPF external type 1, E2 - OSPF external type 2, E - EGP
       i - IS-IS, L1 - IS-IS level-1, L2 - IS-IS level-2, * - candidate default
       U - per-user static route, o - ODR
       T - traffic engineered route

Gateway of last resort is not set

     10.0.0.0/8 is variably subnetted, 25 subnets, 2 masks
O IA    10.69.74.0/24 [110/12] via 10.10.10.1, FastEthernet0/0
O IA    10.69.73.0/24 [110/12] via 10.10.10.1, FastEthernet0/0
O IA    10.69.72.0/24 [110/12] via 10.10.10.1, FastEthernet0/0
O IA    10.0.2.0/24 [110/51] via 10.10.10.1, FastEthernet0/0
O IA    10.69.71.0/24 [110/12] via 10.10.10.1, FastEthernet0/0
O IA    10.0.3.0/24 [110/51] via 10.10.10.1, FastEthernet0/0
O IA    10.69.70.0/24 [110/12] via 10.10.10.1, FastEthernet0/0
O IA    10.51.51.0/30 [110/50] via 10.10.10.1, FastEthernet0/0
O IA    10.69.69.0/24 [110/11] via 10.10.10.1, FastEthernet0/0
O IA    10.0.0.0/24 [110/2] via 10.10.10.1, FastEthernet0/0
C       10.10.10.0/24 is directly connected, FastEthernet0/0
O IA    10.0.1.0/24 [110/51] via 10.10.10.1, FastEthernet0/0
C       10.10.11.0/24 is directly connected, FastEthernet0/1
C       10.10.12.0/24 is directly connected, Loopback2
C       10.10.13.0/24 is directly connected, Loopback3
O IA    10.0.4.0/24 [110/51] via 10.10.10.1, FastEthernet0/0
C       10.10.14.0/24 is directly connected, Loopback4
C       10.1.5.0/24 is directly connected, Loopback0
O IA    10.0.5.0/24 [110/51] via 10.10.10.1, FastEthernet0/0
C       10.10.15.0/24 is directly connected, Loopback5
O IA    10.221.4.0/24 [110/52] via 10.10.10.1, FastEthernet0/0
O IA    10.221.3.0/24 [110/52] via 10.10.10.1, FastEthernet0/0
O IA    10.221.2.0/24 [110/52] via 10.10.10.1, FastEthernet0/0
O IA    10.221.1.0/24 [110/52] via 10.10.10.1, FastEthernet0/0
O IA    10.221.0.0/24 [110/61] via 10.10.10.1, FastEthernet0/0
O E2 192.168.254.0/24 [110/20] via 10.10.10.1, FastEthernet0/0
Dozer#
Dozer#show ip ospf neighbor

Neighbor ID     Pri   State      Dead Time   Address     Interface
10.1.1.1          1   FULL/BDR   00:00:31    10.10.10.1  FastEthernet0/0
Dozer#
```

During

Configuring OSPF authentication is a two-step process. You must activate authentication for the entire OSPF area and set the password *per interface*, as shown in Example 8-3.

Example 8-3 *Configuring OSPF Authentication on Dozer*

```
Dozer#conf t
Enter configuration commands, one per line.  End with CNTL/Z.
Dozer(config)#router ospf 100
Dozer(config-router)#area 10 authentication message-digest
Dozer(config-router)#exit
Dozer(config)#
Dozer(config)#int fa0/0
Dozer(config-if)#ip ospf message-digest-key ?
  <1-255>  Key ID

Dozer(config-if)#ip ospf message-digest-key 1 ?
  md5  Use MD5 algorithm

Dozer(config-if)#ip ospf message-digest-key 1 md5 OSPF-rocks
Dozer(config-if)#^Z
Dozer#
```

After

You are not done yet. Router Oracle needs to be configured identically as well because until you do so, router Dozer is isolated from the network. Dozer wants to speak OSPF with Oracle using MD5 encryption, but Oracle does not yet understand that MD5 is being spoken, so no routes and no neighbors appear. Using **debug** when configuring authentication is also insightful. Example 8-4 shows how no neighbors are found and presents the usefulness of **debug**.

Example 8-4 *Debugging OSPF Authentication*

```
Dozer#show ip ospf neighbor

Dozer#show ip route
Codes: C - connected, S - static, I - IGRP, R - RIP, M - mobile, B - BGP
       D - EIGRP, EX - EIGRP external, O - OSPF, IA - OSPF inter area
       N1 - OSPF NSSA external type 1, N2 - OSPF NSSA external type 2
       E1 - OSPF external type 1, E2 - OSPF external type 2, E - EGP
       i - IS-IS, L1 - IS-IS level-1, L2 - IS-IS level-2, * - candidate default
       U - per-user static route, o - ODR
       T - traffic engineered route

Gateway of last resort is not set

     10.0.0.0/24 is subnetted, 7 subnets
C       10.10.10.0 is directly connected, FastEthernet0/0
C       10.10.11.0 is directly connected, FastEthernet0/1
C       10.10.12.0 is directly connected, Loopback2
C       10.10.13.0 is directly connected, Loopback3
C       10.10.14.0 is directly connected, Loopback4
C       10.1.5.0 is directly connected, Loopback0
```

Example 8-4   *Debugging OSPF Authentication (Continued)*

```
C        10.10.15.0 is directly connected, Loopback5
Dozer#debug ip ospf adj
OSPF adjacency events debugging is on
Dozer#
*Mar  1 08:41:25.883 GMT: OSPF: Rcv pkt from 10.10.10.1, FastEthernet0/0 : Mismatch
Authentication type. Input packet specified type 0, we use type 2
Dozer#
*Mar  1 08:41:27.447 GMT: OSPF: Send with youngest Key 1
*Mar  1 08:41:27.459 GMT: OSPF: Send with youngest Key 0
Dozer#
*Mar  1 08:41:35.887 GMT: OSPF: Rcv pkt from 10.10.10.1, FastEthernet0/0 : Mismatch
Authentication type. Input packet specified type 0, we use type 2
Dozer#
```

The debug messages here are absolutely great, we can see which interface is having the trouble forming an adjacency and why! Example 8-5 shows the debug messages indicating what is wrong.

Example 8-5   *Debug Messages for OSPF Authentication*

```
*Mar  1 08:55:05.895 GMT: OSPF: Rcv hello from 10.1.1.1 area 10 from FastEthernet0/
0 10.10.10.1
*Mar  1 08:55:05.899 GMT: OSPF: End of hello processing
Dozer#
*Mar  1 08:55:07.447 GMT: OSPF: Send with youngest Key 1
*Mar  1 08:55:07.447 GMT: OSPF: Rcv DBD from 10.1.1.1 on FastEthernet0/0 seq 0x1D2A
opt 0x42 flag 0x7 len 32 state INIT
*Mar  1 08:55:07.447 GMT: OSPF: 2 Way Communication to 10.1.1.1 on FastEthernet0/0,
state 2WAY
*Mar  1 08:55:07.451 GMT: OSPF: Neighbor change Event on interface FastEthernet0/0
*Mar  1 08:55:07.451 GMT: OSPF: DR/BDR election on FastEthernet0/0
*Mar  1 08:55:07.451 GMT: OSPF: Elect BDR 0.0.0.0
*Mar  1 08:55:07.451 GMT: OSPF: Elect DR 10.1.5.5
*Mar  1 08:55:07.451 GMT:         DR: 10.1.5.5 (Id)     BDR: none
*Mar  1 08:55:07.451 GMT: OSPF: Send DBD to 10.1.1.1 on FastEthernet0/0 seq 0x1D68
opt 0x2 flag 0x7 len 32
*Mar  1 08:55:07.451 GMT: OSPF: Send with youngest Key 1
*Mar  1 08:55:07.451 GMT: OSPF: First DBD and we are not SLAVE
*Mar  1 08:55:07.455 GMT: OSPF: Rcv DBD from 10.1.1.1 on FastEthernet0/0 seq 0x1D68
opt 0x42 flag 0x2 len 552 state EXSTART
*Mar  1 08:55:07.455 GMT: OSPF: NBR Negotiation Done. We are the MASTER
*Mar  1 08:55:07.459 GMT: OSPF: Send DBD to 10.1.1.1 on FastEthernet0/0 seq 0x1D69
opt 0x2 flag 0x3 len 532
*Mar  1 08:55:07.459 GMT: OSPF: Send with youngest Key 1
*Mar  1 08:55:07.459 GMT: OSPF: Send with youngest Key 1
*Mar  1 08:55:07.463 GMT: OSPF: Database request to 10.1.1.1
*Mar  1 08:55:07.463 GMT: OSPF: sent LS REQ packet to 10.10.10.1, length 144
*Mar  1 08:55:07.463 GMT: OSPF: Send with youngest Key 0
*Mar  1 08:55:07.463 GMT: OSPF: Rcv DBD from 10.1.1.1 on FastEthernet0/0 seq 0x1D69
opt 0x42 flag 0x0 len 32 state EXCHANGE
*Mar  1 08:55:07.467 GMT: OSPF: Send DBD to 10.1.1.1 on FastEthernet0/0 seq 0x1D6A
opt 0x2 flag 0x1 len 32
*Mar  1 08:55:07.467 GMT: OSPF: Send with youngest Key 1
```

Example 8-5 *Debug Messages for OSPF Authentication (Continued)*

```
*Mar  1 08:55:07.467 GMT: OSPF: Send with youngest Key 1
*Mar  1 08:55:07.471 GMT: OSPF: Build network LSA for FastEthernet0/0, router ID
10.1.5.5
*Mar  1 08:55:07.471 GMT: OSPF: No full nbrs to build Net Lsa for interface
FastEthernet0/0
*Mar  1 08:55:07.475 GMT: OSPF: Rcv DBD from 10.1.1.1 on FastEthernet0/0 seq 0x1D6A
opt 0x42 flag 0x0 len 32 state EXCHANGE
*Mar  1 08:55:07.475 GMT: OSPF: Exchange Done with 10.1.1.1 on FastEthernet0/0
*Mar  1 08:55:07.475 GMT: OSPF: Synchronized with 10.1.1.1 on FastEthernet0/0, state
FULL
*Mar  1 08:55:07.503 GMT: OSPF: Send with youngest Key 1
*Mar  1 08:55:07.951 GMT: OSPF: Build router LSA for area 10, router ID 10.1.5.5,
seq 0x8000000E
*Mar  1 08:55:07.983 GMT: OSPF: Send with youngest Key 1
Dozer#
*Mar  1 08:55:12.327 GMT: OSPF: Send with youngest Key 1
*Mar  1 08:55:12.743 GMT: OSPF: Send with youngest Key 1
*Mar  1 08:55:12.859 GMT: OSPF: Build network LSA for FastEthernet0/0, router ID
10.1.5.5
*Mar  1 08:55:12.891 GMT: OSPF: Send with youngest Key 1
Dozer#
*Mar  1 08:55:15.895 GMT: OSPF: Rcv hello from 10.1.1.1 area 10 from FastEthernet0/
0 10.10.10.1
*Mar  1 08:55:15.899 GMT: OSPF: Neighbor change Event on interface FastEthernet0/0
*Mar  1 08:55:15.899 GMT: OSPF: DR/BDR election on FastEthernet0/0
*Mar  1 08:55:15.899 GMT: OSPF: Elect BDR 10.1.1.1
*Mar  1 08:55:15.899 GMT: OSPF: Elect DR 10.1.5.5
*Mar  1 08:55:15.899 GMT:         DR: 10.1.5.5 (Id)    BDR: 10.1.1.1 (Id)
*Mar  1 08:55:15.899 GMT: OSPF: End of hello processing
```

The final configuration for router Dozer would appear as in Example 8-6. Notice that the configuration reflects the two steps that are needed to configure OSPF authentication.

Example 8-6 *OSPF MD5 Authentication: Final Configuration for Dozer*

```
!
interface FastEthernet0/0
 description VLAN 10 TO ORACLE
 ip address 10.10.10.2 255.255.255.0
 no ip directed-broadcast
 ip ospf message-digest-key 1 md5 7 013C35347D46140022475D
!

!
router ospf 100
 network 10.10.0.0 0.0.255.255 area 10
 area 10 authentication message-digest
!
```

Configuring OSPF Authentication on a Virtual Link

In this case, because a segmented area 0 with a virtual link exists, OSPF authentication is configured in both area 0s. That is the right thing to do because through the virtual link, the two area 0s think they are one and the same, and as discussed earlier, OSPF authentication is turned on in an entire area.

However, after checking the network after configuring OSPF authentication, notice that many routes have disappeared from router Neo.

Example 8-7   *Neo's IP Routing Table Is Missing Some Routes That Should Be There*

```
Neo>show ip route
Codes: C - connected, S - static, I - IGRP, R - RIP, M - mobile, B - BGP
       D - EIGRP, EX - EIGRP external, O - OSPF, IA - OSPF inter area
       N1 - OSPF NSSA external type 1, N2 - OSPF NSSA external type 2
       E1 - OSPF external type 1, E2 - OSPF external type 2, E - EGP
       i - IS-IS, L1 - IS-IS level-1, L2 - IS-IS level-2, ia - IS-IS inter area
       * - candidate default, U - per-user static route, o - ODR
       P - periodic downloaded static route

Gateway of last resort is not set

     10.0.0.0/8 is variably subnetted, 12 subnets, 2 masks
C       10.0.2.0/24 is directly connected, Loopback2
C       10.0.3.0/24 is directly connected, Loopback3
C       10.51.51.0/30 is directly connected, Serial0/0
C       10.0.1.0/24 is directly connected, FastEthernet0/0
C       10.1.6.0/24 is directly connected, Loopback0
C       10.0.4.0/24 is directly connected, Loopback4
C       10.0.5.0/24 is directly connected, Loopback5
O IA    10.221.4.0/24 [110/2] via 10.0.1.2, 00:01:07, FastEthernet0/0
O IA    10.221.3.0/24 [110/2] via 10.0.1.2, 00:01:08, FastEthernet0/0
O IA    10.221.2.0/24 [110/2] via 10.0.1.2, 00:01:08, FastEthernet0/0
O IA    10.221.1.0/24 [110/2] via 10.0.1.2, 00:01:08, FastEthernet0/0
O IA    10.221.0.0/24 [110/11] via 10.0.1.2, 00:01:08, FastEthernet0/0
O E2 192.168.254.0/24 [110/20] via 10.51.51.1, 00:01:09, Serial0/0
Neo>
! Where are all the routes from area's 10 and 59???
```

You can see what is going on at router Cypher because that is where you instituted some changes in the form of OSPF authentication. The simple **debug** command in Example 8-8 quickly reveals the root cause!

Example 8-8   *Debug on Router Cypher Reveals a Mismatched Authentication Type*

```
Cypher#debug ip ospf adj
OSPF adjacency events debugging is on
000047: *Mar  1 06:30:59.215 GMT: OSPF: Rcv pkt from 10.51.51.2, Serial0/0 : Mismatch
Authentication type. Input packet specified type 0, we use type 2
Cypher#
000048: *Mar  1 06:31:01.099 GMT: OSPF: Send with youngest Key 1
Cypher#u all
All possible debugging has been turned off
Cypher#
```

Next, determine what the virtual link shows between routers Cypher and Neo in Example 8-9. At first glance, everything seems fine because the virtual link is up. In this case, the virtual link up status means that it can reach router Neo at 10.1.6.6, as discussed in Chapter 4, "Design Fundamentals." However, look further down the display.

Example 8-9 *Displaying the Virtual Link Status Between Cypher and Neo*

```
Cypher#show ip ospf virtual-links
Virtual Link OSPF_VL0 to router 10.1.6.6 is up
  Run as demand circuit
  DoNotAge LSA allowed.
  Transit area 51, via interface Serial0/0, Cost of using 48
  Transmit Delay is 1 sec, State POINT_TO_POINT,
  Timer intervals configured, Hello 10, Dead 40, Wait 40, Retransmit 5
    Hello due in 00:00:09
  Message digest authentication enabled
      No key configured, using default key id 0
Cypher#
```

Notice that OSPF authentication is enabled, but there is no key configured on the virtual link. This is a crucial item in how OSPF operates on Cisco routers. When using OSPF authentication in area 0 and virtual links, the virtual link must be configured for authentication as well. Because the virtual link has not been configured to accept authentication, routing updates are not accepted over the virtual link. Examples 8-10, 8-11, and 8-12 document the process of activating OSPF authentication on a virtual link at the before, during, and after stages.

Before

Example 8-10 *Activating OSPF Authentication on a Virtual Link: Before*

```
!
router ospf 100
 log-adjacency-changes
 area 0 authentication message-digest
 area 51 virtual-link 10.1.6.6
 network 10.0.0.0 0.0.255.255 area 0
 network 10.51.0.0 0.0.255.255 area 51
!
```

During

Example 8-11 *Activating OSPF Authentication on a Virtual Link: During*

```
Cypher#conf t
Enter configuration commands, one per line.  End with CNTL/Z.
Cypher(config)#router ospf 100
Cypher(config-router)#no area 51 virtual-link 10.1.6.6
Cypher(config-router)#area 51 virtual-link 10.1.6.6 authentication-key 0 ?
  LINE  Authentication key (8 chars)
Cypher(config-router)#area 51 virtual-link 10.1.6.6 authentication-key 0 cisco
```

Note that Cisco IOS Software claims the authentication key for the virtual link can only be 8 characters in length. That is incorrect! Passwords can be either shorter or longer.

After

Example 8-12   *Activating OSPF Authentication on a Virtual Link: After*

```
!
router ospf 100
 log-adjacency-changes
 area 0 authentication message-digest
 area 51 virtual-link 10.1.6.6 authentication-key 7 14141B180F0B
 network 10.0.0.0 0.0.255.255 area 0
 network 10.51.0.0 0.0.255.255 area 51
!

Neo#show ip route
Codes: C - connected, S - static, I - IGRP, R - RIP, M - mobile, B - BGP
       D - EIGRP, EX - EIGRP external, O - OSPF, IA - OSPF inter area
       N1 - OSPF NSSA external type 1, N2 - OSPF NSSA external type 2
       E1 - OSPF external type 1, E2 - OSPF external type 2, E - EGP
       i - IS-IS, L1 - IS-IS level-1, L2 - IS-IS level-2, ia - IS-IS inter area
       * - candidate default, U - per-user static route, o - ODR
       P - periodic downloaded static route

Gateway of last resort is not set

     10.0.0.0/8 is variably subnetted, 20 subnets, 2 masks
O IA    10.69.74.0/24 [110/76] via 10.51.51.1, 00:10:09, Serial0/0
O IA    10.69.73.0/24 [110/76] via 10.51.51.1, 00:10:09, Serial0/0
O IA    10.69.72.0/24 [110/76] via 10.51.51.1, 00:10:09, Serial0/0
O IA    10.69.71.0/24 [110/76] via 10.51.51.1, 00:10:09, Serial0/0
C       10.0.2.0/24 is directly connected, Loopback2
O IA    10.69.70.0/24 [110/76] via 10.51.51.1, 00:10:09, Serial0/0
C       10.0.3.0/24 is directly connected, Loopback3
O IA    10.69.69.0/24 [110/75] via 10.51.51.1, 00:10:09, Serial0/0
O IA    10.10.10.0/24 [110/75] via 10.51.51.1, 00:10:09, Serial0/0
O       10.0.0.0/24 [110/65] via 10.51.51.1, 00:29:29, Serial0/0
C       10.51.51.0/30 is directly connected, Serial0/0
O IA    10.10.11.0/24 [110/76] via 10.51.51.1, 00:10:09, Serial0/0
C       10.0.1.0/24 is directly connected, FastEthernet0/0
O IA    10.10.12.0/24 [110/76] via 10.51.51.1, 00:10:09, Serial0/0
O IA    10.10.13.0/24 [110/76] via 10.51.51.1, 00:10:10, Serial0/0
C       10.1.6.0/24 is directly connected, Loopback0
O IA    10.10.14.0/24 [110/76] via 10.51.51.1, 00:10:10, Serial0/0
C       10.0.4.0/24 is directly connected, Loopback4
O IA    10.10.15.0/24 [110/76] via 10.51.51.1, 00:10:10, Serial0/0
C       10.0.5.0/24 is directly connected, Loopback5
Neo#
```

Now that authentication has been enabled on the virtual link, all the routing updates are being exchanged.

Virtual Links and Null Authentication

As just demonstrated, when authentication is enabled for area 0 and a virtual link is present, authentication is automatically enabled on a virtual link, but authentication must then be configured (by you) for the virtual link to operate again. You could configure the same type of authentication as you did in the previous set of examples, or you can configure *null authentication*. This is demonstrated in Example 8-13.

Example 8-13 *Configuring Null Authentication on a Virtual Link*

```
Cypher#conf t
Enter configuration commands, one per line.  End with CNTL/Z.
Cypher(config)#router ospf 100
Cypher(config-router)#no area 51 virtual-link 10.1.6.6
Cypher(config-router)#area 51 virtual-link 10.1.6.6 authentication-key 0 ?
  LINE  Authentication key (8 chars)
Cypher(config-router)#area 51 virtual-link 10.1.6.6 authentication-key null
```

Remember, as with other types of authentication, both ends must be configured identically. However, you should use MD5 for the same reasons that using plaintext is bad practice.

Troubleshooting Virtual Link Authentication

You can run the following commands in addition to what you have already seen to assist you in determining why OSPF is not working correctly:

1 Verify the status of the neighbor relationship between OSPF routers through the use of the **show ip ospf neighbor** command. You might also want to use the **debug ip OSPF adjacency** command.

2 Verify that the authentication key (password) is the same on both routers.

3 Verify that the target IP addresses are correct in the virtual link configuration.

4 Verify that the transit OSPF area ID is correct in the virtual link configuration.

Changing the Virtual Link Password

At some point, you should change the OSPF authentication password to keep your security fresh. This change is a best practice and should be done regularly. The tricky part is changing the authentication without upsetting routing. If you are going against the recommendations in this chapter and using plain text authentication, you must take a brief outage as the network adjusts to the change. However, if you are using MD5, you are in a much better position.

OSPF and the Cisco IOS Software offer a great method that allows this change to happen seamlessly. You essentially configure a new virtual link with a different key and password while leaving the old virtual link in place. Once the new virtual link is up, delete it, and the new one takes its place along with the new passwords. This is another example of the advantage of being able to change keys seamlessly using MD5.

Restricting Access to Network Devices

Managing and securing your network is extremely important. So far this chapter has discussed all the major points in these topics. This section reviews the ways in which you can protect and restrict access to your OSPF network devices while still providing access to legitimate users. This section discusses restricting and protecting access from a logical stand-point and presumes that you have taken the earlier advice of protecting physical access first!

Controlling Access to Network Equipment

It is important to control access to all your network equipment. Most equipment manufac-turers now design their equipment with multiple levels of passwords, typically read and then read/write. This is probably the easiest and most basic step in securing your network.

This section discusses some of the techniques that you must consider regarding Cisco router access and the operation of Cisco router passwords. You can control access to the router using the following methods:

- Console port access
- Telnet access (nonprivileged and privileged)
- Terminal Access Controller Access Control System (TACACS)
- SNMP access
- Controlling access to servers that contain configuration files
- Privilege-level security

You can secure the first two methods by using features within Cisco IOS Software. For each method, you can permit nonprivileged access and privileged access for a user (or group of users). Nonprivileged access allows users to monitor the router but not to configure the router (essentially read-only). Privileged access enables the user to fully configure the router (essentially read-write).

For console port and Telnet access, you can set up the following types of passwords:

- The login password, which allows the user nonprivileged access to the router.
- After accessing the router, the user can enter privileged mode by entering the **enable** command and the proper password. Privileged mode provides the user with full configuration capabilities.

SNMP access allows you to set up different SNMP community strings for both nonprivi-leged and privileged access. Nonprivileged access allows users on a host to send the router SNMP get-request and SNMP get-next-request messages. These messages are used for gathering statistics from the router. Privileged access allows users on a host to send the router SNMP set-request messages to make changes to the router's configurations and operational state.

Console Port Access   A console is a terminal (PC) that is attached directly to the router or switch via the console port. Security is applied to the console by asking users to authenticate themselves via passwords. By default, no passwords are associated with console access. This is why physical security is also important. In the default configuration (that is, no security on the console port), anyone with physical access to the device can access the CLI via the console port and cause problems.

If there is not good physical security and some unauthorized person gains physical access to the console, they are in a position to execute "password recovery" and gain full access to the device.

Telnet: Nonprivileged Mode Password

Each Telnet port on the router is known as a virtual terminal. There is a default number of five virtual terminal (vty) ports on the router, allowing five concurrent Telnet sessions. On the router, the virtual terminal ports are numbered 0 through 4. You can set up nonprivileged passwords for Telnet access via the virtual terminal ports with the following configuration commands. You configure a password for nonprivileged mode (also known as vty) by entering the following commands in the router's configuration file. Remember that passwords are case sensitive. In the following example, the password is ospf4U:

```
line vty 0 4
login
password ospf4U
```

When you log in to the router, the router login prompt is provided, as follows:

```
User Access Verification
Password:
```

You must enter the password ospf4U to gain nonprivileged access to the router. The router response is as follows:

```
Trinity>
```

Nonprivileged mode is signified on the router by the > prompt. At this point, you can enter a variety of commands to view statistics on the router, but you cannot change the configuration of the router.

NOTE   When considering what password format to use—all letters or numbers—it is best to make your passwords an alphanumeric combination with at least one capital letter. Not all cyberthieves are outside your network, and this makes your passwords tougher to crack or guess. For example, the password ospf4U combines all of these suggestions!

Telnet: Privileged Mode Password (Enable)

Configure a password for privileged mode—enable or EXEC—by entering the following commands in the router's configuration file. In the following example, the password is HiredGuns:

```
enable-password HiredGuns
```

To access privileged mode, enter the following command:

```
Trinity> enable
Password:
```

Enter the password HiredGuns to gain privileged access to the router. The router responds as follows:

```
Trinity#
```

Privileged mode is signified by the # prompt. In privileged mode (also known as enable mode), you can enter all commands to view statistics and configure the router.

Telnet Session Timeouts

Setting the login and enable passwords might not provide enough security in some cases. The timeout for an inactive Telnet session (10 minutes by default) provides an additional security measure. If the console is left unattended in privileged mode, any user can modify the router's configuration. You can change the login timeout via the **exec-timeout** *mm ss* command, where *mm* is minutes and *ss* is seconds. The commands in Example 8-14 show what happens before, during, and after changing the timeout to 60 minutes and 0 seconds.

Example 8-14 *Changing the Login Timeout: Before, During, and After*

```
! BEFORE
line vty 0 4
password 7 01070916490E081B
 logging synchronous
 login
!
!
end
! DURING
Zion#conf t
Enter configuration commands, one per line.  End with CNTL/Z.
Zion(config)#line vty 0 4
Zion(config-line)#exec
Zion(config-line)#exec-
Zion(config-line)#exec-t
Zion(config-line)#exec-timeout ?
  <0-35791>  Timeout in minutes

Zion(config-line)#exec-timeout 60 ?
  <0-2147483>  Timeout in seconds
  <cr>
```

continues

Example 8-14   *Changing the Login Timeout: Before, During, and After (Continued)*

```
Zion(config-line)#exec-timeout 60 0
Zion(config-line)#^Z
Zion#
! AFTER
line vty 0 4
 exec-timeout 60 0
 password 7 01070916490E081B
login
!
!
end
```

The **exec-timeout** command is useful, not only from a security standpoint but also from a network management standpoint. To clarify, if a Telnet session is not closed properly, the router still considers that session to be open although no activity is occurring. When a Telnet session is considered open, it reduces the total possible vty sessions (5 maximum); eventually you could inadvertently lock yourself out of the router. As a result, you must reboot the router or gain access via the console port to disconnect these "ghost" sessions. However, if you configure all ports (console, line vty, and aux) with the **exec-timeout** command, after 60 minutes and 0 seconds (as specified in the Example 8-14), the router disconnects the session for inactivity.

Password Encryption

Because protocol analyzers can examine packets (and thus read passwords), you can increase access security by configuring Cisco IOS Software to encrypt passwords. Encryption prevents the password from being readable in the configuration file.

Most passwords on the router are visible via the **write terminal** and **show run** configuration privileged-mode commands. If you have access to privileged mode on the router, you can view all passwords in clear text by default. There is a way to hide clear text passwords. The **service password-encryption** command stores passwords in an encrypted manner so that anyone performing a **write terminal** or **show configuration** cannot determine the clear text password. However, if you forget the password, regaining access to the router requires you to gain physical access.

TIP   Although password encryption is helpful, it can be, and has been, compromised and thus should not be your only network security strategy. This chapter has already covered many of the other possibilities.

The actual encryption process with the **service password-encryption** command occurs when the current configuration is written or when a password is configured. Password encryption is applied to all passwords, including authentication key passwords, the privileged command password, console and vty access passwords, and both OSPF and BGP neighbor passwords. The **service password-encryption** command is used primarily for keeping unauthorized individuals from viewing your password in your configuration file.

Restricting Telnet Access to Particular IP Addresses

To allow only certain IP addresses to use Telnet to access the router, you must use the **access-class** command. The **access-class** *nn* **in** command defines an access list that allows access to the vty lines on the router. The following configuration commands allow incoming Telnet access to the router only from hosts on network 192.85.55.0/24, which is the network operations center (NOC) in this case:

```
access-list 12 permit 192.85.55.0 0.0.0.255
line vty 0 4
access-class 12 in
```

There is an option for **access-class out** which controls to what destination ports on this router may initiate telnet.

Terminal Access Controller Access Control System

Nonprivileged (vty) and privileged (enable) mode passwords are global and apply to every user that accesses the router either from the console port or from a Telnet session. As an alternative, the TACACS provides a way to validate every user on an individual basis before he or she can gain access to the router or communication server.

TACACS was derived from the U.S. Department of Defense and is described in RFC 1492. TACACS is used to allow finer control over who can access the router in vty and enable modes.

When TACACS is enabled in a router, the router prompts the user for a user name and a password. Then the router queries a TACACS server to see if the user provided the correct password. A TACACS server typically runs on a UNIX workstation. Public domain TACACS servers can be obtained via anonymous ftp to ftp.cisco.com in the /pub directory. Use the /pub/README file to find the filename. A fully supported TACACS server is bundled with CiscoWorks Version 3. As a side note one of the interesting ways of configuring tacas is to have a secondary authentication method know as login local should the tacas server go down. Login via local authentication is configured on the router.

The configuration command **tacacs-server** *host* specifies which UNIX host running a TACACS server validates requests that are sent by the router. You can enter the **tacacs-server** *host* command several times to specify multiple TACACS server hosts that a router can validate users against. This use of multiple servers is effective in case a single server fails. In that event, you could potentially be locked out of your network until the server is restored.

Nonprivileged Access

As previously discussed, if all servers are unavailable, you could be locked out of the router. In that event, the following configuration command enables you to determine whether to allow a user to log in to the router with no password (**succeed** keyword) or to force the user to supply the standard login password (**password** keyword):

```
tacacs-server last-resort [password | succeed]
```

The following commands specify a TACACS server and allow a login to succeed if the server is down or unreachable:

```
tacacs-server host 129.140.1.1
tacacs-server last-resort succeed
```

To force users who access the router via Telnet to authenticate themselves using TACACS, enter the following configuration commands:

```
line vty 0 4
login tacacs
```

Privileged Access

This method of password checking can also be applied to the privileged-mode password with the **enable use-tacacs** command. If all servers are unavailable, you could be locked out of the router. In that event, the **enable last-resort [succeed | password]** configuration command enables you to determine whether to allow a user to log in to the router with no password (**succeed** keyword) or to force the user to supply the enable password (**password** keyword). There are significant risks to using the **succeed** keyword. If you use the **enable use-tacacs** command, you must also specify the **tacacs-server authenticate enable** command.

The **tacacs-server extended** command enables a Cisco device to run in extended TACACS mode. The UNIX system must be running the extended TACACS daemon, which can be obtained via anonymous ftp to ftp.cisco.com. The filename is xtacacsd.shar. This daemon enables communication servers and other equipment to talk to the UNIX system and update an audit trail with information on port usage, accounting data, or any other information the device can send.

The **username** *user* **password [0 | 7]** *password* command enables you to store and maintain a list of users and their passwords on a Cisco device instead of on a TACACS server. The number 0 stores the password in clear text in the configuration file. The number 7 stores the password in an encrypted format. If you do not have a TACACS server and still want to authenticate users on an individual basis, you can set up users with the following configuration commands:

```
username rose password 7 rose-pass
username rebekah password 7 rebekah-pass
```

Here, the two users, Rose and Rebekah, are authenticated via passwords that are stored in encrypted format. The definition of usernames and passwords using this command may be used for functions other than local authentication (especially PPP CHAP/PAP authentication).

Privilege Level Security

This feature was introduced by Cisco in Cisco IOS Software Release 10.3 and allows the establishment of 16 levels of access within the router. Default privilege levels are 1 = user and 15 = privileged.

Privilege levels can be used a variety of ways within a router:

- They can be established for both commands and incoming terminal lines.

- Specialized enable passwords can be linked to privilege levels.

- They can be assigned to specialized exec and configure commands to control access.

Privilege Level Command Modes

You can implement a variety of different command modes using privilege levels. All of the following are global configuration commands except **exec**:

```
configuration
controller
exec
hub
interface
ipx-router
line
map-class
map-list
route-map
router
```

Privilege Level Configuration Example

To associate a privilege level with a specific command, you need to configure the router as follows:

```
Trinity(config)#privilege exec level 6 ping
Trinity(config)#privilege exec level 6 clear
```

The preceding two commands, if applied to a router's vty port (the one you Telnet to), allow anyone accessing the router using just the vty command to perform extended pings and a variety of clear commands (that is, counters, interface, router, and so on).

To establish a specific enable password for a privilege level, enter the following command:

```
Trinity(config)# enable password level level # password
```

To associate a privilege level with a terminal line, enter the following commands:

```
Trinity(config)# line vty 0 4
Trinity(config-line)# privilege level level #
```

Nonprivileged Mode (Read-Only)

Use the **RO** keyword of the **snmp-server community** command to provide nonprivileged access to your routers via SNMP. The following configuration command sets the agent in the router to allow only **SNMP GETREQUEST** and **GETNEXTREQUEST** messages that are sent with the community string "public":

```
snmp-server community public RO 1
```

You can also specify a list of IP addresses that are allowed to send messages to the router using the **access-list** option with the **snmp-server community** command. In the following configuration example, only hosts 1.1.1.1 and 2.2.2.2 are allowed nonprivileged-mode SNMP access to the router:

```
access-list 1 permit 1.1.1.1
access-list 1 permit 2.2.2.2
snmp-server community public RO 1
```

Privileged Mode (Read/Write)

Use the **RW** keyword of the **snmp-server community** command to provide privileged access to your routers via SNMP. The following configuration command sets the agent in the router to allow only **SNMP SETREQUEST** messages sent with the community string "private":

```
snmp-server community private RW 1
```

You can also specify a list of IP addresses that are allowed to send messages to the router by using the **access-list** option of the **snmp-server community** command. In the following configuration example, only hosts 5.5.5.5 and 6.6.6.6 are allowed privileged-mode SNMP access to the router:

```
access-list 1 permit 5.5.5.5
access-list 1 permit 6.6.6.6
snmp-server community private RW 1
```

This section describes how to use traffic filters (also known as access lists) to control access to your OSPF router. The use of access lists here is yet another way they can be used within routers in addition to the concepts demonstrated in Chapters 6, "Redistribution," and 7, "Summarization." This is an important feature found within many routers. Filters enable you to deploy an added layer of network security within your network and gain the benefits of a layered secure network.

Traffic filters at their most powerful implementation enable you to control whether router traffic is forwarded or blocked at the router's interfaces. You should use traffic filters to provide a basic level of security for accessing your network. If you do not configure traffic filters on your router, all traffic passing through the router could be allowed onto all parts of your network. This section looks at how to restrict access to your OSPF routers using access lists.

By setting up traffic filters at your router, you can control which traffic enters or leaves your network. Traffic filters are commonly used in firewalls. Typically, a router configured for traffic filtering is positioned between your internal network and an external network such as the Internet. Using traffic-filtering routers enables you to control what traffic is allowed onto your internal network. By combining the routers' filtering capabilities with that of a firewall, you can increase the security of your network. This section explores how you can filter who is allowed to remotely access OSPF routers via Telnet.

TIP   If you are using filters in firewalls, you should always have filters applied to your router as well. This decreases the likelihood that a cyber-thief can gain access to your network.

Traffic-filtering services are provided by access lists (also called *filters*) on many routers. Access lists must be defined on a per-protocol basis. In other words, you should define access lists for every protocol that is enabled on an interface if you want to control traffic flow for that protocol. This section covers the following topics:

- Standard access lists
- Lock-and-key security (with dynamic access lists)

The first section describes standard static access lists, which are the most common type of access lists. Static access lists should be used with each routed protocol that you have configured for router interfaces. Lock-and-key security, available only for IP traffic, provides additional security functions.

Access Lists to Restrict Access

Access lists can be used for many purposes. For example, access lists can be used to:

- Control the transmission of packets on an interface
- Control virtual terminal line access
- Restrict contents of routing updates

Access lists can be used for these and other purposes. The following sections describe how to use access lists to control packet transmission.

Configuring Access Lists for Specific Protocols

To control packet transmission for a given protocol, you must configure an access list for that protocol. Table 8-1 identifies the protocols for which you can configure access lists.

Table 8-1   *Protocols with Access Lists by Range*

Protocol	Range
IP	1–99
VINES	1–100
Extended IP	100–199
Extended VINES	101–200
Ethernet type code	200–299
Transparent bridging (protocol type)	200–299
Source-route bridging (protocol type)	200–299
Simple VINES	201–300
DECnet and extended DECnet	300–399
XNS	400–499
Extended XNS	500–599
AppleTalk	600–699
Ethernet address	700–799
Source-route bridging (vendor code)	700–799
Transparent bridging (vendor code)	700–799
IPX	800–899
Extended IPX	900–999
IPX SAP	1000–1099
Extended transparent bridging	1100–1199

TIP   You should consider configuring access lists for each protocol that you have configured for an interface. Otherwise, the security is only partially applied to each interface within your network.

You must identify every access list by either a name or a number. You assign this name or number to each access list when you define the access list. Cisco IOS Software allows using either names or numbers to identify; some protocols can be identified by either. When a number is used to identify an access list, the number must be within the specific range of numbers that is valid for the protocol.

Although each protocol has its own set of specific tasks and rules required for you to provide traffic filtering, in general, most protocols require taking at least two steps:

Step 1   Create an access list definition.

Step 2   Apply the access list to an interface.

TIP   Some protocols refer to access lists as *filters,* and some protocols refer to the act of applying the access lists to interfaces as *filtering.*

Creating Access Lists

Access list definitions provide a set of criteria that are applied to each packet that is processed by the router. The router decides whether to forward or block each packet based on whether the packet matches the access list criteria.

Typical criteria defined in access lists are packet source addresses, packet destination addresses, or upper-layer protocol of the packet. However, each protocol has its own specific set of criteria that can be defined.

For a given access list, you define each criterion in separate access list statements. These statements specify whether to block or forward packets that match the criteria listed. An access list, then, is the sum of individual statements that all share the same identifying name or number.

TIP   Each additional access list statement that you enter is appended to the end of the access list statements. Also, you cannot delete individual statements after they have been created. You can only delete an entire access list. Not being able to delete individual statements is true of numbered access lists but not true of named access lists. One of the major advantages of named access lists is the ability to delete individual statements.

The order of access list statements is important. When the router is deciding whether to forward or block a packet, the Cisco IOS Software tests the packet against each criteria statement in the order the statements were created. After a match is found, no more criteria statements are checked.

If you create a criteria statement that explicitly permits all traffic, no statements added later are checked. This is usually seen when people allow all other traffic before the hidden explicit deny all at the end of every ACL. If you need additional statements, you must delete the access list and retype it with the new entries. When entering or modifying access lists, you should not modify or alter them on the fly. You can design them on a TFTP server, in a word processor, or on paper. You should not save the changes to the router until you are sure the desired security is working adequately. This provides you with a quick and easy back-out plan in case of errors.

At the end of every access list is an implied "deny all traffic" criteria statement. Therefore, if a packet does not match any of your criteria statements, the packet is blocked.

Applying Access Lists to Interfaces

You can apply only one access list to an interface for a given protocol per direction (that is, inbound or outbound). With most protocols, you can apply access lists to interfaces as either inbound or outbound. If the access list is inbound, when the router receives a packet, Cisco IOS Software checks the access list's criteria statements for a match. If the packet is permitted, the software continues to process the packet. If the packet is denied, the software discards the packet.

If the access list is outbound, after receiving and routing a packet to the outbound interface, the software checks the access list's criteria statements for a match. If the packet is permitted, the software transmits the packet. If the packet is denied, the software discards the packet. The default behavior of Cisco IOS Software is that when it denies a packet it generates an ICMP error message

---

TIP

For most protocols, if you define an inbound access list for traffic filtering, you should include explicit access list criteria statements to permit routing updates. If you do not, you might effectively lose communication from the interface when the implicit "deny all traffic" statement at the end of the access list blocks routing updates.

The guidelines discussed previously apply, in general, to all protocols. However, the specific guidelines for creating access lists and applying them to interfaces vary from protocol to protocol. See the appropriate protocol-specific chapters in the Cisco IOS Software configuration guides and command references (visit www.cisco.com/en/US/products/sw/iosswrel/index.html) for detailed task information on each protocol-specific access list.

User Authentication to Restrict Access

The following methods can be used to configure an authentication query process:

- Use a network access server such as a TACACS+ server. This method requires additional configuration steps on the TACACS+ server but allows stricter authentication queries and more sophisticated tracking capabilities. The syntax for this command is as follows:

    ```
    Trinity(config)# login tacacs
    ```

- Use the **username** command. This method is more effective because authentication is determined on a user basis. Per user local authentication works fine on individual routers but this solution does not scale well since you need to define every individual user on every router. The syntax for this command is as follows:

  ```
  Trinity(config)# username name password password
  Trinity(config-line)# login local
  ```

- Use the **password** and **login** commands. This method is less effective because the password is configured for the port, not for the user. Therefore, any user who knows the password can authenticate successfully. The syntax for these commands is as follows:

  ```
  Trinity(config-line)# password password
  Trinity(config-line)# login local
  ```

You can verify that this operation is successful on the router either by asking the user to test the connection or by using the **show access-lists** command to view dynamic access lists.

Summary

This chapter discussed and proved the importance of consistent network management and security. The more commonly developed and deployed network management models were presented. The section "Simple Network Management Protocol" covered the use of SNMP and described how it fits into today's complex networks as the de facto network management standard. This coverage included components found within an SNMP-managed network such as the NMS, managed devices, and their SNMP agents. This section also covered SNMP's operation, commands, and the various messages that are used by SNMP to communicate with the devices in the network.

You also learned about the various threats against your network in the section about network security. Fortunately, you learned several defenses that are already available for your network. This section also discussed the many reasons that network security should be part of your network design from the beginning as opposed to being an afterthought. The section "Securing Your OSPF Network" covered many different techniques that can be used to increase the overall security of your network. That section also covered the neighbor authentication features that are found in OSPF and described how to configure and deploy your routers to make use of this desirable OSPF feature.

In conclusion, this chapter has covered how important proper network management is to any network. We have peeled back the onion in many places to understand how network management is being performed over the network through SNMP and its various features.

Case Study: IOS Secure Template

You can secure your router and secure OSPF in different ways. This case study applies many of the basic techniques discussed in this chapter as well as some of the more advanced techniques.

This case study is not meant to teach you the ins and outs of the security techniques presented here. Instead, the case study presents ways to secure your router, with brief explanations so that you can decide which commands are appropriate for your network.

This Secure IOS template is a compilation of the one produced by Rob Thomas and combined with the template produced by INRGI (www.inrgi.net/security); both are used with permission and have been modified for our purposes. The configuration commands are in **boldface** text so that they stand out from the supporting comments, which are highlighted for readability. The secure template in Example 8-15 assumes the topology used in Figure 8-16.

Figure 8-16 *Secure Template Topology*

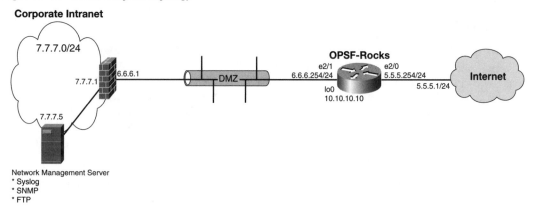

Example 8-15 *Secure IOS Template from http://www.cymru.com/ with Some Commentary*

```
!
John Nagle's algorithm (RFC 896) helps alleviate the small-packet
problem in TCP. The effect is to accumulate characters into larger
chunks, and pace them out to the network at a rate matching the round-trip time of
the given connection. Keepalives ensure that no tcp connections via the router get
hung.
service nagle
service tcp-keepalives-in
service tcp-keepalives-out
!
Provide timestamps in all debug messages and log entries down to the millisecond,
make sure your routers clock is set properly! The 'service password-encryption'
command provides minimal security for user, line, ppp, radius and assorted other
passwords and keys that must be stored in the IOS configuration file.
The command causes passwords in the config file to be encrypted with a reversible
```

Example 8-15 *Secure IOS Template from http://www.cymru.com/ with Some Commentary (Continued)*

> encryption that keeps people from finding your passwords by glancing at your
> configurations.
>
> ```
> service timestamps debug datetime msec show-timezone localtime
> service timestamps log datetime msec show-timezone localtime
> service password-encryption
> ```
>
> Cisco has enabled routers by default to now act as DHCP clients by default, this is
> really not a necessary service to have running so shut it off. Also given the issues
> with TCP & UDP Small Servers make sure they are off! "Chargen" is a character
> generator service that is used to generate a stream of characters for diagnostic
> purposes. The "echo" service merely echos back everything that is sent to it.
> Pointing the "chargen" service at the "echo" service creates a loop which causes an
> enormous amount of traffic to be generated and will eventually overwhelm the router's
> cpu and ram resources, thus we have the makings of a very serious Denial of Service
> Attack (DoS). The easiest way to prevent this kind of attack from happening is to
> disable these services on the router. The commands to do so are "no tcp-small-
> servers" - disables echo, chargen, discard and daytime; "no udp-small-servers" -
> disables echo, chargen and discard.
>
> ```
> no service udp-small-servers
> no service tcp-small-servers
> no service dhcp
> !
> ```
>
> Not all services are bad, in fact this new entry to the service category is quite
> useful, essentially by enabling it your syslog entries will be numbered to ensure
> they are not tampered with to hide hacking from you! Cisco helps us with our servers,
> aren't they nice?
>
> ```
> service sequence-numbers
> !
> hostname OSPF-Rocks
> !
> ```
>
> Logging is a must in almost every case so turn it on! Plus with all the logging we
> are doing in this configuration it might be a good idea to rate limit the log messages
> sent per second to not overwhelm your server, as when you are logging ACLs the
> entries can climb rapidly!
>
> ```
> logging 7.7.7.5
> logging buffered 16384 debugging
> logging rate-limit ?
> !
> ```
>
> Whenever a message is sent to the console port of the router this results in CPU
> interrupt to be delivered and considering the level of logging we have going on,
> disable console logging until needed.
>
> ```
> no logging console
> !
> ```
>
> Of course the most secure password type is enable secret so use it with some CAPITAL
> letters and some Num83r2 as well, it makes brute force attacks harder
>
> ```
> enable secret <PASSWORD>
> no enable password
> !
> ```
>
> Use TACACS+ for AAA. Ensure that the local account is case-sensitive, thus making
> brute-force attacks less effective.
>
> ```
> aaa new-model
> aaa authentication login default group tacacs+ local-case
> aaa authentication enable default group tacacs+ enable
> aaa authorization commands 15 default group tacacs+ local
> aaa accounting exec default stop-only group tacacs+
> aaa accounting commands 15 default stop-only group tacacs+
> ```

continues

Example 8-15 *Secure IOS Template from http://www.cymru.com/ with Some Commentary (Continued)*

```
aaa accounting network default stop-only group tacacs+
tacacs-server host 7.7.7.5
tacacs-server key OSPF-r0ck2
!
```
In the event that TACACS+ fails, use case-sensitive local authentication instead.
Keeps the hackers guessing, and the router more secure, remember security is all
about layers of defense.
```
username <USERNAME> password <PASSWORD>
!
```
Do I really need to explain why you should not use the built-in web server? Sometimes
Cisco takes the web to far, it's a router Jim!
```
no ip http server
!
```
Allows us to use the low subnets and go classless which are areas that have not
typically been used.
```
ip subnet-zero
ip classless
!
```
Why these services are still *on* by default AND in IOS is anyone's guess however for
the security of your network and sanity turn them off
```
no service pad
no ip source-route
no ip finger
no ip bootp server
no ip domain-lookup
!
```
TCP intercept helps prevent SYN-flooding attacks by intercepting and validating TCP
connection requests. In intercept mode, the TCP intercept software intercepts TCP
synchronization (SYN) packets from clients to servers that match an extended access
list. The router responds, if it is a valid connection they are allowed to
communicate
```
ip tcp intercept list 120
!
```
IOS will watch and manage a TCP connection for 24 hours after no activity, why? Who
knows? Regardless it should be changed.
```
ip tcp intercept connection-timeout 60
!
```
Keep half-open sockets open only 10 seconds instead of the default 30 seconds all
the while waiting for a response
```
ip tcp intercept watch-timeout 10
!
```
These commands determine when tcp intercept should deactivate or activate, in this
case 1500 and 6000 respectively, the defaults are not very realistic at 900 and 1100
```
ip tcp intercept one-minute low 1500
ip tcp intercept one-minute high 6000
!
```
Catch core dumps in case of a router crash; very important with a "security router"
as an attack may have been successful so it's good to know what happened. We have
configured our Network Management server beyond our firewall to accept FTP
connections from the router. Make sure you give the core dump files a unique name.
```
ip ftp username rooter
ip ftp password <PASSWORD>
exception core-file secure-router01-core
exception protocol ftp
exception dump 7.7.7.5
```

Example 8-15 *Secure IOS Template from http://www.cymru.com/ with Some Commentary (Continued)*

```
!
```
CEF is an advanced, Layer 3 switching technology inside a router. It defines the
fastest method by which a Cisco router forwards packets from ingress to egress
interfaces. The ip cef command enables CEF globally, not all router support CEF so
check your docs
```
ip cef
!
```
Set the time zone properly. It is best to standardize on one time zone for all routers
and servers, thus making problem tracking easier.
```
clock timezone GMT 0
!
```
Synchronize the routers clock with a local (trusted and authenticated) NTP server.
The SECRETKEY must be the same on both the router and the NTP server. Remember that
NTP is slow to get going properly, it's a cisco thing, so be patient!
```
ntp authentication-key 6767 md5 <SECRETKEY>
ntp authenticate
ntp update-calendar
ntp server 7.7.7.5
!
```
Configure the loopback0 interface as the source of our log messages. This is often
used for routing protocols as well since as a logical interface does not go *down*
thus it is very reliable. Assign an IP address that uniquely identifies this router.
One trick is to allocate a netblock for use as the router loopback netblock.
```
int loopback0
 ip address 10.10.10.10 255.255.255.255
 no ip redirects
 no ip unreachables
 no ip proxy-arp
 !
```
Configure and thus activate the null0 interface as a place to send naughty packets.
This becomes the "roach motel" for packets -- they can route in, but they can't route
out.
```
interface null0
 no ip unreachables
 !
interface Ethernet2/0
 description Unprotected interface, facing towards Internet
 ip address 5.5.5.254 255.255.255.0
 !
```
Do we run CEF verify? Yes if the data path is symmetric. No if the data path is
asymmetric. Use the ip verify unicast reverse-path interface command on the input
interface on the router at the upstream end of the connection. This feature examines
each packet received as input on that interface. If the source IP address does not
have a route in the CEF tables that points back to the same interface on which the
packet arrived, the router drops the packet.
```
 ip verify unicast reverse-path
 !
```
Apply our template ACL, more on what this ACL is covering later in the configuration,
but applying it is crucial to its success.
```
 ip access-group 2010 in
 !
```
Rate limiting traffic to protect the router and by default your infrastructure is
extremely important. The values maybe tweaked to meet your needs but in general we
recommend the following. Allow UDP to use no more than 2 Mb/s of the pipe.

continues

Example 8-15 *Secure IOS Template from http://www.cymru.com/ with Some Commentary (Continued)*

```
 rate-limit input access-group 150 2010000 250000 250000 conform-action transmit
exceed-action drop
!
```

Allow ICMP to use no more than 500 Kb/s of the pipe.

```
 rate-limit input access-group 160 500000 62500 62500 conform-action transmit
exceed-action drop
!
```

Allow multicast to use no more than 5 Mb/s of the pipe.

```
 rate-limit input access-group 170 5000000 375000 375000 conform-action transmit
exceed-action drop
!
```

Disables the sending of ICMP redirect messages to learn routes, let the hackers wonder!

```
 no ip redirects
!
```

Disables the sending of ICMP protocol unreachable and host unreachable messages and once again there is no reason to allow icmp to educate hackers about your network.

```
 no ip unreachables
!
```

IP directed broadcasts are dropped; they are not forwarded. Dropping IP directed broadcasts makes routers less susceptible to denial-of-service attacks

```
 no ip directed-broadcast
!
```

Source routing allows the path to be specified in a packet this could allow the packet to bypass firewalls, etc… disable this feature!

```
 no ip source-route
!
```

Don't pretend to be something you're not. :-)

```
 no ip proxy-arp
!
```

Disables the sending of ICMP mask reply messages. The default for Cisco routers is not to do this but it never hurts to input the command anyway just to be sure!

```
 no ip mask-reply
!
```

Enables IP accounting with the ability to identify IP traffic that fails IP access lists allowing your router to log all naughty business, be sure to check it!

```
 ip accounting access-violations
!
```

If you allow multicast in your network or participate in the MBONE, the following multicast filtering steps will help to ensure a secure multicast environment. These must be applied per interface.

```
 ip multicast boundary 30
 !
```

Keep flow data for analysis. If possible, export it to a cflowd server.

```
 ip route-cache flow
 !
interface Ethernet2/1
 description Protected interface, facing towards DMZ
 ip address 6.6.6.254 255.255.255.0
 !
```

Do we run CEF verify? Yes if the data path is symmetric. No if the data path is asymmetric. See above interface description for more information on this command.

```
 ip verify unicast reverse-path
```

Example 8-15 *Secure IOS Template from http://www.cymru.com/ with Some Commentary (Continued)*

```
!
If we are using Reverse Path Forwarding, comment out the ACL below.
 ip access-group 115 in
 !
The following commands have been described previously, for more information refer
to earlier in the configuration file.
 no ip redirects
 no ip unreachables
 no ip directed-broadcast
 no ip proxy-arp
 ip accounting access-violations
 ip multicast boundary 30
 no ip mask-reply
 ip route-cache flow
 !
Source routing allows the path to be specified in a packet this could allow the
packet to bypass firewalls, etc… disable this feature!
 no ip source-route
 !
Default route to the Internet (could be a routing protocol instead)
 ip route 0.0.0.0 0.0.0.0 5.5.5.1
 !
Route to network on the other side of the firewall
 ip route 7.7.7.0 255.255.255.0 6.6.6.1
 !
The following static routes will Black hole networks that are not supposed to be
routable on the public Internet. Be VERY careful about enabling these when running
TCP Intercept. TCP Intercept command directs the router to act as a TCP socket proxy.
When the router receives the SYN packet the router (instead of the destination)
initially responds with the SYN IACK.  This is where the interaction between TCP
Intercept and black hole routes causes a problem.  If you create black hole routes
for all bogon ranges and point them to the null device, and if someone launches a
SYN flood from a bogon range, then the router will send the SYN IACK to the null
device.  The router isn't clueful enough to realize it has done this, and the TCP
Intercept queue begins to build quite quickly.  The timeouts aren't, by default,
aggressive enough to work through this problem. WARNING - The Internet sometimes
changes without notice to check the validty of this list prior to implementing it.
 ip route 1.0.0.0 255.0.0.0 null0
 ip route 2.0.0.0 255.0.0.0 null0
 ip route 5.0.0.0 255.0.0.0 null0
 ip route 7.0.0.0 255.0.0.0 null0
 ip route 10.0.0.0 255.0.0.0 null0
 ip route 23.0.0.0 255.0.0.0 null0
 ip route 27.0.0.0 255.0.0.0 null0
 ip route 31.0.0.0 255.0.0.0 null0
 ip route 36.0.0.0 255.0.0.0 null0
 ip route 37.0.0.0 255.0.0.0 null0
 ip route 39.0.0.0 255.0.0.0 null0
 ip route 41.0.0.0 255.0.0.0 null0
 ip route 42.0.0.0 255.0.0.0 null0
 ip route 49.0.0.0 255.0.0.0 null0
 ip route 50.0.0.0 255.0.0.0 null0
 ip route 58.0.0.0 255.0.0.0 null0
 ip route 59.0.0.0 255.0.0.0 null0
```

continues

Example 8-15 *Secure IOS Template from http://www.cymru.com/ with Some Commentary (Continued)*

```
ip route 60.0.0.0 255.0.0.0 null0
ip route 70.0.0.0 255.0.0.0 null0
ip route 71.0.0.0 255.0.0.0 null0
ip route 72.0.0.0 255.0.0.0 null0
ip route 73.0.0.0 255.0.0.0 null0
ip route 74.0.0.0 255.0.0.0 null0
ip route 75.0.0.0 255.0.0.0 null0
ip route 76.0.0.0 255.0.0.0 null0
ip route 77.0.0.0 255.0.0.0 null0
ip route 78.0.0.0 255.0.0.0 null0
ip route 79.0.0.0 255.0.0.0 null0
ip route 82.0.0.0 255.0.0.0 null0
ip route 83.0.0.0 255.0.0.0 null0
ip route 84.0.0.0 255.0.0.0 null0
ip route 85.0.0.0 255.0.0.0 null0
ip route 86.0.0.0 255.0.0.0 null0
ip route 87.0.0.0 255.0.0.0 null0
ip route 88.0.0.0 255.0.0.0 null0
ip route 89.0.0.0 255.0.0.0 null0
ip route 90.0.0.0 255.0.0.0 null0
ip route 91.0.0.0 255.0.0.0 null0
ip route 92.0.0.0 255.0.0.0 null0
ip route 93.0.0.0 255.0.0.0 null0
ip route 94.0.0.0 255.0.0.0 null0
ip route 95.0.0.0 255.0.0.0 null0
ip route 96.0.0.0 255.0.0.0 null0
ip route 97.0.0.0 255.0.0.0 null0
ip route 98.0.0.0 255.0.0.0 null0
ip route 99.0.0.0 255.0.0.0 null0
ip route 100.0.0.0 255.0.0.0 null0
ip route 101.0.0.0 255.0.0.0 null0
ip route 102.0.0.0 255.0.0.0 null0
ip route 103.0.0.0 255.0.0.0 null0
ip route 104.0.0.0 255.0.0.0 null0
ip route 105.0.0.0 255.0.0.0 null0
ip route 106.0.0.0 255.0.0.0 null0
ip route 107.0.0.0 255.0.0.0 null0
ip route 108.0.0.0 255.0.0.0 null0
ip route 109.0.0.0 255.0.0.0 null0
ip route 110.0.0.0 255.0.0.0 null0
ip route 111.0.0.0 255.0.0.0 null0
ip route 112.0.0.0 255.0.0.0 null0
ip route 113.0.0.0 255.0.0.0 null0
ip route 114.0.0.0 255.0.0.0 null0
ip route 115.0.0.0 255.0.0.0 null0
ip route 116.0.0.0 255.0.0.0 null0
ip route 117.0.0.0 255.0.0.0 null0
ip route 118.0.0.0 255.0.0.0 null0
ip route 119.0.0.0 255.0.0.0 null0
ip route 120.0.0.0 255.0.0.0 null0
ip route 121.0.0.0 255.0.0.0 null0
ip route 122.0.0.0 255.0.0.0 null0
```

Example 8-15 *Secure IOS Template from http://www.cymru.com/ with Some Commentary (Continued)*

```
ip route 123.0.0.0 255.0.0.0 null0
ip route 124.0.0.0 255.0.0.0 null0
ip route 125.0.0.0 255.0.0.0 null0
ip route 126.0.0.0 255.0.0.0 null0
ip route 127.0.0.0 255.0.0.0 null0
ip route 169.254.0.0 255.255.0.0 null0
ip route 172.16.0.0 255.240.0.0 null0
ip route 192.0.2.0 255.255.255.0 null0
ip route 192.168.0.0 255.255.0.0 null0
ip route 197.0.0.0 255.0.0.0 null0
ip route 201.0.0.0 255.0.0.0 null0
ip route 222.0.0.0 255.0.0.0 null0
ip route 223.0.0.0 255.0.0.0 null0
!
```

Export our NetFlow data to our NetFlow server, 7.7.7.5. NetFlow provides some statistics that can be of use when tracing back to the true source of a spoofed attack. We also use the source as the loopback interface which is a best practice.

```
ip flow-export source loopback0
ip flow-export destination 7.7.7.5 2055
ip flow-export version 5 origin-as
!
```

Log anything interesting to the syslog server. Capture all of the logging output sent from the loopback interface, which makes ID of this router in the various places recording data easy and uniform to identify.

```
logging trap debugging
logging source-interface loopback0
logging 7.7.7.5
!
```

With the ACLs, it is important to log the attempts or activity of naughty folks. Thus, the implicit drop all normal entry at the end of every ACL is replaced (augmented, actually) with an explicit drop all that logs the attempt. You may wish to keep a second list (e.g. 2011) that does not log. During an attack, the additional logging can impact the performance of the router. Simply copy and paste access-list 2010, remove the log-input keyword, and name it access-list 2011. Then when an attack rages, you can replace access-list 2010 on the Internet-facing interface with access-list 2011. Thus allowing the router to concentrate on defending against the attack.

```
!
```

Block SNMP access from any location to the router, except the server (7.7.7.5), which is our Network Mgmt/Syslog server in our template and of course log anyone else that tries to access SNMP info on the router.

```
access-list 20 remark SNMP ACL
access-list 20 permit 7.7.7.5
access-list 20 deny any log
!
```

Multicast - filter out obviously naughty or needless traffic access-list 30 is the Multicast filtering ACL
Link local

```
access-list 30 deny 224.0.0.0 0.0.0.255 log
```

Locally scoped

```
access-list 30 deny 239.0.0.0 0.255.255.255 log
```

sgi-dogfight

```
access-list 30 deny host 224.0.1.2 log
```

rwhod

continues

Example 8-15 *Secure IOS Template from http://www.cymru.com/ with Some Commentary (Continued)*

```
access-list 30 deny host 224.0.1.3 log
ms-srvloc
access-list 30 deny host 224.0.1.22 log
ms-ds
access-list 30 deny host 224.0.1.24 log
ms-servloc-da
access-list 30 deny host 224.0.1.35 log
hp-device-disc
access-list 30 deny host 224.0.1.60 log
Permit all other multicast traffic
access-list 30 permit 224.0.0.0 15.255.255.255 log
!
Block access to the router from everyone except from the Network Mgmt server
(7.7.7.5) or the Firewall (6.6.6.1) and then only if SSH (port 22) or Telnet (port
23) is used, we will log every successful access as well. Of course we will also log
any denied access attempts. This also serves to create an audit trail of all access
to the router through the use of Extended ACLs are used to log some additional data.
access-list 100 remark VTY Access ACL
access-list 100 permit tcp host 7.7.7.5 host 0.0.0.0 range 22 23 log-input
access-list 100 permit tcp host 6.6.6.1 host 0.0.0.0 range 22 23 log-input
access-list 100 deny ip any any log-input
!
Leave one VTY safe for emergency access, just in case. The host 7.7.7.8 is a secure
host in the NOC. If all the VTYs are occupied, this leaves one VTY available and
logging is also happening!
access-list 105 remark VTY Access ACL
access-list 105 permit tcp host 7.7.7.8 host 0.0.0.0 range 22 23 log-input
access-list 105 deny ip any any log-input
!
Configure an ACL that prevents spoofing from within our network, which recognizes
and protects against a hacker gaining access to network via some other means. This
ACL assumes that we need to access the Internet only from the 7.7.7.0/24 network.
If you have additional networks behind 7.7.7.0/24, then add them into this ACL.
access-list 115 remark Anti-spoofing ACL
First, allow our intranet to access the Internet.
access-list 115 permit ip 7.7.7.0 0.0.0.255 any
Second, allow our firewall to access the Internet. This is useful for testing.
access-list 115 permit ip host 6.6.6.1 any
Now log all other such attempts.
access-list 115 deny ip any any log-input
!
Configure an ACL for TCP Intercept. This will protect the hosts on the intranet (e.g.
web servers) from SYN floods.
access-list 120 remark TCP Intercept ACL
access-list 120 permit tcp any 7.7.7.0 0.0.0.255
!
Rate limit (CAR) ACLs for UDP, ICMP, and multicast.
access-list 150 remark CAR-UDP ACL
access-list 150 permit udp any any
access-list 160 remark CAR-ICMP ACL
access-list 160 permit icmp any any
access-list 170 remark CAR-Multicast ACL
access-list 170 permit ip any 224.0.0.0 15.255.255.255
```

Example 8-15 *Secure IOS Template from http://www.cymru.com/ with Some Commentary (Continued)*

```
!
Deny any packets from the RFC 1918, IANA reserved, test, multicast as a source, and
loopback netblocks to block attacks from commonly spoofed IP addresses.
access-list 2010 remark Anti-bogon ACL
This ACL will stop packets that claim they came from the inside network, yet arrives
on the outside (read: Internet) interface. Do not use this if CEF has been configured
to take care of spoofing. uRPF does not_ require the two ACLs.  The two ACLs that
list the internal prefixes, both commented out in my template, are superfluous if
uRPF is used.
! access-list 2010 deny ip 6.6.6.0 0.0.0.255 any log-input
! access-list 2010 deny ip 7.7.7.0 0.0.0.255 any log-input
access-list 2010 deny ip 1.0.0.0 0.255.255.255 any log-input
access-list 2010 deny ip 2.0.0.0 0.255.255.255 any log-input
access-list 2010 deny ip 5.0.0.0 0.255.255.255 any log-input
access-list 2010 deny ip 7.0.0.0 0.255.255.255 any log-input
access-list 2010 deny ip 10.0.0.0 0.255.255.255 any log-input
access-list 2010 deny ip 23.0.0.0 0.255.255.255 any log-input
access-list 2010 deny ip 27.0.0.0 0.255.255.255 any log-input
access-list 2010 deny ip 31.0.0.0 0.255.255.255 any log-input
access-list 2010 deny ip 36.0.0.0 0.255.255.255 any log-input
access-list 2010 deny ip 37.0.0.0 0.255.255.255 any log-input
access-list 2010 deny ip 39.0.0.0 0.255.255.255 any log-input
access-list 2010 deny ip 41.0.0.0 0.255.255.255 any log-input
access-list 2010 deny ip 42.0.0.0 0.255.255.255 any log-input
access-list 2010 deny ip 49.0.0.0 0.255.255.255 any log-input
access-list 2010 deny ip 50.0.0.0 0.255.255.255 any log-input
access-list 2010 deny ip 58.0.0.0 0.255.255.255 any log-input
access-list 2010 deny ip 59.0.0.0 0.255.255.255 any log-input
access-list 2010 deny ip 60.0.0.0 0.255.255.255 any log-input
access-list 2010 deny ip 70.0.0.0 0.255.255.255 any log-input
access-list 2010 deny ip 71.0.0.0 0.255.255.255 any log-input
access-list 2010 deny ip 72.0.0.0 0.255.255.255 any log-input
access-list 2010 deny ip 73.0.0.0 0.255.255.255 any log-input
access-list 2010 deny ip 74.0.0.0 0.255.255.255 any log-input
access-list 2010 deny ip 75.0.0.0 0.255.255.255 any log-input
access-list 2010 deny ip 76.0.0.0 0.255.255.255 any log-input
access-list 2010 deny ip 77.0.0.0 0.255.255.255 any log-input
access-list 2010 deny ip 78.0.0.0 0.255.255.255 any log-input
access-list 2010 deny ip 79.0.0.0 0.255.255.255 any log-input
access-list 2010 deny ip 82.0.0.0 0.255.255.255 any log-input
access-list 2010 deny ip 83.0.0.0 0.255.255.255 any log-input
access-list 2010 deny ip 84.0.0.0 0.255.255.255 any log-input
access-list 2010 deny ip 85.0.0.0 0.255.255.255 any log-input
access-list 2010 deny ip 86.0.0.0 0.255.255.255 any log-input
access-list 2010 deny ip 87.0.0.0 0.255.255.255 any log-input
access-list 2010 deny ip 88.0.0.0 0.255.255.255 any log-input
access-list 2010 deny ip 89.0.0.0 0.255.255.255 any log-input
access-list 2010 deny ip 90.0.0.0 0.255.255.255 any log-input
access-list 2010 deny ip 91.0.0.0 0.255.255.255 any log-input
access-list 2010 deny ip 92.0.0.0 0.255.255.255 any log-input
access-list 2010 deny ip 93.0.0.0 0.255.255.255 any log-input
access-list 2010 deny ip 94.0.0.0 0.255.255.255 any log-input
```

continues

Example 8-15 *Secure IOS Template from http://www.cymru.com/ with Some Commentary (Continued)*

```
access-list 2010 deny ip 95.0.0.0 0.255.255.255 any log-input
access-list 2010 deny ip 96.0.0.0 0.255.255.255 any log-input
access-list 2010 deny ip 97.0.0.0 0.255.255.255 any log-input
access-list 2010 deny ip 98.0.0.0 0.255.255.255 any log-input
access-list 2010 deny ip 99.0.0.0 0.255.255.255 any log-input
access-list 2010 deny ip 100.0.0.0 0.255.255.255 any log-input
access-list 2010 deny ip 101.0.0.0 0.255.255.255 any log-input
access-list 2010 deny ip 102.0.0.0 0.255.255.255 any log-input
access-list 2010 deny ip 103.0.0.0 0.255.255.255 any log-input
access-list 2010 deny ip 104.0.0.0 0.255.255.255 any log-input
access-list 2010 deny ip 105.0.0.0 0.255.255.255 any log-input
access-list 2010 deny ip 106.0.0.0 0.255.255.255 any log-input
access-list 2010 deny ip 107.0.0.0 0.255.255.255 any log-input
access-list 2010 deny ip 108.0.0.0 0.255.255.255 any log-input
access-list 2010 deny ip 109.0.0.0 0.255.255.255 any log-input
access-list 2010 deny ip 110.0.0.0 0.255.255.255 any log-input
access-list 2010 deny ip 111.0.0.0 0.255.255.255 any log-input
access-list 2010 deny ip 112.0.0.0 0.255.255.255 any log-input
access-list 2010 deny ip 113.0.0.0 0.255.255.255 any log-input
access-list 2010 deny ip 114.0.0.0 0.255.255.255 any log-input
access-list 2010 deny ip 115.0.0.0 0.255.255.255 any log-input
access-list 2010 deny ip 116.0.0.0 0.255.255.255 any log-input
access-list 2010 deny ip 117.0.0.0 0.255.255.255 any log-input
access-list 2010 deny ip 118.0.0.0 0.255.255.255 any log-input
access-list 2010 deny ip 119.0.0.0 0.255.255.255 any log-input
access-list 2010 deny ip 120.0.0.0 0.255.255.255 any log-input
access-list 2010 deny ip 121.0.0.0 0.255.255.255 any log-input
access-list 2010 deny ip 122.0.0.0 0.255.255.255 any log-input
access-list 2010 deny ip 123.0.0.0 0.255.255.255 any log-input
access-list 2010 deny ip 124.0.0.0 0.255.255.255 any log-input
access-list 2010 deny ip 125.0.0.0 0.255.255.255 any log-input
access-list 2010 deny ip 126.0.0.0 0.255.255.255 any log-input
access-list 2010 deny ip 127.0.0.0 0.255.255.255 any log-input
access-list 2010 deny ip 169.254.0.0 0.0.255.255 any log-input
access-list 2010 deny ip 172.16.0.0 0.15.255.255 any log-input
access-list 2010 deny ip 192.0.2.0 0.0.0.255 any log-input
access-list 2010 deny ip 192.168.0.0 0.0.255.255 any log-input
access-list 2010 deny ip 197.0.0.0 0.255.255.255 any log-input
access-list 2010 deny ip 201.0.0.0 0.255.255.255 any log-input
access-list 2010 deny ip 222.0.0.0 0.255.255.255 any log-input
access-list 2010 deny ip 223.0.0.0 0.255.255.255 any log-input
access-list 2010 deny ip 224.0.0.0 31.255.255.255 any log-input
Drop all ICMP fragments
access-list 2010 deny icmp any any fragments log-input
Allow IP access to the intranet (firewall filters specific ports)
access-list 2010 permit ip any 7.7.7.0 0.0.0.255
Allow multicast to enter IF you are using multicast. See also access-list 30 for
more specific multicast rules.
access-list 2010 permit ip any 224.0.0.0 15.255.255.255
Our explicit (read: logged everything) deny all else rule
access-list 2010 deny ip any any log-input
!
```

Example 8-15   *Secure IOS Template from http://www.cymru.com/ with Some Commentary (Continued)*

Do not share Cisco Discovery Protocol (CDP) information from your secure router it's just not wise, because CDP contains crucial bits of information about your network topology, device configuration, network devices in use, ip addresses, etc. This command disabled CDP globally. If you require CDP on an interface, use cdp run and disable cdp (no cdp enable) on the Internet-facing interface. In other words use CDP *only* on interfaces where it is needed, *never globally!*

```
no cdp run
!
```

SNMP is VERY important for network management, particularly when in conjunction with MRTG to track usage statistics. To keep SNMP access even more secure treat the COMMUNITY string as a password - keep it difficult to guess by using CAPS, lowercase and Numbers all together. Then include the ACL that we created to further increase security. Notice that we do *not* allow SNMP Read/Write.

```
snmp-server community <COMMUNITY> RO 20
!
```

Introduce ourselves with an appropriately stern banner that reflects the level of security and monitoring applied to our network. It is also important to set the expectations of everyone accessing the router as well as what will happen if attacks are made against it. While we are just showing the Message of the Day (MOTD) Banner it is recommended that you apply the same banner to the console port, aux port, AAA Login, and whenever a user accesses EXEC mode.

```
banner motd %
```
Warning!!! This system is solely for the use of authorized users and only for official purposes. Users must have express written permission to access this system. You have no expectation of privacy in its use and to ensure that the system is functioning properly, individuals using this system are subject to having their activities monitored and recorded at all times. Use of this system evidences an express consent to such monitoring and agreement that if such monitoring reveals evidence of possible abuse or criminal activity the results of such monitoring will be supplied to the appropriate officials to be prosecuted to the fullest extent of both civil and criminal law.
```
%
!
```

Apply a password to the console port of a router. It can often be accessed physical so another layer of security helps. Including the transport input none disables reverse telnet and protects the physical ports against access.

```
line con 0
 exec-timeout 15 0
 transport input none
line aux 0
 exec-timeout 15 0
 transport input none
```
Apply the ACL to the VTY ports that define which systems can attempt to access this router.
```
line vty 0 3
 access-class 100 in
 exec-timeout 15 0
```
Enable SSH connectivity. This is much more secure than telnet. Obviously, you must have an IOS image that supports SSH, and don't forget to generate the key with crypto key generate rsa.
```
 transport input telnet ssh
line vty 4
 access-class 105 in
 exec-timeout 15 0
 transport input telnet ssh
!
```

Case Study: Router and Firewall Deployment

This case study discusses the deployment of Cisco PIX Firewall within a network. A router firewall architecture is a network structure that exists between you and the outside world (for example, the Internet) that is designed to protect your network from intruders (that is, cyber-thieves). In most circumstances, intruders are represented by the global Internet and the thousands of remote networks it interconnects. Typically, a network firewall consists of several different machines, as shown in Figure 8-17.

Figure 8-17 *Typical Firewall Router Deployment*

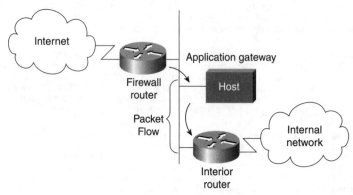

In this network architecture, the router that is connected to the Internet (exterior router) forces all incoming traffic to go to the application gateway. The router that is connected to the internal network (interior router) accepts packets only from the application gateway.

The application gateway institutes per-application and per-user policies. In effect, the gateway controls the delivery of network-based services both into and from the internal network. For example, only certain users might be allowed to communicate with the Internet, or only certain applications might be permitted to establish connections between an interior and exterior host.

The route and packet filters should be set up to reflect the same policies. If the only application that is permitted is electronic mail, then only electronic mail packets should be allowed through the interior router. This protects the application gateway and avoids overwhelming it with packets that it would otherwise discard.

Defending Against Attacks Directly to Network Devices

Any network device that has both the UDP and TCP diagnostic services available should be protected by a firewall or at least have the services disabled. For a Cisco router, this can be accomplished by using the following global configuration commands:

```
no service udp-small-servers
no service tcp-small-servers
```

Controlling Traffic Flow

This section uses the scenario illustrated in Figure 8-18 to describe the use of access lists to restrict traffic to and from a firewall router and a firewall communication server. Notice the communications server that was added to the network architecture to service dial-in users.

Figure 8-18   *Controlling Traffic Flow with the Firewall Router*

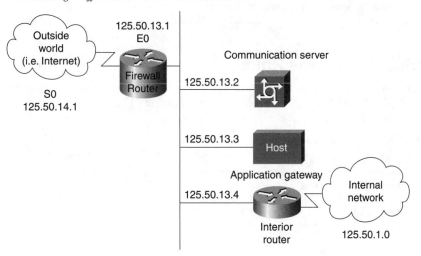

In this case study, the firewall router allows incoming new connections to one or more communication servers or hosts. Having a designated router act as a firewall is desirable because it clearly identifies the router's purpose as the external gateway and avoids encumbering other routers with this task. In the event that the internal network needs to isolate itself, the firewall router provides the point of isolation so that the rest of the internal network structure is not affected.

Connections to the hosts are restricted to incoming File Transfer Protocol (FTP) requests and e-mail services as described in the "Defining Firewall Access Lists" section later in this case study. The Telnet, or modem, connections coming into the communication server are screened by the communication server running TACACS user name authentication, as described in the "Configuring the Communication Server Communications Server" section later in this case study.

TIP	Connections from one communication server modem line to another outgoing modem line (or to the outside world) should be disallowed to prevent unauthorized users from using your resources to launch an attack on the outside world. Because intruders have already passed the communication server TACACS authentication at this point, they are likely to have someone's password. It is an excellent idea to keep TACACS passwords and host passwords separate from one another.

Configuring the Firewall Router

In the firewall router configuration in Example 8-16, subnet 152.50.13.0 of the Class B 152.50.0.0 network is the firewall subnet, and subnet 152.50.14.0 provides the connection to the worldwide Internet via a service provider.

Example 8-16 *Firewall Router Configuration*

```
interface ethernet 0
ip address 125.50.13.1 255.255.255.0
interface serial 0
ip address 125.50.14.1 255.255.255.0
router ospf 500
network 125.50.0.0
```

This simple configuration provides no security and allows all traffic from the outside world onto all parts of your network. To provide security on the firewall router, use access lists and access groups as described in the next section. Perhaps the situation might even warrant the use of OSPF area authentication here.

Defining Firewall Access Lists

Access lists define the actual traffic that is permitted or denied into the internal network, and an access group applies an access list definition to a specific router interface. Access lists can be used to do one of the following items:

- Deny connections that are known to be a security risk and then permit all other connections

- Permit those connections that are considered acceptable and deny all the rest

For a router firewall implementation, the latter is the more secure method, and that is how you will be using your access lists.

In this case study, incoming e-mail and news are permitted for a few hosts, but FTP, Telnet, and rlogin services are permitted only to hosts on the firewall subnet. IP extended access lists (range 100–199) and Transmission Control Protocol (TCP) or User Datagram Protocol (UDP) port numbers are used to filter traffic. When a connection is to be established for e-mail, Telnet, FTP, and so on, the connection attempts to open a service on a specified port number. Therefore, you can filter out selected types of connections by denying packets that are attempting to use that service.

Remember, an access list is invoked after a routing decision has been made but before the packet is sent out on an interface. The best place to define an access list is on a preferred host using your favorite text editor (such as Notepad). You can create a file that contains the **access-list** commands and then cut and paste directly into the router while in configuration mode.

You should remove any instances of an old access list before loading a new or altered version. You can remove access lists with the following command while in configuration mode:

```
no access-list 101
```

The **access-list** command can now be used to permit any packets returning to machines from already established connections. With the established keyword, a match occurs if the TCP datagram has the acknowledgment (ACK) or reset (RST) bit set, as follows:

```
access-list 101 permit tcp 0.0.0.0 255.255.255.255 0.0.0.0 255.255.255.255
established
```

If any firewall routers share a common network with an outside provider, you might want to allow access from those hosts to your network. In this case study, the outside provider has a serial port that uses the firewall router Class B address (125.50.14.2) as a source address so your **access-list** statement to permit them access would be as follows:

```
access-list 101 permit ip 125.50.14.2 0.0.0.0 0.0.0.0 255.255.255.255
```

The following example illustrates how to deny traffic from a user attempting to spoof any of your internal addresses from the outside world:

```
access-list 101 deny ip 125.50.0.0 0.0.255.255 0.0.0.0 255.255.255.255
```

The following access list examples are designed based on many of the well-known port numbers found within the TCP/IP stack. For a list of some of the more common port numbers, refer to Table 8-2.

Table 8-2   *Port Number Assignments*

Port Number	Port Type	Protocol	Keyword (if applicable)
0	TCP & UDP	Reserved	-
1–4	TCP & UDP	Unassigned	-
5	TCP & UDP	Remote Job Entry	RJE
7	TCP & UDP	Echo	ECHO
9	TCP & UDP	Discard	DISCARD
11	TCP & UDP	Active Users	USERS
13	TCP & UDP	Daytime	DAYTIME

continues

Table 8-2 *Port Number Assignments (Continued)*

Port Number	Port Type	Protocol	Keyword (if applicable)
15	TCP & UDP	Who is up or Netstat	NETSTAT
17	TCP & UDP	Quote of the Day	QUOTE
19	TCP & UDP	Character Generator	CHARGEN
20	TCP & UDP	File Transfer (Default Data)	FTP-DATA
21	TCP & UDP	File Transfer (Control)	FTP
23	TCP & UDP	Telnet	TELNET
25	TCP & UDP	SMTP	SMTP
37	TCP & UDP	Time	TIME
39	TCP & UDP	Resource Location Protocol	RLP
42	TCP & UDP	Host Name Server	NAMESERVER
43	TCP & UDP	Who Is	NICNAME
49	TCP & UDP	TACACS	TACACS
53	TCP & UDP	Domain Name Server	DOMAIN
67	TCP & UDP	Bootstrap Protocol Server	BOOTPS
68	TCP & UDP	Bootstrap Protocol Client	BOOTPC
69	TCP & UDP	Trivial File Transfer Protocol	TFTP
70	TCP & UDP	Gopher	GOPHER
75	TCP & UDP	Any private dial-out service	-
77	TCP & UDP	Any private RJE service	-
79	TCP & UDP	Finger	FINGER
80	TCP & UDP	Hypertext Transfer Protocol (HTTP)	WWW
87	TCP	Link, commonly used by intruders	-

Table 8-2   *Port Number Assignments (Continued)*

Port Number	Port Type	Protocol	Keyword (if applicable)
88	TCP & UDP	Kerberos	KERBEROS
89	TCP & UDP	Open Shortest Path First	OSPF
95	TCP	SUPDUP Protocol	SUPDUP
101	TCP	NIC Host Name Server	HOSTNAME
102	TCP	ISO-TSAP	ISO-TSAP
103	TCP	X400	X400
104	TCP	X400-SND	X400-SND
107	TCP & UDP	Remote Telnet Service	RTELNET
109	TCP	Post Office Protocol v2	POP2
110	TCP	Post Office Protocol v3	POP3
111	TCP & UDP	SUN Remote Procedure Call	SUNRPC
113	TCP & UDP	Authentication Service	AUTH
117	TCP & UDP	UUCP Path Service	UUCP-PATH
119	TCP & UDP	USENET Network News Transfer Protocol	NNTP
123 TCP & UDP	Network Time Protocol (NTP)	Well-Known	-
133	TCP & UDP	Unassigned	-
136	-	-	-
137	UDP	NETBIOS Name Service	NETBIOS-NS
137	TCP	Unassigned	-

continues

Table 8-2 *Port Number Assignments (Continued)*

Port Number	Port Type	Protocol	Keyword (if applicable)
138	UDP	NETBIOS Datagram Service	NETBIOS-DGM
138	TCP	Unassigned	-
139	UDP	NETBIOS Session Service	NETBIOS-SSN
144	TCP	NeWS	Well-Known
161	TCP & UDP	Simple Network Management Protocol Q/R	SNMP
162	TCP & UDP	SNMP Event Traps	SNMP-TRAP
177	UDP	X Display Manager Control Protocol	xdmcp
179	TCP & UDP	Border Gateway Protocol (BGP)	Well-Known
194	TCP & UDP	Internet Relay Chat	IRC
195	UDP	DNSIX security protocol auditing	Dnsix
389	TCP & UDP	Lightweight Directory Access Protocol	LDAP
434	UDP	Mobile IP Registration	Mobile-ip
512	TCP	UNIX rexec (Control)	rexec
513	TCP & UDP	UNIX rlogin	rlogin
514	TCP & UDP	UNIX rsh and rcp, Remote Commands	rsh
514	TCP	System Logging	Syslog
515	TCP	UNIX Line Printer Remote Spooling	printer
517	TCP & UDP	Two User Interaction—talk	Well-Known
518	TCP & UDP	ntalk	Well-Known
520	UDP	Routing Information Protocol	RIP

Table 8-2   *Port Number Assignments (Continued)*

Port Number	Port Type	Protocol	Keyword (if applicable)
525	UDP	Time Server	timed
540	TCP	UNIX-to-UNIX copy program daemon	uucpd
543	TCP	Kerberos login	klogin
544	TCP	Kerberos shell	kshell
1993	TCP	SNMP over TCP	-
2000	TCP & UDP	Open Windows	Well-Known
2001	-	Auxiliary (AUX) port	-
2049	UDP	Network File System (NFS)	Well-Known
4001	-	Auxiliary (AUX) port (stream)	-
6000	TCP & UDP	X11 (X Windows)	Well-Known

NOTE   Port 111 is only a directory service. If you can guess the ports on which the actual data services are provided, you can access them. Most RPC services do not have fixed port numbers. You should find the ports on which these services can be accessed and block them. Unfortunately, because ports can be bound anywhere, Cisco recommends blocking all UDP ports except DNS where practical.

Cisco recommends that you filter the finger TCP service at port 79 to prevent outsiders from learning about internal user directories and the names of hosts from which users log in.

The following two **access-list** commands allow Domain Name System (DNS, port 53) and Network Time Protocol (NTP, port 123) requests and replies based on their TCP/IP port addresses:

```
access-list 101 permit udp 0.0.0.0 255.255.255.255 0.0.0.0 255.255.255.255 eq 53
access-list 101 permit udp 0.0.0.0 255.255.255.255 0.0.0.0 255.255.255.255 eq 123
```

The following command denies the Network File Server (NFS) User Datagram Protocol (UDP, port 2049) port:

```
access-list 101 deny udp 0.0.0.0 255.255.255.255 0.0.0.0 255.255.255.255 eq 2049
```

The following commands deny OpenWindows on ports 2001 and 2002 and deny X11 on ports 6001 and 6002. This protects the first two screens on any host. If you have any machine that uses more than the first two screens, be sure to block the appropriate ports.

```
access-list 101 deny tcp 0.0.0.0 255.255.255.255 0.0.0.0 255.255.255.255 eq 6001
access-list 101 deny tcp 0.0.0.0 255.255.255.255 0.0.0.0 255.255.255.255 eq 6002
access-list 101 deny tcp 0.0.0.0 255.255.255.255 0.0.0.0 255.255.255.255 eq 2001
access-list 101 deny tcp 0.0.0.0 255.255.255.255 0.0.0.0 255.255.255.255 eq 2002
```

The following command permits Telnet access from anyone to the communication server (125.50.13.2):

```
access-list 101 permit tcp 0.0.0.0 255.255.255.255 125.50.13.2 0.0.0.0 eq 23
```

The following commands permit FTP access from anyone to the host 125.50.13.100 on subnet 125.50.13.0:

```
access-list 101 permit tcp 0.0.0.0 255.255.255.255 125.50.13.100 0.0.0.0 eq 21
access-list 101 permit tcp 0.0.0.0 255.255.255.255 125.50.13.100 0.0.0.0 eq 20
```

For the following examples, network 125.50.1.0 is on the internal network, as shown in Figure 8-18.

The following access-list commands permit TCP and UDP connections for port numbers greater than 1023 to a very limited set of hosts. Make sure that no communication servers or protocol translators are in this list.

```
access-list 101 permit tcp 0.0.0.0 255.255.255.255 125.50.13.100 0.0.0.0 gt 1023
access-list 101 permit tcp 0.0.0.0 255.255.255.255 125.50.1.100 0.0.0.0 gt 1023
access-list 101 permit tcp 0.0.0.0 255.255.255.255 125.50.1.101 0.0.0.0 gt 1023
access-list 101 permit udp 0.0.0.0 255.255.255.255 125.50.13.100 0.0.0.0 gt 1023
access-list 101 permit udp 0.0.0.0 255.255.255.255 125.50.1.100 0.0.0.0 gt 1023
access-list 101 permit udp 0.0.0.0 255.255.255.255 125.50.1.101 0.0.0.0 gt 1023
```

Standard FTP uses ports above 1023 for its data connections; therefore, for standard FTP operation, ports above 1023 must all be open.

The following **access-list** commands permit DNS access to the DNS server(s) listed by the Network Information Center (NIC):

```
access-list 101 permit tcp 0.0.0.0 255.255.255.255 125.50.13.100 0.0.0.0 eq 53
access-list 101 permit tcp 0.0.0.0 255.255.255.255 125.50.1.100 0.0.0.0 eq 53
```

The following commands permit incoming Simple Mail Transfer Protocol (SMTP) e-mail to only a few machines:

```
access-list 101 permit tcp 0.0.0.0 255.255.255.255 125.50.13.100 0.0.0.0 eq 25
access-list 101 permit tcp 0.0.0.0 255.255.255.255 125.50.1.100 0.0.0.0 eq 25
```

The following commands allow internal Network News Transfer Protocol (NNTP) servers to receive NNTP connections from a list of authorized peers:

```
access-list 101 permit tcp 56.1.0.18 0.0.0.1 125.50.1.100 0.0.0.0 eq 119
access-list 101 permit tcp 182.12.18.32 0.0.0.0 125.50.1.100 0.0.0.0 eq 119
```

The following command permits Internet Control Message Protocol (ICMP) for error message feedback:

```
access-list 101 permit icmp 0.0.0.0 255.255.255.255 0.0.0.0 255.255.255.255
```

Every access list has an implicit deny all (that is, everything not mentioned in the access list) statement at the end of the list to ensure that attributes that are not expressly permitted are denied. When compiled without descriptions of each line's function, the completed access list looks like Example 8-17.

Example 8-17 *The Final Firewall Access List Configuration*

```
access-list 101 permit udp 0.0.0.0 255.255.255.255 0.0.0.0 255.255.255.255 eq 123
access-list 101 deny udp 0.0.0.0 255.255.255.255 0.0.0.0 255.255.255.255 eq 2049
access-list 101 deny tcp 0.0.0.0 255.255.255.255 0.0.0.0 255.255.255.255 eq 6001
access-list 101 deny tcp 0.0.0.0 255.255.255.255 0.0.0.0 255.255.255.255 eq 6002
access-list 101 deny tcp 0.0.0.0 255.255.255.255 0.0.0.0 255.255.255.255 eq 2001
access-list 101 deny tcp 0.0.0.0 255.255.255.255 0.0.0.0 255.255.255.255 eq 2002
access-list 101 permit tcp 0.0.0.0 255.255.255.255 125.50.13.2 0.0.0.0 eq 23
access-list 101 permit tcp 0.0.0.0 255.255.255.255 125.50.13.100 0.0.0.0 eq 21
access-list 101 permit tcp 0.0.0.0 255.255.255.255 125.50.13.100 0.0.0.0 eq 20
access-list 101 permit tcp 0.0.0.0 255.255.255.255 125.50.13.100 0.0.0.0 gt 1023
access-list 101 permit tcp 0.0.0.0 255.255.255.255 125.50.1.100 0.0.0.0 gt 1023
access-list 101 permit tcp 0.0.0.0 255.255.255.255 125.50.1.101 0.0.0.0 gt 1023
access-list 101 permit udp 0.0.0.0 255.255.255.255 125.50.13.100 0.0.0.0 gt 1023
access-list 101 permit udp 0.0.0.0 255.255.255.255 125.50.1.100 0.0.0.0 gt 1023
access-list 101 permit udp 0.0.0.0 255.255.255.255 125.50.1.101 0.0.0.0 gt 1023
access-list 101 permit tcp 0.0.0.0 255.255.255.255 125.50.13.100 0.0.0.0 eq 53
access-list 101 permit tcp 0.0.0.0 255.255.255.255 125.50.1.100 0.0.0.0 eq 53
access-list 101 permit tcp 0.0.0.0 255.255.255.255 125.50.13.100 0.0.0.0 eq 25
access-list 101 permit tcp 0.0.0.0 255.255.255.255 125.50.1.100 0.0.0.0 eq 25
access-list 101 permit tcp 56.1.0.18 0.0.0.1 125.50.1.100 0.0.0.0 eq 119
access-list 101 permit tcp 182.12.18.32 0.0.0.0 125.50.1.100 0.0.0.0 eq 119
access-list 101 permit icmp 0.0.0.0 255.255.255.255 0.0.0.0 255.255.255.255
```

Applying Access Lists to Interfaces

After the access list in Example 8-17 has been loaded onto the router and stored into nonvolatile random-access memory (NVRAM), assign the list to the appropriate interface. In this case study, traffic coming from the outside world via the serial 0 interface of the firewall router is filtered (via access list 101) before it is placed on the subnet 125.50.13.0 (Ethernet 0). Therefore, the **access-group** command, which assigns an access list to filter incoming connections, must be assigned to Ethernet 0, as follows:

```
interface ethernet 0
ip access-group 101 in
```

To control outgoing access to the Internet from the network, define an access list and apply it to the outgoing packets on serial 0 interface of the firewall router. To do this, returning packets from hosts using Telnet or FTP must be allowed to access the firewall subnetwork 125.50.13.0.

Configuring the Communication Server

In this case study, the firewall communication server has a single inbound modem on line 2, as shown in Example 8-18.

Example 8-18 *Comm Server Configuration*

```
interface Ethernet0
ip address 125.50.13.2 255.255.255.0
!
access-list 10 deny 125.50.14.0 0.0.0.255
access-list 10 permit 125.50.0.0 0.0.255.255
!
access-list 11 deny 125.50.13.2 0.0.0.0
access-list 11 permit 125.50.0.0 0.0.255.255
!
line 2
login tacacs
location FireWallCS#2
!
access-class 10 in
access-class 11 out
!
modem answer-timeout 60
modem InOut
telnet transparent
terminal-type dialup
flowcontrol hardware
stopbits 1
rxspeed 38400
txspeed 38400
!
tacacs-server host 125.50.1.100
tacacs-server host 125.50.1.101
tacacs-server extended
!
line vty 0 15
login tacacs
```

Defining the Communication Server's Access Lists

In this example, the network number is used to permit or deny access; therefore, standard IP access list numbers (range 1 through 99) are used. For incoming connections to modem lines, only packets from hosts on the internal Class B network and packets from those hosts on the firewall subnetwork are permitted, as follows:

```
access-list 10 deny 125.50.14.0 0.0.0.255
access-list 10 permit 125.50.0.0 0.0.255.255
```

Outgoing connections are allowed only to internal network hosts and to the communication server. This prevents a modem line in the outside world from calling out on a second modem line, as follows:

```
access-list 11 deny 125.50.13.2 0.0.0.0
access-list 11 permit 125.50.0.0 0.0.255.255
```

Applying Access Lists to Lines

Apply an access list to an asynchronous line with the **access-class** command. In this case study, the restrictions from access list 10 are applied to incoming connections on line 2. The restrictions from access list 11 are applied to outgoing connections on line 2, as follows:

```
access-class 10 in
access-class 11 out
```

Spoofing and Inbound Access Lists

In Cisco IOS Software Release 9.21, Cisco introduced the capability to assign input access lists to an interface. This enables a network administrator to filter packets before they enter the router instead of as they leave the router. In most cases, input access lists and output access lists accomplish the same functionality. However, input access lists are considered more intuitive by some people and can be used to protect some types of IP address from "spoofing," whereas output access lists do not provide sufficient security.

Figure 8-19 illustrates a cyber-thief host that is spoofing, or illegally claiming to be an address that it is not. Someone in the outside world is claiming to originate traffic from network 125.50.13.0. Although the IP address is spoofed, the router interface to the outside world assumes that the packet is coming from 125.50.13.0. If the input access list on the router allows traffic coming from 125.50.13.0, it accepts the illegal packet.

Figure 8-19   *Spoofing Example*

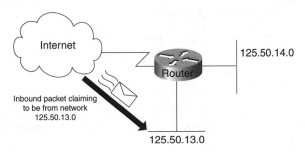

To avoid this spoofing situation, an input access list should be applied to the router interface to the outside world. This access list would not allow any packets with addresses that are from the internal networks of which the router is aware (13.0 and 14.0).

TIP   If you have several internal networks connected to the firewall router and the router is using output filters, traffic between internal networks sees a reduction in performance created by the access list filters. If input filters are used only on the interface going from the router to the outside world, internal networks do not see any reduction in performance.

If an address uses source routing, it can send and receive traffic through the firewall router. For this reason, you should always disable source routing on the firewall router with the **no ip source-route** command.

Additional Firewall Security Considerations

This section addresses some specific topics regarding security and discusses some of the issues surrounding them.

File Transfer Protocol Port

Many sites today choose to block incoming TCP sessions originated from the outside world while allowing outgoing connections. The trouble with this is that blocking incoming connections kills traditional FTP client programs because these programs use the **PORT** command to tell the server where to connect to send the file. The client opens a "control" connection to the server, but the server then opens a "data" connection to an effectively arbitrarily chosen port number (> 1023) on the client.

Fortunately, there is an alternative to this behavior that allows the client to open the data socket, which allows you to have the firewall and FTP as well. The client sends a **PASV** command to the server, receives a port number for the data socket, opens the data socket to the indicated port, and finally sends the transfer.

To implement this, the standard FTP client program must be replaced with a modified one that supports the **PASV** command. Most recent implementations of the FTP server already support the **PASV** command. The only trouble with this idea is that it breaks down when the server site has also blocked arbitrary incoming connections.

Source files for a modified FTP program that works through a firewall are now available via anonymous FTP at ftp.cisco.com. The filename is /pub/passive-ftp.tar.z. This is a version of BSD 4.3 FTP with the PASV patches. It works through a firewall router that allows only incoming established connections.

CAUTION   Use care in providing anonymous FTP service on the host system. Anonymous FTP service allows anyone to access the hosts, without requiring an account on the host system. Many implementations of the FTP server have severe bugs in this area. Also, use care in the implementation and setup of the anonymous FTP service to prevent any obvious access violations. For most sites, anonymous FTP service is disabled.

CHAPTER 9

Troubleshooting OSPF

Nothing has changed, and anything we did change we changed back. — Anonymous

This chapter builds on the design theories and OSPF communication processes discussed throughout the book prior to this chapter. The basis for this chapter is how to go about monitoring OSPF to ensure that it is operating correctly and what to do if it is not. This chapter also covers specific troubleshooting procedures and techniques that you can use to determine the causes of a network problem.

Understanding the commands necessary to troubleshoot and diagnose the inevitable OSPF operational problems requires a strong chapter to provide you with the techniques needed to troubleshoot more effectively when an OSPF-related network problem occurs. This chapter also assists you in developing your network and its related structure to allow you to reduce the duration of any network problem through the use of various types of logging. This information is supplemented by in-depth discussions of various troubleshooting-related commands whose focus is debugging OSPF in support of correcting any problems that might exist.

The Mechanics of Troubleshooting OSPF

This section deals with the inevitable network routing problems that surface from time to time. These problems can take many forms, from straightforward loss of connectivity to the more complex routing loops. You are provided with a variety of "best practices," which can help prepare the network for troubleshooting, ready yourself to respond to a network event, and provide resources that can assist in resolving these issues. Other issues that are not within the scope of this book are mentioned briefly.

Even though additional problems exist that might influence or alter OSPF's operation, such as access list configuration, buffer usage, and queue sizes, these issues are beyond the scope of this book. Consult Cisco.com for information regarding these subjects, as the focus in this chapter is specific to OSPF.

As with any potentially complex problem, certain techniques and methodology have evolved to deal with troubleshooting network-related problems. This troubleshooting methodology is not only applicable to OSPF; it can also be used to assist you with any network problem.

Preparing for Network Failure

Hopefully, this heading really caught your attention! Certainly you do not hear much about preparing for a network failure. Discussion usually revolves around what to do in the *event* of a failure; however, in preparing for the inevitable, you can better respond when the inevitable failure occurs. This makes the old adage "forewarned is forearmed" quite relevant to this chapter. Because you have been warned that a problem is coming, you need the required knowledge to prepare. You can recover from a network failure more easily if you are prepared ahead of time. To see if you are prepared for a network failure, answer the following questions:

- **Do you have an accurate physical and logical map of your internetwork?**—Does your organization or department have an up-to-date internetwork map that outlines the physical location of all the devices on the network and how they are connected, as well as a logical map of network IP address assignments, network numbers, subnet masks, router interfaces, circuit IDs, and so forth? Probably the most important attitude to have with regard to keeping a network map is ensuring that it is a living document synchronized with the changes and evolution of your network. If this advice is not followed, it is of little use in times of stress during a network failure.

- **Do you have an established baseline for your network?**—Has your organization documented the baseline or normal network behavior and performance so that you can compare current problems with a baseline? This documentation is essential to understanding the network and judging the impact of changes to your network. These changes can be related to either a network failure or the introduction of new network service.

- **Do you have a list of all network protocols implemented in your network?**—For each of the routing or routed protocols implemented, do you have a list of the network numbers, IP addresses, router IDs (RIDs), DLCIs, subnetworks, zones, areas, and so on that are associated with them?

- **Do you know which protocols are being routed? For each of these protocols, do you have a correct and current router configuration?**—You also need to keep copies of router configuration files before and after major network changes. This helps ensure that a readily available backup exists in case the change must be reversed. In addition, if a router needs to be replaced, it is much easier to have the known last good and operating configuration if a router or switch is to be replaced. You might even want to keep the network device configurations electronically and in printed form, just in case!

- **Do you know which protocols are being bridged, filtered, or altered in some manner and where this is occurring in your network?**—Are there any filters configured in any of these routers or switches, and do you have a copy of these configurations? What effect are the filters supposed to have?

- **Do you know all the points of contact to external networks, including any connections to the Internet?**—For each external network connection, do you know what routing protocol is being used? Do you have adequate security in place and documented? How are the external networks being advertised into your OSPF network?

- **Is this information stored in a central location so that it is accessible to everyone concerned with the network operation and management?**—Having the information is only half the battle. The information must be available so that if needed, it can be readily accessed to reduce network downtime.

- **Is there a SYSLOG server, network management server, and performance analysis ongoing?**—These servers play an important role in your network. For example, the SYSLOG server allows receipt of router logs, and this becomes extremely important if you have followed the recommendations in the case study in Chapter 8, "Managing and Securing OSPF Networks." One of the best design and troubleshooting tips I can offer is to use Network Time Protocol (NTP) on all your network devices to date stamp and time stamp all logs.

This preparatory section discussed "the where" and provided you with ideas that you should consider when preparing your network. This preparation allows any events to be more easily managed and solved. In the next section, the methodology, or "the how" aspect of troubleshooting an OSPF network, is examined.

Troubleshooting Methodology

Internetworks come in a variety of topologies and levels of complexity, from single-protocol, point-to-point links connecting cross-town campuses to highly meshed, large-scale WANs traversing multiple time zones and international boundaries. The industry trend is quickly advancing toward increasingly complex environments, involving multiple types of media and multiple protocols and often providing interconnection to unknown networks. Convergence of voice and data is quickly becoming more prevalent, and for many in the industry, it is a reality.

Consequently, the potential for connectivity and performance problems arising in internetworks is high, and the sources of such problems are often elusive. The goal of this section is to help you isolate and resolve the most common connectivity and performance problems within your OSPF network. The methodology here is based on years of experience and a firm belief that a systematic approach to troubleshooting is extremely important.

Failures in internetworks are characterized by certain symptoms. These symptoms might be general (such as clients being unable to access specific servers) or more specific (routes not in the routing table). Each symptom can be traced to one or more problems by using specific troubleshooting tools and techniques. After being identified, each problem can typically be remedied by implementing a solution consisting of a series of actions.

What follows describes how to define symptoms, identify problems, and implement solutions as applicable to an OSPF network, but the basics can also apply to any generic network environment. Always apply the specific context in which you are troubleshooting to determine how to detect symptoms and diagnose problems for your specific environment.

When troubleshooting problems within an OSPF networked environment, a systematic approach works best. Define the specific symptoms, identify potential problems, and then finally systematically eliminate each potential problem (from most likely to least likely) until the symptoms disappear.

This process is not a rigid outline for troubleshooting an internetwork. Rather, it is a solid foundation from which you can build a problem-solving process to suit the particular needs of your OSPF environment.

Figure 9-1 documents the seven steps of the problem-solving process.

Figure 9-1   *Troubleshooting Methodology*

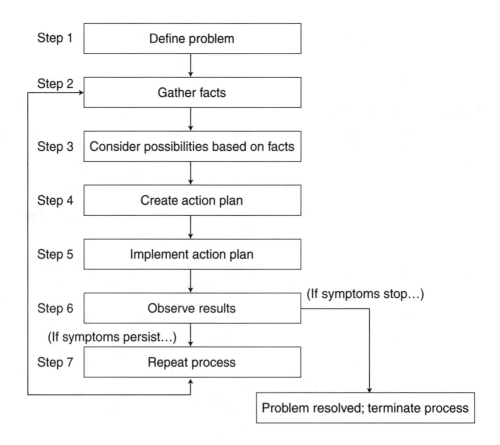

Step 1: Clearly Define the Problem

When analyzing a network problem, make a clear problem statement. You should define the problem in terms of a set of symptoms and potential causes. To do this, identify the general symptoms and then ascertain what kinds of problems (causes) could result in these symptoms.

NOTE	When reporters prepare a story for the newspaper, they try to answer the questions "who, what, when, where, and why." This allows them to retain the most important information and discard the rest. Try and keep these questions in mind during Step 1. They teach you how to stay focused when gathering information about a problem.

Assume, for example, that hosts might not be responding to service requests from clients (the problem). Possible causes might be a misconfigured host, bad interface cards, or missing router configuration commands, which you learn about later in this chapter; however, first you must understand the problem.

Step 2: Gather Facts

Gather the facts you need to help isolate possible causes by asking the following questions of your peers and others:

- **Users that are affected**—What type of problems are they experiencing? Who is affected? What network element do they have in common?

- **Network administrators**—Has anything changed or been added to the network? Did the network work for the user previously?

- **Your peers and associates**—Have the users seen this problem before, or do they know something that might help? Is this a reoccurring or a known network issue?

- **What changed?**—Recent network changes are always a likely problem generator, so it helps to know when changes are being made and by whom.

NOTE	When exploring and gathering facts about the network problem, remember that how you communicate is as important as what you say when communicating to others. For example, you do not want to unknowingly lead people into accidentally providing false data.

Asking questions is a good method of gathering facts, but it is not the only resource available to you. Consider collecting information from the following other sources:

- **Network management system**—What are the indications being reported by your NMS? Is data available that might assist you in the NMS? If your company has spent corporate resources on a NMS, use these resources.

- **Protocol analyzer traces**—What are the characteristics of the traffic? Are you missing something that should be there? (Should you be seeing link-state advertisements [LSAs] but are not?) In this case, it might not be what you see that is important, but what you do not see.

- **Router diagnostic commands**—What does the router tell you is wrong? What do the routers or switches near the affected area report?

- **Cisco IOS Software release notes**—Is what you are experiencing related to new or altered features within Cisco IOS Software? Cisco IOS Software release notes are a great resource in this regard.

- **Cisco bug search**—Could a bug that has already been reported cause what is being experienced? If so, is there a fix for it, or did you just discover it?

- **Remote Monitoring (RMON) probes**—Can you dispatch a probe to reach the location having the problem?

- **Performance analysis tools**—Is this a capacity- or utilization-related issue? Is there a trend going on that long-term monitoring would identify?

You can draw on a variety of different resources to assist you in gathering the facts. A good rule of thumb is that the only dumb question is the one never asked. So tell people to look at what the network is telling you, and utilize various networking-related tools.

Step 3: Consider Possible Problems

The basis for considering a possible problem is tied to the facts you gathered. By using the facts you gathered, you could eliminate potential problems from your list. Armed with your findings and the facts surrounding the problem, you should then use them to discard potential causes of the problem.

For example, depending on the data, you might be able to eliminate hardware as a problem, allowing you to focus on software problems. Another possibility is to let the hardware in question perform a self-test, the results of which are an excellent indicator for you in troubleshooting.

At every opportunity, try to narrow the number of potential problems so that you can create an efficient plan of action. Narrowing the number of possibilities is key to this step. Analyze the data gathered, and use it to reduce the potential causes. This greatly reduces the downtime of the network and increases your accuracy when engaging Step 4. As Sherlock Holmes said, "Eliminate all other factors, and the one which remains must be the truth."

Step 4: Create an Action Plan

Create an action plan based on the remaining potential causes. Begin with the most likely cause, and devise a plan to either prove or disprove that the cause selected was, in fact, the culprit. When creating an action, remember to proceed in steps in which only one variable is manipulated at a time.

For example, you might not see routes to the Internet in your OSPF routing table. You know they are external routes, so look at your ASBR. Verify that your ISP is providing you with the correct routes. If it is, that removes the possibility of an external configuration error as the cause. You can then move on to the next likely cause of the problem.

This approach allows you to reproduce a given solution to a specific problem. If you alter more than one variable simultaneously, you might solve the problem, but identifying the specific change that eliminated the symptom becomes more difficult.

Step 5: Implement the Action Plan

Implement the action plan, performing each step carefully while testing to see if the symptom disappears. You should also have a means of recording your steps during this process. This serves the following purposes during your troubleshooting:

- It provides you with a record of your actions in case you need to recall what was done.

- It ensures that a back-out plan can be implemented immediately, if needed.

- Technical support, if needed, will probably request the information you have been researching.

- After action, reports are always going to require supporting information, and this is a great means of providing it. These reports also help you to write down and learn from the lessons you experienced.

NOTE   Turn on logging in your favorite Telnet client or console program. Take screen shots where applicable. These recorded notes can help prevent duplication or misinterpretation in the wee hours of the night when that cold pizza is turning over in your stomach and you are freezing in the cold data center.

Step 6: Gather Results

Whenever you change a variable, be sure to observe and record the results (if any) because these are the facts of what is now occurring. Generally, you should use the same method of gathering facts that you used in Step 2.

Analyze the results to determine whether the problem has been resolved. If it has, the process is complete. If the problem has not been resolved, continue on to Step 7.

Step 7: Reiterate the Process

If the problem has not been resolved by this step, you must create another action plan based on the next most likely problem in your list. Return to Step 4, and reiterate the process until the problem is solved. Make sure to undo any "fixes" that you made in implementing your first action plan. Remember to change only one variable at a time.

NOTE   Before leaving the generic troubleshooting steps, I would like to suggest a couple of other items regarding troubleshooting for the book audience. First, it can be easy to become overwhelmed by a problem. It can be effective to just take a break. Years ago when I smoked, I could not go more than an hour before I needed a smoke break. Sometimes, while puffing on that cancer stick, I would have a brainstorm that would allow me to go right to the source of the problem.

Second, do not be afraid to ask for help. It makes no sense to suffer through the problem alone and make the clients suffer as well. If you are not making steady progress, get some help! Often, just describing the problem to someone else, even someone who is not technical or well-versed in the issue, can make the difference. Several times, I have struggled with a problem and called tech support. Just explaining the problem on the phone suddenly caused me to know exactly what the root cause was.

Determining That OSPF Is Operating Properly

By this point in the book, you have learned how OSPF operates, what the best design practices are, and how to manage an OSPF network. This section helps you understand how to determine that OSPF is operating properly. Just because the phone is not ringing and the users are not complaining does not mean that OSPF is operating properly. The network could be working without OSPF being the best it can be. By now you should know that OSPF is always looking for a few good engineers to ensure that it excels in your network. You need to ask yourself the following questions before proceeding:

- Is OSPF operating properly and in accordance with your design?
- Are you sure or unsure?
- How and why are you sure or unsure?
- What do you know about how OSPF is operating?

The true test of your OSPF knowledge and a network's design is in how well it operates. This section focuses on the methods needed to determine how well OSPF is operating and provides you with the tools necessary to answer the previously cited questions.

Feeling secure about your network and knowing that your network is operating efficiently are two different things. Many people feel that everything is fine because "the network is up," but going a step further with "the network is up and operating efficiently" is a much better benchmark. This clearly means that as a network engineer, your understanding of the proper functioning of OSPF is crucial.

Monitoring the Operation of OSPF

Having the ability and knowledge to properly monitor OSPF is a crucial part of your network's success or failure. An essential requirement of your network operation is that the status of your routers and their routing protocols is monitored to ensure network availability for all users. Although many different types of network management platforms are available to assist you in this endeavor, there are tools that make this management task easier. At some level, every management platform is based on the following three methods of monitoring:

- **show** commands
- Router SYSLOG files
- SNMP and MIBs

Each of these monitoring techniques requires a different area of understanding to use it. This chapter discusses the various OSPF **show** commands and how to configure the router SYSLOG file to provide you with information regarding OSPF. Chapter 8 discusses SNMP and OSPF MIBs as well as how to use them to better manage an OSPF network. This section uses the network topology and routing in Figure 9-2 to demonstrate the effects of the configuration and command examples.

After understanding the tools needed to monitor a network, you need to look at how you can use DNS to change IP addresses into more legible names, as shown in the next section.

Configuring Lookup of DNS Names

You can configure OSPF to look up Domain Naming System (DNS) names for use in all OSPF **show** command displays. This feature makes it easier to identify a router because the router is displayed by name rather than by its router ID or neighbor ID. Through the use of the **ip ospf name-lookup** command, you can find that some of the more cryptic components displayed by OSPF make a bit more sense, especially if you have used a good naming system, as discussed in Chapter 1, "Networking and Routing Fundamentals."

Use the configuration in Example 9-1 (in the router global configuration mode) so that the OSPF **show** command displays perform a DNS name lookup.

Example 9-1   *Configuring DNS Name Lookup in OSPF* **show** *Command Output*

```
Zion#config terminal
Enter configuration commands, one per line.  End with CNTL/Z.
Zion(config)#ip ospf ?
  name-lookup  Display OSPF router ids as DNS names

Zion(config)#ip ospf name-lookup
```

Figure 9-2   *OSPF Sample Network Topology*

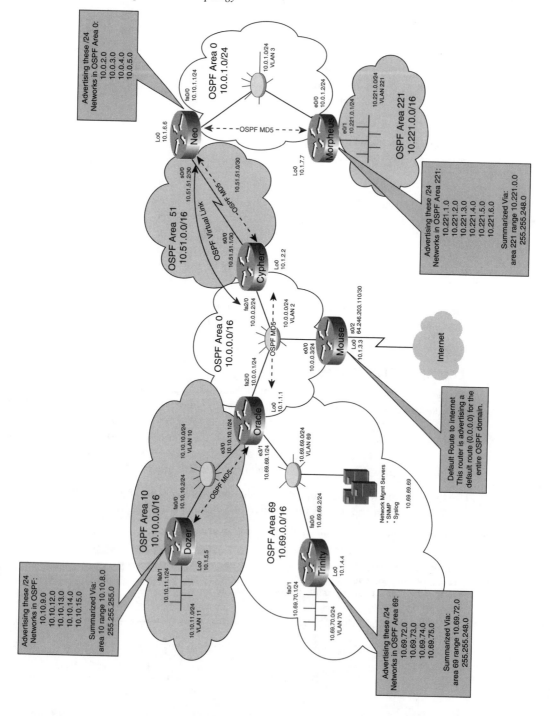

Should you choose to use this configuration command, remember that OSPF displays information based on router ID. Therefore, DNS must have the mapping to the router ID for this to operate correctly. In addition, make sure that the router knows which DNS server to use, as follows:

```
Zion(config)#ip name-server ?
  A.B.C.D  Domain server IP address (maximum of 6)
```

System Logging (SYSLOG)

Logging is an extremely useful troubleshooting tool that enables the router to keep track of events that affect its operation. Several different options are available when configuring this feature. The first concern is that the memory available on the router to keep track and save logs is limited. The use of SYSLOG on the router is tactical in the sense that you can see what is happening only until the memory limitations are reached. A recommended practice is to turn on SYSLOG within the router and deploy it in conjunction with a SYSLOG server. The SYSLOG server allows the router to send all log events to the server, thereby using the gigabit hard drive capacity to store the logs. The storage of these logs is useful from a trend analysis, forensic gathering, and troubleshooting viewpoint.

This flexibility of being able to store log messages is useful because it enables you to see if events occurring within your network are related to the router's operation or if the router has detected a network event. This can help you find trends, system error messages, outages, and a variety of other network events. This section discusses how to configure the router to use logging and how OSPF uses logging to help you troubleshoot the network.

Configuring SYSLOG

The first step in getting the router to start logging requires a decision on your part. Eight possible level settings enable you to limit how the events within the router are logged. To configure the router option, you must enter the global configuration mode, as shown in Example 9-2.

Example 9-2   *Configuring Router Logging Level Settings*

```
Oracle(config)#logging ?
  Hostname or A.B.C.D  IP address of the logging host
  buffered             Set buffered logging parameters
  console              Set console logging level
  exception            Limit size of exception flush output
  facility             Facility parameter for SYSLOG messages
  history              Configure SYSLOG history table
  monitor              Set terminal line (monitor) logging level
  on                   Enable logging to all supported destinations
  rate-limit           Set messages per second limit
  source-interface     Specify interface for source address in logging
                       transactions
  trap                 Set SYSLOG server logging level
```

Table 9-1 shows the different logging message levels.

Table 9-1   *Logging Message Priorities*

Level Name	Level	Level Description	SYSLOG Definition
emergencies	0	System unusable	LOG_EMERG
alerts	1	Immediate action needed	LOG_ALERT
critical	2	Critical conditions	LOG_CRIT
errors	3	Error conditions	LOG_ERR
warnings	4	Warning conditions	LOG_WARNING
notifications	5	Normal but significant condition	LOG_NOTICE
informational	6	Informational messages only	LOG_INFO
debugging	7	Debugging messages	LOG_DEBUG

TIP   The effect of the **log** keyword with the **ip access-list** (extended) command depends on the setting of the **logging console** command. The **log** keyword takes effect only if the logging console level is set to 6 or 7 (lower priority level). If you change the default to a level lower (numerically) than 6 and specify the **log** keyword with the **ip access-list** (extended) command, no information is logged or displayed.

When comparing the preceding example from a router that uses the built-in **help** command to the actual levels of logging listed in Table 9-1, note that the router provides its output in alphabetical order, not level of functionality. You cannot specify your logging level numerically in the router. It must be done in text format, as shown in Example 9-3.

Example 9-3   *Specifying the Logging Level*

```
Oracle(config)#logging console ?
  <0-7>          Logging severity level
  alerts         Immediate action needed       (severity=1)
  critical       Critical conditions           (severity=2)
  debugging      Debugging messages            (severity=7)
  emergencies    System is unusable            (severity=0)
  errors         Error conditions              (severity=3)
  guaranteed     Guarantee console messages
  informational  Informational messages        (severity=6)
  notifications  Normal but significant conditions (severity=5)
  warnings       Warning conditions            (severity=4)
  <cr>

Oracle(config)#
```

The EXEC **show logging** command displays the addresses and levels associated with the current logging setup as well as any other logging statistics. Example 9-4 shows a variety of events that can be reflected within the router's log file.

Example 9-4   *Displaying Log Events*

```
Oracle#show log
SYSLOG logging: enabled (0 messages dropped, 2 messages rate-limited, 0 flushes,
  0 overruns)
    Console logging: level debugging, 36 messages logged
    Monitor logging: level debugging, 0 messages logged
    Buffer logging: level debugging, 38 messages logged
    Logging Exception size (4096 bytes)
    Trap logging: level informational, 42 message lines logged
        Logging to 10.69.69.69, 42 message lines logged

Log Buffer (4096 bytes):
! - Notice here that I have placed a limit on the amount of memory logging can
! use with the router. This is really a very good practice as it helps preserve
! the integrity of the router and as long as you are also using a SYSLOG server
! all the events will be still be logged.

000033: *Mar  1 05:00:55.387 GMT: %SYS-5-RESTART: System restarted --
Cisco Internetwork Operating System Software
IOS (tm) 3600 Software (C3640-JO3S56I-M), Version 12.1(5)T9,
  RELEASE SOFTWARE (fc1)
TAC Support: http://www.cisco.com/tac
Copyright  1986-2001 by cisco Systems, Inc.
Compiled Sun 24-Jun-01 11:26 by cmong
000034: *Mar  1 05:01:42.063 GMT: %OSPF-5-ADJCHG: Process 100, Nbr 10.1.3.3 on
  FastEthernet2/0 from LOADING to FULL, Loading Done
000035: *Mar  1 05:01:43.779 GMT: %OSPF-5-ADJCHG: Process 100, Nbr 10.10.15.1 on
  Ethernet3/0 from LOADING to FULL, Loading Done
000036: *Mar  1 05:01:43.871 GMT: %OSPF-5-ADJCHG: Process 100, Nbr 10.69.74.1 on
  Ethernet3/1 from LOADING to FULL, Loading Done
000037: *Mar  1 05:01:43.983 GMT: %OSPF-5-ADJCHG: Process 100, Nbr 10.1.2.2 on
  FastEthernet2/0 from LOADING to FULL, Loading Done
000038: *Mar  1 06:10:55.539 GMT: %SYS-5-CONFIG_I: Configured from console
  by console
Oracle#
```

The preceding console output is not what you see by default in a Cisco router. It is considered best practice to implement some of the logging commands available to you in Cisco IOS Software. Chapter 8 discussed the importance of these enhancements from a security perspective, and here the operational value is made clear. A typical log entry is as follows:

```
%LINK-3-UPDOWN: Interface Serial0, changed state to down
```

Now consider that your manager is asking you questions. When did the interface go down? How do you know it went down? Is this a valid event? When did those events occur? Did they happen recently? Are they related to problems that are now occurring within the network? Unless you were closely monitoring events in the SYSLOG, it is unlikely that you would be able to answer these questions. You cannot accurately answer these concerns, can you? Certainly you cannot with the information that is contained by default in the logs of a Cisco router. The next section discusses how to make sure each log entry is date and time stamped and given a unique sequence number.

NOTE	A sudden increase in logging output can indicate a security issue where a hacker could be attacking the network, for example, using DOS-style attacks.

Date and Time Stamping

As discussed, it is crucial to know when a SYSLOG entry occurred. You want to ensure that the SYSLOG entries are stamped with the month, date, hour, minute, second, and time zone (programmed into the router) of when the event occurred. The following command shows how to configure the router to automatically date and time stamp all SYSLOG entries on the router and when sent to a SYSLOG server:

```
OSPF_Router(config)#service timestamps log datetime localtime show-timezone
```

Through the use of the router's SYSLOG with date and time stamping, you now see the benefits of troubleshooting your network. You should familiarize yourself with how to see what time the router thinks it is and how to configure the router to operate as previously discussed.

NOTE	If you plan on date and time stamping your log entries, also consider using Network Time Protocol (NTP) to synchronize all the router clocks. This command is out of the scope of this book; however, it can be found in the Cisco documentation.

Logging to the Router's Buffer

To log messages to the router's internal buffer, use the **logging buffered** command while in the router's global configuration mode. This command copies logging messages to an internal buffer instead of writing them to the console terminal. The buffer is circular (that is, FIFO) in nature, so newer messages overwrite older messages after the buffer is filled. The **no** form of this command cancels the use of the buffer and writes messages to the console terminal, which is the default:

```
logging buffered [size]
no logging buffered
```

The *size* argument (optional) sets the size of the buffer from 4096 to 4,294,967,295 bytes. The default is 4096 bytes (4 KB).

NOTE	To display the messages that are logged in the buffer, use the EXEC **show logging** command. The first message displayed is the oldest message in the buffer.

Ensure that you do not make the buffer size too large because the router could run out of memory and not be able to perform other tasks.

TIP

You can use the **show memory** command to view the free processor memory on the router; however, this is the maximum available memory after the router has loaded the Cisco IOS Software and so forth, and should not be considered completely available for use. You should begin by taking the default and seeing if that first meets your needs.

Logging to a SYSLOG Server

The ability to record a router's SYSLOG (system events) at a central location is useful in determining problems that might be occurring or those that did occur on a router you can no longer reach.

To log messages to a SYSLOG server, use the **logging** command in the router's global configuration command mode. This command identifies a SYSLOG server host to receive logging messages. The **no** form of this command deletes the SYSLOG server with the specified address from the list of SYSLOG servers in the router's configuration file. The following is the syntax for the **logging** command as well as for its **no** form:

```
logging host ip address
no logging host ip address
```

There are a variety of places to get this logging software. Some SYSLOG server manufacturers make it available for a fee, and others give it away. The SYSLOG program from Kiwi Enterprises in New Zealand (www.kiwiSYSLOG.com) is flexible and provides automatic archiving of SYSLOGs, notification if certain events occur, and a host of other useful tools. In addition, if you are running UNIX, a SYSLOG daemon is usually included.

By issuing the **logging** command more than once, you build a list of SYSLOG servers that receive logging messages. Example 9-5 shows a section of a router's configuration file.

Example 9-5   *Building a List of SYSLOG Server Logging Messages*

```
logging buffered 8191
logging console critical
logging 175.82.45.6
logging 175.82.56.10
logging 175.82.77.35
```

This particular router has been configured to allocate 8191 bytes to an internal buffer, which records the SYSLOG events. The router has also been configured to send critical events to three SYSLOG servers. Having the capability to send messages to multiple SYSLOG servers is great for large networks. If you choose to implement multiple SYSLOG servers, remember to watch the bandwidth usage!

Logging OSPF Neighbor Changes

Many OSPF issues are caused by OSPF routers losing communication with adjacent/ neighbor routers; it is crucial to know when this happens. Cisco IOS Software has the capability to add a new configuration command in OSPF configuration mode. To activate this functionality, configure your OSPF router with the **debug ip ospf adjacency** command if you want to know when an OSPF neighbor changes without turning on debugging. The **log-adj-changes** command provides a higher-level view of changes to the state of the peer relationship with less output than the **debug** command and thus places less strain on the router.

The During portion of Example 9-6 shows the configuration (in router configuration mode) for a router to generate a SYSLOG message when an OSPF neighbor changes state. The Before and After portions of Example 9-6 show the router before and after this configuration.

Example 9-6   *Configuring a Router to Generate a SYSLOG Message When an OSPF Neighbor Changes State: Before, During, and After*

```
Before
router ospf 100
 area 0 authentication message-digest
 area 10 authentication message-digest
 network 10.0.0.0 0.0.255.255 area 0
 network 10.10.0.0 0.0.255.255 area 10
 network 10.69.0.0 0.0.255.255 area 69
 !
During
Oracle#config terminal
Enter configuration commands, one per line.  End with CNTL/Z.
Oracle(config)#router ospf 100
Oracle(config-router)#log-adjacency-changes ?
  detail  Log all state changes
! - Notice you can add the detail keyword, which will greatly increase the
! level of information provided from this command; we will look at the differences
! in the output so that you can decide which is best for your network. If you are
! troubleshooting OSPF then I recommend using the detail keyword as shown below.
  <cr>
Oracle(config-router)#log-adjacency-changes detail
Oracle(config-router)#
After
router ospf 100
 log-adjacency-changes detail
 area 0 authentication message-digest
 area 10 authentication message-digest
 network 10.0.0.0 0.0.255.255 area 0
 network 10.10.0.0 0.0.255.255 area 10
 network 10.69.0.0 0.0.255.255 area 69
 !
```

The following command output reflects the output that you get when a neighbor changes state. To demonstrate this, router Oracle's fa2/0 interface was shut down, so the neighbor relationship goes down with Router Cypher.

```
000042: *Mar  1 05:47:09.467 GMT: %OSPF-5-ADJCHG: Process 100, Nbr 10.1.2.2 on
FastEthernet2/0 from FULL to DOWN, Neighbor Down: Dead timer expired
```

Assuming that it is important to watch the adjacency process and that you want as much detail as possible, you would add the **detail** keyword to the **log-adjacency-changes** command. Next, reactivate the interface, and watch the adjacency come back up. Notice the high level of detail information provided in Example 9-7.

Example 9-7   *Router Log Output*

```
Oracle#show log
000043: *Mar  1 05:48:57.539 GMT: %OSPF-5-ADJCHG: Process 100, Nbr 10.1.2.2
  on FastEthernet2/0 from DOWN to INIT, Received Hello
000044: *Mar  1 05:48:57.539 GMT: %OSPF-5-ADJCHG: Process 100, Nbr 10.1.2.2
  on FastEthernet2/0 from INIT to 2WAY, 2-Way Received
000045: *Mar  1 05:48:57.539 GMT: %OSPF-5-ADJCHG: Process 100, Nbr 10.1.2.2
  on FastEthernet2/0 from 2WAY to EXSTART, AdjOK?
000046: *Mar  1 05:49:02.543 GMT: %OSPF-5-ADJCHG: Process 100, Nbr 10.1.2.2
  on FastEthernet2/0 from EXSTART to EXCHANGE, Negotiation Done
000047: *Mar  1 05:49:02.555 GMT: %OSPF-5-ADJCHG: Process 100, Nbr 10.1.2.2
  on FastEthernet2/0 from EXCHANGE to LOADING, Exchange Done
000048: *Mar  1 05:49:02.555 GMT: %OSPF-5-ADJCHG: Process 100, Nbr 10.1.2.2
  on FastEthernet2/0 from LOADING to FULL, Loading Done
Oracle#
```

Logging is an important troubleshooting tool that when enhanced with the **log neighbor changes** command can provide you with valuable troubleshooting assistance.

OSPF Troubleshooting Commands

This section is similar in nature to the OSPF configuration commands provided in Chapter 6, "Redistribution." Contained here is a list of the most useful OSPF **show** commands and definitions of their output as well other commands that are useful in helping you troubleshoot an OSPF network. This information is essential for you as you begin implementing your network design. By this point in your network implementation, you should be ready to see if your OSPF network is working as you designed it to.

This section discusses many of the **show** commands that are available for use within Cisco routers. Before reading on, review the OSPF actions and network changes that demand resources from the router, as illustrated in Figure 9-3.

Figure 9-3 *OSPF Resource Utilization*

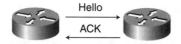

- Hello timer 10 seconds by default
- No LSAs if no link changes state
- CPU utilization determined by SPF frequency

show ip ospf Command

The **show ip ospf ?** command provides you with the means to determine exactly what OSPF **show** commands are available for you within a Cisco router. This is useful because available commands differ with each Cisco IOS Software release. Any time that you use a question mark, it invokes a help menu of the available commands, as demonstrated in Example 9-8. Using the router's built-in help menu is useful in general in case you do not recall the complete syntax of a command. Specifically, with OSPF and the many new commands available, it is useful to explore them all.

Example 9-8 *Displaying the **show ip ospf** Command Options*

```
Oracle#show ip ospf ?
  <1-4294967295>        Process ID number
  border-routers        Border and Boundary Router Information
  database              Database summary
  flood-list            Link state flood list
  interface             Interface information
  mpls                  MPLS related information
  neighbor              Neighbor list
  request-list          Link state request list
  retransmission-list   Link state retransmission list
  summary-address       Summary-address redistribution Information
  virtual-links         Virtual link information
  |                     Output modifiers
  <cr>
```

The **show ip ospf** command displays a variety of general information about the overall OSPF routing process. A lot of good information is available from this command.

To display operational information about OSPF routing processes, use the **show ip ospf** [*process-id*] EXEC command. This command displays specific OSPF process information as Cisco's implementation allows you to operate multiple OSPF processes. Recall the discussion on this point in Chapter 5, "Routing Concepts and Configuration." Therefore, you must specify which OSPF process you want information from. This section uses the network topology and routing in Figure 9-4 to demonstrate the effects of the configuration and command examples.

Figure 9-4   *OSPF Sample Network Topology*

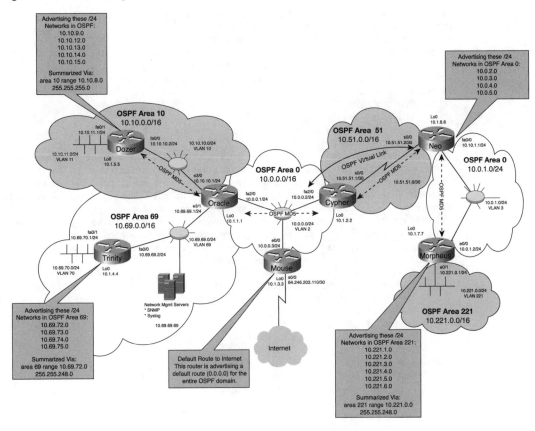

Example 9-9 shows the output from the **show ip ospf** command for Router Oracle.
Comments are included in italics to discuss the more relevant sections of command output.

Example 9-9   *Commented **show ip ospf** Command Output for Router Oracle*

```
Oracle#show ip ospf
 Routing Process "ospf 100" with ID 10.1.1.1 and Domain ID 0.0.0.100
! You can easily see the operation of the entire OSPF process and how
! each area is functioning that the router is operating in to include
! how many router interfaces are present in that area.
Supports only single TOS(TOS0) routes
 Supports opaque LSA
 It is an area border router
! This command will also tell you if the router is acting in a role such as
! an ASBR or ABR (this router is, see below) plus it will identify if
! authentication is configured for a given area, in the example below
! authentication is configured for every area, except area 69.
 SPF schedule delay 5 secs, Hold time between two SPFs 10 secs
```

continues

Example 9-9 *Commented* **show ip ospf** *Command Output for Router Oracle (Continued)*

```
 Minimum LSA interval 5 secs. Minimum LSA arrival 1 secs
 Number of external LSA 0. Checksum Sum 0x0
 Number of opaque AS LSA 0. Checksum Sum 0x0
 Number of DCbitless external and opaque AS LSA 0
 Number of DoNotAge external and opaque AS LSA 0
 Number of areas in this router is 3. 3 normal 0 stub 0 nssa
 External flood list length 0
    Area BACKBONE(0)
        Number of interfaces in this area is 1
        Area has message digest authentication
        SPF algorithm executed 6 times
! From an OSPF operational perspective this command will show you the frequency
! of the SPF algorithm execution, which is a very good indicator of potential
! trouble. Frequent SPF calculations can cause router memory, processor problems
! since the router has to recalculate the LSDB. The full SPF algorithm is run only
! when there is a topology change, as expressed in a router
! link-state advertisement (LSA), not for summary LSAs; they cause a partial SPF
! to be run. This command can be used to determine the number of times the SPF
! algorithm has been executed. It also shows the link-state update interval,
! assuming no topological changes have occurred.
        Area ranges are
        Number of LSA 20. Checksum Sum 0xA441E
        Number of opaque link LSA 0. Checksum Sum 0x0
        Number of DCbitless LSA 0
        Number of indication LSA 0
        Number of DoNotAge LSA 2
        Flood list length 0
    Area 10
        Number of interfaces in this area is 1
        Area has message digest authentication
        SPF algorithm executed 4 times
        Area ranges are
        Number of LSA 17. Checksum Sum 0x9D46A
        Number of opaque link LSA 0. Checksum Sum 0x0
        Number of DCbitless LSA 0
        Number of indication LSA 0
        Number of DoNotAge LSA 0
        Flood list length 0
    Area 69
        Number of interfaces in this area is 1
        Area has no authentication
        SPF algorithm executed 4 times
        Area ranges are
        Number of LSA 16. Checksum Sum 0x7D42B
        Number of opaque link LSA 0. Checksum Sum 0x0
        Number of DCbitless LSA 0
        Number of indication LSA 0
        Number of DoNotAge LSA 0
        Flood list length 0

Oracle#
```

show ip ospf *process-id* Command

Table 9-2 provides additional information regarding the output from the **show ip ospf** *process-id* command in Example 9-9.

Table 9-2   **show ip ospf** *process-id Command Output Definitions*

Field	Description
Routing Process "ospf 100" with a router ID of 10.1.1.1	OSPF process ID and OSPF router ID.
Type of Service	Number of Types of Service supported (Type 0 only).
Type of OSPF Router	Possible types are internal, area border, or autonomous system boundary.
Summary Link Update Interval	Specifies summary update interval in hours:minutes:seconds and time to next update. This field is only included if these types of links (routes) are present in the OSPF domain.
External Link Update Interval	Specifies external update interval in hours:minutes:seconds and time to next update. This field is only included if these types of links (routes) are present in the OSPF domain.
Redistributing External Routes	Lists redistributed routes by protocol. This field is only included if these types of links (routes) are present in the OSPF domain.
Number of Areas	Number of areas in the router, area addresses, and so on.
SPF Algorithm	This is run only for route link-state advertisements (LSAs), not for summary LSAs. This command shows the number of times that the full SPF algorithm has been run.
Link State Update Interval	Specifies router and network link-state update interval in hours:minutes:seconds and time to next update.
Link State Age Interval	Specifies max-aged update deletion interval and time until next database cleanup in hours:minutes:seconds.

show ip ospf interface Command

You can gain much useful information from the **show ip ospf interface** command. In the output of this command, demonstrated in Example 9-10, a specific interface was selected; however, if you do not specify an interface, the resulting output displays information for all interfaces. To display OSPF-related interface information, use the **show ip ospf interface** EXEC command. You can verify that interfaces have been configured in the intended areas. In Example 9-10, the Fast Ethernet interface has been placed in area 0.

TIP   The **show ip ospf interface** command is the first command that I use when I suspect an OSPF problem. It is much easier to catch a config error with this command than to scroll through the config itself.

Example 9-10   show ip ospf interface *Command with the Fast Ethernet 2/0 Interface Specified*

```
Oracle#show ip ospf interface fa2/0
FastEthernet2/0 is up, line protocol is up
  Internet Address 10.0.0.1/24, Area 0
  Process ID 100, Router ID 10.1.1.1, Network Type BROADCAST, Cost: 1
  Transmit Delay is 1 sec, State BDR, Priority 1
  Designated Router (ID) 10.1.3.3, Interface address 10.0.0.3
  Backup Designated router (ID) 10.1.1.1, Interface address 10.0.0.1
! The above portions of the output reveal quite a bit about what and who
! OSPF knows about on the network that this interface is connected to, such as
! the DR/BDR and priority for the election, network type.
  Timer intervals configured, Hello 10, Dead 40, Wait 40, Retransmit 5
! The show ip ospf interface command also gives the timer intervals including the
! Hello interval. These values must match if the OSPF routers are to become
neighbors.
    Hello due in 00:00:03
  Index 1/1, flood queue length 0
  Next 0x0(0)/0x0(0)
  Last flood scan length is 0, maximum is 14
  Last flood scan time is 0 msec, maximum is 0 msec
  Neighbor Count is 2, Adjacent neighbor count is 2
    Adjacent with neighbor 10.1.2.2
    Adjacent with neighbor 10.1.3.3  (Designated Router)
  Suppress hello for 0 neighbor(s)
  Message digest authentication enabled
    Youngest key id is 1
! The above portions of the output discuss the flooding process (see Chapter 3),
! how many and who the OSPF neighbors are attached to the interface displayed,
! and authentication.
Oracle#
```

Table 9-3 describes some fields that are useful in a troubleshooting environment.

Table 9-3   show ip ospf int *Command Output Definitions*

Field	Description
Internet Address	Interface IP address, subnet mask, and area address.
Process ID	OSPF process ID, router ID, link-state cost, and network type (in this case, broadcast).
Transmit Delay	Transmit delay, interface state (whether this router is the DR or BDR), and router interface priority to be used in determining the DR and BDR.

Table 9-3   **show ip ospf int** *Command Output Definitions (Continued)*

Field	Description
State DROTHER	This command means that this router is not acting as either the Designated Router (DR) or the Backup designated router (BDR). Both of these conditions are also possible in this field, and these values are typically only seen on broadcast media.
Priority 1	This value indicates the priority of this router in the DR/BDR election. The default value is 1.
Designated Router	Identifies the DR ID and its respective interface IP address.
Backup Designated router	Identifies the BDR ID and its respective interface IP address.
Timer intervals configured	Configuration values of the OSPF tunable timer intervals. Remember, change these with caution and make sure they match!
Hello	Number of seconds until the next Hello packet is sent out from this interface.
Wait	Indicates how long to wait if the DR fails until the election process begins in order to replace the DR.
Retransmit	If a link-state retransmission list (flooded LSAs but not yet acknowledged) exists, this is the amount of time until it is retransmitted.
Neighbor Count	Count of network neighbors and list of adjacent neighbors.
Adjacent neighbors	Shows all routers that are adjacent to this one. This core router has two adjacencies.

show ip ospf border-routers Command

To display the internal OSPF routing table entries to an Area Border Router (ABR) and Autonomous System Boundary Router (ASBR), use the **show ip ospf border-routers** privileged EXEC command, as demonstrated in Example 9-11.

Example 9-11   **show ip ospf border-routers** *Command Output*

```
Oracle#show ip ospf border-routers

OSPF Process 100 internal Routing Table

Codes: i - Intra-area route, I - Inter-area route

i 10.69.74.1 [10] via 10.69.69.2, Ethernet3/1, ASBR, Area 69, SPF 4
i 10.1.6.6 [49] via 10.0.0.2, FastEthernet2/0, ABR, Area 0, SPF 6
! We can decipher this entry as follows, router Oracle knows there is an
! intra-area route to get to an OSPF Router with a RID of 10.1.6.6 (router Neo)
! and to get to there the next-hop is 10.0.0.2 (router cypher) through Cypher's
! fast Ethernet interface 2/0, the router we are trying to reach is an ABR in
! Area 0 and this route was learned via SPF ID number 6.
i 10.1.2.2 [1] via 10.0.0.2, FastEthernet2/0, ABR, Area 0, SPF 6
Oracle#
```

Table 9-4 describes some fields from this output that are useful in a troubleshooting environment.

Table 9-4 **show ip ospf border-routers** *Command Output Definitions*

Field	Description
Route Type	The type of this route; it is either an intra-area or inter-area route.
Destination	Destination's router ID.
Cost	Cost of using this route, in brackets.
Next Hop	Next hop toward the destination.
Type	The router type of the destination; it is either an ABR, an ASBR, or both.
Area Number	The area ID of the area from which this route is learned.
SPF ID No	The internal identification number of the SPF calculation that installed this route.

show ip ospf database Command

The **show ip ospf database** command displays the contents of the topological database maintained by the router. The command shows the RID and the OSPF process ID. The use of an easy-to-recognize RID, such as a fictitious ID established for a loopback interface, can make troubleshooting more straightforward as can the use of the domain name correlation with a RID, as discussed previously in this chapter.

The various forms of this command deliver information about different OSPF link-state advertisements. Entering a question mark after the **show ip ospf database** EXEC command provides a listing of the various options and arguments that are associated with this command, as demonstrated in Example 9-12.

Example 9-12 **show ip ospf database** *Command Options*

```
Oracle#show ip ospf database ?
  adv-router        Advertising Router link states
  asbr-summary      ASBR summary link states
  database-summary  Summary of database
  external          External link states
  network           Network link states
  nssa-external     NSSA External link states
  opaque-area       Opaque Area link states
  opaque-as         Opaque AS link states
  opaque-link       Opaque Link-Local link states
  router            Router link states
  self-originate    Self-originated link states
  summary           Network summary link states
  |                 Output modifiers
  <cr>

Oracle#
```

Because of the level of detail available with this command, coverage of some of the other forms of this command are examined later in this section.

The output for the **show ip ospf database** command has a certain hierarchy and order to it. The first thing OSPF does is display all data for each OSPF process. Within that display is a display of each OSPF area. Within that display is a display of each area that the applicable LSAs received by that router for that area. It is important to note that this command displays the LSAs received in each area. Also, the command displays each element in numerical order. Therefore, router LSAs (Type 1) are displayed before network LSAs (Type 2), area 0 is displayed before area 1, and so on. Table 9-5 provides a quick review of the types of OSPF LSAs, as covered in Chapter 3, "OSPF Communication."

Table 9-5   *Types of LSAs*

LSA Type Number	LSA Description
1	Router link advertisements
2	Network link advertisements
3	ABR summary link advertisements
4	ASBR summary link advertisements
5	Autonomous System (AS) external link advertisements
7	Not-so-stubby areas (NSSAs)

Use the **show ip ospf database** EXEC command to display lists of information related to the OSPF database for a specific router, as in Example 9-13.

Example 9-13   *Output of* **show ip ospf database** *Command*

```
Oracle# show ip ospf database
            OSPF Router with ID (10.1.1.1) (Process ID 100)

            Router Link States (Area 0)
! -- The command begins with OSPF telling us the RID of the router the command
! is executed on, which OSPF process the database is from. As you review the
! command output notice that the output is segmented by OSPF area, the beginning
! is the core of course, that is area 0!

Link ID         ADV Router      Age         Seq#       Checksum Link count
10.1.1.1        10.1.1.1        1388        0x80000003 0xB845   1
10.1.2.2        10.1.2.2        1396        0x80000006 0x72B9   2
10.1.3.3        10.1.3.3        416         0x80000005 0xC206   2
10.1.6.6        10.1.6.6        6     (DNA) 0x80000003 0xD6A3   7
10.1.7.7        10.1.7.7        66    (DNA) 0x80000002 0x7A93   2
! - The link id refers to the actual link within the OSPF domain. For router
! links only the Link ID and Advertising Router columns will be identical.
! Advertising router is the RID that created and thus advertised the link shown
! in the first column. Age references the age of the LSA of special note here are
! the entries 10.1.6.6 & 10.1.7.7, notice the presence of the DoNotAge bit (DNA).
! The DNA bit is the most significant bit in the LS Age field. By setting this bit
```

continues

Example 9-13 *Output of* **show ip ospf database** *Command (Continued)*

```
! the LSA stops aging, and no periodic updates are sent.
! The next column, sequence number shows the LSA sequence number and is used by OSPF
! to reduce the likelihood of old or duplicate LSAs remaining in the database.
! The last column, Links, displays the number of active networks that this router
! has connected to this area. To really understand this column execute a
! show ip ospf database router <RID>  comand and this more detailed command shows
! and describes each link.
                        Net Link States (Area 0)

Link ID         ADV Router       Age         Seq#        Checksum
10.0.0.3        10.1.3.3         1350        0x80000003 0x8365
10.0.1.1        10.1.6.6         65    (DNA) 0x80000001 0x49C7
! - In this section the Type 2 network LSAs are displayed, if you recall they are
! generated by ABRs and describe the networks that they are connected and for area 0
! there are two ABRs; 10.1.3.3 router Mouse for the center area 0 via 10.0.0.3 and
! 10.1.6.6 is router Neo who connects to area 0 on the right via 10.0.1.1. Notice the
! DNA bit is set for router Neo since it is only accessible via the serial link
! and is considered a demand circuit.

                    Summary Net Link States (Area 0)

Link ID         ADV Router       Age         Seq#        Checksum
10.1.4.0        10.1.1.1         1722        0x80000001 0xCD48
10.1.5.0        10.1.1.1         1272        0x80000001 0xC252
10.10.9.0       10.1.1.1         1272        0x80000001 0x2ADD
10.10.10.0      10.1.1.1         1279        0x80000005 0xDF6
10.10.11.0      10.1.1.1         1275        0x80000001 0x14F1
10.10.12.0      10.1.1.1         1275        0x80000001 0x9FB
10.10.13.0      10.1.1.1         1275        0x80000001 0xFD06
10.10.14.0      10.1.1.1         1275        0x80000001 0xF210
10.51.51.0      10.1.2.2         1399        0x80000003 0x3F0F
10.51.51.0      10.1.6.6         51    (DNA) 0x80000001 0x2D4B
10.69.69.0      10.1.1.1         1730        0x80000003 0xBED0
10.69.70.0      10.1.1.1         1725        0x80000001 0xC1CD
10.69.72.0      10.1.1.1         1725        0x80000001 0xABE1
10.69.73.0      10.1.1.1         1725        0x80000001 0xA0EB
10.69.74.0      10.1.1.1         1725        0x80000001 0x95F5
10.69.75.0      10.1.1.1         1725        0x80000001 0x8AFF
10.221.0.0      10.221.6.1       70    (DNA) 0x80000001 0xE5E
! -- Summary LSAs (type 3) are generated only by Area Border Routers (ABRs) and
! describe inter-area routes to various networks. Remember now that the links
! present in this part of the output should be consider along with those in other
! part to ensure that the router knows every link overall in the domain.
! The highlighted entries above are the summary LSA that describe all the other
! routes that (1) were not described as type 1 or 2 LSAs (2) are connected to
! router Oracle that is the ABR for both area 10 and 69. If you recall that
! PtP serial links do not require the formation of an ABR then you will understand
! that both routers will then advertise the 10.51.51.0 network.

                    Summary ASB Link States (Area 0)

Link ID         ADV Router       Age         Seq#        Checksum
10.69.75.1      10.1.1.1         1725        0x80000001 0x6821
```

Example 9-13   *Output of* **show ip ospf database** *Command (Continued)*

```
                       Router Link States (Area 10)

Link ID         ADV Router      Age        Seq#        Checksum Link count
10.1.1.1        10.1.1.1        1291       0x80000005 0xF2D8    1
10.10.14.1      10.10.14.1      1291       0x80000002 0xCDC7    7

                       Net Link States (Area 10)

Link ID         ADV Router      Age        Seq#        Checksum
10.10.10.2      10.10.14.1      1292       0x80000002 0xC104

                       Summary Net Link States (Area 10)

Link ID         ADV Router      Age        Seq#        Checksum
10.0.0.0        10.1.1.1        1392       0x80000004 0x9B86
10.0.1.0        10.1.1.1        1392       0x80000002 0x8071
10.0.2.0        10.1.1.1        1392       0x80000002 0x757B
10.0.3.0        10.1.1.1        1392       0x80000002 0x6A85
10.0.4.0        10.1.1.1        1392       0x80000002 0x5F8F
10.0.5.0        10.1.1.1        1393       0x80000002 0x5499
10.1.3.0        10.1.1.1        1098       0x80000001 0x7EA1
10.1.4.0        10.1.1.1        1727       0x80000001 0xCD48
10.1.6.0        10.1.1.1        1393       0x80000002 0x3DAE
10.1.7.0        10.1.1.1        1393       0x80000002 0x3CAD
10.51.51.0      10.1.1.1        1393       0x80000003 0x56F8
10.69.69.0      10.1.1.1        1732       0x80000003 0xBED0
10.69.70.0      10.1.1.1        1727       0x80000001 0xC1CD
10.69.72.0      10.1.1.1        1727       0x80000001 0xABE1
10.69.73.0      10.1.1.1        1727       0x80000001 0xA0EB
10.69.74.0      10.1.1.1        1727       0x80000001 0x95F5
10.69.75.0      10.1.1.1        1727       0x80000001 0x8AFF
10.221.0.0      10.1.1.1        1393       0x80000002 0xC0F

                       Summary ASB Link States (Area 10)

Link ID         ADV Router      Age        Seq#        Checksum
10.1.3.3        10.1.1.1        415        0x80000001 0x48D4
10.69.75.1      10.1.1.1        1728       0x80000001 0x6821

                       Router Link States (Area 69)

Link ID         ADV Router      Age        Seq#        Checksum Link count
10.1.1.1        10.1.1.1        1743       0x80000004 0xAC33    1
10.69.75.1      10.69.75.1      1743       0x80000002 0xEF6C    7

                       Net Link States (Area 69)

Link ID         ADV Router      Age        Seq#        Checksum
10.69.69.2      10.69.75.1      1744       0x80000001 0xEB73

                       Summary Net Link States (Area 69)
```

continues

Example 9-13 *Output of* **show ip ospf database** *Command (Continued)*

```
Link ID         ADV Router      Age        Seq#         Checksum
10.0.0.0        10.1.1.1        1394       0x80000004 0x9B86
10.0.1.0        10.1.1.1        1394       0x80000002 0x8071
10.0.2.0        10.1.1.1        1394       0x80000002 0x757B
10.0.3.0        10.1.1.1        1394       0x80000002 0x6A85
10.0.4.0        10.1.1.1        1394       0x80000002 0x5F8F
10.0.5.0        10.1.1.1        1395       0x80000002 0x5499
10.1.3.0        10.1.1.1        1101       0x80000001 0x7EA1
10.1.5.0        10.1.1.1        1280       0x80000001 0xC252
10.1.6.0        10.1.1.1        1395       0x80000002 0x3DAE
10.1.7.0        10.1.1.1        1395       0x80000002 0x3CAD
10.10.9.0       10.1.1.1        1280       0x80000001 0x2ADD
10.10.10.0      10.1.1.1        1284       0x80000005 0xDF6
10.10.11.0      10.1.1.1        1280       0x80000001 0x14F1
10.10.12.0      10.1.1.1        1280       0x80000001 0x9FB
10.10.13.0      10.1.1.1        1280       0x80000001 0xFD06
10.10.14.0      10.1.1.1        1280       0x80000001 0xF210
10.51.51.0      10.1.1.1        1395       0x80000003 0x56F8
10.221.0.0      10.1.1.1        1395       0x80000002 0xC0F

                Summary ASB Link States (Area 69)

Link ID         ADV Router      Age        Seq#         Checksum
10.1.3.3        10.1.1.1        417        0x80000001 0x48D4

                Type-5 AS External Link States

Link ID         ADV Router      Age        Seq#         Checksum Tag
0.0.0.0         10.1.3.3        396        0x80000001 0xAE8F    100
Oracle#
```

Table 9-6 describes the significant fields in this output.

Table 9-6 *Fields in* **show ip ospf database** *Command Output*

Field	Description
Link ID	Router ID number
ADV Router	Advertising router's ID
Age	Link-state age
Seq#	Link-state sequence number (detects old or duplicate link-state advertisements)
Checksum	Fletcher checksum of the complete contents of the link-state advertisement
Link count	Number of interfaces detected for router

show ip ospf database asbr-summary Command

The **show ip ospf database asbr-summary** command provides you with a wealth of relevant information regarding the OSPF database (Type 4 LSAs) on an ASBR. Example 9-14 shows the options that are available with this command.

Example 9-14   **show ip ospf database asbr-summary** *Command Options*

```
Oracle>show ip ospf database asbr-summary ?
  A.B.C.D         Link state ID (as an IP address)
  adv-router      Advertising Router link states
  internal        Internal LSA information
  self-originate  Self-originated link states
  |               Output modifiers
  <cr>

Oracle>
```

Example 9-15 shows sample output from the **show ip ospf database asbr-summary** command when no optional arguments are specified.

Example 9-15   **show ip ospf database asbr-summary** *Command Output*

```
Oracle>show ip ospf database asbr-summary

            OSPF Router with ID (10.1.1.1) (Process ID 100)

            Summary ASB Link States (Area 0)

  LS age: 659
  Options: (No TOS-capability, DC, Upward)
  LS Type: Summary Links(AS Boundary Router)
  Link State ID: 10.1.4.4 (AS Boundary Router address)
  Advertising Router: 10.1.1.1
  LS Seq Number: 80000001
  Checksum: 0x8D84
  Length: 28
  Network Mask: /0
        TOS: 0  Metric: 10

            Summary ASB Link States (Area 10)

  LS age: 1758
  Options: (No TOS-capability, DC, Upward)
  LS Type: Summary Links(AS Boundary Router)
  Link State ID: 10.1.3.3 (AS Boundary Router address)
  Advertising Router: 10.1.1.1
  LS Seq Number: 80000008
  Checksum: 0x3ADB
  Length: 28
  Network Mask: /0
        TOS: 0  Metric: 1

  LS age: 712
  Options: (No TOS-capability, DC, Upward)
  LS Type: Summary Links(AS Boundary Router)
  Link State ID: 10.1.4.4 (AS Boundary Router address)
  Advertising Router: 10.1.1.1
  LS Seq Number: 80000001
  Checksum: 0x8D84
```

continues

Example 9-15   **show ip ospf database asbr-summary** *Command Output (Continued)*

```
      Length: 28
      Network Mask: /0
            TOS: 0   Metric: 10


                        Summary ASB Link States (Area 69)

      LS age: 1820
      Options: (No TOS-capability, DC, Upward)
      LS Type: Summary Links(AS Boundary Router)
      Link State ID: 10.1.3.3 (AS Boundary Router address)
      Advertising Router: 10.1.1.1
      LS Seq Number: 80000008
      Checksum: 0x3ADB
      Length: 28
      Network Mask: /0
            TOS: 0   Metric: 1
  Oracle>
```

Table 9-7 describes some fields from the **show ip ospf database asbr-summary** command output that are useful in a troubleshooting environment.

Table 9-7   **show ip ospf database asbr-summary** *Command Output Definitions*

Field	Description
Router ID	Router ID number.
Process ID	OSPF process ID.
LS age	Link-state age.
Options	Type-of-service options (Type 0 only).
LS Type	Link-state type.
Link State ID	Link-state ID (ASBR).
Advertising Router	Advertising router's ID.
LS Seq Number	Link-state sequence (detects old or duplicate link-state advertisements).
Checksum	LS checksum (Fletcher checksum of the complete contents of the link-state advertisement).
Length	Length in bytes of the link-state advertisement.
Network Mask	Network mask implemented. The network mask for Type 4 LSA is always 0.0.0.0.
TOS	Type of service.
Metric	Link-state metric.

show ip ospf database database-summary Command

When you need a quick snapshot of how the overall LSA processing of OSPF is doing in relation to the LSDB, the **show ip ospf database database-summary** command provides a summary of every type of LSA that has been sent, deleted, or expired because of Maxage; all of this information is displayed on a per-area basis. Example 9-16 shows some sample output from this command.

Example 9-16 **show ip ospf database database-summary** *Command Output*

```
Oracle>show ip ospf database database-summary

              OSPF Router with ID (10.1.1.1) (Process ID 100)

Area 0 database summary
    LSA Type      Count   Delete    Maxage
    Router        5       0         0
    Network       2       0         0
    Summary Net   17      0         0
    Summary ASBR  1       0         0
    Type-7 Ext    0       0         0
    Opaque Link   0       0         0
    Opaque Area   0       0         0
    Subtotal      25      0         0

Area 10 database summary
    LSA Type      Count   Delete    Maxage
    Router        2       0         0
    Network       1       0         0
    Summary Net   18      0         0
    Summary ASBR  2       0         0
    Type-7 Ext    0       0         0
    Opaque Link   0       0         0
    Opaque Area   0       0         0
    Subtotal      23      0         0

Area 69 database summary
    LSA Type      Count   Delete    Maxage
    Router        2       0         0
    Network       1       0         0
    Summary Net   18      0         0
    Summary ASBR  1       0         0
    Type-7 Ext    0       0         0
    Opaque Link   0       0         0
    Opaque Area   0       0         0
    Subtotal      22      0         0

Process 100 database summary
    LSA Type      Count   Delete    Maxage
    Router        9       0         0
    Network       4       0         0
    Summary Net   53      0         0
    Summary ASBR  4       0         0
    Type-7 Ext    0       0         0
```

continues

Example 9-16   **show ip ospf database database-summary** *Command Output (Continued)*

```
  Opaque Link   0       0       0
  Opaque Area   0       0       0
  Type-5 Ext    1       0       0
  Opaque AS     0       0       0
  Total         71      0       0
! - this last line of output of the command provides a summary of all the other
! LSA counts from each individual area all in on simple table.
Oracle>
```

show ip ospf database external Command

The **show ip ospf database external** command provides you with a wealth of relevant information regarding the OSPF database external LSAs. This command has a variety of additional keywords, many of which are useful when OSPF has a large number of external routes coming from many different routers within the OSPF domain. Example 9-17 shows all the available command options.

Example 9-17   **show ip ospf database external** *Command Options*

```
Oracle>show ip ospf database external ?
  A.B.C.D         Link state ID (as an IP address)
  adv-router      Advertising Router link states
  internal        Internal LSA information
  self-originate  Self-originated link states·
  |               Output modifiers
  <cr>

Oracle>
```

In the sample network of Figure 9-4, this command shows you what information is available with regard to the external LSAs in the OSPF routing domain. Example 9-18 shows sample output from the **show ip ospf database external** command when no optional arguments are specified.

Example 9-18   **show ip ospf database external** *Command Output*

```
Oracle>show ip ospf database external

            OSPF Router with ID (10.1.1.1) (Process ID 100)

            Type-5 AS External Link States

  Routing Bit Set on this LSA
! - This line will not appear in every output. Its presence depends on the how
! this external link state information arrived at the router. In Router Oracle's
! case an LSA was used to carry the information from Router Mouse. Compare the
! output of this command with that of Router Mouse so you can see the differences.
  LS age: 1974
  Options: (No TOS-capability, DC)
  LS Type: AS External Link
```

Example 9-18   show ip ospf database external *Command Output (Continued)*

```
       Link State ID: 0.0.0.0 (External Network Number )
       Advertising Router: 10.1.3.3
       LS Seq Number: 80000008
       Checksum: 0xA096
       Length: 36
 ! - We have already discussed much of the information present on the preceding
 ! lines; however, the Length field is an interesting field as it describes the
 ! actual length of the LSA in bytes.
       Network Mask: /0
            Metric Type: 2 (Larger than any link state path)
            TOS: 0
            Metric: 1
            Forward Address: 0.0.0.0
            External Route Tag: 100
 ! - This section of the command output is where the real important
 ! information is located. The network mask in / notation is present,
 ! notice in this case it is 0 bits and we will explain why in a moment.
 ! You can then easily determine if the LSA describes a Type 1 or 2 external route
 ! and then the metric to reach the route. Forwarding address. Data traffic for
 ! the advertised destination will be forwarded to this address. If the forwarding
 ! address is set to 0.0.0.0, data traffic will be forwarded instead to the
 ! advertisement's originator. External route tag, a 32-bit field attached to each
 ! external route. This is not used by the OSPF protocol itself.
 Oracle>
```

Next, review Example 9-19 and see how this information is displayed for Router Mouse, which is the originating router for this external route.

Example 9-19   show ip ospf database external *Command Output for Mouse*

```
Mouse>show ip ospf database external

        OSPF Router with ID (10.1.3.3) (Process ID 100)


                Type-5 AS External Link States

  LS age: 710
  Options: (No TOS-capability, DC)
  LS Type: AS External Link
  Link State ID: 0.0.0.0 (External Network Number )
  Advertising Router: 10.1.3.3
  LS Seq Number: 80000009
  Checksum: 0x9E97
  Length: 36
  Network Mask: /0
        Metric Type: 2 (Larger than any link state path)
        TOS: 0
        Metric: 1
        Forward Address: 0.0.0.0
        External Route Tag: 100

Mouse>
```

Notice that only one external route exists for the whole OSPF domain. Have you figured out why this is the case? Review the routing table for Router Oracle in Example 9-20.

Example 9-20 *Oracle's Routing Table: Just One External Route*

```
Oracle>show ip route
Codes: C - connected, S - static, I - IGRP, R - RIP, M - mobile, B - BGP
       D - EIGRP, EX - EIGRP external, O - OSPF, IA - OSPF inter area
       N1 - OSPF NSSA external type 1, N2 - OSPF NSSA external type 2
       E1 - OSPF external type 1, E2 - OSPF external type 2, E - EGP
       i - IS-IS, L1 - IS-IS level-1, L2 - IS-IS level-2, ia - IS-IS inter area
       * - candidate default, U - per-user static route, o - ODR
       P - periodic downloaded static route

Gateway of last resort is 10.0.0.3 to network 0.0.0.0

     10.0.0.0/8 is variably subnetted, 26 subnets, 3 masks
O       10.69.75.0/24 [110/11] via 10.69.69.2, 00:19:56, Ethernet3/1
O       10.69.74.0/24 [110/11] via 10.69.69.2, 00:19:56, Ethernet3/1
O       10.69.73.0/24 [110/11] via 10.69.69.2, 00:19:56, Ethernet3/1
O       10.69.72.0/24 [110/11] via 10.69.69.2, 00:19:56, Ethernet3/1
O       10.1.3.0/24 [110/2] via 10.0.0.3, 03:03:41, FastEthernet2/0
O       10.0.2.0/24 [110/50] via 10.0.0.2, 03:03:41, FastEthernet2/0
<<<output omitted for brevity>>>
O       10.0.5.0/24 [110/50] via 10.0.0.2, 03:03:43, FastEthernet2/0
O IA    10.221.0.0/21 [110/51] via 10.0.0.2, 00:19:58, FastEthernet2/0
O*E2 0.0.0.0/0 [110/1] via 10.0.0.3, 00:19:58, FastEthernet2/0
Oracle>
```

The highlighted line of the routing table shows a single default route, represented by 0.0.0.0/0, that is being advertised by the next hop, 10.0.0.3, which is the Ethernet interface of Router Mouse. Router Mouse is advertising a default route into OSPF that points to the Internet.

show ip ospf database network Command

The **show ip ospf database network** command provides you with a wealth of relevant information regarding the OSPF database network LSAs. This information is useful when OSPF has large numbers of external routes coming from many different routers within the OSPF domain. Example 9-21 shows the command options that are available with the **show ip ospf database network** command.

Example 9-21 **show ip ospf database network** *Command Output*

```
Oracle>show ip ospf database network ?
  A.B.C.D        Link state ID (as an IP address)
  adv-router     Advertising Router link states
  internal       Internal LSA information
  self-originate Self-originated link states
  |              Output modifiers
  <cr>

Oracle>
```

This command also provides you with information regarding where the routes came from in the network and which routers are part of the network by OSPF area. Example 9-22 shows sample output from the **show ip ospf database network** command when no optional arguments are specified (refer to Figure 9-4 to help you see what is occurring). However, the real reason that you see the area information here is that Oracle is an ABR, and therefore its database is organized by areas.

Example 9-22   **show ip ospf database network** *Command Output*

```
Oracle>show ip ospf database network

             OSPF Router with ID (10.1.1.1) (Process ID 100)

                 Net Link States (Area 0)

    Routing Bit Set on this LSA
    LS age: 1486
    Options: (No TOS-capability, DC)
    LS Type: Network Links
    Link State ID: 10.0.0.3 (address of Designated Router)
    Advertising Router: 10.1.3.3
    LS Seq Number: 8000000C
    Checksum: 0x716E
    Length: 36
    Network Mask: /24
          Attached Router: 10.1.3.3
          Attached Router: 10.1.1.1
          Attached Router: 10.1.2.2

    Routing Bit Set on this LSA
    LS age: 2 (DoNotAge)
    Options: (No TOS-capability, DC)
    LS Type: Network Links
    Link State ID: 10.0.1.1 (address of Designated Router)
    Advertising Router: 10.1.6.6
    LS Seq Number: 80000002
    Checksum: 0x4E97
    Length: 32
    Network Mask: /24
          Attached Router: 10.1.6.6
          Attached Router: 10.1.7.7

                 Net Link States (Area 10)

    Routing Bit Set on this LSA
    LS age: 1521
    Options: (No TOS-capability, DC)
    LS Type: Network Links
    Link State ID: 10.10.10.2 (address of Designated Router)
    Advertising Router: 10.10.14.1
    LS Seq Number: 8000000B
    Checksum: 0xAF0D
    Length: 32
```

continues

Example 9-22 **show ip ospf database network** *Command Output (Continued)*

```
Network Mask: /24
        Attached Router: 10.10.14.1
        Attached Router: 10.1.1.1


                Net Link States (Area 69)


Routing Bit Set on this LSA
LS age: 2037
Options: (No TOS-capability, DC)
LS Type: Network Links
Link State ID: 10.69.69.1 (address of Designated Router)
Advertising Router: 10.1.1.1
LS Seq Number: 80000002
Checksum: 0xB0C5
Length: 32
Network Mask: /24
        Attached Router: 10.1.1.1
        Attached Router: 10.1.4.4

Oracle>
```

The highlighted sections of this command output show the RIDs of all the attached routers for the given network link.

show ip ospf database router Command

The **show ip ospf database router** command provides you with a wealth of relevant information regarding the OSPF database router LSAs. Example 9-23 shows sample output from the **show ip ospf database router** command when no optional arguments are specified. Table 9-8 that follows defines the entries in this output.

Example 9-23 **show ip ospf database router** *Command Output*

```
Trinity>show ip ospf database router

        OSPF Router with ID (10.1.4.4) (Process ID 100)

                Router Link States (Area 69)

Routing Bit Set on this LSA
LS age: 1596
Options: (No TOS-capability, DC)
LS Type: Router Links
Link State ID: 10.1.1.1
Advertising Router: 10.1.1.1
LS Seq Number: 80000010
Checksum: 0x8A4A
Length: 36
Area Border Router
 Number of Links: 1
```

Example 9-23   **show ip ospf database router** *Command Output (Continued)*

```
     Link connected to: a Transit Network
      (Link ID) Designated Router address: 10.69.69.1
      (Link Data) Router Interface address: 10.69.69.1
       Number of TOS metrics: 0
        TOS 0 Metrics: 10

  LS age: 1768
  Options: (No TOS-capability, DC)
  LS Type: Router Links
  Link State ID: 10.1.4.4
  Advertising Router: 10.1.4.4
  LS Seq Number: 80000004
  Checksum: 0x85E6
  Length: 108
  AS Boundary Router
   Number of Links: 7

     Link connected to: a Stub Network
      (Link ID) Network/subnet number: 10.69.75.0
      (Link Data) Network Mask: 255.255.255.0
       Number of TOS metrics: 0
        TOS 0 Metrics: 1

     Link connected to: a Stub Network
      (Link ID) Network/subnet number: 10.69.74.0
      (Link Data) Network Mask: 255.255.255.0
       Number of TOS metrics: 0
        TOS 0 Metrics: 1

     Link connected to: a Stub Network
      (Link ID) Network/subnet number: 10.69.73.0
      (Link Data) Network Mask: 255.255.255.0
       Number of TOS metrics: 0
        TOS 0 Metrics: 1

     Link connected to: a Stub Network
      (Link ID) Network/subnet number: 10.69.72.0
      (Link Data) Network Mask: 255.255.255.0
       Number of TOS metrics: 0
        TOS 0 Metrics: 1

     Link connected to: a Stub Network
      (Link ID) Network/subnet number: 10.69.70.0
      (Link Data) Network Mask: 255.255.255.0
       Number of TOS metrics: 0
        TOS 0 Metrics: 1

     Link connected to: a Transit Network
      (Link ID) Designated Router address: 10.69.69.1
      (Link Data) Router Interface address: 10.69.69.2
       Number of TOS metrics: 0
```

continues

Example 9-23 **show ip ospf database router** *Command Output (Continued)*

```
        TOS 0 Metrics: 1

    Link connected to: a Stub Network
    (Link ID) Network/subnet number: 10.1.4.0
    (Link Data) Network Mask: 255.255.255.0
     Number of TOS metrics: 0
      TOS 0 Metrics: 1

Trinity>
```

Table 9-8 describes some fields from the output in Example 9-23 that are useful in a trouble-shooting environment.

Table 9-8   **show ip ospf database router output** *Command Definitions*

Field	Description
OSPF Router with ID	Router ID number
Process ID	OSPF process ID
LS age	Link-state age
Options	Type-of-service options (Type 0 only)
LS Type	Link-state type
Link State ID	Link-state ID
Advertising Router	Advertising router's ID
LS Seq Number	Link-state sequence (detects old or duplicate link-state advertisements)
Checksum	LS checksum (Fletcher checksum of the complete contents of the link-state advertisement)
Length	Length in bytes of the link-state advertisement
AS Boundary Router	Definition of router type
Number of Links	Number of active links
Link ID	Link type
Link Data	Router interface address
TOS	Type-of-service metric (Type 0 only)

show ip ospf database summary Command

Example 9-24 shows sample output from the **show ip ospf database summary** command when no optional arguments are specified. This command is useful for verifying and checking the contents of the link-state database. Recall that all the LSAs are in this database. Therefore, by viewing the contents of an LSA, you can learn a lot about how OSPF is operating from this detailed information.

Now oddly enough, the use of the **summary** keyword in this command gives the impression that you would be receiving only a summarized description of the link-state database. However, the truth is very different because you get a lot of detailed information of the summarized network LSAs only. That is an important note when viewing this command in that only Type 3 network LSAs are displayed. Nonetheless, it is very detailed output. A review of the output definitions for this command is helpful.

Example 9-24   show ip ospf database summary *Command Output*

```
Oracle>show ip ospf database summary

                OSPF Router with ID (10.1.1.1) (Process ID 100)

                Summary Net Link States (Area 0)

    LS age: 1662
    Options: (No TOS-capability, DC, Upward)
    LS Type: Summary Links(Network)
    Link State ID: 10.1.4.0 (summary Network Number)
    Advertising Router: 10.1.1.1
    LS Seq Number: 80000003
    Checksum: 0xC94A
    Length: 28
    Network Mask: /24
          TOS: 0  Metric: 11

    LS age: 1156
    Options: (No TOS-capability, DC, Upward)
    LS Type: Summary Links(Network)
    Link State ID: 10.1.5.0 (summary Network Number)
    Advertising Router: 10.1.1.1
    LS Seq Number: 8000000B
    Checksum: 0xAE5C
    Length: 28
    Network Mask: /24
          TOS: 0  Metric: 11

    LS age: 1157
    Options: (No TOS-capability, DC, Upward)
    LS Type: Summary Links(Network)
    Link State ID: 10.10.9.0 (summary Network Number)
    Advertising Router: 10.1.1.1
    LS Seq Number: 8000000B
    Checksum: 0x16E7
    Length: 28
    Network Mask: /24
          TOS: 0  Metric: 11
```

Table 9-9 describes some fields from the output in Example 9-24 that are useful in a trouble-shooting environment.

Table 9-9   **show ip ospf database summary** *Command Output Definitions*

Field	Description
OSPF Router with ID	Router ID number.
Process ID	OSPF process ID.
LS age	Link-state age.
Options	Type-of-service options (Type 0 only).
LS Type	Link-state type. In this command, you only see "Summary Links (network)" because these are the LSAs being displayed.
Link State ID	Link-state ID (summary network number).
Advertising Router	Advertising router's ID.
LS Seq Number	Link-state sequence (detects old or duplicate link-state advertisements).
Checksum	LS checksum (Fletcher checksum of the complete contents of the link-state advertisement).
Length	Length in bytes of the link-state advertisement.
Network Mask	Network mask implemented.
TOS	Type of service.
Metric	Link-state metric.

show ip ospf delete Command (Hidden)

The **show ip ospf delete** command is a hidden OSPF command. A hidden OSPF command is not found in Cisco documentation but is still present in Cisco IOS Software if you know the exact syntax. Any use of this command is not supported by Cisco Systems, and it is used at your risk. With that disclaimer in place, review the output in Example 9-25 to see what this command can tell you.

Example 9-25   **show ip ospf delete** *Command Output*

```
Oracle#show ip ospf delete

              OSPF Router with ID (10.1.1.1) (Process ID 100)

    Area BACKBONE(0)

    ROUTER and NETWORK LSDB delete list

      Dest: 10.1.7.0, Type: 0, Metric: 51, ADV RTR: 10.1.7.7
      Path:
```

Example 9-25   show ip ospf delete *Command Output (Continued)*

```
          gateway 10.0.0.2, interface FastEthernet2/0

     Dest: 10.1.6.0, Type: 0, Metric: 50, ADV RTR: 10.1.6.6
     Path:
       gateway 10.0.0.2, interface FastEthernet2/0

     Dest: 10.0.5.0, Type: 0, Metric: 50, ADV RTR: 10.1.6.6
     Path:
       gateway 10.0.0.2, interface FastEthernet2/0

     Dest: 10.0.4.0, Type: 0, Metric: 50, ADV RTR: 10.1.6.6
     Path:
       gateway 10.0.0.2, interface FastEthernet2/0

     Dest: 10.0.3.0, Type: 0, Metric: 50, ADV RTR: 10.1.6.6
     Path:
       gateway 10.0.0.2, interface FastEthernet2/0

     Dest: 10.0.2.0, Type: 0, Metric: 50, ADV RTR: 10.1.6.6
     Path:
       gateway 10.0.0.2, interface FastEthernet2/0

     Dest: 10.1.7.7, Type: 1, Metric: 50, ADV RTR: 10.1.7.7
     Path:
       gateway 10.0.0.2, interface FastEthernet2/0

     Dest: 10.0.1.0, Type: 2, Metric: 50, ADV RTR: 10.1.6.6
     Path:
       gateway 10.0.0.2, interface FastEthernet2/0

     Dest: 10.1.6.6, Type: 1, Metric: 49, ADV RTR: 10.1.6.6
     Path:
       gateway 10.0.0.2, interface FastEthernet2/0

     Dest: 10.1.3.3, Type: 1, Metric: 1, ADV RTR: 10.1.3.3
     Path:
       gateway 10.0.0.3, interface FastEthernet2/0

     Dest: 10.1.2.2, Type: 1, Metric: 1, ADV RTR: 10.1.2.2
     Path:
       gateway 10.0.0.2, interface FastEthernet2/0

     Dest: 10.0.0.0, Type: 2, Metric: 1, ADV RTR: 10.1.3.3
     Path:
       gateway 10.0.0.1, interface FastEthernet2/0

   SUMMARY NET and ASBR LSDB delete list

     Dest: 10.221.0.0, Type: 3, Metric: 51, ADV RTR: 10.1.7.7
     Path:
       gateway 10.0.0.2, interface FastEthernet2/0
```

continues

Example 9-25 **show ip ospf delete** *Command Output (Continued)*

```
        Dest: 10.51.51.0, Type: 3, Metric: 113, ADV RTR: 10.1.6.6
        Path:
          gateway 10.0.0.2, interface FastEthernet2/0

        Dest: 10.51.51.0, Type: 3, Metric: 113, ADV RTR: 10.1.2.2
        Path:
          gateway 10.0.0.2, interface FastEthernet2/0

  TYPE-7 EXTERNAL LSDB delete list

  Area 10

  ROUTER and NETWORK LSDB delete list

    Dest: 10.10.14.0, Type: 0, Metric: 11, ADV RTR: 10.10.14.1
    Path:
      gateway 10.10.10.2, interface Ethernet3/0

    Dest: 10.10.13.0, Type: 0, Metric: 11, ADV RTR: 10.10.14.1
    Path:
      gateway 10.10.10.2, interface Ethernet3/0

    Dest: 10.10.12.0, Type: 0, Metric: 11, ADV RTR: 10.10.14.1
    Path:
      gateway 10.10.10.2, interface Ethernet3/0

    Dest: 10.10.11.0, Type: 0, Metric: 11, ADV RTR: 10.10.14.1
    Path:
      gateway 10.10.10.2, interface Ethernet3/0

    Dest: 10.10.9.0, Type: 0, Metric: 11, ADV RTR: 10.10.14.1
    Path:
      gateway 10.10.10.2, interface Ethernet3/0

    Dest: 10.1.5.0, Type: 0, Metric: 11, ADV RTR: 10.10.14.1
    Path:
      gateway 10.10.10.2, interface Ethernet3/0

    Dest: 10.10.10.0, Type: 2, Metric: 10, ADV RTR: 10.10.14.1
    Path:
      gateway 10.10.10.1, interface Ethernet3/0

  SUMMARY NET and ASBR LSDB delete list

  TYPE-7 EXTERNAL LSDB delete list

  Area 69

  ROUTER and NETWORK LSDB delete list

    Dest: 10.69.75.0, Type: 0, Metric: 11, ADV RTR: 10.1.4.4
    Path:
```

Example 9-25   **show ip ospf delete** *Command Output (Continued)*

```
           gateway 10.69.69.2, interface Ethernet3/1

      Dest: 10.69.74.0, Type: 0, Metric: 11, ADV RTR: 10.1.4.4
      Path:
        gateway 10.69.69.2, interface Ethernet3/1

      Dest: 10.69.73.0, Type: 0, Metric: 11, ADV RTR: 10.1.4.4
      Path:
        gateway 10.69.69.2, interface Ethernet3/1

      Dest: 10.69.72.0, Type: 0, Metric: 11, ADV RTR: 10.1.4.4
      Path:
        gateway 10.69.69.2, interface Ethernet3/1

      Dest: 10.69.70.0, Type: 0, Metric: 11, ADV RTR: 10.1.4.4
      Path:
        gateway 10.69.69.2, interface Ethernet3/1

      Dest: 10.1.4.0, Type: 0, Metric: 11, ADV RTR: 10.1.4.4
      Path:
        gateway 10.69.69.2, interface Ethernet3/1

      Dest: 10.1.4.4, Type: 1, Metric: 10, ADV RTR: 10.1.4.4
      Path:
        gateway 10.69.69.2, interface Ethernet3/1

      Dest: 10.69.69.0, Type: 2, Metric: 10, ADV RTR: 10.1.4.4
      Path:
        gateway 10.69.69.1, interface Ethernet3/1

  SUMMARY NET and ASBR LSDB delete list

  TYPE-7 EXTERNAL LSDB delete list

  EXTERNAL LSDB delete list

      Dest: 0.0.0.0, Type: 5, Metric: 1, ADV RTR: 10.1.3.3
      Path:
        gateway 10.0.0.3, interface FastEthernet2/0
Oracle#
```

show ip ospf events Command (Hidden)

The **show ip ospf events** command is a hidden OSPF command. A hidden OSPF command is not found in Cisco documentation but is still present in Cisco IOS Software if you know the exact syntax. Any use of this command is not supported by Cisco Systems, and it is used at your risk. With that disclaimer in place, review the output in Example 9-26 to see what this command can tell you.

Example 9-26   **show ip ospf events** *Command Output*

```
Zion#show ip ospf events
  862704 Generic: ospf_build_rtr_lsa  0x0
 1612952 Timer Exp:  if_ack_delayed  0x81CE9168
 1731560 Timer Exp:  if_ack_delayed  0x81CE9168
 2885104 Generic: ospf_build_rtr_lsa  0x0
 3632264 Timer Exp:  if_ack_delayed  0x81CE9168
 3730296 Timer Exp:  if_ack_delayed  0x81CE9168
 4888048 Generic: ospf_build_rtr_lsa  0x0
 5650552 Timer Exp:  if_ack_delayed  0x81CE9168
 5772048 Timer Exp:  if_ack_delayed  0x81CE9168
 6709744 Generic: ospf_build_rtr_lsa  0x0
 7661676 Timer Exp:  if_ack_delayed  0x81CE9168
 7780012 Timer Exp:  if_ack_delayed  0x81CE9168
 8713712 Generic: ospf_build_rtr_lsa  0x0
 9679972 Timer Exp:  if_ack_delayed  0x81CE9168
 9790016 Timer Exp:  if_ack_delayed  0x81CE9168
10755568 Generic: ospf_build_rtr_lsa  0x0
11710556 Timer Exp:  if_ack_delayed  0x81CE9168
11819484 Timer Exp:  if_ack_delayed  0x81CE9168
12797424 Generic: ospf_build_rtr_lsa  0x0
13728848 Timer Exp:  if_ack_delayed  0x81CE9168
13791604 Timer Exp:  if_ack_delayed  0x81CE9168
14787056 Generic: ospf_build_rtr_lsa  0x0
15778884 Timer Exp:  if_ack_delayed  0x81CE9168
15785228 Timer Exp:  if_ack_delayed  0x81CE9168
216843248 Generic: ospf_build_rtr_lsa  0x0
217788984 Timer Exp:  if_ack_delayed  0x81CE9168
217809576 Timer Exp:  if_ack_delayed  0x81CE9168
218849264 Generic: ospf_build_rtr_lsa  0x0
219804204 Timer Exp:  if_ack_delayed  0x81CE9168
319833920 Timer Exp:  if_ack_delayed  0x81CE9168
320890096 Generic: ospf_build_rtr_lsa  0x0
321788708 Timer Exp:  if_ack_delayed  0x81CE9168
321819352 Timer Exp:  if_ack_delayed  0x81CE9168
322919664 Generic: ospf_build_rtr_lsa  0x0
323830556 Timer Exp:  if_ack_delayed  0x81CE9168
323837556 Timer Exp:  if_ack_delayed  0x81CE9168
324932848 Generic: ospf_build_rtr_lsa  0x0
325826064 Timer Exp:  if_ack_delayed  0x81CE9168
325844748 Timer Exp:  if_ack_delayed  0x81CE9168
426968560 Generic: ospf_build_rtr_lsa  0x0
427860996 Timer Exp:  if_ack_delayed  0x81CE9168
427869868 Timer Exp:  if_ack_delayed  0x81CE9168
428973552 Generic: ospf_build_rtr_lsa  0x0
429851640 Timer Exp:  if_ack_delayed  0x81CE9168
29871692 Timer Exp:  if_ack_delayed  0x81CE9168
31014384 Generic: ospf_build_rtr_lsa  0x0
31863260 Timer Exp:  if_ack_delayed  0x81CE9168
31869940 Timer Exp:  if_ack_delayed  0x81CE9168
33020400 Generic: ospf_build_rtr_lsa  0x0
33842560 Timer Exp:  if_ack_delayed  0x81CE9168
33855468 Timer Exp:  if_ack_delayed  0x81CE9168
35050992 Generic: ospf_build_rtr_lsa  0x0
```

Example 9-26   show ip ospf events *Command Output (Continued)*

```
35869976 Timer Exp:  if_ack_delayed  0x81CE9168
35887072 Timer Exp:  if_ack_delayed  0x81CE9168
36871664 Generic:  ospf_build_rtr_lsa  0x0
37862584 Timer Exp:  if_ack_delayed  0x81CE9168
37909464 Timer Exp:  if_ack_delayed  0x81CE9168
38899184 Generic:  ospf_build_rtr_lsa  0x0
39879764 Timer Exp:  if_ack_delayed  0x81CE9168
39908296 Timer Exp:  if_ack_delayed  0x81CE9168
40944112 Generic:  ospf_build_rtr_lsa  0x0
41901036 Timer Exp:  if_ack_delayed  0x81CE9168
41919428 Timer Exp:  if_ack_delayed  0x81CE9168
42964464 Generic:  ospf_build_rtr_lsa  0x0
43916160 Timer Exp:  if_ack_delayed  0x81CE9168
43973556 Timer Exp:  if_ack_delayed  0x81CE9168
44976624 Generic:  ospf_build_rtr_lsa  0x0
45931292 Timer Exp:  if_ack_delayed  0x81CE9168
46005164 Timer Exp:  if_ack_delayed  0x81CE9168
46968304 Generic:  ospf_build_rtr_lsa  0x0
47986348 Timer Exp:  if_ack_delayed  0x81CE9168
48017312 Timer Exp:  if_ack_delayed  0x81CE9168
48988656 Generic:  ospf_build_rtr_lsa  0x0
50014796 Timer Exp:  if_ack_delayed  0x81CE9168
50026392 Timer Exp:  if_ack_delayed  0x81CE9168
51024368 Generic:  ospf_build_rtr_lsa  0x0
52010892 Timer Exp:  if_ack_delayed  0x81CE9168
52023776 Timer Exp:  if_ack_delayed  0x81CE9168
53027312 Generic:  ospf_build_rtr_lsa  0x0
54030708 Timer Exp:  if_ack_delayed  0x81CE9168
54051712 Timer Exp:  if_ack_delayed  0x81CE9168
55023088 Generic:  ospf_build_rtr_lsa  0x0
56039700 Timer Exp:  if_ack_delayed  0x81CE9168
57061872 Generic:  ospf_build_rtr_lsa  0x0
58063720 Timer Exp:  if_ack_delayed  0x81CE9168
58088612 Timer Exp:  if_ack_delayed  0x81CE9168
59041264 Generic:  ospf_build_rtr_lsa  0x0
60078940 Timer Exp:  if_ack_delayed  0x81CE9168
60103744 Timer Exp:  if_ack_delayed  0x81CE9168
61056496 Generic:  ospf_build_rtr_lsa  0x0
62077780 Timer Exp:  if_ack_delayed  0x81CE9168
62153688 Timer Exp:  if_ack_delayed  0x81CE9168
63098352 Generic:  ospf_build_rtr_lsa  0x0
64074568 Timer Exp:  if_ack_delayed  0x81CE9168
64164724 Timer Exp:  if_ack_delayed  0x81CE9168
65091056 Generic:  ospf_build_rtr_lsa  0x0
66080572 Timer Exp:  if_ack_delayed  0x81CE9168
66145036 Timer Exp:  if_ack_delayed  0x81CE9168
67124720 Generic:  ospf_build_rtr_lsa  0x0
68089652 Timer Exp:  if_ack_delayed  0x81CE9168
68139692 Timer Exp:  if_ack_delayed  0x81CE9168
69120496 Generic:  ospf_build_rtr_lsa  0x0
70129216 Timer Exp:  if_ack_delayed  0x81CE9168
70145828 Timer Exp:  if_ack_delayed  0x81CE9168
71130608 Generic:  ospf_build_rtr_lsa  0x0
```

continues

Example 9-26   show ip ospf events *Command Output (Continued)*

```
72156628 Timer Exp:  if_ack_delayed  0x81CE9168
72161052 Timer Exp:  if_ack_delayed  0x81CE9168
73147888 Generic:  ospf_build_rtr_lsa  0x0
74153744 Timer Exp:  if_ack_delayed  0x81CE9168
74169712 Timer Exp:  if_ack_delayed  0x81CE9168
75165168 Generic:  ospf_build_rtr_lsa  0x0
76177156 Timer Exp:  if_ack_delayed  0x81CE9168
76190980 Timer Exp:  if_ack_delayed  0x81CE9168
76984816 Generic:  ospf_build_rtr_lsa  0x0
78158580 Timer Exp:  if_ack_delayed  0x81CE9168
78225564 Timer Exp:  if_ack_delayed  0x81CE9168
78998000 Generic:  ospf_build_rtr_lsa  0x0
80174828 Timer Exp:  if_ack_delayed  0x81CE9168
80220220 Timer Exp:  if_ack_delayed  0x81CE9168
81040880 Generic:  ospf_build_rtr_lsa  0x0
82204384 Timer Exp:  if_ack_delayed  0x81CE9168
82213840 Timer Exp:  if_ack_delayed  0x81CE9168
83071472 Generic:  ospf_build_rtr_lsa  0x0
84217704 Timer Exp:  if_ack_delayed  0x81CE9168
84231892 Timer Exp:  if_ack_delayed  0x81CE9168
85098992 Generic:  ospf_build_rtr_lsa  0x0
86242044 Timer Exp:  if_ack_delayed  0x81CE9168
86255308 Timer Exp:  if_ack_delayed  0x81CE9168
87122416 Generic:  ospf_build_rtr_lsa  0x0
88056512 Timer Exp:  if_ack_delayed  0x81CE9168
88250012 Timer Exp:  if_ack_delayed  0x81CE9168
89175536 Generic:  ospf_build_rtr_lsa  0x0
90071728 Timer Exp:  if_ack_delayed  0x81CE9168
90267188 Timer Exp:  if_ack_delayed  0x81CE9168
91221488 Generic:  ospf_build_rtr_lsa  0x0
92066476 Timer Exp:  if_ack_delayed  0x81CE9168
92280260 Timer Exp:  if_ack_delayed  0x81CE9168
93249008 Generic:  ospf_build_rtr_lsa  0x0
94095008 Timer Exp:  if_ack_delayed  0x81CE9168
94281064 Timer Exp:  if_ack_delayed  0x81CE9168
95255024 Generic:  ospf_build_rtr_lsa  0x0
96105104 Timer Exp:  if_ack_delayed  0x81CE9168
96321784 Timer Exp:  if_ack_delayed  0x81CE9168
97063408 Generic:  ospf_build_rtr_lsa  0x0
98137732 Timer Exp:  if_ack_delayed  0x81CE9168
98355340 Timer Exp:  if_ack_delayed  0x81CE9168
99081712 Generic:  ospf_build_rtr_lsa  0x0
100164216 Timer Exp:  if_ack_delayed  0x81CE9168
100381732 Timer Exp:  if_ack_delayed  0x81CE9168
101113328 Generic:  ospf_build_rtr_lsa  0x0
102198892 Timer Exp:  if_ack_delayed  0x81CE9168
102413244 Timer Exp:  if_ack_delayed  0x81CE9168
103130608 Generic:  ospf_build_rtr_lsa  0x0
104222304 Timer Exp:  if_ack_delayed  0x81CE9168
104441684 Timer Exp:  if_ack_delayed  0x81CE9168
105139696 Generic:  ospf_build_rtr_lsa  0x0
--------------Output omitted for brevity--------
Zion#
```

show ip ospf flood-list Command

To display a list of OSPF link-state advertisements (LSAs) waiting to be flooded over an interface, use the **show ip ospf flood-list** EXEC command. This command is most commonly used to observe the effects of the OSPF packet-pacing command, as described in Chapter 3, "OSPF Communication." Packet pacing essentially rate-limits the transmission of LSAs, so being able to "see" how many LSAs are waiting to be transmitted out an interface is important. If packet pacing is not enabled, you cannot see anything when executing this command. Example 9-27 demonstrates sample output from this command.

Example 9-27   **show ip ospf flood-list** *Command Output*

```
Router# show ip ospf flood-list interface ethernet 1
 Interface Ethernet1, Queue length 6
! - Queue length refers to the number of LSAs waiting to be flooded out the interface
on which the command is executed.
 Link state flooding due in 12 msec
! - The time in milliseconds expressed in this line refers to how long before the
next LSA in the queue is transmitted.
 Type  LS ID        ADV RTR         Seq NO      Age  Checksum
    5  9.2.195.0    200.0.0.163     0x80000009  0    0xFB61
    5  9.1.192.0    200.0.0.163     0x80000009  0    0x2938
    5  9.2.194.0    200.0.0.163     0x80000009  0    0x757
    5  9.1.193.0    200.0.0.163     0x80000009  0    0x1E42
    5  9.2.193.0    200.0.0.163     0x80000009  0    0x124D
    5  9.1.194.0    200.0.0.163     0x80000009  0    0x134C
```

OSPF packet pacing is useful in the scenarios described in Chapter 3; use this command to watch the effects on your network. Remember, if an LSA is in the queue here, that topology change has not yet been told to other OSPF routers; you can see a definite cause-and-effect relationship here.

show ip ospf maxage-list Command (Hidden)

The **show ip ospf maxage-list** command is a hidden OSPF command. A hidden OSPF command is not found in Cisco documentation but is still present in Cisco IOS Software if you know the exact syntax. Any use of this command is not supported by Cisco Systems, and it is used at your risk. With that disclaimer in place, review the output in Example 9-28 to see what this command can tell you.

Example 9-28   **show ip ospf maxage-list** *Command Output*

```
Oracle#show ip ospf maxage-list
  AS System 100
  Maxage delete timer due in NEVER
Oracle#
```

show ip ospf neighbor Command

To display OSPF neighbor information on a per-interface basis, use the **show ip ospf neighbor** EXEC command. Example 9-29 shows all avaible options for this command.

Example 9-29 *Displaying* **show ip ospf neighbor** *Command Options*

```
Oracle>show ip ospf neighbor ?
  Ethernet          IEEE 802.3
  FastEthernet      FastEthernet IEEE 802.3
  Hostname or A.B.C.D  Neighbor ID
  Loopback          Loopback interface
  Null              Null interface
  Serial            Serial
  detail            detail of all neighbors
  ¦                 Output modifiers
  <cr>

Oracle>
```

This command provides you with a variety of ways to gain information about an OSPF neighbor. These options are useful in large OSPF areas and allow you to target the specific neighbor that you are concerned about.

Example 9-30 shows the OSPF neighbors from the router's perspective in which it was executed. Therefore, when this command is executed on Router Oracle, the neighbors displayed refer to the routers that are neighbors of Router Oracle and their location out an interface of Router Oracle.

Example 9-30 *Displaying Information About Oracle's OSPF Neighbors*

```
Oracle>show ip ospf neighbor

Neighbor ID    Pri   State       Dead Time   Address      Interface
10.1.2.2        1    FULL/BDR    00:00:37    10.0.0.2     FastEthernet2/0
10.1.3.3        1    FULL/DR     00:00:38    10.0.0.3     FastEthernet2/0
10.10.14.1      1    FULL/DR     00:00:38    10.10.10.2   Ethernet3/0
10.1.4.4        1    FULL/BDR    00:00:36    10.69.69.2   Ethernet3/1
Oracle>
```

When the output refers to Neighbor ID, it is displaying the OSPF RID of the neighbor. You can also see which neighbor is the designated router (DR) and backup designated router (BDR) for each subnet. In the example, Router Mouse (RID 10.1.3.3) is the DR and Router Cypher (RID 10.1.2.2) is the BDR for area 0. The dead-time value is the time in seconds remaining for a Hello to arrive from the neighbor before Cisco IOS Software declares the neighbor dead.

show ip ospf neighbor *ip address* Command

The **show ip ospf neighbor** *ip address* command provides you with detailed information regarding a specific OSPF neighbor as specified by the IP address, as demonstrated in Example 9-31.

Example 9-31   show ip ospf neighbor *ip address Command Output*

```
Oracle>show ip ospf neighbor 10.1.2.2
 Neighbor 10.1.2.2, interface address 10.0.0.2
    In the area 0 via interface FastEthernet2/0
    Neighbor priority is 1, State is FULL, 6 state changes
    DR is 10.0.0.3 BDR is 10.0.0.2.
 ! - IMPORTANT NOTE!!! When the DR and BDR for an area are shown in this command
 ! it is their actual IP Address that is displayed NOT the RID as you would expect,
 ! careful of this when troubleshooting as it can get a bit confusing and I have
 ! no idea why Cisco did this. The short answer to this question is that
 ! RFC 2328 specifies that the DR is known by his interface address and that
 ! is the address in the hello packets and therefore the destination address for
 ! any packets sent to the DR.
    Options is 0x42
 ! -- Hello packet options field contents (E-bit only; possible values are 0 and 2;
 ! 2 indicates area is not a stub; 0 indicates area is a stub)
    Dead timer due in 00:00:34
    Neighbor is up for 06:33:06
 ! -- Dead timer reflects the time before Cisco IOS software will declare
 ! the neighbor dead and neighbor up time is not how long the neighbor router has
 ! been powered on but rather how long the routers have been neighbors, pretty
 ! important if there might be neighbor troubles.
    Index 2/4, retransmission queue length 0, number of retransmission 0
    First 0x0(0)/0x0(0) Next 0x0(0)/0x0(0)
    Last retransmission scan length is 0, maximum is 0
    Last retransmission scan time is 0 msec, maximum is 0 msec
 ! - These remaining lines reference when LSAs will be transmitted and how long
 ! it took to scan the LSDB.
Oracle>
```

show ip ospf neighbor *int ip-address* Command

By adding the interface, you can further clarify where and which neighbor you want to learn about. This command provides the same information as the **show ip ospf neighbor** *ip-address* command and is typically used when you have a high degree of redundancy in your network and thus need to be specific.

show ip ospf neighbor detail Command

The **show ip ospf neighbor detail** command also displays the same information as the **show ip ospf neighbor** *ip-address* command; however, instead of specifying the IP address, you use the keyword **detail** and all the information about every neighbor of the router you are logged into is displayed at once. Example 9-32 shows sample output from the **show ip ospf neighbor detail** command when executed on Router Oracle.

Example 9-32   *Displaying Detailed Information About All of Oracle's OSPF Neighbors*

```
Oracle>show ip ospf neighbor detail
 Neighbor 10.1.2.2, interface address 10.0.0.2
    In the area 0 via interface FastEthernet2/0
    Neighbor priority is 1, State is FULL, 6 state changes
    DR is 10.0.0.3 BDR is 10.0.0.2
    Options is 0x42
    Dead timer due in 00:00:35
    Neighbor is up for 06:35:14
    Index 2/4, retransmission queue length 0, number of retransmission 0
    First 0x0(0)/0x0(0) Next 0x0(0)/0x0(0)
    Last retransmission scan length is 0, maximum is 0
    Last retransmission scan time is 0 msec, maximum is 0 msec
 Neighbor 10.1.3.3, interface address 10.0.0.3
    In the area 0 via interface FastEthernet2/0
    Neighbor priority is 1, State is FULL, 6 state changes
    DR is 10.0.0.3 BDR is 10.0.0.2
    Options is 0x2
    Dead timer due in 00:00:36
    Neighbor is up for 06:35:16
    Index 1/1, retransmission queue length 0, number of retransmission 2
    First 0x0(0)/0x0(0) Next 0x0(0)/0x0(0)
    Last retransmission scan length is 1, maximum is 1
    Last retransmission scan time is 0 msec, maximum is 0 msec
 Neighbor 10.10.14.1, interface address 10.10.10.2
    In the area 10 via interface Ethernet3/0
    Neighbor priority is 1, State is FULL, 6 state changes
    DR is 10.10.10.2 BDR is 10.10.10.1
    Options is 0x2
    Dead timer due in 00:00:37
    Neighbor is up for 06:01:32
    Index 1/2, retransmission queue length 0, number of retransmission 1
    First 0x0(0)/0x0(0) Next 0x0(0)/0x0(0)
    Last retransmission scan length is 1, maximum is 1
    Last retransmission scan time is 0 msec, maximum is 0 msec
 Neighbor 10.1.4.4, interface address 10.69.69.2
    In the area 69 via interface Ethernet3/1
    Neighbor priority is 1, State is FULL, 6 state changes
    DR is 10.69.69.1 BDR is 10.69.69.2
    Options is 0x42
    Dead timer due in 00:00:35
    Neighbor is up for 01:40:57
    Index 2/5, retransmission queue length 0, number of retransmission 0
    First 0x0(0)/0x0(0) Next 0x0(0)/0x0(0)
    Last retransmission scan length is 0, maximum is 0
    Last retransmission scan time is 0 msec, maximum is 0 msec
Oracle>
```

The fields included in this command are also defined in the same way as in the other **show ip ospf neighbor** commands.

show ip ospf virtual-links Command

To display parameters about and the current state of OSPF virtual links, use the **show ip ospf virtual-links** EXEC command. This command provides you with detailed information regarding OSPF virtual links. The information displayed by the **show ip ospf virtual-links** command is useful in debugging OSPF routing operations. Example 9-33 uses comments to define the information from this command.

Example 9-33 **show ip ospf virtual-links** *Command Output*

```
Neo>show ip ospf virtual-links
Virtual Link OSPF_VL0 to router 10.1.2.2 is up
! - This line specifies the OSPF neighbor by RID and if the virtual link to that
neighbor is Up or Down
  Run as demand circuit
! - Virtual links are by design demand circuits and this is why the previous database
commands had the Do Not Age (DNA) bit set!
  DoNotAge LSA allowed.
  Transit area 51, via interface Serial0/0, Cost of using 64
! This line references the transit area through which the virtual link is formed,
the interface through which the virtual link is formed and the cost of reaching the
OSPF neighbor through the virtual link.
  Transmit Delay is 1 sec, State POINT_TO_POINT,
  Timer intervals configured, Hello 10, Dead 40, Wait 40, Retransmit 5
    Hello due in 00:00:03
  Adjacency State FULL (Hello suppressed)
! - This line describes the adjacency state and in this case Hellos are suppressed
because of the run as demand circuit characteristics of a virtual link.
    Index 2/3, retransmission queue length 0, number of retransmission 1
    First 0x0(0)/0x0(0) Next 0x0(0)/0x0(0)
    Last retransmission scan length is 1, maximum is 1
    Last retransmission scan time is 0 msec, maximum is 0 msec
  Message digest authentication enabled
      No key configured, using default key id 0
Neo>
```

show ip ospf stat Command (Hidden)

The **show ip ospf stat** is a hidden OSPF command. A hidden OSPF command is not found in Cisco documentation but is still present in Cisco IOS Software if you know the exact syntax. Any use of this command is not supported by Cisco Systems, and it is used at your risk. With that disclaimer in place, review the output in Example 9-34 to see what this command can tell you.

Example 9-34 **show ip ospf stat** *Command Output*

```
Oracle#show ip ospf stat
  Area 0: SPF algorithm executed 5 times
  Area 10: SPF algorithm executed 4 times
  Area 69: SPF algorithm executed 4 times

  SPF calculation time
Delta T   Intra D-Intra Summ   D-Summ Ext    D-Ext   Total  Reason
00:05:19  0     0       0      0      0      0       0      R, N, SN, SA, X
00:05:09  0     0       0      0      0      0       0      R,
00:04:27  0     0       0      4      0      0       4      R, N, SN, X
00:04:17  0     8       0      0      0      0       8      R, X
00:04:00  0     0       0      0      0      0       0      R, N,
00:03:50  0     4       0      0      0      0       8      R, SN,


  Avg. and Accumulated time of the last 250 process_ase()

                      Avg.     Accumulated
    ASBR-lookup       0,       0

    Forw-Addr-lookup  0,       0

    compare metric    0,       0

    add_ex-route      0,       0

    route_delete      0,       0


  Avg. and Accumulated time of the last 250 add_ex_route

                           Avg.    Accumulated
    ex_delete_route_list   0,      0

    network_update         0,      0

    ex_insert_route_list   0,      0


  Avg. and Accumulated time of the last 250 summary LSA process

                                     Avg. Accumulated
    ABR-lookup                       0,   0

    destination-lookup               0,   0

    add summary route                0,   0

    route_delete & build_inter_route_all  0,   0


Oracle#
```

show ip ospf summary-address Command

The **show ip ospf summary-address** command displays a list of all summary address redistribution information configured under an OSPF process. Example 9-35 shows sample output for the this command.

Example 9-35   **show ip ospf summary-address** *Command Output*

```
Mouse#show ip ospf summary-address

OSPF Process 100, Summary-address

25.25.0.0/255.255.0.0 Metric 20, Type 2, Tag 0
Mouse#
```

clear ip ospf Command

When troubleshooting, sometimes it is important to clear various aspects of OSPF. Cisco IOS Software allows several clear options, ranging from clearing counters to clearing the entire OSPF process! Example 9-36 lists the available options for the **clear ip ospf** command, each of which is discussed in the following sections.

Example 9-36   *Displaying the* **clear ip ospf** *Command Options*

```
Oracle#clear ip ospf ?
  <1-4294967295>  Process ID number
  counters        OSPF counters
  process         Reset OSPF process
  redistribution  Clear OSPF route redistribution
```

clear ip ospf counters Command

You might have seen the **clear ip ospf counters** command in Cisco IOS Software and naturally presumed this command is just like the **clear interface counters** command. Unfortunately, this command resets only one counter. Example 9-37 shows the output of the **show ip ospf neighbor** command for Router Oracle prior to clearing the counter.

Example 9-37   *Displaying OSPF Neighbor Information*

```
Oracle#show ip ospf neighbor 10.1.2.2
 Neighbor 10.1.2.2, interface address 10.0.0.2
    In the area 0 via interface FastEthernet2/0
    Neighbor priority is 1, State is FULL, 6 state changes
    DR is 10.0.0.3 BDR is 10.0.0.2
    Options is 0x42
    Dead timer due in 00:00:38
    Neighbor is up for 00:13:21
    Index 2/4, retransmission queue length 0, number of retransmission 1
    First 0x0(0)/0x0(0) Next 0x0(0)/0x0(0)
    Last retransmission scan length is 2, maximum is 2
    Last retransmission scan time is 0 msec, maximum is 0 msec
Oracle#
```

You can see that this neighbor has changed state six times (exstart, loading, and so on) to become FULL. If you were troubleshooting a neighbor problem, wouldn't it be nice to be able to reset that counter and watch what happens? That is the purpose of the **clear ip ospf counters** command, so review the resulting output in Example 9-38 and see what happens.

Example 9-38 **clear ip ospf counters** *Command Execution and Resulting OSPF Neighbor Information*

```
Oracle#clear ip ospf counters

Oracle#show ip ospf neighbor 10.1.2.2
 Neighbor 10.1.2.2, interface address 10.0.0.2
    In the area 0 via interface FastEthernet2/0
    Neighbor priority is 1, State is FULL, 0 state changes
    DR is 10.0.0.3 BDR is 10.0.0.2
    Options is 0x42
    Dead timer due in 00:00:36
    Neighbor is up for 00:14:23
    Index 2/4, retransmission queue length 0, number of retransmission 1
    First 0x0(0)/0x0(0) Next 0x0(0)/0x0(0)
    Last retransmission scan length is 2, maximum is 2
    Last retransmission scan time is 0 msec, maximum is 0 msec
Oracle#
```

clear ip ospf process Command

In extreme cases, you must completely reset OSPF. In this case, you can use the **clear ip ospf process** command. However, be aware that you should specify the appropriate OSPF process ID. If you do not specify the **pid** option, all OSPF processes are cleared on the router. In Example 9-39, you are attached on the console port of Router Oracle and OSPF is cleared. Notice the resulting messages as all the neighbors go down.

Example 9-39 *Clearing All OSPF Processes*

```
Oracle#clear ip ospf process
Reset ALL OSPF processes? [no]: yes

Oracle#
000048: *Mar  1 11:41:42.738 GMT: %OSPF-5-ADJCHG: Process 100, Nbr 10.1.2.2 on
  FastEthernet2/0 from FULL to DOWN, Neighbor Down: Interface down or detached
000049: *Mar  1 11:41:42.738 GMT: %OSPF-5-ADJCHG: Process 100, Nbr 10.1.3.3 on
  FastEthernet2/0 from FULL to DOWN, Neighbor Down: Interface down or detached
000050: *Mar  1 11:41:42.778 GMT: %OSPF-5-ADJCHG: Process 100, Nbr 10.10.14.1 on
  Ethernet3/0 from FULL to DOWN, Neighbor Down: Interface down or detached
000051: *Mar  1 11:41:42.818 GMT: %OSPF-5-ADJCHG: Process 100, Nbr 10.1.4.4 on
  Ethernet3/1 from FULL to DOWN, Neighbor Down: Interface down or detached
000052: *Mar  1 11:41:47.674 GMT: %OSPF-5-ADJCHG: Process 100, Nbr 10.1.4.4 on
  Ethernet3/1 from LOADING to FULL, Loading Done
000053: *Mar  1 11:41:49.054 GMT: %OSPF-5-ADJCHG: Process 100, Nbr 10.1.2.2 on
  FastEthernet2/0 from LOADING to FULL, Loading Done
000054: *Mar  1 11:41:49.966 GMT: %OSPF-5-ADJCHG: Process 100, Nbr 10.10.14.1 on
  Ethernet3/0 from LOADING to FULL, Loading Done
000055: *Mar  1 11:41:50.586 GMT: %OSPF-5-ADJCHG: Process 100, Nbr 10.1.3.3 on
  FastEthernet2/0 from LOADING to FULL, Loading Done
```

As you can see, this is a powerful command that disrupts all routing until OSPF converges again, so use this command with caution. If you are Telnetted to the router and execute this command, expect to get disconnected!

clear ip ospf redistribution Command

The **clear ip ospf redistribution** command allows you to clear any route redistribution that is going on. The benefit of this command is that it allows a reset of redistributed routes, which is useful in cases where a bad route has been accidentally redistributed into OSPF, and waiting for it to time out is not possible.

Example 9-40   *Using the* **clear ip ospf redistribution** *Command*

```
Oracle#clear ip ospf redistribution ?
  <cr>

Oracle#
```

The next section discusses the uses of the various OSPF **debug** commands.

OSPF debug Commands

The debug privileged EXEC commands can provide a wealth of information about the traffic and events being seen (or not seen) by OSPF. These traffic and events can include, but are not limited to, interface traffic, error messages generated by nodes on the network, protocol-specific diagnostic packets, and other useful troubleshooting data.

CAUTION   Exercise care when using **debug** commands. Many of these commands are processor intensive and can cause serious network problems (such as degraded performance or loss of connectivity). When you finish using a **debug** command, disable it with its specific **no debug** command (or use the **no debug all** command to turn off all debugging).

When to Use debug Commands

Use **debug** commands only for problem isolation; do not use them to monitor normal network operation. The **debug** commands produce a large amount of processor overhead that can disrupt router operation. Try to limit the use of **debug** commands to situations in which you are looking for specific types of traffic or problems and have narrowed your problems to a likely subset of causes. There are a many **debug** commands available. The format of the output varies with each different **debug** command, as follows:

- Some **debug** commands generate a single line of output per packet, and others generate multiple lines of output per packet.

- Some **debug** commands generate large amounts of output, and others generate only occasional output.

- Some **debug** commands generate lines of text, and others generate information in field format.

TIP   Do not be afraid of using the **debug** command. When you need it, you have probably exhausted the **show** commands. But like a surgeon's scalpel, use it carefully. For example, do not just enter the **debug ospf hello** command.

How to Use debug Commands

Adhering to the following procedure minimizes the load created by using **debug** commands because the console port no longer has to generate character-by-character processor interrupts.

To minimize the negative impact on your router of using **debug** commands, follow this procedure:

Step 1   Use the **no logging console** global configuration command on your router. This command disables all logging to the console terminal.

Step 2   Telnet to a router port, and enter the enable EXEC mode.

Step 3   Open another Telnet session with the router and type the **undebug all** command in this second session, but do not press **Enter**. Go back and start the debug session in the first session. When you are ready to stop the debug session, go back to the second session, and press **Enter** to send the command. Eventually the router's CPU will process the command and shut off **debug**. The key sequence **u, all** is the quickest way to turn off all debugging.

Step 4   Use the **terminal monitor** command to copy **debug** command output and system error messages to your current terminal display. This permits you to view **debug** command output remotely, without being connected through the console port.

Step 5   If you intend to keep the output of the **debug** command, spool the output to a file. The procedure for setting up such a debug output file is described in Cisco's Debug Command Reference publication. Certain programs also offer the capability to log everything that is displayed in your current Telnet session. The Windows Telnet application is a good example of a program with this capability.

Timestamping debug Output

You should already be aware of how important it is to date and time stamp debug messages. While mentioned in the previous section on SYSLOG, it is even more important to time stamp **debug** command output. Enter the following command in global configuration:

```
service timestamps debug datetime msec localtime show-timezone
```

Complete OSPF debug Commands

This book refers to specific **debug** commands that are useful when troubleshooting OSPF-specific related problems. Complete details regarding the function and output of **debug** commands are provided in Cisco's Debug Command Reference publication. (Enter "Debug Command Reference" in the search box at Cisco.com, and you can find pointers to the document broken down by Cisco IOS Software release.)

TIP   The **debug** command has many different options available for its use. It also provides you with much information on what is going on within a router. However, it can also hurt the routing processes and normal operation of the router, so use it wisely. Have I stressed this point enough yet?

This section uses the network topology and routing illustrated in Figure 9-5 to demonstrate the effects of the configuration and command examples.

Figure 9-5 *OSPF Sample Network Topology*

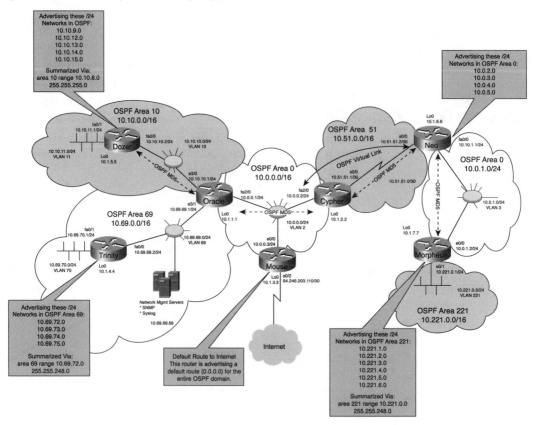

Example 9-41 provides a list of the different types of **debug** commands.

Example 9-41 *OSPF Debug Options*

```
Oracle#debug ip ospf ?
  adj              OSPF adjacency events
  database-timer   OSPF database timer
  events           OSPF events
  flood            OSPF flooding
  hello            OSPF hello events
  lsa-generation   OSPF lsa generation
  mpls             OSPF MPLS
  packet           OSPF packets
  retransmission   OSPF retransmission events
  spf              OSPF spf
  tree             OSPF database tree

Oracle#
```

debug ip ospf adjacency Command

The **debug ip ospf adjacency** command reports the various events that occur in relation to the various adjacencies within OSPF. Example 9-42 shows that the router detected OSPF adjacency problems on the network to which it is connected. The **no** form of this command disables debugging output.

First, check to make sure that the network is converged and that you have all four of the neighbors that Router Oracle is expected to have by reviewing the output in Example 9-42.

Example 9-42 *Verifying Network Convergence on Router Oracle*

```
Oracle#show ip ospf neighbor

Neighbor ID    Pri   State      Dead Time   Address      Interface
10.1.2.2         1   FULL/BDR   00:00:33    10.0.0.2     FastEthernet2/0
10.1.3.3         1   FULL/DR    00:00:10    10.0.0.3     FastEthernet2/0
10.10.14.1       1   FULL/DR    00:00:30    10.10.10.2   Ethernet3/0
10.1.4.4         1   FULL/DR    00:00:33    10.69.69.2   Ethernet3/1
Oracle#
```

Oracle's OSPF is currently operating well, and in area 0, you can see that Router Mouse is the designated router. While you are waiting for something to happen, notice that because you have OSPF authentication turned on, you can see the adjacencies being maintained with authentication as the network is configured, as follows:

```
000095: Jul 21 16:19:02.434 EST: OSPF: Send with youngest Key 1
000096: Jul 21 16:19:02.434 EST: OSPF: Send with youngest Key 1
Oracle#
```

To simulate a change in OSPF adjacencies, remotely reload Router Mouse. With debug OSPF adjacencies on, see what happens in Example 9-43 (comments in italics). Initially nothing happens because Oracle and Mouse are connected via a switch and oracle never "senses" that the Ethernet is going down. However, OSPF sends Hellos and has that timer known as the dead timer, which should detect the loss of Router Mouse.

Example 9-43 *Debug OSPF Adjacencies*

```
000099: Jul 21 16:19:11.353 EST: OSPF: 10.1.3.3 address 10.0.0.3 on
  FastEthernet2/0 is dead
! -- Notice the first debug message that tells us OSPF router with an RID of
! 10.1.3.3 (mouse) reachable via IP Address 10.0.0.3 (mouse e0/0) which is
! located via our routers Fast Ethernet interface 2/0 is dead.
000100: Jul 21 16:19:11.353 EST: OSPF: 10.1.3.3 address 10.0.0.3 on FastEthernet2/
0 is dead, state DOWN
! - Since the neighbor has been declared dead, we take the adjacency state
! immediately to DOWN.
000101: Jul 21 16:19: 11.353 EST: %OSPF-5-ADJCHG: Process 100, Nbr 10.1.3.3 on
  FastEthernet2/0 from FULL to DOWN, Neighbor Down: Dead timer expired
! - Something odd has happened??? Why is OSPF telling us on the 3rd debug message
! that the dead timer has expired? Shouldn't that have been the first message?
! Yes it should of as the dead time expiring is what drives the declaration of
! the neighbor being dead and the resulting down state. Yet IOS is not wrong
```

continues

Example 9-43 *Debug OSPF Adjacencies (Continued)*

```
! here, take a look at the timers in the message header, they are all the same
! down to the millisecond. I told you that setting the time stamps are important!
! All of these happened at the same time, the IOS just displayed them in a
! rather odd order. Go figure.
000102: Jul 21 16:19:12.550 EST: OSPF: Neighbor change Event on
   interface FastEthernet2/0
! - Router Oracle senses that the DR (Router mouse) is dead so a new DR
! election process must take place for area 0.
000103: Jul 21 16:19:12.550 EST: OSPF: DR/BDR election on FastEthernet2/0
000104: Jul 21 16:19:12.550 EST: OSPF: Elect BDR 10.1.2.2
000105: Jul 21 16:19:12.550 EST: OSPF: Elect DR 10.1.2.2
000106: Jul 21 16:19:12.550 EST:          DR: 10.1.2.2 (Id)    BDR: 10.1.2.2 (Id)
! - Remember that the BDR election takes place first and when the DR goes
! missing like this the BDR becomes the DR; this will then leave the area without a
BDR.
000111: Jul 21 16:19:15.666 EST: OSPF: Neighbor change Event on
   interface FastEthernet2/0
000112: Jul 21 16:19:15.666 EST: OSPF: DR/BDR election on FastEthernet2/0
000113: Jul 21 16:19:15.666 EST: OSPF: Elect BDR 10.1.1.1
000114: Jul 21 16:19:15.666 EST: OSPF: Elect DR 10.1.2.2
000115: Jul 21 16:19:15.666 EST: OSPF: Elect BDR 10.1.1.1
000116: Jul 21 16:19:15.666 EST: OSPF: Elect DR 10.1.2.2
000117: Jul 21 16:19:15.666 EST:          DR: 10.1.2.2 (Id)    BDR: 10.1.1.1 (Id)
! - The election of the BDR is now finished and Router Oracle (RID: 10.1.1.1)
! was elected
```

In Example 9-44, you can see that Router Mouse has completed its reload and OSPF once again becomes active.

Example 9-44 *Debug OSPF Adjacency—DR Election*

```
Oracle#
000132: Jul 21 16:20:17.434 EST: OSPF: Rcv DBD from 10.1.3.3 on FastEthernet2/0
   seq 0xFBD opt 0x2 flag 0x7 len 32  mtu 1500 state INIT
000133: Jul 21 16:20:17.434 EST: OSPF: 2 Way Communication to 10.1.3.3 on
   FastEthernet2/0, state 2WAY
000134: Jul 21 16:20:17.438 EST: OSPF: Neighbor change Event on
   interface FastEthernet2/0
000139: Jul 21 16:20:17.438 EST: OSPF: Send DBD to 10.1.3.3 on
   FastEthernet2/0 seq 0x485 opt 0x42 flag 0x7 len 32
000141: Jul 21 16:20:17.438 EST: OSPF: NBR Negotiation Done. We are the SLAVE
! - You can see by the output that Mouse comes up enters INIT and then 2WAY
! at which point the routers are considered neighbors. In order to exchange
! OSPF Database Descriptors Router Oracle becomes the slave in the process.
000142: Jul 21 16:20:17.438 EST: OSPF: Send DBD to 10.1.3.3 on FastEthernet2/0
   seq 0xFBD opt 0x42 flag 0x2 len 572
000144: Jul 21 16:20:17.446 EST: OSPF: Rcv DBD from 10.1.3.3 on FastEthernet2/0
   seq 0xFBE opt 0x2 flag 0x3 len 572  mtu 1500 state EXCHANGE
000145: Jul 21 16:20:17.446 EST: OSPF: Send DBD to 10.1.3.3 on FastEthernet2/0
   seq 0xFBE opt 0x42 flag 0x0 len 32
000148: Jul 21 16:20:17.450 EST: OSPF: Rcv DBD from 10.1.3.3 on
   FastEthernet2/0 seq 0xFBF opt 0x2 flag 0x1 len 32  mtu 1500 state EXCHANGE
```

Example 9-44 *Debug OSPF Adjacency—DR Election (Continued)*

```
000149: Jul 21 16:20:17.450 EST: OSPF: Exchange Done with 10.1.3.3 on
  FastEthernet2/0
! - The exchanging of DBD's is now completed between Routers Mouse & Oracle.
! Don't forget that at the same time Mouse is exchanging information with
! Router Cypher but this debug is being run on Router Oracle so we do not
! see that process.
000150: Jul 21 16:20:17.450 EST: OSPF: Synchronized with 10.1.3.3 on
  FastEthernet2/0, state FULL
000151: Jul 21 16:20:17.450 EST: %OSPF-5-ADJCHG: Process 100, Nbr 10.1.3.3 on
  FastEthernet2/0 from LOADING to FULL, Loading Done
! - The FULL state is achieved so OSPF changes the state to full as
! shown in the load message. The adjacency building process is complete.
Oracle#
```

If an OSPF neighbor relationship is not being formed between two routers, the **debug ip ospf adjacency** command can be used to determine the problem. Any issues of routers not forming adjacencies is easily seen here, thus allowing you to correct the issue. For example, suppose that you misconfigured Router Mouse and told it that network 10.0.0.0 was in area 69 and not area 0. You would see the following in your debug output:

```
000284: Jul 21 17:13:46.861 EST: OSPF: Rcv pkt from 10.0.0.3, FastEthernet2/0,
  area 0.0.0.0 mismatch area 0.0.0.69 in the header
```

If the adjacency were already formed, you would then see it come down as you did before.

debug ip ospf events Command

Use the **debug ip ospf events** EXEC command to display information on the following OSPF-related events:

- Adjacency formation
- Flooding information
- Designated router selection
- Shortest path first (SPF) calculations
- Hello packet processing
- Mismatched Hello timers and other OSPF events
- Mismatched IP subnet masks for routers on the same network.
- Mismatched OSPF dead interval for the router with that configured for a neighbor.

The output from this command duplicates most of what you see from the **debug ip ospf adjacency** command. However, when using the **debug ip ospf events** command, the information is more driven by events, and not all the same details are shown. For example, if you were to reload Router Mouse and watch the adjacency form with Router Oracle again, you would see the much shorter and less descriptive results of Example 9-45.

Example 9-45 **debug ip ospf events** *Command Output*

```
Oracle# debug ip ospf events
000436: Jul 21 17:18:17.280 EST: OSPF: Rcv hello from 10.1.3.3 area 0 from
  FastEthernet2/0 10.0.0.3
000437: Jul 21 17:18:17.280 EST: OSPF: 2 Way Communication to 10.1.3.3 on
  FastEthernet2/0, state 2WAY
000443: Jul 21 17:18:17.280 EST: OSPF: Send DBD to 10.1.3.3 on FastEthernet2/0
  seq 0x17D opt 0x42 flag 0x7 len 32
000446: Jul 21 17:18:17.420 EST: OSPF: Rcv DBD from 10.1.3.3 on FastEthernet2/0
  seq 0x79B opt 0x2 flag 0x7 len 32  mtu 1500 state EXSTART
000447: Jul 21 17:18:17.420 EST: OSPF: NBR Negotiation Done. We are the SLAVE
000448: Jul 21 17:18:17.420 EST: OSPF: Send DBD to 10.1.3.3 on FastEthernet2/0
  seq 0x79B opt 0x42 flag 0x2 len 552
000450: Jul 21 17:18:17.428 EST: OSPF: Rcv DBD from 10.1.3.3 on FastEthernet2/0
  seq 0x79C opt 0x2 flag 0x3 len 552  mtu 1500 state EXCHANGE
000451: Jul 21 17:18:17.428 EST: OSPF: Send DBD to 10.1.3.3 on FastEthernet2/0
  seq 0x79C opt 0x42 flag 0x0 len 32
000454: Jul 21 17:18:17.432 EST: OSPF: Rcv DBD from 10.1.3.3 on FastEthernet2/0
  seq 0x79D opt 0x2 flag 0x1 len 32  mtu 1500 state EXCHANGE
000455: Jul 21 17:18:17.432 EST: OSPF: Exchange Done with 10.1.3.3 on
  FastEthernet2/0
000456: Jul 21 17:18:17.432 EST: OSPF: Synchronized with 10.1.3.3 on
  FastEthernet2/0, state FULL
```

That's a whole lot shorter, isn't it? But it is also considerably less descriptive because this command is more concerned with the events and not the whole adjacency process—an important difference. This command also enables you to see other events as well, such as the periodic OSPF Hello packets, thus ensuring that the adjacencies stay active (see Example 9-46).

Example 9-46 *Displaying Periodic OSPF Hello Packets to Ensure Active Adjacencies*

```
000485: Jul 21 17:18:43.288 EST: OSPF: Rcv hello from 10.10.14.1 area 10 from
  Ethernet3/0 10.10.10.2
000486: Jul 21 17:18:43.292 EST: OSPF: End of hello processing

000487: Jul 21 17:18:45.644 EST: OSPF: Rcv hello from 10.1.4.4 area 69 from
  Ethernet3/1 10.69.69.2
000488: Jul 21 17:18:45.644 EST: OSPF: End of hello processing

000489: Jul 21 17:18:45.664 EST: OSPF: Rcv hello from 10.1.2.2 area 0 from
  FastEthernet2/0 10.0.0.2
000490: Jul 21 17:18:45.664 EST: OSPF: End of hello processing

000491: Jul 21 17:18:47.284 EST: OSPF: Rcv hello from 10.1.3.3 area 0 from
  FastEthernet2/0 10.0.0.3
000492: Jul 21 17:18:47.284 EST: OSPF: End of hello processing
```

Notice how OSPF tells you that a Hello packet was received and processed. This is similar to a positive acknowledge, so everything is fine; however, this command can also tell you when things are not okay, as demonstrated in Example 9-47.

Example 9-47   **debug ip ospf events** *Command Output, Indicating a Problem*

```
Oracle#debug ip ospf events
OSPF events debugging is on
Oracle#
6w4d: OSPF: Rcv hello from 10.1.5.5 area 10 from Ethernet3/0 10.1.1.18
6w4d: OSPF: Mismatched hello parameters from 10.1.1.18
6w4d: OSPF: Dead R 40 C 123, Hello R 10 C 10
```

R is the received dead interval time, and C is the dead interval time configured on the local router. If a router configured for OSPF routing is not seeing an OSPF neighbor on an attached network, do the following:

- Make sure that both routers have been configured with the same IP mask, OSPF Hello interval, and OSPF dead interval.

- Make sure that both neighbors are part of the same area type.

debug ip ospf flood Command

The **debug ip ospf flood** command enables you to view the actions and events that are being generated by OSPF's flooding mechanism. The **no** form of this command disables debugging output. Be careful when using this **debug** command because it can generate a lot of unfiltered traffic when enabled. As Example 9-48 shows, this command allows several options to include access lists.

Example 9-48   **debug ip ospf flood** *Command Options*

```
Cypher#debug ip ospf flood ?
  <1-99>      Access list
  <1300-1999> Access list (expanded range)
  <cr>
```

This **debug** command has an access list option; you should use this command with an access list to reduce the debug message generated and make it more useful.

TIP   Use of the OSPF interface **database-filter all out** command indicates that flood suppression is enabled on this interface. You should use flood suppression (on redundant nonbroadcast multiaccess [NBMA] point-to-point links) to avoid duplicated effort on the router's part during database synchronization by avoiding the use of empty Database Descriptor (DBD) packet.

An access list is used to match the LSA ID, and only the LSA ID permitted by the access list is displayed. For example, if you suspect that the flooding of external LSAs is not working, choose one or two external LSAs and use the access list to identify the traffic that is interesting and to watch the exact operation of flooding on those LSAs.

In Example 9-49, flooding protocol information only for LSAs with an ID of 64.246.203.0/24 is displayed.

Example 9-49 *Using an Access List to Limit Flooding Protocol Information*

```
Oracle#config terminal
Enter configuration commands, one per line.  End with CNTL/Z.
Oracle(config)#access-list 1 permit 64.246.203.0 0.0.0.255
Oracle(config)#^Z
Oracle#
001355: Jul 21 17:45:53.569 EST: %SYS-5-CONFIG_I: Configured from console by console
Oracle#debug ip ospf flood 1
OSPF flooding debugging is on for access list 1
Oracle#
```

Remember the default route to 64.246.203.109 (that is, the Internet) coming from Router Mouse? The access list should identify changes relating only to the LSA with that ID. Review Example 9-50 to see what happens when you take away the default route.

Example 9-50 **debug ip ospf flood** *Command Output*

```
Oracle#
001472: Jul 21 17:50:32.488 EST: Inc retrans unit nbr count index 2 (0/2) to 1/1
001473: Jul 21 17:50:32.488 EST: Set Nbr 10.1.2.2 2 first flood info from 0 (0)
  to 62ADB6EC (8)
001474: Jul 21 17:50:32.488 EST: Init Nbr 10.1.2.2 2 next flood info to 62ADB6EC
001475: Jul 21 17:50:32.488 EST: OSPF: Start FastEthernet2/0 10.1.2.2 retrans
  timer
001476: Jul 21 17:50:32.488 EST: Set idb next flood info from 0 (0) to
  62ADB6EC (8)
001477: Jul 21 17:50:32.488 EST: OSPF: Start FastEthernet2/0 pacing timer
001478: Jul 21 17:50:32.488 EST: Inc retrans unit nbr count index 1 (0/1) to 2/2
001479: Jul 21 17:50:32.492 EST: Set Nbr 10.10.14.1 1 first flood info from 0 (0)
  to 62ADB6EC (8)
001480: Jul 21 17:50:32.492 EST: Init Nbr 10.10.14.1 1 next flood info to 62ADB6EC
001481: Jul 21 17:50:32.492 EST: OSPF: Start Ethernet3/0 10.10.14.1 retrans timer
001482: Jul 21 17:50:32.492 EST: Set idb next flood info from 0 (0) to
  62ADB6EC (8)
001483: Jul 21 17:50:32.492 EST: OSPF: Start Ethernet3/0 pacing timer
001484: Jul 21 17:50:32.492 EST: Inc retrans unit nbr count index 3 (0/3) to 3/3
001485: Jul 21 17:50:32.492 EST: Set Nbr 10.1.4.4 3 first flood info from 0 (0) to
  62ADB6EC (8)
001486: Jul 21 17:50:32.492 EST: Init Nbr 10.1.4.4 3 next flood info to 62ADB6EC
001487: Jul 21 17:50:32.492 EST: OSPF: Start Ethernet3/1 10.1.4.4 retrans timer
001488: Jul 21 17:50:32.492 EST: Set idb next flood info from 0 (0) to
  62ADB6EC (8)
001489: Jul 21 17:50:32.492 EST: OSPF: Start Ethernet3/1 pacing timer
```

Example 9-50   debug ip ospf flood *Command Output (Continued)*

```
001490: Jul 21 17:50:32.520 EST: Create retrans unit
  0x62AD9F34/0x62AD8EF4 2 (0/2) 3
001491: Jul 21 17:50:32.520 EST: OSPF: Set nbr 2 (0/2) retrans to
  4888 count to 1
001492: Jul 21 17:50:32.520 EST: Set idb next flood info from
  62ADB6EC (8) to 0 (0)
001493: Jul 21 17:50:32.520 EST: OSPF: Stop FastEthernet2/0 flood timer
001494: Jul 21 17:50:32.524 EST: OSPF: Set nbr 1 (0/1) retrans to 4812 count to 1
001495: Jul 21 17:50:32.524 EST: Set idb next flood info from
  62ADB6EC (8) to 0 (0)
001496: Jul 21 17:50:32.524 EST: OSPF: Stop Ethernet3/0 flood timer
001497: Jul 21 17:50:32.524 EST: OSPF: Set nbr 3 (0/3) retrans to 4984 count to 1
001498: Jul 21 17:50:32.524 EST: Set idb next flood info from
  62ADB6EC (8) to 0 (0)
001499: Jul 21 17:50:32.524 EST: OSPF: Stop Ethernet3/1 flood timer
001500: Jul 21 17:50:32.524 EST: Dec retrans unit nbr count index 2 (0/2) to 2/2
001501: Jul 21 17:50:32.524 EST: Set Nbr 10.1.2.2 2 first flood info from
  62ADB6EC (8) to 0 (0)
001502: Jul 21 17:50:32.524 EST: Adjust Nbr 10.1.2.2 2 next flood info to 0
001503: Jul 21 17:50:32.528 EST: OSPF: Stop nbr 10.1.2.2 retransmission timer
001504: Jul 21 17:50:35.024 EST: Dec retrans unit nbr count index 1 (0/1) to 1/1
001505: Jul 21 17:50:35.024 EST: Set Nbr 10.10.14.1 1 first flood info from
  62ADB6EC (8) to 0 (0)
001506: Jul 21 17:50:35.024 EST: Adjust Nbr 10.10.14.1 1 next flood info to 0
001507: Jul 21 17:50:35.024 EST: OSPF: Stop nbr 10.10.14.1 retransmission timer
001508: Jul 21 17:50:35.024 EST: Dec retrans unit nbr count index 3 (0/3) to 0/0
001509: Jul 21 17:50:35.024 EST: Free nbr retrans unit
  0x62AD9F34/0x62AD8EF4 0 total 0. Also Free nbr retrans block
001510: Jul 21 17:50:35.024 EST: Set Nbr 10.1.4.4 3 first flood info from
  62ADB6EC (8) to 0 (0)
001511: Jul 21 17:50:35.024 EST: Adjust Nbr 10.1.4.4 3 next flood info to 0
001512: Jul 21 17:50:35.024 EST: OSPF: Stop nbr 10.1.4.4 retransmission timer
Oracle#
```

In the following example, you can see that the OSPF flooding protocol provides a plethora of information on its operation—and this is just for one LSA! The **debug ip ospf flood** command generates information about flooding, which includes sending/receiving update/ acknowledgment packets. The Received and Sending line means that the router has received or sent a packet; the lines that follow give you detailed information about the content of that packet. Use this command with caution.

debug ip ospf hello Command

The **debug ip ospf hello** command displays information about how OSPF Hellos are operating within your OSPF domain. Example 9-51 offers some sample output from this command.

Example 9-51 **debug ip ospf hello** *Command Output*

```
Oracle#
001843: Jul 21 18:02:15.661 EST: OSPF: Rcv hello from 10.1.2.2 area 0 from
  FastEthernet2/0 10.0.0.2
001844: Jul 21 18:02:15.661 EST: OSPF: End of hello processing
001845: Jul 21 18:02:15.737 EST: OSPF: Rcv hello from 10.1.4.4 area 69
  from Ethernet3/1 10.69.69.2
001846: Jul 21 18:02:15.737 EST: OSPF: End of hello processing
Oracle#
```

debug ip ospf lsa-generation Command

The **debug ip ospf lsa-generation** command enables you to view the actions and events that are being generated by OSPF's flooding protocol. The **no** form of this command disables debugging output. The basic syntax for this command is as follows:

[no] debug ip ospf lsa-generation ?

This **debug** command allows several options to include access lists, as previously discussed and as demonstrated in Example 9-52.

Example 9-52 **debug ip ospf lsa-generation** *Command Options*

```
Cypher#debug ip ospf lsa-generation ?
  <1-199>       Access list
  <1300-2699>   Access list (expanded range)
  <cr>

Cypher#
```

In Example 9-53, you can see the OSPF flooding protocol providing a plethora of information on its operation and LSA generation. Router Mouse was configured with IGRP network 25.25.25.0, and that network redistributed into OSPF, where a summary address of 25.25.0.0/16 was configured. The resulting debug of the summary LSA generation is shown in the following example.

Example 9-53 **debug ip ospf lsa-generation** *Command Output*

```
Mouse#debug ip ospf lsa-generation
OSPF summary lsa generation debugging is on
Mouse#
00:31:46: OSPF: Start redist-scanning
00:31:46: OSPF: Scan for redistribution
00:31:46: OSPF: net 25.25.25.0 up, new metric decreases: old 16777215, new 20
00:31:46: OSPF: Generate external LSA 25.25.0.0, mask 255.255.0.0, type 5, age 0,
  metric 20, seq 0x80000001
00:31:46: OSPF: generate external LSA for summary 25.25.0.0 255.255.0.0,
  metric 20
! Mouse has detected the network configured and generated the appropriate LSA
! based on the summary-address in OSPF
00:31:46: OSPF: Generate external LSA 0.0.0.0, mask 0.0.0.0, type 5, age 0,
```

Example 9-53   debug ip ospf lsa-generation *Command Output (Continued)*

```
   metric 1, seq 0x80000001
00:31:46: OSPF: End scanning, Elapsed time 20ms
00:31:51: OSPF: Generate external LSA 0.0.0.0, mask 0.0.0.0, type 5, age 0,
   metric 1, seq 0x80000006
! Don't forget that Mouse is also sending a default route!
Mouse#
```

debug ip ospf monitor Command (Hidden)

The **debug ip ospf monitor** command is a hidden OSPF command. A hidden OSPF command is not found in Cisco documentation but is still present in Cisco IOS Software if you know the exact syntax. Any use of this command is not supported by Cisco Systems, and it is used at your risk. With that disclaimer in place, review the output in Example 9-54 to see what this command can tell you.

Example 9-54   debug ip ospf monitor *Command Output*

```
Oracle#debug ip ospf monitor
OSPF spf monitoring debugging is on
Oracle#
000038: *Feb 28 20:18:06.612 EST: OSPF: Schedule SPF in area 0
      Change in LS ID 10.1.2.2, LSA type R,
000039: *Feb 28 20:18:06.612 EST: OSPF: schedule SPF: spf_time 00:18:06.616
   wait_interval 5s
000040: *Feb 28 20:18:07.204 EST: OSPF: Schedule SPF in area 0
      Change in LS ID 10.0.0.3, LSA type N,
Oracle#
000041: *Feb 28 20:18:11.612 EST: OSPF: Begin SPF at 0x10A820ms, process time 92ms
000042: *Feb 28 20:18:11.612 EST:        spf_time 00:18:06.616, wait_interval 5s
000043: *Feb 28 20:18:11.612 EST: OSPF: Schedule SPF in area 0
      Change in LS ID 10.1.7.7, LSA type SN,
000044: *Feb 28 20:18:11.612 EST: OSPF: Schedule SPF in area 0
      Change in LS ID 10.1.6.6, LSA type SN,
000045: *Feb 28 20:18:11.612 EST: OSPF: Schedule SPF in area 0
      Change in LS ID 10.1.2.2, LSA type SN,
000046: *Feb 28 20:18:11.616 EST: OSPF: End SPF at 0x10A824ms, Total elapsed time 4ms
000047: *Feb 28 20:18:11.616 EST:        Intra: 0ms, Inter: 0ms, External: 0ms

Oracle#
000048: *Feb 28 20:18:15.512 EST: %OSPF-5-ADJCHG: Process 100, Nbr 10.1.2.2 on
   FastEthernet2/0 from LOADING to FULL, Loading Done
Oracle#
000049: *Feb 28 20:18:16.028 EST: OSPF: Schedule SPF in area 0
      Change in LS ID 10.0.0.3, LSA type N,
Oracle#
000050: *Feb 28 20:18:17.120 EST: OSPF: Schedule SPF in area 0
      Change in LS ID 10.1.6.6, LSA type R,
Oracle#
000051: *Feb 28 20:18:20.856 EST: OSPF: Schedule SPF in area 0
      Change in LS ID 10.1.2.2, LSA type R,
000052: *Feb 28 20:18:21.616 EST: OSPF: Begin SPF at 0x10CF34ms,
```

continues

Example 9-54   **debug ip ospf monitor** *Command Output (Continued)*

```
    process time 120ms
000053: *Feb 28 20:18:21.616 EST:        spf_time 00:18:11.620, wait_interval 10s
000054: *Feb 28 20:18:21.616 EST: OSPF: Schedule SPF in area 0
       Change in LS ID 10.1.2.2, LSA type SN,
000055: *Feb 28 20:18:21.616 EST: OSPF: Schedule SPF in area 0
       Change in LS ID 10.1.2.2, LSA type SN,
000056: *Feb 28 20:18:21.616 EST: OSPF: End SPF at 0x10CF34ms,
  Total elapsed time 0ms
000057: *Feb 28 20:18:21.620 EST:        Intra: 0ms, Inter: 0ms, External: 0ms

Oracle#
000058: *Feb 28 20:18:22.852 EST: OSPF: Schedule SPF in area 0
       Change in LS ID 10.1.6.6, LSA type R,
Oracle#
000059: *Feb 28 20:18:26.072 EST: OSPF: Schedule SPF in area 0
       Change in LS ID 10.1.2.2, LSA type R,
Oracle#
000060: *Feb 28 20:18:31.616 EST: OSPF: Begin SPF at 0x10F644ms,
  process time 132ms
000061: *Feb 28 20:18:31.616 EST:        spf_time 00:18:21.620, wait_interval 10s
000062: *Feb 28 20:18:31.616 EST: OSPF: Schedule SPF in area 0
       Change in LS ID 10.1.6.6, LSA type SN,
000063: *Feb 28 20:18:31.616 EST: OSPF: Schedule SPF in area 0
       Change in LS ID 10.1.6.6, LSA type SN,
000064: *Feb 28 20:18:31.616 EST: OSPF: Schedule SPF in area 0
       Change in LS ID 10.1.7.7, LSA type SN,
000065: *Feb 28 20:18:31.616 EST: OSPF: Schedule SPF in area 0
       Change in LS ID 10.1.7.7, LSA type SN,
Oracle#
000066: *Feb 28 20:18:31.624 EST: OSPF: End SPF at 0x10F64Cms,
  Total elapsed time 8ms
000067: *Feb 28 20:18:31.624 EST:        Intra: 0ms, Inter: 4ms, External: 0ms

Oracle#
```

debug ip ospf packet Command

Use the **debug ip ospf packet** EXEC command to display *really really* (yes, using "really" twice is appropriate here) detailed information about each OSPF packet received. The **debug ip ospf packet** command produces one set of information for each packet received. The output varies slightly depending on which type of authentication is used. The following list offers descriptions of fields for the **debug ip ospf packet** command:

- v—Indicates the OSPF version.

- t—Indicates the OSPF packet type. Possible packet types include the following:
  - Hello
  - Data description

- — Link-state request
- — Link-state update
- — Link-state acknowledgment
- l—Indicates the OSPF packet length in bytes.
- rid—Indicates the OSPF router ID.
- aid—Indicates the OSPF area ID.
- chk—Indicates the OSPF checksum.
- aut—Indicates the OSPF authentication type. Possible authentication types are as follows:
  - — 0—No authentication
  - — 1—Simple password
  - — 2—MD5
- auk—Indicates the OSPF authentication key.
- keyid—Indicates the MD5 key ID.
- seq—Indicates the sequence number.
- from—Indicates the interface that received the packet.

Example 9-55 shows sample **debug ip ospf packet** output when MD5 authentication is used.

Example 9-55   **debug ip ospf packet** *Command Output*

```
001924: Jul 21 19:01:40.598 EST: OSPF: rcv. v:2 t:4 l:64 rid:10.1.3.3
        aid:0.0.0.0 chk:0 aut:2 keyid:1 seq:0x1C0 from FastEthernet2/0
! The logging sequence number, date/timestamp, and timezone leads off this output.
001925: Jul 21 19:01:40.698 EST: OSPF: rcv. v:2 t:4 l:64 rid:10.1.2.2
        aid:0.0.0.0 chk:0 aut:2 keyid:1 seq:0x5F3 from FastEthernet2/0
! - This entry and its highlighted portions can be deciphered as from
! OSPF v2 (v: 2), it's a Link State Update packet (t: 4), with a length of
! 64 bytes (l: 64), from Router Cypher (rid: 10.1.2.2)
001926: Jul 21 19:01:42.638 EST: OSPF: rcv. v:2 t:5 l:564 rid:10.1.3.3
        aid:0.0.0.0 chk:0 aut:2 keyid:1 seq:0x1C1 from FastEthernet2/0
! - This entry and its highlighted portions can be deciphered as having
! the packet describe an event in area 0 (aid: 0.0.0.0), then its checksum,
! type of OSPF authentication used, MD5 (aut: 2), which authentication is being
! used, key 1 (keyid: 1), the packet has a sequence number expressed in
! hexadecimal (seq: 0x1C1) and the packet was received on interface Fast Ethernet
2/0.
001927: Jul 21 19:01:42.654 EST: OSPF: rcv. v:2 t:5 l:84 rid:10.10.14.1
        aid:0.0.0.10 chk:0 aut:2 keyid:1 seq:0xA0A from Ethernet3/0
001928: Jul 21 19:01:42.658 EST: OSPF: rcv. v:2 t:5 l:84 rid:10.1.4.4
        aid:0.0.0.69 chk:EBB0 aut:0 auk: from Ethernet3/1
! - Can you decipher these packets?
```

debug ip ospf retransmission Command

The **debug ip ospf retransmission** command displays a list of LSAs that have been flooded but not acknowledged by an OSPF neighbor. The unacknowledged LSAs are retransmitted at intervals until they are acknowledged or until the adjacency with the neighbor is removed. This output can be seen under heavy traffic load and a large number of LSAs that you are trying to exchange.

debug ip ospf spf Command

The **debug ip ospf spf** command enables you to view the actions and events being generated by OSPF's Shortest Path First (SPF) algorithm. OSPF's full SPF contains the following parts:

1 The SPF algorithm calculates the shortest-path tree for the area to figure out all the intra-area routes.

2 All summary LSAs are scanned to calculate the inter-area routes.

3 All external LSAs are scanned to calculate the external routes.

If only the **debug ip ospf spf** command is executed, all information on all three of these steps is shown. This information shows how OSPF decides to add a route from the LSAs and how its cost is calculated. However, you can isolate the **debug** command to display what SPF is doing in each step with specific keywords. Example 9-56 shows the command options that are associated with this **debug** command.

Example 9-56 **debug ip ospf spf** *Command Output*

```
Oracle#debug ip ospf spf ?
  external  OSPF spf external-route
  inter     OSPF spf inter-route
  intra     OSPF spf inter-route
  <cr>

Oracle#
```

Using the additional keywords displays only the step in which you are interested. Furthermore, for partial SPF, only summary or external LSAs are affected, in which case you should execute either **debug ip ospf spf inter** or **debug ip ospf spf external** to monitor the partial SPF.

Because the **debug ip ospf spf** command displays all three SPF calculations at once, output for all three options is provided in the sections that follow.

debug ip ospf spf external Command

Using the **debug ip ospf spf** command with the **external** keyword displays the process that the SPF algorithm takes when external routes are received on the router that is executing the **debug** command. You can specify an access list to display only the calculations for an LSA with a specific LSA ID. Example 9-57 shows the access list options that are available with the **debug ip ospf spf external** command.

Example 9-57   debug ip ospf spf external *Command Options*

```
Oracle#debug ip ospf spf external ?
  <1-99>       Access list
  <1300-1999>  Access list (expanded range)
  <cr>

Oracle#
```

The output in Example 9-58 was generated when the OSPF routing process on Router Mouse was reset. From this output, you can see the calculations the SPF process undergoes in dealing with external routes. The first part of this command output is what you see when Router Mouse goes down and the SPF of Router Oracle needs to be recalculated accordingly.

Example 9-58   debug ip ospf spf external *Command Output*

```
Oracle#
002410: Jul 21 20:13:57.400 EST: OSPF: Started Building Type 5 External Routes
002411: Jul 21 20:13:57.400 EST: OSPF: Start processing Type 5
  External LSA 0.0.0.0, mask 0.0.0.0, adv 10.1.3.3, age 942, seq 0x8000000C,
  metric 1, metric-type 2
002412: Jul 21 20:13:57.404 EST: OSPF: Did not find route to ASBR 10.1.3.3
002413: Jul 21 20:13:57.404 EST: OSPF: ex_delete_old_routes
002414: Jul 21 20:13:57.404 EST: OSPF: ex-Deleting old route 0.0.0.0
002415: Jul 21 20:13:57.404 EST: OSPF: Remove 0.0.0.0 0.0.0.0 10.0.0.3 10.1.3.3
  FastEthernet2/0 18 80000001
002416: Jul 21 20:13:57.404 EST: OSPF: delete lsa id 0.0.0.0, type 5,
  adv rtr 10.1.3.3 from delete list
002417: Jul 21 20:13:57.404 EST: OSPF: Started Building Type 7 External Routes
002418: Jul 21 20:13:57.408 EST: OSPF: ex_delete_old_routes
002419: Jul 21 20:13:57.408 EST: OSPF: Started Building Type 7 External Routes
002420: Jul 21 20:13:57.408 EST: OSPF: ex_delete_old_routes
002421: Jul 21 20:13:57.408 EST: OSPF: Started Building Type 7 External Routes
002422: Jul 21 20:13:57.408 EST: OSPF: ex_delete_old_routes
```

In the remainder of this command output, shown in Example 9-59, you can see the process that SPF undergoes when Router Mouse comes active again and advertises the default route to the Internet.

Example 9-59 debug ip ospf spf external *Command Output*

```
Oracle#
002423: Jul 21 20:14:00.092 EST: %OSPF-5-ADJCHG: Process 100, Nbr 10.1.3.3 on
  FastEthernet2/0 from LOADING to FULL, Loading Done
! Now that adjacency is back routes will be exchanged and in this debug command
! we are watching for the external routes only!
002424: Jul 21 20:14:07.408 EST: OSPF: Started Building Type 5 External Routes
002425: Jul 21 20:14:07.408 EST: OSPF: Start processing Type 5
  External LSA 0.0.0.0, mask 0.0.0.0, adv 10.1.3.3, age 9, seq 0x8000000D,
  metric 1, metric-type 2
002426: Jul 21 20:14:07.412 EST:    Add better path to LSA ID 0.0.0.0,
  gateway 10.0.0.3, dist 1
002427: Jul 21 20:14:07.412 EST:    Add path: next-hop 10.0.0.3,
  interface FastEthernet2/0
002428: Jul 21 20:14:07.412 EST:    Add External Route to 0.0.0.0. Metric: 1,
  Next Hop: 10.0.0.3
002429: Jul 21 20:14:07.412 EST: OSPF: insert route list LS ID 0.0.0.0, type 5,
  adv rtr 10.1.3.3
002430: Jul 21 20:14:07.412 EST: OSPF: ex_delete_old_routes
002431: Jul 21 20:14:07.412 EST: OSPF: Started Building Type 7 External Routes
002432: Jul 21 20:14:07.416 EST: OSPF: ex_delete_old_routes
002433: Jul 21 20:14:07.416 EST: OSPF: Started Building Type 7 External Routes
002434: Jul 21 20:14:07.416 EST: OSPF: ex_delete_old_routes
002435: Jul 21 20:14:07.416 EST: OSPF: Started Building Type 7 External Routes
002436: Jul 21 20:14:07.416 EST: OSPF: ex_delete_old_routes
Oracle#
```

debug ip ospf spf inter Command

Using the **debug ip ospf spf** command with the **inter** keyword displays the process that the SPF algorithm takes when inter-area routes are received on the router that is executing the **debug** command. You can specify an access list to display the calculations for only one LSA with specific LSA ID. Example 9-60 shows the access list options that are associated with this command.

TIP

Inter-area routes are routes to networks in another area, where cost is based on link.

Example 9-60 debug ip ospf spf inter *Command Options*

```
Oracle#debug ip ospf spf inter ?
  <1-99>        Access list
  <1300-1999>   Access list (expanded range)
  <cr>
Oracle#
```

The output in this command was generated when Router Cypher had its fa2/0 interface shut down, and when OSPF went down, the interface was turned back on. This resulted in Router Cypher sending all the routes (LSAs) it knows of; however, through the **debug** command used, you see only inter-area routes Cypher knows about to Router Oracle. Oracle, in turn, executes SPF on all the new LSAs; the resulting calculations appear in Example 9-61.

Example 9-61   **debug ip ospf spf inter** *Command Output*

```
Oracle#debug ip ospf spf inter
OSPF spf inter events debugging is on
Oracle#
002494: Jul 21 20:19:58.575 EST: %OSPF-5-ADJCHG: Process 100, Nbr 10.1.2.2 on
  FastEthernet2/0 from LOADING to FULL, Loading Done
002495: Jul 21 20:19:59.059 EST: OSPF: No change for sum from
  intra-area route 10.1.3.3, mask 0.0.0.0, type 4, age 351, metric 1,
  seq 0x80000001 to area 10
002496: Jul 21 20:19:59.059 EST: OSPF: No change for sum from
  intra-area route 10.1.3.3, mask 0.0.0.0, type 4, age 351, metric 1,
  seq 0x80000001 to area 69
002497: Jul 21 20:19:59.059 EST: OSPF: No change for sum from
  intra-area route 10.0.0.0, mask 255.255.255.0, type 3, age 1403, metric 1,
  seq 0x80000013 to area 10
002498: Jul 21 20:19:59.059 EST: OSPF: No change for sum from
  intra-area route 10.0.0.0, mask 255.255.255.0, type 3, age 1403, metric 1,
  seq 0x80000010 to area 69
002499: Jul 21 20:19:59.059 EST: OSPF: No change for sum from
  intra-area route 10.1.3.3, mask 0.0.0.0, type 4, age 351, metric 1,
  seq 0x80000001 to area 10
002500: Jul 21 20:19:59.059 EST: OSPF: No change for sum from
  intra-area route 10.1.3.3, mask 0.0.0.0, type 4, age 351, metric 1,
  seq 0x80000001 to area 69
002501: Jul 21 20:19:59.059 EST: OSPF: No change for sum from
  intra-area route 10.0.0.0, mask 255.255.255.0, type 3, age 1403, metric 1,
  seq 0x80000013 to area 10
002502: Jul 21 20:19:59.059 EST: OSPF: No change for sum from
  intra-area route 10.0.0.0, mask 255.255.255.0, type 3, age 1403, metric 1,
  seq 0x80000010 to area 69
002503: Jul 21 20:19:59.059 EST: OSPF: sum_delete_old_routes area 10
002504: Jul 21 20:19:59.059 EST: OSPF: sum_delete_old_routes area 69
002505: Jul 21 20:19:59.063 EST: OSPF: running spf for summaries area 0
002506: Jul 21 20:19:59.063 EST: OSPF: Start processing
  Summary LSA 10.51.51.0, mask 255.255.255.252, adv 10.1.2.2, age 1224,
  seq 0x80000002 (Area 0)
002507: Jul 21 20:19:59.063 EST: OSPF: ABR not reachable 10.1.2.2
002508: Jul 21 20:19:59.063 EST: OSPF: Start processing
  Summary LSA 10.51.51.0, mask 255.255.255.252, adv 10.1.6.6, age 1594,
  seq 0x80000008 (Area 0)
002509: Jul 21 20:19:59.063 EST: OSPF: ABR not reachable 10.1.6.6
002510: Jul 21 20:19:59.063 EST: OSPF: Start processing
  Summary LSA 10.221.0.0, mask 255.255.248.0, adv 10.1.7.7, age 1498,
  seq 0x80000008 (Area 0)
002511: Jul 21 20:19:59.063 EST: OSPF: ABR not reachable 10.1.7.7
002512: Jul 21 20:19:59.063 EST: OSPF: sum_delete_old_routes area 0
```

Example 9-61 **debug ip ospf spf inter** *Command Output (Continued)*

```
Oracle#
002513: Jul 21 20:20:09.063 EST:              Exist path: next-hop 10.0.0.3,
  interface FastEthernet2/0
002514: Jul 21 20:20:09.063 EST: OSPF: No change for sum from
  intra-area route 10.1.3.3, mask 0.0.0.0, type 4, age 361, metric 1,
  seq 0x80000001 to area 10
002515: Jul 21 20:20:09.063 EST: OSPF: No change for sum from
  intra-area route 10.1.3.3, mask 0.0.0.0, type 4, age 361, metric 1,
  seq 0x80000001 to area 69
002516: Jul 21 20:20:09.063 EST: OSPF: No ndb for STUB NET old route 10.0.0.0,
  mask /24, next hop 10.0.0.1
002517: Jul 21 20:20:09.063 EST: OSPF: Generate sum from
  intra-area route 10.0.0.0, mask 255.255.255.0, type 3, age 3600,
  metric 16777215, seq 0x80000014 to area 10
002518: Jul 21 20:20:09.067 EST: OSPF: Generate sum from
  intra-area route 10.0.0.0, mask 255.255.255.0, type 3, age 3600,
  metric 16777215, seq 0x80000011 to area 69
002519: Jul 21 20:20:09.067 EST: OSPF: Generate sum from
  intra-area route 10.1.7.0, mask 255.255.255.0, type 3, age 0, metric 51,
  seq 0x80000001 to area 10
002520: Jul 21 20:20:09.067 EST: OSPF: Generate sum from
  intra-area route 10.1.7.0, mask 255.255.255.0, type 3, age 0, metric 51,
  seq 0x80000001 to area 69
002521: Jul 21 20:20:09.067 EST: OSPF: Generate sum from
  intra-area route 10.1.6.0, mask 255.255.255.0, type 3, age 0, metric 50,
  seq 0x80000001 to area 10
002522: Jul 21 20:20:09.067 EST: OSPF: Generate sum from
  intra-area route 10.1.6.0, mask 255.255.255.0, type 3, age 0, metric 50,
  seq 0x80000001 to area 69
002523: Jul 21 20:20:09.067 EST: OSPF: Generate sum from
  intra-area route 10.0.5.0, mask 255.255.255.0, type 3, age 0, metric 50,
  seq 0x80000001 to area 10
002524: Jul 21 20:20:09.071 EST: OSPF: Generate sum from
  intra-area route 10.0.5.0, mask 255.255.255.0, type 3, age 0, metric 50,
  seq 0x80000001 to area 69
002525: Jul 21 20:20:09.071 EST: OSPF: Generate sum from
  intra-area route 10.0.4.0, mask 255.255.255.0, type 3, age 0, metric 50,
  seq 0x80000001 to area 10
002526: Jul 21 20:20:09.071 EST: OSPF: Generate sum from
  intra-area route 10.0.4.0, mask 255.255.255.0, type 3, age 0, metric 50,
  seq 0x80000001 to area 69
002527: Jul 21 20:20:09.071 EST: OSPF: Generate sum from
  intra-area route 10.0.3.0, mask 255.255.255.0, type 3, age 0, metric 50,
  seq 0x80000001 to area 10
002528: Jul 21 20:20:09.071 EST: OSPF: Generate sum from
  intra-area route 10.0.3.0, mask 255.255.255.0, type 3, age 0, metric 50,
  seq 0x80000001 to area 69
002529: Jul 21 20:20:09.071 EST: OSPF: Generate sum from
  intra-area route 10.0.2.0, mask 255.255.255.0, type 3, age 0, metric 50,
  seq 0x80000001 to area 10
002530: Jul 21 20:20:09.075 EST: OSPF: Generate sum from
  intra-area route 10.0.2.0, mask 255.255.255.0, type 3, age 0, metric 50,
  seq 0x80000001 to area 69
```

Example 9-61   **debug ip ospf spf inter** *Command Output (Continued)*

```
002531: Jul 21 20:20:09.075 EST: OSPF: Generate sum from
  intra-area route 10.0.1.0, mask 255.255.255.0, type 3, age 0, metric 50,
  seq 0x80000001 to area 10
002532: Jul 21 20:20:09.075 EST: OSPF: Generate sum from
  intra-area route 10.0.1.0, mask 255.255.255.0, type 3, age 0, metric 50,
  seq 0x80000001 to area 69
002533: Jul 21 20:20:09.075 EST: OSPF: No change for sum from
  intra-area route 10.1.3.3, mask 0.0.0.0, type 4, age 361, metric 1,
  seq 0x80000001 to area 10
002534: Jul 21 20:20:09.075 EST: OSPF: No change for sum from
  intra-area route 10.1.3.3, mask 0.0.0.0, type 4, age 361, metric 1,
  seq 0x80000001 to area 69
002535: Jul 21 20:20:09.075 EST: OSPF: sum_delete_old_routes area 10
002536: Jul 21 20:20:09.075 EST: OSPF: sum_delete_old_routes area 69
002537: Jul 21 20:20:09.075 EST: OSPF: running spf for summaries area 0
002538: Jul 21 20:20:09.075 EST: OSPF: Start processing
  Summary LSA 10.51.51.0, mask 255.255.255.252, adv 10.1.2.2, age 1234,
  seq 0x80000002 (Area 0)
002539: Jul 21 20:20:09.079 EST:      Add better path to LSA ID 10.51.51.0,
  gateway 0.0.0.0, dist 113
002540: Jul 21 20:20:09.079 EST:      Add path: next-hop 10.0.0.2,
  interface FastEthernet2/0
002541: Jul 21 20:20:09.079 EST:      Add Summary Route to 10.51.51.0.
  Metric: 113, Next Hop: 10.0.0.2
002542: Jul 21 20:20:09.079 EST: OSPF: insert route list LS ID 10.51.51.0,
  type 3, adv rtr 10.1.2.2
002543: Jul 21 20:20:09.079 EST: OSPF: Start processing
  Summary LSA 10.51.51.0, mask 255.255.255.252, adv 10.1.6.6, age 1594,
  seq 0x80000008 (Area 0)
002544: Jul 21 20:20:09.079 EST:      Add better path to LSA ID 10.51.51.0,
  gateway 0.0.0.0, dist 113
002545: Jul 21 20:20:09.079 EST:      Add path: next-hop 10.0.0.2,
  interface FastEthernet2/0
002546: Jul 21 20:20:09.079 EST:      Add Summary Route to 10.51.51.0.
  Metric: 113, Next Hop: 10.0.0.2
002547: Jul 21 20:20:09.079 EST: OSPF: insert route list LS ID 10.51.51.0,
  type 3, adv rtr 10.1.6.6
002548: Jul 21 20:20:09.079 EST: OSPF: Start processing Summary LSA 10.221.0.0,
  mask 255.255.248.0, adv 10.1.7.7, age 1498, seq 0x80000008 (Area 0)
002549: Jul 21 20:20:09.079 EST:      Add better path to LSA ID 10.221.0.0,
  gateway 0.0.0.0, dist 51
002550: Jul 21 20:20:09.079 EST:      Add path: next-hop 10.0.0.2,
  interface FastEthernet2/0
002551: Jul 21 20:20:09.083 EST:      Add Summary Route to 10.221.0.0.
  Metric: 51, Next Hop: 10.0.0.2
002552: Jul 21 20:20:09.083 EST: OSPF: insert route list LS ID 10.221.0.0,
  type 3, adv rtr 10.1.7.7
002553: Jul 21 20:20:09.083 EST: OSPF: sum_delete_old_routes area 0
002554: Jul 21 20:20:09.083 EST: OSPF: Generate sum from
  inter-area route 10.221.0.0, mask 255.255.248.0, type 3, age 0, metric 51,
  seq 0x80000001 to area 10
002555: Jul 21 20:20:09.083 EST: OSPF: Generate sum from
  inter-area route 10.221.0.0, mask 255.255.248.0, type 3, age 0, metric 51,
```

continues

Example 9-61 **debug ip ospf spf inter** *Command Output (Continued)*

```
  seq 0x80000001 to area 69
002556: Jul 21 20:20:09.083 EST: OSPF: Generate sum from
  inter-area route 10.51.51.0, mask 255.255.255.252, type 3, age 0, metric 113,
  seq 0x80000001 to area 10
002557: Jul 21 20:20:09.083 EST: OSPF: Generate sum from
  inter-area route 10.51.51.0, mask 255.255.255.252, type 3, age 0, metric 113,
  seq 0x80000001 to area 69
Oracle#
```

debug ip ospf spf intra Command

Using the **debug ip ospf spf** command with the **intra** keyword displays the process that the SPF algorithm takes when intra-area routes are received on the router that is executing the **debug** command. You can specify an access list to display only the calculations for an LSA with specific LSA ID. Example 9-62 shows the access list options associated with this command.

TIP   Intra-area routes are routes to networks within an area, where cost is based on the link.

Example 9-62 **debug ip ospf spf intra** *Command Options*

```
Oracle#debug ip ospf spf intra ?
  <1-99>      Access list
  <1300-1999>  Access list (expanded range)
  <cr>
```

The output in Example 9-62 demonstrates that this command was generated when the OSPF routing process was cleared on Router Cypher. This resulted in Router Cypher sending routes (LSAs); however, through the **debug** command used, you see only all the intra-area routes Cypher knows about to Router Oracle. Oracle, in turn, executes SPF on all the new LSAs; the resulting calculations appear in Example 9-63.

Example 9-63 **debug ip ospf spf intra** *Command Output for Router Oracle*

```
#debug ip ospf spf intra
OSPF spf intra events debugging is on
Oracle#
002564: Jul 21 20:31:40.084 EST: %OSPF-5-ADJCHG: Process 100, Nbr 10.1.2.2 on
  FastEthernet2/0 from LOADING to FULL, Loading Done
002565: Jul 21 20:31:40.132 EST: OSPF: running SPF for area 0
002566: Jul 21 20:31:40.132 EST: OSPF: Initializing to run spf
002567: Jul 21 20:31:40.132 EST: OSPF: No new path to 10.1.1.1
002568: Jul 21 20:31:40.132 EST:  It is a router LSA 10.1.1.1. Link Count 1
002569: Jul 21 20:31:40.132 EST:    Processing link 0, id 10.0.0.3,
  link data 10.0.0.1, type 2
```

Example 9-63   **debug ip ospf spf intra** *Command Output for Router Oracle (Continued)*

```
002570: Jul 21 20:31:40.132 EST:    Add better path to LSA ID 10.0.0.3,
  gateway 10.0.0.1, dist 1
002571: Jul 21 20:31:40.132 EST:    Add path: next-hop 10.0.0.1,
  interface FastEthernet2/0
002572: Jul 21 20:31:40.132 EST: OSPF: insert route list LS ID 10.0.0.3, type 2,
  adv rtr 10.1.3.3
002573: Jul 21 20:31:40.132 EST:  It is a network LSA 10.0.0.3. Router Count 2
002574: Jul 21 20:31:40.132 EST:    Processing router id 10.1.3.3
002575: Jul 21 20:31:40.132 EST:    Add better path to LSA ID 10.1.3.3,
  gateway 10.0.0.3, dist 1
002576: Jul 21 20:31:40.132 EST:    Add path: next-hop 10.0.0.3,
  interface FastEthernet2/0
002577: Jul 21 20:31:40.132 EST:    Processing router id 10.1.1.1
002578: Jul 21 20:31:40.132 EST:    New newdist 1 olddist 0
002579: Jul 21 20:31:40.132 EST: OSPF: delete lsa id 10.1.3.3, type 1,
  adv rtr 10.1.3.3 from delete list
002580: Jul 21 20:31:40.132 EST: OSPF: Add Router Route to 10.1.3.3 via 10.0.0.3.
  Metric: 1
002581: Jul 21 20:31:40.132 EST: OSPF: insert route list LS ID 10.1.3.3, type 1,
  adv rtr 10.1.3.3
002582: Jul 21 20:31:40.132 EST:  It is a router LSA 10.1.3.3. Link Count 1
002583: Jul 21 20:31:40.132 EST:    Processing link 0, id 10.0.0.3,
  link data 10.0.0.3, type 2
002584: Jul 21 20:31:40.136 EST:    Ignore newdist 11 olddist 1
002585: Jul 21 20:31:40.136 EST: OSPF: Adding Stub nets
002586: Jul 21 20:31:40.136 EST: OSPF: Entered old delete routine
002587: Jul 21 20:31:40.136 EST: OSPF: Deleting STUB NET old route 10.1.7.0,
  mask /24, next hop 10.0.0.2
002588: Jul 21 20:31:40.136 EST: OSPF: Deleting STUB NET old route 10.1.6.0,
  mask /24, next hop 10.0.0.2
002589: Jul 21 20:31:40.136 EST: OSPF: Deleting STUB NET old route 10.0.5.0,
  mask /24, next hop 10.0.0.2
002590: Jul 21 20:31:40.136 EST: OSPF: Deleting STUB NET old route 10.0.4.0,
  mask /24, next hop 10.0.0.2
002591: Jul 21 20:31:40.136 EST: OSPF: Deleting STUB NET old route 10.0.3.0,
  mask /24, next hop 10.0.0.2
002592: Jul 21 20:31:40.136 EST: OSPF: Deleting STUB NET old route 10.0.2.0,
  mask /24, next hop 10.0.0.2
002593: Jul 21 20:31:40.136 EST: OSPF: Delete path to router 10.1.7.7 via
  10.0.0.2 spf 73
002594: Jul 21 20:31:40.136 EST: OSPF: Deleting NET old route 10.0.1.0,
  mask /24, next hop 10.0.0.2
002595: Jul 21 20:31:40.136 EST: OSPF: Delete path to router 10.1.6.6 via
  10.0.0.2 spf 73
002596: Jul 21 20:31:40.140 EST: OSPF: Delete path to router 10.1.2.2 via
  10.0.0.2 spf 73
002597: Jul 21 20:31:40.140 EST: OSPF: No ndb for NET old route 10.0.0.0,
  mask /24, next hop 10.0.0.1
002598: Jul 21 20:31:40.140 EST: OSPF: delete lsa id 10.1.7.255, type 0,
  adv rtr 10.1.7.7 from delete list
002599: Jul 21 20:31:40.140 EST: OSPF: delete lsa id 10.1.6.255, type 0,
  adv rtr 10.1.6.6 from delete list
002600: Jul 21 20:31:40.140 EST: OSPF: delete lsa id 10.0.5.255, type 0,
```

continues

Example 9-63 **debug ip ospf spf intra** *Command Output for Router Oracle (Continued)*

```
    adv rtr 10.1.6.6 from delete list
002601: Jul 21 20:31:40.140 EST: OSPF: delete lsa id 10.0.4.255, type 0,
    adv rtr 10.1.6.6 from delete list
002602: Jul 21 20:31:40.140 EST: OSPF: delete lsa id 10.0.3.255, type 0,
    adv rtr 10.1.6.6 from delete list
002603: Jul 21 20:31:40.144 EST: OSPF: delete lsa id 10.0.2.255, type 0,
    adv rtr 10.1.6.6 from delete list
002604: Jul 21 20:31:40.144 EST: OSPF: delete lsa id 10.1.7.7, type 1,
    adv rtr 10.1.7.7 from delete list
002605: Jul 21 20:31:40.144 EST: OSPF: delete lsa id 10.0.1.1, type 2,
    adv rtr 10.1.6.6 from delete list
002606: Jul 21 20:31:40.144 EST: OSPF: delete lsa id 10.1.6.6, type 1,
    adv rtr 10.1.6.6 from delete list
002607: Jul 21 20:31:40.144 EST: OSPF: delete lsa id 10.1.2.2, type 1,
    adv rtr 10.1.2.2 from delete list
002608: Jul 21 20:31:40.144 EST: OSPF: delete lsa id 10.0.0.2, type 2,
    adv rtr 10.1.2.2 from delete list
002609: Jul 21 20:31:41.580 EST: OSPF: Detect change in LSA type 2, LSID 10.0.0.3,
    from 10.1.3.3 area 0
002610: Jul 21 20:31:50.148 EST: OSPF: running SPF for area 0
002611: Jul 21 20:31:50.148 EST: OSPF: Initializing to run spf
002612: Jul 21 20:31:50.148 EST: OSPF: No new path to 10.1.1.1
002613: Jul 21 20:31:50.148 EST:   It is a router LSA 10.1.1.1. Link Count 1
002614: Jul 21 20:31:50.148 EST:   Processing link 0, id 10.0.0.3,
    link data 10.0.0.1, type 2
002615: Jul 21 20:31:50.148 EST:     Add better path to LSA ID 10.0.0.3,
    gateway 10.0.0.1, dist 1
002616: Jul 21 20:31:50.148 EST:     Add path: next-hop 10.0.0.1,
    interface FastEthernet2/0
002617: Jul 21 20:31:50.148 EST: OSPF: delete lsa id 10.0.0.3, type 2,
    adv rtr 10.1.3.3 from delete list
002618: Jul 21 20:31:50.148 EST: OSPF: insert route list LS ID 10.0.0.3, type 2,
    adv rtr 10.1.3.3
002619: Jul 21 20:31:50.148 EST:   It is a network LSA 10.0.0.3. Router Count 3
002620: Jul 21 20:31:50.148 EST:   Processing router id 10.1.3.3
002621: Jul 21 20:31:50.148 EST:     Add better path to LSA ID 10.1.3.3,
    gateway 10.0.0.3, dist 1
002622: Jul 21 20:31:50.148 EST:     Add path: next-hop 10.0.0.3,
    interface FastEthernet2/0
002623: Jul 21 20:31:50.148 EST:   Processing router id 10.1.2.2
002624: Jul 21 20:31:50.148 EST:     Add better path to LSA ID 10.1.2.2,
    gateway 10.0.0.2, dist 1
002625: Jul 21 20:31:50.148 EST:     Add path: next-hop 10.0.0.2,
    interface FastEthernet2/0
002626: Jul 21 20:31:50.148 EST:   Processing router id 10.1.1.1
002627: Jul 21 20:31:50.148 EST:   New newdist 1 olddist 0
002628: Jul 21 20:31:50.148 EST: OSPF: Add Router Route to 10.1.2.2 via 10.0.0.2.
    Metric: 1
002629: Jul 21 20:31:50.152 EST: OSPF: insert route list LS ID 10.1.2.2, type 1,
    adv rtr 10.1.2.2
002630: Jul 21 20:31:50.152 EST:   It is a router LSA 10.1.2.2. Link Count 1
002631: Jul 21 20:31:50.152 EST:   Processing link 0, id 10.0.0.3,
    link data 10.0.0.2, type 2
```

Example 9-63   **debug ip ospf spf intra** *Command Output for Router Oracle (Continued)*

```
002632: Jul 21 20:31:50.152 EST:   Ignore newdist 2 olddist 1
002633: Jul 21 20:31:50.152 EST: OSPF: delete lsa id 10.1.3.3, type 1,
 adv rtr 10.1.3.3 from delete list
002634: Jul 21 20:31:50.152 EST: OSPF: Add Router Route to 10.1.3.3 via
 10.0.0.3. Metric: 1
002635: Jul 21 20:31:50.152 EST: OSPF: insert route list LS ID 10.1.3.3,
 type 1, adv rtr 10.1.3.3
002636: Jul 21 20:31:50.152 EST:   It is a router LSA 10.1.3.3. Link Count 1
002637: Jul 21 20:31:50.152 EST:   Processing link 0, id 10.0.0.3,
 link data 10.0.0.3, type 2
002638: Jul 21 20:31:50.152 EST:   Ignore newdist 11 olddist 1
002639: Jul 21 20:31:50.152 EST: OSPF: Adding Stub nets
002640: Jul 21 20:31:50.152 EST: OSPF: Entered old delete routine
002641: Jul 21 20:31:54.344 EST: OSPF: Detect change in LSA type 1,
 LSID 10.1.6.6, from 10.1.6.6 area 0
002642: Jul 21 20:31:54.852 EST: OSPF: Detect change in LSA type 1,
 LSID 10.1.2.2, from 10.1.2.2 area 0
002643: Jul 21 20:31:59.888 EST: OSPF: Detect change in LSA type 1,
 LSID 10.1.6.6, from 10.1.6.6 area 0
002644: Jul 21 20:32:00.156 EST: OSPF: running SPF for area 0
002645: Jul 21 20:32:00.156 EST: OSPF: Initializing to run spf
002646: Jul 21 20:32:00.156 EST: OSPF: No new path to 10.1.1.1
002647: Jul 21 20:32:00.156 EST:   It is a router LSA 10.1.1.1. Link Count 1
002648: Jul 21 20:32:00.156 EST:   Processing link 0, id 10.0.0.3,
 link data 10.0.0.1, type 2
002649: Jul 21 20:32:00.156 EST:   Add better path to LSA ID 10.0.0.3,
 gateway 10.0.0.1, dist 1
002650: Jul 21 20:32:00.156 EST:   Add path: next-hop 10.0.0.1,
 interface FastEthernet2/0
002651: Jul 21 20:32:00.156 EST: OSPF: delete lsa id 10.0.0.3, type 2,
 adv rtr 10.1.3.3 from delete list
002652: Jul 21 20:32:00.156 EST: OSPF: insert route list LS ID 10.0.0.3,
 type 2, adv rtr 10.1.3.3
002653: Jul 21 20:32:00.156 EST:   It is a network LSA 10.0.0.3. Router Count 3
002654: Jul 21 20:32:00.156 EST:   Processing router id 10.1.3.3
002655: Jul 21 20:32:00.156 EST:   Add better path to LSA ID 10.1.3.3,
 gateway 10.0.0.3, dist 1
002656: Jul 21 20:32:00.156 EST:   Add path: next-hop 10.0.0.3,
 interface FastEthernet2/0
002657: Jul 21 20:32:00.156 EST:   Processing router id 10.1.2.2
002658: Jul 21 20:32:00.156 EST:   Add better path to LSA ID 10.1.2.2,
 gateway 10.0.0.2, dist 1
002659: Jul 21 20:32:00.156 EST:   Add path: next-hop 10.0.0.2,
 interface FastEthernet2/0
002660: Jul 21 20:32:00.156 EST:   Processing router id 10.1.1.1
002661: Jul 21 20:32:00.156 EST:   New newdist 1 olddist 0
002662: Jul 21 20:32:00.156 EST: OSPF: delete lsa id 10.1.2.2, type 1,
 adv rtr 10.1.2.2 from delete list
002663: Jul 21 20:32:00.160 EST: OSPF: Add Router Route to 10.1.2.2 via
 10.0.0.2. Metric: 1
002664: Jul 21 20:32:00.160 EST: OSPF: insert route list LS ID 10.1.2.2,
 type 1, adv rtr 10.1.2.2
002665: Jul 21 20:32:00.160 EST:   It is a router LSA 10.1.2.2. Link Count 2
```

continues

Example 9-63 **debug ip ospf spf intra** *Command Output for Router Oracle (Continued)*

```
002666: Jul 21 20:32:00.160 EST:   Processing link 0, id 10.0.0.3,
  link data 10.0.0.2, type 2
002667: Jul 21 20:32:00.160 EST:   Ignore newdist 2 olddist 1
002668: Jul 21 20:32:00.160 EST:   Processing link 1, id 10.1.6.6,
  link data 10.51.51.1, type 4
002669: Jul 21 20:32:00.160 EST:     Add better path to LSA ID 10.1.6.6,
  gateway 0.0.0.0, dist 49
002670: Jul 21 20:32:00.160 EST:     Add path: next-hop 10.0.0.2,
  interface FastEthernet2/0
002671: Jul 21 20:32:00.160 EST: OSPF: delete lsa id 10.1.3.3, type 1,
  adv rtr 10.1.3.3 from delete list
002672: Jul 21 20:32:00.160 EST: OSPF: Add Router Route to 10.1.3.3 via
  10.0.0.3. Metric: 1
002673: Jul 21 20:32:00.160 EST: OSPF: insert route list LS ID 10.1.3.3,
  type 1, adv rtr 10.1.3.3
002674: Jul 21 20:32:00.160 EST:   It is a router LSA 10.1.3.3. Link Count 1
002675: Jul 21 20:32:00.160 EST:   Processing link 0, id 10.0.0.3,
  link data 10.0.0.3, type 2
002676: Jul 21 20:32:00.160 EST:   Ignore newdist 11 olddist 1
002677: Jul 21 20:32:00.160 EST: OSPF: Add Router Route to 10.1.6.6 via
  10.0.0.2. Metric: 49
002678: Jul 21 20:32:00.160 EST: OSPF: insert route list LS ID 10.1.6.6,
  type 1, adv rtr 10.1.6.6
002679: Jul 21 20:32:00.160 EST:   It is a router LSA 10.1.6.6. Link Count 7
002680: Jul 21 20:32:00.160 EST:   Processing link 0, id 10.1.6.0,
  link data 255.255.255.0, type 3
002681: Jul 21 20:32:00.164 EST:     Add better path to LSA ID 10.1.6.255,
  gateway 10.1.6.0, dist 50
002682: Jul 21 20:32:00.164 EST:     Add path: next-hop 10.0.0.2,
  interface FastEthernet2/0
002683: Jul 21 20:32:00.164 EST:   Processing link 1, id 10.0.5.0,
  link data 255.255.255.0, type 3
002684: Jul 21 20:32:00.164 EST:     Add better path to LSA ID 10.0.5.255,
  gateway 10.0.5.0, dist 50
002685: Jul 21 20:32:00.164 EST:     Add path: next-hop 10.0.0.2,
  interface FastEthernet2/0
002686: Jul 21 20:32:00.164 EST:   Processing link 2, id 10.0.4.0,
  link data 255.255.255.0, type 3
002687: Jul 21 20:32:00.164 EST:     Add better path to LSA ID 10.0.4.255,
  gateway 10.0.4.0, dist 50
002688: Jul 21 20:32:00.164 EST:     Add path: next-hop 10.0.0.2,
  interface FastEthernet2/0
002689: Jul 21 20:32:00.164 EST:   Processing link 3, id 10.0.3.0,
  link data 255.255.255.0, type 3
002690: Jul 21 20:32:00.164 EST:     Add better path to LSA ID 10.0.3.255,
  gateway 10.0.3.0, dist 50
002691: Jul 21 20:32:00.164 EST:     Add path: next-hop 10.0.0.2,
  interface FastEthernet2/0
002692: Jul 21 20:32:00.164 EST:   Processing link 4, id 10.0.2.0,
  link data 255.255.255.0, type 3
002693: Jul 21 20:32:00.164 EST:     Add better path to LSA ID 10.0.2.255,
  gateway 10.0.2.0, dist 50
002694: Jul 21 20:32:00.164 EST:     Add path: next-hop 10.0.0.2,
```

Example 9-63   **debug ip ospf spf intra** *Command Output for Router Oracle (Continued)*

```
          interface FastEthernet2/0
002695: Jul 21 20:32:00.164 EST:    Processing link 5, id 10.0.1.1,
          link data 10.0.1.1, type 2
002696: Jul 21 20:32:00.164 EST:    Add better path to LSA ID 10.0.1.1,
          gateway 10.0.1.1, dist 50
002697: Jul 21 20:32:00.164 EST:    Add path: next-hop 10.0.0.2,
          interface FastEthernet2/0
002698: Jul 21 20:32:00.164 EST:    Processing link 6, id 10.1.2.2,
          link data 10.51.51.2, type 4
002699: Jul 21 20:32:00.168 EST:    Ignore newdist 113 olddist 1
002700: Jul 21 20:32:00.168 EST: OSPF: Add Network Route to 10.0.1.0 Mask /24.
          Metric: 50, Next Hop: 10.0.0.2
002701: Jul 21 20:32:00.168 EST: OSPF: insert route list LS ID 10.0.1.1,
          type 2, adv rtr 10.1.6.6
002702: Jul 21 20:32:00.168 EST:    It is a network LSA 10.0.1.1. Router Count 2
002703: Jul 21 20:32:00.168 EST:    Processing router id 10.1.6.6
002704: Jul 21 20:32:00.168 EST:    New newdist 50 olddist 49
002705: Jul 21 20:32:00.168 EST:    Processing router id 10.1.7.7
002706: Jul 21 20:32:00.168 EST:    Add better path to LSA ID 10.1.7.7,
          gateway 10.0.1.2, dist 50
002707: Jul 21 20:32:00.168 EST:    Add path: next-hop 10.0.0.2,
          interface FastEthernet2/0
002708: Jul 21 20:32:00.168 EST: OSPF: Add Router Route to 10.1.7.7 via
          10.0.0.2. Metric: 50
002709: Jul 21 20:32:00.168 EST: OSPF: insert route list LS ID 10.1.7.7,
          type 1, adv rtr 10.1.7.7
002710: Jul 21 20:32:00.168 EST:    It is a router LSA 10.1.7.7. Link Count 2
002711: Jul 21 20:32:00.168 EST:    Processing link 0, id 10.1.7.0,
          link data 255.255.255.0, type 3
002712: Jul 21 20:32:00.168 EST:    Add better path to LSA ID 10.1.7.255,
          gateway 10.1.7.0, dist 51
002713: Jul 21 20:32:00.168 EST:    Add path: next-hop 10.0.0.2,
          interface FastEthernet2/0
002714: Jul 21 20:32:00.168 EST:    Processing link 1, id 10.0.1.1,
          link data 10.0.1.2, type 2
002715: Jul 21 20:32:00.168 EST:    Ignore newdist 60 olddist 50
002716: Jul 21 20:32:00.168 EST: OSPF: Adding Stub nets
002717: Jul 21 20:32:00.172 EST: OSPF: Add Network Route to 10.0.2.0 Mask /24.
          Metric: 50, Next Hop: 10.0.0.2
002718: Jul 21 20:32:00.172 EST: OSPF: insert route list LS ID 10.0.2.255,
          type 0, adv rtr 10.1.6.6
002719: Jul 21 20:32:00.172 EST: OSPF: Add Network Route to 10.0.3.0 Mask /24.
          Metric: 50, Next Hop: 10.0.0.2
002720: Jul 21 20:32:00.172 EST: OSPF: insert route list LS ID 10.0.3.255,
          type 0, adv rtr 10.1.6.6
002721: Jul 21 20:32:00.172 EST: OSPF: Add Network Route to 10.0.4.0 Mask /24.
          Metric: 50, Next Hop: 10.0.0.2
002722: Jul 21 20:32:00.172 EST: OSPF: insert route list LS ID 10.0.4.255,
          type 0, adv rtr 10.1.6.6
002723: Jul 21 20:32:00.172 EST: OSPF: Add Network Route to 10.0.5.0 Mask /24.
          Metric: 50, Next Hop: 10.0.0.2
002724: Jul 21 20:32:00.172 EST: OSPF: insert route list LS ID 10.0.5.255,
          type 0, adv rtr 10.1.6.6
```

continues

Example 9-63 **debug ip ospf spf intra** *Command Output for Router Oracle (Continued)*

```
002725: Jul 21 20:32:00.172 EST: OSPF: Add Network Route to 10.1.6.0 Mask /24.
  Metric: 50, Next Hop: 10.0.0.2
002726: Jul 21 20:32:00.172 EST: OSPF: insert route list LS ID 10.1.6.255,
  type 0, adv rtr 10.1.6.6
002727: Jul 21 20:32:00.176 EST: OSPF: Add Network Route to 10.1.7.0 Mask /24.
  Metric: 51, Next Hop: 10.0.0.2
002728: Jul 21 20:32:00.176 EST: OSPF: insert route list LS ID 10.1.7.255,
  type 0, adv rtr 10.1.7.7
002729: Jul 21 20:32:00.176 EST: OSPF: Entered old delete routine
Oracle#
```

debug ip routing Command

Use the **debug ip routing** EXEC command to display information about how the routing table is updated. All routing protocols can update the routing table, so it is not OSPF-specific. Example 9-64 shows sample output generated by this command.

Example 9-64 **debug ip routing** *Command Output*

```
Oracle#
002377: Jul 21 19:59:15.092 EST: RT: del 10.51.51.0/30 via 10.0.0.2,
  ospf metric [110/49]
002378: Jul 21 19:59:15.092 EST: RT: delete subnet route to 10.51.51.0/30
002379: Jul 21 19:59:15.092 EST: RT: add 10.51.51.0/30 via 10.0.0.2,
  ospf metric [110/113]
002380: Jul 21 19:59:20.092 EST: RT: del 10.1.7.0/24 via 10.0.0.2,
  ospf metric [110/51]
002381: Jul 21 19:59:20.092 EST: RT: delete subnet route to 10.1.7.0/24
002382: Jul 21 19:59:20.092 EST: RT: del 10.1.6.0/24 via 10.0.0.2,
  ospf metric [110/50]
002383: Jul 21 19:59:20.092 EST: RT: delete subnet route to 10.1.6.0/24
002384: Jul 21 19:59:20.092 EST: RT: del 10.0.5.0/24 via 10.0.0.2,
  ospf metric [110/50]
002385: Jul 21 19:59:20.092 EST: RT: delete subnet route to 10.0.5.0/24
002386: Jul 21 19:59:20.092 EST: RT: del 10.0.4.0/24 via 10.0.0.2,
  ospf metric [110/50]
002387: Jul 21 19:59:20.092 EST: RT: delete subnet route to 10.0.4.0/24
002388: Jul 21 19:59:20.092 EST: RT: del 10.0.3.0/24 via 10.0.0.2,
  ospf metric [110/50]
002389: Jul 21 19:59:20.092 EST: RT: delete subnet route to 10.0.3.0/24
002390: Jul 21 19:59:20.096 EST: RT: del 10.0.2.0/24 via 10.0.0.2,
  ospf metric [110/50]
002391: Jul 21 19:59:20.096 EST: RT: delete subnet route to 10.0.2.0/24
002392: Jul 21 19:59:20.096 EST: RT: del 10.0.1.0/24 via 10.0.0.2,
  ospf metric [110/50]
002393: Jul 21 19:59:20.096 EST: RT: delete subnet route to 10.0.1.0/24
002394: Jul 21 19:59:20.100 EST: RT: del 10.51.51.0/30 via 10.0.0.2,
  ospf metric [110/113]
002395: Jul 21 19:59:20.100 EST: RT: delete subnet route to 10.51.51.0/30
002396: Jul 21 19:59:20.100 EST: RT: del 10.221.0.0/21 via 10.0.0.2,
  ospf metric [110/51]
```

Example 9-64   **debug ip routing** *Command Output (Continued)*

```
002397: Jul 21 19:59:20.100 EST: RT: delete subnet route to 10.221.0.0/21
002398: Jul 21 19:59:20.100 EST: %OSPF-5-ADJCHG: Process 100,
  Nbr 10.1.2.2 on FastEthernet2/0 from LOADING to FULL, Loading Done
002399: Jul 21 19:59:30.100 EST: RT: network 10.0.0.0 is now variably masked
002400: Jul 21 19:59:30.100 EST: RT: add 10.51.51.0/30 via 10.0.0.2,
  ospf metric [110/49]
002401: Jul 21 19:59:35.232 EST: RT: metric change to 10.51.51.0 via 10.0.0.2,
  ospf metric [110/49] new metric [110/113]
002402: Jul 21 19:59:59.295 EST: RT: add 10.0.1.0/24 via 10.0.0.2,
  ospf metric [110/50]
002403: Jul 21 19:59:59.295 EST: RT: add 10.0.2.0/24 via 10.0.0.2,
  ospf metric [110/50]
002404: Jul 21 19:59:59.295 EST: RT: add 10.0.3.0/24 via 10.0.0.2,
  ospf metric [110/50]
002405: Jul 21 19:59:59.295 EST: RT: add 10.0.4.0/24 via 10.0.0.2,
  ospf metric [110/50]
002406: Jul 21 19:59:59.295 EST: RT: add 10.0.5.0/24 via 10.0.0.2,
  ospf metric [110/50]
002407: Jul 21 19:59:59.299 EST: RT: add 10.1.6.0/24 via 10.0.0.2,
  ospf metric [110/50]
002408: Jul 21 19:59:59.299 EST: RT: add 10.1.7.0/24 via 10.0.0.2,
  ospf metric [110/51]
002409: Jul 21 19:59:59.303 EST: RT: add 10.221.0.0/21 via 10.0.0.2,
  ospf metric [110/51]
Oracle#
```

Summary

This chapter discussed a troubleshooting methodology that can be used to facilitate the isolation and resolution of OSPF-related network issues. This methodology, according to Cisco Systems, was divided into seven recommended steps.

The importance of logging and how to configure general router logging as well as OSPF-specific logging was covered. At the same time, you learned about date and time stamping of log entries and how to give these entries sequence numbers. This is not only another method of keeping track of their order but also a way of increasing the security of your OSPF network.

A variety of excellent commands are available to assist you in verifying and trouble-shooting the operation of your OSPF network.

A number of OSPF **show** commands were covered, with comments and pointers on their display and the operation of OSPF. In addition to the **show** commands, you learned about all the possible OSPF **debug** commands, with plenty of examples of their operation and function. Both sections were full of useful comments and observations that have application and usefulness in a real OSPF network.

Case Study: In the Trenches with OSPF

This case study is intended to describe a real-world case where this problem actually occurred and to identify how it was corrected. The case study then outlines some lessons to help prevent the problem from happening again. The troubleshooting model introduced earlier in this chapter is used throughout this case study as a process to reference when performing network troubleshooting.

Recently, a large broadcast storm occurred in an OSPF enterprise network, affecting a region of the network that consisted of approximately 50 geographically separate sites consisting of over 75 routers serving approximately 3000 users. This condition brought all user WAN traffic in the impacted area to a standstill.

Through the course of troubleshooting, we identified how and why localized broadcasts were erroneously being propagated across the WAN, resulting in a dramatic degradation in network performance. Additionally, several Cisco OSPF router configuration problems were identified and corrected during the course of troubleshooting.

Problem No. 1

When troubleshooting in any type of networking environment, a systematic methodology works best. The seven steps outlined throughout this section help us to clearly define the specific symptoms associated with network problems, identify potential problems that could be causing the symptoms, and then systematically eliminate each potential problem (from most likely to least likely) until the symptoms disappear.

This process is not a rigid outline for troubleshooting an internetwork. Rather, it is a foundation from which we can build a problem-solving process to suit our particular internetworking environment. The following troubleshooting steps detail the problem-solving process:

Step 1   Clearly define the problem.

Step 2   Gather facts.

Step 3   Consider possible problems.

Step 4   Create an action plan.

Step 5   Implement the action plan.

Step 6   Gather results.

Step 7   Reiterate the process, if needed, in Steps 4–7.

The customer has called the Network Operations Center (NOC) and reported a network slowdown at a number of critical sites. The situation is even more urgent because the customer is preparing to run the end-of-inventory reconciliation report. The network must be available at this critical time or the customer will lose money.

Step 1: Define the Problem

The first step in any type of troubleshooting and repair scenario is to define the problem. What is actually happening is sometimes different from what is reported; therefore, the truth in this step is defining the actual problem. We need to do two things: identify the symptoms and perform an impact assessment.

The customer called us and explained that the network response was extremely slow. This, of course, was a rather vague and broad description from a network operations standpoint. Due to the nature of the problem report (that is, it can sometimes be difficult to define *slow*), a clear understanding of the problem was required before we could proceed with developing an action plan. This was accomplished by gathering facts and asking several questions of the user who reported the problem. According to the users, the general symptoms were as follows:

- Slow response (including a 30–40 percent packet loss) while connecting to any device on the WAN from the downtown location (see Figure 9-5). We confirmed the slow response by executing a ping from Router B to Router C and received an 800-millisecond round-trip delay. A normal network round-trip delay for other routers in our network had consistently been in the range of 100 to 150 milliseconds.

- Nearly 100 percent utilization was found on Router B's Frame Relay permanent virtual circuit (PVC) to Router C. Our long-distance carrier's Frame Relay network group, which had been monitoring Frame Relay switch statistics at our request, first noticed this.

- We were informed that impact on user productivity was so great that several users were sent home because they could not reliably access critical network resources.

- Other users reported that their ability to run inventory reports was being impaired and the deadline was quickly approaching.

Step 2: Gather Facts

After the problem is defined, we next begin gathering the facts surrounding the problem. This step provides the facts that were gained in this network case study.

Before starting to troubleshoot any type of networking problem, it is helpful to have a network diagram. Figure 9-6 shows the diagram that we used.

Figure 9-6 *Case Study WAN Diagram*

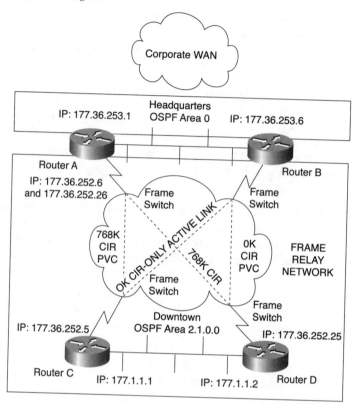

Following the previously mentioned troubleshooting methodology, we collected as many facts as possible and made some general observations by connecting to the routers in question. We gathered facts from several sources on the router, including the Cisco log buffer, and used various Cisco **show** commands. Our observations revealed the following facts and occurrences within the network.

Router B in Figure 9-5 reported high traffic input to the Ethernet segment at headquarters. This caused the Ethernet connectivity to become so unstable that the links would become unavailable for brief periods. Consequently, OSPF adjacencies were being reformed repeatedly. Example 9-65 is an excerpt from the SYSLOG on Router A.

Example 9-65 *Router A SYSLOG Excerpt*

```
Mar 1 00:08:17 UTC: %LINEPROTO-5-UPDOWN: Line protocol on Interface Ethernet0,
changed state to down
Mar 1 00:08:29 UTC: %LINEPROTO-5-UPDOWN: Line protocol on Interface Ethernet0,
changed state to up
Mar 1 00:08:35 UTC: %LINEPROTO-5-UPDOWN: Line protocol on Interface Ethernet0,
changed state to down
Mar 1 00:08:39 UTC: %LINEPROTO-5-UPDOWN: Line protocol on Interface Ethernet0,
changed state to up
```

As you can see by the SYSLOG entries, Ethernet connectivity was being lost for brief periods of time. The router was definitely showing us a contributing factor to the problems that were being reported by our customer.

Missing OSPF Adjacencies

No OSPF neighbors were formed between Routers A and C, A and D, or B and D. The only link that was actively carrying routed traffic was between Routers C and B. Unfortunately, this circuit was a 0-kbps CIR Frame Relay link. This meant that all traffic between Routers C and B was being marked as discard eligible (DE) by the Frame Relay switches in the Frame Relay cloud. (That is, all traffic between Router C and B was set at such a low priority for packet delivery and could be dropped at any time.) As discussed later in this case study, the Cisco router commands to show this information are **show ip ospf neighbors** and **show frame pvc**. Example 9-66 shows output for the **show frame pvc** command. Note that the number of input packets and the number of DE packets are the same.

Example 9-66   **show frame pvc** *Command Output*

```
ROUTER_C#show frame pvc
PVC Statistics for interface Serial0/0:0.2 (Frame Relay DTE)
DLCI = 700, DLCI USAGE = LOCAL, PVC STATUS = ACTIVE, INTERFACE = Serial0/0:0.2
        input pkts 31341659     output pkts 12061107     in bytes 757769644
        out bytes 2564616415     dropped pkts 0     in FECN pkts 17
        in BECN pkts 0     out FECN pkts 0     out BECN pkts 0
        in DE pkts 31341659     out DE pkts 0
        out bcast pkts 2690375     out bcast bytes 250333218
        pvc create time 15w5d, last time pvc status changed 4w2d
```

Output Drops

A large number of output drops were noted on Router C's only active OSPF WAN interface (the one with the 0-KB CIR Frame Relay PVC). Output drops signify that the router is processing a very large number of outbound frames. In this case, the circuit could not accommodate the vast amount of data that the router was trying to output into it, so as a result, the router was dropping frames. This observation is important because it directly influences the number of retransmits that the router sends and contributes to slow end-user throughput. This happens in a router when the circuit and router are overloaded with a large amount of input or output traffic. As discussed later in this case study, the Cisco command to see this happening is **show interface serial** *interface number*. The next section covers the numbers of input and output drops in the output of this useful command.

Input Drops

Large numbers of input drops were observed on Router B's only active WAN interface (0-KB CIR Frame Relay PVC). Input drops signify that the router is processing a large number of inbound frames. The router could not keep up with the data stream because there was so much inbound traffic. Consequently, the router was dropping many inbound frames, resulting in large numbers of input drops being reported. This observation is important because it directly affects the number of retransmits that the router sends, contributing to slower end-user throughput. As discussed previously, the Cisco router command to use is **show interface serial** *interface number*. Example 9-67 shows the output of Router B's WAN interface.

Example 9-67 **show interface serial** *Command Output for Router B*

```
ROUTER_B#show int s0/0:0
Serial0/0:0 is up, line protocol is up
      Hardware is DSX1
      Description: Frame Relay Circuit to Downtown
      MTU 1500 bytes, BW 1536 Kbit, DLY 20000 usec, rely 255/255, load 6/255
      Encapsulation FRAME-RELAY IETF, loopback not set, keepalive set (10 sec)
      LMI enq sent 11212, LMI stat recvd 11212, LMI upd recvd 0, DTE LMI up
      LMI enq recvd 0, LMI stat sent 0, LMI upd sent 0
      LMI DLCI 0 LMI type is ANSI Annex D frame relay DTE
   Broadcast queue 0/64, broadcasts sent/dropped 983815/57443, interface broadcasts
1035677
      Last input 00:00:00, output 00:00:00, output hang never
      Last clearing of "show interface" counters 1d22h
      Input queue: 0/75/421238 (size/max/drops); Total output drops: 32333
      Queueing strategy: weighted fair
      Output queue: 0/64/32333 (size/threshold/drops)
      Conversations 0/51 (active/max active)
      Reserved Conversations 0/0 (allocated/max allocated)
      5 minute input rate 50000 bits/sec, 19 packets/sec
      5 minute output rate 42000 bits/sec, 8 packets/sec
      1493015 packets input, 320768751 bytes, 0 no buffer
      Received 0 broadcasts, 2 runts, 0 giants, 0 throttles
      48 input errors, 35 CRC, 13 frame, 0 overrun, 0 ignored, 2 abort
      2335606 packets output, 845399484 bytes, 0 underruns
      0 output errors, 0 collisions, 1 interface resets
```

Gather More Facts

In an attempt to gather more facts to form an action plan, we needed to know if the problem was hardware or software related. Through the use of Telnet, we determined that we could successfully connect to all routers, although the performance was slow. This ruled out the possibility of a complete hardware failure on any of the routers. We then began to shift focus to the router configurations. Our initial examination of Router A's configuration showed that PVCs to C and D were defined, configured, and active (line up and line protocol up). Example 9-68 shows the observed configuration.

Example 9-68 *Abbreviated Configurations*

```
ROUTER_A# show running-config
!
interface Serial1
description Frame Relay PVCs Downtown to Router C
no ip address
encapsulation frame-relay IETF
```

Example 9-68 *Abbreviated Configurations (Continued)*

```
bandwidth 56
no fair-queue
frame-relay lmi-type ansi
!
interface Serial1.1 point-to-point
description 768K CIR PVC to router C
ip address 177.36.252.6 255.255.255.252
frame-relay interface-dlci 700
!
interface Serial2
description Frame Relay PVCs Downtown to Router D
no ip address
encapsulation frame-relay IETF
bandwidth 56
no fair-queue
frame-relay lmi-type ansi
!
interface Serial2.1 point-to-point
description 768K PVC to Router D
ip address 177.36.252.26 255.255.255.252
frame-relay interface-dlci 701
!
router ospf 204
network 177.36.253.0 0.0.0.255 area 0
network 177.36.252.2 0.0.0.0 area 2.1.0.0
network 177.36.252.24 0.0.0.0 area 2.1.0.0
area 2.1.0.0 authentication
area 2.1.0.0 stub
```

Step 3: Consider Possible Problems

Soon after our initial observations were made and the facts were gathered, we determined that hardware did not seem to be a problem. However, we recognized that we had to confront two problems:

- **Routing issues**—No OSPF adjacencies were being created on three of the four WAN links. Consequently, these links were not passing any routed customer information. Because we had previously ruled out hardware as an issue, we decided it would be necessary to confront this problem from a software configuration standpoint.

- **Performance issues**—A large number of output drops and input drops on the WAN link seemed to be directly related to user slowdowns. However, a circuit problem could not be fully ruled out at this time. If the circuits were truly being overutilized, they could potentially require an upgrade in speed. However, we determined that increasing the circuit speed might require more investigation after the routing issues were fully resolved.

Step 4: Create an Action Plan

Based on the previous troubleshooting methodology, we decided to use a "divide and conquer" approach by breaking up the problem into two pieces: routing issues and performance issues.

As part of our action plan, we decided to correct the routing issues first and then tackle the performance issues. We also decided to change only one variable at a time (that is, only make one router configuration change at a time) to clearly understand the solution after it was discovered.

Step 5: Implement the Action Plan

One of the best troubleshooting commands to use for dealing with OSPF routing issues is **show ip ospf neighbors**. The output of this command displays useful information about OSPF adjacencies in any OSPF network. And as we know, OSPF routing is highly influenced by adjacencies.

The initial output of this command on Router A and Router B gave some useful information, as shown in Example 9-69.

Example 9-69 **show ip ospf neighbors** *Initial Command Output on Router A*

```
ROUTER_A# show ip ospf neighbors
177.36.253.6    1    FULL/DR    00:00:32    177.4.255.32    Ethernet1
```

The findings here indicate that Router A was adjacent with Router B and vice versa (see Example 9-70). Router B was fully adjacent with Router C's backup link (0-KB CIR). These links were running at 0 KB CIR, and all packets going into the network were being marked discard eligible. This helped us to understand why performance was so slow.

Example 9-70 **show ip ospf neighbors** *Initial Command Output on Router B*

```
ROUTER_B# show ip ospf neighbors
177.36.253.1    1    FULL/BDR-    00:00:32    177.4.255.31    Ethernet1
177.36.252.5    1    FULL/ -      00:00:32    177.65.252.45   Serial2.1
```

Later, you will see that when the routing issues were corrected, the output of the same command on Router A yields the results in Example 9-71.

Example 9-71 **show ip ospf neighbor** *Command Output*

```
ROUTER_A# show ip ospf neighbors
177.36.252.1     1    2WAY/DROTHER    00:00:32    177.4.255.32    Ethernet1
177.36.252.5     1    FULL/ -         00:00:34    177.65.252.1    Serial1.1
***FULL T1 (768K CIR) Link to ROUTER C
177.65.252.25    1    FULL/ -         00:00:32    177.65.252.29   Serial2.1
***FULL T1 (768K CIR) Link to ROUTER D
```

Step 6: Gather Results

In this step, we begin to gather the results of the action plan that we created to deal with the reported network problem.

The first step in determining why the adjacencies were not being formed over the WAN links is to confirm that OSPF was enabled on them. By using the **show ip ospf interfaces** command, we quickly determined that indeed OSPF was not enabled on the WAN interfaces for Router A. Specifically, OSPF was not enabled for the WAN links to Routers C and D. As noted in the preceding command output, Ethernet0 on Router A had correctly formed an adjacency with Router B. Example 9-72 shows the output of the **show ip ospf interfaces** command.

Example 9-72 **show ip ospf interfaces** *Command Output*

```
ROUTER_A# show ip ospf interface
Ethernet0 is up, line protocol is up
Internet Address 177.2.255.1/24, Area 0
Process ID 202, Router ID 177.36.252.1 Network Type BROADCAST, Cost: 10
Transmit Delay is 1 sec, State DROTHER, Priority 1
Designated Router (ID) 177.2.255.4, Interface address 177.2.255.4
Backup Designated router (ID) 177.32.252.6, Interface address 177.2.255.5
Timer intervals configured, Hello 10, Dead 40, Wait 40, Retransmit 5
Hello due in 00:00:02
Neighbor Count is 1, Adjacent neighbor count is 1
Adjacent with neighbor 177.36.253.6 (Designated Router)
Serial0 is up, line protocol is up
 OSPF not enabled on this interface
Serial0.1 is up, line protocol is up
 OSPF not enabled on this interface
Serial1 is up, line protocol is up
 OSPF not enabled on this interface
Serial1.2 is up, line protocol is up
 OSPF not enabled on this interface
```

This message **OSPF not enabled on this interface** explained why OSPF would not form an adjacency—it had simply not been enabled!

Step 7: Reiterate the Process, If Needed, in Steps 4–7

Our action plan was successful, and we had identified errors in the router configurations that needed to be corrected. The question then became "How do I turn on OSPF on the WAN interfaces s0.1 and s1.2 of Router A?" A new solution was achieved in the following three steps:

Step 1   Determine the networks that belong to s0.1 and s1.2. This was done by using the Cisco commands **show ip int s0.1** and **show ip int s0.2**. The output from those commands yields the IP address of each interface and the subnet mask that each has configured.

Step 2   Add the network number(s) obtained in Step 1 to the OSPF process as well as the area number to Router A's configuration.

Step 3   Enable area authentication because the design specification requires simple cleartext OSPF authentication.

At this point, it is necessary to reiterate the troubleshooting process and its steps to now begin making the changes to the router's configuration identified in the preceding three-step process. We return to Step 4.

Step 4: Create a New Action Plan

Remember that it is important to change only one variable at a time while executing an action plan. Additionally, it is considered good practice to log any changes that you are making to the router's configuration. Many terminal tools allow the terminal output to be redirected into an ASCII file. A recommended practice is to create an audit trail for later retrieval and reference. This information is also good if you ever have to write an after-action report or a case study!

The action plan was developed to implement steps described previously to enable OSPF on the identified routers and observe the results after these actions had taken effect.

Step 5: Implement the New Action Plan

Identifying the steps needed to enable OSPF, we formulated a new action plan that consisted of taking the actions in Example 9-73 to the router's configuration.

Example 9-73   *Configuring Authentication*

```
ROUTER_A#conf t
Enter configuration commands, one per line. End with CNTL/Z
ROUTER_A(config)#router ospf 202
ROUTER_A(config-router)#network 177.36.252.0 0.0.0.255 area 2.1.0.0
ROUTER_A(config-router)# area 2.1.0.0 authentication
```

After entering these commands, interfaces s0.1 and s1.2 began to "speak" OSPF and attempted to form an adjacency. The relevant new OSPF configuration in Router A is shown in Example 9-74.

Example 9-74   *New OSPF Configuration on Router A*

```
!
router ospf 202
network 177.2.254.0 0.0.0.255 area 0
network 177.36.252.0 0.0.0.255 area 2.1.0.0
area 2.1.0.0 authentication
!
```

Step 6 Revisited: Gather Results

We confirmed that the serial links were now "talking" OSPF by once again using the **show ip ospf interface** command. As we discovered, the routers were speaking OSPF but were not forming adjacencies over the WAN link. This condition was confirmed by the neighbor and adjacency, the counts for which were zero—as indicated by the output in bold that follows.

TIP   Under a normal **show interface** command, the up status reported refers to the data link layer keepalive packet. The same is true when performing a **show ip ospf interface** command.

Example 9-75   **show ip ospf interface** *Command Output*

```
ROUTER_A#show ip ospf interface
Serial0.2 is up, line protocol is up
Internet Address 177.36.252.6/30, Area 2.1.0.0
Process ID 202, RouterID 177.36.252.26, Network Type POINT_TO_POINT, Cost:1
Transmit Delay is 1 sec, State POINT_TO_POINT,
Timer intervals configured, Hello 10, Dead 40, Wait 40, Retransmit 5
Hello due in 00:00:03
Neighbor Count is 0, Adjacent neighbor count is 0
Adjacent with neighbor 177.3
Serial1.2 is up, line protocol is down
Internet Address 177.36.252.26/30, Area 2.1.0.0
Process ID 202, RouterID 177.36.252.26, Network Type POINT_TO_POINT, Cost:1
Transmit Delay is 1 sec, State POINT_TO_POINT,
Timer intervals configured, Hello 10, Dead 40, Wait 40, Retransmit 5
Hello due in 00:00:08
Neighbor Count is 0, Adjacent neighbor count is 0
```

Our past experiences in troubleshooting OSPF led us to believe that this was still some sort of configuration problem because hardware had been ruled out earlier in the troubleshooting process.

Step 7: Reiterate Steps 4–6

We then issued the **show ip ospf neighbors** command again to ensure that the adjacencies had been properly formed. See Example 9-76.

Example 9-76   **show ip ospf neighbors** *Command Output*

```
ROUTER_A#show ip ospf neighbors
Neighbor ID     Pri    State     Dead Time     Address        Interface
177.32.252.6     1     FULL/DR   00:00:37      177.2.254.5    Ethernet0
177.36.254.5     1     INIT/ -   00:00:34      177.36.252.5   Serial0.2
177.36.254.25    1     INIT/ -   00:00:35      177.36.252.25 Serial1.2
```

However, over a period of minutes, we realized that the OSPF neighbor state had not changed from INIT. This meant that each router has seen its neighbor's Hello packets but could not mutually agree on the parameters with which to form an adjacency. We were getting closer to resolving the problem, but something else was still wrong.

We decided that we needed more information to correct this problem, so we turned on OSPF event debugging. Executing the troubleshooting command **debug ip ospf events** while in the Enable mode of a router does this. OSPF debugging allows us to uncover the inner workings of the OSPF process in an effort to determine why adjacencies were not properly formed, as demonstrated in Example 9-77.

Example 9-77   *Activating the* **debug ip ospf events** *Command*

```
ROUTER_A# debug ip ospf events
OSPF events debugging is on
ROUTER_A# ter mon
```

NOTE   The **ter mon** command stands for "terminal monitor" and is a useful Cisco IOS Software command that allows the output from a debug session to be displayed on the current user's terminal. To disable **ter mon**, use the **ter no mon** command.

Some more useful information now began to appear on the output from the **debug ip ospf events** command. The debug output informed us of the following authentication key problem:

```
OSPF: Rcv pkt from 177.36.252.5, Serial0.2: Mismatch Authentication Key-Clear Text
OSPF: Rcv pkt from 177.36.252.25, Serial1.2: Mismatch Authentication Key-Clear Text
```

After speaking with our network design team, we received the correct OSPF authentication key and placed it on Serial0.2 and Serial1.2 on router A. Almost instantly, the OSPF adjacencies were formed and the states were FULL. The output in Example 9-78 shows the relevant configuration modification and the resulting OSPF events.

Example 9-78   *Configuration of Router A*

```
ROUTER_A#conf t
Enter configuration commands, one per line. End with CNTL/Z.
ROUTER_A(config)#int s0.2
ROUTER_A(config-subif)#ip ospf authentication-key secretkey
ROUTER_A(config-subif)#
OSPF: Receive dbd from 177.36.253.6 seq 0x2503
OSPF: 2 Way Communication to neighbor 177.36.254.5
OSPF: send DBD packet to 177.36.252.5 seq 0x22C3
OSPF: NBR Negotiation Done We are the SLAVE
OSPF: send DBD packet to 177.36.252.5 seq 0x2503
OSPF: Receive dbd from 177.36.254.5 seq 0x2504
OSPF: send DBD packet to 177.36.252.5 seq 0x2504
OSPF: Database request to 177.36.254.5
```

Example 9-78   *Configuration of Router A (Continued)*

```
OSPF: sent LS REQ packet to 177.36.252.5, length 864
OSPF: Receive dbd from 177.36.254.5 seq 0x2505
OSPF: send DBD packet to 177.36.252.5 seq 0x2505
OSPF: Database request to 177.36.254.5
OSPF: sent LS REQ packet to 177.36.252.5, length 1080
OSPF: Receive dbd from 177.36.254.5 seq 0x2506
OSPF: Exchange Done with neighbor 177.36.254.5
OSPF: send DBD packet to 177.36.252.5 seq 0x2506
OSPF: Synchronized with neighbor 177.36.254.5, state:FULL
OSPF_ROUTER_A(config-subif)#
OSPF: Neighbor 177.36.254.25 is dead
OSPF: neighbor 177.36.254.25 is dead, state DOWN
OSPF: Tried to build Router LSA within MinLSInterval
OSPF: Rcv pkt from 177.36.252.25, Serial1.2 : Mismatch Authentication Key - Clear
Textint s1.2
OSPF_ROUTER_A(config-subif)#ip ospf authentication-key secretkey
OSPF: Rcv pkt from 177.36.252.25, Serial1.2 : Mismatch Authentication Key - Clear
Text
OSPF_ROUTER_A(config-subif)#
OSPF: 2 Way Communication to neighbor 177.36.254.25
OSPF: send DBD packet to 177.36.252.25 seq 0xCC5
OSPF: Receive dbd from 177.36.254.25 seq 0x794
OSPF: NBR Negotiation Done We are the SLAVE
OSPF: send DBD packet to 177.36.252.25 seq 0x794
OSPF: Receive dbd from 177.36.254.25 seq 0x795
OSPF: send DBD packet to 177.36.252.25 seq 0x795
OSPF: Receive dbd from 177.36.254.25 seq 0x796
OSPF: send DBD packet to 177.36.252.25 seq 0x796
OSPF: Receive dbd from 177.36.254.25 seq 0x797
OSPF: Exchange Done with neighbor 177.36.254.25
OSPF: Synchronized with neighbor 177.36.254.25, state:FULL
```

Step 6 Visited Again: Gather Results

We then confirmed that the OSPF adjacency states were now correct because they were
both FULL. This meant that the OSPF link-state databases for all routers were 100 percent
synchronized with each other, and most importantly, routing was now working correctly, as
shown in the output of Example 9-79.

Example 9-79   *Confirming Routing Between OSPF Neighbors*

```
ROUTER_A#show ip ospf neighbor

Neighbor ID      Pri    State      Dead Time    Address      Interface
177.32.253.6      1    FULL/DR     00:00:31    177.2.254.5    Ethernet0
177.36.254.5      1    FULL/ -     00:00:39    177.36.252.5   Serial0.2
177.36.254.25     1    FULL/ -     00:00:30    177.36.252.25  Serial1.2
```

By executing some trace routes, we confirmed that the primary links (768-kbps Frame Links) were now routing traffic through the proper primary path, namely Router A. Example 9-80 shows the final relevant OSPF router configuration for Router A.

Example 9-80 *Router A: Final OSPF Configuration*

```
!
router ospf 202
network 177.2.254.0 0.0.0.255 area 0
network 177.36.252.0 0.0.0.255 area 2.1.0.0
area 2.1.0.0 authentication
area 2.1.0.0 stub
!
```

This was a solid fix relating to the originally reported routing problem. However, users were still complaining of a slowdown.

Problem #2: Performance Issues

In Step 3, we identified that there were, in fact, two problems being seen in the network. These two problems (routing and performance) were causing the customers' slowdowns. At this point, we have successfully resolved problem No. 1 and its routing issues. We must now resolve the second problem: network performance.

Step 1: Define the Problem

At this point, the network was routing according to design, but a high percentage of traffic was still coming into Router A from the LAN segment downtown. Users downtown were still complaining of a slowdown, so we had a clear problem definition. We used the trouble-shooting model again to develop and implement an action plan.

Step 2: Gather Facts

We observed that there were still a significant amount of output drops on Router C and Router D. Example 9-81 shows the output for Router C.

Example 9-81 **show interface** *Command Output for Router C*

```
ROUTER_C#show int s0/0:0
Serial0/0:0 is up, line protocol is up
Hardware is DSX1
Description: Frame Relay Circuit to Headquarters
MTU 1500 bytes, BW 1536 Kbit, DLY 20000 usec, rely 255/255, load 6/255
Encapsulation FRAME-RELAY IETF, loopback not set, keepalive set (10 sec)
LMI enq sent 16732, LMI stat recvd 16732, LMI upd recvd 0, DTE LMI up
LMI enq recvd 0, LMI stat sent 0, LMI upd sent 0
LMI DLCI 0 LMI type is ANSI Annex D frame relay DTE
Broadcast queue 0/64, broadcasts sent/dropped 983815/57443, interface broadcasts
1035677
Last input 00:00:00, output 00:00:00, output hang never
```

Example 9-81   **show interface** *Command Output for Router C*

```
Last clearing of "show interface" counters 1d22h
Input queue: 0/75/48 (size/max/drops); Total output drops: 1500632
Queueing strategy: weighted fair
Output queue: 0/64/19 (size/threshold/drops)
Conversations 0/51 (active/max active)
Reserved Conversations 0/0 (allocated/max allocated)
5 minute input rate 50000 bits/sec, 19 packets/sec
5 minute output rate 42000 bits/sec, 8 packets/sec
1493015 packets input, 320768751 bytes, 0 no buffer
Received 0 broadcasts, 2 runts, 0 giants, 0 throttles
48 input errors, 35 CRC, 13 frame, 0 overrun, 0 ignored, 2 abort
2335606 packets output, 845399484 bytes, 0 underruns
0 output errors, 0 collisions, 1 interface resets
```

This output is useful in troubleshooting suspected utilization issues. The statistics that are presented here show, for example, if the circuit is taking errors. Additionally, it describes what kinds of errors the circuit is seeing. In this case, the output showed a large number of output drops.

The vast number of output drops was a signal that there was a lot of unnecessary traffic being routed across the WAN links. Essentially, a vicious cycle of repeated retransmits was formed, further aggravating the problem.

Step 4: Create an Action Plan

Troubleshooting WAN performance issues can be difficult. As any good network engineer can tell you, without the proper tools, solving these types of problems is generally a hit-or-miss process. However, solid experiences in the "trenches" of network troubleshooting can help isolate the problem and eventually resolve performance problems.

The action plan was to identify and correct why the router was dropping so many packets. From our past experiences and help from Cisco documentation, drops can be corrected by increasing the output queue on the WAN interface or by turning off WFQ (Weighted Fair Queuing) by issuing the **no fair-queue** command.

NOTE   Weighted Fair Queuing (WFQ) is a packet prioritization technique that Cisco routers use by default on all serial interfaces. It is a strategy that allows data streams to be prioritized in a fair fashion. WFQ is on by default only on links under 2 Mbps, as discussed in the following document:

www.niall.demon.co.uk/Cisco/Queuing/Weighted_Fair_Queuing/
weighted_fair_queuing.html

For more information on WFQ, see the following URL:

www.cisco.com/univercd/cc/td/doc/product/software/ios113ed/113ed_cr/ fun_c/
fcprt4/fcperfrm.htm#37357

Step 5: Implement the Action Plan

Hold Queues

In an effort to control the number of drops on Router C and Router D, the hold queues were increased to 300 on Router C and Router D. Our experiences with other routers in our network showed that this process worked well. Example 9-82 highlights the steps needed to do this.

Example 9-82 *Increasing Hold Queues*

```
ROUTER_C#conf t
Enter configuration commands, one per line. End with CNTL/Z.
ROUTER_C(config-if)#hold-queue 300 out
ROUTER_C(config-if)#no fair-queue
```

In this particular situation, this change had negligible performance impact, and we found that at times performance got somewhat worse. It appeared that we now were dropping fewer frames and saturating an overloaded circuit with even more traffic as a result.

It soon became clear that we needed to better understand the traffic flow between downtown and headquarters. We reasoned that if we could determine the source and destination IP addresses being passed, we might be able to isolate the problem.

IP Accounting

Because we had no access to a "sniffer" or probe on these circuits, we enabled IP accounting on the serial interface of Router C to determine if a particular address was generating the majority of the traffic. Router C was chosen because it was closest to the impacted users downtown, and we believed that it could provide us with the most relevant information for this problem. Example 9-83 shows the steps to do this.

Example 9-83 *Enabling IP Accounting*

```
ROUTER_C# conf t
Enter configuration commands, one per line. End with CNTL/Z.
ROUTER_C(config)#int s0/0:0.1
ROUTER_C(config-if)#ip accounting
```

The results showed a tremendous amount of the utilization (approximately 30 percent) was coming from a system on the LAN segment. In particular, these packets were directed broadcasts from this device (destination 177.2.4.255). Directed broadcasts are a special type of broadcast that are often used in the Microsoft Windows WINS environment. Directed broadcasts can create a problem if an excessive number of them are transgressing the WAN environment. By contrast, normal broadcasts (that is, destination 255.255.255.255) stay on the local LAN and do not impact WAN routing or performance. Example 9-84 shows the relevant **show ip accounting** command output.

Example 9-84   **show ip accounting** *Command Output*

```
ROUTER_C# show ip accounting
Source        Destination     Packets    Bytes
177.1.1.7     177.2.4.255     100322     53732122
```

TIP   When examining network performance problems, the **ip accounting** command should not be used arbitrarily because it imposes extra overhead (that is, CPU and memory) on the router. However, it is a useful tool that can help isolate performance issues quickly, especially if you do not have immediate access to a probe or sniffer device for packet analysis.

Step 6: Gather Results

Site documentation showed us that the Ethernet segments connected to the downtown site were multinetted (that is, they had multiple logical IP segments on the same physical wire). Figure 9-7 shows the downtown LAN topology.

Figure 9-7   *Downtown LAN Topology*

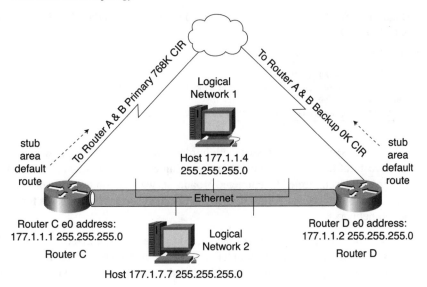

Downtown LAN Topology: Two Logical
Networks on 1 Physical Segment:

*Problem: Routers C and D configured as
OSPF stub & only for Logical Network 1*

IP Accounting Data Analysis

Because Router C and Router D both had been configured as an OSPF stub area, they automatically forwarded any unknown packets through their default router (serial interface), namely to Router A.

The impact was an extremely high traffic load on Router C and Router D's WAN links to Router A. Previously, this was seen on the 0-KB CIR links to Router B.

This problem was resolved once secondary addresses were put on Router C and D, which correctly reflected the multinetted configuration of the downtown location.

NOTE   Secondary IP addresses, although usable in a variety of situations, are generally used when there are not enough host addresses for a particular network segment. For example, the downtown subnetting allows up to 254 hosts per logical subnet, but in some cases, on one physical subnet, 300–500 host addresses are needed. Using secondary IP addresses on the router allows two logical subnets to use one physical subnet.

Example 9-85 shows the commands needed to put the secondary IP addresses on Router C and Router D.

Example 9-85   *Configuring Secondary IP Addresses*

```
ROUTER_C#config terminal
Enter configuration commands, one per line. End with CNTL/Z
ROUTER_C#int e0
ROUTER_C#ip address 177.1.7.1  255.255.255.0 secondary
```

When these secondary addresses were in place, Routers C and D knew to keep localized broadcast traffic local. The **show ip accounting** command was again run on the Cisco routers, which confirmed that directed broadcasts were no longer being propagated through the Cisco routers, because both Router C and D had correct IP addresses for all local multinetted networks.

Performance greatly improved, as evidenced by the now-stabilized number of drops, and we confirmed that PVC utilization had returned to normal levels. We made a phone call to the users who reported the initial problem, and the users confirmed that their performance had been restored.

Case Study Conclusion and Design Tips

An essential approach in troubleshooting and eventually correcting this problem was to follow a structured troubleshooting methodology. Using the seven steps to troubleshooting as a guide, we corrected these problems in an orderly, efficient fashion.

Through the course of troubleshooting this case study, we found the value of the following key Cisco IOS Software commands to help resolve OSPF and performance-related problems:

- **show ip ospf neighbors**
- **show ip interfaces**
- **debug ip ospf events**
- **ip accounting** and **show ip accounting**

We discovered that OSPF stub area configurations have some dangers if a misconfigured network interface or router port is on the local LAN that the router attaches to. In most cases, the benefit of having a smaller routing table generally outweighs the drawbacks of using stub areas, but it is important to understand the implications that can be caused by OSPF stub area misconfigurations. We also found that it is critical to have the correct authentication key to form an adjacency. For Cisco router performance problems, we examined why output drops were occurring and learned how to control them by raising output hold queues and turning off WFQ.

In conclusion, this case study demonstrates that if you follow a structured troubleshooting methodology with solid fundamentals, and dig deep into the trenches, you can divide and conquer any networking problem.

Case Study: OSPF Issues and Teasers

This case study is intended to describe common OSPF issues that have been encountered by many engineers around the world. I have tried to bring in useful information and examples from many sources into a single case study that has but one purpose. I put this information at the end of the chapter as a section to help you figure out what the problem might be. I want to give you some quick possibilities that can enable you to solve your OSPF problem. With what you have learned so far in this book, I am sure that you will! Good luck.

Cisco has some excellent flow charts that are included here to help you troubleshoot OSPF; some are useful and some are not. I thought the good ones would be a useful addition to this section and the philosophy of empowering you, the reader, to go forth and solve your OSPF issues! Figure 9-8 is the first introductory flow chart that starts the documentation of the most common OSPF issues encountered by the TAC.

Figure 9-8 *OSPF Common Issues*

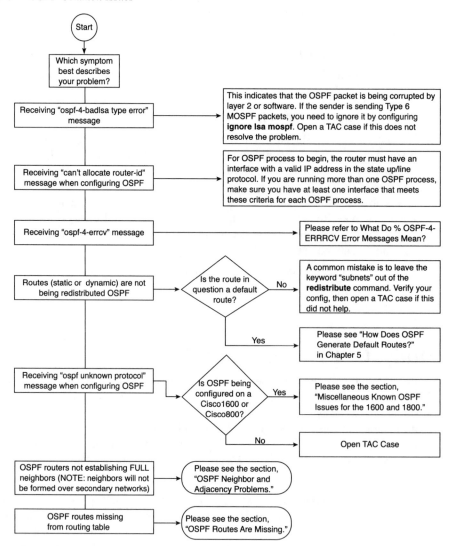

OSPF Error Messages

This section contains some of the more common OSPF error messages and the meaning of these messages. If you learn about any more, please let me know. My e-mail address is in the front of the book.

What Do %OSPF-4-ERRRCV Error Messages Mean?

The %OSPF-4-ERRRCV error message indicates that an OSPF router has received an invalid OSPF packet. The cause of the error is included in the error message itself. Possible causes are as follows:

- Mismatched area ID

- Bad checksum

- OSPF not enabled on the receiving interface

- Bad version

- Invalid type

- Bad link-state update advertisement count

- Bad link-state update length

The first three items in the list are the most common causes of the %OSPF-4-ERRRCV error message; they are discussed in more detail at the following URL:

www.cisco.com/warp/public/104/19.html

What Does the Adv router not-reachable Error Message Mean?

When you see the Adv router not-reachable error message on the top of a link-state adver-tisement (LSA), it means that the router advertising the LSA is not reachable through OSPF. There are several reasons for this message, most of which deal with misconfigu-ration or a broken topology. The following document explains some of the more common reasons for this error message:

www.cisco.com/warp/customer/104/26.html (available to registered users)
www.cisco.com/warp/public/104/26.html (available to non-registered users)

OSPF Is Having Neighbor and Adjacency Problems

OSPF routers might not be establishing neighbor relationships or adjacencies properly. The result is that link-state information is not properly exchanged between routers, and therefore their routing tables are inconsistent. There are a number of possible OSPF neighbor relationship problems; however, for the purposes of this example, we focus on the problem of when the OSPF neighbor list is empty. Some of the possible causes for the OSPF neighbor list being empty are as follows:

- OSPF is not enabled on the interface, or a network router configuration command is misconfigured or missing.

- Mismatched Hello or dead timers, E-bits (set for stub areas), area IDs, authentication types, or network masks.

- Access list is misconfigured and might be blocking OSPF Hellos.
- Virtual link and stub area configurations are mismatched.
- OSPF is not enabled on the interface.
- Interface is defined as passive.
- Mismatched Hello/dead interval.
- Mismatched authentication key.
- Mismatched area ID.
- Layer 2 is down.
- Interface is defined as passive under OSPF.
- Mismatched subnet number/mask over a broadcast link.
- Mismatched authentication type (plaintext versus MD5).
- Mismatched stub/transit/NSSA options.
- No network type is defined over NBMA (Frame Relay, X.25, SMDS, and so on).
- Frame-relay/dialer-map statement is missing the keyword **broadcast** on both sides.

The preceding list provides some items to review if you are having OSPF communication issues between routers. Depending on the OSPF communication state, you can also use the flow chart shown in Figure 9-9 to proceed.

OSPF Stuck in INIT

When OSPF is stuck in the init state, some lower-layer issues are typically not allowing the Hello packets to be exchanged. The init state indicates that a router sees Hello packets from the neighbor, but two-way communication has not been established. A Cisco router includes the router IDs of all neighbors in the init (or higher) state in the neighbor field of its Hello packets. For two-way communication to be established with a neighbor, a router must also see its own router ID in the neighbor field of the neighbor's Hello packets. Some common reasons for the OSPF stuck in INIT problem are as follows:

- One side is blocking the Hello packet.
- One side is translating (NAT) OSPF Hellos.
- One side multicast capabilities are broken.
- Must be a Layer 2 problem.
- The **dialer map** or **frame-relay map** command is missing the **broadcast** keyword.
- Router sending Hellos to contact neighbor on NBMA but have received no reply.
- Neighbor Hellos are getting lost in the NBMA cloud.
- Neighbor received our Hello but is rejecting it for some reason (Layer 2).

Figure 9-9   *OSPF Neighbor States*

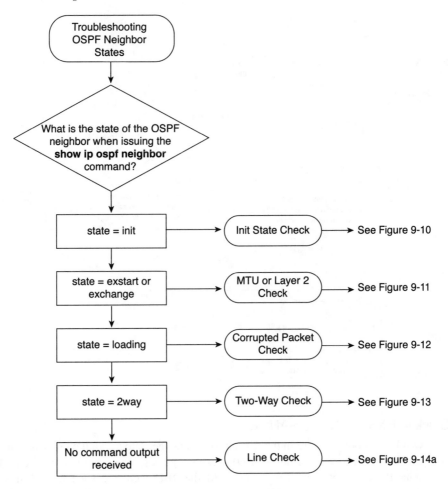

In addition to checking the preceding items, you can also follow the flow chart shown in Figure 9-10.

Figure 9-10 *OSPF Stuck in INIT State*

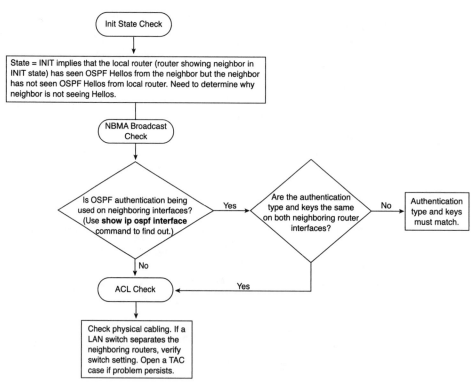

OSPF Stuck in EXSTART/EXCHANGE

OSPF neighbors that are in the Exstart or Exchange state are in the process of trying to exchange database descriptor (DBD) packets. The adjacency should continue past this state. If it does not, there is a problem with the DBD exchange, such as MTU mismatch or the receipt of an unexpected DBD sequence number. Some possible causes of the OSPF stuck in EXSTART/EXCHANGE problem are as follows:

- If the neighbor is bay router, adjust the interface MTU to match other vendors. OSPF sends the interface MTU in a database description packet. If there is any MTU mismatch, OSPF does not form an adjacency. See the following URL:

  — www.cisco.com/en/US/tech/tk648/tk365/
    technologies_tech_note09186a0080093f0d.shtml#4

- Neighbor RIDs are identical

- Unicast is broken:
  - Wrong VC/DLCI mapping in frame/ATM environment in a highly redundant network.
  - MTU problem, cannot ping across with more than certain length packet.
  - Access list blocking unicast. After 2-way OSPF send unicast packet except p2p links.
  - NAT is translating unicast packet.
- Between PRI and BRI/dialer and network type is point-to-point.

In addition to checking the preceding items, you can also follow the flow chart shown in Figure 9-11.

Figure 9-11 *OSPF Stuck in EXSTART/EXCHANGE State*

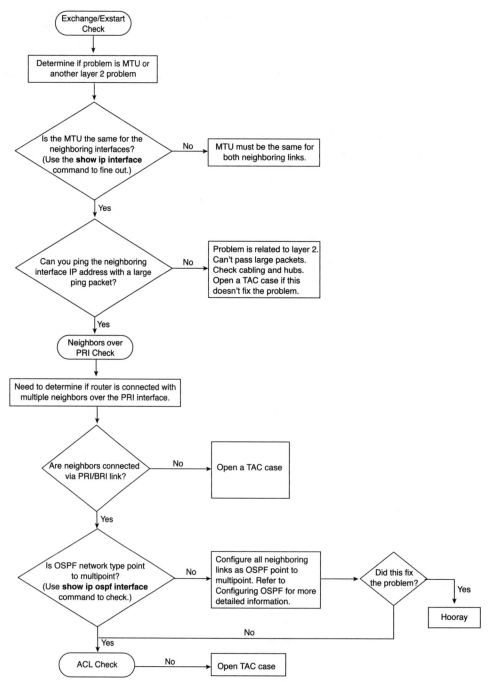

OSPF Stuck in LOADING

In the LOADING state, routers send link-state request packets. During the adjacency, if a router receives an outdated or missing link-state advertisement (LSA), it requests that LSA by sending a link-state request packet. Neighbors that do not transition beyond this state are most likely exchanging corrupted LSAs. This problem is usually accompanied by a %OSPF-4-BADLSA console message. Some of the possible causes are as follows:

- LS request is being made and neighbor is sending bad packet or corrupt memory:
  - Execute a **show ip ospf request-list** *neighbor RID interface* command to see a bad LSA.
  - show log will show OSPF-4-BADLSATYPE message.
- LS request is being made and neighbor is ignoring the request.
- MTU mismatch problem. Old IOS does not detect it (RFC 1583).

In addition to checking the preceding items, you can also follow the flowchart shown in Figure 9-12.

Figure 9-12   *OSPF Stuck in LOADING State*

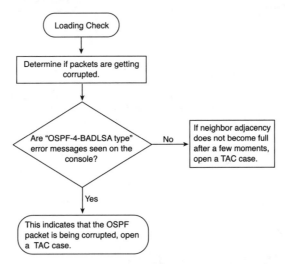

OSPF Stuck in TWO-WAY

The flowchart in Figure 9-13 documents some possible causes of this problem.

Figure 9-13 *OSPF Stuck in TWO-WAY State*

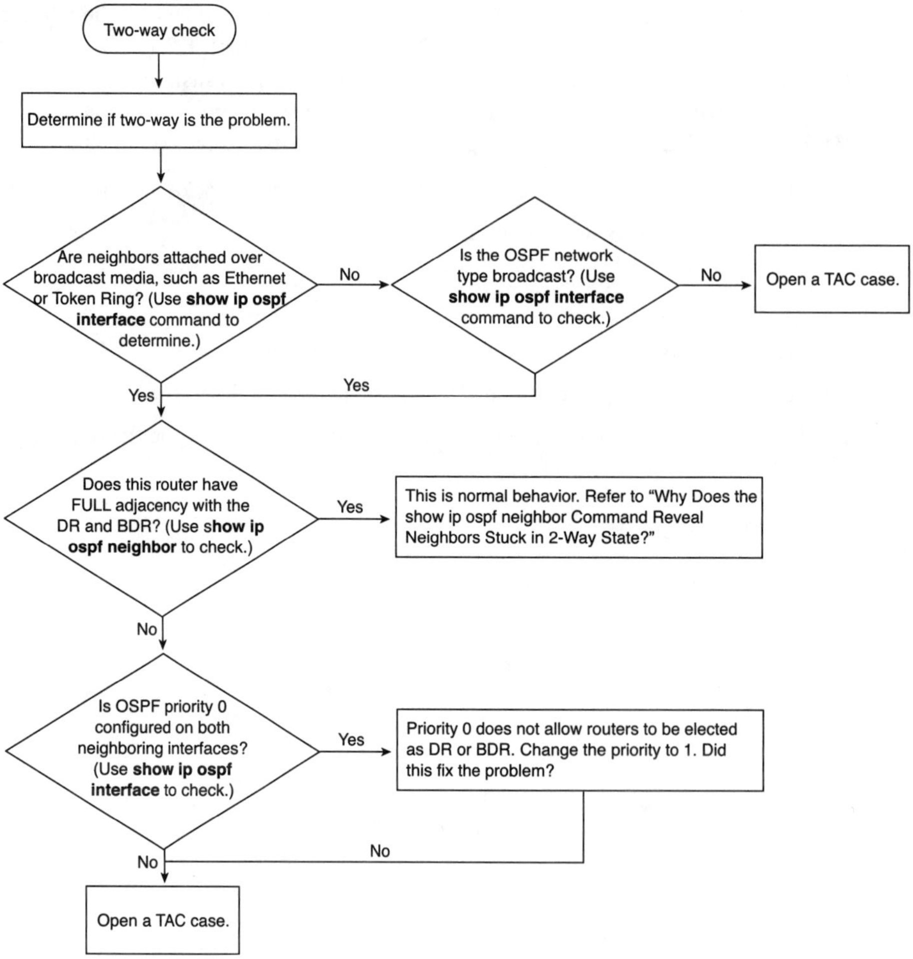

OSPF Routes Missing from Routing Table

A common problem when using OSPF is routes in the database that do not appear in the routing table. In most cases, OSPF finds a discrepancy in the database, so it does not install the route in the routing table. You often see the "Adv Router is not-reachable" message (meaning that the router advertising the LSA is not reachable through OSPF) on top of the link-state advertisement (LSA) in the database when this problem occurs. Example 9-86 shows sample output.

Example 9-86   **show ip ospf database** *Command Ouptut*

```
Router# show ip ospf database
Adv Router is not-reachable
LS age: 418
Options: (No TOS-capability, DC)
LS Type: Router Links
Link State ID: 172.16.32.2
Advertising Router: 172.16.32.2
LS Seq Number: 80000002
Checksum: 0xFA63
Length: 60
 Number of Links: 3
```

There are several reasons for this problem, most of which deal with misconfiguration or a broken topology. When the configuration is corrected, the OSPF database discrepancy goes away and the routes appear in the routing table. This case study explains some of the more common reasons that can cause the discrepancy in the database. OSPF routes and networks are not being advertised to other routers. Routers in one area are not receiving routing information for other areas. Some hosts cannot communicate with hosts in other areas, and routing table information is incomplete.

Some common causes for OSPF routes to be missing from the routing table are as follows:

- OSPF routers are not establishing neighbors.

- Routing information is not redistributed correctly into OSPF (remember the subnets).

- An ABR is not configured in an area, which isolates that area from the OSPF backbone.

- An interface network type mismatch exists on Frame Relay WAN.

- The area is configured as a stub area.

- A misconfigured route is filtering.

- The virtual link is misconfigured.

OSPF Routes Are in the Database but Not in the Routing Table

Sometimes, OSPF routes are present in the link-state database but are not present in the IP routing table. This odd set of circumstances necessitates determining why that is. Some of the possible reasons are as follows:

- One side is numbered, and the other is unnumbered.

- IP addresses are flipped, dual serial.

- Forwarding address is not known or is known via external/static (O E1, O E2) - route sum and redistribute connections?

- Different mask or IP address in point-to-point.

- **distribute-list in** is configured.
- Backbone area became discontiguous.
- OSPF is enabled on secondary but not on primary.
- The contiguous flow charts in Figures 9-14a through 9-14g document how to determine why routes are not present in the database.

Figure 9-14a *OSPF Link State Check*

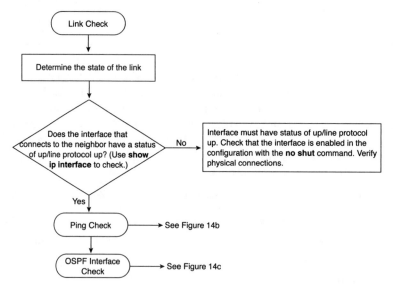

Figure 9-14b *OSPF Link State Check*

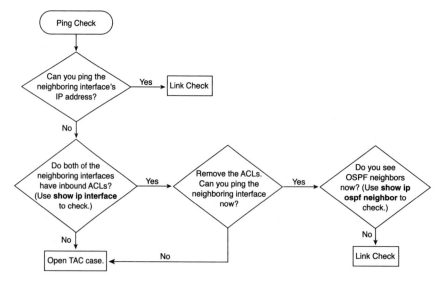

Figure 9-14c *OSPF Link State Check*

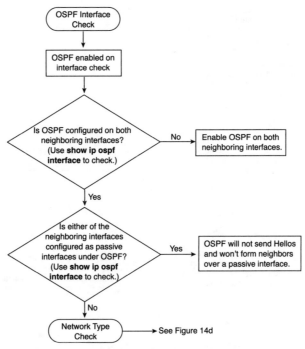

Figure 9-14d *OSPF Link State Check*

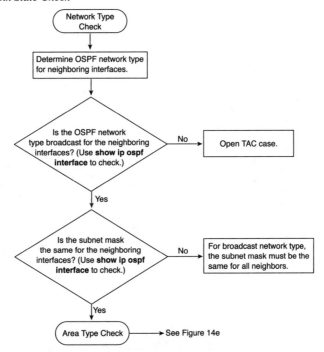

Figure 9-14e *OSPF Link State Check*

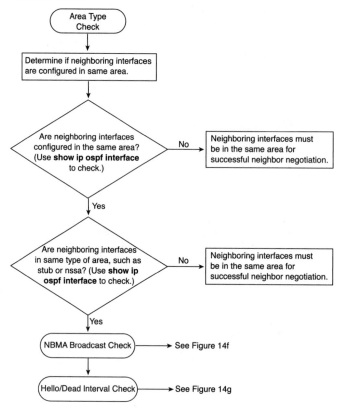

Figure 9-14f *OSPF Link State Check*

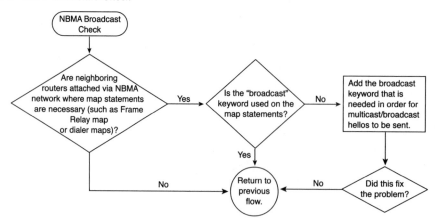

Figure 9-14g *OSPF Link State Check*

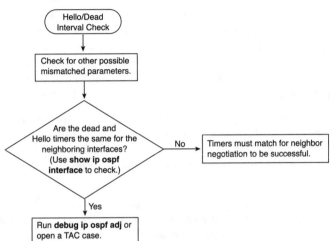

Miscellaneous Known OSPF Issues

This section contains discussions on a variety of OSPF issues that can assist you in determining the solutions to your OSPF problems.

Why Doesn't My Cisco 1600 Router Recognize the OSPF Protocol?

The Cisco 1600 router requires the PLUS feature set image of Cisco IOS Software to run OSPF. This can also be found by searching for the 1600 feature matrix. For more information, see the following section of the "Release Notes for Cisco IOS Release 11.2(11) Software Feature Packs for Cisco 1600 Series Routers":

www.cisco.com/univercd/cc/td/doc/product/software/ios112/fp112rn/4821_02.htm

Why Doesn't My Cisco 800 Router Run OSPF?

Cisco 800 routers are not designed to run OSPF, so they do not support it. See the "Cisco 800 Series Router Applications Overview" to learn how a Cisco 1600 or higher model router is needed to support OSPF at the following URL:

www.cisco.com/warp/public/cc/pd/rt/800/prodlit/800sr_ov.htm

Why Is the **ip ospf interface-retry 0** Configuration Command Added to All Interfaces?

When OSPF is configured on a router, the router interfaces are polled and interfaces that are up are enabled with OSPF. As interfaces become more complex and the number of interfaces increases, the time for interfaces to come up also increases, and there is a slight chance that OSPF will poll the interface before its state is fully up. This can result in the interface being up, but OSPF not being enabled on it. The default number of times that OSPF polls the interfaces has been increased from 0 to 10 to avoid this situation.

If you are running OSPF and upgrading to Cisco IOS Software Release 12.0(8)S, notice that the **ip ospf interface-retry 0** command is automatically added to every interface. This value is the old default value. The new default number of retry times is 10. The router displays the old behavior so that the command shows up in the configuration.

NOTE   The **ip ospf interface-retry 0** command is harmless, and OSPF continues to function normally regardless of whether you change the interface retry value.

Only configure **ip ospf interface-retry 10** on all interfaces if you do not want this command to appear in your router's configuration. Because 10 is the new default value, the command no longer appears in the configuration.

How Do I Produce a Stable OSPF Network with Serial Links Flapping?

You can do nothing in the OSPF process to stabilize a network with flapping serials. You need to address the real problem and fix the flapping serial lines. If you want to patch the problem for a while, you could set the keepalives on the serial interfaces higher than 10 seconds, especially in point-to-point environments. Summarization is also an alternative to this problem.

OSPF Routing Issues

Figures 9-15a through 9-15e document the general methodology for resolving a variety of OSPF routing issues. Through the use of these flow charts you can methodically isolate and determine the source of the routing issue that your network might be experiencing.

When your routing table contains missing routes, it is best to begin by determining what is known about the routes.

Figure 9-15a *OSPF Routing Issues Flow Chart: Route Check*

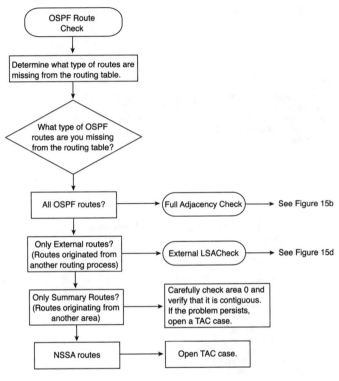

Are the adjacencies at the level of communication that they need to be?

Figure 9-15b *OSPF Routing Issues Flow Chart: Full Adjacency Check*

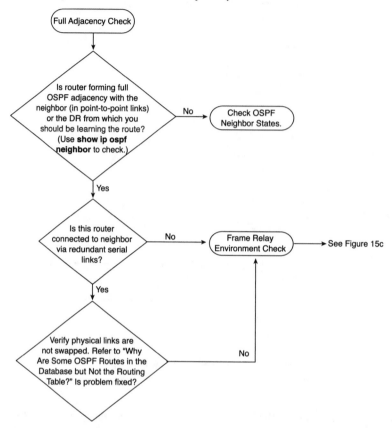

As discussed, OSPF does operate differently when operating over serial interfaces. Therefore, you must verify that OSPF is operating as expected.

Figure 9-15c *OSPF Routing Issues Flow Chart: Frame Relay Environment Check*

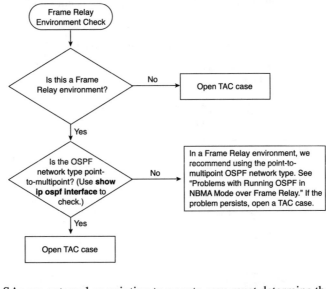

If the LSAs are external or pointing to a route, you must determine the validity of them.

Figure 9-15d *OSPF Routing Issues Flow Chart: External LSA Check*

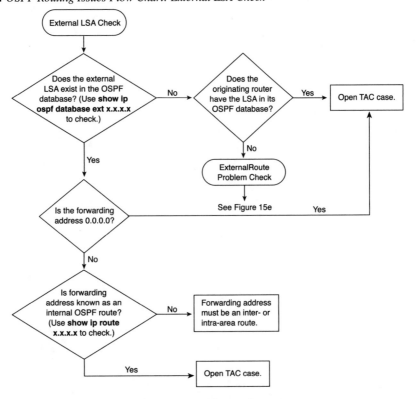

The final step is to determine why the external route is not in the routing table or OSPF database.

Figure 9-15e *OSPF Routing Issues Flow Chart: External Route Problem Check*

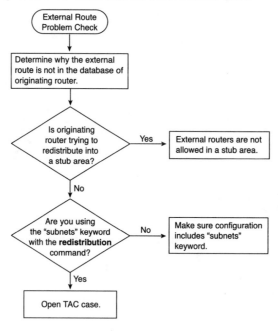

CHAPTER 10

BGP and MPLS in an OSPF Network

If you would make a man happy, do not add to his possessions but subtract from the sum of his desires.—Seneca

This chapter describes the interaction between OSPF and BGP. Why include coverage of BGP in an OSPF book? What do they have to do with each other? The answer is more complicated than you might expect.

This chapter also covers some of the new capabilities and evolving extensions of OSPF as it grows to embrace new technologies such as MultiProtocol Label Switching (MPLS).

Review of Interior Gateway Protocols and Exterior Gateway Protocols

The world of TCP/IP is both logical and a little bit magical. Logical in the way that it adheres to well-defined inflexible rules; Class A IP addressing schemes use a default mask of 255.0.0.0; Layer 3 addresses are thirty-two bits in length subdivided into four octets containing eight bits each. Without routing protocols, packets don't reach their final destination. The routing of packets through a network infrastructure is where the magical part comes into play.

Because packets have both a source and destination address, it would seem that with appropriately intelligent routers factored into the mix, packets could find their way without much assistance through a network. This is not always the case, even with the most finely designed router hardware playing "traffic cop." Without a routing protocol present to lend a hand, the routers will never learn how to get the packets to their destinations.

You need to remember that a router has absolutely no idea how to reach networks that it is not physically connected to. It learns routes to networks in distant lands via the information passed to it by a routing protocol.

You might think that static routes would get the packets where they are going. Unfortunately, you most likely will not have access to all the routers the packets will need to travel across to get to the finish line. Moreover, static routes would have to be manually changed or removed if an interface (or router) were eliminated from the picture because of hardware failure or administrative intervention.

Dynamic routing protocols step in and save the day when static routes are not flexible and responsive enough for an interconnected network. Static routes have their place in the networking world, and they perform quite well in certain circumstances; however, they are limited in their usefulness when networks begin to grow larger in scale. Imagine the number of static routes that would need to be maintained on a network that spanned three countries and consisted of 200 routers. Starting to see how maintaining all those static routes would be futile and an ineffective use of valuable resources?

Of the many possible dynamic routing protocols available (Chant with me, "OSPF is the best!"), you will find that routing protocols are classified for use in two different scenarios: those routing protocols used inside (interior) and those used outside (exterior) an autonomous system (AS). To simplify this, consider OSPF used within a company's network. When the company wants to connect to the Internet, which is *outside* its AS, then OSPF is not the answer. Instead, a different type of routing protocol known as an Exterior Gateway Protocol (EGP) is required. Soon you will see why OSPF is not suited to this task. The list that follows summarizes the characteristics of and differences between Interior Gateway Protocols and Exterior Gateway Protocols:

- **Interior Gateway Protocols (IGPs)**—A classification that describes the use of a dynamic routing protocol in situations where routing tables (or databases) need to be built and maintained within the confines of an AS. Examples of common IGPs include OSPF, Enhanced IGRP (EIGRP), Intermediate System-to-Intermediate System (IS-IS) and Routing Information Protocol (RIP).

- **Exterior Gateway Protocols (EGPs)**—A classification that describes the use of a dynamic routing protocol in situations where routing protocols need to handle the gargantuan task of building and maintaining routing tables (or databases) between one or more autonomous systems and the Internet.

See the difference? You can summarize these definitions by saying that routing within an AS is considered *interior in nature* and that routing between your AS and others is *exterior in nature.*

Although this might seem simplistic, it is accurate. Nevertheless, do not let that fool you into thinking that EGPs are easier to use or understand than IGPs; nothing is further from the truth. Remember, BGP (Border Gateway Protocol) is considered an EGP. Moreover, anyone who knows anything about BGP will tell you that there is nothing "simple" or "easy" when it comes to deploying BGP. The next section describes the roles that IGPs and EGPs play in a network.

Role of IGPs and EGPs in a Network

If you have ever helped design or maintain a corporate LAN or WAN, you know the limitations imposed by the various types of routing protocols.

An IGP such as OSPF can scale well in a topology that spans more than one area, but OSPF is a link-state routing protocol. This means that as the state of links within the areas experience change, those changes are broadcast to the neighboring routers, which in turn cause the link-state databases to be recalculated. This might not seem important, but consider what would happen if OSPF had to deal with the hundreds of thousands of routers that connect together to form the Internet. The limitations of an IGP such as OSPF become apparent when you consider that each of those thousands of routers could each be in an OSPF area.

You also have to consider that OSPF requires the presence of an area 0 to act as the transit area for routing updates. If the Internet had a single area 0, what do you think would happen if something went wrong and it became unreachable?

Figure 10-1 shows the concept of where an IGP operates. The routers have identical routing tables within the AS, and OSPF is the IGP.

Figure 10-1   *IGP Routing Within an AS*

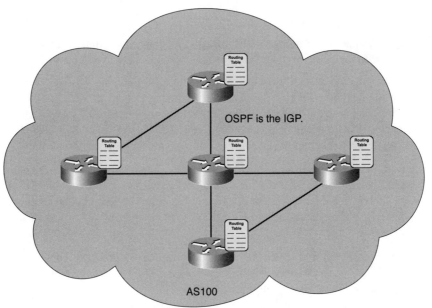

With BGP, you must be introduced to the concept of autonomous systems. The Internet is a collection of them; they are each individual networks. A more formal description of an autonomous system is

> An internetwork that is part of the Internet and has a single routing policy. Each autonomous system is assigned an autonomous system number that is globally unique.

Realistically and functionally, an autonomous system is a network running an IGP such as OSPF within itself (that is, internal). All the routers in that network or in that IGP's domain are considered part of the autonomous system. BGP is not concerned with what is going on inside autonomous systems.

The best way to understand how an EGP such as BGP differs from an IGP such as OSPF is to examine the methods that each uses when passing routing update information.

IGP updates (such as OSPF) contain the following:

- Destination network address
- Route metric
- Next-hop router identity

EGP updates (such as BGP) contain the following:

- Network number
- Community
- Local Preference
- AS path accumulation (a list of networks that the routing announcement has passed through, and through which the network is presumed reachable)

A BGP update generally contacts only a single AS-Path and AS-Set. Also, BGP updates contain next hops and metrics. The real difference between IGPs and EGPs is that an IGP provides next-hop reachability for destinations in your AS, and EGPs provide next-hop reachability for destinations outside of your AS. Also, IGPs converge quickly and support fewer routes, whereas EGPs converge slowly and support many routes.

An EGP such as BGP is designed to scale, enabling it to handle the large number of routes and have routing policies that are required when two or more autonomous systems connect. You have probably heard about BGP and think that it is just another routing protocol designed to handle large numbers of routes. While true, this is only a small piece of what BGP does.

Consider for a moment that the Internet is just a large number of companies, typically service providers or telecommunication companies. These companies have some characteristics in common, specifically the following:

- They have routers and connections in many cities and countries.
- They are for-profit businesses.
- Frequently, they are competitors with each other.
- They often connect to each other.

Think about how peculiar it is for competitors to connect their business together—imagine two department stores sharing some shelf space together? Rather odd, isn't it? That is the

Internet. These companies are often huge and have many concerns, so they need a routing protocol that can meet many of the following needs:

- Has a routing table to share that is over 110,000 routes in size.

- Ensures that your profitability is not affected by increased connectivity.

- Alters the flow of packets based on cost savings (That is, this link is cheaper to have, so use it first.)

- Provides multiple paths between locations to ensure reliability.

- Keeps the shareholders and lawyers happy.

You might consider this last one to be a tongue-in-cheek quip; however, many books often mention technology this and technology that when the truth is that it all results in making businesses more profitable. A network is a business enabler and as such, it must bring value to a company's profitability.

Back to network engineering. The Internet uses BGP to handle routing updates between the spider web of routers that connect together throughout the world to bring us websites, e-mail, FTP sites, MP3 files, and best of all, streaming video. Just how does BGP manage to pull this off? Consider the network depicted in Figure 10-2, which presents two companies, each of which is an AS.

Figure 10-2 *BGP Is the EGP Connecting Different Autonomous Systems*

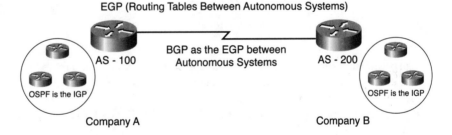

This simple demonstration of connecting two autonomous systems shows exactly how the Internet connects. To understand what the Internet looks like, make this drawing several magnitudes larger and more interconnected. To complete the example, make it a collection of companies all over the world, with many connections within their own networks and to others. That is the Internet. Take a look at Figure 10-3. Insert the name of your favorite Internet service provider (ISP) or telecommunications company in each cloud; then arrange them by country until they span the globe. This represents just a small section of the World Wide Web. To review, inside each cloud is a company's network running an IGP such as OSPF, and to connect externally to each other, they use BGP.

Figure 10-3 *The Internet*

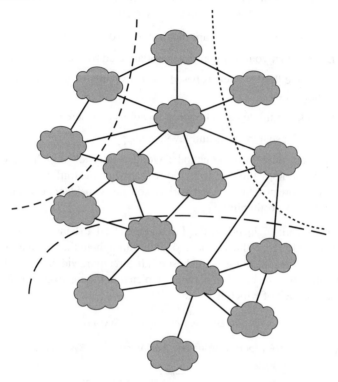

The use of BGP enables each company to apply various policies and route filters as needed. The other point to understand is that the number of routes present on the Internet is currently approximately 112,000, and as discussed, an IGP is not designed to handle that many. Are you starting to understand why IGPs and EGPs stick to what they do best?

This leads to the question—Why not just use BGP everywhere? The answer is convergence speed. For example, BGP is slow when compared to OSPF.

Introduction to BGP

BGP is running in thousands of networks, almost as many as OSPF. When it runs, it relies heavily on the other IP routing protocols in use in the network, specifically the IGP. The main purpose of this section is to help you understand exactly how BGP relies on OSPF, and how OSPF supports and augments BGP operations and features.

To better set your expectations of this discussion of BGP, this section covers the points that aid in understanding this technology and how it interacts with OSPF. Clearly, there is much more information to impart on BGP, but that is beyond the scope of this book. I recommend that you consider *BGP4 Inter-Domain Routing in the Internet* by John Stewart.

Characteristic Overview of BGP

BGP went through different phases and improvements from the earliest version, BGP-1, in 1989 to today's version, BGP-4, deployment of which started in 1993. BGP can be categorized as an EGP. In contrast, OSPF is an IGP. The difference between them is that, although an IGP is designed to populate your routing tables with the routes from your own network or autonomous system, BGP is designed to populate your routing tables with routes from other networks. Put simply, an IGP routes within a network, whereas an EGP such as BGP routes between them.

BGP assumes that routing within an autonomous system is done through an IGP routing protocol such as OSPF. BGP uses TCP as its transport protocol. This ensures that all the transport reliability such as retransmission is taken care of by TCP and does not need to be implemented in BGP itself.

BGP was designed to operate in networks that had the following characteristics:

- Networks implementing route aggregation have this handled by BGP4 via CIDR.
- Complex routing policies.
- Large routing tables.
- Different autonomous systems that needed to be connected.

To address these requirements, certain tradeoffs were required to make BGP viable:

- **Slow convergence**—Scalability is so important that it takes some time to become peers and share large numbers of routes.
- **Reliable Connectivity**—Through the use of TCP, every BGP is reliable in nature, resulting in a CPU-intensive protocol.

The Internet consists of a rapidly increasing number of hosts interconnected by constantly evolving networks of links and routers. Inter-domain routing in the Internet is coordinated by BGP, which allows each AS to choose and develop its own routing policies that are the basis for selecting the best routes and when propagating routing information to others. These routing policies are determined and constrained by the contractual commercial agreements between companies, as represented by an AS number.

For example, an AS sets its policy so that it does not provide transit services between its providers. In other words, a company can have redundant connections to the Internet through provider A and provider B. This company can create a routing policy that says, "Do not allow traffic from provider A to reach provider B via my network and vice versa." In Figure 10-4, you can see how a company has become the customer of two different service providers, thus giving themselves redundant connections to the Internet.

Figure 10-4 *Dual-Homed to the Internet*

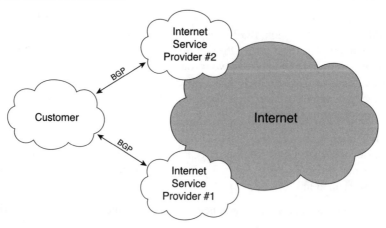

This is an excellent design and is more commonly know as having a *dual-homed network*. Although BGP is useful and ideally suited for connecting your company's network to the Internet, it is not always necessary. To clarify, it is not always a good idea or appropriate to use BGP when the following situations are present:

- There is no need to have an external routing policy.

- There is limited bandwidth on the connection over which you are considering running BGP.

- Your company has only a single connect to another AS, another company, or the Internet.

- Your router connecting to the Internet has limited memory or processor power— remember that BGP takes a lot of router resources.

In many of these cases, a simple static route can achieve the level of connectivity necessary for your network.

Operational Overview of BGP

BGP uses TCP as its transport protocol, which provides connection-oriented reliable delivery. In this way, BGP assumes that its communication is reliable; therefore, it does not need to implement any retransmission or error recovery mechanisms. BGP uses TCP port 179. Two routers speaking BGP form a TCP connection with one another and exchange messages to open and confirm the connection parameters. These two routers are called *peer routers* or *neighbors*.

After the TCP connection is made between peers, full routing tables are exchanged. Because the connection is reliable, BGP routers need to send only incremental updates after the initial exchange of routes. Periodic routing updates are also not required on a reliable link, so triggered updates are used. BGP sends *keepalive* messages, similar to the Hello messages sent by OSPF.

In BGP, there are different kinds of messages that routers send to each other. Routers that are sending messages to each other are said to be *peers*.The route descriptions that are included with these messages are called *attributes*. These attributes control how BGP deals with routes that have been marked with these attributes. Receipt of different types of BGP messages triggers different actions within the BGP process on a router.

BGP compares attributes for like prefixes received from different neighbors. Cisco routers use a decision process that can contain up to 13 steps to pick out the best path to a destination prefix.

On routers running Cisco IOS Software, BGP has a complex series of route characteristics it uses to determine the Path Preference. If you want to learn more, read the document, "BGP Best Path Selection Algorithm," at Cisco.com.

Preventing Routing Loops

BGP sends updates that deal only with that part of the routing table affected by the topology change. This way, changes are sent incrementally, thus keeping update traffic to a minimum.

BGP routers exchange network reachability information or *path vectors,* which are made up of path attributes, including a list of the full path (of BGP AS numbers) that a route should take in order to reach a destination network.

NOTE   BGP allows policy decisions at the AS level to be enforced. This setting of policies, or rules, for routing is known as *policy-based routing*.

The term path vector comes from the fact that BGP routing information carries a sequence of AS numbers. (Public AS numbers are assigned by the Internet Assigned Numbers Authority [IANA], and Private AS numbers are in the 64512 through 65535 range.) An AS_path attribute is the sequence of autonomous system numbers a route has traversed to reach a destination. This AS_path attribute is mandatory, which means it is carried by all BGP updates. The AS-Path attribute is an ordered list of autonomous systems used by BGP to inform the router what networks the traffic to this destination will flow over. In Figure 10-5, you can see how the AS Path tracks the route to reach networks.

Figure 10-5   *Tracking the AS Path of a Route*

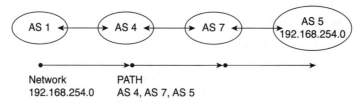

The list of autonomous systems is prepended as the route passes through BGP peers. *Prepending* is the act of adding the AS number to the beginning of the list. BGP routers look at the list to see if it is already a part of the sequence. If so, a loop is assumed, and the BGP router will not accept the route. If not, the AS number is prepended, and the route is forwarded to the next hop. BGP can prepend additional AS numbers to lessen the preference of a route. Figure 10-6 illustrates how BGP prevents routing loops.

Figure 10-6   *Preventing Routing Loops with BGP*

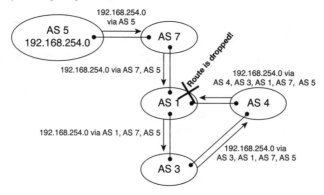

Types of BGP

Yes, this is an interesting heading for this section, and no, do not become overly concerned because the concept is straightforward. Strangely enough, BGP comes in both EGP and IGP flavors; the Internal Border Gateway Protocol (iBGP) can run inside the AS and provide updates for External Border Gateway Protocol (eBGP). This arrangement works out quite well because BGP does not "play nice" with traditional IGPs. iBGP and eBGP are similar to each other. However, there are a number of ways in which iBGP and eBGP operate differently: the propagation of next-hop address, the requirement of full mesh, the assumption of synchronization, propagating Local Preference, and the assumption of directly connected or not.

As illustrated in Figure 10-7, a neighbor connection between two routers can be established within the same AS, in which case BGP is called iBGP. A peer connection can also be established between two routers in different autonomous systems. BGP is then called eBGP.

Figure 10-7 *iBGP and eBGP*

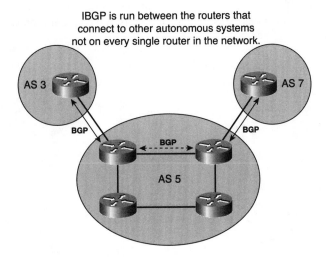

Static Versus Dynamic Injection of Routes

Dynamically injected information can be further divided into the following methods:

- Purely dynamic, where all IGP routes are redistributed into BGP (**redistribute** command)

- Semidynamic, where only certain IGP routes are to be injected into BGP (**network** command)

These methods are considered dynamic because they disappear from BGP advertisements if the routes fail or become unstable.

To statically inject information into BGP, IGP routes (or aggregates) that need to be advertised to other peers are manually defined as static routes and then redistributed into BGP. Static routes disappear from the routing table if the outbound interface or the next-hop address becomes unreachable. This is one of the reasons that static routes to null 0 are popular in BGP because it is an interface that will not go down.

BGP and OSPF Interaction

BGP and OSPF work together in a network to provide reachability (that is, routing) information to routers about networks outside the OSPF network. In a provider network, BGP populates the routing table, with the address of the eBGP neighbor, as the next hop for routes to exterior autonomous systems. OSPF is used within the AS to provide the internal routing throughout the network; BGP and OSPF rely upon each other at various places to provide optimal and effective routing.

All this is interesting conceptually, but take a moment to visualize a possible network that uses both OSPF and BGP and connects to the Internet through two different providers at two different locations. This network topology and configuration is common and is shown in Figure 10-8.

Figure 10-8   *Typical OSPF and BGP Network Implementation*

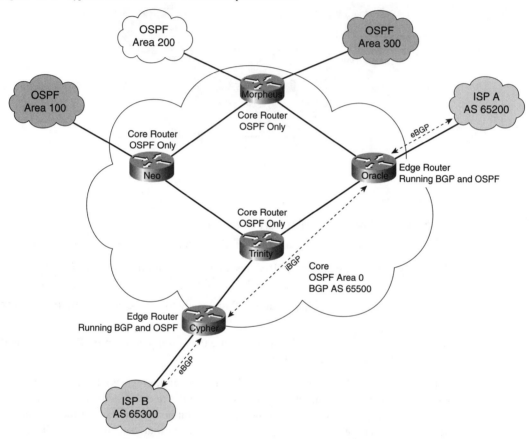

In the figure, the edge routers are the only routers running BGP in the core, and all other routers are running OSPF. The edge routers (Cypher and Oracle) use iBGP to communicate to each other through Router Trinity, which is speaking only OSPF. There is no need for Trinity to use BGP at this point. Routers Cypher and Oracle are then using eBGP to speak to ISPs A and B, respectively.

In a typical network, users need to access the Internet to check the latest golf scores. Because the performance of Tiger Woods is so amazing, the users have two connections to the Internet. OSPF needs to know that there are two ways to get there. (In Chapter 5, "Routing Concepts and Configuration," you learned about the various ways to accomplish this.)

There are many issues with regards to making the network in Figure 10-7 function effectively. BGP is a subject for a whole other book. This chapter highlights some of the issues you need to be aware of when running OSPF and BGP in the same network. Refer to other resources that are more dedicated to BGP. One good resource is the following case study ("BGP Case Studies Section 5") that you can find at Cisco.com at www.cisco.com/warp/public/459/bgp-toc.html.

Routing Dependencies and Synchronization

One of the first caveats to discuss is the requirement that for BGP to advertise a route, such as one within an AS, to other external autonomous systems, BGP must be able to conduct the recursive lookup into the IGP routing table and see those routes. This check-and-balance system helps to ensure reachability and that BGP is advertising networks that can be reached. This requirement of BGP is crucial. Why? Consider that BGP is not and was not designed to run inside a large private enterprise network, rather it is designed for the Internet.

This means that if a user in Australia wants to view information on a web server in Turkey to help plan an upcoming holiday trip, the packets making up the request does not need to flow all the way to Turkey before learning that the network the web server is located on is unavailable. Thus, BGP says that network must be available and seen before it can be advertised to other ISPs, thereby allowing the network to be seen in Australia. Remember, bandwidth is expensive, and you want to serve customers so that they can actually get to their destinations. If the network being accessed by the vacation taker is unavailable, you want those packets to be stopped sooner rather than later by withdrawing the network in question from the global routing table.

BGP keeps its own table for storing BGP information received from and sent to other routers. This table is separate from the IP routing table in the router, similar to how OSPF keeps its routing table separate via the LSDB. The router can be configured to share information between the two tables. You can see in Figure 10-9 that the routing protocols depend on each other to ensure optimal routing results.

Figure 10-9 *OSPF/BGP Dependencies*

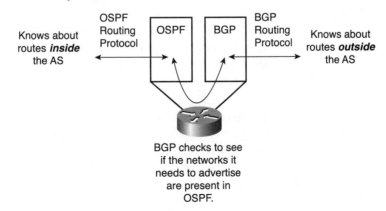

This is the default behavior of BGP and is known as *synchronization*. This can be expressed in a simple operational rule as follows:

> BGP will not advertise routes to external neighbor (via eBGP) destinations that BGP has learned about from an iBGP neighbor unless the IGP (such as OSPF) also knows about them. This is the default behavior of Cisco's BGP code. It is not RFC complaint behavior, and other routers (read Juniper) don't act like this.

BGP must be synchronized with the IGP (OSPF) in the AS in such a way that it waits until the IGP has propagated routing information across your AS before advertising routes to other autonomous systems. The use of synchronization ensures that BGP does not advertise and thus accept data destined to networks that IGP (OSPF) does not yet know about. If it did, the traffic would be black holed (that is, tossed into the bit bucket). To successfully check synchronization with OSPF, BGP performs a two-step process:

1 BGP checks the destination network prefix to see if it knows where to send the packets. BGP looks for the next-hop router, which would be the next hop along the route for the packets to reach the destination network.

2 BGP checks the IGP routing table to see if the destination network prefix exists.

If BGP is successful in these two steps, it announces the network prefix to its eBGP peers. Here's a crucial point to note at this stage:

> In Cisco IOS Software, synchronization is on by default. Cisco decided to keep the synchronization requirement on by default because as the more stub (that is, one connection to the Internet) autonomous systems connect to the Internet, the greater the chances of resulting suboptimal routing. Cisco is relying upon experienced network engineers to know when to shut off synchronization.

You are probably wondering why these synchronization points were emphasized? Synchronization seems like a good thing doesn't it? Remember the "it depends" rule discussed earlier in this book? Synchronization is a great example of this rule, as you will see in the next two sections.

Synchronization Is Good

If you recall, Cisco wanted to make it easy for one connection's autonomous systems to connect to the Internet without causing routing problems. Leaving synchronization on in this situation is good design choice.

NOTE   When you have one connection to the Internet, it is not necessary to use BGP; just have a default route. Nevertheless, for purposes of this demonstration, when synchronization is good, please take this at face value!

When you have one route to the Internet, you should be advertising a default route within your network that points to the Internet. Thus, your routing table will contain all the prefixes for your internal networks that OSPF will know about, as well as a default route to the Internet.

The operational rule of synchronization said that the network must be present in the IGP before it can be advertised. That step is easy to pass in this case because if the network were not present in the IGP (that is, OSPF), there would be larger problems.

The two verification steps of synchronization also need to be passed. The first step is to check and inform the router on the destination prefix's next-hop router. When you have one router connecting to the Internet, it definitely knows what the next hop is for each of the internal prefixes you are using, so another pass.

The second step is to check the IGP to make sure the destination prefix exists. Because there is a default route present in the Internet router, certainly that rule is passed.

This is a simplistic and not realistic view of how and why synchronization can be an effective tool to ensure your routing is optimal and working correctly.

Synchronization Is Bad

Many network engineers feel that synchronization is not necessary and is in fact deprecated. Even though Cisco defaults it to on, numerous recommendations suggest that it be shut off. Specifically, ISPs are strongly encouraged to turn off synchronization, but more on that later. Take a look at the network originally presented in Figure 10-8 and add a route advertisement from ISP B, as shown in Figure 10-10.

Figure 10-10 *Synchronization Is Bad!*

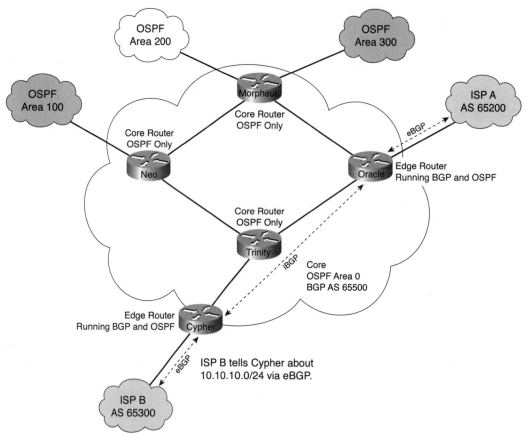

Take the propagation of this advertised network prefix through the process of how BGP will handle it:

1 The advertisement arrives via eBGP to Router Cypher as a network ISP B can reach.

2 Router Cypher advertises this new network via iBGP to Router Oracle. Remember that Router Trinity is running only OSPF, not BGP.

3 Router Oracle advertises this new network to ISP A and traffic destined to 10.10.10.0/24 begins flowing to Router Oracle.

4 A packet comes into Router Oracle destined to the new 10.10.10.0/24 network. Oracle promptly checks its BGP table and sees that the network is there. Oracle promptly forwards the packet to Router Trinity because that is the next hop to reach Router Cypher.

5 Router Trinity receives a packet destined to 10.10.10.0/24, which a network OSPF knows nothing about, so the packet is promptly dropped. This drop is because the IGP and BGP are not synchronized. OSPF was never told about 10.10.10.0/24.

Okay, so most people would say let's just tell OSPF about the network and then everything will work! Although there is a grain of truth to that belief operationally, it is still considered a bad thing to do. Consider the following points:

- BGP is used to connect to the Internet.

- The Internet routing table is over 110,000 routes in size.

- If you redistribute a BGP database of that many routes into OSPF, the results would be disastrous.

- OSPF was designed to operate as an IGP, and thus simply cannot handle the resulting updates and size required for the Internet routing table.

- This type of redistribution can cause IGPs to inform BGP of routes that it just learned from BGP. This is yet another reason you should not redistribute BGP into an IGP.

This is why many ISPs turn off synchronization and instead rely on a fully meshed group of iBGP peers. This would work if you turned on BGP on Router Trinity and allowed it to communicate through iBGP to Routers Oracle and Cypher. The packets then coming from Router Oracle to Trinity would result in Trinity seeing the next-hop address to reach network 10.10.10.0/24 as Router Cypher.

There are two situations where turning synchronization off is okay: if all the routers in the forwarding path are running BGP (this is the situation you have just described) or if the AS is a nontransit AS. There is one more little caveat concerning the integration of routing between OSPF and BGP and that is the next hop, which is discussed in the next section.

Next-Hop Reachability

The IGP's job in a network that has BGP routing enabled is to provide routers with information on the best path to reach that BGP next hop for the destination network. This is called *recursive routing*, or noted as a recursive lookup in the routing table. Determining the next hop is based on the following criterion:

- For eBGP sessions and iBGP sessions, the BGP next hop is the router advertising the route.

- For routes injected into the AS through eBGP, the next hop is carried unaltered into iBGP.

- A recursive lookup is used to find the correct route.

- When using a Frame Relay or ATM hub and spoke topology, the next hop is the address of the router that originated the route. This is a problem for a route that goes from spoke to spoke. Because there is no virtual circuit (VC) between the spokes, the route fails.

Figure 10-11 shows an example of understanding the importance of the next hop in BGP. Having the correct next hop to the destination network is crucial to the proper operation of BGP. If this next hop is not valid and reachable through the IGP, routing will not operate correctly.

Figure 10-11 *BGP Next-Hop Determination*

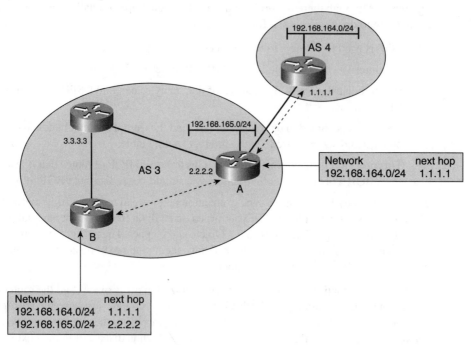

In Figure 10-11, the router in AS 4 advertises network 192.168.164.0/24 to Router A in AS 3 with the next hop set as 1.1.1.1 (the advertising router's interface). BGP has a rule that specifies that the next hop of eBGP-learned routes should be carried without modification into iBGP.

Because of this BGP rule, Router Oracle in AS 3 advertises 192.168.164.0 to its iBGP peer (Router Cypher) with a next hop attribute of 1.1.1.1. As a result, according to Router Cypher, the next hop to reach 192.168.164.0/24 is 1.1.1.1, instead of 2.2.2.2. For that reason, the network configuration must ensure that Router Cypher can reach 1.1.1.1 through an IGP (OSPF). Otherwise, Router Cypher will drop packets destined for 192.168.164.0 because the next-hop address is inaccessible.

TIP   Use the **next-hop-self** command in BGP routers so that all BGP traffic between peers routes through the router that advertised the network, thus maintaining optimal routing at all times.

In this example, you would configure in BGP the **next-hop-self** command between Routers Cypher and Oracle. Thus, when router Oracle advertises 192.168.164.0/24 to Router Cypher, it will set the next hop to reach that network as 2.2.2.2 (Oracle's interface IP address). OSPF knows how to reach 2.2.2.2 through Router Trinity, and this routing would continue to operate properly.

The other big advantage of using **next-hop-self** is that you do not have to put border interface /30s into your IGP. You can just put loopbacks into your IGP, and the BGP next hops will point to the loopbacks.

The next section expands on how OSPF conducts redistribution (as discussed in Chapter 6, "Redistribution," to understand some of the caveats surrounding redistributing OSPF into BGP.

Redistributing OSPF into BGP

By now you should know how bad it is to redistribute BGP into OSPF. Performing redistribution the other way, however, is acceptable and in many cases necessary to ensure the networks found in OSPF are advertised through BGP out to other external destinations— the Internet, for example.

This is an extremely important section, and if you ever plan on doing redistribution between OSPF and BGP, you should definitely read this section and RFC 1403 prior to planning such a move. Remember that the Internet is an ever-changing landscape, with routes appearing and disappearing at the blink of an eye. Redistributing this information into an IGP would cause the IGP routers to have a nervous breakdown trying to keep their routing tables reconciled.

RFC 1403 outlines the behavior of OSPF to BGP redistribution. This RFC defines the various network design specifications and considerations to keep in mind when designing Autonomous System Boundary Routers (ASBRs) that will run BGP with other ASBRs external to the AS and OSPF as its IGP. Within this RFC, you can find some guidelines and recommendations for the exchange of routing tables between OSPF and BGP and vice versa.

TIP   I do not recommend redistributing BGP into OSPF as a permanent situation in a network. I acknowledge that in some limited and temporary circumstances this might be necessary but do not let it become permanent!

RFC 1403 also covers the mapping of routing metrics between BGP and OSPF—this is useful information. This RFC also defines the various network design specifications and considerations to remember when designing ASBRs that run BGP with other ASBRs external to the AS and using OSPF as the IGP.

Now on to the redistribution portion of the discussion. Routes can be filtered during OSPF to BGP redistribution with the help of the **route-map** command. The default behavior is to not redistribute any routes from OSPF into BGP. In other words, the simple **redistribute** command, such as **redistribute ospf 100** under **router bgp 100**, is a bad idea.

Specific keywords such as **internal**, **external**, and **nssa-external** are required to redistribute respective routes. There are four cases of redistributing OSPF routes into BGP discussed in the sections that follow:

- Redistributing OSPF Internal (Intra- and Inter-Area) Routes into BGP
- Redistributing OSPF External (Type 1 and 2) Routes into BGP
- Redistributing both Internal and External Routes into BGP
- Redistributing OSPF NSSA-External Routes into BGP

The network diagram shown in Figure 10-12 applies to the first three examples for discussion.

Figure 10-12 *Redistributing OSPF and BGP*

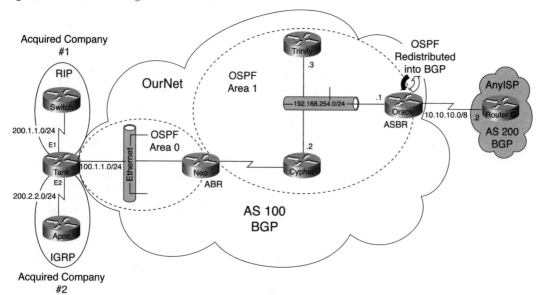

The company you are working for is called "OurNet" and you have currently deployed OSPF as the IGP and BGP (AS100) as the EGP. You just connected the network to your service provider, AnyISP (AS200), and implemented redistribution of OSPF into BGP on router Oracle. However, the AnyISP engineers report they do not see your internal network on their Router ISP_A, as shown by the routing table in Example 10-1.

Example 10-1 *urNet Does Not Appear in ISP's Routing Table*

```
ISP_A#show ip route
Codes: C - connected, S - static, I - IGRP, R - RIP, M - mobile, B - BGP
       D - EIGRP, EX - EIGRP external, O - OSPF, IA - OSPF inter area
       N1 - OSPF NSSA external type 1, N2 - OSPF NSSA external type 2
       E1 - OSPF external type 1, E2 - OSPF external type 2, E - EGP
       i - IS-IS, L1 - IS-IS level-1, L2 - IS-IS level-2, * - candidate default
       U - per-user static route, o - ODR

Gateway of last resort is not set

C    10.0.0.0/8 is directly connected, Serial0
```

The first thing to check is if Router Oracle has learned all the routes, as done in Example 10-2. If it does not know the routes, it could not possibly be expected to tell AnyISP!

Example 10-2 *Oracle's IP Routing Table: All Routes Accounted For*

```
Oracle#show ip route
Codes: C - connected, S - static, I - IGRP, R - RIP, M - mobile, B - BGP
       D - EIGRP, EX - EIGRP external, O - OSPF, IA - OSPF inter area
       N1 - OSPF NSSA external type 1, N2 - OSPF NSSA external type 2
       E1 - OSPF external type 1, E2 - OSPF external type 2, E - EGP
       i - IS-IS, L1 - IS-IS level-1, L2 - IS-IS level-2, ia - IS-IS inter area
       * - candidate default, U - per-user static route, o - ODR
       P - periodic downloaded static route

Gateway of last resort is not set

O E2 200.2.2.0/24 [110/20] via 192.168.254.2, 00:25:53, Ethernet0
O E1 100.1.1.0/24 [110/20] via 192.168.254.2, 00:25:53, Ethernet0
O IA 131.108.1.0/24 [110/20] via 192.168.254.2, 00:25:53, Ethernet0
O 100.1.1.0/24 [110/20] via 192.168.254.1, 00:25:53, Ethernet0
C    192.168.254.0/24 is directly connected, Ethernet0
C    10.0.0.0/8 is directly connected, Serial1
```

Router Oracle sees all the routes so you need to recheck the configuration of Router Oracle in Example 10-3 to see what is happening.

Example 10-3 *Configuration of Router Oracle*

```
hostname Oracle
!
interface Ethernet0
 ip address 192.168.254.1 255.0.0.0
!
interface Serial1
 ip address 10.10.10.1 255.0.0.0
!
router ospf 1
 network 192.168.254.0 0.0.0.255 area 1
!
```

continues

Example 10-3 *Configuration of Router Oracle (Continued)*

```
router bgp 100
 redistribute ospf 1
 neighbor 10.10.10.2 remote-as 200
 !
end
```

As mentioned earlier, the use of keywords must be specified when conducting redistribution. Notice in the highlighted line of Example 10-3 that Cisco IOS Software takes the command, thus leading you to the erroneous conclusion that redistribution will take place.

This caveat is a great concept to be aware of, as many experts like to try and stump people with it.

The following sections look at how to configure redistribution of the various types of OSPF routes listed previously using the different keywords.

Redistributing OSPF Internal (Intra- and Inter-Area) Routes into BGP

Perhaps you do not necessarily want to redistribute the external routes that you know about in the networks of the companies you just acquired, as represented by the RIP and IGRP networks to the far left of Figure 10-12.

In this case, only the OSPF intra-area and inter-area routes are going to be redistributed into BGP. These are the routes that are found in Area 0 (inter-area) and the routes in Area 1 (intra-area).

NOTE   Remember that these designations are how they are viewed from Router Oracle's perspective, and one router's intra-area route is another's inter-area route! It's all a matter of perspective.

To redistribute OSPF intra-area and inter-area routes, use the **internal** keyword along with the **redistribute** command under **router bgp**. Example 10-4 shows the new configuration of Oracle that redistributes only the intra-area route (100.1.1.0/24) and inter-area route (192.168.254.0/24) into BGP.

Example 10-4 *Configuring Redistribution of Intra-Area and Inter-Area Routes into BGP*

```
hostname Oracle
!
interface Ethernet0
 ip address 192.168.254.1 255.0.0.0
 !
interface Serial1
```

Example 10-4 *Configuring Redistribution of Intra-Area and Inter-Area Routes into BGP (Continued)*

```
 ip address 10.10.10.1 255.0.0.0
 !
router ospf 1
 network 192.168.254.0 0.0.0.255 area 1
 !
router bgp 100
 redistribute ospf 1 match internal
 neighbor 10.10.10.2 remote-as 200
 !
end
```

After making the configuration change, Router C starts learning about these two internal OSPF routes from BGP, as shown in Example 10-5.

Example 10-5 *ISP's Routing Table Reveals Discovery of the Inter-Area and Intra-Area Routes Configured for Redistribution into BGP*

```
ISP_A#show ip route
Codes: C - connected, S - static, I - IGRP, R - RIP, M - mobile, B - BGP
       D - EIGRP, EX - EIGRP external, O - OSPF, IA - OSPF inter area
       N1 - OSPF NSSA external type 1, N2 - OSPF NSSA external type 2
       E1 - OSPF external type 1, E2 - OSPF external type 2, E - EGP
       i - IS-IS, L1 - IS-IS level-1, L2 - IS-IS level-2, * - candidate default
       U - per-user static route, o - ODR

Gateway of last resort is not set

B    100.1.1.0.0/24 [20/20] via 10.10.10.1, 00:01:23
B    192.168.254.0/24 [20/0] via 10.10.10.1, 00:01:23
C    10.0.0.0/8 is directly connected, Serial0
```

Redistributing OSPF External (Type 1 and 2) Routes into BGP

Now, instead of redistributing the internal OSPF routes, redistribute just the external routes from the acquired companies. Perhaps, they have good lawyers that negotiated Internet access for their employees; however, employees of the parent company do not have access. Although this might seem a little far-fetched, it could happen and probably has.

Configuring external redistribution is a bit more complicated than internal redistribution. Look at the configuration in Example 10-6, which shows the configuration of external routes for redistribution into BGP on Router Oracle.

During

Example 10-6 *Configuring External Routes for Redistribution into BGP*

```
Oracle(config-router)#redistribute ospf 100 match external ?
  1          Redistribute external type 1 routes
  2          Redistribute external type 2 routes
  external   Redistribute OSPF external routes
```

continues

Example 10-6 *Configuring External Routes for Redistribution into BGP (Continued)*

```
      internal       Redistribute OSPF internal routes
      match          Redistribution of OSPF routes
      metric         Metric for redistributed routes
      nssa-external  Redistribute OSPF NSSA external routes
      route-map      Route map reference
      <cr>


Oracle (config-router)#redistribute ospf 100 match external
Oracle (config-router)#
```

You can select **match external**, which will "automagically" tell the router you want to redistribute all external routes. However, if you want to redistribute only type 1 or perhaps type 2, use the number keyword. Example 10-7 shows the resulting configuration.

After

Example 10-7 *Configuring Type 1 and Type 2 External Routes for Redistribution into BGP*

```
hostname Oracle
!
interface Ethernet0
 ip address 192.168.254.1 255.0.0.0
!
interface Serial1
 ip address 10.10.10.1 255.0.0.0
!
router ospf 1
 network 192.168.254.0 0.0.0.255 area 1
!
router bgp 100
 redistribute ospf 1 match external 1 external 2
 neighbor 10.10.10.2 remote-as 200
!
end
```

Router Oracle's configuration shows **redistribute OSPF 1 match external 1 external 2**; the redistribution configuration command entered was **redistribute ospf 1 match external**. This is normal because OSPF automatically appends "external 1 external 2" in the configuration. It matches both OSPF external 1 and external 2 routes, and it redistributes both routes into BGP as discussed previously, so do not become alarmed when you see something other than what you typed present in the configuration.

After making the configuration change, ISP_A starts learning about these two OSPF external routes from BGP, as shown in Example 10-8.

Example 10-8 *ISP's Routing Table Reveals Discovery of the Type 1 and Type 2 External Routes Configured for Redistribution into BGP*

```
ISP_A#show ip route
Codes: C - connected, S - static, I - IGRP, R - RIP, M - mobile, B - BGP
       D - EIGRP, EX - EIGRP external, O - OSPF, IA - OSPF inter area
       N1 - OSPF NSSA external type 1, N2 - OSPF NSSA external type 2
       E1 - OSPF external type 1, E2 - OSPF external type 2, E - EGP
       i - IS-IS, L1 - IS-IS level-1, L2 - IS-IS level-2, * - candidate default
       U - per-user static route, o - ODR

Gateway of last resort is not set

B    200.1.1.0.0/24 [20/20] via 10.10.10.1, 00:01:33
B    200.2.2.0.0/24 [20/0] via 10.10.10.1, 00:01:33
C    10.0.0.0/8 is directly connected, Serial0
```

Redistributing Both Internal and External Routes into BGP

In this example, you want to configure OSPF to redistribute into BGP both internal and external (type 1 and type 2) routes. This is simple; stack the keywords onto each other as follows and everything will work:

```
Oracle (config-router)#redistribute ospf 100 match internal external
```

Redistributing OSPF NSSA-External Routes into BGP

This is a special case in which only Not-So-Stubby Area (NSSA) routes are redistributed into BGP. This example is similar to how you redistributed only OSPF External (Type 1 and 2) routes into BGP. The only difference is that BGP is now matching NSSA-external routes instead of just external routes. Example 10-9 shows the options possible to redistribute OSPF routes.

During

Example 10-9 *Redistribute OSPF Routes*

```
Oracle(config-router)#redistribute ospf 100 match external ?
  1              Redistribute external type 1 routes
  2              Redistribute external type 2 routes
  external       Redistribute OSPF external routes
  internal       Redistribute OSPF internal routes
  match          Redistribution of OSPF routes
  metric         Metric for redistributed routes
  nssa-external  Redistribute OSPF NSSA external routes
  route-map      Route map reference
  <cr>

Oracle (config-router)#redistribute ospf 100 match external nssa-external
Oracle (config-router)#
```

The automatic assumption you want to redistribute both types 1 and 2 external NSSA routes is made with this configuration example. Again, if you want to specify the specific type you want to redistribute, append the numeric keyword as appropriate.

Conclusions About BGP

So far in this chapter, you have learned about several particular instances of potential issues when routing with OSPF and BGP. There are many more caveats that you should consider when implementing BGP. These caveats are beyond the scope of this book but are so important that you should definitely investigate them.

The next section discusses how OSPF is being used to provide enhancements to some of the new traffic engineering protocols that are sweeping the Internet.

Case Study: BGP

I have talked a lot about the reliance of BGP to the underlying IGP routing and presence of the routes to ensure effective and proper routing is taking place. This case study is courtesy of I-NAP Ltd. (www.i-nap.co.uk), an ISP in the United Kingdom who provides a full range of connectivity services. I helped them resolve this issue, and they have graciously allowed the situation and resulting solution to be included here.

I-NAP and I hope that this case study demonstrates the use of BGP and its operational requirements to help you better understand the concepts presented in this chapter.

Problem Description

When executing a **traceroute**, the path taken is through the level 3 Internet link; this is suboptimal, as shown in the **traceroute** output in Example 10-10.

Example 10-10 traceroute *Output Reveals Suboptimal Path*

```
UK1#traceroute www.linx.net
Type escape sequence to abort.
Tracing the route to www.linx.net (195.66.232.34)
  1 fe1-0-0.gate-L3.london.ix-nap.net (195.50.116.25) [AS 9057] 0 msec 0 msec 0 msec
  2 gigabitethernet1-0.core1.London1.Level3.net (212.187.131.13) [AS 9057] 0 msec 0
msec 4 msec
  3 pos2-0.metro1-londencyh00.London1.Level3.net (212.113.0.113) [AS 9057] 0 msec 0
msec 4 msec
  4 collector.linx.net (195.66.225.254) [AS 702] 0 msec 4 msec 0 msec
  5 www.linx.net (195.66.232.34) [AS 5459] 4 msec *  0 msec
UK1#
```

The expected route to www.linx.net should be through the LINX router (212.54.190.254), as shown in the output of **show ip bgp 195.66.232.34** for the IP Address associated with the

Linx web server (see Example 10-11). As you can see, the UK1 router has a BGP entry for the network in question, yet is it not known through the Linx router, as you would expect.

Example 10-11 show ip bgp *Command Output Shows the Best Path*

```
UK1#show ip bgp 195.66.232.34
BGP routing table entry for 195.66.224.0/19, version 736399
Paths: (3 available, best #2)
  Not advertised to any peer
  9057 5459
    195.50.116.25 from 195.50.116.25 (212.113.2.234)
      Origin IGP, metric 100000, localpref 100, valid, external, ref 2
  5459
    195.66.225.254 from 212.54.190.254 (212.54.190.254)
      Origin IGP, metric 0, localpref 200, weight 200, valid, internal, best, ref 2
  6461 2529 5459
    213.161.64.169 from 213.161.64.169 (208.185.157.253)
      Origin IGP, metric 97, localpref 100, valid, external, ref 2
UK1#
```

The Linx router is directly connected to the Linx peering point, thus the five hops the UK1 router is taking to reach the web server is clearly suboptimal in nature.

You would expect the routing to be optimal as the weight is set to the LINX router (212.54.190.254) as its local preference, and clearly BGP wants to prefer that route as best.

Clearing the BGP neighbors has no effect, though, as the suboptimal routing returns when they resume peering. Example 10-12 shows the **traceroute** results.

Example 10-12 *traceroute Results*

```
UK1#traceroute www.linx.net

Type escape sequence to abort.
Tracing the route to www.linx.net (195.66.232.34)

  1 fe1-0-0.gate-L3.london.ix-nap.net (195.50.116.25) [AS 9057] 0 msec 4 msec 0 msec
  2 gigabitethernet1-0.core1.London1.Level3.net (212.187.131.13) [AS 9057] 0 msec 4
msec 0 msec
  3 pos2-0.metro1-londencyh00.London1.Level3.net (212.113.0.113) [AS 9057] 0 msec 4
msec 0 msec
  4 collector.linx.net (195.66.225.254) [AS 702] 0 msec 0 msec 0 msec
  5 www.linx.net (195.66.232.34) [AS 5459] 0 msec *  0 msec
```

The Linx router has the entry highlighted in Example 10-13 for the network in question.

Example 10-13 *Output of Show BGP*

```
Linx_Rtr>show ip bgp 195.66.232.34
BGP routing table entry for 195.66.224.0/19, version 14874
Paths: (8 available, best #3)
  Advertised to non peer-group peers:
    212.54.190.1 212.54.190.2
```

continues

Example 10-13 *Output of Show BGP (Continued)*

```
       4589 5459
         195.66.225.43 from 195.66.225.43 (195.66.225.43)
           Origin IGP, metric 1, localpref 200, weight 200, valid, external, ref 2
           Community: 367460362 367460366 367461052 743243777 743243786 743243796
       4589 5459
         195.66.224.43 from 195.66.224.43 (195.40.0.93)
           Origin IGP, metric 1, localpref 200, weight 200, valid, external, ref 2
           Community: 367460362 367460366 367461052 743243777 743243786 743243796
       5459
         195.66.225.254 from 195.66.225.254 (195.66.232.254)
           Origin IGP, metric 0, localpref 200, weight 200, valid, external, best, ref 2
       5378 5459
         195.66.224.20 from 195.66.224.20 (213.38.244.241)
           Origin IGP, metric 20, localpref 200, weight 200, valid, external, ref 2
           Community: 352467986 352469274
       2914 5413 5413 5459
         195.66.224.139 from 195.66.224.139 (129.250.0.38)
           Origin EGP, metric 263, localpref 200, weight 200, valid, external, ref 2
       2914 5413 5413 5459
         195.66.224.138 from 195.66.224.138 (129.250.0.9)
           Origin EGP, metric 264, localpref 200, weight 200, valid, external, ref 2
       5378 5459
         195.66.225.20 from 195.66.225.20 (213.38.244.240)
           Origin IGP, metric 20, localpref 200, weight 200, valid, external, ref 2
           Community: 352467986 352469274
       2529 5459
         195.66.224.13 from 195.66.224.13 (195.66.224.13)
           Origin IGP, localpref 200, weight 200, valid, external, ref 2
Linx_Rtr>
```

So all the BGP routes are correct, and clearly BGP wants to prefer the proper route, yet it is not doing so. The assumption that you would make here is that BGP is operating properly, and the root cause of this issue lies somewhere else.

At this point, you should check I-NAP's IGP, which is OSPF (of course) and see what it believes is correct. Remember that because the Linx router is connected to the Linx peering point, the 195.x.x.x network should be seen in the IP routing table because the Linx router has an interface in that subnet.

Checking the IP routing table on the UK1 router reveals that the route is present and being advertised from the Linx router (212.54.190.254), as shown in Example 10-14.

Example 10-14 *Output of Show Ip Route*

```
UK1#show ip route 195.66.232.34
Routing entry for 195.66.224.0/19, supernet
  Known via "bgp 16334", distance 200, metric 0
  Tag 5459, type internal
  Last update from 195.66.225.254 00:48:59 ago
  Routing Descriptor Blocks:
```

Example 10-14 *Output of Show Ip Route (Continued)*

```
  * 195.66.225.254, from 212.54.190.254, 00:48:59 ago
        Route metric is 0, traffic share count is 1
        AS Hops 1

UK1#
```

Looking at the BGP configurations, there is a missing command—yep, you guessed it; the **next-hop self** command is missing from the Linx router's BGP configuration.

From the Linx router's perspective, what is happening in BGP is as follows:

The route is sent from the eBGP peers to the iBGP peers.
The Linx router will not change the next-hop IP address of the route by default unless **next-hop-self** is configured.

Adding the **next-hop self** command into the Linx router and then running another traceroute confirms that the situation has resolved itself, as shown in Example 10-15.

Example 10-15 *Confirming that* **next-hop-self** *Resolves the Issue of Suboptimal Routing*

```
UK1#traceroute www.linx.net

Type escape sequence to abort.
Tracing the route to london.linx.net (195.66.232.34)

  1 linx (212.54.160.247) 0 msec 4 msec 0 msec
  2 collector.linx.net (195.66.225.254) [AS 5459] 0 msec 0 msec 0 msec
  3 london.linx.net (195.66.232.34) [AS 5459] 4 msec *  0 msec
UK1#
```

Alternatively, you could have added the 195.x.x.x subnet into the Linx router's BGP configuration through a **network** statement; though this would work, because you are at a peering point, this method is not allowed.

MPLS and OSPF

This section discusses how OSPF and Multiprotocol Label Switching (MPLS) work together in many of today's more complex internetworks. To facilitate your understanding of how these two rather unique and somewhat different networking technologies interoperate, you most likely should understand the fundamentals of what MPLS is and why it is being deployed.

Background of MPLS

In the early 1990s, the core of the Internet was connected mostly by T1 circuits between various routers with a handful of T3 circuits. This, of course, is a far cry from what the Internet is today, but this was many years ago in Internet time.

There was some benefit to these simpler times. There were only a handful of routers and links to manage and configure. Traffic was manageable, and in the event that some links became congested while others did not, humans manually adjusted the routing parameters to alter the routing sufficiently to lessen the problem. These actions were the first attempts at *traffic engineering,* and they were based on altering routing protocol metrics.

By the mid-1990s, the core of the Internet had grown substantially in size and bandwidth. The projections at that time showed that growth would continue at an unprecedented rate. This was the time just before the dot.com boom when everyone wanted to connect to the Internet and the groundwork for the success of Cisco Systems was being laid.

Unfortunately, not everything was perfect at this time. These growth projections were scary in that the hardware technology needed to actually make the speeds possible and processing that large number of packets per second were not yet envisioned. The routers of that day were not able to keep pace. The level of interconnectivity had increased to such a point that the Internet was truly becoming a vast web of links, routers, switches, and peering points that spanned the globe. In many ways, this was a good thing; however, for those responsible for traffic engineering, changing and altering routing metrics were becoming too complex. A solution was needed. Network scientists and engineers worldwide came together in the Ether (and even sometimes in person) to give birth to several ideas and finally what they touted as the ultimate solution. MPLS was that solution. MPLS takes the best of many technologies that are slowly going way. For example, ATM-like services are available in MPLS to meet the needs for traffic engineering, and MPLS allows for the switching of packets before Layer 3 of the OSI reference model. This means no more route lookups in the huge Internet routing table!

Today, the Internet is a different place, and MPLS is slowly becoming part of it. Stories abound that both shout its benefits and point out its shortcomings. The usefulness of MPLS depends on the needs of your network. (The "it depends" rule surfaces again.) Although MPLS fans and naysayers might balk or nod their heads in agreement, read on to understand why MPLS is not the solution for all our networking problems.

At the time of the development of MPLS, hoards of hardware engineers were at work diligently developing newer and faster technologies to implement in the routers and switches found throughout networks. Yes, these bright individuals beat the problem found in hardware and today some extremely fast network devices are available for use. It is commonly believed that MPLS significantly enhances the forwarding performance of label-switching routers. It is more accurate to say that exact-match lookups, such as those performed by MPLS and ATM switches, have historically been faster than the longest match lookups performed by IP routers. However, recent advances in silicon technology allow ASIC-based route-lookup engines to run just as fast as MPLS or ATM virtual path identifier/virtual circuit identifier (VPI/VCI) lookup engines. Considering that the same ASICs do CEF lookup for both MPLS and IP on the GSR platform, it follows that the speed is indeed, exactly the same.

At the same time, service providers were hard at work laying thousands of miles of optics and cables to meet the upcoming traffic needs as everyone connected to the Internet in a glorious flurry of TCP/IP packets. The dot-coms were here, and if you were not connected or if you were not planning on being connected, surely you were going to be left behind. Cisco stock was splitting every year, and surely the nerds would inherit the riches of the world! Okay, so Bill Gates got rich, but for the majority of us, a funny thing happened.

One day, in a place that has not been identified, someone asked a fundamental business question regarding all this Internet hoopla—"Where are the profits?" The painful realization was that billions of dollars were spent worldwide, investments were made, projections given, but at some point, someone asked to see the profits from all this spending. Pop! As simple as that the bubble burst. Today, the traditional, and might I add *proven*, business model has reasserted itself. These are the days when you make do until you have to upgrade—and even perhaps a bit longer. These are the days you look to technology to save you money, and if it does not, you do not buy. The simple but proven concept of spending money to make a profit is back. What about the Internet? It is still here and still advancing; however, a lot has changed. Gone are many of the companies that built thousands of miles of fiber connections crossing the globe, and those that are left are barely profitable. Many places have excess bandwidth, and although the smart are surviving, the bold and stupid have disappeared from the headlines as we all wonder what will happen next.

What is going on with MPLS? MPLS has not been displaced by faster routers or pushed aside because of easy availability of bandwidth. MPLS is now being looked at to solve some specific networking problems and as a way to enhance services. These enhancements will provide increased profitability for ISPs, and that is key to their success. ISPs need to develop new revenue-generating services; the MPLS forwarding infrastructure can remain the same while new services are built by simply changing the way packets are assigned to a path in MPLS.

For example, packets could be assigned to a label-switched path based on a combination of the destination subnetwork and application type, a combination of the source and destination subnetworks, a specific quality of service (QoS) requirement, an IP multicast group, or a VPN identifier. In this manner, new services can easily be migrated to operate over the common MPLS forwarding infrastructure.

One of the most common scenarios involves companies that want to provide services to many remote offices and yet do not want to build and maintain a unique network that is solely theirs. Businesses now look at the Internet as fast and reliable, so why not use it for business traffic? The nervous and paranoid say there are those dreaded hackers that can read their packets online. More likely, hackers will not deploy a sniffer at the local CO but instead hack your server because you forgot to apply the recent security patch! Some bright person developed the idea of VPNs over the Internet. Companies said they could live without connectivity for a little while and the occasional slow day if it saves them money while increasing productivity and services! Today, companies are connecting offices by the dozen to the Internet and then connecting themselves together through VPNs, so the Internet is saved and MPLS finds a future.

What Is the Benefit of MPLS?

The usefulness of MPLS can be and is a hotly debated topic; however, it offers some benefits and solves some problems that have not yet been addressed by other competing technologies. The advantages and benefits of MPLS can be easily listed as follows:

- **MPLS separates the routing and forwarding planes**—This is a key advantage of MPLS and ensures that it is not tied to a specific L2 or L3 technology.

- **MPLS enables some key applications**—This allows for increased services (and fees), such as video on demand.

- **MPLS provides for Layer 2 integration**—ATM, Frame Relay, Ethernet, it does not matter: MPLS works over them all, which is a great thing because it means you do not have to build a new infrastructure to use it.

- **MPLS allows for traffic engineering and QoS support**—If you have a large customer that wants to make sure their VPNs or video conferencing works over your network, MPLS can support you.

- **MPLS enabled virtual private networks**— fast and even more private VPNs for the security conscious.

- **MPLS solves the hyper-aggregation of IP traffic problems**—In normal IP networks, traffic tends to congregate at one link as many smaller links come together, but MPLS fixes this and allows for specific traffic engineering solutions.

- **MPLS solves the N2 Scalability problem**—IP over ATM fully meshed requires a lot of real circuits, thus increasing your route table size. MPLS label-switching requirements are much smaller.

- **Bandwidth speeds**—Because of Segmentation And Reassembly (SAR) requirements at speeds of OC48 (2.488 Gbps)and greater, ATM currently cannot support them. MPLS allows those speeds via Packet over Sonet.

Why Not IP Routing or ATM Switching?

Perhaps you are wondering how MPLS got to the point where it solves so many of today's tough networking problems. Why not IP Routing or ATM switching?

IP routing has several powerful factors working against it:

- Connectionless environment

- Lacks effective and adaptable traffic engineering services
- Lacks effective quality of service / class of service
- Provides Best Effort Routing services only
- Slow and cumbersome hop-by-hop routing decision

ATM switching also has a few factors and issues that it needs to overcome as well:

- Strong drive toward an IP-based world
- Lack of acceptance in the LAN segment
- Per port costs too high for LAN deployment
- More difficult to manage ATM networks
- Scalability issues (N2 challenge)
- ATM cell tax (percentage of the cell required for ATM operation)
- SAR overhead
- Split control plane (that is, ATM and routing)

The real benefit of MPLS is that it provides a clean separation between routing (that is, control) and forwarding (that is, moving data). This separation allows the deployment of a single forwarding algorithm—MPLS—that can be used for multiple services and traffic types. With MPLS, you need one box instead of two.

Does all this mean that you better run out and deploy MPLS in your network or be left behind? Absolutely not. MPLS is a solution waiting for those that have the need. If you review the problems MPLS solves and benefits associated with it, you can see that currently large complex Enterprise networks are those that need MPLS. Though there are many of those around, there are many medium-sized or smaller networks that will not need to consider MPLS until it becomes affordable or their networks grow extensively. In the end though, it depends on whether MPLS will work for you.

Conventional Best Effort Routing

Before looking at the basics of MPLS, refresh your memory on some aspects of conventional Best Effort Routing. This will enable you to understand the way in which MPLS creates its paths and provides for increased services, with OSPF as the IGP:

- Link-state advertisements (LSAs) are sent from each router to every other router within the IGP area.
- Each router uses these LSAs to build a routing table.
- Forwarding decisions are based on the contents of these routing tables.

A typical network using OSPF will behave as shown in Figure 10-13. When packets are sent with a Destination Address of network A (on the right) for them to get there, proper OSPF will have sent lots of LSAs so that all routing tables are all converged. Remember, there is no guarantee (unless the application is giving you on) that the packets will arrive to the destination and you do not have any control on the path they take.

Figure 10-13 *Conventional Best Effort Routing*

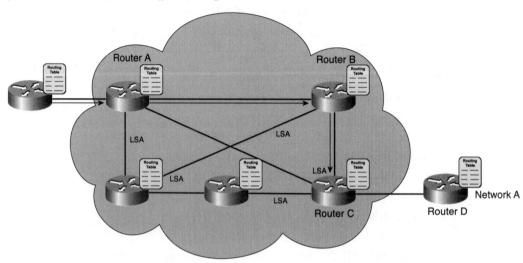

Traffic by default will follow a pattern that is determined in relation to the OSPF metrics along the way. Remember the metrics for OSPF? In Figure 10-13, the traffic pattern would be

> Router A => Router B => Router C => Router D

In Figure 10-13, traffic bound for Network A is flowing across the backbone links between Routers A, B, and C.What happens when the traffic pattern needs to be engineered to bypass Router B?

Rerouting traffic destined for Network A by raising metrics along the path between Routers A and B will have the effect of forcing traffic to use the link between Router A and Router C, as is seen in Figure 10-14.

Rerouting traffic by raising metrics along the path between Routers A and C has the desired effect of forcing the traffic destined for D to use the link between Routers A and C but has the unintended effect of causing traffic destined for Router B to also follow the same path.

Because IGP route calculation was topology driven and based on a simple additive metric such as the link cost, the traffic patterns on the network were not taken into account when OSPF calculated its forwarding table. As a result, traffic was not evenly distributed across the network's links, causing inefficient use of expensive resources. Some links became congested, while other links remained underutilized. This might have been satisfactory in a sparsely connected network, but in a richly connected network (that is, bigger, more thickly meshed and more redundant), it is necessary to control the paths that traffic takes in order to balance loads.

Figure 10-14 *Rerouted Traffic*

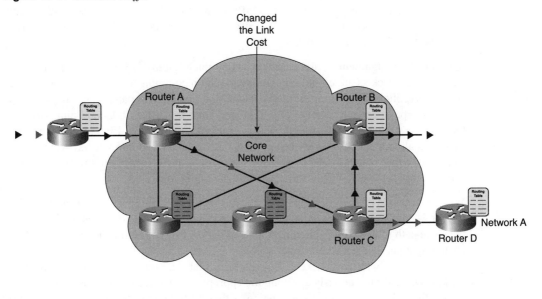

MPLS Overview

As ISP networks became more richly connected, it became more difficult to ensure that a metric adjustment in one part of the network did not cause problems in another part of the network. Traffic engineering based on metric manipulation offers a trial-and-error approach rather than a scientific solution to an increasingly complex problem. IP packets that are placed in the network are examined at each router. The router matches the IP address in each packet with a prefix in the routing table. This computational intensive process is repeated at each router along the path.

MPLS solutions provide network administrators with the tools to fine-tune the network through traffic engineering, allowing system operators to precisely control the consumption of provisioned backbone bandwidth.

MPLS combines the best aspects of high-speed switching with the intelligence of routing. MPLS uses labels to simplify packet forwarding and adds a level of control without affecting performance. Discussion of the formatting and placement of labels occurs a bit later in this chapter, but for now it is only important to know that the labels are used to forward packets.

MPLS label forwarding occurs when

1 The Label Switch Router (LSR) performs a label lookup on an incoming packet, swaps the incoming label for an outgoing label, and forwards the packet to the next LSR along the Label Switch Path (LSP).

2 The Label Edge Router (LER) sits on the entrance and exit of the LSP and respectively adds and removes the MPLS label to and from the packet. The entrance and exit points of the LSP are typically also the same entry/exit points to the core of the MPLS enabled network.

MPLS Label assignment occurs based on a common grouping or Forwarding Equivalency Class (FEC). Packets are classified together based on common attributes, such as source addresses (policy based routing), source and destination address pairs, destination address, and even type of service (ToS) or Differentiated Service (DiffServ) Code Point (DSCP) bits. After a packet is classified, all packets grouped into the same FEC receive similar treatment along the LSP. For MPLS, packets must be classified into "flows" which are categories of packets that need to be treated the same way. A category of this type is termed Forwarding Equivalency Class (FEC) in MPLS terminology.

When a packet is classified, an MPLS LER inserts the MPLS label in between the MAC (Layer 2) and Network (Layer 3) headers. All packets belonging to the same FEC follow the same path in the MPLS domain. A labeled packet is forwarded inside the network by switching it purely based on its label, that is, the Layer 3 header is not examined at all. The core LSRs simply receive packets, read the MPLS labels, swap labels, and forward the packets while simultaneously applying the appropriate service. The MPLS lookup and forwarding scheme allows network engineers the ability to fine-tune and explicitly control packet routing based on source and destination addresses (or other FEC classification criteria), allowing for the seamless introduction of new IP services.

Table 10-1 provides a quick primer on the key terms associated with MPLS.

Table 10-1   *MPLS Terminology*

MPLS Term	Definition
MPLS Domain	A network that has MPLS enabled.
Forwarding Equivalency Class (FEC)	Packets are classified into "flows" or categories. All packets in the same FEC follow the same path in an MPLS domain.
Label	A label is a short, fixed length, locally significant identifier that identifies an FEC.
Label Information Base (LIB)	A database that keeps track of labels and the interfaces they are assigned to. This database is also known as the LFIB where the F is Forwarding because it tells the router where and which label to use to forward a packet.
Label Switch Path (LSP)	A specific path for traffic through an MPLS network. There are two types of LSPs: Topology Driven LSP and Traffic Engineered LSP.
Label Switch Router (LSR)	LSRs forward traffic purely based on labels. This type of MPLS-enabled router has only interfaces that *only* accept MPLS labeled packets. These types of routers are found in the core area of an MPLS domain.

Table 10-1   *MPLS Terminology (Continued)*

MPLS Term	Definition
Label Edge Router (LER)	LERs are on the border of the MPLS domain and traditional IP networks. This type of MPLS enabled router has both MPLS and non-MPLS interfaces, which allow it to accept unlabeled and labeled packets. There are two categories of LERs, which are dependent upon their placement in the MPLS domain—Ingress LER and Egress LER.
Forwarding	A labeled packet is forwarded inside the network based purely on its label.

The next section discusses what an actual MPLS label is and the information that it contains.

Label Structure

The label in MPLS is the heart of the technology. A label is defined in the MPLS Internet Draft as the following:

> A label is a short, fixed length, locally significant identifier that is used to identify a FEC. The label that is put on a particular packet represents the Forwarding Equivalence Class to which that packet is assigned.

Figure 10-15 illustrates the structure of an MPLS label.

Figure 10-15 *Structure of an MPLS Label*

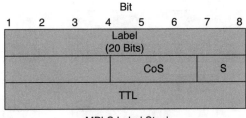

MPLS Label Stack

The fields in the MPLS label can be described as follows:

- The Label field (20-bits) carries the actual value of the MPLS label. The label value gives the necessary information for MPLS to forward the entire packet throughout the MPLS domain.

- The CoS field (3-bits) can affect the queuing and discard algorithms applied to the packet as it is transmitted through the network.

- The Stack (S) field (1-bit) supports a hierarchical label stack so that multiple labels can be stacked together. The presence of this bit is set to a value of one for the last entry in the stack of labels, otherwise the default is zero.

- The TTL (time-to-live) field (8-bits) provides conventional IP TTL functionality.

This section discussed the contents and function of an MPLS label. However, you still need to learn where such labels are placed, and that is the subject of the next section.

Label Placement

Many people say MPLS operates at Layer $2^1/_2$ of the OSI reference model. This is insightful as the placement of the MPLS label is after the Layer MAC Header and before the Layer 3 IP Header. Remember that MPLS is Layer 2-independent—in other words, MPLS can be integrated over any Layer 2 technology. Refer to Figure 10-16 to see where MPLS places the label, which is dependent upon the Layer 2 technology in use.

Figure 10-16 *MPLS Label Placement in a Packet*

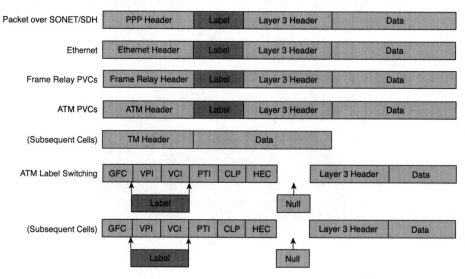

As you can see, regardless of the Layer 2 technology, the MPLS label falls between the Layer 2 header and the Layer 3 header, which is why some people refer to it as Layer $2^1/_2$.

MPLS Addresses Traffic Engineering

MPLS is a technology that was designed to address an ever-changing set of problems. One of the issues MPLS was designed to address that did *not* change was how MPLS can improve the traffic engineering within a network.

Recall that traffic engineering in the world of routing has some serious problems when used in large, complex internetworks. The goal would be to balance (that is, engineer) the traffic across different links to spread the traffic load in such a way that it reduces the congestion levels.

Look at Figure 10-17, which clearly illustrates the more common issues associated with trying to perform traffic engineering. In this figure, the network illustrated has large (OC-12) connections on the edge of the network coming onto a core network that is comprised of smaller bandwidth links (OC-3). Why are the large capacity links not in the core? Although their presence (on the edge) is against accepted best-practice network design, the reality is that is often the way networks are implemented. Networks are designed to make money, and in this case the designers are gambling that not everyone on the edge will be active on the network at the same time. However, they know that many will be (but not all), so they want to perform traffic engineering to spread the traffic load around the network.

Figure 10-17 *Problems with Traffic Engineering*

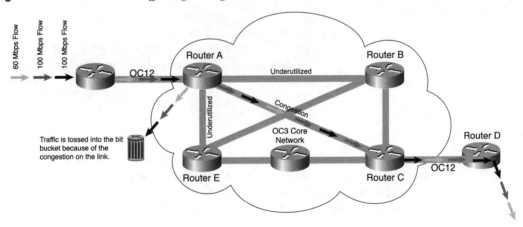

Figure 10-17 shows that the link between Router A and Router C will quickly become congested because it cannot handle the amount of traffic coming into the network from Router A. The issue comes into sharp focus when you learn that the Router A-to-Router B link is underutilized, as is the Router A-to-E link.

The common thinking is that altering the metrics of routing protocols could easily handle this scenario and perhaps in some cases it could. The trouble is that in the real world, the situation is not likely to be so clear and the result is that some links will be underutilized.

The solution to this problem is to use MPLS. When looking at how to relieve the congestion and underutilization, you saw in Figure 10-17 the use of MPLS will clearly assist you. Take a minute to review what you have learned about IP routing and MPLS before demonstrating the solution.

Increasingly, the major role of the IGPs such as OSPF is to give MPLS topology information so that MPLS can set up LSPs. Edge IP routers (LERs in MPLS terminology) can then assign user traffic based on filter criteria, BGP communities, policy routing, and so on.

Thus, you can see that in Figure 10-18 the OSPF network now uses MPLS. Through the classification of inbound traffic into the network, the various MPLS paths can be developed to *spread* the load throughout the network.

Figure 10-18 *MPLS Enabled Traffic Engineering*

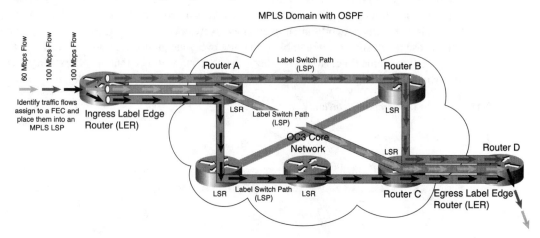

In conventional IP routing using traffic engineering, a router typically considers two packets in the same engineered path unless each router is configured to differentiate between them in some manner. As the packet traverses the network, each router in turn re-examines the packet and assigns it to a traffic engineered path.

In MPLS, the assignment of a particular packet to a FEC is done once, as the packet enters the network. At subsequent hops, there is no further analysis of the packet's header. Rather, the label is added as an index into a table, which specifies the next hop and a new label. The old label is replaced with the new label, and the packet is forwarded to its next hop.

Looking up the Label Path

The label lookup procedure consists of finding an exact match, which is significantly less complex than looking for the longest prefix match like conventional IP routing does. Label switching has a number of advantages over conventional Layer 3 forwarding:

- Because a packet is assigned to a FEC when it enters the network, the ingress LSR may use, in determining the assignment, any information it has about the packet, even if that information cannot be gleaned from the network layer header. For example, packets arriving on different ports might be assigned to different FECs. Conventional forwarding, on the other hand, can consider only information, which travels with the packet in the packet header.

- Another advantage of MPLS label switching is that it can be done by switches that are capable of doing label lookup and replacement but are either not capable of analyzing the network layer headers or are not capable of analyzing the network layer headers at adequate speed.

- The identity of a packet's ingress router does not travel with the packet. A packet that enters the network at a particular router can be labeled differently than the same packet entering the network at a different router. As a result, forwarding decisions that depend on the ingress router can be easily made. This cannot be done with conventional forwarding.

- The considerations that determine how a packet is assigned to a FEC can become increasingly complicated, without any impact at all on the transit LSRs that merely forward labeled packets.

- Finally, the way labels are assigned and the capability to carry a stack of labels attached to the packet. Simple unicast IP routing does not use the label stack, but other MPLS applications rely heavily on it. Such applications are traffic engineering, virtual private networks, fast rerouting around link failures, and so on. On some networks, all traffic, including normal IP, is label switched to hide hops and enable TE for all traffic. L3 and Global Crossing are good examples.

Put this all together in Figure 10-19 and trace the path of a packet through an MPLS network to see how labels are assigned, and so forth. As the packet enters the network, it is first classified and then assigned to a label applicable to the LSP to reach its destination. As the packet travels throughout the network, the label changes and is swapped around until the egress router removes the MPLS label and again uses the Destination IP Address to determine how it should be routed.

The next section discusses a sample network where OSPF will be configured. Then you use MPLS as well within the network.

Figure 10-19 *MPLS in Action*

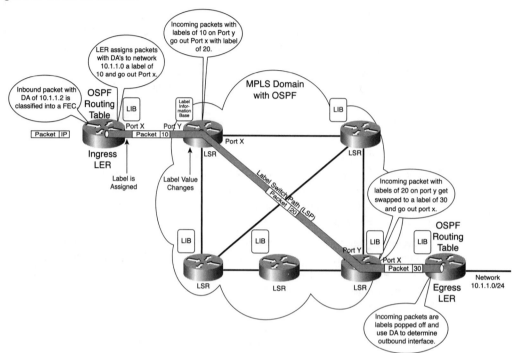

Configuring OSPF and MPLS

An MPLS network is commonly a backbone network composed of MPLS-enabled routers called LSRs. Generally, the network consists of a core LSR with an edge LSR responsible for applying labels to packets. In combination, these routers take on the roles of classifying packets, assigning them to a label path and switching as needed.

In order to properly set up MPLS in an OSPF network, you must first make some assumptions and take some steps. The setup mechanism of an MPLS network is as follows:

- Routing tables of the different LSRs are computed using an IGP. A link-state protocol such as OSPF is used to deploy MPLS Traffic Engineering. OSPF provides the underlying reachability information upon which MPLS builds the paths.

- A label distribution protocol (LDP) advertises the bindings between routes and labels. These bindings essentially map a network to a Label Switch Path (LSP). Recall in Figure 10-19 that to reach a destination network, label 10 was first used on the ingress LER—this is what is happening here.

These bindings are checked against the routing table. If the route (prefix/mask and next hop) learned through the LDP matches the route learned through OSPF in the routing table, an entry is created in the label forwarding information bases (LFIB) on the LSR. Remember the LFIB is just another term for LIB.

Until this point, you have learned about how MPLS operates in general terms. The way in which Cisco Systems has actually implemented MPLS is the next topic of discussion along with coverage of some of the steps it takes to forward a packet in their implementation of MPLS. The LSR uses the following steps to forward a packet:

1 The edge LSR receives an unlabeled packet, the Cisco Express Forwarding (CEF) table is checked, and a label is imposed on the packet if needed. This LSR is called the *ingress LSR*.

2 Upon the arrival of a labeled packet at the incoming interface of a core LSR, the LFIB provides the outgoing interface and the new label (number) that will be associated with the outgoing packet. This process is repeated as the packet flows through the MPLS domain until it is ready to exit.

3 The router before the last LSR (the penultimate hop) pops the label and transmits the packet without the label. The last hop is called the *egress LSR*.

NOTE   The penultimate hop is the last LSR to remove, or "pop," labels on packets in an MPLS network and then forward the unlabeled packets to the egress LSR.

Figure 10-20 illustrates this network setup.

Configuring MPLS

This configuration for this example was developed and tested using the software and hardware versions of Cisco IOS Software Releases 12.0(11)S and 12.1(3a)T on Cisco 3600 routers:

Step 1   Set up your network as discussed in this book using OSPF. Remember that MPLS needs a standard IP connection in order to establish forwarding bases to track the labels.

Step 2   Ensure that OSPF is working correctly and complete connectivity exists in your network. These commands are underlined in the configurations in Example 10-16.

Step 3   Enable **ip cef** (for better performances, use **ip cef distributed** when available) in the global configuration mode (shown as shaded in the configurations in Example 10-16).

Step 4   Enable **mpls ip** on each interface (shown as shaded in the configurations in Example 10-16).

Figure 10-20 *Basic Cisco MPLS Network with OSPF*

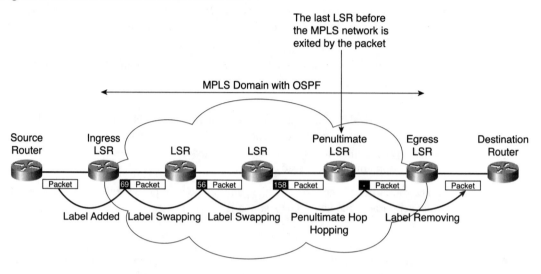

<table>
<tr><td>**NOTE**</td><td>The LSRs must have (up) Loopback interfaces with an address mask of 32 bits, and these interfaces must be reachable through the global IP routing table.</td></tr>
</table>

Example 10-16 details the configurations of the core routers in the OSPF network with MPLS enabled, as shown in Figure 10-21.

Figure 10-21 *OSPF Network with MPLS Enabled*

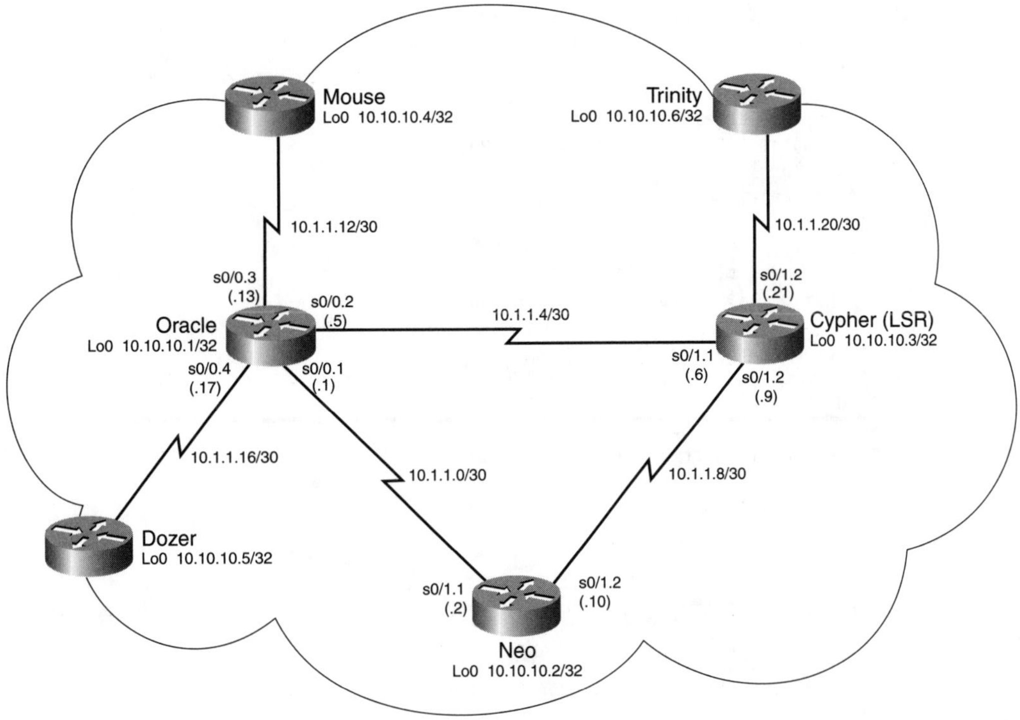

Example 10-16 *MPLS Configurations in the OSPF Network*

```
Cypher
Current configuration:
!
version 12.0
!
hostname Cypher
!
ip cef
!
interface Loopback0
 ip address 10.10.10.3 255.255.255.255
!
interface Serial0/1
 encapsulation frame-relay
!
interface Serial0/1.1 point-to-point
 ip address 10.1.1.6 255.255.255.252
 mpls ip
 frame-relay interface-dlci 301
!
```

continues

Example 10-16 *MPLS Configurations in the OSPF Network (Continued)*

```
 interface Serial0/1.2 point-to-point
  ip address 10.1.1.9 255.255.255.252
  mpls ip
 !
 interface Serial0/1.3 point-to-point
  ip address 10.1.1.21 255.255.255.252
  mpls ip
  frame-relay interface-dlci 306
 !
 router ospf
   network 10.1.1.0 0.0.0.255 area 9
   network 10.10.10.0 0.0.0.255 area 9
 !
 ip classless
 !
 end
```
```
Neo
Current configuration:
 !
 version 12.1
 !
 hostname Neo
 !
 ip cef
 !
 interface Loopback0
  ip address 10.10.10.2 255.255.255.255
 !
 interface Serial0/1
  encapsulation frame-relay
 !
 interface Serial0/1.1 point-to-point
  ip address 10.1.1.2 255.255.255.252
  mpls ip
  frame-relay interface-dlci 201
 !
 interface Serial0/1.2 point-to-point
  ip address 10.1.1.10 255.255.255.252
  mpls ip
  frame-relay interface-dlci 203
 !
 ip classless
 !
 router ospf
   network 10.1.1.0 0.0.0.255 area 9
   network 10.10.10.0 0.0.0.255 area 9
 !
 end
```
```
Oracle
Current configuration : 2366 bytes
 !
 version 12.1
 !
 hostname Oracle
```

Example 10-16 *MPLS Configurations in the OSPF Network (Continued)*

```
!
ip cef
!
interface Loopback0
 ip address 10.10.10.1 255.255.255.255
!
interface Serial0/0
 encapsulation frame-relay
!
interface Serial0/0.1 point-to-point
 ip address 10.1.1.1 255.255.255.252
 mpls ip
 frame-relay interface-dlci 102
!
interface Serial0/0.2 point-to-point
 bandwidth 512
 ip address 10.1.1.5 255.255.255.252
 mpls ip
 frame-relay interface-dlci 103
!
interface Serial0/0.3 point-to-point
 ip address 10.1.1.13 255.255.255.252
 mpls ip
 frame-relay interface-dlci 104
!
interface Serial0/0.4 point-to-point
 ip address 10.1.1.17 255.255.255.252
 mpls ip
 frame-relay interface-dlci 105
!
!
router ospf
   network 10.1.1.0 0.0.0.255 area 9
   network 10.10.10.0 0.0.0.255 area 9
!
ip classless
!
end
```

Verifying OSPF and MPLS Operation

It is important to verify the operation of OSPF because OSPF must be fully converged to allow MPLS to operate correctly. To illustrate this sample configuration, look at a particular destination, for example, 10.10.10.4 (loopback interface of router Mouse) on the Cypher LSR. First, check the IP route for this destination in the IP routing table, as shown in Example 10-17.

Example 10-17 *Verifying Operation*

```
Cypher#show ip route 10.10.10.4
Routing entry for 10.10.10.4/32
  Known via "ospf 9", distance 110, metric 391, type intra area
  Redistributing via ospf 9
  Last update from 10.1.1.5 on Serial0/1.1, 00:05:34 ago
  Routing Descriptor Blocks:
  * 10.1.1.5, from 10.10.10.1, 00:05:34 ago, via Serial0/1.1
      Route metric is 391, traffic share count is 1
```

Router Cypher does indeed know how to get to Router Mouse through OSPF. To check that CEF is working properly and that tags will be swapped correctly, look at the output in Example 10-18.

Example 10-18 *Verifying CEF Operation and Tag Swapping*

```
Cypher#show ip cef 10.10.10.4 detail
10.10.10.4/32, version 154, cached adjacency to Serial0/1.1
0 packets, 0 bytes
  tag information set
    local tag: 20
    fast tag rewrite with Se0/1.1, point2point, tags imposed {22}
  via 10.1.1.5, Serial0/1.1, 0 dependencies
    next hop 10.1.1.5, Serial0/1.1
    valid cached adjacency
    tag rewrite with Se0/1.1, point2point, tags imposed {22}
```

The next step is to ensure that MPLS also knows the proper path to take. The MPLS forwarding table is the label-switching equivalent of the IP routing table for standard IP routing. It contains incoming and outgoing labels and descriptions of the packets. You can check it using the **show mpls forwarding-table** command, as shown in Example 10-19.

Example 10-19 *Displaying the MPLS Forwarding Table*

```
Cypher#show mpls forwarding-table
Local  Outgoing    Prefix          Bytes tag  Outgoing   Next Hop
tag    tag or VC   or Tunnel Id    switched   interface
16     Untagged    6.6.6.7/32      0          Se0/1.3    point2point
17     Pop tag     10.1.1.12/30    0          Se0/1.1    point2point
18     Pop tag     10.10.10.1/32   0          Se0/1.1    point2point
19     Pop tag     10.10.10.6/32   782        Se0/1.3    point2point
20     22          10.10.10.4/32   48         Se0/1.1    point2point
21     21          10.10.10.5/32   182        Se0/1.1    point2point
22     Pop tag     10.1.1.16/30    0          Se0/1.1    point2point
```

Example 10-20 shows how to display MPLS forwarding table details.

Example 10-20 *Displaying the MPLS Forwarding Table: Detailed Information*

```
Cypher#show mpls forwarding-table 10.10.10.4 32 detail
Local  Outgoing    Prefix            Bytes tag  Outgoing   Next Hop
tag    tag or VC   or Tunnel Id      switched   interface
20     22          10.10.10.4/32     48         Se0/1.1    point2point
            MAC/Encaps=4/8, MTU=1520, Tag Stack{22}
            48D18847 00016000
            No output feature configured
       Per-packet load-sharing, slots: 0 1 2 3 4 5 6 7 8 9 10 11 12 13 14 15
```

When using this command, MPLS label is referred to as a "tag." This is because Cisco first called MPLS Tag Switching, and the Cisco IOS Software CLI engineers have not yet caught up, so do not let this confuse you. The label bindings are the labels associated with a particular destination, and you can see them using one of the commands in Example 10-21 (depending on what Cisco IOS Software release and which label distribution protocol you are using).

Example 10-21 *Displaying MPLS Label Bindings*

```
Cypher#show mpls ldp bindings 10.10.10.4 32
   10.10.10.4/32, rev 77
           local binding:  label: 20
           remote binding: lsr: 10.10.10.1:0, label: 22
           remote binding: lsr: 10.10.10.6:0, label: 24

Cypher#show tag-switching tdp bindings 10.10.10.4 32
   tib entry: 10.10.10.4/32, rev 77
           local binding:  tag: 20
           remote binding: tsr: 10.10.10.1:0, tag: 22
           remote binding: tsr: 10.10.10.6:0, tag: 24
```

Labels for each forwarding class have been established at each LSR, even if they are not on the preferred (shortest) path. In this case, a packet destined to 10.10.10.4/32 can go by 10.10.10.1 (with label 22) or by 10.10.10.6 (with label 24). The LSR chooses the first solution because it is the shortest one. This decision is made using the standard IP routing table (which in this case has been built using OSPF).

That is all it takes to deploy simple MPLS within an OSPF network. The commands shown allow you to perform some basic functionality checks and to see the routes in both OSPF and MPLS.

Summary

This chapter discussed how OSPF as an IGP routing protocol interacts with other protocols. The most widely used protocol is BGP, which connects many networks together and to the Internet. The use of the MPLS is increasing; the many problems affiliated with standard IP routing that MPLS addresses and resolves was discussed. However, there is reliance on the part of both of these protocols on OSPF; therefore, ensuring the effective operation and design of OSPF is a crucial piece of any network.

PART IV

Additional OSPF Resources

Overview of the OSPF RFCs

Teamwork: If everyone is moving forward together, then the success takes care of itself.—Successories

This appendix discusses in detail the background and evolution of the OSPF protocol by tracing the Request for Comments (RFCs) relating to OSPF. The functional environment of OSPF is of great importance in order to understand the workings of the protocol and design of a network in which it will operate properly. In the real world, you might need this information because you are

- Responsible for testing OSPF interoperability between equipment manufacturers
- Studying for advanced certifications
- Writing an actual OSPF code implementation
- Troubleshooting a possible bug
- Writing a book, white paper, or teaching
- Developing or writing code for a router or UNIX platform

From the established beginnings of OSPF, the evolution and modifications applied to OSPF can be traced through the RFCs. Each RFC relating directly and indirectly to the protocol is summarized and discussed as needed in this appendix.

Overview of OSPF-Related RFCs

To properly reference the technical standards used in the design and evolution of OSPF, each of them are briefly discussed in chronological order as they were standardized by the IETF.

The following is a list of the RFCs that have been published by the IETF relating to the OSPF protocol. Each RFC contains a brief summary of its contents and purpose. Furthermore, the tracking of the RFC evolution includes information on those that are current and those that have been made obsolete. This enables you to understand where you can go for additional reading or research. Figure A-1 provides a timeline of the development and evolution of OSPF and is a great reference to see how OSPF has grown over the years to become the most popular Interior Gateway Protocol (IGP) in use today.

Figure A-1   *OSPF Evolution*

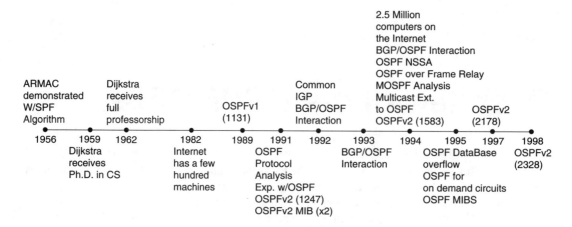

- RFC 1131: *OSPF Specification Version 1* (J. Moy, Oct. 1989)

- RFC 1245: *OSPF Protocol Analysis* (J. Moy, July 1991)

- RFC 1246: *Experience with the OSPF Protocol* (J. Moy, July 1991)

- RFC 1247: *OSPF Version 2* [obsoletes 1131] (J. Moy, July 1991)

- RFC 1248: *OSPF Version 2 Management Information Base* (F. Baker & R. Coltun, July 1991)

- RFC 1252: *OSPF Version 2 Management Information Base* [obsoletes 1248] (F. Baker & R. Coltun, July 1991)

- RFC 1253: *OSPF Version 2 Management Information Base* [obsoletes 1252] (F. Baker & R. Coltun, Aug. 1991)

- RFC 1364: *BGP OSPF Interaction* [obsoletes 1247 and 1267] (K. Varadhan, Sept. 1992; IAB; L. Chapin, Oct. 1992)

- RFC 1370: *Applicability Statement for OSPF* (IAB; L. Chapin, Oct. 1992)

- RFC 1371: *Choosing a "Common IGP" for the IP Internet* (IESG; P. Gross, Oct. 1992)

- RFC 1403: *BGP OSPF Interaction* [obsoletes 1364] (K. Varadhan, Jan. 1993)

- RFC 1583: *OSPF Version 2* [obsoletes RFC1247] (J. Moy, March 1994)

- RFC 1584: *Multicast Extensions to OSPF* (J. Moy, March 1994)

- RFC 1585: *MOSPF: Analysis and Experience* (J. Moy, March 1994)

- RFC 1586: *Guidelines For Running OSPF Over Frame Relay Networks* (O. deSouza and M. Rodriguez, March 1994)

- RFC 1587: *The OSPF NSSA Option* (V. Fuller & R. Coltun, March 1994)

- RFC 1745: *BGP4/IDRP for IP-OSPF Interaction* (K. Varadhan, S. Hares, Y. Rekhter, Dec. 94)
- RFC 1765: *OSPF Database Overflow* (J. Moy, March 1995)
- RFC 1793: *Extending OSPF to Support Demand Circuits* (J. Moy, April 1995)
- RFC 1850: *OSPF Version 2 Management Information Base* [obsoletes 1253] (F. Baker & R. Coltun, Nov. 1995)
- RFC 2178: *OSPF Version 2* [obsoletes 1583] (J. Moy, July 1997)
- RFC 2328: *OSPF Version 2* [obsoletes 2178] (J. Moy, April 1998)

The discussion of the RFCs is somewhat brief and limited when the standard allows for an easy summary of its contents. The importance of this information is to show you how OSPF evolved. If you need, verify correct operation of the protocol, the RFCs are the standards, and the implementation either complies to the standard or it does not. If you require further information or want to read an RFC in its entirety, refer to the following websites for locations of the various RFCs:

www.ietf.org
www.internic.net
www.cisco.com/warp/public/459/index.shtml
www.rfc-editor.org
www.ccprep.com/resources/RFCs/index.asp

The next step is to begin reviewing the individual RFCs chronologically. It is always good to start at the beginning as it gives you a sense of history, even if some of the applications therein are no longer viable.

RFC 1131: OSPF Specification

First published back in 1989, RFC 1131 was the first RFC that introduced OSPF to the networking community. There is not a lot to gain by discussing this RFC because it has been rendered obsolete several times over. However, this is where OSPF began and consider that this was barely over 10 years ago.

RFC 1245: OSPF Protocol Analysis

OSPF version 1 was published in RFC 1131 on October 1, 1989. Between that time and the release of this RFC in July 1991, OSPF version 2 was developed but had not yet become a standard. The Internet Architecture Board (IAB) and the Internet Engineering Steering Group (IESG) required two reports in order for OSPF version 2 to advance to Draft Standard Status. This RFC and the next one (RFC 1246) summarize the key features of OSPF version 2. In addition, it analyzes how the protocol will perform and scale in the Internet.

The requirements of this RFC are briefly summarized in the following list. The remaining sections of the RFC document how OSPF version 2 satisfies these requirements:

- What are the key features and algorithms of the protocol?

- How much link bandwidth, router memory, and router CPU cycles does the protocol consume under normal conditions?

- For these metrics, how does the usage scale as the routing environment grow? This should include topologies at least an order of magnitude larger than the current environment.

- What are the limits of the protocol for these metrics (that is, when will the routing protocol break)?

- For which networking environments is the protocol well suited, and for which is it not suitable?

These requirements are actually exceptional questions that help determine the operating specifications of the protocol within a production environment.

RFC 1246: Experience with the OSPF Protocol

This RFC is the second of two reports on the OSPF protocol version 2. These reports are required by the IAB/IESG for an Internet routing protocol to advance to Draft Standard.

The requirements of this RFC are briefly summarized in the following list. The remaining sections of the RFC document show how OSPF version 2 satisfies these requirements:

- The specification for the routing protocol must be well written so that independent, interoperable implementations can be developed solely based on the specification. For example, it should be possible to develop an interoperable implementation without consulting the original developers of the routing protocol.

- A Management Information Base (MIB) must be written for the protocol. The MIB must be in the standardization process but does not need to be at the same level of standardization as the routing protocol. From these MIB definitions, SNMP can be used to determine the operation of OSPF.

- The security architecture of the protocol must be set forth explicitly. The security architecture must include mechanisms for authenticating routing messages and might include other forms of protection.

- Two or more interoperable implementations must exist. At least two must be written independently.

- There must be evidence that all features of the protocol have been tested, running between at least two implementations. This must include that all the security features have been demonstrated to operate and that the mechanisms defined in the protocol actually provide the intended protection.

- There must be significant operational experience. This must include running in a moderate number of routers configured in a moderately complex topology and must be part of the operational Internet. All significant features of the protocol must be exercised. In the case of an IGP, both interior and exterior routes must be carried (unless another mechanism is provided for the exterior routes). In the case of an Exterior Gateway Protocol (EGP), it must carry the full complement of exterior routes.

The information presented in this RFC was compiled through a variety of sources. Because many of the goals and examples of the RFC require direct knowledge of the protocols operation, if you require further information, refer to the complete document.

RFC 1247: OSPF Version 2

In RFC 1247, certain configurations of the OSPF virtual links might cause routing loops. To correct this problem, a new bit has been added, called bit "V," to the routers' links advertisement. A new algorithm parameter has been added to the OSPF area structure, which indicates if the area supports virtual links. New calculations are to be performed only by the area border routers, which examine all the summary links.

In RFC 1247, an OSPF router cannot originate separate autonomous system (AS) external link advertisements for two networks that have the same IP address but different subnet masks. The link-state ID settings have been altered to allow the host bit portion of the network address to also be set.

The metric, *LSInfinity*, can no longer be used in router link advertisements to indicate unusable links. By doing this, it removes any possible confusion within an OSPF area about which links are reachable. In addition, it also assists MOSPF.

A lot more from this RFC needs to be discussed because it has been replaced by RFC 2328.

RFC 1248: OSPF Version 2 Management Information Base

This RFC defines the experimental portion of the MIB. Specifically, it defines objects for managing OSPF version 2 via SNMP. Additional information regarding the content of this RFC will not be provided because it quickly became obsolete twice through the publication of RFCs 1252 and 1253, respectively.

RFC 1252: OSPF Version 2 Management Information Base

This RFC defines the experimental portion of the MIB. Specifically, it defines objects for managing OSPF version 2. This RFC replaced RFC 1248, which contained some minor errors in referring to "experimental" and "standard-mib." This demonstrates that, although authors try hard and even have excellent technical and peer reviewers, errors do happen. Additional information regarding the content of this RFC is not provided, as it quickly became obsolete after the introduction of RFC 1253.

RFC 1253: OSPF Version 2 Management Information Base

This RFC defines the experimental portion of the MIB. Specifically, it defines objects for managing OSPF version 2. This memo replaces RFC 1252, which contained an error in the "standard-mib" number assignment in Section 5.

This RFC discusses network management and which RFCs were used as the basis for defining the new MIB objects associated with OSPF. A thorough discussion is then presented so that you can fully comprehend the standards of the MIBs implemented with OSPF. The entire OID structure is provided in the ASN.1 format as well. This makes the OSPF MIB implementation extremely easy for programmers to code and for easy data retrieval by network managers or a network management system.

RFC 1364: BGP OSPF Interaction

This RFC defines the various network design specifications and considerations to keep in mind when designing Autonomous System Border Routers (ASBRs) that will run BGP with other ASBRs external to the AS and OSPF as its IGP. Within this RFC, you can find some guidelines and recommendations for the exchange of routing tables between OSPF and BGP and vice versa.

TIP   Please be aware that I never recommend redistributing BGP into OSPF as a permanent situation in a network. I acknowledge that in some limited and temporary circumstances this might be necessary but don't let it become permanent!

The mapping of routing metrics between BGP and OSPF is also covered, and this is a useful reference. This RFC also defines the various network design specifications and considerations to consider when designing ASBR that will run BGP with other ASBRs external to the AS and OSPF as its IGP.

RFC 1370: Applicability Statement for OSPF

This is probably one of the few RFCs that actually seems to encourage comments and suggestions. The purpose of this RFC was driven by the requests of users and vendors who wanted IP routers to have the capability to "interoperate" through the use of an IGP. However, this RFC is rather out of date; although, it is useful for reference if you write OSPF code because it is kind of a how-to guide for OSPF coding.

RFC 1371: Choosing a "Common IGP" for the IP Internet

I am often asked, "Which routing protocol should I use in my network?" or "Why should I choose OSPF as my IGP?" This RFC provides some excellent answers to these questions and is worth reading if you are involved in network design or implementation. The authors of this RFC did an excellent job in providing a summary regarding the business case and relevance of such an RFC. They provided the rationale behind making an overwhelming endorsement of OSPF as the IGP of choice for IP networks.

RFC 1403: BGP OSPF Interaction

This RFC is a republication of RFC 1364 to correct some editorial problems. See the RFC 1364 entry for a review of its contents and applicability.

RFC 1583: OSPF Version 2

This RFC is similar to RFC 1247, which it deprecates. In fact, they are backward-compatible and will interoperate with each other. The differences between them involve OSPF virtual links and some enhancements and clarifications, both minor in nature.

Some of the more general changes that were not discussed in detail but are mentioned and discussed in the RFC are the following: TOS encoding updated, flushing anomalous network links advertisements, summarizing routes into stub areas, summarizing routes into transit areas, and a variety of small changes.

At this point in OSPFs evolution, it has been five years since its inception. In this RFC, you see a more mature and advanced routing protocol taking shape in the form of OSPF v2.

RFC 1584: Multicast Extensions to OSPF

Implementations of OSPF up until this RFC supported only Unicast traffic, which is when a message is sent to a single network destination, as opposed to multicast, which is when a message is sent to a section of network addresses.

During the time of the writing of this RFC (1993–1994, which coincided with the Internet and network growth boom), the need to broadcast packets using the multicast technique was required; therefore, this RFC was developed.

This RFC is extremely detailed and is over 100 pages long, allowing the complete detailing of the features and modification necessary for the deployment of the multicast feature. It is also within this RFC that a new acronym was developed—MOSPF. This new acronym stands for Multicast Open Shortest Path First (MOSPF), which allowed engineers to intelligently reference the difference between routers running OSPF using Unicast and those running the new OSPF Multicast implementation.

By implementing this new standard, OSPF gained the capability to forward multicast packets from one IP network to another. A new Link-State Advertisement (LSA) is used to determine the exact location of all the autonomous system's members. This RFC provides the information necessary to understand the operation of this new feature and its specific LSA, the group-membership-LSA. Also presented is how the link-state database operates to include the building, pruning, and caching of routes.

A potential area of concern was seen as a result of this new feature. When OSPF forwards multicasts between areas, incomplete routes are built; this might lead to routing inefficiency. To correct that problem, OSPF summary link advertisements or OSPF AS external link advertisements can approximate the neighbors needed for routing. The RFC provides a good description of this issue and the resulting methodology needed to compensate.

Discussion is provided on the compatibility between network devices running MOSPF and original Unicast implementations of OSPF. This includes some of the issues surrounding a network operation if this mixed topology were put in place. You can find additional practical information on this subject in RFC 1585, *MOSPF: Analysis and Experience*.

RFC 1585: MOSPF: Analysis and Experience

This RFC immediately followed the 100+ page RFC 1584 that fully detailed all relevant information regarding the ability of allowing OSPF to perform multicasting. This RFC is rather short and was written to fulfill the requirements imposed by the IETF Internet Routing Protocol Standardization Criteria as detailed in RFC 1264.

This RFC provides excellent justification on why it was written by providing a brief discussion surrounding the basic operation of MOSPF and how it uses the Internet Group Management Protocol (IGMP) to monitor multicast group membership. This information is retrieved from the LAN and then forwarded out by the router by the OSPF flooding protocol through the use of the new group-membership-LSA. The specific benefits that result from this process and detailed operation are provided.

The six primary characteristics of the multicast datagram's path are also provided, as well as some of the more interesting miscellaneous features.

The RFC further details the testing the author conducted and how MOSPF was implemented during these tests. Further discussion is provided on the scaling characteristics of MOSPF and some of the known difficulties surrounding it.

NOTE   Cisco routers do not currently support MOSPF because of scaling issues. At least that was the initial reason provided by Cisco when this book was first published. However, it is more likely that MOSPF is not currently supported because of PIM's capability to work with any IGP—OSPF, IS-IS, and so on. Allowing two different proposals in one area of technology is consistent with the observation that the ultimate test of a standard is whether it is accepted in practice: This implies that it is appropriate for the IETF to defer to the user community when it is unable to reach consensus on advancing one proposal in preference to an alternative. In this case, it appears that PIM is the multicast standard of choice.

RFC 1586: Guidelines for Running OSPF over Frame Relay Networks

This RFC specifies a set of guidelines for implementing the OSPF routing protocol to bring about improvements in how the protocol runs over Frame Relay networks. The authors show the techniques that can be used to prevent the "fully meshed" connectivity that had been required by OSPF until the publication of this RFC. The benefits of following the guidelines detailed in this RFC allow for more straightforward and economic OSPF network designs. This RFC differs from many of the others in that it does not require changes to be made to the protocol itself but rather the RFC suggests better ways to configure OSPF.

The reason behind this RFC is that OSPF considers Frame Relay (FR) networks as non-broadcast multiple access (NBMA). OSPF does this because FR can support more than two connected routers but FR does not offer any broadcast capabilities. The following quote from the RFC addresses this issue:

> OSPF characterizes FR networks as non-broadcast multiple access (NBMA) because they can support more than two attached routers, but do not have a broadcast capability [2]. Under the NBMA model, the physical FR interface on a router corresponds to a single OSPF interface through which the router is connected to one or more neighbors on the FR network; all the neighboring routers must also be directly connected to each other over the FR network. Hence OSPF implementations that use the NBMA model for FR do not work when the routers are partially interconnected. Further, the topological representation of a multiple access network has each attached router bi-directionally connected to the network vertex with a single link metric assigned to the edge directed into the vertex.
>
> We see that the NBMA model becomes more restrictive as the number of routers connected to the network increases. First, the number of VCs required for full-mesh connectivity increases quadratically with the number of routers. Public FR services typically offer performance guarantees for each VC provisioned by the service. This means that real physical resources in the FR network are devoted to each VC, and for this the customer eventually pays. The expense for full-mesh connectivity thus grows quadratically with the number of interconnected routers. We need to build OSPF implementations that allow for partial connectivity over FR. Second, using a single link metric (per TOS) for the FR interface does not allow OSPF to weigh some VCs more heavily than others according to the performance characteristics of each connection. To make efficient use of the FR network resources, it should be possible to assign different link metrics to different VCs.

These rather expensive limitations can result in reducing the value and cost effectiveness of FR as network size increases. The RFC proposes a set of solutions that do not greatly increase the complexity of OSPF's configuration. A brief list of their recommendations is provided, though I recommend further reading in the actual RFC if more in-depth information is required.

One of the recommendations is to expand the operation of an OSPF interface to allow the protocol to understand its function (point-to-point, broadcast, NBMA). In other words, allow OSPF to support both logical and physical interfaces.

The other recommendation proposed by the RFC is to use the NBMA model as OSPF's mode of operation for small homogenous networks.

NOTE   Cisco's recommendations for how to use the NBMA model can be found at

www.cisco.com/warp/public/104/3.html#11.0

They consider point-to-point a good option because of the reduced OSPF operations required (that is, there are no DR or neighbor statements).

RFC 1587: The OSPF NSSA Option

This RFC provides a description of a new type of optional OSPF area, the "*not-so-stubby*" area or NSSA. This optional stubby area is similar in operation to the existing stubby areas, but it has the additional capability to import external OSPF routes from the AS to which it belongs.

This RFC is good reading and its authors should be commended for bringing some of the real world into their discussion on the "not-so-stubby" area discussion. This RFC details a problem seen with the implementation of OSPF at the time of its writing. They provide a good scenario and supporting documentation about the issue this RFC addresses.

Within this RFC, the authors propose adding a new option bit, referred to as the "N" bit and a new type of LSA area definition. This new "N" bit would assist in identifying routers that belong to an NSSA and allow them to agree upon the area's topology. The new LSA would allow for external route information to be exchanged within the area.

Discussion is provided on the new LSA and how it compares to existing LSAs and how the new LSA will operate. The need for NSSA area border routers to have a default route is also discussed and justified.

Reading more about this RFC is recommended because it provides a good insight into how the OSPF protocol has matured and responded to the needs of its users. To assist you in clarifying that point, the following excerpt is provided from the RFC.

Why Was a Not-So-Stubby Area Needed?

Wide-area transit networks (such as the NSFNET regionals) often have connections to moderately-complex "leaf" sites. A leaf site may have multiple IP network numbers assigned to it.

Typically, one of the leaf site's networks is directly connected to a router provided and administered by the transit network while the others are distributed throughout and administered by the site. From the transit network's perspective, all of the network numbers associated with the site make up a single "stub" entity. For example, BARRNet has one site composed of a class-B network, 130.57.0.0, and a class-C network, 192.31.114.0. From BARRNet's perspective, this configuration looks something like Figure A-2.

Figure A-2 *BARRNet Wide-Area Transit Network*

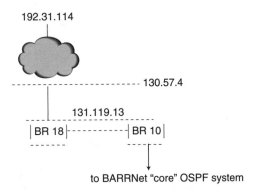

192.31.114

130.57.4

131.119.13

BR 18 --------- BR 10

to BARRNet "core" OSPF system

The "cloud" consists of the subnets of 130.57 and network 192.31.114, all of which are learned by RIP on router BR18. Topologically, this cloud looks very much like an OSPF stub area. The advantages of running the cloud as an OSPF stub area are:

- Type-5 routes (OSPF external link-state advertisements (LSAs)) are not advertised beyond the router labeled BR10. This is advantageous because the link between BR10 and BR18 may be a low-speed link or the router BR18 may have limited resources.

- The transit network is abstracted to the "leaf" router BR18 by advertising only a default route across the link between BR10 and BR18.

- The cloud becomes a single, manageable "leaf" with respect to the transit network.

- The cloud can become, logically, a part of the transit network's OSPF routing system.

- Translated type-5 LSAs that are sent into the backbone from the cloud (which is a separate stub area) may be considered "leaf" nodes when performing the Dijkstra calculation.

However, the current definition of the OSPF protocol [1] imposes topological limitations, which restrict simple cloud topologies from becoming OSPF stub areas. In particular, it is illegal for a stub area to import routes external to OSPF; it is not possible for routers BR18 and BR10 to both be members of the stub area and to import the routes learned from RIP or other IP routing protocols as type-5 (OSPF external LSAs) into the OSPF system. In order to run OSPF out to BR18, BR18 must be a member of a non-stub area or the OSPF backbone to import routes other than its directly-connected network(s). Since it is not acceptable for BR18 to maintain all of BARRNet's external (type-5) routes, BARRNet is forced by OSPF's topological limitations to run OSPF out to BR10 and to run RIP between BR18 and BR10.

RFC 1745: BGP4/IDRP for IP-OSPF Interaction

This RFC has been included in this list in order to be as complete as possible, thereby helping you understand and be able to reference all the many sources of information available on OSPF.

This RFC provides the technical information necessary to design and deploy a network or implement an ASBR that will be running Border Gateway Protocol (BGP4) or Inter-Domain Routing Protocol (IDRP) for IP as your EGP with OSPF as your IGP. This document details the settings necessary between the fields and attributes of OSPF and the other protocols. BGP4 is referenced in RFC 1654.

RFC 1765: OSPF Database Overflow

This RFC deals with an undesirable occurrence known as OSPF Database Overflow. For OSPF to operate properly, a complete link-state database must be within each OSPF router in an area. The condition known as a *database overflow* occurs when the link-state database becomes too large for the router to handle. This RFC allows for the handling of unanticipated database overflows and gives some recommendations on how to configure your network if you anticipate database overflow.

One way of handling database overflow is to encase routers having limited resources within OSPF stub areas or NSSAs. AS-external-LSAs are omitted from these areas' link-state databases, thereby controlling database size.

However, unexpected database overflows cannot be handled in the this manner. This RFC describes a way of dynamically limiting database size under overflow conditions.

The method used to recover from unexpected database overflow is discussed in detail, and if you are interested or believe you are experiencing this condition, consult the RFC.

RFC 1793: Extending OSPF to Support Demand Circuits

The author of this RFC did an excellent job in summarizing its contents. A direct quote of selected sections taken from the RFC provides you with an excellent overview of this RFC and its contents. The following section comes directly from RFC 1371:

> This memo defines enhancements to the OSPF protocol that allow efficient operation over "demand circuits". Demand circuits are network segments whose costs vary with usage; charges can be based both on connect time and on bytes/packets transmitted. Examples of demand circuits include ISDN circuits, X.25 SVCs, and dial-up lines.

The periodic nature of OSPF routing traffic has until now required a demand circuit's underlying data-link connection to be constantly open, resulting in unwanted usage charges. With the modifications described herein, OSPF Hellos and the refresh of OSPF routing information are suppressed on demand circuits, allowing the underlying data-link connections to be closed when not carrying application traffic.

Demand circuits and regular network segments (e.g., leased lines) are allowed to be combined in any manner. In other words, there are no topological restrictions on the demand circuit support. However, while any OSPF network segment can be defined as a demand circuit, only point-to-point networks receive the full benefit. When broadcast and NBMA networks are declared demand circuits, routing update traffic is reduced but the periodic sending of Hellos is not, which in effect still requires that the data-link connections remain constantly open.

While mainly intended for use with cost-conscious network links such as ISDN, X.25 and dial-up, the modifications in this memo may also prove useful over bandwidth-limited network links such as slow-speed leased lines and packet radio.

RFC 1850: OSPF Version 2 Management Information Base

This RFC defines a portion of the MIB for managing the OSPF routing protocol. It had been over four years and 12 additional RFCs detailing many features of OSPF to include a new version. This RFC was needed to handle the many new enhancements to the protocol and includes over 20 new features or changes. Some of these are rather minor, such as name changes or clarifications, and you are referred to the RFC for specific details. Some of the more important modifications are as follows:

- Support for status entries were added.
- Range of the link-state database MIB was extended to include the multicast (group-membership-LSA) and NSSA (NSSA-LSA).
- The OSPF external link-state database was added.

RFC 2178: OSPF Version 2

At over 211 pages, this RFC is a document that explains the smallest and most detailed internal workings of the OSPF protocol. Armed with this document, you could program the code necessary for OSPF to operate on any type of network equipment it supports. The RFC also takes you through every step of its operation to include those that are not apparent to the user. However, this RFC was made obsolete by RFC 2328, which is discussed in more detail.

RFC 2328: OSPF Version 2

This is the document that most modern-day OSPF implementations are based on. This RFC is almost a book by itself. At 244 pages, it surpasses all the previous OSPF RFCs in length and detail. Remember, though, that this is the standard and that how a company such as Cisco implements OSPF can vary a bit from the standard. But by purchasing this book, you are all set.

Any CCIE, network designer, or CIO who is considering an OSPF network should have this document available for their design specification. This RFC is definitely written for an advanced and specific target audience within the networking arena. The differences between this RFC and the previous are detailed in Appendix G of the document.

The differences between RFC 2178 and RFC 1583 are explained in Appendix G of the RFC. All differences are backward-compatible in nature. Implementations following this RFC and of those following RFC 1583 can interoperate:

- **Section 1: Introduction**—Briefly explains the history and background of the OSPF. It also includes a brief description of some of the more important design goals surrounding its use and operation.

- **Section 2: Link-State Database**—Goes into great detail regarding the layout and operation of OSPF's database. It includes information regarding its functionality and usage.

- **Section 3: Splitting the AS into Areas**—Details the methods and procedures regarding the segmentation of autonomous systems into various OSPF areas. It also discusses some of the unique characteristics the routers within an area will have regarding the OSPF protocol.

- **Section 4: Functional Summary**—Contains information regarding the overall functionality of the protocol and includes the operation of the shortest path algorithm.

- **Section 5: Protocol Data Structures**—Describes in detail the terms of its operation on various protocol data structures. Discussion is provided, as well as the top-level OSPF data structures. Areas, OSPF interfaces, and neighbors also have associated data structures that are described later in this specification.

- **Section 6: The Area Data Structure**—Discusses the characteristics of areas and how the protocol operates within that structure.

- **Section 7: Bringing Up Adjacencies**—Discusses, in general terms, the purpose and function of how OSPF forms adjacencies with the majority of routers that are neighbors.

- **Section 8: Protocol Packet Processing**—RFC discusses the general processing of routing protocol packets and their importance. The packet header of these routing protocol packets is also broken down for the reader.

- **Section 9: The Interface Data Structure**—Details their purpose and place within the operation of the protocol of an interface.

- **Section 10: The Neighbor Data Structure**—Covers the protocol's capability to converse with other routers that are considered its neighbors. This discussion includes additional information on adjacencies and how they are part of this structure.

- **Section 11: The Routing Table Structure**—Details the structure of the routing table and how the information provided within it can be used to forward packets correctly.

- **Section 12: Link-state Advertisements**—Discusses the functions of the five distinct types of link-state advertisements and how they form into the link-state database. Additional information regarding the link-state header structure is provided.

- **Section 13: The Flooding Procedure**—Provides an overview of how link-state update messages provide the mechanism for flooding advertisements throughout an area.

- **Section 14: Aging the Link-state Database**—Describes in detail the process of how a link-state advertisement uses its age field after it is placed in the database to determine which advertisement is most current.

- **Section 15: Virtual Links**—Provides information on the purpose and operation of virtual links and the part they play in ensuring the connectivity of different areas through the backbone.

- **Section 16: Calculation of the Routing Table**—Details the OSPF routing table calculation.

RFC 2370: Opaque LSA Option

Because you are reading this book, you obviously recognize how OSPF has increasingly been deployed in a variety of different networks. This increase has required OSPF to be extended into a variety of areas, yet more flexibility was needed. Enter the Opaque LSA. These new types of LSAs are designed to provide a method of carrying information that can be used as follows:

- Encapsulating application-specific information in a specific Opaque type, either type 9, 10, or 11

- Sending and receiving application-specific information

- If required, informing the application of the change in validity of previously received information when topological changes are detected

The interesting thing is that the actual use of these Opaque LSAs is not defined by this RFC but left open for use as needed. This type of LSA is distributed using the link-state mechanism for flooding and uses a standard LSA Header followed by a 32-bit application specific information field. The type of Opaque in use defines the scope of how and where the flooding will take place within a network.

- Link-state type 9 denotes a link-local scope. Type-9 Opaque LSAs are not flooded beyond the local (sub)network.

- Link-state type 10 denotes an area-local scope. Type-10 Opaque LSAs are not flooded beyond the borders of their associated area.

- Link-state type 11 denotes that the LSA is flooded throughout the AS. The flooding scope of type-11 LSAs are equivalent to the flooding scope of AS-external (type-5) LSAs. Specifically, type-11 Opaque LSAs are

  — Flooded throughout all transit areas

  — Not flooded into stub areas from the backbone

  — Not originated by routers into their connected stub areas

  As with type-5 LSAs, if a type-11 Opaque LSA is received in a stub area from a neighboring router within the stub area, the LSA is rejected.

RFC 2676: QoS Routing Mechanisms and OSPF Extensions

As of this publication, RFC 2676 is an experimental standard. This RFC describes a set of extensions to OSPF that allow OSPF to support QoS determined routes. The required framework for this support is discussed as well as the information needed by OSPF, information format, manageability, and the algorithms needed.

RFC 2740: OSPF for IPv6

This RFC details the changes necessary to OSPF in order to operate within an IPv6 network. The document describes the fundamental features of OSPF that remain unchanged. There have been changes to OSPF that are required to cope with the new features and changes found within IPv6 (for example, the longer addressing structure and inherent security). All these result in new LSAs being required and some other changes.

RFC 2844: OSPF over ATM and Proxy PAR

The RFC provides a great summary on its purpose: This memo specifies, for OSPF implementers and users, mechanisms describing how the protocol operates in ATM networks over PVC and SVC meshes with the presence of Proxy-PAR. These recommendations require no protocol changes and allow simpler, more efficient, and cost-effective network designs. It is recommended that OSPF implementations should be able to support logical interfaces, each consisting of one or more virtual circuits and used either as numbered logical point-to-point links (one VC), logical NBMA networks (more than one VC), or Point-to-MultiPoint networks (more than one VC), where a solution simulating broadcast interfaces is not appropriate.

Summary

This appendix discussed the evolution of the OSPF protocol by tracing its path through the RFCs. Each RFC was examined and briefly discussed to include whether it is still relevant in today's networks. RFC 2328 is the most current OSPF RFC.

Now that you have a complete picture concerning the technical resources and documentation surrounding OSPF, you should familiarize yourself with the functional environment and hierarchy used by OSPF, as discussed in the text.

INDEX

Symbols

/16, 38

/24, 38

? (question mark), invoking Cisco IOS help menu, 550

Numerics

2-way communication exchange process
troubleshooting neighbor stuck in 2-way state, 156–157
troubleshooting neighbor stuck in exstart/exchange state, 151–156

2-way state (neighbors), 119, 134

A

ABRs, 78
configuring, 273–274
inter-area route summarization, 411
inter-area traffic, controlling, 269–270
routing table, displaying, 555–556

access lists
applying to interfaces, 504
configuring, 501–502
creating, 503
SNMP, 462

activating OSPF, 271–272
ABR considerations, 273–274
ASBR considerations, 274–275
backbone router considerations, 275
network command, 272

adaptability as network design goal, 166

adding routers to OSPF networks, 85–88

addressing, 180
bit splitting, 184
discontiguous subnets, 185–186

naming schemes, 186
public versus private, 180–181
summarization, 181–182
VLSM, 185

adjacencies, 82
DRs, 83–84
selection process, 84–85
event logging, 591–593
troubleshooting, 136–138
versus neighbor relationships, 82–83

administrative distances, 341–342
altering, 313–314

agents (SNMP), 452

aggregates, 39

aggregation, 33

algorithms, distance vector, 55

allocating IP addresses, 184

altering
administrative distance, 313–314
LSA default behavior
blocking LSA flooding, 131
group pacing, 128–129
configuring, 130
ignoring MOSPF LSAs, 132
LSA retransmissions, 132
LSA transmission delay, 133
packet pacing, 131
routes to control redistribution, 397

analyzing network design requirements, 168–169
convergence, 170–171
deployment, 169
load balancing, 170

ANSI (American National Standards Institute)
X3S3.3 committee, 54

APNIC (Asia Pacific Network Information Centre), 21

application layer (OSI), 9

D

E

F

G

H

M

N

R

S

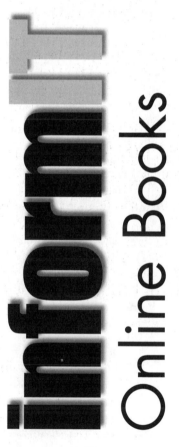

☐ **YES!** I'm requesting a **free** subscription to *Packet*™ magazine.

☐ No. I'm not interested at this time.

☐ Mr.
☐ Ms.

First Name (Please Print) _____ Last Name _____

Title/Position (Required) _____

Company (Required) _____

Address _____

City _____ State/Province _____

Zip/Postal Code _____ Country _____

Telephone (Include country and area codes) _____ Fax _____

E-mail _____

Signature (Required) _____ Date _____

☐ I would like to receive additional information on Cisco's services and products by e-mail.

1. Do you or your company:
A ☐ Use Cisco products   C ☐ Both
B ☐ Resell Cisco products   D ☐ Neither

2. Your organization's relationship to Cisco Systems:
A ☐ Customer/End User   E ☐ Integrator   J ☐ Consultant
B ☐ Prospective Customer   F ☐ Non-Authorized Reseller K ☐ Other (specify):
C ☐ Cisco Reseller   G ☐ Cisco Training Partner   _____
D ☐ Cisco Distributor   I ☐ Cisco OEM

3. How many people does your entire company employ?
A ☐ More than 10,000   D ☐ 500 to 999   G ☐ Fewer than 100
B ☐ 5,000 to 9,999   E ☐ 250 to 499
c ☐ 1,000 to 4,999   f ☐ 100 to 249

4. Is your company a Service Provider?
A ☐ Yes   B ☐ No

5. Your involvement in network equipment purchases:
A ☐ Recommend   B ☐ Approve   C ☐ Neither

6. Your personal involvement in networking:
A ☐ Entire enterprise at all sites   F ☐ Public network
B ☐ Departments or network segments at more than one site   D ☐ No involvement
C ☐ Single department or network segment   E ☐ Other (specify):
                                                            _____

7. Your Industry:
A ☐ Aerospace   G ☐ Education (K–12)   K ☐ Health Care
B ☐ Agriculture/Mining/Construction U ☐ Education (College/Univ.) L ☐ Telecommunications
C ☐ Banking/Finance   H ☐ Government—Federal   M ☐ Utilities/Transportation
D ☐ Chemical/Pharmaceutical   I ☐ Government—State   N ☐ Other (specify):
E ☐ Consultant   J ☐ Government—Local   _____
F ☐ Computer/Systems/Electronics

CPRESS

PACKET

Packet magazine serves as the premier publication linking customers to Cisco Systems, Inc. Delivering complete coverage of cutting-edge networking trends and innovations, *Packet* is a magazine for technical, hands-on users. It delivers industry-specific information for enterprise, service provider, and small and midsized business market segments. A toolchest for planners and decision makers, *Packet* contains a vast array of practical information, boasting sample configurations, real-life customer examples, and tips on getting the most from your Cisco Systems' investments. Simply put, *Packet* magazine is straight talk straight from the worldwide leader in networking for the Internet, Cisco Systems, Inc.

We hope you'll take advantage of this useful resource. I look forward to hearing from you!

Cecelia Glover
Packet Circulation Manager
packet@external.cisco.com
www.cisco.com/go/packet

PACKET

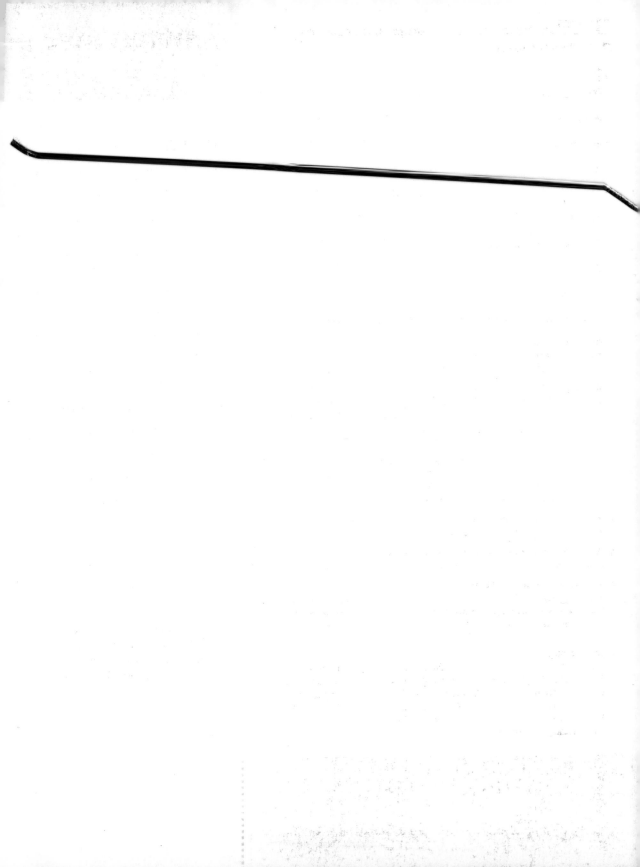